Substance Abuse, Addiction, and Treatment

Marshall Cavendish
Reference
New York

Copyright © 2012 Marshall Cavendish Corporation

Published by Marshall Cavendish Reference

An imprint of Marshall Cavendish Corporation

All rights reserved.

Website: www.marshallcavendish.us

This publication represents the opinions and views of the authors based on personal experience, knowledge, and research. The information in this book serves as a general guide only. The author and publisher have used their best efforts in preparing this book and disclaim liability rising directly and indirectly from the use and application of this book.

Other Marshall Cavendish Offices:

Marshall Cavendish International (Asia) Private Limited, 1 New Industrial Road, Singapore 536196 • Marshall Cavendish International (Thailand) Co Ltd. 253 Asoke, 12th Flr, Sukhumvit 21 Road, Klongtoey Nua, Wattana, Bangkok 10110, Thailand • Marshall Cavendish (Malaysia) Sdn Bhd, Times Subang, Lot 46, Subang Hi-Tech Industrial Park, Batu Tiga, 40000 Shah Alam, Selangor Darul Ehsan, Malaysia

Marshall Cavendish is a trademark of Times Publishing Limited

All websites were available and accurate when this book was sent to press.

Library of Congress Cataloging-in-Publication Data

Substance abuse, addiction, and treatment.
 p. cm.
Includes bibliographical references and indexes.
ISBN 978-0-7614-7943-7
1. Substance abuse. 2. Substance abuse--Treatment. I. Title.
RC564.3.S83 2012
362.29--dc22   2011009226

Printed in Malaysia

15 14 13 12 11   1 2 3 4 5

Consultants

Michael J. Kuhar, PhD, Charles Howard Candler Professor of Pharmacology, Emory University, Atlanta, Georgia

Howard Liddle, EdD, Director, Center for Treatment and Research on Adolescent Drug Abuse, University of Miami Medical School, Miami, Florida

Marshall Cavendish
Publisher: Paul Bernabeo
Production Manager: Michael Esposito
Indexer: Cynthia Crippen, AEIOU, Inc.

PHOTOGRAPHIC CREDITS
Front Cover: istock/Nicholas Monu

Ardea: Dennis Avon 82; **Brookhaven National Laboratory:** 35, 61, 268; **The Brown Reference Group plc** 226; **Corbis:** Annie Griffiths Belt 217, Ariel Skelley 332, Bettmann 85, 127, Bill Varie 105, Bob Krist 39, Bojan Brecelj 260, Chris Collins 176, Chuck Savage 53, Clouds Hill Imaging Ltd. 192, David H. Wells 241, David Turnley 89, Douglas Kirkland 329, Ed Kashi 196, 211, 324, 336, Howard Sochurek 170, Hutchings Stock Photography 245, Images.com 158, James Leynse 334, James Marshall 10, Jeffrey L. Rotman 177, Jennie Woodcock/Reflections Photolibrary 25, Jim Cummins 253, Jim McDonald 309, Jon Feingersh 300, L. Clark 56, Lawrence Manning 156, Lester V. Bergman 194, Owen Franken 66, Reuters 295, Richard Hutchings 77, 160, Richard T. Nowitz 215, Robert Holmes 327, Roy Morsch 203, Steve Chenn 292, Tom Stewart 148, Tom & Dee Ann McCarthy 99, 135, 152, Tom Wagner 321, Zach Gold 275; **Corbis Royalty Free:** 204, 248, 257, Charles Gupton 22; **Corbis Saba:** Ricki Rosen 180; **Corbis Sygma:** Elder Neville 138, J. B. Russell 110, Pascal Parrot 33; **Digital Vision:** 120; **Dynamic Graphics:** Communication 58; **Getty Images:** 318, Bruce Ayres 155, John Bradley 25; Stewart Cohen 140; **Imagingbody.com:** 51; **National Library of Medicine:** 116; **IAAA:** 37; **Ogilvy & Mather** 244; **PHIL** 297; **PhotoDisc:** Keith Brofsky 146, Steve Mason 69; **Rex Features:** Action Press 330, Burger/Phanie Agency 232, 285, Frank Monaco 59, Garo/Phanie 133, IPC Magazines 228, Oy Lehtikuva 150; Phanie Agency 187, 281, Raphael Cardinael 276, Reso 206, Richard Gardner 30, Shout 209, Sipa Press 65, 162, 234, 287, 314, Stephen Meddle 162, The Sun 174, Tim Clark 230; **Rutgers University Center for Alcohol Studies:** 185, 213; **Science Photo Library:** 190, Garry Watson 188; **Topham Picturepoint:** 19, 124, Bill Bachmann/The Image Works 122, Bob Daemmrich/The Image Works 16, 72, 237, 242, 290, Eastcott/Momatiuk/The Image Works 250, Esbin-Anderson/The Image Works 305, John Griffin/The Image Works 93, 200, Mike Silluk/The Image Works 13, uppa.co.uk 46; **U.S. Customs:** James R. Tourtellotte 336.

Contents

Foreword

Drug use has occurred in every society throughout the world, from ancient times to today. Societies and their members have many reasons for using drugs and for wanting to avoid substance abuse. The two major reasons for using drugs are therapeutic and social–recreational. Therapeutic reasons for drug use involve prescription and nonprescription drugs for healing or to prevent health problems. Some drugs are used therapeutically to treat drug problems, for example, by administering medications to prevent drug abuse or to control addiction, but certain therapeutic purposes stretch the definition of medical need. Some drugs are used to improve a person's self-image (for example, to increase height or reduce weight), to help people deal with the stress and tension of everyday life, and to enhance physical and mental performance.

Social and Recreational Use of Drugs

Other reasons for drug use are defined as nonmedical. Some societies use drugs as part of religious ceremonies. Examples include peyote (mescaline) and magic mushrooms (psilocybin and psilocin). Drugs have sometimes been used by artists and musicians because they believe drugs enhance their creativity or artistic performance. But the primary occurrence of the nonmedical use of drugs is in a social or recreational context. Social drug use is common in most societies, but it usually is limited to a few types of drugs.

Drinking alcohol and smoking or chewing tobacco are legal forms of social drug use, at least for people over certain age limits. Smoking marijuana might be considered by some people to be social drug use, but in most societies marijuana is illegal in the general population. In some societies, consumption of coca leaf, betel nut, and khat is allowed, but these drugs are often illegal in other societies. Most societies permit the use of some drugs for social reasons, but they put limits or boundaries on social drug use that becomes harmful or has destructive results, such as binge drinking and drunk driving.

Recreational drug use may reflect a social context, but often recreational use involves drugs that society has declared illegal. Both social and recreational drug use, when they consist of low to moderate doses of legal drugs and when done occasionally (certainly not daily), are viewed by most societies as acceptable and a choice that adults should be allowed to make. Society usually declares certain drugs illegal due to the increased risk they have of causing harm to users or other people in society. Social and recreational use of illegal drugs is more dangerous when the use involves higher doses, occurs on a regular basis, or includes substances that are toxic or addictive. This type of drug use is called drug abuse or drug addiction.

Prevention and Control of Drug Use

The most interesting, and perhaps confusing, aspect of drug abuse is that society can influence and encourage as well as prohibit or control the use of drugs. That is especially the case with social and recreational drug use. Society can make people aware of trendy and popular drugs and inaccurately portray seemingly desirable drug effects. Society can also influence beliefs about the lack of harmful effects from using certain drugs. It can encourage the use of illegal drugs or the dangerous use of legal drugs. Society promotes attitudes about drug use in advertising, in mass media (movies, television, music, books, and the Internet), in the specific types of drug use it attempts to prohibit or control, and in the types of drug use it does not control.

While certain aspects of a society seem to encourage drug use, other aspects act to prevent or control drug use. Most often, society attempts to control dangerous types of drug use or harmful effects. This is done by passing laws and regulations that prohibit or curtail the use of certain drugs, educating people about the dangers of drug use, testing people to identify if they are drug users, and imprisoning or providing treatment to those people who misuse drugs or become addicted.

Some societies prohibit the use of alcohol and tobacco by young people but not adults. Most prohibit alcohol use by anyone engaged in some activity or work that becomes dangerous if that person's physical or mental abilities are impaired or reduced by alcohol. Society more recently has tried different ways to control adult tobacco use. Some examples include prohibiting smoking in public places, requiring that tobacco products carry warning messages about the dangers of use, and making smokers pay more for health insurance. Society has not decided to control caffeine use.

Drug Abuse and Society

The 108 articles included in *Substance Abuse, Addiction, and Treatment* will help readers understand how and why drugs are used by individuals and society and the problems and dangers that can occur from the inappropriate use and abuse of drugs. Readers will find information on the predisposing, enabling, and reinforcing factors that lead to experimental and continual drug use, and on behaviors involving drugs that lead to adverse reactions and dangerous outcomes such as overdoses and addictions. Articles contained herein will also inform readers of the efforts being made through scientific research, medical practice, therapeutic processes, and social policy to address the impact, both personal and society-wide, of the abuse of drugs.

Explore this book with the realization that substance abuse is a complex phenomenon, sometimes involving confusing meanings and conflicting behaviors. The focus of life should be on optimal health and well-being without drugs. Drugs can be helpful as medicines when used to treat health problems under a physician's supervision. Drug use, however, becomes harmful and dangerous when drugs are used for nonmedical reasons, especially when social or recreational use involves illegal drugs, or when the abuse of legal drugs becomes part of a person's everyday life.

Details on the most widely abused substances can be found in the single-volume *Drugs of Abuse*. Additional information on these topics is also available in the three-volume set *Drugs and Society* and the online *Drugs and Society* database at www.marshallcavendishdigital.com.

Michael Montagne, PhD, Massachusetts College
of Pharmacy and Health Sciences,
Boston, Massachusetts

Consultants and Contributors

Michael J. Kuhar, PhD, Charles Howard Candler Professor of Pharmacology, Emory University, Atlanta, Georgia

Howard Liddle, EdD, Director, Center for Treatment and Research on Adolescent Drug Abuse, University of Miami Medical School, Miami, Florida

---

Peter J. Ambrose, PharmD, School of Pharmacy, University of California, San Francisco, California

David E. Arnot, PhD, Institute of Cell, Animal, and Population Biology, University of Edinburgh, UK

Sudie E. Back, PhD, Dept. of Psychiatry, Yale University, New Haven, Connecticut

Ronald A. Beard, PhD, Center for Drug and Alcohol Studies, University of Delaware, Wilmington, Delaware

Denise Biron, MS, MA, School of Psychology and Counseling, Regent University, Norfolk, Virginia

Yvonne Bonomo, PhD, Dept. of Drug & Alcohol Studies, St. Vincent's Hospital, Melbourne, Australia

Kirk J. Brower, MD, Dept. of Psychiatry, University of Michigan Addiction Research Center, Ann Arbor

R. Andrew Chambers, MD, Dept. of Psychiatry, Yale University, New Haven, Connecticut

Martin Clowes, BSc, Nottingham, UK

Cynthia A. Conklin, PhD, University of Pittsburgh Medical Center, Pittsburgh, Pennsylvania

Gerard J. Connors, PhD, Director, Research Institute on Addictions, University at Buffalo, Buffalo, New York

Ross Coomber, PhD, Dept. of Sociology, University of Plymouth, Plymouth, UK

Nancy Costikyan, MSW, Division on Addictions, Harvard Medical School, Boston, Massachusetts

Hans S. Crombag, PhD, Dept. of Psychological and Brain Sciences, Johns Hopkins University, Boston, Massachusetts

Dennis C. Daley, PhD, University of Pittsburgh Medical Center, Pittsburgh, Pennsylvania

Dena Davidson, PhD, Institute of Psychiatric Research, Indiana University School of Medicine, Indianapolis

William DeJong, PhD, Dept. of Social and Behavioral Sciences, Boston University, Boston, Massachusetts

Anthony N. Donato, BA, MPP, Division on Addictions, Harvard Medical School, Boston, Massachusetts

Christopher Donohue, PhD, Dept. of Psychiatry, University of Minnesota, Minneapolis, Minnesota

Amy S. Elkavich, BA, Center for Community Health, University of California, Los Angeles, California

Cele Fichter-DeSando, MPM, CPS, University of Pittsburgh, Pittsburgh, Pennsylvania

Dwayne W. Godwin, PhD, Wake Forest University Baptist Medical Center, Winston-Salem, North Carolina

Andrew D. Hathaway, PhD, Centre for Addiction and Mental Health, Toronto, Ontario, Canada

Leanne Hides, PhD, Orygen Research Centre, University of Melbourne, Melbourne, Australia

Wendy A. Horan, BSc, Croydon, Surrey, UK

Richard G. Hunter, PhD, Emory University, Yerkes Primate Research Center, Atlanta, Georgia

William Ingless, BA, Nottingham, UK

Jason Jaworski, PhD, Neurosciences Division, Emory University, Yerkes Research Center, Atlanta, Georgia

Judith L. Johnson, PhD, School of Psychology and Counseling, Regent University, Virginia Beach, Virginia

Maher Karam-Hage, MD, Dept. of Psychiatry, University of Michigan Medical School, Ann Arbor, Michigan

Linda P. King, MSW, PhD, Research Institute on Addictions, University at Buffalo, Buffalo, New York

Matt G. Kushner, PhD, Dept. of Psychiatry, University of Minnesota, Minneapolis, Minnesota

Nathan Lepora, PhD, London, UK

Francesco Leri, PhD, Dept. of Psychology, University of Guelph, Guelph, Ontario, Canada

Daniel I. Lubman, PhD, Department of Psychiatry, University of Melbourne, Melbourne, Australia

Eric Maurer, Dept. of Psychiatry, University of Minnesota, Minneapolis, Minnesota

John McMahon, PhD, Centre for Alcohol and Drug Studies, University of Paisley, Paisley, UK

Meryl Nadel, PhD, Social Work Department, Iona College, New Rochelle, New York

Daniel J. O'Connell, PhD, Center for Drug and Alcohol Studies, University of Delaware, Newark, Delaware

Tami C. O'Connell, BS, Division of Rehabilitation Services, State of Maryland

Kenneth Perkins, PhD, Western Psychiatric Institute and Clinic, University of Pittsburgh, Pittsburgh, Pennsylvania

Kelly B. Philpot, PhD, Emory University, Yerkes Primate Research Center, Atlanta, Georgia

Maureen D. Reynolds, PhD, University of Pittsburgh, Pittsburgh, Pennsylvania

Paula D. Riggs, MD, University of Colorado Health Sciences Center, Denver, Colorado

Mary Jane Rotheram-Borus, PhD, Neuropsychiatric Institute, University of California, Los Angeles, California

Henry Russell, MA, London, UK

Harry Shapiro, DrugScope, London, UK

Sandra Sletten, MEd, Dept. of Psychiatry, University of Minnesota, Minneapolis, Minnesota

Lis Stedman, BA, Chelmsford, Essex, UK

Antonio Tejero-Pociello, PhD, Unitat de Toxicomanies, Servei de Psiquiatria, Hospital de la Santa Creu i Sant Pau, Barcelona, Spain

Paul G. Thompson, London, UK

Christian Thurstone, MD, University of Colorado Health Sciences Center, Denver, Colorado

J. Scott Tonigan, PhD, University of New Mexico, Albuquerque, New Mexico

Patricia L. Torchia, LCPC, CADC, Prairie Psychotherapy Associates, Springfield, Illinois

Michael Vanyukov, PhD, Center for Education and Drug Abuse Research, University of Pittsburgh, Pennsylvania

Samantha Walker, PhD, Prevention Research Center, Pacific Institute for Research and Evaluation, Berkeley, California

Chris Woodford, MSc, Burton-on-Trent, Staffordshire, UK

Joycelyn S. Woods, MA, President, National Alliance of Methadone Advocates, New York, New York

Murat Yücel, PhD, Orygen Research Centre, University of Melbourne, Melbourne, Australia

Zhiwei Zhang, PhD, NORC, University of Chicago, Chicago, Illinois

Abstinence

Abstinence involves the complete avoidance of a drug or alcohol, a common aim for many people recovering from addiction. Some researchers argue for controlled use as a more achievable alternative to abstinence.

Many people regard abstinence as the only valid goal of treatment for alcoholics and addicts. For drugs, the reasoning is not difficult to understand, since drug use is an illegal activity in almost all countries. However, to understand why abstinence is advocated for alcohol, it is necessary to understand the models of alcohol problems, in particular the disease model.

The disease model makes some basic assumptions about the nature of alcoholism. Briefly, it suggests that alcoholics suffer from an abnormal and uncontrollable craving that leads them to drink, and that once they begin drinking they have no control over their consumption. Thus, it follows that alcoholics cannot drink in safety. Couple this with the belief that the disease is progressive (that is, it continually gets worse) and irreversible, and the only possible or safe outcome is for the alcoholic to abstain for the rest of his or her life. This assumption is generally made whether one believes the disease was acquired or inherited. Further, it tends to be generalized to drugs and other addictive behaviors.

Sobriety

The organization Alcoholics Anonymous (AA) believes that the alcoholic needs to stop drinking and remain that way for life, but makes a distinction between abstinence and sobriety. AA views abstinence as an absence of alcohol, whereas sobriety is viewed as a state of both mental and spiritual well-being. This state is achieved by the AA member working through a program known as the twelve steps. Working through the program entails self-examination and a corresponding change in attitudes and behavior, facilitated by a relationship with the AA group and a belief in a higher power (such as God). Thus, whereas abstinence is negative (merely a removal of alcohol), sobriety involves gaining a positive outlook and behavioral pattern that will enhance the life of the alcoholic. However, while sobriety may be a positive goal, it also highlights one of the major problems that face those who wish to stop drinking—significant lifestyle changes.

Problems with abstinence as a goal

Alcoholics and addicts often socialize with others who follow similar lifestyles. Even if the friends are not actively encouraging the alcoholic or addict to indulge, merely being in the company of others who are getting intoxicated can represent a major temptation to relapse. This temptation is acute for alcoholics, since alcohol is so commonly used in Western society. Indeed, recovering alcoholics often fear that their social life will be over; it may take a considerable time for them to feel they can socialize where alcohol is present without being at great risk.

Alan Marlatt, an American psychologist, highlights a second problem of abstinence as a goal. In his research on relapse, he suggests that the inflexibility of the goal leads to a belief on the part of the alcoholic that any drinking, regardless of how slight, is proof of a return to full-blown alcoholic relapse. Marlatt argues that this outcome, rather than being a physiological process, is in fact a psychological process arising from a belief in the disease model. He calls this phenomenon the "abstinence violation effect." Thus, someone who has remained abstinent for over a year and then takes a drink would view this act as a failure; instead, one might describe this behavior as a substantial reduction in volume and frequency of consumption.

The categorization of other nonsubstance-based behaviors as addictions also brings into question the appropriateness of abstinence as the only treatment goal for addiction. Abstinence for behaviors such as overeating and overexercising is not only inappropriate but dangerous. Other goals, such as moderation management, harm reduction, and controlled use have come into the treatment repertoire of addiction and have also filtered into the treatment of chemical addictions.

Alternative treatment goals

The best known of the alternative treatment goals is controlled drinking. In a famous experiment of the 1970s, Mark and Linda Sobell, psychologists at

NATURAL RECOVERY

Natural recovery, in which alcoholics and addicts recover without the aid of treatment, is a new topic of study. Part of the reason for its neglect by researchers was the dominance of the disease theory of addiction; an implication of this theory is that alcoholics and addicts cannot recover without the aid of treatment. However, increasing numbers of reports were suggesting that some alcoholics and addicts were recovering without the aid of treatment. Since by definition they did not appear in treatment agencies, how could they be contacted and studied?

For some researchers, the solution was to advertise in the media for volunteers who fulfilled the criteria of natural recovery. This research made a number of discoveries. First, natural recovery was indeed a possible route out of addiction for both alcoholics and opiate addicts. Second, natural recoverers were found to be either abstinent or controlled users. Thus, both outcomes were possible. Third, despite beliefs to the contrary, natural recoverers had dependency problems that were equally as severe as those who had attended treatment. Fourth, a major reason for not seeking treatment was the stigma associated with addiction treatment.

While these studies were informative, the general consensus was that natural recovery was a rare event. However, a large-scale Canadian study by Mark and Linda Sobell in 1996 found that, rather than being rare, natural recovery was the most common route out of addictive behaviors. Estimates of its frequency have suggested that between 60 and 85 percent of those who recover from addiction do so without treatment. However, some of these studies have included smoking and other behaviors that do not have a tradition of formal treatment. In spite of this caveat, it is clear that natural recovery is far more common than was originally thought possible.

Patton State Hospital in California, carried out a study aimed at testing the feasibility of teaching controlled drinking to alcoholics. The evidence that was beginning to emerge in the 1960s suggested that the disease model of alcoholism was flawed (alcoholics were recovering without treatment and controlled drinking was therefore a possibility). The study caused a furor at the time, but it was also a success, although not necessarily in the manner that was expected. The Sobells' writing about the study later pointed out that many of the study group had in fact opted for abstinence. Their interpretation of the results of the study was that controlled drinking was possible for alcoholics, but that abstinence was the more common outcome, and patients were more likely to remain abstinent when they felt that they had a choice of outcome. They argued that this choice appears to enable the patient to take ownership of the goal and hence ensures greater adherence to it.

Other goals have arisen out of pragmatic rather than theoretical or ideological positions. The present approach to drug use is a prime example of this. Harm reduction practices, such as needle exchange, arose out of the need to prevent the further spread of HIV/AIDS rather than a desire to give alternative treatments to addicts. Nevertheless, the approach is now firmly established in drug treatment programs.

Abstinence is sometimes essential

For some alcoholics and addicts, there are sound medical reasons why abstinence is essential. In cases where there is severe liver damage, further consumption of alcohol will only exacerbate the problem, and abstinence is strongly recommended. Similarly, for patients with severe cognitive impairments due to Wernicke's encephalopathy or Korsakoff's psychosis, further consumption will only increase the damage. Abstinence is also necessary in cases where moderation cannot be achieved.

J. McMAHON

SEE ALSO:

Alcoholics Anonymous ● Biopsychosocial Theory of Addiction ● Disease Theory of Addiction

Acupuncture

Acupuncture is an alternative therapy that is sometimes used to treat patients suffering withdrawal effects from drug addiction. Although it is not a proven treatment, some people seem to find relief from this type of therapy.

Acupuncture is a medical therapy that involves the insertion of needles, usually made of stainless steel, into specific body points in order to relieve pain or improve health. It was first practiced in China more than 2,500 years ago. From there it spread throughout the rest of Asia; by the late twentieth century, it was in use throughout the world. It is now popular as a treatment for certain forms of drug addiction because it appears in some cases to ease both withdrawal symptoms and further cravings.

How acupuncture works

According to the Chinese, the body's life force, or chi, is balanced by positive and negative components. Disruptions to either of these components can cause an obstruction in the flow of the vital force, which can result in a disease either along the pathway or in the organ to which the pathway leads. The body has 12 of these pathways, or meridians, each associated with a major organ. More than 365 points along the meridians are used for treatment by needle therapy, and acupuncturists undergo rigorous training during which they learn the correct procedures for needle insertion and manipulation and the proper duration of every treatment.

The needles used in acupuncture may be slightly arrowheaded or may have extremely fine points. The typical insertion is 0.1 to 0.4 inch (3–10 mm) in depth; a few treatments require insertions up to almost 10 inches (25 cm) deep. Once inserted, a needle is usually left in place for 5 to 20 minutes; it may sometimes be twisted. Because of the body's meridian system, the acupuncturist frequently inserts needles at a considerable distance from the point on

Up to five needles are placed at points in the outer ear during acupuncture treatment for withdrawal.

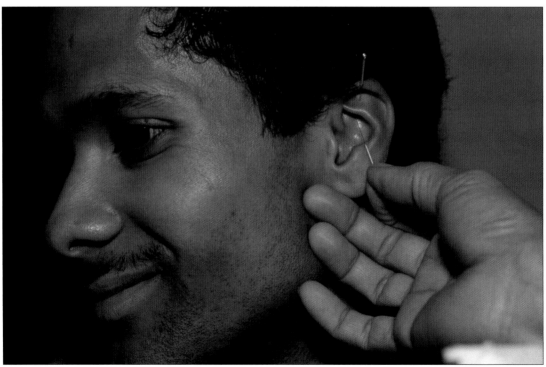

which they are intended to act; for example, a needle inserted in the pad of the thumb is expected to reduce pain in the abdomen, while insertions in the lung meridian aim to stem nosebleeds, reduce swollen joints, heart pains, and depression, and restore the ability to stretch the arms above the head.

Science has so far failed to explain exactly how acupuncture works. Some Japanese acupuncturists contend that needle therapy affects the autonomic nervous system, which is responsible for the body's automatic functions, such as breathing and heart-beat. In China, physicians believe that acupuncture works by means of nerve impulses and a mechanism that they are unable to specify.

In the West, some doctors have speculated that the needle insertions stimulate the production of endorphins or enkephalins, natural painkillers that bind to the opiate receptors in the brain. Others have suggested that the minor stimulation of acupuncture selectively acts on impulse transmission to the central nervous system, thus closing certain neurological "gates" and blocking the transmission of pain impulses from other parts of the body. According to another body of opinion, the analgesia caused by acupuncture is no more than a placebo effect, although that does not detract from its effectiveness. While claims by Chinese practitioners that acupuncture can actually cure certain diseases remain unsubstantiated, Western medical researchers do not dismiss the possibility that it might.

Treating disease and addiction

Acupuncture has been used successfully in the treatment of a wide variety of illnesses, both on its own and in combination with traditional Western medicine. Among the conditions most responsive to acupuncture are acute and chronic musculoskeletal pain, respiratory ailments such as sinusitis and bronchitis, irritable bowel syndrome, male infertility, and some forms of impotence. When applied to the outer ear, acupuncture has been used to help people quit smoking tobacco and to cope with withdrawal from alcohol, cocaine, and opiate dependency. In a famous case in 1972, H. L. Wen, a neurosurgeon in Hong Kong, noticed that the application of acupuncture with electrical stimulation (AES) eliminated withdrawal symptoms in a narcotics addict on whom he had been about to operate. He repeated the treatment on 40 other addicts, and all but one were cured of their withdrawal symptoms. This form of treatment was later successfully extended in the mid-1970s to alcoholics and cocaine addicts. In 1985, the National Acupuncture Detoxification Association (NADA) was established in New York.

Not everyone is convinced of the effectiveness of acupuncture for treating addiction, but the treatment is undeniably less expensive than conventional Western drug-based treatments. It appeals to both self-help groups and people who do not like the idea of medical detoxification.

Although acupuncture has been used for managing withdrawal for more than 30 years, there has been little scientific evidence of its efficacy and few clinical evaluations of its role in treatment. A controlled study of the use of acupuncture was set up at Yale University and reported its results in 2000. The trial involved cocaine addicts who had four acupuncture needles inserted into one of their outer ears five times a week over the course of eight weeks. Those who received acupuncture specifically for withdrawal, rather than the control groups who had needles inserted at random points or were given relaxation therapy, spent less time in treatment for their addiction. Half of them were free of cocaine in their urine by the last week of the trial.

A larger study by the same group of researchers two years later was less conclusive about the use of acupuncture as a primary treatment for cocaine addiction. Patients had managed to cut their use of the drug but still took fairly high amounts. One significant finding related to how often the patients had attended counseling sessions as part of the trial. Attendance at these sessions was generally poor compared with the first trial and may have been a factor in the results.

Despite these findings, acupuncture may prove useful to some patients as part of a broader treatment program. Its painkilling effects and general use in relaxing the body may help some people through the difficulties of withdrawal, which can only be beneficial in their bid to overcome addiction.

H. RUSSELL

SEE ALSO:
Causes of Addiction, Biological • Detoxification • Smoking Cessation • Withdrawal

Addiction

The root causes of drug addiction are complex and the influences on the course of an addiction are many and varied. Determining exactly what addiction is continues to spark much scientific research and debate.

Addiction is an acquired condition where an individual persistently pursues and obtains some form of reward at the expense of other important motivations or activities, and to the detriment of his or her own mental or physical health. The term *addiction* is commonly invoked in regard to intake of drugs, although it is increasingly also used in relation to other reward-directed behaviors including food intake, sex, gambling, and video-game playing. The vast majority of scientific and medical knowledge about addiction focuses on substance use.

Addictions to drugs and alcohol have long been recognized as particularly common and destructive forms of addiction. Also, drug addiction is uniquely amenable to scientific investigation since it involves the delivery to the brain of a chemical made outside the body. This chemical may be viewed as the disease-causing agent, and it can be studied in terms of its particular molecular structure and its characteristic patterns of effects in the brain. In contrast, addictions to sex, food, and other activities, while involving many of the same brain systems as in drug addiction, do not involve clearly discernable and unitary disease-causing agents that can be easily separated from the great complexity of naturally occurring processes in the brain.

Drug addiction is an acquired condition. This concept is essential to understanding how it represents both changes in a person's behavior and in brain function. Addiction does not happen overnight. Instead, it requires repetitions of episodes of drug intake, with each episode contributing to a progressive worsening of the condition. The speed of this process or the number of drug-intake episodes required is determined by a wide array of factors. These include the type of addictive drug; amount (doses) of drug delivered per intake episode; the route of delivery, for example, oral ingestion, smoking, or intravenous injection; psychological conditions at time of drug intake; the age of the individual; the individual's gender; the presence of underlying mental illness; history of traumatic life events; genetic makeup of the individual; and probably many other biological factors that have not yet been clearly identified. Drug availability is also a prerequisite for drug intake and thus the initiation and maintenance of the addictive process.

The nature of addiction

The view of drug addiction traditionally held by psychiatrists and other health care providers as a medical illness, rather than a social, legal, or moral problem, has gained popular attention. Nevertheless, the exact nature of addiction is still debated among many groups in society, partly because it involves a philosophical question of whether or not a biological process can truly alter the free will of an individual. It is clear, however, is that drug addictions represent a very destructive force in individuals and society as a whole. When taking into account all forms of drug addiction and the effects of both legal drugs such as alcohol and nicotine and illegal drugs such as cocaine and heroin, substance use is the leading root cause of all preventable psychiatric and medical sickness, injury, early death, and health care expenditures in the United States. Smoking, for example, is a leading cause of early cancer, heart disease, and brain injury from stroke, while the shared use of needles for the intravenous injection of drugs is a major causative factor in the spread of human immunodeficiency virus (HIV) and some forms of hepatitis. Virtually all of the symptoms associated with major psychiatric illnesses, including schizophrenia, depression, bipolar disorder, and anxiety disorders, can be at least temporarily produced by various forms of substance intoxication or withdrawal.

In advanced addictions, the motivations to acquire and use substances often consume vital financial resources or the ability to work and care for loved ones. Such losses of occupational and social function can lead to homelessness and alienation and are themselves risk factors for depression and suicide.

Chemical dependency units provide medical services to people suffering from drug addictions.

instances of compromised work or school obligations, breaking the law, or increased risk of physical harm caused by activities such as driving while under the influence of alcohol.

Substance dependence, the psychiatric diagnosis for advanced drug addiction, involves evidence that for the last year the substance use has become a habitual behavior over which the individual has little control; at the same time the substance use produces a pattern of more serious consequences. Substance dependence is thus diagnosed by the criteria of the American Psychiatric Association's *Diagnostic and Statistical Manual of Mental Disorders,* 4th edition (DSM-IV), as a constellation of signs that includes at least three of the following: tolerance to the intoxicating effects of the drug; symptoms of withdrawal when the drug use is temporarily discontinued; increases in either the amount of drug or duration of use associated with each drug-intake episode; persistent desire to stop or reduce the drug use despite not being able to do so; increasing the amount of time and effort spent acquiring the drug; reduction or stopping of important social, school, work, or recreational activities in favor of those associated with drug use; and persistent drug use despite awareness that the drug use has caused physical or mental health problems.

Diagnoses of drug addiction

While a wide array and interplay of biological, psychological, and social forces contribute to the process and speed of becoming addicted, the psychiatric diagnosis of drug-addiction-related or substance-use disorder is made in a graded fashion according to the degree to which the substance use represents an uncontrollable habit causing impairment and distress. Occasional use of a substance that produces no observable detrimental effects is not regarded as a medically diagnosable problem. This pattern is variously termed as recreational, experimental, casual, or social drug use.

The diagnosis of substance abuse is made when an individual demonstrates over a year a pattern of recurrent substance use that produces problems on multiple occasions. These problems may include

Mechanisms of addiction

A long-standing scientific debate has centered on the question of whether or not the primary mechanisms responsible for addiction can be best understood in terms of negative or positive reinforcement. In negative reinforcement, individuals take a drug to relieve themselves of some form of aversive (negative or punishing) stimuli, uncomfortable symptoms, or some other negative outcome. One example of this is the taking of a narcotic medication to relieve surgical pain. In positive reinforcement, drug intake is desired because of the pleasurable effects produced by the drug, such as the "buzz" obtained from having a beer.

Most addictive drugs can produce both positive and aversive effects, depending to some extent on the time phase after drug intake. During drug intake, and in the minutes to hours afterward, the drug enters the bloodstream and reaches the brain, increasing to levels that produce a characteristic profile of intoxicating effects. These effects may include changes in thinking, perception, attention, memory, or mood, and often involve some sense of pleasure such as a feeling of euphoria. Bodily effects may also occur, including changes in heart rate, blood pressure, and motor activity. According to the positive reinforcement view of addiction, repeated drug use occurs because of a desire to attain the drug-induced euphoric effects.

At some more distant time after drug intake, the body begins to make progress in the breakdown and elimination of the substance so that the brain levels of the drug begin to fall and soon return to zero. During this phase, commonly known as withdrawal, other mental and bodily effects of the drug use can emerge, many of which are opposite from those experienced during intoxication. Often this includes a loss or reversal of the initial pleasurable effects, leading to a general feeling of displeasure called dysphoria. According to the negative reinforcement view of addiction, repeated drug use occurs because of a desire to alleviate the dysphoric withdrawal effects caused by previous drug intake.

Tolerance and sensitization

Since most addictive drugs are associated with both euphoric and dysphoric effects, both positive and negative reinforcement might simultaneously contribute to the process of addiction. However, their relative contributions may differ depending on the stage of the addiction process and the phenomena of tolerance and sensitization. In tolerance, repeated intake of the same drug and dose produces a progressive decrease in certain drug effects. For example, regular drinkers usually require more drinks to feel the effects of alcohol than occasional drinkers. Because individuals often experience tolerance to the euphoric effects of addictive drugs, drug users who are becoming addicted are observed to take drugs in progressively greater doses to attain the same level of positive reinforcement. Eventually, even very high doses of the drug or near continuous intake no longer produce the same level of euphoric effects, suggesting that the importance of positive reinforcement in maintaining drug use decreases with progressive addiction. In sensitization, repeated intake of the same drug and dose produces a progressive increase in certain drug effects. Often, sensitization occurs with respect to the aversive effects of drugs encountered in withdrawal such that with continued drug use, a period of withdrawal becomes increasingly uncomfortable. This observation suggests that the importance of negative reinforcement in maintaining drug intake might increase with progressive addiction.

Effects on the brain

The recognition of tolerance and sensitization as important features of the process of addiction has influenced brain research and new theories about the nature of addiction. Abused drugs produce a whole array of physical effects in the brain that change the way brain cells (neurons) communicate information. These changes are seen as alterations in several areas, including expression of the genetic code inside neurons that programs for cell form and function; molecules (receptors) inside and on the surface of neurons involved in detecting and acting on chemical messengers of information; the electrical signaling and energy consumption properties of neurons and groups of neurons; the release of interneuronal chemical messengers (neurotransmitters); and the number and shape of neuron parts, such as axons, dendrites, and synapses, involved in interneuronal communication. Some of these brain changes occur temporarily during drug intake to produce the characteristic intoxicating effects of the drug, or during the withdrawal phase, while others represent more permanent alterations; the more permanent changes are termed *neuroplastic*. Because of the highly adaptive nature of brain tissue, most of these changes are corrected; however, with repeated drug intake the more permanent alterations become increasingly irreversible and accumulate until an individual response to drugs or other drug-related behaviors has been greatly changed. Both tolerance and sensitization have been linked with many of these drug-induced brain alterations, and to the extent that they involve progressive changes in response to repeated drug intake, they represent signs of the more permanent alterations. However, many of the essential features of drug addiction are not fully explained by the concepts of positive and negative reinforcement, and tolerance and sensitization as described above, suggesting that theories about how drug-induced neuroplasticity causes addiction require further development.

Different types of addictive drugs have different intoxication and withdrawal effects, and in some cases, such as with cocaine and opiates, the effects are quite opposite. In addition, the particular forms of tolerance and sensitization characteristically observed with each type of drug may differ substantially. These differences are attributed to the unique molecular structures of each of the abused drugs, which cause them to act in a variety of ways on neuronal receptors, neurons, and alternate brain regions. Since addiction is a common disorder produced by these different drugs, the process of addiction should encompass brain effects that these drugs have in common, rather than their divergent properties.

A common brain effect attributable to all known addictive drugs is that they cause release of the neurotransmitter dopamine into a deep brain region called the nucleus accumbens. Dopamine release into the nucleus accumbens is also important in the maintenance and control of natural motivations, including desire for food, sex, and other resources and activities important to living. Together, these findings provide very strong evidence that drug addiction involves a common action of substances in particular brain circuits involved in motivation. Another key observation is that laboratory animals display locomotor sensitization when given one of a variety of addictive drugs. With repeated daily intake of the same drug and dose, animals will move around more vigorously and for longer periods on each successive day after they receive the drug. The brain systems involved with the initiation and control of motor activity in locomotor sensitization also involve dopamine release and are anatomically connected with and structurally similar to the nucleus accumbens. These observations suggest that addiction may be viewed as a sensitization of motivational processes caused by the repeated action of addictive drugs on dopamine-related systems producing long-term neuroplastic effects in the nucleus accumbens and related brain regions. The sensitization of motivation in drug-addicted individuals corresponds to the increasing desire for and activity spent acquiring and using the drug, at the expense of other natural motivations and activities necessary for healthy living. As an individual's motivations are increasingly dominated by drug use, he or she experiences a sense of loss of free will to stop using,

and begins to accumulate what might become a long list of medical and psychological injuries, potentially leading to death.

Persistence of addiction

The concept of addiction as a drug-induced form of sensitization in brain motivation systems accounts for several important observations about human addiction not fully addressed by traditional notions of positive and negative reinforcement associated with drug intoxication and withdrawal. It is generally observed that once advanced addiction has occurred, the motivational effects of the drug, that is, the desire for the drug, persist for months and years after the last drug use. This persistent desire, commonly called craving, continues and often increases long after the individual has suffered through drug withdrawal and its associated aversive effects. Drug craving and associated triggers, such as the environmental stimuli that remind the addict of prior drug use and produce intense craving, are the major cause of relapse to drug use in recovering addicts. Craving is often experienced as a more powerful motivation for returning to drug use than the desire to attain the pleasurable intoxicating effects of the drug itself, which in many cases of advanced addiction has greatly diminished.

The recognition of long-term craving as a factor in advanced addiction and persistent risk of relapse is supported by observations that short-term medication and psychological treatments used to specifically treat the aversive symptoms during drug withdrawal or the psychological state of the individual in early abstinence have little proven benefits for long-term recovery. Current research on understanding and treating addiction focuses on how drug-induced neuroplasticity in motivation systems produces long-term craving and how new medications or psychological treatments might correct these effects.

R. A. CHAMBERS

Addictive Behavior

The behaviors associated with addiction are the result of an escalating need to take a drug or repeat an activity. Although the individual may know that the behavior is unhealthy, he or she feels unable to resist its repetition.

Addiction can lead an individual to behave in ways that are inappropriate and irresponsible, such as drinking alcohol while at work or while operating machinery.

According to many researchers, an individual may become addicted to any activity, substance, object, or behavior from which he or she derives pleasure. Typically, most addictions begin with the repetition of an initially rewarding behavior, such as drinking alcohol. If the individual continues to find the activity rewarding, the behavior may become a habit. While habitual behavior is by definition repeated, it is normally not the main focus for the individual, and it is rarely associated with significant personal cost if discontinued. However, if a person finds himself or herself saying "I should stop this, but I feel compelled to continue," then the behavior is more likely to be compulsive in nature.

Addiction differs from compulsion in that it inevitably escalates. Even though a person understands that a certain behavior is excessive, such as drinking too much alcohol, he or she feels driven to repeat it and is unable to stop the behavior. As the addiction process continues, the person feels less able to control his or her behavior, resulting in increasing personal costs. The completion of the behavior gradually becomes more important than other activities, and the behavior is pursued despite various conflicting interests, as in the case of someone drinking in the evening rather than studying for an exam. As the addiction progresses, the negative consequences, such as problems with schoolwork and physical and mental health problems, increase. The addicted individual is forced to choose between continuation of his or her valued behavior and significant family, social, medical, and legal costs. It is this conflict—between wanting to continue the behavior and knowing that one should not—that is the core feature of addictive behavior.

The root of the term *addiction* comes from the Latin *addicere*, which means "to enslave." This enslavement is inherently damaging, as it is invariably related to significant physical, psychological, or social harms. The term *addiction* is used widely throughout society but is mostly applied in a pejorative sense, implying social disapproval. However, the scope of addictions and addictive behaviors is much wider than that suggested by the stereotypical portrayal of an addict—an alcoholic lying in the gutter or a junkie stealing to get his or her next fix. Instead, addictive behavior may encompass a range of habits and compulsions.

Models of addiction

While most people broadly agree on what addictive behavior involves, there is a lack of consensus regarding a unifying model of addiction, in part due to the differing ideas about addiction within medical, social, economic, and political settings. Its definition varies widely and in relation to the conceptual model proposed. For many centuries, addiction was viewed as sinful or demonic behavior and, as such, a sign of a lack of moral character. This moral model of addiction highlighted personal responsibility in choosing to continue an addictive behavior, such as repeated drunkenness, and emphasized that punishment was a justifiable intervention for addressing this violation of social norms.

The temperance model arose from the prohibition movement in the late nineteenth century. The emphasis was not on the individual but on the drug, highlighting the destructive and addictive properties of substances. The movement declared that moderation was impossible, and abstinence was the only alternative. These ideas formed the underlying ideology of the Prohibition era in the United States during the 1920s, when it was illegal to produce or consume alcohol in bars.

Following the repeal of Prohibition in 1933, and in keeping with contemporary advances in medicine, an alternative model based on a disease perspective was adopted. This disease model, first advocated in the work of Benjamin Rush in the 1800s, viewed addiction as a progressive, irreversible, relapsing medical disease that could be arrested but not cured by lifelong abstinence.

With the founding of Alcoholics Anonymous (AA) in 1935, an alternative spiritual model emerged that emphasized the acknowledgment that an addicted individual is powerless over his or her drinking. Drinkers must seek some other force that is stronger than both themselves and their addiction, such as the belief in a higher power and the support of others.

This ongoing debate regarding terminology led the World Health Organization (WHO) to propose abolishing the term *addiction* in 1964. Instead, WHO introduced the term *drug dependence* to encompass both the physical and psychological aspects of problematic substance use. This concept of addictive behavior is incorporated within modern diagnostic classifications (*see* table on p. 18). Under this definition, drug dependence is viewed as a disorder, and dependence on a substance is considered a valid medical diagnosis. Within this illness model, prolonged use of drugs of abuse can lead to both physical and psychological dependence. Physical dependence is characterized by the need to take increasing amounts of the drug in order to get the same subjective effect as before (such as needing to drink more to feel relaxed) together with the experience of a withdrawal syndrome when drug use ceases. Psychological dependence is characterized by intense cravings, compulsive drug-seeking, and drug-taking, with an apparent loss of control over these behaviors. For the addicted individual, these behaviors become all-consuming, leading to the progressive neglect of alternative interests as the time spent obtaining, using, or recovering from drugs increases.

Although physical and psychological dependence commonly co-occur in chronic substance users, it is possible to be physically dependent on a drug without being psychologically dependent, and vice versa. For example, problem behaviors, such as gambling, may produce psychological dependence without an associated physical component. Although the present classification of dependence is an important and useful concept, it fails to account fully for all the various manifestations of addictive behavior.

Over the past few decades, a neurobiological model of addiction has been proposed, based on genetic and psychological investigations of addictive processes in animals and humans. This model uses a variety of sophisticated imaging techniques to see how drugs impact the brain. More recently, an integrated model has developed that attempts to incorporate aspects from a variety of theoretical perspectives. This biopsychosocial model emphasizes that biological, psychological, social, and cultural factors are all important when considering a comprehensive model of addiction, and that clinicians should assess these different areas when considering appropriate interventions for individuals with addictive disorders.

Is there an addictive personality?

While there remains support in some settings for the idea of an addictive personality—that is, a specific dysfunctional personality type that inevitably leads to the adoption of certain types of addictive behaviors—extensive research over the past 50 years has

---

CRITERIA USED FOR DIAGNOSING SUBSTANCE DEPENDENCE

A maladaptive pattern of substance use, leading to clinically significant impairment or distress, as manifested by three (or more) of the following, occurring at any time in the same 12-month period:

- Tolerance (as defined by: a need for markedly increased amounts of the substance to achieve intoxication or desired effect; or, markedly diminished effect with continued use of same amount of the substance).

- Withdrawal (as defined by: characteristic substance-specific withdrawal syndrome; or, the same substance is taken to relieve or avoid withdrawal symptoms).

- Substance is often taken in larger amounts or over a longer period than was intended.

- There is a persistent desire or unsuccessful efforts to cut down or control substance use.

- Considerable time is spent in activities necessary to obtain or use the substance, or to recover from its effects.

- Important social, occupational, or recreational activities are given up or reduced because of substance use.

- Continued use despite knowledge of persistent or recurrent adverse consequences.

The American Psychiatric Association's criteria for defining dependence on a substance are found in the fourth edition of the *Diagnostic and Statistical Manual of Mental Disorders* (DSM-IV).

failed to provide any evidence for its existence. In 1987, the Royal College of Psychiatrists in the United Kingdom concluded that "the best evidence is that no single underlying trait or unique constellation of personality features can be identified as predisposing to drug misuse." There appears to be some support, however, for antisocial and perhaps anxiety traits as factors in addictive behaviors. In addition, there is evidence for an increased risk of addiction among individuals with certain personality traits, such as impulsiveness, shyness with strangers, and fear of uncertainty, and certain behavioral tendencies, such as sensation-seeking and risk-taking.

Causes of addictive behaviors

The cause of addictive behaviors is a complex area that requires consideration of genetic, family, psychological, sociocultural, and economic factors. One of the key environmental factors that has a major impact on the incidence of addictive behaviors is availability. There is a proven relationship between cost, legal constraints, income, drug accessibility, and drug consumption. In this regard, governments have a key role in determining acceptability and availability of certain behaviors through advertising, taxation, and legislation. Cultural factors are also critical in terms of prevailing attitudes toward drug use. For example, ritualized use of alcohol in Jewish culture is thought to help to explain the low rates of alcohol-related problems in the community, whereas high rates of alcoholism in the Irish community are thought to relate to alcohol's principal role within social settings in which refusing a drink, for example, may be considered an insult. Other cultural risk factors include disenfranchised indigenous groups, with increased rates of addiction related to disconnection from their traditional cultural values and associated community dysfunction.

Social factors implicated in the development of addictive behaviors include heightened levels of stress, trauma, and alienation within society. Peer influence is also suggested to be a key factor in initiating substance use, especially in adolescence. A number of other variables are also thought to be

Gambling is a potentially addictive activity. Sufferers of gambling addiction experience an overwhelming need to repeat this activity that is similar to the need for drugs experienced by substance addicts.

important factors, including genetic risk (family studies have shown that risk of alcoholism is substantially increased among relatives of alcoholics); cognitive deficits, such as poor attention and inhibitory control; psychological problems, such as anxiety or depression; and certain personality traits (as discussed above).

Research into the effects of substance use on adolescent brain development has suggested that behavioral responses to acute drug use in adolescents are different from those in adults. For example, adolescents experience less sedation with alcohol compared with adults, but they are more sensitive to the damaging toxic effects of drugs on the nervous system. These differing effects on brain function have significant implications for the maturation of emotional and cognitive control systems, as well as for the development of future dysfunction. Recent brain imaging studies have demonstrated that specific brain regions, especially within the frontal

parts of the brain, are directly affected by long-term exposure to drugs of abuse. In particular, two frontal regions have been implicated, the anterior cingulate cortex and orbitofrontal cortex, both of which are critically involved in regulating and preventing potentially harmful behaviors. Dysfunction within these regions has been proposed as a key mechanism underlying addiction, although as yet it is unclear whether these brain abnormalities are related to an underlying vulnerability to develop addictive behaviors or are largely a consequence of the addictive process.

Animal models have demonstrated that drugs of abuse act on a specific brain system that encourages behaviors leading to rewards such as water, food, and sex, and thus promotes behaviors that sustain life. Activation of this reward system results in the experience of pleasure and leads to further motivation to continue the associated behavior. However, artificial rewards, such as drugs of abuse, also activate this system, and with repeated drug use, the reward system responds so overwhelmingly that the behavior is powerfully reinforced (encouraged), and the individual continues this unhealthy behavior. Nondrug addictive behaviors, such as problematic eating and gambling, may also involve similar mechanisms.

Addictive behavior is characterized by a pre-occupation with an activity, such as gambling, or a substance, such as alcohol, with subsequent lack of interest in other activities. As his or her addiction progresses, the addicted individual places an increasingly greater priority on this behavior, often to the detriment of important work or interpersonal relationships. The person may become abusive, defensive, and aggressive toward the environment and anything or anyone who interferes with the successful pursuit of the obsession. For some, this may result in recurrent legal problems and sometimes incarceration. In addition, significant cravings may develop, as well as a recurrent compulsive pattern of engaging in the behavior, to the point that the addicted individual appears to have lost control. Often he or she will deny any associated problems or consequences of his or her behavior, even though the negative effects are clear to everyone else. If the individual does decide to abstain from the behavior, withdrawal symptoms often occur.

Factors that sustain addiction

It has been suggested that a number of factors—including biological, psychological, and sociocultural factors—maintain addictive behavior. Any unresolved issue that initially led to the development of an addiction, such as depression or family dysfunction, that has not been adequately addressed may maintain the behavior. Distinct psychological and neurobiological factors have also been implicated in the maintenance of addictive processes.

Drugs of abuse increase the probability of a particular response and influence ongoing behavior by hijacking the natural reward system of the brain. In addition, through the development of physical dependence, a further incentive to continue drug use is the avoidance or relief of painful or unpleasant states, such as withdrawal or anxiety. Although withdrawal is rarely fatal, it is often extremely uncomfortable and severe enough to become a major hurdle for many drug users. Avoidance of withdrawal symptoms may become a powerful motivation to continue drug

use. Furthermore, with repeated substance use, neuroadaptations (changes in brain activity) occur within distinct brain regions. In their incentive-sensitization theory, Terry Robinson and Kent Berridge at the University of Michigan propose that chronic drug use leads to neuroadaptations in the brain's reward system, rendering it sensitized, that is, over-responsive to drugs and stimuli associated with drug use, such as drug equipment or environments. They propose that with ongoing drug use, drug-related stimuli (cues) become increasingly influential and are able to induce excessive drug craving. In support of this model, drug cues have been shown to significantly increase activity within the brain's reward system in animal models and to produce craving in addicted individuals.

Conclusions

There is a lack of consensus among models that describe the cause of addictive behavior. No definitive treatment currently exists, and clinically addiction is managed as a chronic relapsing disorder. Consequently, a significant international research effort has focused on understanding the mechanisms underlying addictive behavior, as well as improving treatment and prevention strategies. What is clear is that some drugs appear to be more addictive in certain societies or environments, in certain individuals, and at certain times. Addiction is therefore a complex and multifaceted condition involving both internal factors, such as genetics, neurochemistry, learning, and personality, and external factors, such as the environment, culture, spirituality, and economics. Addictive behaviors interweave physical, neurobiological, psychological, and social components that are uniquely blended in each affected individual. Therefore, all addicted individuals must be treated as unique, and their own particular needs and vulnerabilities must be appropriately identified and addressed.

M. YÜCEL, D. LUBMAN

Adolescents and Substance Abuse

Adolescence is a time during which individuals may be particularly vulnerable to abusing substances. Peer pressure, feelings of loneliness, and having parents who use substances may all influence a young person to try drugs.

Use of alcohol and drugs is typically presented as a problem rooted in an individual's lack of will power or other personal or family deficits. Yet there are national trends in the rates of use of different substances, types of substances, and subgroups who are at risk that strongly suggest that the likelihood of drug use depends on when an adolescent was born, where he or she lives, with whom he or she spends time, and how many community resources and jobs are available.

National trends

Drug use comes in waves, with rhythmic increases and decreases over time. In the United States the popularity of heroin in the 1920s was followed by marijuana in the 1930s and heroin again in the 1950s. The rates of illicit drug use rose steadily through the mid-1960s and early 1970s, with a diversification in the range of substances available. Rates of substance use varied substantially in different regions of the country. Use of all illicit drugs was at its highest in 1979, with overall marijuana use increasing dramatically. These rates were associated with a rise in student protests, an endorsement of liberal lifestyles, and a greater acceptance of drug use (especially of marijuana) by both adults and young people. A decrease in use followed the peak rates of 1979 until 1992; 1992 reflected the lowest annual rate of any illicit drug use in the United States. Overall drug use steadily increased again until 1997, followed by gradual decline but with substantial variations according to substance.

An ongoing annual survey carried out by the University of Michigan (*Monitoring the Future*) tracks drug usage rates and perception of risk for 8th, 10th, and 12th graders in the United States. The survey is conducted anonymously and is designed to gain a clear overview of adolescent drug trends, identify dangerous drug usage and addiction, and ascertain the need for treatment. Results from the 2010 survey reveal that adolescent use of a variety of illicit drugs increased in the previous year. For adolescents there has also been a decline in the mean age of initial drug use, more adolescents were trying drugs earlier, and the drug use rates for boys and girls were similar (whereas reports prior to 2002 showed differences in the rate of illicit substance use for male and female adolescents).

Types of drugs and their use among adolescents

Since 1975, the medical health profession has documented studies proving the harmful effects of cigarette smoking and smokeless tobacco. According to the 2010 survey 42 percent of 12th graders have tried cigarettes and nearly 11 percent are daily users. Long-term alcohol abuse leads to liver damage and lowered inhibitions that may lead to risky or dangerous behavior (drug use, unsafe sex, driving while intoxicated, and so on). About 70 percent of 12th graders have used alcohol and more than half have been drunk, while 35 percent of 8th graders have used alcohol and 16 percent have been drunk at least once.

Marijuana is the most commonly and widely used illegal drug by adolescents. Though marijuana usage among adolescents does not necessarily signify use or future use of harder drugs, marijuana has come to be understood as a gateway drug. A gateway drug is perceived as a less harmful drug that leads the user to try more harmful illegal substances. In 1979, 50 percent of 12th graders used marijuana, but overall usage declined after a brief surge in the 1990s. The majority of students in high school report that marijuana is easy to acquire if they want it, making it the most accessible illicit drug.

Inhalants are readily available and easily purchased by younger adolescents. Inhalant usage tends to decrease with age due to the availability of other, stronger drugs that become more desirable. Inhalant usage has dropped substantially since a peak in the 1990s, more so among older adolescents.

Ecstasy began to be widely used in the 1980s and its use increased in the mid-1990s; its use subsequently dropped slightly and then rose dramatically at the end of the century. In the early 2000s this club drug dropped in use, reflecting an increased fear of the damage it can cause, but it registered increasing popularity in 2010. Ecstasy is called a club drug because it is widely used at concerts, dance parties, clubs, and bars. Some side effects of Ecstasy are hallucinations, high blood pressure, increased heart rate, dehydration, and sometimes death. During the period 2000 to 2003, an increase in the use of tranquilizers emerged, with use by 8th and 10th graders increasing in 2010 over 2009.

Adolescents living in rural environments reported an increased likelihood of abusing or being dependent on drugs. Rural adolescents have also shown a greater likelihood of alcohol consumption and drunkenness among 8th graders than urban youth; higher rates of all drugs except marijuana and Ecstasy for 10th graders; and usage exceeding the rate of 12th grade urban adolescents for cocaine, inhalants, crack, amphetamines, and

cigarettes. Reports also reveal greater ease in acquiring marijuana in rural environments. However, overall illicit drug abuse and dependency for all persons above the age of 12 is higher in urban areas. Urban and low-income inner-city environments exhibit wide distribution rates and are the primary markets for many major drugs. Individuals living in urban environments are more likely to try any illicit drug than those individuals living in more rural areas.

School transitions are key time points for the initiation of drug use; whether a school district has a junior high school or goes from elementary to high school will influence the rate of substance use. For example, if the transition from grade school to high school is between 8th and 9th grade, the rate of alcohol use will jump dramatically during that transition. If there is a transition to junior high at 7th grade, initiation is likely to be earlier.

Runaway and homeless adolescents are at risk for drug and alcohol abuse. There are approximately

During adolescence the need to be accepted by one's peers is very important. Fear of rejection may place pressure upon a young person to accept drugs that they might otherwise refuse.

733,000 to 1.2 million runaway adolescents in the United States, and approximately 5 percent of all adolescents between the ages of 12 and 17 are homeless nationwide. Homeless and runaway adolescents are most common in major cities but are located throughout the country, with diverse ethnic backgrounds and multiple health and behavior problems. Substance use can be a factor in becoming a runaway or homeless adolescent, with an increase in risk of substance use once an adolescent leaves or is forced to leave home. Homeless and runaway youth are also at risk of prostitution or drug trafficking in order to feed or shelter themselves while on the streets, increasing their risk of sexually transmitted diseases through unprotected sex or intravenous drug use.

Patterns of use

Substance use varies by year and region of the country, and the consequences of substance use are linked to the types of drug used. It is therefore clear that developmental factors have a substantial impact on individual patterns of use. Since the 1970s, substance use has followed a pattern: young people typically start with alcohol and move to drugs they consider to be less harmful. There is also a different sequence in the initiation of use that a few young people move through, using a more serious drug than the one they initially used. The sequence is: alcohol use, marijuana, amphetamines, club drugs, barbiturates, heroin, and injection. The age of initiation is older for each drug in the sequence, and fewer young people use the drugs the further they go in the sequence. Only about 2 percent of adolescents ever inject any drug.

Not all adolescents try drugs, but all adolescents are exposed to substances and will probably be offered an illegal substance at some point during adolescence. The types of illegal substances, the frequency of the offers, and the pressure to use drugs vary based on environmental and developmental factors.

Misperceptions of peer norms

Many adolescents think that their peers are using far more drugs than they actually are. Young people's misperceptions of their peers' behaviors act as a disinhibitor of their own behavior. The most effective substance abuse prevention programs provide accurate knowledge of the percentage of young people using substances and the frequency of use.

Peer pressure and influence

For adolescents, fitting in with peers is very important; school life can be difficult if one is judged for one's choice of friends or activities. Having little ability in sports, being overweight, or wearing braces might place adolescents at risk of being picked on or rejected by their peers. Fear of peer rejection may lead adolescents to accept a drug when offered, because they believe that their peers will think they are as cool if they try it. Low self-esteem places adolescents at risk of substance abuse; without confidence and satisfaction with themselves, adolescents may try drugs without concern for their own well-being.

Feeling alone and depressed

The physiological changes accompanying puberty significantly increase the probability that adolescents feel depressed and anxious, particularly girls. The emerging independence of a physically mature youth who is financially, legally, and emotionally dependent on parents often elicits conflict. Parents and adolescents often perceive their conflicts as emerging from intra- and interpersonal differences when, in fact, normal developmental processes are unfolding. Such processes increase risk for both depression and problem behaviors. The desire to feel better about themselves and forget their problems can encourage young people to experiment with drugs in an attempt to bury their negative feelings. Some experts contend that adolescents are self-medicating when using nonprescription drugs.

Parent who uses drugs or alcohol

If children have a parent who uses a drug, the adult has demonstrated that substance use is acceptable. The probability of substance use therefore increases if the parent uses. The relationship an adolescent has with his or her parents plays a crucial role in his or her potential for risky behavior and drug use. If adolescents are able to talk to their parents and parents are open and honest with their children, the risk of their children using drugs is lower than for those who do not have such a relationship with their parents. It can be difficult to talk to parents about drugs and what they do to the body and mind, but honest interaction between parents and adolescents concerning drugs will allow a safe environment to voice questions and gain valuable information. These talks can help adolescents make educated decisions about whether or not to try drugs or associate with other adolescents who use illegal substances.

Unstructured time

Because adolescents are free from the adult responsibilities of having a job and supporting themselves and a family, there is a large amount of free time available to them aside from school. Adolescents who are bored with doing the same thing after school and on weekends, such as watching TV or hanging out in the neighborhood, may turn to drugs as an escape from the monotony and predictability they experience on a daily basis. The most effective parental response to decrease their children's drug use is to actively monitor their time, friends, and activities.

Stages of drug use

There are various stages of drug use that indicate the level of abuse taking place in an adolescent life. Experimentation or recreational use is infrequent and most often done with other adolescents and is not necessarily an indicator of long-term use. Regular use includes a heightened tolerance for drugs and an increase in the amount of drugs used to reach the high first achieved during experimentation; it may lead to use of harder drugs. Daily use requires even more of the drug to reach a desired effect and often leads to use of harder drugs and drug abuse, problems in school, distance from family members and friends, and can include infractions with the law (possible arrest). This process may finally lead to drug dependency, when the adolescent needs drugs to function in daily life, has heightened paranoia, exhibits a high level of denial when confronted with evidence of abuse, and will probably begin to use harder drugs. This stage of drug use is consistent with drug abuse and drug addiction, and frequently abusers exhibit high levels of depression, suicidal thoughts, familial alienation, and risk behaviors such as unsafe (unprotected or nonconsensual) sex.

Drugs vary in their effects on humans, depending on the quantity introduced into the body, the desired outcome (effective dose in terms of the proper use of the drug), a toxic amount (negative side effects) or a lethal amount (overdose). The stronger the dose (amount of the drug taken in) and the greater the concentration level of a drug, the greater the risks of negative side effects and overdose. Injecting a drug into the body by way of a blood vein accelerates the delivery of the drug into the body. Sharing needles increases the risk of contracting and transmitting diseases, such as HIV, AIDS, and hepatitis.

Drug addiction is a physical and psychological condition; the human brain is altered by the use of drugs. The user craves the drug and is dependent on it, regardless of negative outcomes. An addicted person compulsively searches out drugs. Someone who is addicted to drugs has a chronic (habitual or routine) health problem that will most often cause them to relapse if they try to stop using drugs without help. Some individuals may try a drug a few times without becoming addicted and have no negative consequences, while another individual may try a drug only once and become addicted or suffer permanent damage to their motor and cognitive skills.

Treatment

Detoxification (detox) is the initial phase users experience once they stop taking drugs. During this period, an addicted person stops taking a drug and allows the body to remove or run out of the toxic substance that has been taken in. Withdrawal is a result of detox; the body craves the drug it has become dependent upon. Detox can result in cold flashes, vomiting, stomach pain, headaches, diarrhea, restlessness, and bone and muscle pain. These symptoms can persist from days to weeks, depending on the drug. Detoxification alone is not proven as a successful method of treatment; a long-term substance abuse treatment program is also necessary to assist those who want to quit and succeed.

Deciding to stop taking drugs, seeking help, and participating in a treatment program are proven more effective than quitting the drugs without the assistance of substance abuse treatment. Treatment combined with the absence of drugs in the body is a successful method of avoiding drug-use relapse. Substance abuse treatment programs help a drug user decrease the chances of further damage to the body and help an addict live a more normal, drug-free life.

Drug treatment for adolescents can be successful if the program is designed for their age group, involves their family, is accepted by their community,

Young teenagers may be influenced by older friends to smoke and drink alcohol. Learning how to resist offers of cigarettes and alcohol can have a positive effect in preventing use of harder drugs.

lifestyles, drug abuse hotlines, and outpatient clinics for anyone who needs them.

Approximately 19 percent of secondary schools in the United States employ drug testing for their student body, but research shows that the rates of drug use were identical to the rates at schools without a drug testing policy. Schools will often improve their academic achievement and decrease adolescent drug use if peer groups openly discuss the dangers of drugs with each other and their teachers or counselors. A setting that offers support and treatment will increase the chances of adolescents and teens staying away from and ceasing the intake of illicit substances. Treatment services that are easily available and cater to this specific age group have a greater rate of success.

Treatment programs that prevent drug use are available in many different formats and are accessible for all ages. Asking for help is the first step to freeing oneself from addiction and drugs. This is a very difficult step to take because there are strong fears of being perceived as weak or a failure. A doctor, school counselor, parent, or friend can help an adolescent find the right prevention program. Treatment should also meet the needs of an adolescent whose drug use began as a means of coping with depression, loneliness, or other stressful situations. Adolescents with multiple life stressors, such as mental illness, homelessness, and history of sexual abuse, will require additional services focusing on these issues in addition to substance abuse treatment.

After they stop taking drugs, addicted adolescents will initially still find themselves in situations that invite drug use. Going to a friend's house after school, hanging out at the mall, or going to a party on a Saturday night may create a risk of relapse. Adolescents and teens can gain valuable coping skills through treatment programs that will help them maneuver safely through tough or tempting environments without giving in to drug use. In addition to treatment, the support of family and friends will decrease the risk of relapse and promote healthy, drug-free behavior.

A. ELKAVICH, M. J. ROTHERAM-BORUS

and is acknowledged by their school. A program that caters to adolescents and teenagers will focus on the struggles adolescents will inevitably encounter in various environments and social situations. Substance abuse treatment programs can focus on one specific drug (heroin only) or encompass treatment for a number of drugs (alcohol, inhalants, cocaine, and so on). Most often, treatment will include valuable tools to help adolescents and teens gain a positive attitude about keeping themselves off drugs, strengthening family relationships, and learning how to decline drugs when offered. Parents who learn about the drugs to which their adolescents and teens are addicted can help clarify the negative effects of the drugs and can better lend support during tough situations. Community involvement can entail a media campaign promoting drug-free

SEE ALSO:
Children • Drug Use, Life Patterns • Gateway Drugs • Peer Influence

Alcoholics Anonymous

Alcoholics Anonymous (AA) is a worldwide mutual-help organization dedicated to individuals seeking relief from drinking problems. Since its beginnings in the 1930s, AA has grown to include groups in more than 150 countries.

Alcoholics Anonymous (AA) meetings are where people with drinking problems come together to help one another abstain from alcohol. According to the organization, AA is "a fellowship of men and women who share their experience, strength, and hope with each other that they may solve their common problem and help others to recover from alcoholism. The only requirement for membership is a desire to stop drinking....Our primary purpose is to stay sober and help other alcoholics to achieve sobriety."

History

AA was founded in Akron, Ohio, in 1935, as the outgrowth of a meeting between Bill W., a New York stockbroker, and Dr. Bob S., an Akron surgeon (as part of the tradition of anonymity, the founders are referred to only by their first name and the initial of their surname). Bill had recently achieved sobriety and Dr. Bob was still drinking when the pair first met. Together they recognized the value and importance of a mutual-help approach to alcoholism, and the organization grew from that point.

The basic text of AA is a book entitled *Alcoholics Anonymous* (known in AA as "the Big Book"). Written by Bill and first published in 1939, it outlines AA's philosophy and methods. The second core text used in AA is *Twelve Steps and Twelve Traditions*. Published in 1953, this volume provides interpretations of principles of personal recovery from alcoholism. AA also publishes a wide variety

Sharing experiences with a group of other alcoholics is a key method to recovery in AA. Some meetings are open to everyone, while others are limited to people willing to introduce themselves as alcoholics.

TABLE 1: THE TWELVE STEPS OF ALCOHOLICS ANONYMOUS

Step 1	We admitted we were powerless over alcohol—that our lives had become unmanageable.
Step 2	Came to believe that a Power greater than ourselves could restore us to sanity.
Step 3	Made a decision to turn our will and our lives over to the care of God as we understood Him.
Step 4	Made a searching and fearless moral inventory of ourselves.
Step 5	Admitted to God, to ourselves, and to another human being the exact nature of our wrongs.
Step 6	Were entirely ready to have God remove all these defects of character.
Step 7	Humbly asked Him to remove our shortcomings.
Step 8	Made a list of all persons we had harmed, and became willing to make amends to them all.
Step 9	Made direct amends to such people when possible, except wherever to do so would injure them or others.
Step 10	Continued to take personal inventory and when we were wrong promptly admitted it.
Step 11	Sought through prayer and meditation to improve our conscious contact with God as we understood Him, praying only for knowledge of His will for us and the power to carry that out.
Step 12	Having had a spiritual awakening as the result of these steps, we tried to carry this message to alcoholics and to practice these principles in all our affairs.

Source: Alcoholics Anonymous (1976).

---

of pamphlets designed to help people understand what AA does and to provide information to particular interest groups, such as older alcoholics, members of the clergy and armed services, and people in correctional facilities. A more detailed account of the history of AA can be found in the book *Not-God: A History of Alcoholics Anonymous* by the historian Ernest Kurtz.

The growth of AA since 1935 has been remarkable. There are more than 100,000 AA groups worldwide (around 50 percent are in the United States), and membership exceeds 2,000,000 people.

Basic principles

The AA program is built around the working of the Twelve Steps, which present a sequential plan for recovery from alcoholism. The first step entails admitting powerlessness over alcohol. This step is followed by belief in a power greater than oneself that can restore balance to one's life (often referred to as a Higher Power, which for many AA members is God). Later steps deal with such matters as conducting a moral inventory, making amends to people harmed by one's drinking, engaging in prayer and meditation to improve conscious contact with

one's Higher Power, and, in Step 12, practicing these steps in all of one's affairs and carrying the message of the Twelve Steps to others. All twelve steps are detailed in Table 1 *(above)*.

Traditionally, the working of the steps is accomplished with the aid of a sponsor, who is an AA member who has already worked through the Twelve Steps. This one-to-one service helps the individual to practice "step-work," which is considered to be a life-long process. In addition to these programmatic aspects, AA places strong emphasis on the fellowship of the program. Fellowship refers to the experiencing of the program and includes helping others, building relationships, and sharing the joys and hardships associated with the recovery process. The guiding principles for fellowship are stated in the Twelve Traditions (*see* Table 2, p. 29).

The AA meeting

There are a number of aspects common to all AA meetings. The meeting typically lasts about one hour, usually in rented space in a building or in a place of religious worship. Meetings often open with a reading of the Serenity Prayer, which goes as follows: "God, grant me the serenity to accept the things

I cannot change, the courage to change the things I can, and the wisdom to know the difference." The prayer is followed by a reading from the Big Book.

A chairperson guides the meeting. This role is typically rotated among the group's membership on either a daily or weekly basis. Attendees who are visiting or who are newcomers to the group will introduce themselves, using their first name only. In some cases, they will identify themselves as an alcoholic ("Hi. My name is John, and I'm an alcoholic."). Members introduce themselves by their first name only to retain anonymity. Anonymity is important not only to protect an individual from the stigma that may be attached to alcoholism, but also to discourage any possible desire for personal recognition that could impair the effectiveness of AA. This tradition of anonymity therefore extends to members dealing with the media.

During each meeting, a basket for donations is passed around, and those in attendance can give or not, as they wish. AA groups are entirely self-supporting and do not accept external funds. Individual members, however, may not contribute more than $2,000 per year.

A noteworthy aspect of AA meetings is that they are not open discussion groups. Cross talk, such as a group discussion or commenting on experiences unrelated to alcoholism, is strongly discouraged. Most meetings close with a recitation of *The Lord's Prayer*, typically with group members holding hands in a circle.

Different kinds of meetings

Within the basic structure, AA meetings follow a wide variety of formats. Probably the most common distinction is between an open and a closed meeting. As the term suggests, open meetings can be attended by any individual, whether they have a drinking problem or not. Closed meetings are available only to those individuals who are willing to introduce themselves as alcoholic if called on to share their history of drinking during the meeting.

Whether open or closed, AA meetings can use several formats. In discussion meetings, participants are asked to share their experiences, generally in the context of a particular topic (such as gratitude, or a reading from the core AA literature). At speaker meetings, one or several members will tell their stories. The recommended format for such storytelling is to describe life before membership in AA, what led to joining AA, and what life is like now as a result of membership in AA. Finally, a considerable number of specialty AA groups have been formed, especially in larger population centers. These groups include meetings for men, meetings for women, meetings for individuals in particular professions, meetings for individuals belonging to particular ethnic or religious groups, and meetings for gays and lesbians.

Does AA work?

There is no question that AA has helped many individuals in their recovery from alcoholism. A number of studies have shown a positive relationship between participation in AA and abstinence from alcohol. Individuals who join AA and remain involved appear to have good prospects for recovery.

While attendance at AA meetings is associated with recovery, closer involvement in AA may be a stronger predictor of positive outcome. That is, when individuals are actively participating in AA, rather than simply attending meetings, they seem to do better. Examples of this involvement include reading the core AA literature, getting a sponsor, telling their story at a meeting, working the twelve steps, and serving as a sponsor.

While participation in AA brings many positive prospects for many people, AA does not work for everybody. Many individuals initiate contact with AA but do not maintain their involvement. In some cases, the individual may not be ready to make changes in his or her drinking habits. In other cases, there may not be a good match between the individual and the philosophy and format of AA. Other options are available for such individuals, including mutual-help organizations with other orientations or emphases, and formal alcohol treatment programs.

Al-Anon

Programs based on the Twelve Steps have been developed to address the needs of the family of the alcoholic. The largest and best-known of these programs is Al-Anon. The purpose of Al-Anon is to assist the loved ones (family and friends) of alcoholics to recover from the effects of living with the problem

TABLE 2: THE TWELVE TRADITIONS OF ALCOHOLICS ANONYMOUS

Tradition 1	Our common welfare should come first; personal recovery depends upon AA unity.
Tradition 2	For our group purpose there is but one ultimate authority—a loving God as He may express Himself in our group conscience. Our leaders are but trusted servants; they do not govern.
Tradition 3	The only requirement for AA membership is a desire to stop drinking.
Tradition 4	Each group should be autonomous except in matters affecting other groups or AA as a whole.
Tradition 5	Each group has but one primary purpose—to carry its message to the alcoholic who still suffers.
Tradition 6	An AA group ought never endorse, finance, or lend the AA name to any outside facility or enterprise, lest problems of money, property, and prestige divert us from our primary purpose.
Tradition 7	Every AA group ought to be fully self-supporting, declining outside contributions.
Tradition 8	Alcoholics Anonymous should remain forever nonprofessional, but our service centers may employ special workers.
Tradition 9	AA, as such, ought never be organized; but we may create service boards or committees directly responsible to those they serve.
Tradition 10	Alcoholics Anonymous has no opinion on outside issues; hence the AA name ought never be drawn into public controversy.
Tradition 11	Our public relations policy is based on attraction rather than promotion; we need always maintain personal anonymity at the level of press, radio, and films.
Tradition 12	Anonymity is the spiritual foundation of all our traditions, ever reminding us to place principles before personalities.

Source: Alcoholics Anonymous (1976).

drinking of a relative or friend. There are more than 24,000 Al-Anon meetings in 115 different countries, and the only requirement for membership is that a relative or friend is or was a problem drinker.

Al-Anon believes that alcoholism is a family illness, and that the recovery process can be helped by changing the family's attitudes to drinking problems. Al-Anon seeks to accomplish this aim by practicing the Twelve Steps, by welcoming and comforting the families of alcoholics, and by giving understanding and encouragement to the alcoholic family member. Regarding this last activity, Al-Anon advocates detachment from the alcoholic's drinking behavior. Consistent with the Twelve Steps, Al-Anon members accept their powerlessness to control the alcoholic.

Alateen

Alateen is an organization that evolved from, and remains closely aligned to, Al-Anon. Over 2,300 Alateen groups worldwide focus on the needs of young people. These groups are sponsored by members of Al-Anon, and as with Al-Anon, the only requirement for membership is that a family member or friend be a problem drinker. Alateen meetings are often held in the same buildings as Al-Anon meetings. During meetings, young people have the opportunity to share their experiences, strengths, and hopes with each other, discuss their difficulties, and learn ways to cope with the problems they face. One of the key facts that Alateen members learn is that compulsive drinking is a disease and that they can detach themselves from the loved one's drinking while still loving that individual. They also learn that they are not the cause of anyone else's alcoholism, and that they are not responsible for the actions of anyone except themselves.

G. J. CONNORS, J. S. TONIGAN

SEE ALSO:
Abstinence • Alcoholism • Alcoholism Treatment • Binge Drinking • Narcotics Anonymous • Step Programs

Alcoholism

More people abuse alcohol than any other type of drug. Dependence on alcohol is called alcoholism, and its effects can have a profound impact on the health of the abuser and the lives of family and colleagues.

Women are less likely to become alcoholics than men, but it takes less alcohol to make a woman drunk.

Alcoholism, also known as alcohol dependence, is a primary, chronic disorder whose development and manifestations are influenced by genetic, psychological, and environmental factors. More than 14 million people in the United States, including around 1 in every 13 adults, abuse alcohol or are alcoholics. Rates of alcohol problems are highest among young adults between the ages of 18 and 29 and lowest among adults 65 years and older. Men are four times as likely to become alcohol dependent or experience alcohol-related problems than are women. Among major U.S. ethnic groups, rates of alcoholism and alcohol-related problems vary.

Alcoholism as an addiction is an involuntary disability associated with a specific common set of characteristics by which such individuals differ from the norm and which places them at a disadvantage. Like many other disorders, alcoholism has a generally predictable course and has recognized symptoms. For clinical and research purposes, formal diagnostic criteria for alcoholism have been developed. Such criteria are included in the *Diagnostic and Statistical Manual of Mental Disorders*, fourth edition, published by the American Psychiatric Association.

People with this disorder have a preoccupation with the drug alcohol; they continue drinking despite repeated alcohol-related problems, such as losing a job or getting into trouble with the law; and they have distortions in thinking, most notably denial. Denial is broadly defined to include a range of psychological maneuvers designed to reduce awareness of the fact that alcohol use is the cause of

CHILDREN OF ALCOHOLICS

Alcoholism does not only impact the alcoholic; it can also have a devastating effect on the family. According to the National Association for Children of Alcoholics, the number of people in the United States who have an alcoholic parent is estimated at 28 million, of which 11 million are under 18 years of age. Living with an alcoholic places family members under stress, to which they react in different ways. In young children, depression and anxiety may manifest itself through crying, nightmares, bed wetting, and being afraid to go to school. Teenagers can develop phobias, become extremely self-conscious or perfectionistic about the things they do, and may avoid contact with other people. Schoolwork often suffers even if the child is smart and academically capable.

Some of these problems arise from changes in family dynamics, which may include an increase in conflict, physical or emotional abuse, lack of organization, marital strain, financial difficulties, and frequent moving. Children of alcoholics often lack order in their lives but are expected to carry responsibilities that would not be expected of their contemporaries.

Enlisting the support of a nonalcoholic relative or adult can help children cope with the problems of an alcoholic parent. Research has shown that children with a support structure are more independent and can handle emotional situations better. Teaching social skills and building self-esteem are important components in making the child feel less isolated among his or her peers.

an individual's problems rather than a solution to those problems. Denial becomes an integral part of the disease and a major obstacle to recovery.

Not all heavy drinkers meet the definition of the term *alcoholic*. The majority of heavy drinkers drink in short, intense bouts often described as binges. This group of drinkers can suffer the same medical consequences of intoxication as alcoholics, but they are more likely to be the victims of unexpected events, such as car crashes, accidents, and violence.

The symptoms of alcoholism

Symptoms of alcoholism include alcohol craving, increased tolerance, physical dependence, and impaired control over drinking. Cravings are associated with a strong need, or compulsion, to drink. People who drink large amounts of alcohol repetitively over time become tolerant to its effects. That is, alcoholics develop a need for increasing amounts of alcohol in order to feel its effects, which are caused by adaptational changes of central nervous system (CNS) cells. Although alcoholics develop a tolerance for alcohol, they always manifest some degree of intoxication and impairment with a high enough dose. People may die of respiratory depression secondary to alcohol overdose, even in the

presence of tolerance. The physical dependence accompanying tolerance is profound, and withdrawal produces adverse effects that may lead to death. Those tolerant of alcohol are generally cross-tolerant to many other CNS depressants (for example, barbiturates, benzodiazepines, and other sedatives).

A continuum of symptoms accompanies alcohol withdrawal, usually beginning 12 to 48 hours after cessation of intake. The mild withdrawal syndrome includes tremor, weakness, sweating, hyperreflexia (overactive reflexes), and gastrointestinal symptoms. Some patients have generalized convulsive seizures, usually not more than two in short succession (alcoholic epilepsy, or rum fits). In more serious cases, alcoholic hallucinosis may follow abrupt abstinence from prolonged excessive use of alcohol. Symptoms of hallucinosis include auditory illusions and hallucinations, which are frequently accusatory and threatening; the patient is usually apprehensive and may be terrified by the hallucinations and vivid frightening dreams. The syndrome resembles schizophrenia, but thought is usually not disordered, and the history is not typical of schizophrenia. Symptoms do not resemble the delirious state of an acute organic brain syndrome as much as does delirium tremens (a later, more severe stage of withdrawal) or other pathologic reactions associated with withdrawal. Consciousness remains clear, and the signs of physical instability seen in delirium tremens are usually absent. When hallucinosis occurs, it generally precedes delirium tremens. Hallucinosis is usually temporary. Recovery usually occurs in one to three weeks and recurrence is likely if the patient resumes drinking.

Withdrawing alcoholics are suggestible to many sensory stimuli, particularly to objects seen in dim light. Inner-ear disturbances may cause them to believe that the floor is moving, the walls are falling, or the room is rotating. As the delirium progresses, resting tremors of the hand may develop, sometimes extending to the head and trunk. Delirium tremens usually begins 48 to 72 hours after alcohol withdrawal, with anxiety attacks, increasing confusion, poor sleep patterns (with frightening dreams or nocturnal illusions), marked sweating, and profound depression. Fleeting hallucinations that arouse restlessness, fear, and even terror are common. Typical of the initial delirious, confused, and disoriented state is a return to a habitual activity. For example, the alcoholic frequently imagines that he or she is back at work and attempts to perform some related activity. Delirium is also accompanied by increases in autonomic processes and is shown by increased pulse rate and temperature. Appreciably elevated temperature in delirium tremens is a sign of a poor prospect for recovery. Symptoms vary among patients but are usually the same for a particular patient with each recurrence. Although delirium tremens may be fatal, the course is usually self-limited, terminating in a long sleep. Delirium tremens should begin to resolve within 12 to 24 hours.

Progression of alcoholism

Alcoholism is often progressive and fatal. That is, the disorder persists over time with cumulative detrimental changes in physical, psychological, and emotional areas. The complications and long-term effects of alcohol dependency include organic complications involving the brain, such as memory loss or, in extreme cases, Wernicke-Korsakoff's syndrome (*see* box on p. 34), cirrhosis of the liver, pancreatitis (inflammation of the pancreas), heart disease, and other organ dysfunction. Long-term dependence is also associated with significant damage to occupational, social, and interpersonal

areas, including sexual dysfunction. Other detrimental effects may be suicide, homicide, motor vehicle crashes, and other traumatic events. Finally, alcohol may cause premature death through overdose.

Alcoholism is a primary disorder and thus is not a symptom of an underlying disease state. When alcoholism coexists with other conditions, such as depression or anxiety disorders, therapies applied to them are ineffective until the alcoholism is treated.

Risk factors associated with alcoholism

Genetic influences. Many scientific studies, including research conducted on twins, adopted children, and family studies, have shown that genetic factors influence vulnerability to alcoholism. Indeed, alcoholics were six times more likely than nonalcoholics to report a family history of alcoholism. The classic twin study involves comparing the differences in identical twins, who share 100 percent of their genes, and fraternal twins, who share 50 percent of their genes, while assuming that each twin pair shares similar familial environments. An adoption study is a simple yet powerful method for establishing the existence of genetic influences. Adoption studies allow for a clean separation of genetic and environmental sources of influence. That is, the adopted child is reared in an environment separate from the biological parents. Thus, adopted children of alcoholics and nonalcoholics reared away from their biological parents can be compared to determine the extent to which biological and environmental influences contribute to the development of alcoholism. Family studies allow researchers to examine both the family environment and the genetic contribution of biological parents. Taken together, these studies demonstrate the importance of genetic factors. Children of alcoholics are about four times more likely than the general population to develop alcohol problems. Children of alcoholics also have a higher risk for many other behavioral and emotional problems. Genetic factors seem to have a stronger influence on male risk for alcoholism than on female risk for alcoholism. However, not all children of alcoholics automatically develop alcoholism, and a person with no family history of alcoholism can become alcohol dependent.

Age of onset. Another risk factor is the age at which an individual begins to drink alcohol. Individuals who have their first drink of alcohol before the age of 15 are substantially more likely to become alcoholic than those who have their first drink after the age of 20. Early onset alcoholics typically have a family history of alcoholism, higher levels of hostility, and more emotional problems, and tend to have shorter periods of abstinence between heavy drinking episodes than late onset alcoholics. Drinking at an early age is not only associated with increased rates of alcoholism but is also predictive of increased rates of other drug abuse and dependence, mental health problems, and educational underachievement.

Personality factors. Personality factors have also been found to relate to alcoholism. Two types of alcoholism have been defined on the basis of heritable personality traits: Type I and Type II alcoholism (as described by Cloninger, Sigvardsson, and Bohman in *Alcohol Health and Research World,* 1996). Categorization of Type I and Type II

Many alcoholics have a poor diet, which can compromise their health. For those on the street, a meal at a soup kitchen may be the only source of nutrition. Although alcohol is a source of carbohydrates, it is nutritionally worthless and lacks essential minerals and vitamins.

alcoholism is based on an individual's levels of these traits: harm avoidance, novelty seeking, and reward dependence. Low harm avoidance identifies a person as being confident, relaxed, optimistic, and uninhibited, whereas a high harm-avoidance person is more likely to be cautious, apprehensive, pessimistic, and inhibited. Traits associated with novelty seeking include impulsiveness, flexibility, and an inability to focus attention. Reward dependence reflects emotional dependence and a desire to help others. Type I alcoholism is associated with high harm avoidance, low novelty seeking, and high reward dependence. Type II alcoholism is associated with low harm avoidance, high novelty seeking, and low reward dependence.

Type I is classified as milieu-limited alcoholism, and Type II as male-limited alcoholism. Type I alcoholism was found to affect both men and women, required the presence of both genetic and environmental risk factors, occurred later in life after years of heavy drinking, and could take on either a mild or severe form. Type II alcoholism was found to have a strong genetic component, to affect mainly sons of alcoholics, and to be influenced weakly by environmental factors. The onset of Type II alcoholism began during adolescence or early adulthood, was characterized by moderate severity, and was typically associated with criminal behavior. Compared with Type I alcoholics, Type II alcoholics exhibit more severe dependence symptoms, alcohol-related problems, and other coexisting psychopathologies.

Environmental factors. Environmental factors also contribute to the development of alcoholism and include the community, family environment, and peer groups. The availability of alcohol in the environment contributes to how much access a person has to alcohol, and the culture within the community contributes to how socially acceptable drinking is for men and women. Both of these aspects of community may contribute to age of onset of alcohol use and drinking patterns. Aspects of family life also affect the risk for alcoholism. For example, families with an alcoholic parent who is depressed or has other psychological problems, where both parents abuse alcohol and other drugs, where the parents' alcohol abuse is severe, or where family conflicts lead to aggression and violence all have high risk for alcohol abuse and alcoholism. Such family

ALCOHOLISM AND BRAIN DISORDERS

There are many brain disorders associated with alcoholism. Wernicke-Korsakoff's syndrome is a brain disorder that is usually associated with heavy drinking over a long period. The disorder comprises Wernicke's encephalopathy, characterized by a staggering gait and confusion, and Korsakoff's psychosis, a loss of short-term memory that leaves sufferers struggling to remember events that have occurred only moments before. Although it display similarities to dementia, Wernicke-Korsakoff's syndrome is actually caused by lack of thiamine (vitamin B1), which affects the brain and nervous system. Excessive use of alcohol is often the cause of vitamin B1 deficiency, which arises because many heavy drinkers have poor eating habits and their nutrition is inadequate. As a result, the diet of an alcoholic may not contain enough essential vitamins. Another cause of this deficiency may be the effect that alcohol has on the digestive system. Alcohol can inflame the stomach lining and impede the body's ability to absorb the key vitamins it receives.

Cerebellar deterioration may occur in alcoholics (as well as in other malnourished persons). Its pathologic and clinical features are probably identical to the cerebellar involvement of Wernicke's encephalopathy. An inability to coordinate voluntary muscular movements involved in standing and walking evolves over weeks or months but can appear suddenly. Computed tomography imaging (CT scan) shows degeneration of the superior vermis and anterior cerebellar lobes. The disorder is lessened by taking supplements of thiamine and other B vitamins.

Marchiafava-Bignami disease is a rare demyelination (deterioration of the protective sheath) of the corpus callosum that occurs in chronic alcoholics, predominantly among men. Although originally attributed to the effects of a crude red wine in Italy, this disorder has occurred in many countries and with many alcoholic beverages. Patients become agitated and confused, with signs of progressive dementia. Some patients recover over several months. However, in other patients, seizures and coma develop and may precede death.

Pathologic intoxication is a rare syndrome. It is characterized by repetitive, automatic movements and extreme excitement with aggressive, uncontrolled irrational behavior after ingesting a relatively small amount of alcohol. The episode may last for minutes or hours and is followed by a prolonged period of sleep with amnesia of the event on awakening.

environments have been linked to inadequate parental monitoring, discipline, supervision, and communications during adolescence which in turn may lead to association with deviant peer groups and academic problems.

Most of the research conducted in the area of alcoholism has been confined to specific scientific areas of study (for example, genetic, psychosocial, and environmental) with few studies making links across fields. Much of the current understanding about alcoholism is therefore confined within specific spheres of influence. However, researchers are focusing on ways to bridge these distinct areas by identifying specific genetic-environmental interactions that could be relevant for designing early interventions for behaviors that predispose a person to alcohol abuse and dependence.

Is alcoholism treatable?

In the past, alcoholism carried a tremendous public and social stigma. This was a barrier to many people who needed to seek help but were fearful of employer, family, or social retribution. This stigma has lessened greatly as the result of increased awareness that alcoholism is a medical condition, and that as such, it requires professional treatment to be overcome.

The first step in the treatment for alcoholism is detoxification. During the detoxification phase,

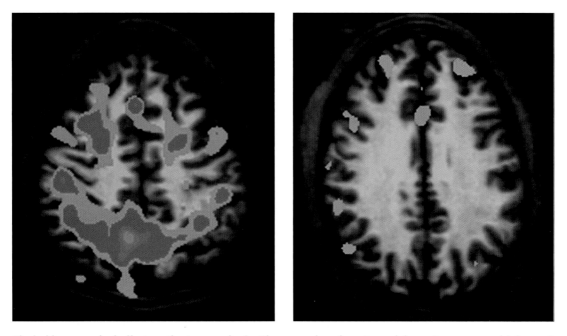

Alcohol has a marked effect on the teenage brain. The scans show how two adolescents, one a nondrinker and the other a heavy drinker, perform during mental agility tests. The scan of the heavy drinker (right) shows how areas of the brain associated with memory and learning, shown by the pink and red areas in the brain of the nondrinker (left), fail to function. Instead, other areas of the brain try to compensate for this loss of ability.

alcohol is withdrawn. Benzodiazepines are often used in the treatment of alcohol withdrawal symptoms such as seizures and episodes of delirium tremens. After correction of nutritional deficiencies associated with excessive alcohol intake, the patient may require one or more courses of treatment, including therapy and medication.

There are a variety of treatment options available to people suffering from alcoholism. Although in-patient treatments are available, they usually require admission into a hospital for a period of 28 days or more. Inpatient treatments often require frequent meetings each week involving physicians, substance abuse counselors, others who are alcohol dependent, and family members. Though similar to inpatient treatment, outpatient treatment programs afford greater flexibility, as patients are not required to leave their home or family, or take leave from work. Various types of psychotherapy have been recommended, but group therapy is generally believed to be superior to one-on-one therapy. Alcoholism treatment programs and self-help groups such as Alcoholics Anonymous are effective in many cases.

Some alcoholics remain sober one year after treatment, while others have periods of sobriety alternating with relapses. The longer an individual abstains from alcohol, the more likely that person is to remain sober. However, some alcoholics are unable to stop drinking for any length of time. Many people relapse one or more times before achieving long-term sobriety. Relapses are common and do not mean that a person has failed or cannot eventually recover from alcoholism. If a relapse occurs, it is important that the alcoholic tries to stop drinking again and to get whatever help is needed to abstain from alcohol. Ongoing support from family members and others can be important in recovery.

S. WALKER

SEE ALSO:

Abstinence • Alcoholics Anonymous • Alcoholism Treatment • Binge Drinking • Delirium Tremens • Denial • Disease Theory of Addiction • Driving While Impaired • Heart and Circulatory Diseases • Intervention • Liver Diseases • Recovery • Relapse • Withdrawal

Alcoholism Treatment

Alcoholism is lethal—95 percent of untreated alcoholics die as a direct result of the condition or medical complications arising from it. However, there are a wide range of treatment programs available that can help the alcoholic recover.

How alcoholism is understood and defined guides what type of treatment is offered and how that treatment is implemented. There are many varying opinions and theories about what factors contribute to the development of alcoholism. Research has revealed that these factors can be behavioral, biological, social, and environmental. There are many questions yet to be answered about alcoholism: how it develops, why it manifests in some people and not in others, the cause of variation in severity of alcoholism, and why there is such variation in abstinence rates. Many experts within various disciplines are attempting to answer these questions and others.

Whatever definition of alcoholism is chosen, it appears that there are three essential components. First, the drinking does serious harm to the drinker, whether physical, emotional, financial, and so on. Second, the drinker continues to drink despite negative consequences. Third, this pattern of drinking continues over an extended period of time and becomes progressively worse.

Alcohol use and abuse is best viewed on a continuum. At one end is the social, occasional use of alcohol; in the middle is the overuse and possible abuse of alcohol; and at the other end is full-blown alcoholism. What factors contribute to the progression from social drinking to problem drinking to alcoholism is unknown. It appears that for each person, in each situation, there are individual factors that contribute to whether a person will become a social drinker, a problem drinker, or an alcoholic.

Alcoholism is a serious condition that often requires some type of professional treatment. More than 19 million Americans (7.7 percent of the population aged 12 or older) needed treatment in 2009 for an alcohol use problem. Many die each year from the direct and indirect causes of alcoholism. Research has shown that only 4 percent of alcoholics stay sober for the next year if they try to quit on their own, whereas 50 percent of alcoholics stay sober for the next year if they go through treatment. Seventy percent of alcoholics stay sober for the next year if they go through treatment and regularly attend Alcoholics Anonymous (AA) meetings. Ninety percent of alcoholics stay sober for the next year if they go through treatment, regularly attend Alcoholics Anonymous meetings, and go to aftercare once a week.

Over the centuries, professionals, clergy, and laypersons have argued about whether alcoholism is the result of a moral deficit, a bad habit, or a disease. There are records dating back to 1700 BCE of legislative attempts to control the use of alcohol. The belief that alcohol abuse is an indication of moral inferiority was present in many ancient cultures as well as today. For this reason harsh sanctions have been levied against those who abuse alcohol. In some cases, these sanctions have included public executions, torture, or incarceration. Many in present-day society view alcohol use and alcoholism as an individual choice. However, the World Health Organization (WHO) and the American Psychiatric Association (APA) have both defined alcoholism as a disease. Alcoholics Anonymous, which was formed in the 1930s as a model of treatment, stresses that alcoholism is a physical, spiritual, and mental disease.

Assessment of condition

Treatment for alcoholism can begin only when the alcoholic is willing to acknowledge that there is a problem. This is a difficult step for alcoholics to take, and often they have to be forced into a realistic examination of their drinking habits and consequences. One of the defining attributes of alcoholism is denial. Denial is a mechanism whereby individuals are able to convince themselves that they actually do not have a problem. Sometimes they are able to accomplish this by blaming others, sometimes by ignoring warning signs, and sometimes by lying to themselves and others. Denial is one of the first defenses that must be broken through in order to get an alcoholic into treatment.

One method used by clinicians to assist families who are concerned about their loved one's use of alcohol is an intervention. An intervention can be a highly effective way to break through an alcoholic's denial defense. An intervention should only be conducted by a trained professional because of the often emotionally charged circumstances and issues being discussed. Any person who has a relationship with the alcoholic and has potential to influence his or her willingness to seek treatment may participate in the intervention. This could include a spouse, children, parents, siblings, close friends, employer,

physician, or others. One objective of the intervention is to have the alcoholic hear how drinking is affecting those people close to them. This should be done in as nonconfrontational a manner as possible, and it is the responsibility of the interventionist to keep everyone on track. Usually the interventionist has met prior to the actual intervention with all involved parties, except the alcoholic, to establish parameters. The intervention is usually a surprise to the alcoholic.

The primary goal of an intervention is to get the alcoholic into treatment. For this reason, an appropriate treatment facility should already have been contacted and be holding a bed. Once the alcoholic has heard from everyone and has been given a reasonable understanding of the consequences, he or she is given a choice—go to treatment or face the consequences. These consequences could include marital separation, loss of employment, declining health, loss of rights to see children, and so on. Alcoholics agreeing to seek treatment are told that there is a bed waiting and their bag is already packed; they are then escorted to treatment. If the alcoholic is unwilling to seek treatment, the interventionist will encourage the family to seek treatment and enforce all appropriate consequences.

An assessment is usually done face-to-face, over the telephone, or by questionnaire. Whatever method is used, it is important to remember that a major defensive structure in an alcoholic is denial, and that denial can influence the ability to be forthright when answering questions about lifestyle and alcohol use. For this reason, many treatment providers assess an alcoholic's condition at several different points during treatment. An alcoholic's condition may be assessed by an interventionist, a physician, a counselor, or another professional.

Research has demonstrated that repeated, excessive, and prolonged use of alcohol is toxic to the human body. A thorough assessment of an alcoholic includes a physical examination. A physical examination is necessary to determine if alcohol use has caused damage to the

Posters that emphasize the positive side of not drinking alcohol, such as enjoying sports and talking with friends, are found in the corridors of most schools. Advice and help for drinking problems can be sought from the school nurse or staff teaching drug-awareness programs.

TREATMENT OPTIONS

Type	Length	What influences decision	Benefit
Detoxification	2–10 days medical setting or social setting	Medical examination is necessary for those who require medication or intense medical monitoring	Physical safety of patient
Short-term	10–28 days	Availability of beds, private or public funding	Allows for short period of abstinence under supervision
Long-term	30 days–1 year	Severity of condition and other treatment needs (housing, employment, and so on)	Allows for longer period of abstinence with additional supports
Inpatient (IP)	Short- or long-term	Availability of beds, private or public funding	Allows for 24-hour monitoring to enhance compliance
Outpatient (OP)	Short- or long-term	Client needs, current level of functioning, support structure in place	Allows clients to be in work or educational pursuits with support and monitoring
Professional	IP/OP short-term or long-term	Any setting in which persons with academic and professional training work with patients	Factors of alcoholism include coexisting mental illness, often requiring professional treatment
Self-help	Ongoing	Alcoholics Anonymous (AA) most universally known	Worldwide availability of meetings and support
Group therapy	All settings	Useful for dealing with trauma-based issues such as physical or sexual abuse	Private setting for exploring painful memories
Individual therapy	All settings	Useful for dealing with trauma-based issues such as physical or sexual abuse	Private and confidential setting for exploring painful memories

neurological systems of the body or to the heart, liver, pancreas, or other organs. Testing for cirrhosis of the liver and hepatitis are usually conducted, in addition to routine screening for tuberculosis and HIV.

Determination of type of treatment

Once an alcoholic decides to seek treatment, there are several options (*see above*). The type of treatment is determined by the alcoholic and a treatment provider. One of the primary methods of gaining information to assist in treatment planning is through a clinical interview. During the clinical interview, the interviewer will ask questions designed to provide background information on the client's current and previous level of functioning. Level of functioning usually includes ability to care for one's self, attendance at work or school, changes in relationships with family and friends, appetite changes, sleep patterns, and so on. During a clinical interview, the alcoholic will be assessed for other treatment needs, including medical, vocational, employment, and housing. Typically, a clinical interview is designed to gain historical information regarding the client's family structure, incidences of previous sexual or physical abuse, medical history, academic and occupational history, and relationship history. This information is used to gain a more thorough understanding of the client's life and to assist in all phases of treatment planning. An alcoholic who has stable employment and a safe living environment may be recommended for intensive outpatient counseling in a group and individual format, whereas an alcoholic who has nowhere to live and no marketable job skills may be recommended for inpatient treatment followed by a brief placement in a transitional living situation. In the best scenario, the type of treatment is decided by a thorough assessment of the individual and his or her unique needs. However, treatment decisions are often made in response to insurance requirements, fiscal constraints, and bed availability.

Detoxification

Detoxification is primarily a medical issue, and decisions about what type of detoxification are best for a person should be made under medical supervision or after consultation with a medical professional. There are several options for detoxification. A person can detox at home, in a hospital, or in a treatment setting (usually called social detox). Detoxification at home is rarely recommended due to potential complications and should only be attempted with extreme caution.

Detoxification involves terminating the use of alcohol abruptly. This abrupt change in consumption of alcohol can cause serious physical complications. The symptoms that occur during detoxification are often referred to as withdrawal symptoms. These symptoms may include fever, chills, nausea, vomiting, tremors, seizures, or hallucinations. Alcohol detoxification and withdrawal can be deadly. It is important to follow professional advice in seeking the best detoxification option for each individual.

Patients at a detox clinic undergo group therapy as part of their treatment for alcoholism. Treating alcoholism can involve the use of medical and psychological therapies backed by outpatient services once the alcoholic leaves the clinic. Medical supervision is essential for chronic alcohol users because they face the risk of collapse.

SPECIALTY SUBSTANCE ABUSE TREATMENT IN 2009

23.5 million persons aged 12 or older needed treatment for an illicit drug or alcohol use problem. Of these, 2.4 million received specialty treatment.

949,000	Treatment for alcohol use only
739,000	Treatment for illicit drug use only
756,000	Treatment for both alcohol and drugs

Of 1.8 million youths aged 12 to 17 in need of treatment, 150,000 received treatment at a specialty facility.

Source: Substance Abuse and Mental Health Services Administration. 2010. Results from the 2009 National Survey on Drug Use and Health.

Individuals who are known to have heart conditions such as high blood pressure should always be withdrawn from alcohol in a medical setting. People who have a history of seizures or complications from withdrawal should also be detoxed in a medical setting. In a medical setting, the person is typically given a tranquilizer such as Librium to ease the experience of withdrawal symptoms and lessen the severity of symptoms. This medication is begun immediately upon admission to the hospital and is gradually tapered until the person is discharged. A person is never discharged from a medical detox while still taking tranquilizers to assist withdrawal.

If medical detoxification is not necessary, a brief period (usually 2 to 10 days) is spent in a treatment setting known as a social detox. In this setting, the person has his or her vital signs monitored, is under constant observation, and can get professional help if needed. No medication is used to assist with withdrawal except standard over-the-counter remedies such as Tylenol, Advil, or antacids.

What to expect during treatment

Alcoholism treatment begins with detoxification. During detoxification, the person is introduced to the disease concept of alcoholism, twelve-step recovery programs (AA or Narcotics Anonymous), individual or group counseling, and other support services. A thorough physical, mental, and social history is gathered from the person, and a treatment plan is written and reviewed. A treatment plan usually includes goals in all domains of primary functioning. These domains include housing, employment or education, health and wellness, social and recreational activities, relationship and family goals, and spiritual goals. The treatment plan will also usually contain recommendations regarding type of ongoing treatment, length of treatment, and support services.

Following detoxification, the person will progress to either an inpatient or outpatient facility for short-term or long-term treatment. The decision about what type of treatment is best is usually made with a treatment professional and the person in treatment working together. Inpatient treatment is a highly structured program of daily activities and services designed to enhance recovery and improve overall health. A typical day will begin early; activities will be scheduled until bedtime. There are groups with a variety of topics, individual counseling, self-help meetings, educational opportunities, visits, and free time, all scheduled around a meal and snack schedule with opportunities for a full night's rest. Inpatient treatment may be provided on a short- or long-term basis. In long-term inpatient treatment, patients typically progress through a series of phases or levels that give them opportunities for additional privileges and responsibilities.

Outpatient treatment is structured, but the person has the opportunity to live at home and continue working or attending school. Outpatient treatment usually begins with an aftercare group that meets one to three times per week. A relapse prevention group is required, with meetings two to three times per week. Attendance at a minimum number of self-help (AA/NA) meetings is required. The person in outpatient treatment may also seek individual counseling as appropriate.

Aftercare programs are tailored to meet the needs of the people seeking services. A person leaving short-term intensive inpatient treatment requires structured aftercare services at a different level from a person who has completed long-term inpatient treatment with a gradual reentry program.

Halfway houses are designed to meet the treatment needs of recovering alcoholics between an inpatient setting and home. A typical halfway house program lasts from three to six months.

A halfway house is a residence where 10 to 30 people who are recovering from alcoholism live together. Living quarters may be similar to dormitory style with community restrooms, kitchen, and leisure facilities. Residents are required to be working or attending school. Mandatory groups, individual meetings, and twelve-step meetings are required in order to maintain eligibility for placement at a halfway house.

Transitional houses are the least structured environment. Typically there are mandatory house meetings weekly, employment must be maintained, and twelve-step attendance is required at least three times weekly. Aside from those activities, the residents are free to come and go and have limited structure.

Co-occurring conditions

Many people who suffer from alcoholism often need treatment for other coexisting conditions. These conditions may include forms of mental illness such as depression or anxiety or more serious mental illnesses such as bipolar disorder or schizophrenia. A diagnosis of a co-occurring mental illness should only be tentative until the person has maintained a period of sobriety during which the symptoms of the mental illness can be separated from use, abuse, and withdrawal symptoms from alcohol.

People who enter alcoholism treatment may be wealthy, poor, or anywhere between. The socio-economic status of the person will partially determine what other types of conditions may need to be treated. A person who has maintained stable employment with a good income and benefits has better access to health care than the underemployed. People who have become unemployed or homeless because of their alcoholism may not have seen a doctor or a dentist for years. They may have rotting teeth, poor nutrition, undiagnosed hypertension or heart disease, and many other health complications that can arise from a lack of personal care. All people who suffer from alcoholism are at risk for liver diseases, including hepatitis and cirrhosis, and neurological difficulties associated with the impact of alcohol on the brain.

Relapse

Relapse is a major concern for people leaving alcoholism treatment. A relapse may be defined as a return to drinking following a period of abstinence. Relapse prevention programs are popular, and every type of treatment program includes education about the dangers of relapse. A relapse can be brief and involve as little as one drink, or it may propel a person back into a pattern of heavy drinking. However, not everyone who relapses returns to previous levels of drinking, and sometimes people relapse following a long period of sobriety.

As with all areas of alcoholism treatment, the treatment and monitoring of relapse should be individualized as much as possible. How the relapse is handled and how the person views his or her relapse can determine the final outcome of a relapse episode. Someone who gets drunk one night after discharge from treatment but uses that experience to reinforce what he or she learned in treatment and as a motivation to maintain sobriety has not failed but has in fact strengthened his or her path to success. A person who relapses and feels like a failure, becomes demoralized, and contemplates suicide is in a much more dangerous position. These types of differences make thorough assessment, followed by appropriate treatment, the best course of action for anyone who relapses.

D. E. BIRON

American Society of Addiction Medicine (ASAM)

The American Society of Addiction Medicine is an organization dedicated to educating physicians and improving the treatment of individuals suffering from alcoholism and other addictions.

Physicians from across the United States cooperate within the American Society of Addiction Medicine (ASAM) to improve the quality and availability of health care for people affected by addiction. Members of ASAM are physicians from all medical specialties. They are engaged in private practice, serve as corporate medical directors, and work in group practice or other clinical settings. A number are also involved in research and medical education.

Aims, methods, and origins
A primary focus of ASAM is to inform the medical community and the public about the seriousness of addiction and its treatment. Addiction is often perceived as a weakness of character or an unwillingness to stop using drugs. One of the society's aims is to get physicians, health insurers, health care organizers, and policymakers to recognize addictive disorders as biopsychosocial medical disorders. Members work together in an organized effort to compile sources of credible, scientifically validated, and up-to-date information about addictive disorders and appropriate diagnoses and treatments. For example, ASAM sponsors various conferences and has published major reference manuals for addiction, including *Principles of Addiction Medicine* and the nationally recognized *Patient Placement Criteria* (PPC).

Among the conferences, the ASAM's annual medical scientific conference provides the most current addiction information in a clinically relevant format. Courses, workshops, lectures, and presentations provide an opportunity for participants to interact with addiction experts. Another conference sponsored by ASAM is the Buprenorphine and Office Based Treatment of Opioid Dependence. The target audience of this convention includes physicians who wish to qualify to use buprenorphine, an opiate, for opioid addiction treatment.

The society started out in 1954 as the New York City Medical Society on Alcoholism. Its first president was Ruth Fox, a physician who was interested in the problems of alcohol addiction. Education on the treatment of alcoholism and other dependencies increased tremendously over the next few decades with the establishment of other similar societies, and especially with the new National Institute on Drug Abuse/National Institute on Alcohol Abuse and Alcoholism (NIDA/NIAAA) Career Teacher Program for medical school faculty in 1970. A number of name changes followed to reflect interest in other types of addictions, until the society was officially labeled ASAM in 1989 and was admitted to the American Medical Association (AMA) House of Delegates as a voting member in June 1988.

ASAM members actively advocate legal changes concerning drug enforcement and addiction treatments at both the national and state levels of public policy. The California Little Hoover Commission, for example, has accepted expert testimony from many ASAM members concerning the prevalence of drug addiction and the cost of addiction to the economy and taxpayers of California. In an effort to bring an evidence-based understanding of addiction and treatment into public policy, ASAM members developed and provided information in an easily understandable format for educators and legislators. Collective efforts of this nature in other states encourage legislators to evaluate current drug treatment facilities and drug enforcement policies in their communities. ASAM also promotes research and prevention methods for addiction.

K. PHILPOT

SEE ALSO:
College on Problems of Drug Dependence (CPDD) ● National Institute on Alcohol Abuse and Alcoholism (NIAAA) ● National Institute on Drug Abuse (NIDA)

Antisocial Personality Disorder

Antisocial personality disorder (APD) is a type of mental disorder characterized by aggressive, manipulative, and often criminal behavior. People with APD are also very likely to suffer from drug addictions.

Psychopaths (coldly calculating criminals) and sociopaths (selfish and egocentric people who lack conscience) often suffer from APD. The disorder usually begins with problems in childhood, and it affects many more men than women. Although APD is strongly linked with alcohol and drug abuse, it remains uncertain whether one problem causes the other or whether they simply occur together.

What is APD?

Personality is the collection of characteristics that makes people who they are. During childhood and adolescence, most people develop personalities that will enable them to lead more or less happy and fulfilled lives as part of society. Some people, however, form personalities that repeatedly bring them into conflict with those around them and with society as a whole. This problem is sometimes described (and formally diagnosed) as a personality disorder. The American Psychiatric Association's *Diagnostic and Statistical Manual of Mental Disorders* (DSM) recognizes 10 different personality disorders.

Antisocial personality disorder (APD), which is one of the personality disorders defined in the DSM, can be broadly described as antisocial behavior that shows an extreme lack of respect for other people. People who suffer from APD tend to be deceitful and calculating and are often aggressive and intimidating. Although they can be charming, they make friendships and relationships purely to suit their own needs and are usually emotionally "cold" people. They act very impulsively, need constant stimulation, and become bored very quickly. They also tend to have a history of antisocial and often criminal behavior.

In order to meet the DSM definition of APD, a person must have suffered from at least three of the following symptoms since the age of 15: repeatedly coming into conflict with the law; conning for pleasure or profit, or repeated lying; failure to plan ahead (impulsive behavior); repeatedly assaulting other people; recklessness; poor behavior at work; and knowingly and deliberately inflicting pain on others. They must be at least 18 and must have shown signs of conduct disorder, another mental disorder defined in DSM involving aggressive, destructive, unlawful, or disruptive behavior during childhood.

Various studies in the United States and Europe show that APD affects around 1 to 3 percent of the population, which makes it a relatively rare condition. By comparison, around 25 percent of the population suffer some form of substance dependence and almost 20 percent suffer from depression. Men are much more likely to suffer from APD than women; in one study, eight times more men than women were diagnosed. Up to 80 percent of men and 65 percent of women in prison meet the DSM criteria for APD, although fewer than half the people diagnosed with APD end up in prison.

Links to substance abuse

A number of research studies have shown strong links between APD and substance abuse. Alcoholics are up to 21 times more likely to suffer from APD, for example, while somewhere between half and three-quarters of APD sufferers abuse alcohol and half abuse other drugs. One study found APD sufferers were 13 times more likely to suffer a substance abuse disorder at some point in their lives. Having APD also tends to produce earlier and more severe alcoholism and drug abuse, while drug abuse in adolescence significantly increases the risk of developing APD later in life. Drug abuse is also more likely to produce APD rather than other types of personality disorders. APD sufferers do not abuse any one drug more than any other but are likely to use multiple substances. In short, the antisocial behavior seen in APD can be caused (or exacerbated) by substance abuse, but substance abuse can also occur (or be exacerbated) if someone has APD. Most of the time, however, the APD seems to occur first.

Various explanations have been offered for the link between APD and substance abuse. One obvious connection is the overlap between the criteria used

ADDICTED TO MURDER

Serial killers are generally psychopaths, and most psychopaths meet the clinical diagnosis of antisocial personality disorder. The reverse is not true, however; not all of the people suffering from APD are psychopaths and not all psychopaths become serial killers.

According to research published by the Federal Bureau of Investigation (FBI), addiction can play a major role in the life of serial killers. Sex addiction and substance abuse have both been found to be significant. One study found that around 70 percent of serial killers come from families that have a history of alcoholism. Many other factors are believed to contribute to the development of psychopathology, including physical and sexual abuse and the gradual retreat into a fantasy life.

for diagnosing both. For example, some drug users resort to threatening or criminal behavior to obtain money to satisfy their addiction. Another explanation is that APD sufferers tend to be people with a low boredom threshold who seek the stimulation that substance abuse appears to offer. Drugs such as alcohol might seem to offer easy relief from the boredom, impulsiveness, and irritability that typically characterize APD. Environmental factors might also explain the link: people with APD, with higher risk of poor schooling, unemployment, and imprisonment, might be more likely to abuse substances as a result.

Causes of APD

Researchers have identified a number of biological risk factors that seem to make someone more likely to suffer from APD. People with APD are more likely to have dysfunctions in the frontal lobes of their brains (the areas responsible for such things as planning future behavior), deficiencies in the production of the serotonin neurotransmitter (which regulates mood), and increased testosterone (the male sex hormone). There is some evidence that they may have suffered brain damage at birth, and dietary factors may also play a role. There are strong indications of a genetic component in more serious cases of APD, with a high risk of people suffering from APD if family members already have the disorder.

A number of other risk factors seem to make people more likely to suffer from APD. Personal risk factors include having conduct disorder during childhood, being male, suffering other mental disorders (including substance abuse), and having cognitive problems or low educational ability. Family difficulties can also play a part; poor parenting, parents who are substance abusers, and problems such as divorce and adoption all increase the risk. APD (and the conduct disorder from which it can develop) also seems to be associated with peer group pressures. Environmental problems, such as poverty and unemployment, also increase the risk.

It remains uncertain whether these risk factors are causes that lead to the development of APD, effects that occur because someone already suffers from APD, or simply associations that occur alongside APD but are not causally related. Many of the risk factors identified for APD are also risk factors for substance abuse, so the link between the two is not altogether surprising.

Treatment

Personality is a deeply ingrained part of who a person is, and personality disorders are generally among the most difficult mental disorders to treat. APD is no exception. Most people who seek treatment for APD do so because of other problems associated with the disorder (such as marital conflicts, substance abuse, or another mental problem such as depression). Psychotherapy is sometimes successful in helping APD sufferers to understand how their personalities cause their problems and to modify their behavior accordingly. Medication can also play a role, for example, in helping to stabilize the aggressive or reckless moods that can lead to antisocial behavior. Generally, however, people with APD respond poorly both to medication and psychotherapy.

C. WOODFORD

SEE ALSO:
Causes of Addiction, Biological • Causes of Addiction, Psychological and Social • Conduct Disorder • Mental Disorders

Arrestee Drug Abuse Monitoring Program (ADAM II)

The Arrestee Drug Abuse Monitoring Program collects data on the use and prevalence of drugs of abuse. This information is used to improve understanding of the links between drugs and crime.

The Arrestee Drug Abuse Monitoring Program (ADAM II) grew from the Drug Use Forecasting System (DUF). Developed in 1987, DUF had three main aims—to help forecast drug epidemics, to determine the drug use of arrestees, and to offer treatment services. Beginning in 1998, the National Institute of Justice initiated a major redesign of the program and renamed it the Arrestee Drug Abuse Monitoring (ADAM) Program. ADAM was developed to track trends in the prevalence and types of drug use among arrestees in urban areas. ADAM extended the DUF system by increasing the number of data collection sites and improving the quality of the data. The first data collections for the ADAM program were in 2000. ADAM encountered funding issues and research collection ceased in 2003. In 2007, the program was re-established under the sponsorship of the Office of National Drug Control Policy (ONDCP), and is now referred to as ADAM II. The data collected through the ADAM II program provide a picture of drug abuse in the adult male arrestee population nationwide and are central to estimating drug use trends in local areas, understanding the correlation between drug use and crime, and gaining insight into the drug market activity of the target population.

ADAM operated in 35 sites, with affiliate sites in ten additional locations. The program expanded for a short time across international boundaries. Envisioned as a partnership among criminal justice organizations across the world, the international program was known as the International Arrestee Drug Abuse Monitoring Program (I-ADAM). By offering standardized surveillance systems, I-ADAM enabled accurate comparisons across countries to evaluate the relationship between drug use and crime and examined variations in illicit drug use and their associated risk factors that are neither country nor culturally specific. I-ADAM had partners in eight countries: Australia, Chile, United Kingdom, Malaysia, Netherlands, Scotland, South Africa, and Taiwan. Funding issues ended this collaboration along with the ADAM program. In 2011, ADAM II is operating in 10 of the original ADAM sites: Atlanta, GA; Charlotte, NC; Chicago, IL; Denver, CO; Indianapolis, IN; Minneapolis, MN; New York, NY; Portland, OR; Sacramento, CA; and the District of Columbia.

Program mission

ADAM II strives to support the continued development and growth of a valid and reliable database on the drug use and involvement of male arrestees from communities across the United States. The program makes every effort to provide timely information about drugs and crime, patterns of drug use, emerging drug trends, drug markets, the effects of law enforcement on drug use, and treatment needs of the male arrestee population. It develops national and local partnerships to directly and indirectly encourage and support research that will build knowledge about drugs, crime, and related social issues. ADAM II research has the potential to identify important information about related public health and safety issues, such as domestic violence, sexually transmitted diseases, and the acquisition and use of firearms. The data can also highlight the effects of law enforcement and criminal justice strategies, such as community policing and drug courts, as well as guide and strengthen local and national social policy.

Procedures

Data are collected in booking facilities during two 14-day periods each year. ADAM II sites collect data according to the same standardized procedures as the ADAM program. This allows for data comparison across the two programs. Trained interviewers collect

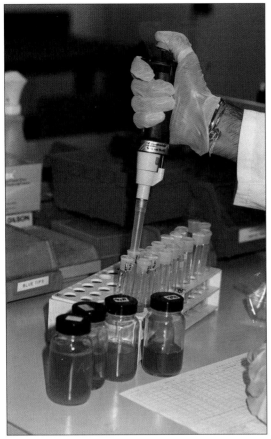

Testing arrestees' urine for a number of different drugs of abuse is an important source of data for the ADAM II program.

voluntary anonymous data and urine specimens from adult male arrestees. Face-to-face interviews generally last 20 to 25 minutes and take place within 48 hours of the interviewee's arrest. The interview covers demographic (age, employment, housing, education, and insurance coverage) and charge information, as well as drug use history, current use, recent participation in buying and selling drugs, lifetime drug treatment, and mental health treatment. For those with any illegal drug use in the prior 12 months, additional detailed information on arrests, treatment, housing, and drug and alcohol use for the last year is also collected. In addition to the drugs tested for through urinalysis, the interview collects data about the use of other synthetic narcotics, MDMA, LSD and other hallucinogens, inhalants,

antidepressants, and other substances. Information that could be used to identify an interviewee is not collected.

Arrestees are asked about their prior 12-month and prior 30-, 7- and 3-day use of marijuana, cocaine, crack, heroin, methamphetamine, and other drugs they may specify. It is critical for ADAM II to verify the self-reported drug use of respondents; therefore, urine samples are collected and sent to a central laboratory for analysis. In 2009, 86 percent of all arrestees interviewed agreed to supply a urine sample. The laboratory conducts tests for marijuana, cocaine, opiates, barbiturates, Phencyclidine (PCP), methamphetamine, amphetamine, methadone, Oxycodone, Propoxyphene (Darvon), and benzo-diazepines. Any test resulting positive for ampheta-mines is confirmed using a technique called gas chromatography, which eliminates false positives resulting from over-the-counter preparations. For most drugs, the urine test can detect substances used in the previous two to three days. Marijuana and PCP may be detected up to several weeks after use, depending on the frequency and quantity of use.

In 2009, at the time of arrest, between 56 percent (Charlotte) and 82 percent (Chicago) of arrestees across sites tested positive for the presence of some substance. Many (12 to 28 percent of all arrestees in 2009) tested positive for multiple substances. Marijuana continues to be the most commonly detected illegal substance among ADAM II participants in all but Atlanta, where the same number of arrestees test positive for cocaine use.

ADAM II continues as an essential complement to other drug survey research. The program has captured data on a population that is unique to other research on drug use and remains an important source of information on the basic characteristics, drug use, and drug market participation of arrestees—a population often more heavily involved in drugs than other groups surveyed. The program continues to provide vital information for influencing and guiding social policy and change.

P. L. TORCHIA

SEE ALSO:
Drug Testing • Prison Drug Use and Treatment • Research, Medical • Treatment

Attention Deficit Disorder

Attention deficit disorder (ADD) is a mental disorder that makes people impulsive, inattentive, and usually hyperactive as well. Sufferers from ADD are also at a higher risk of experiencing a substance use disorder.

Attention deficit disorder (ADD) is an immensely disruptive mental disorder whose sufferers cannot focus their attention in the normal way. One National Institutes of Health publication describes ADD vividly as like "living in a fast-moving kaleidoscope, where sounds, images, and thoughts are constantly shifting." ADD has many different behavioral symptoms (effects of the disorder on a person's behavior), which vary with the age of the sufferers. Infants may be restless or sleepless, constantly crying, or refusing affection. Older children may be aggressive, restless, disruptive at school, sullen, and withdrawn. They may also be low achievers despite high ability, physically clumsy, irritable, and uncooperative, and may move around constantly. By adulthood, many sufferers have learned coping strategies that help them to manage behaviors of this kind so ADD, whether diagnosed or not, may be much less apparent in older people. Nevertheless, the disorder might appear as restlessness, poor concentration, a tendency to blurt out inappropriate remarks, and an inability to follow projects through to a conclusion.

Most infants cry a lot, most children can be naughty, and most adults have periods of restlessness, which seems to suggest that most people might warrant a diagnosis of ADD. However, the American Psychiatric Association's *Diagnostic and Statistical Manual of Mental Disorders* (DSM) definition of ADD requires all these behaviors to be long term, excessive, and highly disruptive. They must also affect a person's whole life rather than just one part of it. Disruptiveness or poor concentration at school because a person does not respect his or her teacher, for example, would probably not indicate ADD.

The DSM definition of ADD is based on three broad types of behavioral problems: inattention, hyperactivity, and impulsivity. Inattention includes such symptoms as not listening when spoken to directly, not paying attention to detail, often losing things, or being easily distracted. Hyperactivity includes fidgeting, excessive running around or climbing, and nonstop talking. Impulsivity includes blurting out answers or interrupting people when they are talking. To meet the DSM diagnosis of ADD, behaviors such as these need to occur for at least six months; there must be some evidence that problems of this kind occurred before age seven; there must be a significant impairment in the person's work, home, or school life; and the symptoms must occur in at least two distinct settings (not just at school, for example).

Epidemiological studies (research into how many people suffer diseases in the wider population) suggest that around 3 to 5 percent of the population has ADD. Yet some researchers believe far more people (perhaps twice as many) suffer from the disorder and simply have not been properly diagnosed. As many as three million school-aged children—at least one per classroom—are thought to have ADD in the United States. Many more boys than girls are diagnosed, with estimates varying from a ratio of around 2:1 to as high as 9:1.

Types of ADD

Many different behavioral symptoms are involved in ADD, and the disorder varies dramatically from person to person. The most noticeable difference is that around one-third of sufferers do not show signs of the hyperactivity described in the DSM classification. This suggests that there are at least three subtypes of ADD: the most common is the combined subtype, in which sufferers show both inattention and hyperactivity; a less common subtype involves mainly inattentive and withdrawn behavior, but no hyperactivity; and a much rarer subtype involves only hyperactive behavior. ADD without hyperactivity (often seen as day-dreaming) seems to affect girls more than boys, while ADD with hyperactivity seems more common in boys.

Some researchers think there may be as many as six or more variations of ADD and that the term will one day be used as a general description for a whole cluster of different disorders. One problem with the

MEDICATION CONTROVERSY

Concerns have been raised about the numbers of children taking medication for ADD ever since the disorder was first treated with medication in 1937. The amphetamine-like stimulant drug Ritalin (methylphenidate) was developed in 1955 and became popular for treating ADD (or hyperkinetic behavior, as it was then known) in the 1960s. However, by 1995, around 6 million Ritalin prescriptions were being issued in the United States each year and around 2.5 million children were taking the drug. The United States accounted for more than 90 percent of the drug's manufacture and consumption.

In 1996 the United Nations (UN) issued a warning that methylphenidate use had spiraled out of control because of its "controversially extensive use" in treating ADD. According to the UN, "the use of Ritalin is being actively promoted by an influential parent association, which has received significant financial contributions from the preparation's leading United States manufacturer." Some doctor and parent groups have since mounted vociferous backlash campaigns against Ritalin and other ADD medications, arguing that the drugs might lead to abuse, addiction, or long-term health problems. Others contend that ADD medications have been used safely for over half a century and cite studies showing that ADD sufferers who receive medication show benefits and improvements in most cases.

current system of diagnosis and classification is that ADD sufferers with hyperactivity, by their very nature, are much more likely to be spotted, diagnosed, and treated than inattentive ADD sufferers. This might explain why so many more boys are diagnosed with ADD than girls. If boys are more likely to develop hyperactive ADD, and girls are more likely to develop inattentive ADD, boys with ADD may simply be more noticeable, even if equal numbers of girls have the disorder. The concern is that many people with inattentive forms of the disorder (boys as well as girls) may not be diagnosed or treated.

Over the years ADD has gone by a variety of other names. It is sometimes referred to as attention-deficit hyperactivity disorder (ADHD), although the terms ADD and ADHD largely mean the same thing. Other names for ADD include hyperkinesis and hyperkinetic syndrome (implying lots of movement) and minimal brain damage, minimal cerebral dysfunction, and minor cerebral dysfunction (suggesting brain damage as a cause).

Diagnosis

Unlike a physical illness, ADD must be diagnosed by looking at how a person behaves in different settings. Children are typically diagnosed when they show disruptive behavior either at home or at school. A trip to the physician usually results in a thorough and systematic evaluation of the child's behavior, including interviews with parents and teachers and detailed psychological tests. The first thing the physician is likely to do is a full medical examination to try to establish that eyesight, hearing, or other physical problems are not to blame.

A major difficulty in diagnosing ADD is that symptoms of inattention or hyperactivity can be caused by other learning difficulties, emotional problems, and other mental disorders. It would be counterproductive to diagnose ADD, for example, if a child had become distracted and inattentive because of bullying at school, a family problem such as divorce, or substance abuse. Comorbidity (when a person has two or more different disorders at the same time) is extremely common in ADD sufferers. According to some studies, comorbidity occurs in up to 97 percent of cases, with over half of all ADD sufferers having four or more other disorders. Common comorbid disorders include anxiety, depression, and substance abuse. Roughly half of all ADD sufferers also have oppositional defiant disorder (angry outbursts, temper tantrums, and irritability typically directed at parents and teachers), which can lead to conduct disorder (general troublemaking and antisocial behavior in childhood) and other problems. Around a third of ADD sufferers also have a learning disability.

A diagnosis of ADD can be a mixed blessing for sufferers and families. On one hand, it can be a huge relief to realize that behavior ascribed to laziness or poor parenting is actually caused by a recognized medical problem. On the other hand, it may prove hard to come to terms with a disability that is very difficult to treat and that may have lifelong consequences. Families may go through a process similar to bereavement, passing through stages of mourning and denial before finally accepting the diagnosis.

Causes

ADD involves many different types of disruptive behavior and may even consist of a number of quite distinct disorders, so it is perhaps not surprising that research has not identified a single underlying cause of the problem. ADD originally went under names such as minimal brain damage, reflecting the idea that it was caused by birth complications or largely undetectable brain damage in early life. That theory failed to explain more than a small proportion of cases, however, and has now largely fallen into disfavor as an overall explanation. Another once-popular theory was that food additives (such as colorings and preservatives) and refined sugar made children hyperactive. Although nutritional factors may be important, they still explain only a small number of cases. One purported cause of ADD that has been definitively ruled out is poor parenting and teaching, although it is the case that good parenting and teaching can help children to manage the problems of living with ADD.

A complete explanation of what causes ADD may be far off, but some things are already clear. The disorder tends to run in families, and links between ADD and some genes have been discovered. Genetic and family studies suggest that the disorder has a biological basis, while neurological studies are seeking to explain how and why this produces disruptive behavior. One theory is that ADD sufferers have reduced activity in those parts of the brain (the frontal lobes and basal ganglia) believed to control attention and planning and believed to inhibit disruptive and impulsive behavior.

ADD and substance abuse

The type of brain damage thought to produce ADD can also be caused in other ways. For example, alcohol abuse during pregnancy can lead to fetal alcohol syndrome (FAS) in childhood, which can have very similar symptoms to ADD. Perhaps because they are impulsive and more likely to associate with people who have educational problems, ADD sufferers are much more likely to become substance abusers. One study found that around half of all ADD sufferers abuse substances at some time in their lives, although other studies have reported lower figures. ADD sufferers' substance abuse is likely to start earlier in life, last longer, and have less chance of mitigation. Although ADD is sometimes cited as a cause of substance abuse, scientific studies do not support this definitively. From current research it is possible to say only that there is a link between ADD and substance abuse, not what the connection is or why it occurs.

Treatment

With its complex range of disturbed and disruptive behaviors, ADD cannot be treated as simply as a physical problem such as a toothache or a broken leg. Behavioral patterns can be very difficult to change, so treatment involves the learning of coping strategies and has to be tailored carefully to the needs of individual sufferers. Typically, treatment involves a combination of individual therapy (which might involve such things as helping sufferers to understand the disorder and counseling them to cope with its problems), educational intervention (such as special classes), family therapy (in which the whole family tries to support the sufferer), and medication. Prescribed medications include stimulant drugs, such as Ritalin, Dexedrine, and Adderall, and antidepressants, such as selective serotonin reuptake inhibitors (SSRIs) and tricyclic antidepressants. Types of medications and doses are always tailored to the specific needs of individual patients. Around half of all children diagnosed with ADD learn to manage the disorder in adulthood without medication.

C. WOODFORD

SEE ALSO:
Conduct Disorder • Mental Disorders

Aversion

Aversion therapies used to promote abstinence from drugs or alcohol attempt to create strong associations between the taking of these drugs and very unpleasant experiences and sensations such as vomiting or electric shocks.

Aversion therapy is based on the simple premise that the positive and negative consequences of an action, termed an outcome, can shape behavior. This premise suggests that if someone performs a behavior that results in a good outcome, the probability of that behavior being repeated will increase. Conversely, if someone performs a behavior that results in a bad outcome, the probability of that behavior being repeated will decrease. For example, if the first time someone drinks alcohol he or she has an enjoyable time, then the likelihood of him or her drinking again will be high. If he or she has a bad time, however, vomiting, getting into a fight, or getting injured, then the likelihood of drinking again will be less. Aversion therapy attempts to have the alcoholic or addict associate consumption with negative (or aversive) outcomes. Rather than being a cognitive or counseling technique, aversion is a behavioral modification treatment.

As a treatment (or deterrent) for drug and alcohol problems, aversion has been used for centuries. The Roman scholar Pliny (23–79 CE) reported that the ancient Romans would put snakes into the wine of habitual drunkards in an attempt to reduce their consumption. In medieval times, drunkards were placed in the stocks, imprisoned, or beaten to reduce their consumption.

Uses of aversion

Aversion is a general premise and is not confined to substance use or addiction. One can find aversion in all spheres of human activity. The philosophy underpins the imprisonment of those who break the law as well as past use of corporal punishment in the home and schools. If a behavior such as driving while intoxicated results in a negative outcome (a driving ban or imprisonment), then its frequency should be reduced.

The premise underpinning aversion is not new; the recognition that consequences shape behavior has been around for centuries. The difference today is that the scientific theory and principles are applied to

aversion therapy rather than punishment. Aversion therapy is not punishment and works on very different principles. However, in one basic respect it is similar: the aim of both punishment and aversion therapy is that the alcoholic or addict will come to associate the consumption of his or her drug of choice with a negative outcome.

Theoretical basis

The origins of the theoretical basis for aversion treatment lie in the research carried out by the Russian physiologist Ivan Pavlov (1849–1936), who showed that associations could be conditioned between a nonvoluntary behavior and a stimulus. Pavlov showed that dogs could be made to salivate at the sound of a bell by repeatedly sounding the bell just before presenting the dogs with food. The dogs learned to associate the bell with food and behaved toward it in the same way they would toward food, that is, they salivated, indicating they were conditioned.

This deceptively simple principle is at the heart of aversion therapy. The therapy's aim is to condition a noxious reaction (for example, vomiting) with consuming alcohol or drugs. One question that might arise is how this technique could possibly be effective when alcoholics and addicts already have so many negative outcomes, including vomiting. The answer to this lies in what psychologists call temporal contiguity. This term refers to how close together two events occur. Pavlov found that if he sounded the bell several minutes before or after presenting food, dogs formed no associations between the bell and the food. He established that there was only a short window of time when the bell could be sounded and conditioning would occur. Thus, the bell and the food needed to be contiguous (close together) temporally (in time).

It is true that alcoholics and addicts often suffer severe negative outcomes from their substance use. However, these outcomes tend to be removed from the actual behavior of consumption. A hangover, for example, occurs the day after a bout of excessive drinking. Because of this delay, the associations between the action of consumption and the consequences tend to be very weak, as it is the desired effects that happen immediately. Aversion therapy attempts to reverse this process.

The practice of aversion therapy

Aversion therapy has largely been supplanted by cognitive and counseling therapies, although it is still practiced in some medical establishments. The real peak of aversion treatment was the 1930s, mainly in Europe. Two types of unpleasant stimuli were used in these treatments: electric shocks and emetics (substances that induce vomiting).

In the procedure for the electric shock treatment, the patient has electrodes attached to his or her skin. He or she is then allowed to see, smell, and taste alcohol. While doing so, the patient receives mild electric shocks, enough to be unpleasant but not dangerous.

The alternative treatment is to give the client an emetic before taking him to a room that contains bottles of alcohol. After about six to eight minutes (the time that it takes the emetic to produce vomiting), the therapist gives the patient a glass of alcohol. The patient is asked to smell the alcohol, then take a sip, roll it around his or her mouth, and spit it out. Vomiting should then ensue.

In both of these treatments, the patient undergoes at least five sessions. Eventually, the sight, smell, and taste of alcohol should be associated with unpleasant outcomes. Evidence suggests that this form of treatment is as efficient as other forms of treatment for alcohol problems. It has been less commonly used for drug problems, however, and the evidence for its efficacy in drug treatment is less clear.

The research into aversion therapy appears to show that the emetic form of treatment works better than electric shocks. Some commentators have argued that the reason for this is that humans and animals have evolved an aversion to noxious substances as a survival technique to avoid poisoning. Humans and animals rarely, however, experience electric shocks produced by naturally occurring phenomena. Vomiting food that has gone bad is more natural than electric shocks, and electric shocks are therefore more difficult to condition.

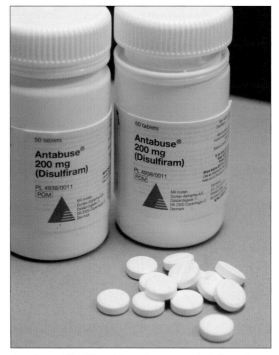

Antabuse (disulfiram) is a pharmaceutical drug that uses aversion to treat alcoholism. It works by causing people to feel ill and vomit if they drink alcohol.

Critics of the treatment suggest that it is a rather barbaric procedure. On a more theoretical note, they point to two problems. The first is that the sight, smell, and even taste of alcohol are not particularly important for alcoholics. They drink almost entirely for effect, and this association is difficult to reverse. Second, if they do start to drink again, then without the noxious stimuli, the associations with negative outcomes will soon become extinct and, indeed, more difficult to condition in the future.

While these criticisms have some validity, advocates of the treatment argue that aversion therapy is, or at least should be, only one element of a wider treatment program. It would be unusual to find aversion therapy as a stand-alone treatment. Instead it would normally accompany counseling and relapse-prevention treatment.

J. McMahon

SEE ALSO:
Conditioning • Cognitive Behavior Therapy • Counseling • Treatment

Binge Drinking

There is disagreement over the definition of binge drinking. What is certain, however, is that the consumption of large quantities of alcohol on regular occasions is damaging to health and is a possible sign of alcoholism.

Historically, alcohol-treatment clinicians have used the term *binge drinking* to describe an extended period of heavy drinking, sometimes lasting several days. Extreme drinking at this level is often evidence of alcoholism or severe alcohol dependence.

Recently, researchers have used the term to describe alcohol consumption that meets or exceeds a specified threshold. Often, this threshold is defined as five or more drinks on a single occasion. Some researchers have argued that the threshold for women, who experience more alcohol-related problems at lower consumption levels, should be four or more drinks. This is sometimes called the "5/4-plus" definition.

By this new definition, a binge drinker is a person who drinks beyond the specified threshold at least once in a two-week period. In some studies, the specified time period is 30 days. These varying definitions make cross-study comparisons difficult.

The terminology debate

The new definition of binge drinking has sparked a major controversy among researchers, prevention specialists, and clinicians. Many clinicians have complained that it obscures an important distinction between extreme, out-of-control consumption and lower, though still problematic, levels of heavy alcohol use. To avoid this confusion, the *Journal of Studies in Alcohol*, a leading journal in the field, disallows the newer use of the term *binge*, requiring instead the phrase "heavy, episodic drinking" to describe this level of drinking. Likewise, the National Institute on Alcohol Abuse and Alcoholism (NIAAA), a U.S. federal agency that funds alcohol research, has never endorsed the new use of the term.

Prevention specialists have noted that the public also tends to think that a binge-drinking episode involves a level of extreme drinking that far exceeds the research definition. As a result, the specialists note, when survey research is briefly summarized in the press, the public can get a distorted picture of current drinking norms, which might then serve to encourage high levels of alcohol consumption.

Defenders of the newer definition explain that binge drinkers are more likely to report a range of problems due to alcohol. That is true, but beyond very low levels, increase in alcohol consumption corresponds with an increase in the risk of alcohol-associated problems. Thus, whatever cut-off point is chosen to define binge drinking, people who drink at that level or higher will on average report more alcohol-related problems than those who do not.

Critics of the research definition also argue that it does not necessarily demarcate "heavy" from "moderate" drinking, as it does not account for time elapsed when drinking, or take account of body weight and whether people are eating while drinking. The phrases "in a row" and "on a single occasion" are meant to suggest a relatively short time frame, but people who space their drinks over a single occasion that lasts several hours might still be labeled a binge drinker, even though their blood alcohol concentration (BAC) might not reach levels associated with mental or physical impairment. The BAC a drinker reaches can be estimated from the number of drinks consumed, the duration of the drinking episode, and that individual's gender and body weight. One study estimated that 30 percent of drinkers whose consumption exceeded the 5/4-plus binge-drinking threshold had an estimated BAC of less than 0.06 percent, the point at which the NIAAA declares that alcohol-induced impairment generally begins.

In the United States, prevention specialists on college campuses often report having trouble accepting the newer binge definition because it undermines their credibility with many students who think of a binge as being a more extreme level of drinking. The ensuing battle over terminology often short-circuits a potentially more useful discussion about the harmful consequences of drinking large quantities of alcohol within short time periods.

The research definition of binge drinking provides a crude measure for assessing high-risk drinking, because it classifies a person as either a binge drinker

Binge drinking among students may be influenced by the prevalence of events such as happy hours.

or a nonbinge drinker. If the measure is used to assess the impact of a prevention or treatment program, then it is possible that fairly dramatic reductions in alcohol consumption could go undetected. Program evaluations should instead rely on continuous measures of consumption, based, for example, on the maximum number of drinks consumed on a single occasion during the last two weeks or the average number of drinks consumed per week.

The consumption of large quantities of alcohol on a single occasion is an important indicator of a person's alcohol habit. For years, researchers have been asking study participants whether they have consumed five or more drinks in a row in the past two weeks. If this research is continued, it will enable a greater understanding of long-term trends. There is a consensus that calling this level of drinking a binge should discontinue, but no alternative term has emerged. Here, the phrase "heavy drinking" will be used.

Prevalence in the United States

The 2009 National Survey on Drug Use and Health, sponsored by the Substance Abuse and Mental Health Services Administration (SAMHSA), reported that 23.7 percent of Americans (about 59.6 million people) aged 12 or older participated in heavy drinking, which was defined as having five or more drinks on the same occasion on at least one day in the previous 30 days. In an earlier study of adults 18 years and older, the 2001 Behavioral Risk Factor Surveillance System reported that 14 percent had at least one heavy drinking episode in the past 30 days. For this study, heavy drinking was defined as having five or more drinks on a single occasion. The heavy drinking rate was far higher for men (22 percent) than women (7 percent). Among drinkers of legal age (21 years and older), the heavy drinking rate declined with increasing age: 21 to 25 years, 32 percent; 26 to 34 years, 21 percent; 35 to 54 years, 14 percent; 55 years and over, 4 percent. Among underage drinkers aged 18 to 20, the heavy drinking rate was 26 percent.

Among different ethnic and racial groups, Hispanics had the highest heavy drinking rate at 17 percent. White respondents were next highest at 15 percent, while African American respondents had a rate of only 10 percent. Rates for other demographic groups were not reported.

Heavy drinking behavior decreased with higher education levels. Respondents who had only some high school education had a heavy drinking rate of 38 percent, whereas those who had graduated from college had a rate of 20 percent.

The 2010 Monitoring the Future Study on adolescent drug use, sponsored by the National Institute on Drug Abuse, reports on substance use in grades 8, 10, and 12. The study found that the gradual declines in teen drinking and drunkenness that became manifest in all grades in 2002 were continuing in 2010. Heavy drinking among 12th graders was far below peak levels reported in the early 1980s. For this study, heavy drinking was defined as having five or more drinks in a row in the last two weeks. In 2002, for students in grade 8, the heavy drinking rate was 12 percent. For students in grade 10, the rate was significantly higher, at 22 percent. For those in grade 12, the rate was 29 percent.

Prevalence in Europe

In 1995 the European School Survey Project on Alcohol and Other Drugs (ESSPAOD) collected survey data from students aged 15 to 16 in 22 European countries. The study defined heavy drinking as consuming five or more drinks in a row. Students in several nations reported heavy drinking rates far above the rate of 24 percent established in 1995 for U.S. students in grade 10. Only three countries had heavy drinking rates below the U.S. rate, while 19 had a higher rate, of which 13 exceeded the U.S. rate by 10 or more percentage points.

The highest heavy drinking rates were found among students in Denmark (61 percent), Finland (51 percent), United Kingdom (50 percent), Ireland (47 percent), and Ukraine (46 percent). The lowest heavy drinking rates were found in Portugal (14 percent), Hungary (23 percent), Slovenia (23 percent), Croatia (27 percent), and Slovakia (29 percent).

Consequences

Extreme binge drinking can result in alcohol poisoning. Symptoms of alcohol poisoning include vomiting, unconsciousness, cold, clammy, or pale skin, and slow or irregular breathing. A severe overdose can starve the brain of oxygen or cause the victim to choke on his or her own vomit, resulting in death.

Heavy alcohol use is associated with increased risk of injury due to automobile accidents, fires, falls, and interpersonal violence. This increased risk is due to reductions in cognitive function, physical coordination, and disinhibition, leading to greater risk taking. Longer-term medical consequences can result if such use becomes an established pattern.

Alcohol-related consequences among U.S. college students have been studied extensively. By one estimate, more than 1,400 U.S. college and university students die each year from alcohol-related causes, with approximately 80 percent of these deaths as a result of driving while intoxicated. Each year, college student drinking is implicated in roughly 500,000 nonfatal injuries, 600,000 assaults, and 70,000 sexual assaults.

The 2001 CAS showed that 20 percent of U.S. college students who drank reported having five or more alcohol-related problems since the beginning of the school year (about six months prior to the survey). Earlier CAS surveys revealed that frequent heavy drinkers were several times more likely to do something they regret, miss a class, have unprotected sex, argue with friends, get hurt or injured, damage property, and so on. Students who drink at this level are also more likely to drive after drinking.

Environmental factors

Environmental factors affect heavy drinking rates. One factor is the price of alcohol. Higher prices discourage consumption among all types of drinkers, including young heavy drinkers. Extensive research has shown that increasing prices will result in decreased alcohol-related problems. Another major factor is retail outlet density. Several studies have established a strong relationship between the per capita number of alcohol licenses or retail outlets and alcohol consumption and alcohol-related problems. The underlying mechanism of the relationship is unclear.

A 2002 study demonstrated that heavy drinking by U.S. college students under age 21 years was lower in communities where laws establish age 21 as the legal minimum age to sell alcohol. It was also lower in jurisdictions where four or more of the following six laws were in place: keg registration, a 0.08 percent BAC per se law (that defines the legal limit by which alcohol-impaired driving is defined), and restrictions on happy hours, open containers, beer sold in pitchers, and billboards and other advertising.

W. DeJong

SEE ALSO:

Alcoholism • Adolescents and Substance Abuse • Driving While Impaired • National Institute on Alcohol Abuse and Alcoholism (NIAAA)

Biopsychosocial Theory of Addiction

The biopsychosocial theory provides the most comprehensive explanation for addiction, drawing on biological, psychological, and social factors to explain the complex interactions that can lead an individual to become addicted.

The biopsychosocial theory of addiction contends that multiple factors contribute to alcohol and drug use and abuse in both adults and adolescents. These factors could include the individual's physical make-up, how he or she thinks, feels, and behaves, and the social environment in which he or she lives. The model takes into account the combined effects of a person's biology, psychological state, and social environment. It should be noted that there is no specific combination of factors that can be used to identify who will become addicted to any type of substance. Rather, this model suggests that one needs to be aware of the interaction of these factors in order to prevent and treat addiction problems. The following defines some important factors in each of the aspects of this model as applied to adolescents.

Biological factors in adolescence

A biological explanation of addiction would suggest that there is some physical condition or abnormality that makes an individual more vulnerable to substance use problems. Some key physiological factors in adolescent addiction are hormonal changes, genetic links, family history of substance-related problems, developmental level, and psychiatric disorders. Adolescence is a time when significant body changes are rapidly occurring. In particular, hormonal changes influence the effect of alcohol and other substances in the biological system. This influence may affect absorption of the drug into the body, which is a key factor in the overall drug experience. Body weight and the level of fatty tissue affect the absorption rates of many substances. In response, the rate of absorption impacts the physical reaction within the system. Lower body weight and higher fatty tissue contributes to a greater drug effect. This combination makes teenagers, and especially young women, susceptible to high absorption rates into the bloodstream. The result is an intensified response to a substance. Individual drug sensitivity may also explain a vulnerability to addiction. The degree to which an adolescent experiences the euphoric effects of drugs may influence the extent to which a drug is reinforcing. If a person has enhanced experiences with substances, he or she may be at a greater risk for heavier and more frequent usage.

Hormones and genetics

Risk-taking or sensation-seeking behaviors in young adults have also been associated with hormonal changes and genetic influences. Substance use is a common risk-taking activity during teenage years. It is frequently associated with other behaviors that can result in negative health outcomes. Such high-risk behaviors may include premature or unprotected sexual activity, driving while under the influence of substances, aggression, and suicide. Initial drug sensitivity may also be influenced by genetic makeup. There has been considerable research, particularly with regard to alcoholism, suggesting that this disorder may be inherited. Additionally, temperament attributes, such as hyperactivity, are inheritable and may contribute to early drinking.

Rates of substance disorders in offspring have been explored by various types of studies involving twins and adopted children in families with problematic substance use. These studies have provided some support for a genetic link to substance-use disorders. However, that connection has not been clearly identified. At issue is the difficulty of determining the influence of growing up in an environment of substance-use problems and identifying a specific genetic marker that is biologically inherited.

The age of the adolescent may also influence the vulnerability and sensitivity to drugs. If biological functions are not fully developed, drugs can remain in the system for longer periods of time. For example, when drugs are introduced into the body,

Research into the incidence of drug and alcohol addictions in twins and adopted children has suggested that some people may have a genetic predisposition to addictions such as alcoholism.

the enzyme system is responsible for the biochemical reactions in the cell. This process may be less effective in younger adolescents and can result in a more intense and extended drug reaction. Such powerful responses can be reinforcing and may contribute to earlier onset of problematic drug use.

The adolescent brain is also in transition. The forebrain is of particular interest in substance abuse research. The frontal cortex is the area that interprets drug actions and relays the messages to other parts of the brain. The relationship to adolescent brain development and the immediate and long-term biological implications of substance use have yet to be fully understood.

Comorbidity

Adolescent substance-use disorders have also been associated with other psychiatric problems such as depression, disruptive behavior disorders (DBD), and posttraumatic stress disorders (PTSD). High rates of comorbidity (having at least one other psychiatric disorder in addition to a substance-use disorder) have been established in the young adult population. Research carried out in 2000 suggested that about two out of three adolescents with substance-use disorders also had at least one other

psychiatric disorder. The relationship of substance use, abuse and dependence, and other mental health disorders remains unclear with regard to the types of drugs used, genetic influences of either disorder, any patterns concerning which disorders come before any others, and whether one type of disorder is the cause of another.

The biological sciences have established various connections to substance-use disorders that may make some individuals susceptible to having problems with substance use. It is important, however, to note that any biological vulnerability to any type of drug does not mean that an individual will develop an addictive lifestyle. Although physical addiction in adolescence is less likely than in adulthood, early use of substances has been associated with dependence problems later in life. The biopsychosocial model clearly stresses the importance of the biological makeup of an individual within his or her environment. The physical characteristics of an adolescent may contribute to substance use and place a young adult at risk for an addictive lifestyle.

Psychological factors

One of the major psychological factors associated with substance abuse is personality. *Personality* is a term that describes the unique features of a person. It reflects the ways in which an individual thinks, feels, and behaves. Some examples of personality characteristics that may contribute to problem substance use are his or her own view of drugs, the degree to which a person has a positive or negative sense of him- or herself, and how an individual acts under pressure or in stressful situations. An assessment of an individual's psychological framework may serve to identify addictive tendencies and provide direction for behavioral change.

Drug experiences may vary among people due to the unique characteristics of an individual's personality. Although there is a physiological response to drugs, the extent to which a person will experience the drug may be related to his or her previous drug knowledge and practices. The effect may also be heightened by thoughts, beliefs, and attitudes about using substances. These factors contribute to an adolescent's anticipation of what will occur when using drugs, which is termed drug expectancy. For example, if an adolescent expects to feel more relaxed when using alcohol or marijuana, this attitude may enhance and reinforce the anticipated drug response.

Many adolescents use alcohol and other drugs to feel good. This practice may be a coping behavior to deal with stress, to self-medicate unpleasant feelings, or to create pleasure and excitement in their lives. It is important in a psychological model to understand the emotions underlying the drug addiction. If such sentiments can be identified, then interventions may assist young adults in identifying and reducing stress and the need to use drugs to feel good. When drugs are used for pleasure, then it is important to explore what is exciting, fulfilling, and reinforcing in life that could serve as alternatives to substance use. Encouraging other activities will promote positive physical and psychological health outcomes.

Adolescents face many tasks as they grow to adulthood, including developing social skills, establishing independence from parents, seeking friendships and intimate partners, and developing inner confidence. It has been suggested that young adults who have difficulty meeting role expectations and developing basic personality attributes, such as trust, independence, and self-assuredness, are more at risk to turn to drug use. The inability to keep pace with the maturation process makes these adolescents more vulnerable to addiction and other serious behaviors and acts, including aggression and suicide.

Many aspects of the biopsychosocial model of addiction have overlapping explanations. Although sensation seeking may have a biological origin, it is also considered a personality trait. Sensation seeking is an important characteristic because it has been associated with substance use. Thrill and adventure seeking, experience seeking, disinhibition, and an inclination toward boredom have been identified as categories of sensation-seeking behavior. People who possess one or more sensation-seeking traits may have a more intense reaction or greater sensitivity to drugs. Some would suggest that risk-taking behavior is an essential part of adolescent growth and assists in the maturation process. Although this behavior may constitute a part of a young adult's rite of passage, it places the adolescent at risk for engaging in activities with detrimental outcomes such as addiction.

The biological sciences have not provided any cures and only clues to the physical origins of addictions. Studying biological vulnerability in conjunction with psychological characteristics is a more fruitful approach for understanding and then preventing and treating substance disorders in adolescents.

Social factors
The final component of the biopsychosocial model of addiction focuses on how adolescents interact with everyone around them. Two important relationship categories in young adulthood are family and peers. Other social influences to be considered are ethnic and cultural differences, school setting, employment, and the social settings of leisure activities.

Under the best circumstances, family relationships are more often than not tested during the adolescent years. Family conflict or tension may be a natural consequence as young adults seek increasing independence from parental influence. Parenting styles contribute to the living environment of the family. Extremes of protectiveness or hands-off parenting may lead to feelings of anger and resentment in youth. It has been suggested that turning to drugs may be an act of defiance and rebellion against overprotective or negligent parents.

The abuse of alcohol by one or both parents increases the chances of alcohol problems in young adults, compared with young adults living without any parental alcoholism. There are many possible explanations for this situation. An individual's genetic makeup cannot be discounted as a factor, but it does not explain all types of alcohol difficulties. It has been suggested that such issues as marital conflict, violence in the family, absence of positive role modeling, lack of support and nurturance, inconsistent parenting practices, and family stresses such as financial difficulties all may influence the initiation and ongoing drinking of adolescents in alcoholic home environments.

Sensation seeking is a common feature of growing up, but taking drugs is more likely to have a negative outcome than trying dangerous sports.

The importance and influence of peers increase as escape from parental control intensifies. Family values may be challenged or disregarded due to a greater reliance on the selection and opinions of an adolescent's friends. If a teenager becomes disconnected from his or her family, there is an increased chance that he or she will enter into drug experimentation and ongoing use. This is especially tempting when friends are participating in substance use. The earlier an individual drinks alcohol or uses other substances, the greater the chances of later problems related to addictive behaviors.

Cultural factors
Cultural attitudes surrounding the use of substances, with particular reference to family drinking customs, may impact where and how much alcohol is consumed. Some ethnic groups consider drinking a part of the family dining experience. A sizable amount of alcohol may be consumed with food, but

drunkenness is not considered an acceptable behavior. Other cultures may encourage drinking at bars as a way of meeting friends and socializing. Drinking in public places, however, may encourage the consumption of larger amounts of alcohol. Heavy drinking may also be reinforced by peer encouragement that results in an adolescent feeling a greater sense of belonging. There is not a singular distinct belief about the cause of alcoholism within most complex societies. Different attitudes and beliefs attribute alcohol and other drug use to such origins as immorality, disease, or deviant behavior. Greater cultural sanctions regarding drinking may be related to a group's view of the cause of substance abuse.

Alcohol and other drugs have also been associated with poor school performance and delinquent behavior. Research has established an association between poor academic progress and drug use. Disruptive behavior disorders, particularly conduct disorders, are frequently linked with substance abuse disorders. Conduct disorders include such serious behaviors as causing harm to other people or animals, damage to property, deceitfulness, theft, and serious rule violations. Adolescents involved in such activities often jeopardize and limit their chances of completing high school. Family functioning, peer connections, cultural attitudes and beliefs, and school performance are only a few examples of factors in the social environment that influence a person's use of substances.

The biopsychosocial model suggests that the simultaneous consideration of multiple causes of addictive behavior is a more powerful approach to preventing and treating substance use disorders than any singular factor. The model is a comprehensive view of the biological, psychological, and social environment of the individual. The task faced by adolescents and their families, teachers, physicians, and mental health professionals is identifying and putting together all the important pieces that contribute to the addiction puzzle.

L. P. KING

Causes of Addiction, Biological

The cause of drug addiction is a subject of intense examination. Investigations into the biological factors that influence the probability, cause, and development of addiction are an important area of research.

Profound addiction displaces the normal motivations of life, such as home, family, career, and self-care. Homeless addicts are particularly vulnerable to picking up diseases that can further compromise their health.

The word *addiction* derives from the Latin *addico* (to bind oneself over as a slave); the term is appropriate for the large segment of the population that experiences an enslavement to drugs. In 2009 in the United States 8.7 percent of people age 12 years or older were estimated to be users of addictive drugs, with 6.8 percent of the population characterized as heavy alcohol users.

Addiction is a complex state involving a number of contributing factors, including those that are biological, psychological, and social. The term *addiction* generally refers to a situation in which getting a drug and taking it comprise a dominant behavioral force in the life of the addict. While substance abuse may lead to addiction, substance abuse may occur independently. The American Psychiatric Association publishes a manual that is used by health care professionals as an aid for the diagnosis of drug abuse, dependency, and other mental disorders. A basic difference between substance abuse and addiction is the disruption of the normal motivational structure of an individual's personality. Normal motivation is rather varied, and it depends on the personal reward system of each individual. Some motivations will be relatively more important than others. They may also vary according to the state of the individual at the moment—those motivations that possess the highest reward for the individual will tend to influence behavior the most. For example, a rat in a laboratory can be taught (conditioned) to press a button (the behavior) for water (the reward). If the rat is thirsty (high motivation), it will press the button more in order to obtain the reward than if it is not thirsty (low motivation). As the reward is made less important, the motivation to perform the behavior will be reduced.

For addicts, the euphoria produced by abused drugs rapidly climbs the motivational hierarchy, and addicted individuals become highly motivated to seek and administer the substance that drives their addiction. The ability of drug-seeking behaviors to disrupt and displace the normal motivational choices and behaviors of an individual is known as motivational toxicity. The displacement is a reduction in the individual's engagement in normally motivating rewards, such as food, sex, or career.

Effects on nervous system

The intensity of the desire to abuse a drug is related to the effect of the drug on the neural pathways of the brain. Research suggests that many abused substances act upon a region of the brain known as the mesolimbic dopamine system, part of the brain's reward pathway. The chemical changes produced by the particular substance on these pathways can lead to drug abuse and addiction.

Many factors may influence the initial abuse of a drug, but it is the potent effects of drugs on the central nervous system that promote the abuse, which leads to addiction. Addiction involves a downward spiral of changes in the brain's modulatory systems that results in compulsive drug use. Obtaining and taking the drug begins to dominate the addict's behavior. When normal psychological and social control of behavior is no longer possible in the face of continued drug abuse, the addiction is fully developed. A paradox in the transition to drug addiction is that drug abuse can intensify even as the drug begins to lose its ability to produce pleasurable (so-called hedonic) responses. This discovery has led some researchers to propose that the brain may have a hedonic set point (like a thermostat) that is disrupted by the effects of drugs on the brain, and that drug use may be an attempt to restore the levels of brain chemicals that have been disrupted.

While the direct effect of drugs on nerve cells in the central nervous system is a major reason for drug abuse, it may not be the sole cause of addiction. Studies have shown that if drugs are administered passively to animals (without the animal working for the drug), an addictive pattern is less likely to be established or is weaker, suggesting that there is something about the self-administering behaviors that is important to establishing a pattern of addiction.

Initial drug use

How does an individual become addicted? Drug abuse can begin at a young age, and individuals may try drugs due to a number of risk factors (situations in their lives that promote abuse). One key to preventing abuse is to diminish the effect of particular risk factors. There is no single risk factor that predicts the development of drug addiction, but common ones include behavioral problems at home and school, experiencing academic failure in early grades, anger and hostility, a sensitivity to peer pressure, inadequate supervision by a parent or guardian, lax attitudes within the local community toward drugs, high availability of drugs, and having family members or friends who use drugs.

One theory of drug initiation is the gateway hypothesis. This view suggests that substances such as alcohol and cigarettes taken at early ages increase the likelihood that the individual will move on to illegal drugs. Alcohol, because of its effect on lowering normal personal inhibitions, may lead to using other drugs in combination. Also, drugs with lesser abuse potential, such as marijuana, have been shown to lead to the abuse of harder drugs such as cocaine and heroin. Despite the popularity of this idea and continued research, the data are conflicting. Much of the confusion is caused by the perspective from which the questions are asked. Studies have found that most individuals who try drugs with low addiction potential do not in turn become addicts. However, many drug users do report using drugs that have less addiction potential before moving on to new drugs (for example, individuals who have tried heroin and cocaine have probably used tobacco and alcohol). This finding suggests that an escalation, or developmental progression, of drug abuse may occur in some individuals. In the case of marijuana (a commonly cited gateway drug), it may be that the risk factors that lead to initial abuse are similar to those that lead to the abuse or addiction to harder drugs. Using marijuana may also expose someone at risk to the black-market trade in other illicit substances, apart from the effects that marijuana has on the brain.

Why do some people become drug dependent, while others who have similar life experiences and risk factors do not? The human genetic code, or DNA, may hold part of the answer. One very

FOOD AND CRAVING

Cravings for drugs and food can be triggered by external stimuli. Scientists have discovered that the smell and taste of food alone can prompt a response in the dopamine system, which is the brain's pleasure and reward center. Eating food prompts the release of dopamine in the striatum area of the brain (shown by the red-yellow tracer signal). Drug addicts and obese people have been found to have fewer dopamine receptors than nonaddicts. In a study, volunteers were deprived of food and injected with a radiotracer that binds to dopamine receptors. Ritalin blocks the reabsorption of dopamine into nerve cells and was used to indicate changes in dopamine levels during the experiment. Two controls were set up to test the response to a placebo and Ritalin without food. The subject was then allowed to see, smell, and taste the food without swallowing. In the Ritalin + food scan, increased levels of

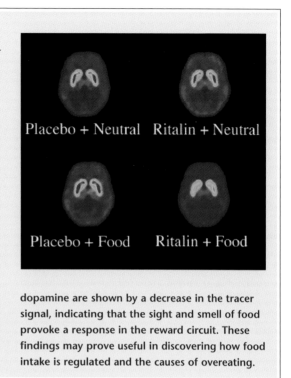

Placebo + Neutral   Ritalin + Neutral

Placebo + Food   Ritalin + Food

dopamine are shown by a decrease in the tracer signal, indicating that the sight and smell of food provoke a response in the reward circuit. These findings may prove useful in discovering how food intake is regulated and the causes of overeating.

effective way to understand the roles of genes in substance abuse is the study of identical twins. Studies of the incidence of alcoholism in twins have shown that the likelihood of identical twins (who share the same DNA) both becoming alcohol dependent is significantly greater than with fraternal twins (who share only some of the same DNA), suggesting a genetic component to alcoholism. Researchers have shown that dependence on cocaine follows a similar pattern, with pairs of identical twins being nearly 40 percent more likely to abuse cocaine than pairs of fraternal twins. In addition, one identical twin is 35 percent more likely to become addicted if his or her twin becomes addicted. While such studies are compelling, it is difficult to know whether the identical twins possess genes that relate specifically to alcohol sensitivity, metabolism, or to their psychological makeup.

Dopamine is a neurotransmitter, or chemical operating in the brain to transmit messages. Because of the central role of the dopamine system in drug actions, genetic variations in the way that system functions may contribute to abuse and addiction.

One such potential link occurs in the genes encoding certain types of dopamine receptors (receptors bind neurotransmitters or drugs, and are responsible for their effects on brain circuits). Many drugs increase the amount of dopamine that is available to affect the receptors, resulting in euphoria. There are at least five types of dopamine receptors (D1 to D5), and the D2 receptor gene is found on chromosome 11. Dopamine D2 receptors are important because they control the amount of dopamine released into the synapse (the space between adjoining neurons). There are two forms, or alleles, of this gene that are responsible for the number of D2 receptors that are made. The A1 allele is found in a much smaller percentage of the population than the A2 form. A person with the A1 allele usually has a significantly reduced number of D2 dopamine receptors in the brain, and several studies (though not all) have linked this difference with alcohol abuse.

A prevalence of the A1 allele has also been associated with brain disorders (one example is autism), raising the possibilities that either the A1 allele is a genetic contributor to drug abuse, or that the allele may be associated with underlying brain disorders that may themselves contribute to drug abuse and addiction. Studies have shown that a number of brain disorders are associated with drug dependence, including bipolar disorder, depression, schizophrenia, and anxiety disorders. These associations suggest the possibility that for some individuals, drugs are used to relieve the symptoms of the disorder or the subjective dysfunction that it causes.

Conditioning factors

Another factor related to substance dependence is the environment. Laboratory rats that are exposed to a drug in a particular place will consistently return to the location where the drug (and the euphoric experience caused by the drug) was received. This behavior indicates that a form of conditioning, or learning, has occurred (referred to as conditioned place preference). Such behavior helps to explain the response of human addicts whose drug cravings intensify when they are exposed to places where they have previously taken drugs, or even when viewing items associated with taking drugs. This response can also extend to hearing stories told by other addicts at recovery meetings. A related phenomenon is aversion, where unpleasant experiences can be paired with a specific location. Aversive conditioning is the basis of alcohol treatment with the drug Antabuse (disulfiram), which works to disrupt the metabolism of alcohol and produces nausea when alcohol is consumed.

Neuroadaptation

Drugs change the brain in many ways—a process often referred to as neuroadaptation. Exposure to drugs over time causes the normal levels of many of the brain's neurotransmitter systems to be altered, and the remarkable ability of the brain to adapt and modify its responses to the world under normal circumstances is overwhelmed by the effect of the drug. For example, the brain responds to the depressive effects of alcohol by raising the threshold for such inhibition in the brain through a process known as tolerance so that more alcohol becomes necessary to achieve intoxicating effects.

Repeated exposure to stimulants and opiates can produce a response called sensitization, in which subsequent doses produce more intense effects.

Sensitization is thought to occur through neuro-adaptations of a part of the brain called the meso-limbic system and is related to a reduction in the ability of the D2 receptors to reduce the amount of dopamine in the synapse, resulting in an overload.

Withdrawal is a well-known and serious consequence of ceasing to take certain drugs. In the cases of opiates and alcohol, the physical withdrawal symptoms can be severe and dangerous. Effects experienced by the addict include anxiety, bad moods, and sleep disruption. Withdrawal is thought to be connected to the neuroadaptational responses of the brain that occurred when taking the drug. Tolerance contributes to the severity of withdrawal by changing the set points (normal response levels) of the affected neurotransmitter systems. When the drug is withdrawn, these adaptive changes persist. For example, if the drug has had an inhibitory effect on a neural pathway, sudden withdrawal can cause the neurons to overreact to normal levels of excitatory neurotransmitters. The severity of such symptoms depends on the particular drug, but may include delirium tremens, seizures, hallucinations, rapid heartbeat, high blood pressure, rapid breathing, and fever—in essence, the addicted individual has become physically dependent upon the drug, and biological aversion to the drug's absence may contribute to a return to drug use.

Conclusion

Progress is being made in understanding addiction at many levels, ranging from the basic societal risk factors for early substance abuse down to the cellular, molecular, and genetic mechanisms responsible for the brain's response to drugs. Addiction results from the ability of certain drugs to take over the brain's capacity to adapt to change, and a deeper understanding of these processes promises to transform the way society treats addiction. These new treatments may act at multiple levels to compensate or reduce the effects of long-term drug use on the affected brain cells and circuits, or they may reduce the impact of environmental influences in relapse.

D. W. GODWIN

SEE ALSO:
Aversion • Causes of Addiction, Psychological and Social • Hereditary and Genetic Factors • Neurotransmission • Sensitization

Causes of Addiction, Psychological and Social

Drug use is influenced by more than just the way in which a person's body reacts to a substance. Psychological and social pressures also play a key part in the reasons for trying drugs and maintaining their use.

Drug abuse is caused by multiple factors. By itself, no single factor can cause someone to abuse drugs. Rather, different factors work together to make someone more likely to develop a problem. Addiction is a complex mix of biology, psychology, and social environment. It is impossible to say that any particular combination of these three factors will result in a person becoming an addict. However, there are some combinations that will make addiction a possible outcome.

The influence of biology

Nobody can predict how an individual will develop psychologically as he or she grows from a child to an adult. To some extent, characteristics of behavior and temperament can be explained by genetic inheritance. Certain people are born with genes that make them more likely to abuse substances. Others have a natural temperament that increases their risk of developing a drug abuse problem. People with this temperament tend to be interested in dangerous activities, less afraid of harm, and less concerned about what others think of them.

Certain people are also born with a natural tolerance for a drug. This natural tolerance enables people to experience the pleasurable effects of a drug with fewer adverse effects when they first start using. For example, people with this natural tolerance frequently do not feel nauseous when they first drink alcohol, use heroin, or smoke tobacco. Instead, they feel the positive effects right away and are more likely to keep using the substance.

On the other hand, certain people are more likely to experience the negative effects of a substance and will be less likely to continue using. For example, some people have decreased activity of the enzymes that break down alcohol. This decreased activity leads to a buildup of a chemical called acetaldehyde after drinking. Acetaldehyde, in turn, makes people dizzy, flushed, and nauseous. Therefore, people who lack the activity of this enzyme are less likely to become addicted to alcohol. This biological trait is most common in Asian populations.

Certain emotional or psychiatric problems that may have a significant biological component are also risk factors. These problems include antisocial personality disorder, anxiety disorders, attention deficit hyperactivity disorder, bipolar disorder, borderline personality disorder, conduct disorder, depression, learning disorders, oppositional defiant disorder, poor self-esteem, and poor social skills. In fact, almost half of people with an addictive disorder meet criteria for another psychiatric disorder. Of these psychiatric disorders, conduct disorder (a pattern of serious misbehavior in juveniles) is most associated with drug abuse. People with conduct disorder are five times more likely to develop alcohol or drug dependence than the general population.

Self-medication

The fact that psychiatric disorders are more common in people with addictions has led to the idea that people with addictions medicate their psychiatric symptoms with drugs and alcohol. This idea is commonly called the self-medication hypothesis. The self-medication hypothesis proposes, for example, that someone with attention deficit hyperactivity disorder might be more likely to use tobacco because of nicotine's ability to help certain people improve their attention span. Another example would be that people with insomnia as a consequence of an anxiety or mood disorder might be more likely to use sedating drugs, such as alcohol or marijuana, to help them sleep. People with physical pain sometimes develop a dependence on certain painkilling medications.

While the self-medication hypothesis can explain why some people abuse drugs, it does not explain drug abuse as a whole. For example, the hypothesis does not explain the drug use of people who do not have a psychiatric disorder. Even when someone does have anxiety or depression, it is often impossible to distinguish which came first, the drug use or the mental disorder. The distinction is important because many drugs of abuse cause anxiety, depression, or psychosis and can, therefore, mimic psychiatric symptoms. Withdrawal from drugs or alcohol also mimics many emotional and psychiatric problems, such as anxiety, irritability, and depression. In that situation, what is really being self-medicated is the drug dependence itself.

Another variable that predisposes people to alcohol or drug abuse is gender. With the exception of tobacco, men are much more likely to abuse drugs and alcohol. This finding is true throughout the world. For example, in the United States, men are around five times more likely than women to develop alcoholism. There is no clear explanation for this statistic. Some think that it may reflect the existence of more cultural taboos against women drinking or using drugs. Women also have less tolerance to alcohol and are, therefore, more sensitive to its effects. This decreased tolerance is due to two factors. First, women have less of the enzyme alcohol dehydrogenase in their stomachs. This enzyme is

important in breaking down alcohol. Because women have less of this enzyme, they absorb more alcohol into their bodies when they drink. Second, when alcohol is absorbed, it is dissolved into water within the body. Women have a lower percentage of water in their bodies and, therefore, reach higher blood-alcohol levels for the amount they drink.

Effects of the social environment

Environmental factors affecting drug use can be individual, familial, or societal. An example of an individual factor is academic failure. Another example is an individual's attitude toward drugs. Teenagers who have positive beliefs about drugs or who believe that "everyone else is doing it" are more likely to use drugs themselves.

Environmental factors can also be influenced by one's family. For example, parents who abuse drugs are more likely to have children who abuse drugs. By using drugs, parents model behavior that their children can learn and mimic. Furthermore, parents make alcohol, drugs, and tobacco more available to their children by keeping such substances in the house. Whenever the availability of a substance increases, its use also increases. In addition, if children see their parents using drugs, they are more likely to believe that everyone else is using drugs or that drugs are not very harmful. Such beliefs are individual risk factors for drug abuse. For similar reasons, having siblings who abuse drugs is also a risk factor for teenage drug abuse.

Having parents who are either too lenient or too harsh is also a risk factor. Being too lenient includes using limited discipline and having minimal supervision of a child's activities. Being too lenient can also decrease the consequences of misbehavior, including drug use. As a result, drug use increases. Conversely, being too harsh can be expressed by anger, negative communication patterns, and physical or sexual abuse. These behaviors decrease the bond between children and parents. By contrast, a warm and close relationship between children and parents tends to decrease drug use.

The early relationship, or attachment, between infants and parents also can affect one's risk of developing drug abuse. More than two hundred years ago, the British physician Thomas Trotter proposed that people weaned from breast-feeding too

FACTORS FOR SUBSTANCE ABUSE IN THE ELDERLY

While the vast majority of drug and alcohol use begins before the age of 20, there is also a significant increase in alcohol-related problems at about the age of 60. The risk factors typically associated with this increase are the following: a family history of alcoholism, loss of a spouse or friends, medical illness, past history of alcohol abuse, and retirement. The overall explanation for these factors is that older adults who lose their daily structure and social supports are more likely to develop problematic alcohol use. Despite the overall increase in alcohol use, the elderly remain much less likely to abuse illicit substances.

Boredom and lack of interest in learning may lead to a child failing school tests. Poor academic achievement can be a significant risk factor in whether an adolescent develops an addiction problem.

early were more likely to develop alcohol dependence later in life. A study published in the *American Journal of Psychiatry* in 1999 has since supported this hypothesis by showing that boys weaned before three weeks of age had an increased risk of developing alcohol dependence later in life. However, the underlying connection between breast-feeding and alcoholism is still unclear.

Scientists have characterized the different types of attachment to see if certain types are more likely to lead to later emotional and behavioral problems. Attachment is measured by carefully observing infants' reactions when they are separated and then reunited with their caretakers. In a secure attachment, the infant demonstrates visible pleasure after being reunited with the familiar adult. In the three types of insecure attachment, infants do one of the following upon reuniting with their caretaker: they ignore the caretaker, get angry, or act confused.

The insecure attachment characterized by getting angry more commonly leads to behavior problems with peers and teachers in the early school years. The explanation for these problems is that children develop the ability to trust others early in life. If they do not develop a trusting relationship with their main caretaker, they then view subsequent relationships with similar mistrust, even if there is no basis for that mistrust. Eventually, they more often develop a negative view of themselves and others.

This early difficulty getting along with peers and teachers can either become a pattern of continued behavior or can be improved by positive experiences later in life. If the behavior becomes a pattern, it can lead to academic failure, peer rejection, association with other delinquent peers, and poor self-esteem. These consequences, in turn, are risk factors for drug abuse. In fact, adults and teenagers who recall insecure attachments to their caretakers are more likely to have drug abuse problems.

On the other hand, the consequences of insecure attachments can be lessened by warm and trusting relationships later in life. This finding may partially account for the ability some people have to succeed in life despite adverse experiences as a child. It is also important to note that infants derive a certain amount of emotional support from an insecure attachment, and that an insecure attachment is usually much better than having no attachment at all.

Environmental influences also include certain societal factors. Common societal beliefs affect the acceptability and availability of drugs as well as laws about drugs. These things, in turn, influence teenage drug abuse. For example, adolescents are more likely to abuse drugs if drugs are readily available. Teenagers are also more likely to use drugs if their peers abuse drugs or if the society in which they live does not think drugs are harmful. In fact, the perceived harmfulness of a drug often predicts future trends of drug abuse. When the perceived harmfulness of a substance decreases, the use of the substance increases.

Having friends who use drugs is one of the biggest risks for teenage drug use. There are a number of possible explanations for this finding. Teenagers with friends who use drugs are likely to experience peer pressure to use and also have more access to drugs through their friends. They are also more likely to receive the message that drug use is more common than it actually is.

Government legislation also affects drug use. Laws prohibiting drugs tend to decrease their overall use. Legislation taxing alcohol and tobacco also decreases the use of these substances. Whenever the cost of a substance increases, its use goes down, even among people who have an addiction.

Easy access to cheap liquor can have a strong influence on the consumption rate of drinkers.

Furthermore, whenever the availability of a substance increases, its use will also increase. Therefore, consumption of alcohol increases when there are more stores selling alcohol and when they are open longer hours.

Geography also plays an important role in the development of drug abuse. For example, cocaine and heroin tend to be more available in urban areas. Consequently, use of these substances is much increased within large cities. On the other hand, methamphetamine tends to be more available in rural areas of the United States. The reasons for methamphetamine's prevalence in rural areas are that the drug is easily made in illicit laboratories and that some of the chemicals necessary to make this drug are commonly found in the farming industry.

Overlap between factors
Biological and environmental influences frequently overlap. One reason is that environmental factors produce biological changes in the body. For example, child abuse and emotional trauma can alter blood levels of cortisol, epinephrine, and norepinephrine, which are associated with stress. Trauma has also

been shown to alter brain and thyroid functioning. Some of these changes have been shown to last for years after the actual trauma.

On the other hand, psychological attributes can affect environmental events. For example, a difficult temperament or disruptive behavior caused by attention deficit hyperactivity disorder may elicit anger and negative communication patterns from parents and other adults. Thus, biological and environmental factors exert a mutual influence on each other.

Because of the connection between biological and environmental factors, addictions are increasingly viewed as a medical problem. This viewpoint supposes that, in some people, a combination of factors alters the part of the brain that produces the feeling of pleasure. This part of the brain is called the reward system, and typically produces pleasure in response to things that promote survival, such as food and sex. However, in addictions, a reward system develops that overreacts to substances of abuse. This view is consistent with the finding that addictions are very difficult to stop without outside help and that people do not intentionally develop an addiction.

Viewing addictions as primarily a medical problem does not mean that treatment must consist of only biological therapies, such as medication. Psychotherapy, for instance, also produces biological changes in the body. Biological changes also stem from other common aspects of addiction recovery, such as establishing a regular sleep pattern or managing stress.

Reducing the risks

Knowledge about the risk and protective factors of drug abuse has led to increased interest in drug-abuse prevention. Prevention programs that intervene at the individual level frequently educate teenagers about the effects of drugs or attempt to improve their academic performance. Prevention programs often employ role playing in which teenagers practice how to refuse an offer of drugs. By practicing, they are prepared when actually faced with peer pressure to use.

Drug prevention programs also intervene at the familial level by helping parents develop good relationships with their children and appropriate supervision and discipline strategies. If applicable, helping parents with their own addiction problems will also decrease their children's substance abuse.

Other prevention programs target societal risk and protective factors. One such intervention attempts to establish conservative norms of drug use. Studies show that teens usually overestimate the amount of drug use around them. Some prevention programs combat this belief by showing teens that most of their peers do not actually use drugs. Prevention programs similarly try to increase the perceived harmfulness of a substance. If they can convince the community that drugs are indeed harmful, they are also likely to decrease drug use.

Other societal interventions involve governmental legislation. For example, age limits for buying alcohol and tobacco tend to decrease teenage drug use. Legislation in the United States banning smoking in public places, such as restaurants, also decreases overall smoking rates. The explanation for this finding is that smoking bans decrease the availability of tobacco, increase its perceived harmfulness, and make people who have already quit smoking less likely to relapse. Furthermore, laws making certain substances illegal decrease overall drug use by making substances less available and increasing their perceived harmfulness.

The vast majority of drug and alcohol problems start in adolescence. In fact, it is very rare for most drug and alcohol problems to start after the age of 20. Drug and alcohol use usually peaks when people are in their 20s. After this age, people typically decrease their drug and alcohol use as they develop careers or have families. Therefore, if prevention programs can delay the onset of drug use by several years, they are likely to make a large impact on the number of people who eventually develop a drug-abuse problem. The explanation for this finding is that it frequently takes time for the body to become addicted to a substance. Therefore, the earlier people start abusing a substance, the more time they have to become dependent. Once a drug user is dependent, the more difficult it is to stop.

C. THURSTONE, P. RIGGS

SEE ALSO:

Addiction • Addictive Behavior • Biopsychosocial Theory of Addiction • Causes of Addiction, Biological • Dual Diagnosis • Mental Disorders • Prevention • Protective Factors • Risk Factors • Trauma and Addiction • Vulnerability

Children

Relationships established in the early part of one's life can influence how an individual copes with the pressures of growing up. Positive factors in childhood can prevent teenagers from indulging in risky behaviors such as drug use.

The use of alcohol, tobacco, and other drugs among young people can lead to many problems. Substance use at any age is related to addiction, injury, disease, family and legal problems, imprisonment, and death. Among children, substance use can also lead to many other problems, including school failure, delinquent behavior, isolation, negative social attitudes, medical problems, depression, violence, and suicide. Research has shown that the earlier substance use is started, the more likely a person is to develop alcohol or other drug problems later in life.

Trends in drug use in adolescents

According to national surveys carried out in 2009, 10 percent of young people aged 12 to 17 reported current use of illicit drugs, with marijuana the major illicit drug used. The rate of current alcohol use among youths aged 12 to 17 was 14.7 percent. Youth binge and heavy drinking rates in 2008 and 2009 were similar, at 8.8 and 2 percent respectively. Past month tobacco use for the same cohort was 11.6 percent, with cigarette use declining since 2002 but use of smokeless tobacco increasing from 2.0 percent in 2002 to 2.3 percent in 2009.

Risk factors

To prevent substance use and its related problems among children and teenagers, it is important to identify risk factors associated with an increased likelihood of substance use and dependency. A risk factor is any condition or element that increases harm or danger. Risk factors associated with substance use are those conditions or elements that increase the harm or danger to the child by increasing the likelihood of future use of substances. Examples of risk factors include having family members who abuse substances, school failure, poor coping skills, and association with friends who use. Risk factors can be associated with all aspects of life and include factors associated with the individual, peers and friends, family, school, community, and the environment.

Prevention and protection factors

Many children who are at risk do not develop substance-use problems later on. These children have protective factors in their life to prevent them from becoming involved with harmful substances. Identifying risk factors helps in identifying those children who are vulnerable to substance use and who may be in need of extra protection. Just as there are risks associated with substance use, there are also protective factors or conditions that can help prevent a child from beginning the use of substances. Examples of protective factors include a positive outlook, healthy family relationships, clear rules and boundaries, and involvement in healthy social and recreational activities. Protective factors can also be categorized in the areas of individual, family, peer, school, community, and environment.

Individual factors

Individual risk factors are those that are associated with the physical, emotional, and mental health of the individual child or adolescent. Having a parent or family member who is an alcohol or drug abuser increases a child's risk due to a possible genetic or familial predisposition, but also because the child sees substances used in an abusive manner to cope or solve problems. Children who are thrill seekers, who are unable to cope with stress and problems, and who are unable to express anger in a healthy manner are all at risk of developing problems with substances. For many children, alcohol and other drugs provide an escape from anger and stress and a seemingly easy way to feel better about life. A young person is less likely to know that alcohol and other drugs can cause addiction and are dangerous and risky ways to solve problems.

Individual protective factors are those characteristics or traits that are naturally present in the child or that can be taught or reinforced. Children who are at ease socially and are able to communicate well with both children and adults are not as easily frustrated and are protected from turning to

Strong family relationships where parents and children interact and share activities are influential in preventing children from becoming involved in substance use when they reach their teens.

substances to solve their social and communication problems. Children who are taught how to solve problems, who feel as if they have control, and who know where to get help are less likely to use alcohol or drugs to solve their problems.

Family factors

Children learn their earliest behaviors and attitudes within the family setting. Children who do not have positive, loving family relationships to guide and help them are at greater risk because they feel that no one cares about them or their behavior. If a child has parents or brothers and sisters who use drugs or alcohol, the child learns that substance use and abuse are normal and acceptable parts of growing up. Children who do not have any family guidance or supervision do not learn that substance use can be unhealthy and dangerous.

Families can establish guidelines and rituals that protect children from substance use. A number of studies have shown that constantly changing rules can impair the parents' ability to monitor their child's activities and leave the child uncertain of the limits of acceptable behavior. A parent's own drug use can also lead to a lack of supervision that allows children to mix with peers who may encourage them to try drugs. On the other hand, families who eat dinner together and have time for talking and sharing activities are less likely to have children with substance abuse problems. Communication is important in defining relationships between parents and children and establishing security and trust.

Peer factors

Children interact with friends, classmates, and peers on a frequent basis and can be positively and negatively impacted by others in their age group. Peer influence occurs through bonding and friendship, social activities, and the setting of what are determined to be acceptable attitudes and behaviors. If children or adolescents have friends who use alcohol, tobacco, or other drugs, they are more likely to use substances. Children who do not have many friends or positive relationships with peers may turn to substances to attract friends, to become accepted, or to cope with loneliness.

Adolescents who associate with others who break rules, act aggressively, or rebel against authority are more likely to be at risk for using substances because they see their friends doing dangerous things as part of their normal routine.

Children can learn social skills and self-confidence from belonging to a healthy peer group. Children who are involved in structured peer activities such as sports, clubs, and so on, can be protected because they have a place to go where alcohol and drugs are not part of the activity. Children who have many different types of friends may be protected in that they do not have to choose dangerous friends in order to be part of a group.

School factors

School policies, safety, sense of belonging, and academic performance all play a part in the level of risk associated with children becoming involved with substances. Children who are frequently absent from school and who are experiencing school failure are at risk of using substances. If children go to schools without clear rules and policies against the use of drugs, there is a greater risk because there is no consequence or discipline to keep children from harm. Schools with a great deal of violence, bullying, and chaos are risky environments through a lack of supervision and increased opportunities for children to be exposed to, and engaged in, dangerous activities.

Schools can offer prevention and protection from substance use in the form of accurate information, codes of conduct, and opportunities to explore the world in a safe environment. Children who feel they can contribute to the school by participating in academic and social activities are protected through their ability to see themselves as competent individuals who are able to interact with adults and peers. If schools offer clear expectations, written policies, guidance, help for problems, and a safe environment, children are less likely to be exposed to substances or see the use of drugs in a positive light.

Community

The community where a child lives and plays has an influence on how much risk a child is at for substance use. Communities that tolerate and accept drug use put their children at risk by failing to set and follow clear rules and guidelines for acceptable behavior. Some communities are uneducated or unaware about the presence of substance use in their community. Children who do not have any place to play or who lack services such as education, health care, shopping, or transportation in their community are at greater risk because they do not have the choices that might offer them healthy alternatives to using substances.

Like the school, the community can provide a safe place for children to grow and play while learning acceptable behaviors for interaction and participation without substance use. When a community has a pleasant, clean atmosphere with plenty of adult supervision and role models, children are offered protection by having another safe place to go in addition to their family and school. Communities that involve children in events like community picnics and block parties protect their children by offering them a way to be accepted and interact without alcohol or drugs.

Environmental factors

Laws, community standards, cultural norms, and codes of conduct can decrease or increase the risks present in the larger environment in which a child lives and interacts. If there are not adequate laws and standards in place to provide a safe world or environment, then the risk of children becoming involved with substances increases. Governments, communities, schools, and businesses that do not establish laws and rules to keep children safe put children at risk for trying dangerous and unhealthy behaviors.

Protection can also come from external sources, such as law enforcement, legislators, and governing bodies. Laws that set a minimum drinking age and purchase age for alcohol and tobacco protect children from being exposed to risky behaviors before they have the physical and emotional maturity to handle them. Neighborhood groups, schools, religious organizations, and law enforcers who collaborate to protect children provide acceptance, security, and a way to live without using dangerous substances.

C. FICHTER-DESANDO

SEE ALSO:
Adolescents and Substance Abuse • Family Environment • Prevention • Protective Factors • Risk Factors

Clinics

There are many different services available for people who seek help with their addiction problems. Most will use a specialized clinic that can provide a number of therapy options to suit the severity of the addiction.

Clinics are the main places where people with substance abuse problems go to seek help for addiction. Such places are variously referred to as centers, facilities, or clinics. There are a range of treatment options that can be offered, depending on the needs of the individual, the resources available, the severity of the addiction, the existence of other mental health problems, and the degree of interest in changing the addictive behavior. Patients are assigned to different levels of care based on any one or more of these variable characteristics.

Most clinics require an initial telephone assessment, which can be very brief or detailed, depending on the clinic's philosophy and range of services. The initial assessment is usually followed by an appointment at the clinic for a more detailed evaluation of problems. The appointment also includes discussion of the treatment program, payment information, and future scheduling options, such as when to start treatment or whether to extend the evaluation for a few more sessions. The intensity of treatment can be determined after the evaluation, generally starting at the least intensive and going up to the most intensive, depending upon the needs of the patient. The range of options includes outpatient treatment, intensive outpatient (IOP), and partial hospitalization.

Oupatient clinics
Outpatient treatment is the least restrictive environment in the continuum of care. This type of treatment comprises a broad range of services from professionals of various backgrounds, including psychotherapists, psychologists, psychiatrists, and certified addictions counselors (usually doctors) specializing in treating addiction. Outpatient services can also be provided at clinics, centers, and in medical office settings, each providing different levels of intensity and catering to a different population or subpopulation. Private practice is a variant of outpatient treatment and is the least restrictive of all professional settings. The professional therapist or counselor usually provides a range of services to the patient, including assessment and evaluation of problem areas, guidance and assistance with problem resolution, and motivational intervention to induce change in a desirable direction. People providing these services are licensed or certified in the state in which they practice and are usually monitored by a state governing board to ensure consumer protection. Many treatment centers offer outpatient programs. The intensity of the program is measured by the number of times a person uses the facility's services. Most programs consist of a combination of group therapy once a week with individual therapy once or twice a week. The maximum number of sessions undertaken is three per week and the minimum is once every other week.

Intensive outpatient clinics
Intensive outpatient (IOP) treatment is usually a step above the outpatient level of intensity and is defined as a minimum of three contacts per week. Sessions can be a combination of group and individual therapies. Some clinics offer educational groups called didactics as part of an IOP program. In general, IOP services consist of a three-hour session three or four times a week. Some of these programs are held in the evenings to accommodate people who are working or who might have child care or other scheduling problems. Most clinics try to include the spouse, partners, or family members in the program and often have a separate and dedicated family day, which can be a crucial element of the recovery program. On average, around 50 percent of addiction cases have a co-occurring mental disorder, such as depression, anxiety, or insomnia, that may have resulted from addiction or that may have influenced the addict's initial use of drugs. Some clinics integrate physical and mental health treatment by having available in-house staff or on-call physicians, psychiatrists, or addiction specialists to tackle any of these disorders when they occur in addiction patients.

Partial hospitalization

Partial hospitalization is a more intensive program that often consists of a full day of multidisciplinary professional services. A patient arrives in the morning and remains at the facility all day but goes home at night. Day treatment is a less intense variant of partial hospitalization for substance abuse or addiction and consists of a four-hour block of services as many as five or six times a week for a specified period, usually one month. Again, most clinics involve the spouse or partner and family in the program. Clinics often have specialized staff available to deal with health and mental problems arising from the addiction. Also included in this type of treatment is a comprehensive detoxification, or "detox," from all mood-altering substances. Nurses and physicians (who can be psychiatrists or general physicians specializing in addiction) are responsible for conducting, supervising, and administering medications as appropriate.

Undergoing detoxification

The first step in recovery after making the decision to "get clean" is to clear the body of toxic substances. This process—called detoxification, or detox—usually occurs in a supervised medical setting. The body has to be withdrawn safely from all chemicals to prevent serious medical complications. Doctors, nurses, and other staff work in centers that specialize in the detox process. The amount of time an individual remains in detox varies from person to person and depends on what substances have been used, the length of use, and the symptoms to be treated. The methods used for this process encompass social and medical treatments that address physical and emotional or everyday welfare problems, and specific treatments aimed at a particular type of drug addiction, such as rapid opiate detox for heroin, OxyContin, and other narcotics. Medications such as buprenorphine (Buprenex), Suboxone, and methadone are used for managing withdrawal from opiates to prevent patients from having to undergo full inpatient treatment, which sometimes occurs if partial hospital detox fails. Other medications include tranquilizers of the benzodiazepine family (for example, Ativan, Valium, or Librium), which are commonly used to calm the anxiety and withdrawal that a person experiences when he or she stops or

Group therapy sessions at which individuals can talk about their addiction problems are a feature of many outpatient treatment programs. Groups usually meet once a week for a specified period.

reduces use of a substance. Care must be taken with patients detoxing from chronic alcohol abuse as the sudden cessation of alcohol intake can cause life-threatening withdrawal effects.

Co-occurring disorders

When mental illness and substance disorders coexist, both disorders are often considered as primary conditions and must be treated by an integrated dual program, as required by federal and professional societies' guidelines. These phenomena are often referred to as co-occurring disorders to highlight the fact that the disorders are separate conditions and can occur in multiples (not only dual disorders but sometimes triple or quadruple disorders). Each disorder can exist independently of the others, or exacerbate one another, which is usually the case. This category of diagnosis is reserved for those seeking treatment for substance abuse and a co-existing disorder. The Center for Substance Abuse Treatment (CSAT) of the Substance Abuse and Mental Health Services Administration (SAMHSA) defines dual diagnosis, or co-occurring disorder, as "the simultaneous existence of a substance-use disorder interacting with one or more independent mental disorders or a cognitive, physical, sensory, or developmental disability. The disorder or disability is of a type and severity that exacerbates the substance-use disorder or other conditions, and complicates treatment of the substance-use disorder, or interferes with functioning in age-appropriate social roles."

Methadone maintenance clinics

A subtype of clinic is the opioid dependence treatment clinic, often referred to as a methadone clinic. These clinics use a substitute medication that acts on the same systems of receptors in the brain as opioids but has a different pharmacology and longer duration of effect in the body, producing a less euphoric effect and therefore having less potential for abuse. Most methadone clinics are found in major metropolitan areas and are heavily regulated by the federal government. Regulation is necessary to protect against misuse or diversion of medication from treatment settings to the street and ultimately into the hands of addicted individuals. Methadone has been used for the treatment of millions of opioid-dependent patients for more than 35 years. The effects of methadone on the health of these people has probably been studied more thoroughly than those of any other medication throughout medicine. Mary Jeanne Kreek, one of the best-known and leading researchers in the field of methadone maintenance treatment, has summed up the findings: "The most important medical consequence of [ongoing] methadone treatment, in fact, is the marked improvement in general health and nutritional status observed in patients as compared with their status at time of admission to treatment. Most medical complications observed in methadone

maintenance patients are either related to ongoing preexisting chronic disease, especially chronic liver disease, the onset of which occurred prior to entry into methadone treatment, or to coexisting new diseases or illnesses or to ongoing polydrug or alcohol use."

In general, people actually become healthier in methadone maintenance treatment—just how healthy depends on the individual's condition before treatment and how well the person takes care of him- or herself during treatment. People with certain medical conditions may feel body or bone aches and pains. Sometimes these aches are just a consequence of growing older. However, such afflictions often go unnoticed during a stressful life of opioid addiction. A landmark study that began in the mid-1970s by researchers at the University of California at Los Angeles followed male heroin addicts admitted to a court-ordered drug treatment program in California during the early 1960s. Interviews were conducted with the men in 1974 and 1975. They were interviewed again in the mid-1980s. The final report presented the findings of a 33-year follow-up, carried out in 1996 and 1997. Of the 581 men in the original study, the researchers found that 284 had died. Of these, 21.6 percent died as the result of drug overdoses or from poisoning by adulterants added to the drug. Another 38.6 percent had died from cancer or from heart or liver disease. Three died from AIDS. Homicides, suicides, or accidents killed 55 of the group. Disturbing as these numbers were—the death rates were higher, by several orders of magnitude, than those for the general population—the struggles of the men who were still living were equally troubling.

Due to multiple societal and economic shifts, it has been difficult for communities and governments (local, state, and federal) to keep substance-abuse clinics viable on a long-term basis without changes in how and to whom they provide their services. However, a list of locally available physicians, clinics, and centers specializing in treating addictions can be obtained by contacting SAMHSA.

M. KARAM-HAGE

SEE ALSO:
Continuum of Care • Detoxification • Medical Care • Treatment • Treatment Centers

Cocaine Addiction Treatment

While most methods for treating cocaine addiction involve some form of psychotherapy, considerable research is being carried out into the use of medications that will help cocaine addicts to abstain.

Among high-school seniors in the United States, approximately 8 percent have used cocaine at least once in their lifetime. Because of its reinforcing effects, such as feelings of euphoria, elevated energy, and increased self-confidence, cocaine has a high potential for addiction. Over time, cocaine use can lead to serious neurological, cardiovascular, behavioral, and cognitive impairment. In addition, cocaine users are at high risk for overdose and may experience seizures, stroke, and pulmonary complications. These issues underscore the need for effective treatments for cocaine addiction.

Difficulties in treating cocaine addiction

There are a number of difficulties in treating cocaine addiction. First, many cocaine users do not seek professional treatment. Some individuals do not consider their cocaine use a problem. Others may feel embarrassed or ashamed about their drug use and have difficulty admitting that it causes problems in their life. Because cocaine is an illegal substance, people may also be concerned about any legal consequences of admitting their drug use. Finally, some health insurance companies do not cover the cost of substance abuse treatment, which is often long-term and expensive. As a consequence of cocaine use, many individuals have serious financial problems or are unemployed and are thus unable to pay for their treatment. All of these factors decrease the likelihood that people addicted to cocaine will seek professional treatment for their problem.

Another difficulty in treating cocaine addiction is the fact that most individuals with cocaine addiction also meet diagnostic criteria for other psychiatric disorders. That is, they have comorbid (co-occurring) disorders. Commonly co-occurring disorders include alcohol dependence, post-traumatic stress disorder, major depression, attention deficit hyperactivity disorder (ADHD), and personality disorders. Comorbid psychiatric disorders affect the clinical presentation, severity of substance use, motivation for treatment, and ability to abstain from cocaine.

Finally, cocaine is a drug that is characterized by highly reinforcing properties, strong cravings, and high relapse rates. Cocaine is a short-acting drug, so the feelings of euphoria do not last long. In order to try to keep the high going, individuals may frequently readminister the drug until their supply disappears. The average cocaine binge lasts between 12 hours and 7 days. During this time, the individual is usually "missing in action" and is difficult, if not impossible, to reach and reengage in treatment.

Medical care

Individuals addicted to cocaine sometimes first present for treatment in a hospital emergency room. Signs of cocaine toxicity, such as hyperthermia (high temperature), seizures, psychosis, and tachycardia (rapid hearbeat), are a serious concern and must be carefully monitored by medical staff. If left untreated, symptoms of cocaine toxicity can result in death.

Following the cessation of cocaine use, withdrawal symptoms may be present for several weeks. These symptoms may include depression, fatigue, apathy, and hypersomnia (excessive sleeping). These withdrawal symptoms can complicate proper diagnosis because they can mimic symptoms of other psychiatric disorders, such as major depression. It can be difficult to discern whether the depressive symptoms are a result of the cocaine use, a separate disorder that contributes to the cocaine use, or a withdrawal symptom that will diminish as the person progresses through the withdrawal stage.

In addition to comorbid psychiatric disorders, individuals addicted to cocaine sometimes have comorbid medical conditions, such as HIV infection and hepatitis, that warrant assessment and treatment.

Psychotherapy and behavioral therapy

Psychotherapy and behavioral approaches are the most widely used forms of cocaine addiction treatment. In particular, cognitive behavioral therapies (CBT) have been shown to be effective in the treatment of cocaine addiction. One of the guiding principles behind CBT is the idea that we feel the way we think. So if we change how we think, we will change how we feel and behave.

Relapse prevention (RP) is a type of therapy that combines cognitive and behavioral skills interventions with lifestyle modifications. RP helps individuals to develop awareness of high-risk situations (people, places, and things that increase the risk for using cocaine); feelings of self-control and confidence; and a repertoire of coping skills. A technique called cognitive restructuring is used to help (1) identify maladaptive or harmful ways of thinking, such as the thought "I need a hit to get through the day," or "I will feel better if I use"; (2) to challenge those thoughts, for example, by asking if it is really true that you need a hit; and (3) substitute harmful ways of thinking with more positive, adaptive ways of thinking, such as the thought "I want a hit, but I don't need a hit. Using is just going to make me feel worse in the long run."

Voucher-based treatment programs have also been helpful in treating cocaine addiction. In this type of treatment, individuals are given vouchers that can be exchanged for items such as movie tickets or groceries. Being given these vouchers depends upon the cocaine user staying abstinent.

Another type of therapy that uses CBT principles is motivational enhancement (ME). ME is particularly useful in helping to decrease ambivalence about quitting and to increase internal motivation to stop using drugs. It is well known that most individuals in treatment for cocaine addiction are ambivalent about quitting. While they know cocaine is detrimental to their lives, the reinforcing properties of the drug make it difficult to quit. ME helps cocaine users to think more about their future goals, for example, having a family, a good job, and good physical health, and to consider whether using cocaine will help or hinder them in reaching those goals.

Although research shows that psychotherapy and behavioral treatments can be very effective in treating cocaine addiction at least for some, most studies also show that treatment is complicated by high rates of drop out and relapse. In addition to these approaches, many individuals also find self-help groups, such as Cocaine Anonymous, useful in their recovery. Major lifestyle changes are often necessary, such as breaking off relationships with dealers and drug-using friends, discarding drug paraphernalia, and changing one's telephone number or geographic location. These changes enable individuals addicted to cocaine to achieve and maintain abstinence.

Pharmacotherapies

At present, no pharmacotherapy—that is, medication—has been approved by the U.S. Food and Drug Administration to treat cocaine addiction. The majority of past research in this area has focused on dopaminergic (DA) agonist agents and antidepressant medications, but the results have been modest. Dopamine is a neurochemical associated with cocaine's "rush." Cocaine works by binding to the dopamine transporter and preventing its reuptake (reabsorption by the nerve cells). A number of negative side effects, such as headache, hypotension, and psychosis, have been associated with DA agents.

Unlike DA agents, antidepressants have relatively few and minor negative side effects. However, their onset of action is delayed, and it can take 10 to 20 days before the medication takes effect. Success in treating cocaine addiction with antidepressants has also been modest. A number of other agents, such as carbamazepine, disulfiram, and buprenorphine, have also been tested but with little success.

A new vaccine for cocaine addiction, TA-CD, is being tested. The vaccine works by blocking the pleasurable, reinforcing effects of cocaine. It is then less likely that the individual will use cocaine since the effects being sought after will not occur. Preliminary tests have shown that the vaccine is safe and well tolerated. Other research investigating the combination of drugs such as buprenorphine and disulfiram for cocaine addiction are also underway.

Researchers have begun to design psychotherapies to address specific comorbid diagnoses. For example, therapies to treat cocaine addiction and post-traumatic stress disorder have been developed, and the preliminary results show promise. Finally, gender-specific treatments are also being explored to meet the differing needs of cocaine-addicted men and women.

S. E. Back

SEE ALSO:
Addictive Behavior • Cognitive Behavior Therapy • Dual Diagnosis • Relapse • Research, Medical • Treatment

Cognitive Behavior Therapy

Psychological therapies provide important tools in the treatment of drug and alcohol addictions. One effective form of therapy is cognitive behavior therapy (CBT), which treats addictions as learned behaviors.

Cognitive behavior therapy (CBT) is the most commonly used form of psychological therapy for the treatment of drug addictions. Addiction treatment agencies choose this form of therapy because of its proven efficacy and because of the relative shortness of the time needed for treatment. This form of psychological therapy is also the most frequently used method in the treatment of many mental problems, including behavioral addictions such as pathological gambling. The focus of CBT is the observable behavior of a person, not only in the actions this person performs, but also in his or her covert behaviors, that is, what he or she really thinks and how this person interprets reality. CBT is based on a theory called social learning. This theory argues that people learn different ways of behavior from society, including the use and abuse of substances, rather than possessing them naturally. An individual may learn to use drugs through a number of processes, which psychologists term modeling, operant conditioning, and classical conditioning.

Modeling

The process known as modeling reflects how people learn new skills by observing and listening to others and then copy what they have seen and heard. For example, children learn language by listening to and copying their parents. The same process may be true for many substance abusers. By seeing parents use alcohol, an individual may learn to cope with problems by drinking, and teenagers often begin smoking after watching their friends use cigarettes.

Operant conditioning

The name given to the process by which behavior (the operant) obtains rewards is operant conditioning. Experiments have shown that laboratory animals will perform certain tasks to obtain substances that many humans abuse, such as cocaine, opiates, and alcohol. A laboratory rat, for example, will repeatedly press a lever that enables it to receive a dose of cocaine. One reason for this behavior is that exposure to such drugs is pleasurable and animals will attempt to maintain these sensations of pleasure, a concept known as reinforcement. The effects of drugs may be positively or negatively reinforcing. Cocaine may be used because it alters a person's awareness so that he or she feels, for example, powerful, euphoric, energetic, or stimulated. These "good" outcomes are known as positive reinforcement. Cocaine may also make a person feel less depressed or anxious. This relief from "bad" feelings is called negative reinforcement.

The reinforcing effects of any drug of abuse vary widely from individual to individual. People with family histories of substance abuse, a high need for sensation seeking, or a concurrent psychiatric disorder may find any kind of drug particularly reinforcing. It is therefore necessary that professionals taking charge of these patients understand that an individual may use any drug for a combination of reasons that are specific and important to them.

Classical conditioning

Classical conditioning reflects a theory of behavior famously demonstrated by the Russian physiologist Ivan Petrovich Pavlov (1849–1936). He demonstrated that, over time, repeatedly pairing one stimulus with another could elicit a reliable response. In his most famous experiment, Pavlov investigated salivation in dogs. Immediately before the dogs were fed, Pavlov rang a bell. He repeated the process several times. He rang the bell without presenting any food and discovered that the dogs still salivated. They had learned to associate the sound of a bell ringing with food to the extent that their bodies prepared for digestion. Like the pairing of food with the sound of a ringing bell, any drug of abuse may become paired with another stimulus, such as the sight of money or drug administration paraphernalia, particular places, particular people, certain times of the day or week, or certain feelings. In classical conditioning, exposure to those cues alone is sufficient to elicit very intense cravings or urges that are often followed by drug taking.

According to the theory of social learning, a child may learn to use alcohol to cope with problems by seeing a parent do the same. This process, called modeling, is one of several ways in which addiction can be learned.

Craving for drugs or for reinforcing behaviors, as in the case of pathological gambling, are among the most important factors psychologists take into account when working with CBT. Usually craving implies a strong desire for and a willingness to go on taking a drug despite the user's knowledge that doing so will cause personal harm. When a drug user craves a drug in this way, he or she may be regarded as an addict.

Functional analysis

CBT assumes that the purpose of any behavior is to arrive at a certain consequence. Discovering which behaviors relate to specific consequences is termed functional analysis—a key method in the treatment of addiction using CBT. After a functional analysis, the therapist and client are both able to identify the cues and stimuli that lead to addictive behavior. Usually these kinds of cues and stimuli are considered high-risk situations in which an addict confronted with such a situation feels the desire to take drugs and may relapse.

Motivational interviewing

CBT gives the addict the skills to cope with high-risk situations, craving, stress, and so on, without drugs. However, CBT can never be effective if the patient is not able to establish a good working alliance with the therapist. In order to create a good working alliance, the style with which the therapist conducts the interview is extremely important.

W. R. Miller, a psychologist working at the University of New Mexico, has demonstrated that a confrontational style of dealing with an addict has an anti-therapeutic effect. It increases the resistance of the patient to beginning treatment and increases his or her mixed feelings toward quitting drugs. If the therapist, however, adopts a supportive style throughout the course of therapy, the patient is more likely to be motivated to quit drug taking. Support is especially important in the first stages of treatment, where a confrontational style may cause a patient to assume a rigid and defensive manner, preventing him or her from recognizing the destructive consequences of addiction.

The stages of change model

The scientists J. O. Prochaska and C. C. DiClemente from the University of Maryland have developed a model to understand how addicts change from compulsive addiction to a drug-free lifestyle. The first stage of change is called precontemplation. In this stage, addicted people take drugs regularly with no awareness of the negative consequences the behavior has on their lives. The second phase of change is called contemplation. In this phase, while the addict takes drugs with no attempt to remain abstinent, he or she begins to become aware of the destructive consequences that addictions have. The third stage is called preparation for change. In this stage, an individual makes a commitment to change behavior patterns and develops a plan and strategy for doing so. In the fourth stage, called action, the individual implements the plan for change and takes steps to alter current behavior patterns and begin creating a new drug-free style of living. The final stage is called maintenance, where the new behavior patterns are sustained and consolidated into a drug-free lifestyle.

It is important that a therapist working with a drug addict uses a therapeutic strategy that accommodates the addict's particular stage of change and adjusts as the addict moves to another stage. It is also important to consider that most addicts rarely follow the process of change in a linear way, passing through each stage one after the other. During a course of therapy, an addict will usually make backward movements as well as forward. This does not necessarily mean that the addict is not motivated to abstain from drug taking; it may, in fact, simply be the best they can do at a particular time. Allowing for backward as well as forward movements is also important for the well-being of the therapist, since it reduces the risk of "burn-out," which can occur when a therapist tries to make a patient change while only finding resistance.

The relapse prevention model

Since 1985, Alan Marlatt, a CBT psychologist working at the University of Washington, has developed the most comprehensive model for understanding how addicted people relapse and how CBT can be used to prevent it. Marlatt's main contribution to the field of addiction treatment is in reminding addicts and therapists that relapse is not only possible in the process of change but also very probable. In his model for training patients in relapse prevention, he helps to identify all the high-risk situations that can lead addicts to relapse into addictive ways of behavior and to pinpoint apparently irrelevant decisions that can lead to relapse. The model also helps addicts to learn coping strategies for dealing with such difficulties. The most important therapeutic factor, and also the most difficult to achieve after the treatment, is that the addict learn and integrate a new drug-free style of living into his or her own daily life.

In this type of therapy relapse is never considered a catastrophic event. Instead, the model educates the patient to consider any relapse as a new opportunity to learn from experience and then to try to avoid similar behavior. If an addict who has made a commitment to remain abstinent relapses, he or she experiences a state known as the abstinence violation effect. This emotional state is usually characterized by a sense of feeling guilty and sad. When this occurs, the probability of a future or immediate full-blown relapse is very high. In Marlatt's approach to therapy, relapse remains a constant possibility for which addicts must prepare themselves by maintaining a high level of vigilance for warning signs.

Effectiveness of CBT

Addictive behaviors show a high resistance to change, which makes them very difficult for mental-health professionals to treat. However, many studies, especially those by Bruce Rounsaville and Kathleen Carroll at Yale University, prove that CBT is effective in the treatment of both drug and behavioral addictions. Although the working alliance between patient and therapist and the quality of the therapist's training are important factors in the efficacy of CBT, the most important factor, as in the case of any other psychological therapy, is the ability of CBT to retain the patient in treatment. Retention is without any doubt the most important variable regarding the effectiveness of any psychological therapy.

A. TEJERO-POCIELLO

SEE ALSO:
Addictive Behavior • Compulsive Behaviors • Conditioning • Counseling • Defense Mechanisms • Reinforcement • Relapse • Treatment

Cold Turkey

Cold turkey is a common method for achieving freedom from addiction, but it often requires a short period during which the drug user will experience a range of unpleasant side effects. For some drugs, abrupt withdrawal can be fatal.

Cold turkey is a method of withdrawing from an addictive drug by ceasing its use completely and abruptly. The phrase "cold turkey," when it was first coined in the early twentieth century, originally referred only to heroin but has since come to mean the abrupt withdrawal from any addictive substance. One suggested origin for the phrase is the food cold turkey, since it requires little preparation. Another possible origin is that heroin addicts in withdrawal are covered by gooseflesh, where the skin resembles a plucked turkey. Other expressions for opioid withdrawal include dopesickness and "kicking the habit," which refers to the leg-muscle spasms that begin around 12 hours after the last dose of heroin.

Symptoms of withdrawal

The withdrawal symptoms of cold turkey depend on the addictive substance. Heroin users suffer flulike symptoms, such as sneezing, weakness, depression, diarrhea, and vomiting, that may last for a week to 10 days after stopping. Withdrawal from nicotine (in tobacco) can cause headaches, irritability, sleeplessness, and anxiety. For some addictive drugs, the abrupt cessation of use can be fatal. The most common drugs that have this effect are barbiturates, which are sedatives used to calm nervous disorders and help induce sleep. Often the withdrawal symptoms of an addictive drug are compounded by psychological dependence, where users associate taking the drug with their lifestyle or how they conduct themselves in certain situations.

Because the effects of cold turkey are unpleasant, doctors and addicts have developed several methods for relieving the symptoms. Heroin users can substitute heroin with methadone, a drug that alleviates the withdrawal symptoms and for which the dose required can slowly be reduced. Cigarette smokers can use nicotine replacement therapy, where the cigarettes are replaced with patches or gum, whose dose can also be reduced gradually. Other medications have become available that alleviate the withdrawal symptoms of some addictive drugs. These therapeutic drugs include clonidine, to relieve the physical symptoms of heroin withdrawal, and Zyban, which helps combat the urge to smoke.

Causes of cold turkey

Withdrawal symptoms are caused by changes in brain chemistry that occur after prolonged exposure to an addictive substance. The brain contains many receptors that respond to neurotransmitters (chemicals that regulate how a person feels, breathes, digests food, as well as many other processes not under conscious control). Addictive drugs mimic these neurotransmitters, inducing effects that a person finds enjoyable or pleasant. After prolonged exposure to such substances, the brain responds by making the receptors less sensitive or fewer in number, causing the user to need a larger dose for a similar effect. With further exposure the user becomes progressively more tolerant and depends on the drug to feel normal. When the drug is not taken, the user feels unpleasant symptoms that are often opposite to the original desired effect. The suffering of these symptoms while the brain returns to its former unaddicted state is the period of cold turkey.

Pregnancy and cold turkey

Suffering cold turkey while pregnant can be very harmful to the mother and child. In cases of heroin addiction, sudden withdrawal can cause termination in newly pregnant women and premature birth in more advanced pregnancies. While drug addiction during pregnancy is harmful, the results of withdrawal are usually considered more dangerous. However, all babies born to an addicted mother will have to endure a period of cold turkey. Neonatal Abstinence Syndrome results in an extremely distressed and sick newborn child.

N. LEPORA

SEE ALSO:
Nicotine Replacements • Pregnancy and Fetal Addiction • Withdrawal

College on Problems of Drug Dependence (CPDD)

The College on Problems of Drug Dependence is devoted to the study of drug use, bringing together behavioral scientists, health professionals, biochemists, and public health experts in one forum.

The College on Problems of Drug Dependence is the oldest existing scholarly body in the United States, and the largest in the world, specifically devoted to the study of drug abuse and dependence. The CPDD was founded in 1929 as the Committee on Problems of Drug Dependence, in association with the National Academy of Sciences. It became an independent body in 1976 and evolved into the College on Problems of Drug Dependence in 1991.

The College provides a means for professionals across assorted fields to communicate ideas and information about drug dependence, both at its annual meetings and in its sponsored journal, *Drug and Alcohol Dependence*. The College also supports testing facilities for the assessment of abuse liability of various drugs in animal models of drug use and abuse at a number of universities across the United States. In addition, the CPDD is involved in coordinating clinical and basic research to assess the abuse liability of both medically useful and illicit or recreational drugs; it does so in cooperation with government and a number of national and international organizations. The CPDD also provides consultative expertise to individuals and organizations concerned with drug dependence.

Organizational relationships
Perhaps the most significant organizational relationship CPDD has is with the National Institute on Drug Abuse (NIDA), the section of the National Institutes of Health devoted to drug abuse research and treatment. Many, if not most, CPDD members receive funding and support from NIDA. This is a natural relationship, given the way that scientific funding is organized in the United States, and has generally been an effective one. While there are concerns about the lack of independence that such a relationship with a government body might create, the College has usually stayed close to the balance of

scientific opinion regardless of the political emphases of the time. A good example of this is the fact that the CPDD has consistently supported drug treatment as the best solution to problems associated with drug abuse, even while successive U.S. presidential administrations were supporting an expanding "war on drugs," emphasizing law enforcement and even military means to prevent the drug trade while providing relatively less monetary support for drug treatment. On the negative side, however, the organization's study of drug abuse is separated from the study of alcohol abuse, which has its own research society, the Research Society on Alcoholism. This situation has resulted from the political decision to create both NIDA and the National Institute on Alcohol Abuse and Alcoholism. This separation has little legitimate scientific basis, given that substance abuse—of which alcoholism is one form—seems to involve the same underlying biological and psychological mechanisms regardless of whether or not the substance is legal. The organizational division has not kept many individual researchers from working in both fields, however, nor has it prevented the CPDD from discussing alcohol at meetings and in publications, which speaks to the scientific integrity of the individual scientists involved, as well as the flexibility of the organization.

The CPDD plays an important role in the United States and the world as a mediator among scientists, industry, government, and the public on issues relating to drug abuse and dependence. It is a valuable resource for all of these parties as it provides an organizational framework for exchange of information.

R. G. HUNTER

SEE ALSO:
American Society of Addiction Medicine (ASAM) ● National Institute on Alcohol Abuse and Alcoholism (NIAAA) ● National Institute on Drug Abuse (NIDA)

Compulsive Behaviors

Compulsive behaviors account for many conditions often described as addictions, such as gambling and shopping. However, the underlying motives for these behaviors can be very different from those involved in drug addiction.

Drug addiction can involve compulsive behaviors—repeated actions that people feel forced to carry out against their wishes. Compulsive behaviors are not only a symptom of drug taking, however. Psychiatrists recognize a number of mental disorders, from overeating to pathological gambling, in which compulsive behaviors are a prominent feature. Although the different types of compulsive behaviors have things in common, it is uncertain whether they are fundamentally related. Treatments for compulsive behaviors vary from patient to patient and from one disorder to another but usually involve a combination of medication and psychotherapy.

Describing compulsive behaviors

The term *addiction* is generally used to describe a person's dependency on a drug. Addicts often feel compelled to keep taking drugs even when it is unwise or harmful for them to do so. However, in psychiatry, the word *compulsion* usually describes types of behaviors that do not involve drugs. In the eating disorder bulimia nervosa, people eat excessive amounts of food in sudden binges and then use laxatives or make themselves vomit to avoid putting on weight. Compulsions often occur alongside obsessions. While compulsions are repetitive actions, obsessions are repetitive thoughts or feelings that people simply cannot stop. Also related to compulsions are impulses, more immediate calls to action that can force people to do damaging or destructive things. Kleptomania (when people feel compelled to steal things) and pyromania (setting fires) are caused by impulses like this.

Obsessive-compulsive disorders

Some compulsions involve doing one thing over and over again, such as repeatedly checking that doors are locked, counting or saying words, or rearranging things on a shelf. Obsessive-compulsive disorder (OCD) is a mental disorder in which obsessive thoughts generally lead to compulsions of this kind. For example, if a person is obsessed with the idea of uncleanness, he might develop a compulsion to wash his hands many times a day or constantly until they bleed. Addictions generally lead to pleasure, but people with OCD carry out their compulsions because the actions relieve tension, and they feel a crippling sense of anxiety or panic if they try to stop.

For this reason, psychiatrists group OCD with anxiety disorders (such as phobias and stress disorders) in the American Psychiatric Association's *Diagnostic and Statistical Manual of Mental Disorders* or DSM (the standard classification of mental disorders). Many people become obsessed with things or carry out repetitive behaviors from time to time, but that does not necessarily mean they have OCD. The DSM defines the obsessions and compulsions in OCD as much more extreme than ordinary, everyday behavior. They must cause extreme distress, be very time consuming, or cause a great deal of disruption to a person's life before they can be truly considered as OCD.

OCD affects around 2 to 3 percent of the population, which makes it relatively more common than better-known disorders such as schizophrenia or bipolar disorder (manic-depressive illness). Although OCD affects equal numbers of men and women, males generally develop the disorder in childhood (typically between the ages of 6 and 15), whereas women tend to develop it in their 20s. OCD is more common among better-educated people from backgrounds of higher socioeconomic status, although this may simply reflect the fact that such people can more easily afford, or are more likely to seek, psychiatric treatment.

Most people who develop OCD suffer from perhaps a single obsession and a single compulsion. Someone obsessed with the idea that a sudden disaster is about to happen might check doors and windows and electrical appliances over and over again before leaving home each day. However, the rest of a person's life might be completely unaffected by these fairly well-defined obsessions and compulsions. Obsessions and compulsions can some-

might experience a sudden desire to gamble or steal things, most people can suppress those impulses; people with an impulse-control disorder, by contrast, give way to impulses that are usually harmful to themselves or other people.

Five specific types of impulse-control disorders are recognized in DSM: intermittent explosive disorder, in which someone repeatedly carries out serious attacks on people or property; kleptomania, in which people feel compelled to steal things even when they can afford to buy them or have no need of the things themselves; pathological gambling; pyromania, in which people take pleasure from setting fires for no real reason; and trichotillomania, in which a person repeatedly pulls out his or her hair.

Although fire setting may seem quite unrelated to hair pulling or stealing, these compulsive behaviors are grouped together because they have important things in common. Immediately before an episode of compulsive behavior, the sufferers feel a huge buildup of tension and an overwhelming desire to begin the behavior. If they try to resist this impulse, the tension increases still further. Once they give way to the impulse, they feel a huge sense of pleasure or relief. However, the impulse soon takes hold of them again and locks them in a vicious circle of compulsive behavior. Even if the compulsive behavior is itself pleasurable, sooner or later it disrupts or harms the person's life.

Understanding compulsive behaviors

Obsessive-compulsive and impulse-control disorders are not the only examples of compulsive behaviors. In fact, depending on how compulsive behavior is defined, quite a wide range of other disorders involve compulsive behavior of one kind or another. The binge eating disorder bulimia nervosa could be described as compulsive eating, for example. Alcoholism could be described as compulsive drinking. Sexual disorders, which have their own category in the DSM classification, often involve compulsions to engage in unusual kinds of sexual behavior.

Some apparently compulsive behaviors are only now being formally recognized in DSM. Compulsive shopping, for example, is similar to impulse-control disorders. It starts with a feeling of tension, culminates in a person making many sudden purchases of things he or she probably does not want or need,

Like humans, birds engage in compulsive behaviors, such as feather plucking and tearing at the skin, in response to stress, anxiety, or a lack of stimulation.

times affect a person's life in a more general way if he or she suffers from an obsessive-compulsive personality disorder. Such a person might be so preoccupied with making lists, rules, or schedules for doing things that she never actually does them; or she might be a workaholic or perfectionist who never quite gets things done or meets the absurdly high standards that she has set. Unlike a person with OCD, a person with obsessive-compulsive personality disorder would suffer problems in many different areas of his or her life.

Impulse-control disorders

The compulsions found in OCD are carried out to relieve tension and seem to be different in kind from the impulse-type compulsions found in such things as pathological gambling. Impulsive problems of this kind are more like addictions that lead to the continuation of pleasure, and they are usually known as impulse-control disorders. Although many people

which relieves the anxiety, and ends with feelings of emptiness until the whole process starts again.

If all these things involve compulsive behavior, why are they not simply grouped together under the same heading by psychiatrists and treated as one thing? The answer is that, although they have some things in common, it is far from clear that they are caused by the same triggers or that people who suffer from them should be treated in exactly the same way. Eating disorders, for example, seem to be strongly connected with changing social and cultural attitudes about ideal body shape and weight. Although OCD and impulse-control disorders are both connected with the relief of anxiety and tension, OCD usually results in ongoing misery, while impulse-control disorders such as pathological gambling can generate temporary excitement and pleasure. Separating these disorders from one another and studying their similarities and differences not only gives a much clearer scientific understanding of their causes and effects, it also produces more effective treatments.

Causes

Different types of compulsive behaviors may have very different causes, although a complex interplay of genetics, brain structure, irregular neurotransmitter production, and personality and social factors is probably involved in all cases.

Although the genetic evidence is so far unclear, the idea that compulsive behavior is caused by biological problems in the brain is supported by studies that show it is likely to run in families. There is evidence to suggest that patients suffering from OCD may have abnormalities in parts of their brain (structures such as the frontal lobes, basal ganglia, and cingulum bundle) that control repeated behaviors.

Neurotransmitters also seem to play a key role in compulsive behaviors. OCD sufferers tend to have unusually low levels of the neurotransmitter serotonin, which explains why medications that increase levels of serotonin (such as antidepressant SSRI drugs) are effective in treating the disorder. Dopamine neurons in the midbrain (which control such things as motivation, reward, and motor control) seem to play a role in other compulsive behaviors, as well as in drug addictions. Some researchers believe compulsive behaviors affect the same "reward pathways" as the addictive behaviors

caused by drug taking. Research has found that midbrain dopamine neurons fire when the brain is uncertain of the rewards that it will receive (such as during gambling or other impulse-control behaviors). This discovery suggests dopamine neurons may be involved in perpetuating compulsive behaviors. Another intriguing finding comes from the treatment of Parkinson's disease (a debilitating brain disorder caused by dopamine deficiency in the basal ganglia). Parkinson's patients who are treated with L-dopa (which increases levels of dopamine) sometimes develop such unusual behaviors as compulsive gambling and shopping.

Comorbidity (when people have two or more disorders at once) is also an important factor. Around half of all pathological gamblers also have drug or alcohol problems, whereas some studies of substance abusers have found that 10 to 30 percent are also gamblers. Compulsive disorders of all kinds are very likely to occur with other mental disorders, including anxiety, depression, and antisocial personality disorder.

Treatments

Although treatment for compulsive behavior varies from person to person, and from disorder to disorder, it typically involves a combination of medication and psychotherapy. OCD is widely treated with drugs such as clomipramine (a relatively inexpensive, older-style tricyclic antidepressant), as well as newer SSRI antidepressants such as Prozac (fluoxetine). In psychotherapy (sometimes known as talking treatment), the patient works with a therapist over a period of time to gradually modify behavior. A compulsive hand washer might be slowly exposed to dirtier and dirtier objects and encouraged to refrain from washing his or her hands for increasingly long periods of time. Behavioral therapy is also used to treat compulsive problems such as pathological gambling and sex addiction. The long-term outlook for people with compulsive behaviors is generally very good. Most OCD sufferers who receive treatment show partial or complete relief from symptoms after lengthy periods of therapy.

C. WOODFORD

SEE ALSO:

Addictive Behavior • Cognitive Behavior Therapy • Dual Diagnosis • Mental Disorders

Conditioning

Conditioning theory describes a process whereby certain stimuli become associated with certain responses. This theory has been used to explain some of the causes of addiction and has provided the basis for treatment techniques.

Conditioning theory is the earliest and most primitive theory of learning. Originally developed using animals, it has been generalized to humans. Its contribution to understanding substance use and addiction has been very influential, both in terms of explaining the causes and maintenance of addictive behavior and in its treatment. There are two main theories of conditioning: classical conditioning and operant conditioning.

Classical conditioning

Classical conditioning was discovered by Ivan Pavlov, a Russian physiologist. He was investigating salivation in dogs when he discovered that they salivated not only in the presence of food but also in anticipation of food being presented. He suggested that the dogs were responding to signals, or cues, that food was about to be presented; that is, they were learning. To test this proposition Pavlov carried out a famous experiment that forever linked his name with dogs.

A dog is presented with food (an unconditioned stimulus), which causes it to salivate (an unconditioned response). The dog is then presented with food just after a bell is rung (a neutral stimulus). After this latter process has been repeated several times, the neutral stimulus (the bell) becomes a conditioned stimulus. Salivation now occurs in response to the bell, regardless of whether or not food is presented. Salivation, which was an unconditioned response, becomes a conditioned response.

What has happened during the experiment is that the dogs have learned. Dogs salivate in the presence of food, a natural reflex reaction that produces a substance to aid digestion. When the bell was sounded immediately prior to the food being produced, the dogs learned to expect food and began to salivate in anticipation. As a result, the dogs salivate, not because there is food present, but because the bell has sounded. This is not a natural reaction but a conditioned, or learned, one. If a bell is sounded, dogs will not normally salivate, but after conditioning they will. Also, if a bell is sounded and food is not presented, the dogs will continue to salivate. However, in this case the dogs would eventually cease to react to the bell; that is, the conditioned behavior would be extinguished.

An important point of classical conditioning is that it tends to work on instincts or involuntary behavior. It is believed that classical conditioning is at the root of many of the phobias that people suffer from or the fetishes that they have. If sexual arousal or normal fear in the presence of danger is paired with other neutral stimuli, then fetishes or phobias can result.

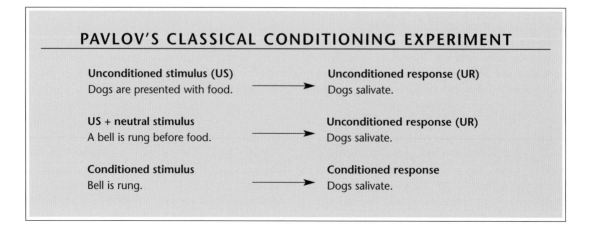

PAVLOV'S CLASSICAL CONDITIONING EXPERIMENT

Unconditioned stimulus (US) Dogs are presented with food.	→	Unconditioned response (UR) Dogs salivate.
US + neutral stimulus A bell is rung before food.	→	Unconditioned response (UR) Dogs salivate.
Conditioned stimulus Bell is rung.	→	Conditioned response Dogs salivate.

A pigeon in a Skinner box learns to associate the pressing of a colored lever with the delivery of a food pellet. This is a form of operant conditioning.

Operant conditioning

Operant conditioning tends to act on voluntary behaviors. If an action results in a good outcome, then the probability of that action being repeated is increased; conversely, if an action results in a negative outcome, then the probability of that action being repeated is decreased. Good outcomes can be a reward, such as food or pleasure, and are known as positive reinforcement. However, good outcomes can also be the end of or decrease of a noxious condition, such as a decrease in anxiety or the removal of pain. This is known as negative reinforcement.

The classic experiments in this field were largely carried out with animals, although there have been some studies conducted with humans. The most famous experiments were carried out with pigeons in a "Skinner box." This device was invented by the influential U.S. psychologist B. F. Skinner; in its most basic form, it consists of a box with a mesh front (so that the pigeon can be observed) and a lever attached to a device that can deliver food pellets.

A characteristic of pigeons is that they peck at anything and, when placed in the Skinner box, a pigeon would peck at the walls, the floor, the mesh, and the lever. However, when the pigeon pecked at the lever, a pellet of food would be delivered. The pigeon would continue to peck at everything until, after some time, it learned that pecking at the lever would release food. Soon the pigeons were just pecking at the lever. They had learned to associate the behavior of pecking the lever with a reward (food), and so the behavior was reinforced.

During the reinforcement process, the immediacy of reinforcement and the schedule of reinforcement are important. If the pigeon had pecked at the lever and the pellet of food had not been delivered for a couple of minutes, the pigeon would have found it harder to make a connection between the two events. In the meantime, the pigeon may have pecked the floor and the cage front, and the association with food and the lever would have been less strong. It has also been found that if the behavior is not reinforced soon after learning has taken place, then the behavior will cease. This situation, however, does not occur immediately; the pigeon will continue to peck at the lever for some time in the expectation of a reward.

Random reinforcement

Psychologists have found that they can vary the schedule of reinforcement (for example, rewarding every tenth peck) and the pigeon will continue to peck. However, extinction of the behavior will occur if reinforcement takes too long to happen. The most powerful schedule of reinforcement, where extinction of the behavior is the most difficult, occurs when the reward is random and there is no pattern to the reinforcement. Any peck could produce results, and the pigeon continues its behavior long after reinforcement has ceased.

This type of reinforcement and the powerful learning that occurs has been used to explain gambling. Every time a gambler playing a slot machine pulls the lever he or she is hoping to win (to be reinforced), and sometimes this actually occurs. Thus, like the pigeons, gamblers can continue for long periods with no reinforcement, as the next pull (or peck) of the lever may be the one that produces a positive result.

Conditioning and substance use

Although classical and operant conditioning have been used separately to explain addictive behavior, it is in combination that they supply the most convincing explanations. However, before exploring this issue, it is important to determine what is actually being conditioned. There are three distinct theories, all with some evidence to support them. The first, oldest, and most widely accepted is that substance users experience a conditioned withdrawal from the substance. That is, when placed in the presence of alcohol or drugs, the user will experience some discomfort (anxiety and craving) that will increase the likelihood that he or she will consume the substance. The second theory suggests that, rather than withdrawal, it is a druglike effect that is induced, such that the person experiences a slight intoxication as if he or she had already consumed the substance. In the disease model, which suggests that there is a loss of control when substances are consumed, this is known as the priming effect. In simple terms, the intoxicating effect may break down any inhibitions to consume more of the substance.

Opponent process theory

The final model, opponent process theory, is more complex. It suggests that all organisms seek homeostasis (a stable state of being). However, in the presence of alcohol or drugs, an effect like that of Pavlov's dogs takes place. In other words, the body prepares for the consumption of these substances by making adjustments in the opposite direction from the effect of the drug. In this way, the drug will have less effect and homeostasis may be preserved (although this is generally not the case with an addicted person, who continues to use the drug so that intoxication rather than homeostasis ensues). This particular model is less popular as an explana-

tion of addiction, but it is a useful nonphysiological explanation of tolerance: addicts show fewer effects from substances or need more of the substance to gain the same effect. This theory has been used as an explanation for why drug overdoses occur. If addicts are using a substance in unfamiliar surroundings, then the cues that initiate the opponent process will not be present. Hence the body will not have made its usual adjustments, and the drug will have a more powerful effect. Evidence such as this has been used by psychologists to argue against the disease model of addiction, suggesting instead that addiction is a learned behavior rather than a physical abnormality.

However, what represents a cue to consume (conditioned stimulus) will vary from individual to individual. Some obvious cues are the sight and smell of alcohol and drugs and drug-taking paraphernalia (needles and syringes, and so on). Other cues may include people, places, and times of day.

Nevertheless, even if a physiological response such as craving is elicited by some cue, that is only part of the story. The other part is supplied by operant conditioning. It is believed that positive reinforcement is sufficient explanation for why people initiate substance use; that is, they do it because they get pleasure. However, patterns of use are maintained by a different but related mechanism, negative reinforcement. At some time, a person may discover that alcohol or drugs can ameliorate or eradicate negative feelings, such as anxiety or depression; hence these feelings can become cues for drug taking. If a cue then elicits craving or anxiety (classical conditioning), and an association with substance use and feeling better has been formed, then conditions may be set for problematic use. Alcohol or drug use will in itself create conditions in which negative moods and feelings will be more frequent, and if consumption relieves these feelings, then a cycle of addiction is set up. Thus researchers believe that, while positive reinforcement has a large part to play in the initiation of substance abuse, negative reinforcement has a greater role in its maintenance, as the alcoholic or addict consumes the substance to relieve the withdrawal symptoms.

It may seem puzzling that a person is caught in this cycle when it is obvious that the alcohol or drugs are fueling the negative feelings. The answer to this dichotomy is again reinforcement, in particular the immediacy of reinforcement. The negative feelings are delayed. They do not occur until the alcohol or drugs are wearing off. On the other hand, the reinforcement (feeling better) happens very quickly after consumption. Thus, the negative feelings of hangover have less effect on consumption than the more immediate positive reinforcement of the pleasurable feelings of use.

Conditioning and treatment

The aim of treatment based on conditioning theory is to extinguish the links between the conditioned cues and the conditioned response. When used for phobias, this type of treatment is generally called desensitization. In substance-use treatment, it is called cue exposure or cue reactivity. There are a number of different forms of the treatment, but they all have the same basic aims, and the treatment usually works on both the classical and operant elements of conditioning.

In the first stage of treatment, the clients may be asked to imagine that they are in the presence of alcohol or drugs, or they may be shown pictures depicting alcohol or drugs. The aim is to elicit the conditioned response (withdrawal or craving). The person may then be asked to use relaxation techniques to combat these negative feelings. This stage and later stages of the treatment are attempting to do two things. First, they attempt to demonstrate that the negative feelings can be handled without the aid of substances. Second, since no alcohol or drugs will be consumed, the link between the cue and the reaction should be weakened and, after time, extinguished. It has been found that, to be effective, this exposure to the cues must last for at least 45 minutes. The reason for this is that the responses will abate naturally given sufficient time. Hence if the exposure is too short, the absence of responses will not be experienced and learned by the alcoholic or addict.

The next stage of treatment is actually to expose the alcoholic or addict to his or her drug of choice but in a safe environment. This is usually done by having the drug in a glass box where it can be seen but not touched. All other parts of the procedure are the same as the previous stage. In later stages the alcoholic or addict will be able to actually touch the drug and then handle it.

From this point, a divergence occurs in treatment between alcohol and drug treatment and between abstinence and controlled-drinking–oriented treatments. Drug and alcohol abstinence treatments will normally stop at the stage of being able to handle the substance. In controlled-drinking treatments, the next stage would be to have the drinker take a sip of the alcohol and, again using relaxation techniques, wait for the aroused craving to subside. The rationale is that, as with craving, loss of control is a learned effect. Extinguishing the link between the cues and the response will thus allow the drinker to regain some control over his or her drinking.

Effectiveness of treatment

The evidence for the effectiveness of this treatment is mixed, as it is with all addiction treatment. Cue exposure suffers from one large drawback, which is that many therapists regard it as unethical, since it exposes people to the substance that has caused them so many problems. Proponents of the approach point to the fact that desensitization is a well-established treatment for other disorders, such as phobias, and that there is a solid theoretical base for the role of conditioning in both phobias and addiction. Regardless of the ethics, cue exposure suffers from another problem, which is discovering what cues are the most important for the individual. The deceptive simplicity of the theory masks the complexity of the available cues in any given environment. For example, there is a wide range of possible cues in a bar: the sight of alcohol, its smell, the sound of voices talking excitedly, or the music on the jukebox. The cues are not limited to the actual sight, smell, and taste of the alcohol. Because of this complexity, cue exposure is often seen as a treatment that may be ineffective, especially if it is viewed as a stand-alone intervention. However, as part of a more comprehensive program of treatment, it can be an important component. There is no doubt that drug abusers, if they are to recover successfully, need to be able to handle exposure to substances without resorting to their use.

J. McMahon

SEE ALSO:

Conduct Disorder

Conduct disorder is an official diagnosis established by both the American Psychiatric Association and the World Health Organization. It describes a pattern of serious misbehavior that involves breaking important societal rules.

Conduct disorder is a behavioral condition found in young people. It consists of at least one of the following tendencies: harming people or animals, destroying someone else's property, stealing and lying, and other serious rule breaking.

Examples of harm to others include bullying, fighting, and sexual assault. Intentional destruction of someone else's property sometimes includes arson. Stealing and lying can encompass car theft, forgery, and shoplifting. Other rule violations include breaking curfew, running away from home, and truancy.

Up to 10 percent of young people have conduct disorder, which is much more common among boys than girls. The condition usually starts before age 16 but does not continue into adulthood in at least half of all cases. Children and adolescents with conduct disorder usually do not think about the feelings of others. They are often unrepentant about what they have done, except when acting sad will help them avoid punishment. Acts of aggression are common because they think others are trying to hurt them.

People with conduct disorder tend to get frustrated easily and to behave recklessly. They often perform poorly in school, especially in subjects requiring communication skills, such as reading and writing, and they are more likely to make suicide attempts. Children and adolescents with conduct disorder are more likely to abuse substances, such as alcohol and tobacco. In fact, symptoms of conduct disorder frequently precede symptoms of drug abuse. Studies also show that aggressive teens are more likely to abuse drugs and that many teens get arrested for crimes committed while intoxicated.

Causes of conduct disorder

The exact cause of conduct disorder is uncertain, but multiple factors combine to create the problem. These factors can be broadly divided into those that are biological and those that are environmental. Biological causes can stem from a person's genetic inheritance or from a child's exposure to tobacco before birth or to lead as a toddler. Exposure to either of these substances can lead to problems such as impulsivity and deficits in verbal skills that are common in conduct disorder.

Environmental causes depend much on the family in which a child grows up. Children with little parental supervision are more likely to develop conduct disorder. Parental discipline that is too harsh, too lenient, or inconsistent also contributes to conduct disorder. Sometimes parents are too lenient or too harsh because of their own problems, such as poverty, depression, and marital conflict. Children who suffer physical or sexual abuse are also likely to develop conduct disorder.

The early relationship that infants have with their parents, known as attachment, has been studied to see how it contributes to conduct disorder. Attachment is assessed by observing how infants react when they are separated from and then reunited with their caregiver. There are two main types of attachment, secure and insecure. Infants with a secure attachment show clear pleasure when reunited with their caregiver. Infants with an insecure attachment react with anger, confusion, or indifference.

Children with a secure attachment seem to trust their caregivers to respond to their needs and therefore tend to have a positive view of themselves and others. This attitude leads to good relationships in and outside the home. On the other hand, infants with an insecure attachment have difficulty trusting their parents to take care of them. This lack of trust can make a child think negatively about himself or herself and others. Such thoughts help lead to the kinds of misbehaviors seen in conduct disorder.

Children with an insecure attachment are more likely to develop behavior problems in school. This pattern of misbehavior can lead to further academic failure and peer rejection, themselves risk factors for developing conduct disorder. However, the pattern can be altered by having new, caring relationships with adults and peers that shape a more positive view of oneself and others. This change, in turn, can decrease a person's risk of developing conduct disorder.

Aggressive behavior among children can be changed by teaching positive methods of resolving conflict.

Environmental causes also include the influence of the society in which a youth lives. Youths who are unpopular with their peers, for example, are more likely to develop conduct disorder. People with friends, parents, or siblings who have conduct disorder are also more likely to develop conduct disorder themselves.

How conduct disorder is treated

Interventions for conduct disorder typically target individual, family, and social domains. Individual interventions usually help young people learn new ways of behaving and thinking. For example, instead of fighting, they learn how to resolve conflict by talking or by seeking the help of an adult. Constructive ways to deal with anger and problem-solving skills can also be taught.

Ways of thinking that contribute to behaviors of conduct disorder are also targeted. Young people with conduct disorder frequently think that other people are threatening them even when they are not. The misperception can lead to retaliation and subsequent fighting. Adolescents with the disorder also frequently think that no one understands them, which can lead to difficulty developing positive relationships with coaches, parents, peers, or teachers. This difficulty then perpetuates behaviors of conduct disorder. However, if the initial thoughts that "everyone is out to get me" or "no one understands me" are altered, then the individual's disobedience and aggression can also be altered. Therefore, psychotherapists frequently try to understand and alter the ways of thinking that lead to rule-breaking behavior.

Intervention in the family domain includes working with the youth's parents. In this intervention, parents learn to communicate clear rules of behavior to their children. They then practice providing effective punishments for bad behavior and rewards for good behavior. Instruction is also given on the importance of developing a warm, nurturing relationship with their children. Such things are likely to decrease the serious misbehaviors of conduct disorder. Another intervention targets the social environment. In this intervention, social influences that help perpetuate the disorder are changed, for example, by working with the school system to improve an adolescent's chances of academic success.

Additional treatments

Depending on their needs, young people with conduct disorder frequently receive a combination of interventions. Such patients also frequently require additional treatment for other problems such as attention deficit disorder, anxiety disorders, bipolar disorder, depression, and substance abuse. These disorders are more common in youths with conduct disorder and sometimes mimic conduct disorder. For example, adolescents with depression, anxiety, or substance withdrawal often feel very irritable. Their irritability, in turn, causes them to misbehave. Therefore, it is important to assess for these conditions whenever treating a youth's misconduct.

Medical conditions such as thyroid problems can also cause behavior problems and should also be assessed. Medications are sometimes used to treat conduct disorder. Medication is also used to treat conditions such as anxiety, depression, and bipolar disorder that frequently occur along with conduct disorder. However, medications are almost never used by themselves to treat conduct disorder.

C. THURSTONE, P. RIGGS

SEE ALSO:

Adolescents and Substance Abuse • Attention Deficit Disorder • Children • Family Environment • Mental Disorders

Continuum of Care

Continuum of care describes the sequence of addiction treatment processes by which a person with an addiction is helped from one stage of recovery to another. This continuity can be vital to the success of treatment.

Continuum of care is a generic term used by various drug and alcohol treatment providers, mental health service providers, and therapeutic community (TC) treatment providers to denote a continuing arrangement of treatment services. The specific approach concerning philosophy, activity, and staff involvement contrasts strongly among these different service providers. The services offered generally include outpatient counseling services, continuous treatment teams, and aftercare. Most service providers would agree that continuum of care arrangements are effective for monitoring a client's progress and subsequently providing early intervention if recovery is threatened. This last aspect is especially important for young drug addicts participating in continuum of care programs.

Outpatient counseling services

Outpatient programs have often been used for treating clients who have completed residential programs. Outpatient counseling is usually associated with traditional medical treatment programs. The overall philosophy is based on teaching the client about alcoholism and addiction by way of educational and group counseling sessions. In most cases, professional staff members serve as the primary teachers, instructors, and agents for change. Although the emphasis on treatment involves a measure of self-help, traditional outpatient programs primarily consist of psychiatric sessions, psychosocial assessment sessions, clinical team assessments, and educational sessions about the disease model of addiction or an understanding of the developmental stages of alcoholism and addiction, or a combination of both. While this approach demands an education about addiction and an involvement with positive community support systems such as Alcoholic Anonymous (AA) or Narcotics Anonymous (NA), the weekly sessions are usually limited to one individual or group contact a week or sometimes a combination of the two.

Upon successful completion of the typical eight-to-twelve week educational sessions, the client severs his or her relationship with staff and peers. Outpatient programs that are not used as a continuum of care for residential program graduates are usually reserved for highly motivated addicted clients who have some measure of stability.

Continuous treatment teams

In an effort to provide continuum of care services to mental health patients, most mental health agencies have adopted a continuous treatment method that uses an intensive case-management approach. Similar to the outpatient method, continuous treatment uses psychiatric sessions, psychosocial assessments, and clinical team assessments. While both outpatient and continuous treatment methods use a measure of self-help, the continuous treatment approach involves extensive client monitoring, early intervention, and staff involvement consisting of home visits, employment checks, and family sessions, as appropriate.

The philosophy of continuous treatment brings together medical, clinical, pharmacological, psychiatric, and professional mental health personnel. For some years, mental health organizations have sought to modify the ways in which they move people back into the community. For example, continuous treatment personnel encourage the use of self-help programs, such as AA and NA, for people dually diagnosed as having an addiction and a mental illness. Clients are referred to as patients and are treated primarily from a doctor-patient perspective. Continuous treatment bases a client's successful completion of a program on psychiatric, pharmacological, or medication achievements and social stability factors rather than the rigid time frames associated with a typical treatment program.

Aftercare services

Aftercare services by definition are generally linked to traditional outpatient services, and while outpatient and aftercare services operate as continuum of care components, the term *aftercare* is specifically used by therapeutic community professionals to denote an

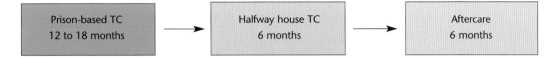

Therapeutic communities and aftercare are typical components of continuum of care arrangements.

all-inclusive arrangement for residents who have completed a prison-based or halfway house TC program. A therapeutic community is a drug-free residential treatment facility for people suffering from alcoholism or addiction. Halfway houses are establishments for people recovering from addiction who are not stable enough to live independently. Aftercare is the third stage of the TC continuum of care arrangement. The diagram above illustrates a typical model used by the Delaware Department of Correction. The program design consists of a prison-based TC, a halfway house, and aftercare.

Unlike the outpatient and continuous treatment philosophies, aftercare uses the treatment participants as the teachers, instructors, and agents for change, and uses paraprofessionals, many of whom are former drug users and program graduates, as staff members. Therapeutic community treatment participants are referred to as family members or community members rather than clients or patients.

While the continuum of care arrangements in aftercare services focus on traditional clinical concerns, such as reestablishing family ties, identifying positive and sober support systems, securing adequate employment, obtaining sufficient housing, and other socially stabilizing factors, the treatment activity and approach differ from continuous treatment and outpatient services quite drastically. All aftercare participants are graduates of TC residential programs, with an average length of stay ranging from 6 to 18 months. While continuum of care services are essential to all treatment populations, most TC participants have an extensive history of involvement with drug and alcohol addiction, criminal activity, unemployment or underemployment, and inadequate education, thereby requiring greater exposure to treatment opportunities. Uniquely, aftercare entails the continuation of the TC program's concepts, terminology, personal accountability, and specialized treatment techniques.

The TC approach is based on honesty, openness, and accountability. As such, the aftercare participants are expected to honor and uphold these principles without the constraints imposed upon them by residential pressures. Once a principle is broken or disregarded, it is the aftercare participant's obligation to confront his or her peers regarding this error in an open group meeting. In line with TC residential principles, aftercare participants are regarded as their "brother's keepers."

Continuum of care evaluation

Extensive evaluation studies of the effectiveness of Delaware's Department of Correction TCs and traditional work-release programs have been conducted by the University of Delaware's Center for Drug and Alcohol Studies (UD-CDAS) program. The continuum of care study consisted of four groups: prison-based TC graduates, halfway house TC graduates, prison-based and halfway house continuum of care graduates, and traditional work-release comparison group offenders. The preliminary follow-up data reviewed the following variables: the number of clients drug free by self-report, the number that were drug free as confirmed by urine testing, the number that were drug free at 18 months, and the number that were arrest free at 18 months. According to the UD-CDAS evaluation, the majority of people graduating from the combined prison-based and halfway house TC care arrangement were drug free and arrest free at 18 months. The table opposite shows the specific 18-month follow-up outcome.

Does continuum of care work?

The State of Delaware Statistical Analysis Center states in its *Sentencing Trends and Correctional Treatment in Delaware*, April 10, 2002, sentencing accountability commission report, "The maximum potency of treatment is likely to be realized with

THERAPEUTIC COMMUNITY OUTCOME AT 18-MONTH FOLLOW-UP				
Variable	Comparison group	Prison-based group	Halfway house group	Prison-based and halfway house group
Drug-free self report and urine testing	18%	25%	30%	53%
Arrest free	41%	43%	54%	63%

Source: University of Delaware, Center for Drug and Alcohol Studies

offenders who participate in a full continuum of treatment." The report further notes that the positive cumulative effect of TC and halfway house treatment increases as graduates move into and complete the aftercare treatment component. The Delaware Department of Correction study compares two different prison-based programs and a combined prison-based and halfway house continuum of care treatment arrangement. The findings show that offenders who complete the continuum of care arrangement return to prison less often than individuals who complete only the prison-based programs.

Youth continuum of care
The effectiveness of aftercare services for young people has not yet been evaluated. Investigations by juvenile correction experts Richard Dembo, Linda Williams, and James Schmeidler report that "aftercare services are a vital link in the service continuum" and yet "these services are infrequent, underdeveloped, and tend to be narrowly focused on problem areas, such as school placement or peer networks." The team concludes that repeated interventions over a protracted period, which are reinforced by improvements in the social, vocational, and educational skill levels of the individuals in treatment, are most likely to be successful. In particular, the transition from treatment to the community in general is an ongoing and potentially long process and therefore requires ongoing supportive services.

Overall, youth continuum of care programs should be based on practices that have been shown to be effective—from treatment to the wider community.

Most often these services include family counseling; case-management services involving school, family, and community issues; and peer counseling services, as appropriate. Family counseling services appear quite productive providing that the services are long term. It is not surprising that when a young person returns to his or her former environment, he or she will experience setbacks. Aftercare continuum of care arrangements should therefore include well-structured interventions.

Conclusion
Continuum of care treatment strategies should be designed to accommodate the needs of the specific treatment population. Most important, these efforts need to be consistent, supportive, and directed toward specific goals that are related to the client's particular needs. Third-party evaluation studies clearly show that continuum of care arrangements are beneficial in helping individuals overcome addiction. Although youth aftercare has received only limited evaluation, preliminary findings strongly support a comprehensive approach. All in all, ongoing process and outcome evaluation studies support continuum of care treatment strategies for people recovering from addictions.

R. A. BEARD, D. J. O'CONNELL

SEE ALSO:
Addiction • Alcoholism Treatment • Clinics • Cocaine Addiction Treatment • Halfway Houses • Heroin Addiction Treatment • Prison Drug Use and Treatment • Rehabilitation • Therapeutic Communities • Treatment Centers

Counseling

More than 16 percent of U.S. citizens will experience a substance use disorder (SUD) during their lives. Counseling is a psychological therapy that is proven to be effective in helping people overcome such disorders.

Counseling is commonly used in the treatment of psychiatric illnesses, including substance use disorders (SUDs). These include abuse or dependence on alcohol, marijuana, opiates, and stimulants including cocaine, inhalants, or club drugs. Many people have problems with more than one type of substance. People with SUDs may also have psychiatric disorders; 37 percent of people with alcoholism and 53 percent with a drug use disorder have a lifetime disorder such as depression, bipolar illness, an anxiety disorder, schizophrenia, or a personality disorder. SUDs have many negative effects on the person and family and cost society several hundred billion dollars per year.

Counseling is provided in treatment settings such as detoxification units, rehabilitation programs, hospitals, intensive outpatient programs, standard outpatient programs, or by private counselors. While counseling is sometimes sought voluntarily, it often occurs as a result of pressure from the legal system or a referral by an employee assistance counselor or a medical, mental health, or social service professional. Some people seek counseling due to pressure from family or a loved one. Research shows that clients who enter treatment as a result of pressure from others do as well as those who enter voluntarily. External pressure is one of the most effective strategies to get some people with SUDs to seek counseling.

The counseling process and goals
Counseling is a process in which a substance abuser meets with a trained professional to discuss the SUD and what to do about it. In individual counseling, the person meets privately with a counselor; in group counseling, he or she meets with the counselor and a small group of other substance abusers (between

Counseling can take the form of individual, family, or group therapy sessions.

6 and 10 people); in family counseling, other family members attend sessions. Counseling may be provided as part of a total program that includes group education, self-help groups, and medications.

Goals of counseling vary and depend on the severity of the problem, the motivation of the person, and the presence of significant social or psychological problems. In some cases, the goal is to help the person decide whether or not an SUD exists and, if so, what to do about it. In other cases, it involves helping the person stop substance use, learn ways to stay sober, and make personal or lifestyle changes needed for a life of abstinence from all substances. Sometimes, the goal of counseling with the family is to help the members develop strategies to pressure or influence a reluctant family member to enter counseling.

Individual counseling sessions last up to an hour. Group or family sessions last between one and two hours. The number of sessions attended depends on the treatment setting, the substance abuser's motivation, and his or her ability to pay. For example, during a three-to-six-week rehabilitation or partial hospital program, the person will receive 10 or more group counseling sessions per week in addition to individual and family counseling. In outpatient counseling, sessions are held once a week initially, then taper off to biweekly or monthly. The cost of counseling sessions are covered by insurance policies. For those with low incomes, most states provide services for free or at a nominal cost.

Models of counseling

Several models of counseling have proven to be effective in studies sponsored by the National Institute on Drug Abuse (NIDA) and the National Institute on Alcohol Abuse and Alcoholism (NIAAA). NIDA models include individual drug counseling, group drug counseling, contingency management, cognitive behavior therapy, relapse prevention, cue extinction, and family therapy. NIAAA models include motivational enhancement therapy, twelve-step facilitation therapy, coping skills training, and family therapies. While each model varies in terms of the theory upon which it is based or the counseling strategies used, most aim to help the person get sober, stay sober, and reduce relapse risk. For example, many counseling models help the person identify and change negative thinking or

upsetting feelings that lead to relapse, identify and manage urges to drink alcohol or ingest drugs, resist pressures from others to use substances, develop recovery supports, identify and manage warning signs of relapse, and learn steps to take if a relapse occurs.

Pros and cons of counseling

Counseling can help a person decide whether or not he or she has a problem. It helps many increase their motivation to change, initiate sobriety, or sustain it over time. Counseling leads to stopping or reducing substance use. Sometimes, substance use is reduced before it is stopped completely. Counseling may also lead to improvement in any area of life—family, social relationships, self-esteem, psychological status, spirituality, ability to maintain a job or stay in school, and financial condition.

Counseling has potential risks and personal costs, however. It requires motivation, a commitment of time and money, and psychological effort because personal issues and problems are discussed. Stopping substance use often leads initially to anger, anxiety, depression, and sleep problems. In addition, feelings of guilt and shame are common as the person examines the impact of the SUD on his or her life and family. Feedback from a counselor or a counseling group on negative behaviors can also be distressing.

The counselor

The successful counselor possesses certain attitudes, knowledge, and skills. Helpful attitudes include empathy, sensitivity to the struggles of the person with the SUD, being nonjudgmental, and accepting that success may come in small steps for some people. The successful counselor's client will feel heard, understood, accepted, and valued. Areas of knowledge needed by couselors include types, effects, and methods of substance use; causes, effects, signs, and symptoms of SUDs; treatment strategies; the recovery process; relapse causes; prevention and intervention strategies; psychiatric illnesses; impact on the family; support groups; the twelve-step program of Alcoholics Anonymous (AA) or Narcotics Anonymous (NA); and resources for people with SUDs. Counselors also need knowledge of human behavior and how culture, gender, and sexual identity affect addiction and recovery. Skills

COUNSELING WITH MIKE, AN ALCOHOLIC

Mike is a 32-year-old, married father of sons ages eight and nine. He sought treatment on the advice of his boss after missing many days of work due to hangovers. Mike was interviewed alone and with his wife by a counselor and was evaluated by a physician. Based on these interviews, Mike was diagnosed with alcohol dependence and marijuana abuse. He had a 10-year history of alcohol problems, high tolerance to alcohol, experience of many blackouts or periods in which he could not remember what he said or did while drinking, and problems with his wife and job.

Mike's goals were to stop drinking alcohol and using marijuana. Although he had two brief relapses (a two-day and a four-day drinking binge), Mike has now been sober for over 5 months. He attended 10 individual and four family counseling sessions. He attends two Alcoholics Anonymous (AA) meetings each week and has a sponsor who guides him in using the twelve-step

program of AA and helps him work on staying sober. Counseling helped Mike learn to accept the need for total abstinence, identify triggers for substance use, learn ways to resist giving in to strong cravings to drink, and learn to refuse offers to drink. Mike's counselor also helped him learn to manage boredom and to get interested in leisure activities to occupy the time in which he used to drink on weekends.

Mike's wife and children attended sessions with him to talk about their experiences. These helped Mike see that his drinking upset his wife and made his sons worry about his health and behavior. Mike's wife goes to open AA meetings with him, and attends Al-Anon meetings herself (these are for family members affected by alcoholism). Both Mike and his wife feel that counseling has been beneficial to him and to the family. His sons learned about alcoholism as a disease and now know that their father has to work at his recovery.

needed include the ability to assess for SUDs, form a working alliance with the client, educate him or her about substance abuse and recovery, help the client to identify and prioritize problems, help him or her to learn recovery skills, and help increase motivation to change. For group counselors, skill is also needed in keeping the group on task and addressing problems such as one member dominating the discussions. The family counselor needs skills in assessing the family and engaging the members of the session in identifying and working on goals.

Effectiveness of counseling

Effectiveness of counseling is measured by its impact on substance use and functioning of the client. Hundreds of studies of treatment have shown that treatment is effective in helping clients to stop or reduce substance use, improve relationships with family or others, improve employment status, improve mental, physical, or spiritual health, and reduce high-risk behaviors such as crime and using dirty hypodermic needles.

One large study of alcoholics found that they drank on an average of 80 percent of days and consumed an average of 17 drinks per day prior to treatment. One year after treatment, these same alcoholics drank on only 20 percent of days and consumed an average of three drinks per day. Heroin addicts seeking HIV testing who received counseling had lower rates of drug use, fewer arrests, and were four times more likely to be abstinent from heroin compared with those who did not receive counseling. Cocaine-addicted pregnant women who received counseling delivered much healthier babies than those not in counseling. Their babies weighed more and required fewer days in neonatal care. Many studies show that prisoners who receive treatment for an SUD while in prison are less likely to return to prison than those who do not receive treatment.

D. C. DALEY

SEE ALSO:
Alcoholism Treatment • Cognitive Behavior Therapy • Family Therapy • Treatment

Craving

Although the feelings associated with craving may vary from drug to drug and from one individual to another, craving is, in general, one of the most difficult obstacles for addicts overcoming their addiction.

Craving is a subjective experience—like the experience of anger or love—and is therefore difficult to define. Drug- and alcohol-dependent individuals describe their cravings as a persistent and intrusive preoccupation with thoughts about using drugs or alcohol that arise when they try to abstain. Cravings can be frustrating and can linger for months or even years after an individual has stopped using drugs or alcohol. Both addicts and treatment providers alike believe that craving is a major reason that dependent individuals find it difficult to break their dependency. The assumption that craving leads to relapse makes craving a major focus of study for researchers who are interested in developing new treatments for addiction. There are a number of addiction models that attempt to explain the underlying causes of craving and its relation to drug and alcohol use.

Causes

Models of addiction loosely fit into one of two categories: first, those that emphasize the role of negative withdrawal symptoms in maintaining addiction, and second, those that emphasize the positive mood states experienced when an individual takes drugs or alcohol. According to withdrawal-based models, cravings are triggered in two ways. They are either triggered directly during withdrawal or they are triggered indirectly by conditioned withdrawal long after an individual has recovered from the symptoms of withdrawal itself.

Conditioning takes place when a physical experience like the sickness brought on during withdrawal is repeatedly paired with cues (stimuli) in the environment. For example, former heroin addicts report feeling physically sick, as if in withdrawal, when entering a neighborhood where they used to use drugs and have experienced withdrawal in the past. The neighborhood acts as a cue that brings on a milder form of withdrawal illness and induces craving. This model assumes that the craving arises from the desire to stave off the withdrawal illness by using drugs or alcohol again.

Positive mood states

Models that emphasize the positive mood states induced by drugs and alcohol argue that cravings are triggered either by ingesting drugs or alcohol or by conditioned drug effects. In this model, the cues that are repeatedly paired with taking drugs come to induce effects that are similar to the positive mood effects induced directly by drugs. For example, when an abstinent alcoholic enters a bar where he or she frequently drank alcohol, he or she may feel an immediate lift in mood and start to crave a drink. This model assumes that the craving arises from the desire to experience the positive mood effects of drugs or alcohol. What these models have in common is the assumption that when cravings occur, drug taking or drinking will follow.

Researchers, however, have not been able to demonstrate that craving always leads to drug use. When alcoholics are asked to identify the reason for their first relapse after treatment, craving is rarely the primary reason they provide. The same lack of association between craving and relapse is also found with heroin addicts, cocaine addicts, and cigarette smokers. More complicated models of craving take into account the fact that cravings will not always result in drug taking. These models attempt to identify the circumstances in which craving is more likely to pose a threat to recovery.

Craving cues

The most common cues that cause craving are things like the sight, smell, and taste of drugs or alcohol. Former drinking buddies or drinking environments can also serve as powerful inducers of craving for alcohol. Internal mood states such as anxiety or depression can also trigger craving. In short, cues are objects, people, environments, and internal mood states that were repeatedly present when an addict used drugs or alcohol, or when he or she experienced withdrawal. The greater the number of cues that are present at any one time, the more likely the individual is to experience craving.

PHYSICAL DEPENDENCE

Physical dependence arises when the body cannot function normally unless the substance being abused is present; this dependence is recognized only when withdrawal symptoms become apparent. Repeated use of a drug over time results in tolerance. Tolerance to a drug means that the amount of the drug that once produced an effect like euphoria (a positive mood state) no longer produces that effect. The user must take more of the drug to achieve the same effects. Tolerance is the result of physical changes in the body that take place to accommodate the continual presence of the drug. Once tolerance has been established and the individual tries either to use less of the drug or to stop using it all together, he or she experiences withdrawal. The person now needs the drug in order to feel normal.

The symptoms of withdrawal are different for different types of drugs, but they are always experienced as negative. Withdrawal from heroin, for example, has similar symptoms to severe influenza. Withdrawal from alcohol can be life-threatening because of the possibility of grand mal seizures (a form of epilepsy). Many theories of drug dependence are based on the fact that avoidance of withdrawal is a powerful motivator that causes people to continue using drugs even when aware of the harm they do.

Treatments

There are two traditional approaches for treating craving: cue-exposure treatments and medication. The rationale for the development of cue-exposure treatment comes from theories that emphasize the role of conditioned cues in eliciting craving. If the repeated pairing of cues with withdrawal or drug-taking results in the capacity of cues to induce craving, then to cure craving it is necessary to break these connections. Specifically, repeated exposure to cues in the absence of withdrawal or drugs should eliminate or extinguish the capacity of cues to induce craving. Breaking the association between cues and drug taking is one of the targets of cue-exposure treatments. Patients undergoing treatment for alcoholism, for example, are asked to repeatedly look at and sniff their favorite alcoholic beverage without actually drinking it. Initially the sight and smell of the alcoholic beverage elicit strong cravings to drink alcohol. With repeated exposure to the alcohol cue in the absence of drinking, however, the cravings begin to fade and eventually disappear. Cue-exposure treatments also attempt to break the chain of behaviors that lead to drug use. Any belief on the part of the addict that drugs will make them feel good are downplayed by the therapist, while the belief that it is possible to resist taking drugs in the presence of powerful cues is strengthened.

Medications have also proved useful for blocking cravings. Naltrexone is one medication that has shown promise for treating alcoholism. When alcoholics take naltrexone, they are much less likely to drink alcohol than alcoholics who are given a sugar pill (placebo). One of the ways in which naltrexone is thought to work is by blocking the craving for alcohol. Abstinent alcoholics report that, while taking naltrexone, they no longer think about drinking alcohol. Exactly how naltrexone acts on the brain is not completely understood.

Smokers trying to quit smoking cigarettes also report powerful cravings. Cravings for cigarettes can be reduced by providing the smoker with nicotine, the addictive ingredient in tobacco. Nicotine is taken into the body in the form of gum, a nasal spray, or a patch that rests on the skin of the smoker. Receiving nicotine in this way is much less harmful to smokers than inhaling the nicotine from cigarettes. When smokers use nicotine replacement treatments, the amount of nicotine can be gradually reduced over time, until the body's physical dependence on nicotine is eliminated.

D. DAVIDSON

SEE ALSO:
Abstinence • Addictive Behavior • Conditioning • Relapse • Smoking Cessation • Withdrawal

Defense Mechanisms

There are many different defense mechanisms that a person can use to avoid difficult or painful situations and experiences. Defense mechanisms also play a part in the origins and maintenance of addiction.

Defense mechanisms or ego defense mechanisms are derived from a psychoanalytic theory developed by the Austrian neurologist Sigmund Freud (1856–1939). Freud described the human personality as being divided into three parts: the id, ego, and superego. In this theory the ego is responsible for dealing with threats and dangers that may arouse anxiety. The ego has two options for coping in these situations: it may choose to solve a problem and address the threat or danger, or it may choose to deny, falsify, or distort reality as a means of avoiding the anxiety. Defense mechanisms are the young ego's unconscious way of making the latter choice.

In youth, since the ego is not yet fully developed, it is too weak to handle the demands placed upon it, and so resorts to these defenses to protect itself. Through the physical changes and environmental influences that occur with maturity, the ego goes through graded and synchronized experiences that give it the opportunity to shed its defense mechanisms and replace them with more realistic and efficient mechanisms. If the ego does not shed its youthful defenses, they become irrational. The defense mechanisms of youth distort, hide, or deny reality and hinder psychological development in adults. Additionally, they use psychological energy that could be better used for more effective ego activity. If a defense becomes too influential, it can negatively affect flexibility and adaptability. If the defense fails, there is no safety net, and the person is flooded by anxiety, resulting in a nervous breakdown.

The defense mechanisms discussed in this article include repression, displacement, sublimation, dissociation, projection, reaction formation, fixation, regression, denial, minimization, rationalization, intellectualization, and avoidance. This is not an exhaustive list but does review the primary defenses.

Repression

Repression is the most common of the defense mechanisms; it is often thought of as the parent of all defenses. It is also the basis for many of Freud's theories. Repression prevents a threatening thought from intruding into awareness. It is not the same as forgetting; the information is not lost, it is merely tucked away into the subconscious mind.

Repression forces a dangerous memory, idea, or perception out of consciousness and sets up a barrier against any form of recall. This barrier may include associated memories that alone would be harmless, but which, when coupled with other memories, could trigger recollection of the repressed traumatic experience or idea, resulting in anxiety. An alcoholic may suppress the memory of emotions related to a drunk-driving accident that caused somebody's injury or death.

Displacement and sublimation

Displacement is a form of repression. It permits the repressed idea to find a place for expression, though it may be less satisfying than carrying out the preferred action. Displacement often takes the form of outward physical or verbal aggression, turned toward a less dominant or threatening target. A stereotypical act of displacement is that of an individual who comes home from a job where he is dominated and stressed by his employer, who then copes with the resulting anger by physically or emotionally abusing his wife. A common and more socially acceptable location for the expression of repressed feelings is in dreams. With the same example given above, the individual would not be abusive to his spouse but would, instead, dream that he is punishing his boss.

Related to displacement is sublimation, which is a healthy redirection of an emotion to a socially acceptable outlet. Sublimation is used, for example, when a person who has experienced the painful loss of a child or loved one as a result of a drunk driver joins an organization that promotes the idea of having designated drivers (such drivers abstain from alcohol at a social event, for example, in order to drive their friends safely home).

Repressions are necessary for normal personality development. Everyone uses repressions to some extent, but they become problematic when they are used to the exclusion of other ways of adapting. Repressions may contribute to physical ailments, such as arthritis, asthma, and ulcers. Repressions may lift if the source of threat disappears, but this does not occur automatically. A person must test reality to find out if the fear continues to have any foundation. If a person never gets or takes the chance to discover that the fear is no longer relevant, the fear is carried over to adulthood.

Dissociation, projection, and reaction formation

Closely related to repression is the process of dissociation, which involves the splintering or distortion of memories, usually related to some type of strong trauma or intensely painful event. Dissociation is a failure to integrate all thoughts, emotions, bodily sensations, and knowledge of the

A man who shows aggression toward his family may be displacing aggression he feels toward a more dominant person, such as his employer.

event. Thus, one may remember what happened but forget how one felt as a result. The individual may discuss the event as though it happened to someone else. Dissociation may be seen, for example, in the case of a person who witnesses a murder. The witness would describe details of the situation as though they were seen through someone else's eyes, and the description would be void of emotion.

Projection occurs when a person seeks relief from anxiety by attributing its cause to the external world. The purpose of projection is to transform neurotic or moral anxiety into objective anxiety. Projection changes an internal danger, which is difficult to handle, to a more manageable external danger. This defense typically arises when the anxiety-provoking situation involves an act that would typically cause guilt. The person attributes blame to an outside person or source instead of accepting responsibility for the deed. A person using this defense may say, "If my wife didn't nag at me all the time, I wouldn't drink." Defenses such as this are common. People learn very early that punishment and self-blame can be avoided by inventing plausible excuses for misdeeds.

Reaction formation begins when a person attempts to compensate for an unacceptable behavior or thought by concentrating on and displaying the opposite behavior. One instinct is hidden or masked by the other. Behaviors that are triggered by reaction formation are exaggerated and overdone, and are constantly on display. An example of this in youth is the boy who finds a girl attractive and, instead of admitting his attraction and risk being laughed at by his friends, picks on her and teases her. The risk of this reaction in adults is that the person will actually convince himself that his reactive thinking is true, so the real desire remains latent and unresolved.

Fixation and regression

In fixation a person becomes stuck at a stage of psychological growth. The person is so overcome by the fear of hardships or hazards that may lie ahead that he or she avoids taking the next step. The dangers of this defense are insecurity, failure, and punishment.

When a person reacts to fear by retreating to an earlier, more pleasurable level of development, he or she is said to regress. Any flight from controlled and realistic thinking constitutes a regression. Even healthy, well-adjusted people regress at times. Common examples are nail biting, thumb sucking, excessive eating, alcohol or tobacco use, daydreaming, or property destruction. Many regressive behaviors are so commonplace that they are actually mistaken for signs of maturity. When they occur in adults, however, they are all forms of regression.

Denial and minimizing

Denial is often a person's first reaction when faced with a sudden and disastrous event. It is one of the most common defense mechanisms and probably the easiest to understand. It is the act of refusing to accept or recognize the realities of a threatening thought or situation. If the denial is not soon replaced by acceptance, it may become especially serious. In the case of medical diagnosis, for example, a person's illness may go untreated and worsen if the person remains in denial. The same is true in cases of addiction. If a person denies his or her problem, it is left untreated and will continue to result in further anxiety-invoking consequences.

Closely related to denial is the defense of minimizing. With minimizing, the person accepts what has happened, but in a more diluted form. This defense is especially common in cases of addiction, and it is not confined to the addicted person. A man may admit that his spouse drinks regularly but deny seriousness because she goes to work every day and cooks dinner every night.

Rationalization and intellectualization

At times, a person seeks a reason or excuse for his behavior that he considers more socially and personally acceptable. This process is known as rationalization. The driver who receives a ticket for driving under the influence of alcohol may rationalize that the ticket was given because the police were out to get him or were just trying to fulfill their monthly quota. This defense works extremely well at ridding the person of any guilt or responsibility for the behavior, and it serves to maintain self-esteem. However, it also tempts the individual to hide from reality.

Related to rationalization is intellectualization, which is the act of avoiding unacceptable emotions by focusing on the intellectual aspects of the

situation. For example, upon the death of a loved one, a person may focus on the details of the funeral, instead of allowing him- or herself to feel the emotions of grief. A person using intellectualization can discuss a painful event in a very calm and sterile manner, yet he cannot tell you what he really feels.

Avoidance

Most common in cases of phobias is the defense of avoidance. Avoidance is the act of avoiding any situation that may arouse unpleasant feelings, memories, or impulses. For example, a person who is afraid of flying may refuse to travel by plane. In another example, a person will not drink any alcoholic beverage, even in a socially appropriate manner, out of fear of becoming addicted like his or her parent, or may avoid social situations where alcohol may be present out of fear of having to witness the behavior of an intoxicated person.

Defense mechanisms themselves are not unhealthy. In fact, they can be very helpful when someone is especially vulnerable to the effects of stress and anxiety. It is the timing with which these mechanisms are employed that can be problematic. If defenses are used as a temporary means on the route to more effective ways of coping, there is no problem. If, however, defense mechanisms are an adult's only means of coping and no effort is made toward healthy adaptation, then psychological growth becomes stunted and the person fails to mature.

Breaking down unhealthy defenses is best done through the process of psychotherapy. Through psychotherapy, a person is able to resolve conflicted emotions that cause anxiety and dependence on the defenses. Therapy also provides for the development of healthier coping skills, which are necessary to prevent the emotional breakdown that would occur if the individual were stripped of defenses and left with no other means of adaptation. Psychotherapy may include the use of exposure therapies or desensitization, relaxation training and other cognitive activities, and environmental alterations and avoidances.

P. L. TORCHIA

SEE ALSO:
Cognitive Behavior Therapy • Counseling • Denial • Mental Disorders • Stress

Delirium Tremens

Delirium tremens is a potentially fatal form of alcohol withdrawal characterized by trembling, insomnia, hallucinations, and delusions. It is also referred to as DTs and less commonly as Saunders-Sutton syndrome or Morel's disease.

The term *delirium tremens* is attributed to Thomas Sutton, an English physician who used it in 1813 to describe the shaking delirium associated with the withdrawal of alcohol. It is one of a cluster of unpleasant mental and physical symptoms that are collectively known as alcohol withdrawal syndrome.

Causes

Delirium tremens occurs most commonly in patients with a long history of alcohol use and a prior history of difficulty during withdrawal from the use of alcohol. Alcoholics with a prior incidence of delirium tremens are predisposed to future episodes. The repeated consumption of alcohol has been shown to disturb the balance of chemical messengers (neurotransmitters) in the brain and may also affect the level of protein targets to which the neurotransmitters bind in order to achieve their effects on the brain. The brain responds to repeated consumption of alcohol by adapting the sensitivity of these protein targets in a process called tolerance. When consumption of alcohol is discontinued, the adaptations developed during prolonged drinking are suddenly unopposed, leading to a greater excitability of brain circuits. Delirium tremens is particularly associated with a rebound overexcitability of the sympathetic nervous system.

Signs and symptoms

The symptoms of delirium tremens may vary depending on the individual, the severity of alcoholism, and the duration of withdrawal. Shaking begins around six hours after the last drink. Other symptoms usually appear from three to five days after abstaining from or reducing the consumption of alcohol and can last for several days. Mental symptoms may include disorientation, irritability, insomnia, and terrifying hallucinations. Visual hallucinations are the most common type experienced during alcohol withdrawal. Patients may believe that they see or feel insects or worms crawling on walls or over their skin, a phenomenon known as formication. Auditory hallucinations are less common. Physical symptoms may include tremor, seizures, agitation, sweating, rapid breathing and heart rate, blood pressure abnormalities, difficulty in regulating body temperature, severe muscle cramps, vomiting, and gastritis.

Incidence and mortality

While estimates vary, delirium tremens affects approximately 5 percent of individuals undergoing withdrawal from alcohol. Death rates of those affected by this form of withdrawal are less than 5 percent if recognized and treated early but can be up to 35 percent if left untreated. Individuals with fever or electrolyte imbalances, or concurrent illnesses such as hepatitis, pancreatitis, or pneumonia that may obscure diagnosis and treatment, are the most likely to die from delirium tremens. It is not uncommon for an alcoholic patient to develop acute alcohol withdrawal symptoms and delirium tremens after a few days of hospitalization, or during recovery from routine surgery.

Treatment

Sedatives are used to control the acute symptoms of delirium tremens. The drugs of choice act to increase inhibitory chemical transmission in the brain through gamma-aminobutyric acid (GABA) receptors, which reduces the sympathetic hyperactivity associated with the disorder. Benzodiazepines such as diazepam (Valium) are commonly used in treatment and are usually administered intravenously to achieve a more rapid effect, along with fluids and electrolytes. Drug treatments are gradually reduced during the week following the beginning of treatment to reduce the chance of rebound seizures.

D. W. GODWIN

SEE ALSO:
Alcoholism • Alcoholism Treatment • Cold Turkey • Detoxification • Rehabilitation • Tolerance • Withdrawal

Denial

Admitting to a drug or alcohol problem is a key step on the road to overcoming addiction. For some, it can be the hardest part of the process, as it involves breaking down barriers that have been set up deep in the unconscious mind.

Many people who abuse alcohol and other drugs are unwilling or unable to admit, to themselves and to others, that their substance use is a problem that needs to be addressed. Not admitting that a problem exists and not taking steps to address the problem have been thought by psychiatrists to reflect denial or resistance. Traditionally, researchers have argued that a primary challenge in working with a substance abuser is to confront this denial and resistance in order to break through it. Successful confrontation is presumed to set the stage for the individual to take action regarding his or her substance use disorder.

Denial

Overcoming denial is a cornerstone of many models of rehabilitation for persons with substance use disorders. In 1970 Morris Chafetz, founding director of the National Institute on Alcohol Abuse and Alcoholism, wrote that "denial constitutes the main method by which alcoholics deal with life." Similar impressions have been offered regarding people who abuse drugs other than alcohol. Counselors who work with alcoholics and drug abusers say that denial is among the most difficult problems they face in working with their patients. In fact, one proposed definition of alcoholism, published in 1992 in the *Journal of the American Medical Association*, identified denial as a major obstacle to recovery from substance use disorders.

The concept of denial is rooted in the psychoanalytic literature on defense mechanisms, which are defined as unconscious processes used by an individual to alleviate emotional conflict and anxiety. A primary component of denial is a distorted perception of reality in which a person negates or refuses awareness of the problem.

Dan Anderson, a pioneer of the Minnesota Model of addiction treatment developed at the Hazelden Foundation, provided one of the more comprehensive discussions of denial. He used the term *denial* to designate "a wide repertoire of psychological defenses and maneuvers that alcoholic persons

unwittingly set up to protect themselves from the realization that they do in fact have a drinking problem," or, by extension, a problem with any psychoactive substance. As with defense mechanisms more generally, Anderson sees denial as an unconscious process. Moreover, denial can also operate within the substance abuser's family or other support systems. In these situations, the spouse, other family members, and friends will similarly deny to themselves and others that the substance abuser is in need of help, sometimes through a sense of shame but also through a strong desire to try to control the situation.

Anderson identified a number of the most typical defensive maneuvers. One, not surprisingly, is simple denial, where the person insists that his or her substance use is not a problem, despite evidence to the contrary. In a second maneuver, termed minimizing, the person acknowledges a small problem but dismisses it as not being serious. Another maneuver is rationalizing, where the abuser provides excuses or justifications to account for or excuse the substance abuse. Finally, a frequent form of denial is hostility. In this case, the substance abuser responds in an angry and irritated manner to people who attempt to discuss the substance abuse with him or her. The substance abuser's objective here is to dissuade others from bringing up the issue.

In discussing these manifestations of denial, Anderson also described two of its other features. First, denial is automatic and should not be characterized as lying or being willfully deceptive. Instead, the denial is an outgrowth of a firmly entrenched state of self-delusion. The second feature of denial, according to Anderson, is that it is progressive. He argues that "by the time an individual's illness is sufficiently advanced that the problem appears serious to others, an elaborate system of defenses has usually been built up." Thus, as the severity of alcoholism or drug abuse increases, the complexity and intractability of the denial increases comparably.

Resistance

A related term frequently encountered in discussions of substance abuse is *resistance,* a concept originally developed by the psychologist Sigmund Freud about patients who remained silent on issues relevant to their case. Counselors generally use the term *resistance* to refer to patient behaviors that they view as counter to or disruptive of the process of treatment. Resistance occurs on both conscious and unconscious levels. While resistance may have the goal of avoiding uncomfortable feelings such as anxiety or guilt, resistance can also refer to a patient who lacks motivation to change behavior. Representative of this view are psychologists Arnold Lazarus and Allen Fay, who state that resistant patients are neither people who "do not want help" nor "deliberate saboteurs," but are instead people for whom exploration and change are difficult, painful, and even dangerous.

Reconceptualizing denial and resistance

The concepts of denial and resistance are frequently used to explain why drug-use patients do not succeed in treatment. In this view, it is the patients' traits of denial and resistance that account for treatment failure. However, there are significant difficulties in validating the ways these traits account for the failure of treatment. According to William Miller, a psychologist at the University of New Mexico, one observation that has not been substantiated by research models is that denial is more frequently seen among alcoholics than among other clinical populations (such as anxious or depressed patients), and that denial is directly related to treatment outcome.

Miller and his colleague Stephen Rollnick have argued that the use of concepts such as denial and resistance has not advanced our knowledge about addictive behavior or its treatment. As an alternative, they have focused on improving motivation—often seen as the flip side of denial and resistance—and increasing the occurrence of behaviors helpful to resolving the substance use problem as an important step in the treatment of addictive behaviors. Motivational counseling involves the use of a variety of techniques to help individuals mobilize their own resources to overcome their ambivalence and initiate changes in their behavior. A "motivational intervention" might be any operation that increases the probability of entering, continuing, and complying with an active strategy for change. In 1985 Miller outlined a series of motivational interventions that potentially could be used to promote change, including giving advice, providing feedback, setting goals, role-playing, manipulating external contingencies, providing choices, and decreasing the attractiveness of problem behavior. These and other strategies have been summarized as building blocks that can be applied as part of the counselor's effort to engender productive change in an individual's addictive behavior.

Goals of intervention

Because many substance abusers are characterized by lack of awareness of a drug problem (despite evidence that drug use is contributing to dysfunction), one important goal of motivational interventions with such patients is to make more salient the effects of their drug use on their lives. Among people who are ambivalent about the level of the problem or about making change, a major goal of motivational interventions is to emphasize the advantages of reduced or zero use and the disadvantages of continued use at existing levels, and to thus encourage the taking of steps that will lead to making changes.

Providing choice is another possible intervention for people not thinking or just starting to think about changing their drug use. Identifying options for the patient may help diffuse the resentments that arise when a counselor, family member, or friend has applied pressure on the individual to stop using alcohol and drugs and to seek treatment. If the person believes he or she has a choice in directions that can be taken, then the belief that he or she can influence and guide the course of action may result in initiating critical steps toward change. Similarly, a person wavering about change may use the availability of several options as a way of initiating steps toward making change.

G. J. CONNORS

SEE ALSO:
Addictive Behavior • Alcoholism • Alcoholism Treatment • Counseling • Defense Mechanisms • Recovery • Treatment

Dependence

Dependence describes a state in which an individual cannot function normally without using a drug of abuse. Although several different criteria are used to diagnose this state, not all need be present for a person to have a dependence.

The concept of dependence has a fairly recent history in the study of alcohol and drug abuse. The dependence syndrome was originally proposed by the British psychologists Griffith Edwards and Milton Gross in 1974. A key definition of dependence is the degree of difficulty experienced in refraining from whatever a person is dependent upon, be it alcohol, drugs, gambling, exercise, or surfing the Internet. Although this may be a useful general definition, it does not make clear what actually constitutes dependence, nor does it help in the diagnosis and measurement of the degree of dependence. Edwards and Gross studied addiction and put together a list of the defining features. They called this list a *syndrome*, a medical term describing a number of signs and symptoms that tend to cluster together. To have this syndrome there is no need to show signs of all the elements or have them to the same degree.

Critics of the dependence syndrome, and there are many, suggest that it was hastily formulated, mainly as a reaction to psychological research suggesting that addiction was not a disease and could therefore be treated by nonmedical agencies. Further, critics suggest that the dependence syndrome is merely a reformulation of the disease model in a slightly more acceptable fashion. The addiction field is replete with passionate loyalties to theoretical models and treatment approaches, and so these criticisms are probably overly harsh. What is certain, however, is that in spite of criticisms, the dependence syndrome has gained acceptance throughout the world and is almost certainly the most commonly used model of addictive behavior.

The dependence syndrome

There are seven elements in the dependence syndrome. It is described here for alcohol, as it was originally intended, but its generalization to other substances and behaviors is obvious.

Narrowing of the drinking repertoire. Most people have a number of different drinking repertoires, that is, they will drink different types of alcohol, different amounts, and at a different rate depending on the occasion. For example, one might drink quite differently at a party than at a business lunch. As someone becomes dependent, the distinction between occasions begins to blur and the person drinks in a similar fashion, usually to excess, regardless of the occasion. It is easy to see how this behavior could apply to other drugs and activities. For example, an overeater might binge at every meal rather than have light snacks occasionally.

Salience of drink-seeking behavior. Drink-seeking behavior refers to the amount of time spent thinking about, searching out, and consuming alcohol. The time associated with drinking may acquire increasing prominence in a person's life. Again, this description can be applied to other activities, for example, the dependent Internet surfer may spend increasing amounts of time thinking about being on the Internet as well as actually surfing.

Increased tolerance to alcohol. Tolerance is defined as the amount of a substance required to gain a given state. For the alcoholic, the same amount of alcohol will have less effect than it had previously, and more alcohol will be needed to gain the same effect. This is a feature of all addictive behaviors: increasing amounts are needed to gain satisfaction.

Repeated withdrawal symptoms. Withdrawal symptoms vary from substance to substance and from behavior to behavior. For example, in alcohol problems, there is the classic triad of shaking, sweating, and anxiety. Irritability, restlessness, and low mood have manifested in gamblers who refrain, and similar symptoms have been found in people who stop exercising (even if they do not exercise to extremes).

Subjective awareness of a compulsion to drink. In this element of the syndrome, the person reports feeling an overwhelming craving to indulge. In the disease model, this craving was seen as a core element of addiction, and was regarded as evidence that there was something abnormal about alcoholics and drug addicts. Again, however, this element can be seen in both chemical and behavioral addictions.

Avoidance of withdrawal symptoms by further drinking. In the classic relief-drinking repertoire, people drink not to feel good but in order to feel less bad. Although it is clear that continued alcohol or drug use will lead to even worse feelings and withdrawal, the lure of the short-term gain (relief from withdrawal) tends to win over the threat of longer-term discomfort.

Reinstatement of dependence after abstinence. The idea that drinkers cannot renounce their habit is seen by critics as a restatement of the old adage "once an alcoholic, always an alcoholic." While there is evidence that many who have had alcohol problems relapse to their previous severity of addiction, others do not and have been able to maintain a drinking behavior that is free from the problems associated with dependence.

Dependence may occur not only in relation to drugs but also to activities such as playing video games.

Benefits of the dependence syndrome

One benefit of identifying the dependence syndrome was that it provided a framework that allowed dependence to be diagnosed and measured. It offered an alternative to self-diagnosis or the controversial disease model, and established a scientific standard. A number of approaches have been developed for both alcohol and drugs that can discriminate between those who are dependent and those who are not and also between degrees of dependence. Cut-off points vary, but a fairly conservative estimate suggests that if someone is exhibiting signs of three of the seven elements, he or she is probably dependent.

A second benefit of recognizing the syndrome was that it eradicated the distinction between physical and psychological dependence originally introduced by E. M. Jellinek (the cofounder of the Center of Alcohol Studies at Yale University) in his disease model. Instead, the syndrome recognizes that there are both physical and psychological elements to dependence. For example, withdrawal is a physical reaction to abstinence, while drink-seeking behavior is psychological.

Dependence does not always need to have negative connotations. The psychologist B. S. Tuchfeld, for example, suggests that in order for an alcoholic or addict to recover, he or she needs to develop a positive dependency to replace the negative one. For many who do recover, transference of dependency to a self-help group such as Alcoholics Anonymous is often observed. Some may take up time-consuming hobbies, while others may throw themselves into work. This dependency is, to some extent, a desire to fill the time that was devoted to pursuing an addiction. It is not always recognized that dependency is a time-consuming pursuit involving thinking about taking the substance, acquiring the substance, and consuming it. Thus, abstinence can leave a gap in dependent persons' lives, not just because they no longer have the substance or behavior to alter the way they feel, but also because much of their time was occupied by their dependency.

Some criticisms

Although the dependence syndrome attempted to define and measure addiction scientifically, and as such was welcomed by many, the concept has also received much criticism. One critique contends that there is a lack of evidence to underpin the concept. Nick Heather, a British psychologist, suggests that some of the elements, such as subjective compulsion to drink, are flawed. This argument puts forward the view that alcoholics justify their drinking (or gamblers their gambling, and so on) by suggesting that they cannot control it because they suffer from an uncontrollable craving, which means they are dependent. Hence, people who cannot control their drinking are dependent and people who are dependent cannot control their drinking, which is a tautology, or a circular argument. Another criticism concerns the concept's neglect of environmental factors, which clearly play a part in substance use. The dependence syndrome locates the problem within the individual, whereas the weight of evidence suggests that environmental factors, such as poverty and deprivation, have a large part to play in addiction.

Studies of Vietnam soldiers

Sociologist Lee Robins conducted a study of Vietnam War veterans that clearly implicates the environment. In her 1975 study she found that roughly one in five American soldiers in Vietnam were addicted to narcotics. She identified a group of around 450 men who had tested positive for drugs before leaving Vietnam and traced them after their return to the United States. She found that once back home, only about 7.5 percent remained addicted, with the rest either stopping use altogether or using only occasionally. Robins argued that the drug use, and the dependence on it, was a reaction to a high-stress situation and the easy availability of high-grade drugs. Once troops had left the war environment, the need for the drugs was reduced or removed. What is remarkable about this study is that the recovery rate of this group is many times that of addicts who have developed their dependency at home. A second remarkable finding of this study is that around 45 percent of the sample used narcotics occasionally after returning home, without any signs of reinstated dependency. Robins declared that this finding was contrary to the conventional wisdom.

Perhaps the largest criticism of the dependence syndrome is that it is couched in medical terms. Research by scientists working in other disciplines, such as psychology and sociology, suggests that there are other explanations for excessive substance use that do not require a medical explanation. Psychologists suggest that one issue that has been continually underrated is the concept of pleasure or reward. There is little doubt that most people start drinking or taking drugs for the simple reason that they find it enjoyable. Some argue that the pursuit of this aspect of drug taking can maintain the behavior long after the enjoyment has ceased. Work on expectancy (the belief about the outcome of a particular action) has shown that the more positive outcomes a person expects, the more he or she will drink. Indeed, it has been a consistent finding of this research that alcoholics have higher expectations of good outcomes than lighter drinkers. The types of outcomes expected are tension relief, sexual enhancement, social facilitation, and assertiveness. Other explanations for addiction can be found in conditioning. This concept has been used to explain elements such as craving and tolerance that would appear to be strictly physiological.

Is dependence a useful concept?

The final criticism of the concept asks how useful it is. If dependence can be diagnosed, and its severity measured, how does that help? One way in which it might help is that (as in other fields of treatment) it might predict the prognosis, that is, the outcome of treatment. One might believe that the greater the degree of severity, the worse the prognosis, and indeed a great deal of evidence would support that belief. However, others may believe that the greater the severity, the better the outcome, since alcoholics and addicts would feel compelled to change before things got even worse. Again, there is a great deal of evidence to support that belief. There is also a great deal of evidence that suggests that prognosis is unrelated to severity of dependence. So if the outcome from dependence cannot be predicted, how can it be used? The only secure prediction seems to be the severity of withdrawal and the amount of medication required to alleviate it.

J. MCMAHON

SEE ALSO:
Abstinence • Addiction • Addictive Behavior • Conditioning • Craving • Disease Theory of Addiction • Tolerance • Withdrawal

Depression

Depression and addiction are often strongly linked. Approximately 30 percent of people suffering from depression have also suffered from an addiction to drugs or alcohol at some point in their lives.

Depression is a mental illness characterized by a profoundly sad mood and feelings of emptiness. It affects around 19 million people per year in the United States; roughly one person in six will experience some kind of depressive disorder in the course of his or her life. The effectiveness of drug treatments in treating depression strongly suggests that biological factors play a major role in its cause. Depression can also play a major role in addiction, both by causing addiction in vulnerable people and by helping to lock people into a cycle of addictive behavior.

What is depression?

Much more than simply "having the blues," depression is a serious mental illness that can utterly disrupt someone's life for weeks, months, or even years. Although depression is especially common in the elderly, it can occur at any age and it is becoming increasingly widespread in children and adolescents. In its most devastating form, depression can drive despairing sufferers to suicide. However, there are many effective treatments for depression; about 80 percent of patients show some improvement and many can be cured completely.

Depression is often referred to as an affective disorder because it dramatically alters a person's affect (a psychiatrist's term for mood): persistent sad or empty mood is the major symptom of depression. Other symptoms may include a lack of interest in hobbies and activities, thoughts of death and attempts to plan suicide, and feelings of guilt, hopelessness, or worthlessness. Although depression is essentially a mental illness, it also has a number of physical symptoms. These can include feelings of tiredness or fatigue, disrupted patterns of sleeping and eating, difficulty in concentrating and remembering, and a loss of libido (sex drive).

Depressive disorders

There are broadly two different types of depressive illness: depression that occurs by itself and depression that occurs with mania (out-of-control, excitable behavior). If depression occurs alone, it can range in seriousness from major depression (a very disrupting and disabling condition) to dysthymia (a milder, less disruptive form of depression).

Mania and depression are opposite extremes (or poles) of mood, so depression alone is often referred to as unipolar depression (a mood that stays at one extreme) while depression with mania is called bipolar disorder (because it swings back and forth between the two extremes, the lows and highs of depression and mania). Although much less common than depression, bipolar disorder is usually much more disruptive and typically requires either hospitalization or continuous medication. Just as dysthymia is a less-severe form of depression, there is also a milder form of bipolar disorder known as cyclothymia, which involves regular mood swings between mild mania and mild depression. Unlike depression, mania never occurs alone; patients with mania always suffer from depression as well.

Treatments

People with mild forms of depression are sometimes treated with psychotherapy alone. Cognitive behavior therapy (CBT) is an increasingly popular method that starts from the idea that depression is caused by the way people think about themselves when negative things happen to them. Treatment involves learning better ways of reacting to the stresses of everyday life.

For the majority of people suffering from depression, a combination of psychotherapy and drug treatment proves the most effective treatment. While the drugs help to relieve the symptoms of the illness itself, the psychotherapy offers a way of learning better strategies for coping with the stressful and traumatic events that can trigger depression in especially vulnerable people. There are three main types of antidepressant drugs in common use today: tricyclic antidepressants (TCAs), monoamine oxidase inhibitors (MAOIs), and selective serotonin reuptake inhibitors (SSRIs).

Patients with a very severe depression that does not respond to either psychotherapy or medication may be treated with electroconvulsive therapy (ECT). Two electrodes are attached to the scalp and deliver a short (0.5 to 4-second) electric shock to the brain. ECT is typically administered several times a week for several weeks and produces dramatic improvements in 80 to 90 percent of patients. Although ECT became highly controversial in the latter part of the twentieth century, its effectiveness in treating severe depression has since returned it to favor.

Causes

Psychiatrists once tended to divide depression into two general types: endogenous (caused from within by a person's biological or psychological makeup) and reactive (caused through a reaction to such outside life events as the death of a loved one). This basic division is related to the wider nature-nurture debate in which psychologists try to find out how inherited, genetic factors (nature) work with environmental and developmental factors (nurture) to produce different types of human behavior.

The effectiveness of different sorts of treatments also seems to confirm the idea that depression can be caused in several different ways. The success of psychotherapy suggests that depression is a psychological disorder caused by cognitive problems (negative thoughts) and behavioral problems (learning to become "helpless"), while the success of drug treatments and ECT suggest depression is a biological disorder of the brain.

Modern genetic research has demonstrated that depression and bipolar disorder tend to run in families, while studies of brain chemistry and the development of new types of antidepressant drugs have led to new theories of how depression may actually arise. The MAOIs and SSRIs, for example, are believed to work by increasing the availability of mood-enhancing neurotransmitters (the brain's chemical messengers) such as serotonin. Evidence such as this seems to confirm the idea of depression as a biological disorder, but that does not mean that biological factors are always the cause. Many researchers now view depression as an essentially biological disorder to which some people have a genetic predisposition and which can be triggered by environmental factors such as stressful life events.

Depression in children and adolescents

Depression is becoming more and more common in children and adolescents. According to the National Institute of Mental Health, 2.5 percent of children and 8.3 percent of adolescents suffer from the illness. The seriousness of the problem is reflected in suicide rates for young people. In the United States, the suicide rate in children aged 10 to 14 was 0.9 percent per 100,000 in 2007. The reason for the increase in childhood depression is unclear. It might reflect social pressures on young people to grow up more quickly or it might be a problem that has always existed but whose seriousness is only now being discovered. Either way, the issue is receiving increasing amounts of attention from mental health professionals.

Depression and addiction

Depression and addiction often go hand-in-hand: either disorder increases the risk of a person suffering from the other disorder. Studies have found that around a third of people with depression have had a drug or alcohol problem at some point in their lives, while alcoholics are three times more likely to suffer depression than nondrinkers. Smokers are twice as likely to suffer from major depression as nonsmokers, although the vast majority of smokers never suffer from depression. Depression is also strongly linked with other kinds of addiction, including sex addiction and compulsive gambling.

The precise reasons that depression and addiction are so strongly connected remain the subject of much research and debate. It could be that addiction provides distraction or relief from the symptoms of depression. It might be that the genetic factors that make some people vulnerable to depression also make them more likely to develop addictions when they turn to alcohol or drugs for relief. Or it might be that both depression and addiction involve similar brain systems and pathways or related behavioral and cognitive processes.

C. WOODFORD

SEE ALSO:
Addictive Behavior • Cognitive Behavior Therapy • Compulsive Behaviors • Counseling • Mental Disorders • Suicide • Vulnerability

Detoxification

Detoxification is a natural process by which the human body rids itself of toxins. In the context of drug use, detoxification is the elimination of drugs of abuse from the body in conjunction with the treatment of withdrawal symptoms.

In the context of recovery from drug dependency, detoxification, or detox, is the process of halting consumption of the drug of abuse and allowing the body to eliminate the drug by natural processes. In some cases, careful medication or alternative therapies, such as acupuncture, can help treat withdrawal symptoms. Other therapies can accelerate the elimination of a drug from the body.

Detox is not a cure for addiction; rather, it is a means of getting the patient to a clean state in which the drug is no longer in the body in significant amounts and the symptoms of physical dependence have subsided. Rehabilitation programs can then improve the chances of the former user remaining abstinent, as can a restructuring of the former user's life so as to avoid or remove influences and situations that would tempt the user back to the drug. Many of the former user's social contacts will be associated with his or her drug abuse, so successful recovery usually means finding new associates.

Unless drug abuse poses an immediate threat to the user's life, the detox and rehabilitation program should only start once the user is firmly resolved to become free of a drug. Halfhearted attempts at detox and recovery are likely to fail and thus reduce the user's confidence in his or her ability to succeed.

Once the decision to detoxify has been made, the medical team will discuss the best approach and the requirement for medical support. If the user is physically dependent on more than one drug, it might be safer to detoxify from one drug at a time while managing the other dependencies with pure prescription versions of street drugs.

Elimination

The body starts the process of elimination immediately after the administration of any drug. The kidney excretes water-soluble drugs in urine, while enzymes in the liver convert water-insoluble drugs into water-soluble metabolites that pass into bile and leave the body through the bowel. Other elimination routes are in sweat, sebum (skin oils), and milk in the case of a nursing mother. Elimination gets rid of drugs dissolved in the bloodstream. Drugs in the brain must first pass through the blood-brain barrier and into the blood before the liver and kidneys can process them. Significant amounts of fat-soluble drugs also become tied up in fat deposits around the body, so their elimination is slowed by the need for them to pass into the blood before they can be processed. Since many psychoactive drugs rely on high fat-solubility to get them through the blood-brain barrier, total elimination from fat deposits is the focus of some detox therapies. A sauna is one means of promoting reduction of drugs in fat deposits.

Detoxification often features a dietary regime with fresh fruit and vegetables to ensure a good flow of fecal waste to carry away toxins in bile, and plenty of fluids to flush toxins through the kidneys. Mineral and vitamin supplements help correct deficiencies caused by prolonged periods of poor nutrition that are typical of long-term drug abusers. These deficiencies are not only important for general health but also for efficient functioning of the enzyme systems that take part in detoxification.

Withdrawal symptoms

Detoxification from physiologically addictive drugs may require medication to combat the symptoms of withdrawal. Withdrawal occurs because the body has become used to overstimulation of drug-sensitive receptors and has responded by decreasing the number or activity of those receptors. These receptor systems take time to return to their normal activity level after withdrawal of the drug. Until they do, the symptoms are the opposite of the effects of the drug. Hence, withdrawal from a painkilling drug such as an opiate causes an increased sensitivity to pain.

Opiates

Unassisted withdrawal from an opiate such as heroin is most uncomfortable because of the role of opiate receptors in fighting pain. The pain response normalizes over five to seven days. Opiate receptors also cause sedation, so withdrawal of an opiate can cause up to three weeks of insomnia accompanied by weakness, lethargy, and anxiety. Diarrhea increases discomfort as the opiate receptors that suppress bowel activity are understimulated.

The traditional method for heroin detox is substitution by a less addictive opioid, such as methadone, followed by slow reduction of the dosage of methadone. The success of this approach is limited by the fact that methadone is addictive in its own right, and attempts at heroin detox often lead to indefinite maintenance with methadone.

The other extreme is ultra-rapid opiate detoxification, or UROD. This procedure uses a general anesthetic to obliterate pain, while an opioid antagonist such as naloxone or naltrexone strips all traces of opiate from receptors. The doctor usually implants a pellet of naltrexone under the skin to maintain a concentration of opiate antagonist that prevents heroin from having any effect during the high-risk period immediately after detoxification.

A more moderate approach uses an opiate partial agonist, such as buprenorphine. Such a drug stimulates the opiate receptors sufficiently to avoid withdrawal symptoms but does not produce a high. It also reduces the effects of heroin if the patient's resolve weakens and he or she uses heroin. Over time, the patient can gradually reduce the dosage of buprenorphine without suffering from withdrawal symptoms.

CNS depressants and stimulants

Withdrawal from central-nervous-system (CNS) depressants such as alcohol, benzodiazepines, and GHB (gamma-hydroxybutyrate) is less uncomfortable than withdrawal from opiates, but it is potentially more dangerous. These drugs act by boosting the action of GABA (gamma-aminobutyric acid) in slowing brain activity. The GABA system becomes less active through prolonged use of such drugs, so sudden withdrawal causes hyperactivity in the brain that can lead to epileptic fits and life-threatening symptoms including seizures and heart-rhythm disturbances.

Withdrawal from these drugs is usually managed by administering a diminishing dosage of another CNS depressant to reduce the risk of seizures and heart failure. Lorazepam helps in the withdrawal of

This patient is participating in detoxification and rehabilitation at the Milo Shaheed Trust in Quetta, Pakistan. Readily available heroin from neighboring Afghanistan increased the number of heroin addicts in Pakistan needing treatment.

alcohol, GHB, and fast-acting benzodiazepines such as Xanax. Withdrawal from benzodiazepines prescribed for anxiety, such as Valium, can be assisted by switching to a less addictive, slower acting drug such as flurazepam, then slowly reducing the dosage.

CNS stimulants such as Ecstasy, cocaine, and various amphetamines cause little physical dependence, so there is seldom a need for medical supervision. The absence of these mood-lifting drugs can cause depression, so a course of antidepressants can help relieve these symptoms.

M. CLOWES

SEE ALSO:

Addiction • Cocaine Addiction Treatment • Tolerance • Withdrawal

Diagnosing Substance Abuse

Before a person enters treatment for a substance use disorder, he or she is assessed according to criteria that determine the level of use of and dependence on the substance. The patient can then be sent for the correct type of treatment.

Use, misuse, harmful use, abuse, dependence, and *addiction* are all terms that are commonly used in everyday language. In ordinary conversation, these labels often refer to taking substances in ways that other people disapprove. For example, most parents disapprove of their children smoking marijuana, so many parents would consider any use of marijuana as abuse. The terms *harmful use, abuse,* and *dependence,* however, also have highly specific definitions as medical diagnoses.

What is meant by a diagnosis?

Diagnosis refers to a medical judgment about the cause or explanation of a person's symptoms, distress, or problem behaviors. Coughing is an example of a symptom that could be caused by several different conditions such as the common cold, pneumonia, or lung cancer. Making a correct diagnosis is important because it guides the type of treatment the patient needs. To determine which disease is causing the cough, the physician first takes a history by asking the patient questions about the symptom, examines the patient by listening to breathing sounds with a stethoscope, and orders tests such as a chest X-ray. The physician then compares the findings and results of the history, examination, and tests to known criteria for each possible diagnosis. A diagnosis is ultimately made by matching the patient's findings and results to specific diagnostic criteria.

Similarly, using a substance could be a symptom of harmful use, abuse, or dependence, but it is not always diagnostic of them. To make a diagnosis, other criteria must also be present. Making a correct diagnosis is important in deciding the best form of treatment for the condition.

How a diagnosis is classified

Diseases and other medical diagnoses can be classified in a variety of ways. One way classifies them according to the organ system they predominantly affect. Thus, there are diseases of the respiratory system, the heart and circulatory system, the digestive system, and so on. Medical diagnoses are also classified according to their cause. Infection, abnormal growth of cells, genetic abnormalities, trauma, and exposure to radiation and poisons are causes of various medical conditions. Another classification system distinguishes between physical disorders and mental disorders. Mental disorders include mood disorders, anxiety disorders, eating disorders, psychotic disorders, and substance use disorders.

Mental disorders are often characterized by particular behaviors, such as binge eating (as in bulimia) or repeatedly taking substances in a way that harms oneself or others (as in abuse and dependence). The distinction between mental and physical disorders, however, is somewhat artificial because many mental disorders are either known or thought to have physical causes involving the brain or genetics. Substance dependence is an example of a mental disorder that is caused in part by genetic factors and in part by exposure of the brain to toxic substances. Accordingly, the U.S. National Institute on Drug Abuse refers to substance use disorders as diseases of the brain. However, psychological and social factors can also cause and perpetuate substance use disorders, so it is best to consider them as complex disorders.

The American Psychiatric Association's *Diagnostic and Statistical Manual of Mental Disorders,* 4th edition (DSM-IV, 1994) and the World Health Organization's *International Classification of Diseases,* 10th edition (ICD-10, 1993) are the American and worldwide standards for defining and diagnosing all medical diseases and mental disorders, including substance abuse, harmful use, and dependence. These books provide the most widely accepted criteria for determining if an individual's pattern of taking substances qualifies for a diagnosis of abuse, harmful use, or dependence. Both books are periodically updated as the nature and causes of various diagnoses become better understood.

The term *addiction* is generally, although not always, used interchangeably with *dependence,* but *addiction* does not appear in either ICD-10 or

---

TABLE 1
DSM-IV CRITERIA OF SUBSTANCE DEPENDENCE

A pattern of substance use leading to significant impairment or distress as manifested by three or more of the following in the same one-year period:

(1)   Tolerance (physiological dependence)

(2)   Withdrawal (physiological dependence)

(3)   More substance taken than intended

(4)   Persistent desire or unsuccessful efforts to cut down or control use

(5)   Large time expenditure on substance-related activity

(6)   Important social, work, or leisure activities reduced or replaced by substance use

(7)   Continued substance use despite knowing that physical or psychological problems are
        caused or worsened by use

ICD-10 CRITERIA FOR SUBSTANCE DEPENDENCE

Three or more of the following at some time during the previous year:

(1)   Tolerance

(2)   Withdrawal (physiological dependence)

(3)   Difficulties in controlling substance use in terms of onset, termination, or levels of use

(4)   Large time expenditure on substance-related activity; OR
        Progressive neglect of alternative pleasures or interests in favor of substance use

(5)   Continued substance use despite overtly harmful physical or psychological consequences

(6)   A strong desire or compulsion to use substance

Source: Criteria paraphrased and simplified from DSM-IV (1994, 2000) and ICD-10 (1993)

DSM-IV. Likewise, terms such as *addictive disease, addictive behaviors,* and *chemical dependency* do not appear in these systems of classification. Therefore, the discussion that follows uses the terms *abuse, harmful use,* and *dependence* and for the most part avoids the other terms.

Criteria for substance dependence

The criteria for diagnosing substance dependence according to the DSM-IV and ICD-10 are presented in Table 1. The two diagnostic systems are more similar than different. For example, the tolerance and withdrawal criteria (Criteria 1 and 2, respectively) are identical in both diagnostic systems. The criterion of tolerance (Criterion 1) is fulfilled when a user needs larger amounts of a substance to obtain the same effects previously experienced with smaller amounts, or when the user experiences diminished effects over time with the same amount of drug use. Withdrawal

(Criterion 2) refers to newly experienced physical or psychological symptoms of distress that occur when the user either stops or reduces use of a particular substance. Specific withdrawal symptoms differ by drug class. Tolerance and withdrawal often occur together. They indicate that the body has adapted to (or changed in response to) repeated substance use, so that more of the substance is needed to feel its effects and prevent withdrawal symptoms. Thus, users may increase their drug use due to tolerance and withdrawal. Because the body changes in its response to a drug after repeated exposure, tolerance and withdrawal are often referred to by the following terms, which generally mean the same thing: *physical dependence, physiological dependence,* and *pharmacological dependence.* DSM-IV recognizes the distinction between substance dependence and physiological dependence. Thus, if someone diagnosed with alcohol dependence also has evidence of either tolerance or withdrawal, then the correct diagnosis is specified as "alcohol dependence with physiological dependence"; in the absence of tolerance or withdrawal, the diagnosis is "alcohol dependence without physiological dependence." Physiological dependence and its two synonyms are sometimes contrasted with psychological dependence, which is characterized by a compulsion to take a drug for its psychological effects and not simply to avoid withdrawal symptoms. These distinctions can lead to confusion, especially when *dependence* is used without a qualifier such as *substance, physiological,* or *psychological.* Throughout this article, when *dependence* is used by itself without a qualifier, it refers to substance dependence.

It is important to note that a diagnosis of substance dependence does not require fulfillment of all criteria. Rather, in either system the user must meet three or more criteria within the same twelve-month period to qualify for the diagnosis. The criteria for dependence are identical across the following substances: alcohol, amphetamines, cannabis, hallucinogens, inhalants, nicotine, and sedatives and hypnotics. In addition, DSM-IV includes a diagnosis of polysubstance dependence to describe people who use three or more substances (not including nicotine) and are not dependent on any one of those substances but do meet criteria for dependence when the group of substances is considered together.

Criteria for substance abuse and harmful use

In DSM-IV, substance abuse is diagnosed by repeated use resulting in adverse consequences (*see* Table 2). Four categories of adverse consequences are listed in Criterion A: impaired performance at work, home, or school; recurrent use when physically dangerous (for example, driving while intoxicated); recurrent legal problems; and persistent or recurrent social or interpersonal problems. If any one category is true, then Criterion A is fulfilled.

In ICD-10, the category that most closely resembles DSM-IV substance abuse is harmful use, defined as a pattern of psychoactive substance use that is causing or has caused actual physical or mental damage to health. DSM-IV abuse and ICD-10 harmful use are similar in that they are both defined by adverse consequences in the absence of other criteria for dependence. They are also similar because they cannot be diagnosed in the presence of

dependence; that is, ICD-10 harmful use and dependence and DSM-IV abuse and dependence are mutually exclusive diagnoses. One cannot, for example, be diagnosed with both ICD-10 harmful cocaine use and dependence. As with substance dependence, the criteria for abuse and harmful use are identical across the following substances: alcohol, amphetamines, cannabis, hallucinogens, inhalants, and sedative-hypnotics. By contrast, however, harmful use and abuse differ markedly because ICD-10 harmful use requires a consequence of actual physical or mental damage, whereas DSM-IV substance abuse requires only adverse social consequences or the risk of physical damage. Not surprisingly, therefore, studies reveal that the same individuals do not necessarily meet criteria for both abuse and harmful use.

Determination of abuse and dependence

Health care professionals make a diagnosis of substance abuse or dependence after interviewing and examining the patient, ordering tests such as urine drug screens, talking with people who know the patient (with the patient's consent), and reviewing past medical, legal, or educational records (also with the patient's consent). Questionnaires filled out by the patient may also be helpful. During the clinical interview, a detailed history of a patient's use of substances is obtained, including times of first and last use, patterns of use over time (amounts, frequency, duration), adverse consequences of use, tolerance, withdrawal symptoms, means employed to control use, desire to change pattern of use, and previous attempts to stop using. Because patients often tend to minimize or deny the extent of their substance use, the clinician will ask for permission to speak with family members, employers, teachers, and other significant people about a patient's patterns of use and consequences. Past medical, legal, or educational records also help gather further information to make or rule out a diagnosis of substance abuse or dependence. A physical examination may yield either evidence or health consequences of use. An examination of the skin, for example, may reveal needle marks from injecting drugs. Alcohol-dependent individuals may have enlarged livers on physical examination. A mental status examination may reveal psychological indicators of use such as depression, panic attacks, or

---

TABLE 2
DSM-IV CRITERIA OF SUBSTANCE ABUSE

A. A pattern of substance use leading to significant impairment or distress as manifested by one or more of the following in the same one-year period:
(1) Recurrent substance use that impairs performance at work, school, or home
(2) Recurrent substance use in physically dangerous situations (for example, driving a car when impaired)
(3) Recurrent legal problems resulting from substance use
(4) Continued substance use despite social problems related to substance use

B. Has never met criteria for substance dependence for this particular substance

---

ICD-10 CRITERIA FOR HARMFUL USE

A. A pattern of substance use that is causing or has caused actual physical or mental damage to health
B. No concurrent diagnosis of substance dependence for the same class of substance

---

Source: Criteria paraphrased and simplified from DSM-IV (1994, 2000) and ICD-10 (1993)

---

suicidal thoughts. People who abuse or are dependent on substances also have an increased risk for attempting suicide.

How diagnosis is used to decide on treatment

Decisions about treatment for substance use disorders are based on at least three aspects of diagnosis. First, does the patient meet criteria for dependence rather than abuse or harmful use? This diagnostic distinction influences the selection of a treatment goal. Because dependence is distinguished by impaired control and compulsive use, treatment must address those symptoms for recovery to occur. Therefore, the treatment goal for dependence is most often complete abstinence from all substances of abuse and dependence, because impaired control is usually thought of as irreversible.

For patients diagnosed with abuse or harmful use, the goal of treatment is harm reduction. Although abstinence is the surest way to reduce harm, and abstinence from illicit substances is always recommended, controlled use of substances such as alcohol without adverse consequences is theoretically possible, because impaired control is not part of the definition of abuse and harmful use.

Second, does the patient meet criteria for substance dependence with physiological depen-

dence because of the presence or history of withdrawal symptoms? If yes, then withdrawal symptoms will require assessment and medical treatment in some cases. Alcohol withdrawal, for example, may require medications in order to prevent complications such as seizures. Third, what specific substances are part of the diagnosis? Methadone, for example, is a medication used in the treatment of heroin dependence, but not in the treatment of alcohol dependence. Disulfiram is a medication used in the treatment of alcohol dependence but not heroin dependence. When heroin dependence and alcohol dependence co-occur in the same individual, then both methadone and disulfiram may be prescribed. Other factors that influence treatment selection include the severity of the consequences associated with the diagnosis, the co-occurrence of other medical and mental disorders, social support for treatment, access to treatment, and a patient's willingness to have treatment.

K. J. BROWER

SEE ALSO:
Addiction • Addictive Behavior • Dependence • Dual Diagnosis • Mental Disorders • Multiple Addiction • Tolerance • Treatment • Withdrawal

Disease Theory of Addiction

The disease theory regards addiction not as a moral problem influenced by an individual's will or control but as a disease arising from a physical or mental predisposition or acquired as a result of using an addictive substance.

Society's view of substance use has taken many forms over the centuries, from approval to condemnation. It is easy to believe that the present view is the only logical one. Attitudes change, however, with new discoveries and social conditions. A prime example of changing attitudes is the disease model of addiction, a relatively recent view of a behavior (substance use) that has been around for thousands of years.

Prior to the nineteenth century, both alcohol and drugs (in particular, opiates) were seen as good substances, praised by the clergy and laity alike. Opiates were used to treat all ailments (real or imaginary), and drinking alcohol was safer than drinking the water in most cities before proper sewerage systems were built. As a result, both alcohol and opiates tended to be consumed in prodigious amounts, certainly at levels that are far higher than today. Those who were prone to overconsumption were regarded as weak-willed or sinful but were not felt to be a threat to society. Offenders could be dealt with quite easily within the existing judicial system by whipping or the stocks, or, for the more persistent, jail. In some areas, the church, instead of the judicial system, would have been regarded as the proper authority to deal with drunkards. In other areas, both the civil and ecclesiastical authorities would deal with drunkards; thus they could be punished twice.

The above approach is referred to as the moral model of addiction. Those who subscribe to the moral model suggest that people overindulge because they are bad or sinful and need to be taught the error of their ways through punishment or, in more religious societies, by preaching and sermons designed to bring them back to the fold. Some remnants of this model can still be seen in modern society's attitudes toward drunkenness and more particularly to drug use.

The origins of the disease model

Science emerged in the eighteenth century as a method for explaining the world and, to a lesser extent, human behavior. Independently of each other, two physicians, Thomas Trotter in the United Kingdom and Benjamin Rush in Philadelphia, began to write about inebriety (drunkenness). Both began to refer to the condition as a disease. Trotter suggested that it was a disease of the mind, while Rush called it a disease of the will. Both concluded that no rational person would deliberately engage in a behavior that was both antisocial and harmful to him- or herself. Hence, individuals must be consuming substances against their will. Unlike normal people, they had no control over their consumption; logically, they must therefore have a disease.

It is hard now to comprehend just how radical this suggestion was at the time. The two physicians were suggesting that behavior was not being governed by goodness or badness (sinfulness) but was instead caused by processes over which the individual had no control. The implication was that sermons or punishments would not only have no effect in changing the person's behavior, they were also punishing sufferers for being sick. Thus, it would be like punishing a person for having tuberculosis.

Some commentators regard this period as a time of enlightenment, resulting in the sick being treated rather than punished. Others regard it as a time when any behavior that ran contrary to society's norms, including antisocial behaviors, was excused as a disease. Some go further and suggest that this was when the medical profession began to replace priests in the role of arbiters of what was good and how society should behave, what people should eat, and so on.

This radical change of thinking had little immediate effect; it was not for another 150 years that the disease model was widely accepted in the United States. Some changes did occur in the interim. The first formal efforts to create a home for alcoholics occurred in Boston in 1841, with the provision of temporary accommodation for reforming male alcoholics. The first reform center, however, was the New York State Inebriate Asylum, which was opened in 1864 but ceased to be used for treating alcoholism after only three years. Nevertheless, by the end of the century, fifty inebriate asylums had opened across the United States. It was not until the American Medical Association declared that alcoholism was a disease in 1958, however, that there was wide acceptance of this position.

The contribution of Jellinek

E. M. Jellinek is regarded by many as the father of the modern disease model. His research produced two major concepts, the stages of the disease and the species of diseases. The stages of the disease had a major impact on how alcoholism (and addictions in general) were viewed. According to Jellinek, there are four stages in alcoholism: the presymptomatic stage, in which

An engraving of scenes from the New York State Inebriate Asylum, founded by Joseph Edward Turner, which opened in 1864. It was the first example of a center built specifically to treat alcoholics.

there are no problems with alcohol; the early warning stage, which is characterized by blackouts (amnesic episodes), guilt, and increasing drunken episodes; the crucial stage, characterized by failed attempts at controlling use; and the chronic stage, in which there are mental and physical complications and increasingly lengthy binges. Many of these symptoms can be seen in heavy drinkers, but Jellinek distinguished heavy drinkers from real alcoholics by their ability to control their drinking, that is, to stop at will or to decide whether or not to drink.

Jellinek suggested that, although there were points at each of these stages at which the alcoholic could stop drinking, the majority of alcoholics would continue to the chronic stage. It was at this stage, when physical and mental damage had occurred, that change would be most likely to occur. Another physician, Max Glatt, working in the United Kingdom, drew a curve depicting Jellinek's stages as a descent into alcoholism and a rise back to sobriety. It was from this diagram, which was hung on the wall of every treatment agency, that the term "hitting bottom" originated. Hitting bottom was seen as the only means of change for the alcoholic.

The second contribution of Jellinek was the concept of the species (or types) of alcoholism. Jellinek was both aware of and fascinated by the fact that different countries had different drinking patterns and different drinking problems. He argued that there are five types of alcoholism, which he named for the first five letters of the Greek alphabet; alpha, beta, gamma, delta, and epsilon. However, of these he stated that only the gamma and delta species are true alcoholism. Gamma alcoholism is to be found predominantly in peoples of Anglo-Saxon descent, and is the most damaging in physical, financial, and social terms. This species will be described in more detail below. The delta alcoholic tends to be found mainly in the wine regions of France and some other wine-growing nations. The main characteristic of this species is that, while its members are seldom drunk, they are seldom entirely sober—they drink regularly throughout the day (wine with lunch and dinner)—but seldom enough to be intoxicated. It is only when there is an enforced period of abstinence that withdrawal symptoms will be seen and a diagnosis of alcoholism may be made.

People in France and Italy drink wine with their main meals from an early age but seldom drink to excess.

Types of disease models

Three basic types of disease models have been proposed at various times. They all tend to share the same basic characteristics, but each proposes a different etiology, or underlying mechanism that causes the condition.

The first and oldest model is that there is some, often unspecified, preexisting physical abnormality. This model suggests that alcoholics or addicts are born with an inherent flaw in the way their body reacts with substances. The manual for Alcoholics Anonymous (AA), for example, begins with a discussion by William D. Silkworth of what form the disease takes. In this section, called the Doctor's Opinion, Silkworth suggests that the alcoholic is allergic to alcohol and that this is the reason alcoholics drink and behave in an abnormal fashion. This pronouncement led to much speculation that alcoholics and addicts were genetically programmed to be addicted. For many years, research found no evidence for this proposition and the model's support waned, although AA continued to promote it. Research using more advanced technology, such as gene probes, has since found that there may indeed be a genetic component to addiction, if not strictly an "alcoholic gene." The exact mechanism for this is still unclear, and a genetic predisposition would appear to be only one prerequisite for a complex behavior.

The second model suggests that addiction, which includes alcoholism, is a psychopathology, or mental illness. To some extent, the mental illness model has echoes of the original theories of Trotter and Rush, who suggested a disease of the mind or will. Many theories have been proposed to support this model. For example, the work of the psychologist Sigmund Freud has been used to suggest that addicts become fixated at the stage of child development referred to as the oral stage, which is characterized by self-destructiveness and a lack of self-control. The influence of Freud continues today in the language of addiction. A typical view of the alcoholic, for example, is that he or she is in denial (refuses to admit the problem) and practices projection (blames others). Another theory that continues to be given credence, at least with the general public, is the addictive personality, where some people are prone to be addicted to numerous substances (such as alcohol, drugs, and tobacco) and behaviors (such as eating, exercise, gambling, and using the Internet). No convincing evidence has been produced that unequivocally supports this model, because it is difficult to separate what is cause and what is consequence. Does having a particular type of personality predispose a person to addiction, or does addiction cause a person to exhibit certain personality traits?

The third and final model suggests that addiction can be acquired through alcohol or drug use. Unlike the other two models, this theory suggests that the disease does not precede and cause the problematic use but is instead a consequence of it. This model tends to be given more credence than the others, both by professionals working in the addiction field and by the general public. One example is the current view of heroin and crack cocaine and how addictive they are. This model is the forerunner of the dependence syndrome developed by Griffith Edwards and Milton Gross in 1974.

117

Characteristics of the disease models

Although there are differences between the above models, four essential elements are common to all disease models. These elements are based on Jellinek's concept of the gamma alcoholic, which he regarded as one of the two types of true alcoholic.

The first characteristic is that addiction is a discrete entity; that is, a person either is or is not an addict. Thus, addicts are different (either physically or psychologically) from nonaddicts. In the first model above (and in some formulations of the second model), addicts can never be normal in respect to alcohol or drug use, and normal alcohol or drug users can never be addicts. Even in some formulations of the third model, addicts are viewed as qualitatively different from nonaddicts rather than quantitatively different: that is, they are considered to be different by what they are rather than by what they do.

The second characteristic is that the addict suffers from loss of control and abnormal craving. These symptoms are often regarded as the hallmark of addiction. It is suggested that addicts have great difficulty abstaining from alcohol or drugs because of an abnormal craving. Once they do begin to consume, the lack of control means that they cannot stop.

The third characteristic is that the abnormal craving and loss of control are irreversible. In this view, once a person becomes an addict, he or she is always an addict. The only recovery possible is permanent abstinence, since, even after a long period of abstinence, the mechanisms of abnormal craving and loss of control are still present, and any consumption will result in a return to the prior state of addiction.

The fourth and final characteristic is that, left untreated, the disease is progressive. Jellinek described this progression in his phases of alcoholism, and Glatt depicted it in a diagram that showed graphically that without treatment addiction would result in insanity or death.

Critique

There is little doubt that the disease model has brought benefits to alcoholics and addicts. To some extent, it has reduced the stigma experienced by sufferers and has opened the door to treatment rather than punishment. It is the mainstay of the belief system of AA and Narcotics Anonymous (NA),

which have helped many addicts to recover from a hopeless state. However, the disease model has been criticized on the grounds that there is both little evidence to support it and that it may in fact be detrimental to recovery.

Much of the evidence directly opposes rather than supports the model. For example, a famous study of alcoholics found that they could control their craving and consumption. In this experiment, they were given the opportunity to work in exchange for alcohol and to consume it when and as they wanted. Instead of being constantly drunk, it was found that the subjects worked and consumed alcohol selectively, sometimes saving some for consumption at a later time. Other studies have found that alcoholics (both treated and untreated) have returned to patterns of problem-free consumption. These people are in the minority but nevertheless represent a significant number. Finally, a new topic in addiction research is natural recovery, where addicts change their behavior without the aid of treatment. Many studies have found that this is a common route out of addiction. Indeed, one large-scale Canadian study in 1996 found that not only is natural recovery common, it is by far the most common form of recovery. All of these findings undermine the validity of the disease model.

In respect to treatment, the present view is that the disease model sees the addict as someone who has no control over his or her behavior and hence requires treatment to recover. This strategy is often criticized as engendering feelings of helplessness and encouraging a denial of responsibility. In contrast, the modern view of treatment is that in order for recovery to occur, the client needs to take responsibility for his or her behavior and to be empowered to change. Moreover, rather than enforced abstinence, the client should have a choice of possible outcomes, that is, abstinence, reduction in consumption, or controlled drinking. By doing so, the client is felt to have greater ownership of his or her recovery and is more motivated to succeed.

J. MCMAHON

SEE ALSO:
Abstinence • Biopsychosocial Theory of Addiction • Causes of Addiction, Biological • Dependence • Jellinek Classification • Recovery

Dosage

Determining the safe dosage for a particular drug requires a system of trials that monitor unexpected reactions. By comparing the effects of different doses and administration intervals, researchers can decide the best regime for use.

A narrow definition of the term *dosage* is taken to mean the amount of a medication, toxicant, drug, or other chemical administered to, or taken by, an organism, expressed as some function of the organism and of time (for example, milligrams per kilogram of body weight per day). More simply it is the amount of a substance, such as a drug, that is taken at any one time. Unless otherwise noted, liquid dosages are given in units of drops, while tablets and capsules are considered as one unit each.

Clinical trials

Drugs that are intended to treat humans must be tested in the body. These tests, called clinical trials, determine whether a drug is safe and effective, at what doses it works best, and what side effects it causes—information that guides health professionals and, for nonprescription drugs, consumers in the proper use of medicines. Clinical testing is not the only way to discover the effect a drug might have on people. Alert observation of unexpected reactions in patients and careful monitoring of results can often suggest drug effects and lead to more formal study. However, such observations are usually not reliable enough to serve as the basis for scientifically valid conclusions. Controlled clinical trials, in which results observed in patients being administered the drug are compared with the results in similar patients receiving a different treatment, are the best way to determine the actions of a new drug. Controlled clinical trials are therefore the only legal basis used by the Food and Drug Administration (FDA), the federal agency responsible for the regulation and approval of new medications, to conclude that a new drug has shown "substantial evidence of effectiveness."

It is important to test drugs on the people they are intended to help. It is also important to design clinical studies that ask, and answer, the right questions about drugs under investigation. Several types of studies are performed to achieve that aim. For example, the dosage regimen is a formalized schedule by which drugs are administered, including the amount of drug, the number of doses per time period, and the time between doses. The dose is a specified quantity of a drug, prescribed to be taken at a specified interval. Sometimes dose-escalation trials are needed to determine the amount that delivers the best balance of high efficacy and fewest side effects. Dose-escalation trials are clinical studies that monitor the effects of a gradually increasing dosage of a drug. In this kind of clinical trial, researchers look for the largest quantity of the substance that can be tolerated in volunteers without the occurrence of an adverse reaction. A dose-ranging trial is a clinical trial involving groups of volunteers given different quantities of a substance, or the same quantity but at different intervals. Results are compared to determine which quantities and intervals give the best results and produce the fewest adverse reactions. A dose-response relationship is the phenomenon by which increased doses of a drug lead to increased effects, such that the response to a drug is directly related to the dose administered.

Dosage in addiction treatments

Dosage levels are important in addiction treatment when an individual is trying to give up a particular substance and a physician needs to substitute a safer drug to wean the addict gradually without precipitating major symptoms of withdrawal or triggering dependency on the new drug. For alcohol withdrawal the most commonly used medications are the benzodiazepine class of drugs (for example, chlordiazepoxide, diazepam, lorazepam, and oxazepam), which are used because of their high efficacy and low risk potential. These drugs act in the nervous system on the GABA (gamma-aminobutyric acid) group of receptors, which are responsible for calming brain activity and are present in 60 percent of the brain's cells. People who are already dependent on benzodiazepines, obtained either by prescription or by purchasing them on the street, are prescribed phenobarbital (a barbiturate) in doses of 5 to 10

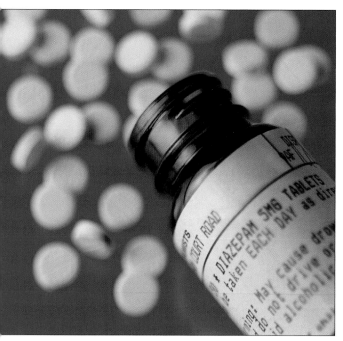

The instructions given to patients about drug dosage levels and frequency are determined during clinical trials. These instructions may also include warnings about possible side effects and interactions with other drugs.

milligrams per kilogram of body weight per day to replace the benzodiazepines in the brain. Sudden cessation of these drugs can trigger withdrawal or even a seizure if the patient is left without an alternative medication.

The dose is also important for people who need to take a medication called Antabuse (disulfiram). This medication blocks the metabolism of alcohol and results in the accumulation of a metabolic product called acetaldehyde. A buildup of acetaldehyde can provoke a toxic reaction in the individual if he or she continues to drink. The toxic reaction intensifies if the patient is taking 250 milligrams or more of Antabuse, although up to 1,000 milligrams may be needed in certain individuals to produce the reaction. This type of reaction is called an aversive reaction in that it is thought to help deter the individual from using alcohol while taking Antabuse. If the individual drinks a few sips of alcohol, he or she will feel a flushing of the face, high blood pressure, nausea, headaches, and other unpleasant

sensations. The reaction quickly reminds the individual about the Antabuse, therefore prompting him or her to stop and think about the consequences of drinking more. Some people continue to drink despite the reaction; they are referred to as compulsive drinkers, as they cannot stop their behavior despite the unpleasant experience.

A particular type of medicine used in addiction treatment is referred to as an antagonist. A specific dose needs to be administered before the antagonist is able to counter the stimulating effect of another drug (the agonist) on the receptor sites where these substances usually work. Examples of antagonist medicines are naltrexone and naloxone, both of which block the opioid receptors where morphine, heroin, and opioid painkillers act agonistically to lessen the pain that people experience after a trauma to the body. Naltrexone is used in two different doses and for two different purposes. One use (50 to 100 milligrams per day) is to aid recovery from alcoholism—drinking alcohol will not produce the same pleasurable effect. The other use of naltrexone is as an opioid receptor antagonist; it is given to people who are in treatment to prevent them from experiencing a high when using opioids (morphine, heroin, and opioid-related painkillers).

In other situations medications, can be used to maintain a person on a certain level of replacement for the addiction, as is the case in methadone clinics. Methadone clinic patients are given daily doses of methadone that range between 80 and 200 milligrams to keep them from desiring the use of street drugs like heroin or prescription medicines (morphine, oxycodone, hydrocodone, hydromorphone, and so on). In Europe and more recently in the United States, another drug substitute is now in use as a replacement therapy: buprenorphine is a unique type of drug that, at a dosage of between 8 and 16 milligrams a day, provides relief equivalent to 60 to 100 milligrams of methadone per day. This medicine has a good safety profile and does not cause the same high that people might get from heroin or even methadone when taken in high doses.

M. KARAM-HAGE

SEE ALSO:
Overdose • Toxicity

Driving While Impaired

Driving under the influence of alcohol or drugs is a reckless behavior that can cause injury or death. Vigorous law enforcement is beginning to make drunk driving socially unacceptable and personally costly to offenders.

Driving while impaired (DWI), also known as driving under the influence (DUI), refers to the act of being in control of a motor vehicle while intoxicated by drink or drugs. Drunk driving is a significant problem in the United States: it has been estimated that one in three people will be affected by an impaired driving incident at some point in their lives. The National Highway Traffic Safety Administration, which conducted a comprehensive survey in 2007, reported a dramatic decline since 1973 in the number of drivers with a blood alcohol concentration (BAC) above the legal limit. Nonetheless, 16,885 alcohol-related traffic fatalities occurred in 2005, which represented 39 percent of total traffic fatalities that year.

A link between alcohol and traffic accidents has been observed since the earliest days of the motor car. However, little was done about the problem until the early 1970s, when surveys revealed that alcohol was responsible for more than 50 percent of all fatal traffic accidents and 33 percent of serious injuries involving collisions.

Driving while impaired is an irresponsible action that can lead to financial penalties, jail, injury, and death. People who drive under the influence often have a false sense of their own abilities and feel that nothing will happen to them, particularly if they have driven without incident in the past. Because alcohol can compromise short-term thinking, a person may also regard leaving his or her car and arranging a cab as inconvenient, or may not have enough money to get home on public transportation.

Blood alcohol concentrations

The group most often involved in a fatal crash are young male drivers, who are about twice as likely as female drivers to have a BAC of 0.1 percent or greater. Blood alcohol concentrations are measured in grams of alcohol per deciliter of blood and are given as g/dl or a percentage (0.1 g/dl = 0.1 percent). Values in the range 0.01 to 0.07 percent are classed as impaired, more than 0.08 percent as intoxicated. Most states have accepted 0.08 percent as the legal threshold since 2003, although some still hold to the previous level of 0.1 percent. Canada also sets 0.08 percent as its threshold for intoxication, but levels in Europe are much lower, ranging from 0.02 to 0.05 percent. More vigorous restrictions of 0.04 percent are set under federal law for commercial vehicle drivers, and all states set a limit of 0 to 0.02 percent for drivers under 21.

Alcohol's effects as a central nervous system depressant are well known. Even the slightest amount will have some effect on the body, depending on the age, sex, build, metabolism, and rate of intake of the drinker. A BAC of 0.02 percent can be reached after drinking two standard drinks in an hour. At this level, a driver will experience difficulty maintaining lane position and attending to traffic signals and will be less aware of other vehicles and road users. As the BAC increases, controlling the vehicle becomes harder; a driver will brake more frequently, steer erratically, and change gear incorrectly. Between 0.08 and 0.1 percent BAC, drivers show visible signs of drunkenness, such as the inability to walk in a straight line, stand on one leg, or follow an object moved in front of the eyes—tests used by police officers to gauge impairment.

There is no general level at which impairment of ability to drive begins. Studies involving closed courses or driving simulators have shown that there is considerable variation in drivers' abilities to respond to situations at various blood alcohol concentrations. What is clear, however, is that the probability of being involved in an accident rises exponentially with increasing levels, such that a driver with a BAC of 0.02 percent is 100 times more likely to be involved in a collision than a driver who has not had a drink.

Behaviors of impaired drivers

The majority of crashes relating to drunk driving are caused by errors in information processing by the driver. Even at low BACs, drivers have trouble controlling the vehicle, are less aware of road conditions and other road users, and are less able to perceive risks. Attempting to perform another action while driving, such as changing a CD or lighting a cigarette, can reduce the driver's attention still further. There is also a tendency for drivers to fall asleep at the wheel at low alcohol levels.

The second biggest cause of accidents relates to judgment errors. Drivers may have a reduced perception of distances between vehicles and the speed at which they or other drivers are traveling. However, fewer accidents occur as a result of decreased motor skills than is usually imagined, despite the more obvious symptoms of drunkenness that are exhibited at this level of intoxication. However, not all drivers found to be intoxicated at the site of a crash are necessarily responsible for the accident. In some instances, the error may have been someone else's fault, but the driver's own drinking impeded his or her ability to avoid a collision.

The pattern of crashes indicates that most drunk driving accidents relate to heavy drinking during leisure time. Three times as many fatal crashes occur in the evening than during the day, and the figure is five times higher for all alcohol-related accidents. On weekends, alcohol accounts for 54 percent of

fatal crashes, compared with 31 percent during the week. In 2002, 68 percent of the people killed in crashes had a BAC exceeding 0.08 percent. Of these, 56 percent were drivers and 12 percent were intoxicated pedestrians or bicyclists. Motorcyclists make up the greater part of the fatality toll at 31 percent, followed by light truck drivers (23 percent), passenger car drivers (22 percent), and heavy truck drivers (2 percent).

Young people face a greater risk of being involved in a traffic accident than older people. Although the legal age at which alcohol can be bought in the United States is 21, nearly one-quarter of drivers aged between 15 and 20 killed in crashes had been drinking alcohol. Children under 15 also suffer the effects of alcohol; nearly two-thirds of victims were riding with a drunk driver and 20 percent of these were not properly restrained by a seat belt or child seat at the time of the accident.

Drugged driving

While alcohol is a recognized cause of traffic accidents, there is a growing awareness of the effects of other drugs. Overall, 10.5 million Americans over the age of 12 admitted driving under the influence of illegal drugs during 2009, according to the National Survey on Drug Use and Health. The rate of driving

Sobriety tests can be used by police officers to test whether drivers suspected of drunk driving are capable of handling their vehicles. Failure to meet standards of response will result in the driver's arrest.

under the influence of illicit drugs was highest among young adults aged 18 to 25. Most often the drug used is marijuana, which is prevalent among teenage drivers, who find it easier to obtain than alcohol. The role of marijuana in accidents has been difficult to determine. There is no evidence that the number of traffic incidents has increased because of the effects of marijuana. However, it is well known that marijuana affects coordination and cognitive and perceptual ability. Unlike with alcohol, drivers under the influence of marijuana retain insight over their performance and tend to compensate for the drug's effects by driving more cautiously. There remains, however, a slowness in reaction times and an inability to keep to a straight trajectory. The problem of determining whether the drug has any effect on traffic accidents is compounded by the frequent use of marijuana and alcohol together.

Stimulants, such as cocaine and amphetamines, also figure among the statistics for fatal crashes. Although this type of drug does not decrease driving performance while the user is high, drivers are more likely to speed and take unnecessary risks than marijuana users. The depressed phase that follows the high can also cause a driver to become sleepy and less alert to road conditions.

Prescription drugs, particularly tranquilizers, antidepressants, and antihistamines, are also implicated in a number of accidents. Despite warnings against driving or operating machinery, people often continue to do both while taking this type of medication. Drivers can be arrested for DWI even if they are legally taking a prescribed drug. Sedatives and antihistamines can cause drowsiness, lack of alertness, and difficulties in visual tracking, while hypnotics can linger in the system and impair skills 24 hours after use. Pressure from regulatory agencies has led to the development of drugs that cause less impairment or clear the system more quickly.

Testing for impairment

When a driver is stopped by police under suspicion of driving under the influence of drink or drugs, he or she may be asked to perform a number of sobriety tests. These vary across states but usually include walking in a straight line, standing on one leg, placing a finger on the nose, pupil reaction, and measurement of pulse rate. Officers may also check for skin marks, hyperactivity, drowsiness, and apathy. The officer may then ask the driver to blow into a breathalyzer at the scene or at the police station after arrest, where the driver may also be required to give a blood sample. Breathalyzers used in the field detect only alcohol, but many police stations now have sophisticated devices that can determine the presence of a number of other drugs. In the United States, anyone arrested for DWI immediately has his or her license revoked for a set period that varies among states. Refusing to take a breath or blood test can result in an automatic driving ban of one year, even if found not guilty of driving under the influence. Driving while a license has been revoked carries a jail sentence unless the driver has been granted a hardship license because driving is necessary for work or medical reasons. Licenses are not automatically returned at the end of the period of suspension. A driver will often have to prove that he or she has undergone an alcohol or drug abuse education program, has valid insurance, or must submit to regular urine tests. For the worst offenses, a driver may have to take lessons at an approved driving school and then retake the driving test.

Penalties and punishments

In all countries there is a sliding scale of punishments for DWI, depending on whether the incident is a first-time or repeat offense, the level of alcohol or drugs in the body, and the degree to which any damage or injury has occurred. A first offense in which the BAC is above 0.08 percent will generally incur a minimum fine and a driving ban of at least a year. Second offenses may carry a short jail sentence, followed by probation and a ban of two or more years. Subsequent offenses will prompt longer sentences and the possibility of a lifetime ban. If injury or death occurs, the penalties become more severe; drivers can face mandatory sentences up to life imprisonment if someone is killed. Offenders are also hit financially, having to pay for counseling courses, higher insurance costs, and, increasingly, the costs of damages to accident victims, which can run to millions of dollars.

W. A. HORAN

SEE ALSO:
Binge Drinking • Drug Testing

Drop-in Centers

Informal meeting places are ideal for people to discuss issues about drugs and addiction. These drop-in centers can also provide practical advice about obtaining services and recreational activities.

Drop-in centers are gathering places designed for patients of mental health or addiction services to meet for socialization, relaxation, self-help, and mutual support. It is not certain when the term *drop-in center* began to be used to refer to places that provide services for addiction and substance abuse recovery. Drop-in center services are offered to any patient of mental health or addiction problems, past or present, mostly for 18 years of age or older, but some are designed specifically for younger people, whose parents have to consent for their child to attend. Centers are usually established in a central but discrete location to encourage people to walk in and yet keep a low profile, thus reducing any stigma that might be associated with addiction or treatment. A drop-in center provides an opportunity for patients to make friends and socialize with people who accept them as peers without prejudice or prejudgment based on their appearance or history of problems or social skills.

Many activities are offered at a drop-in center, including meals, games, arts and crafts, sports, field trips, shopping trips, television, parties, music, dancing, life-skills classes, and support groups. The services provided differ widely among localities, states, and even countries. Some centers are meant only for socialization and support and have minimal staffing, if any is available at all. Others are fully staffed to provide treatment for some of the most serious addictions to alcohol, Ecstasy, crack cocaine, heroin, and other drugs of abuse.

Provision of services
Some centers in downtown areas of big cities operate around the clock, offering shelter for homeless people and providing respite beds for around eight hours at a time per participant. Such hostels have showers and public restrooms, information and referral services for other housing programs, and laundry facilities. Other centers promote prevention, education, and harm reduction strategies, such as teaching about safe sexual practices and other risk avoidance tactics. Some also provide relapse prevention strategies or needle exchange programs to reduce the risk of contracting blood-transmitted diseases, such as HIV or hepatitis B and C, through sharing needles. As a result of the destructive process that follows the continued use of drugs and alcohol, many of these patients have no home to go to, so it would be of limited help to provide them only with a place to socialize. Therefore, short-term respite shelters have been established in several of these centers to provide temporary shelter for individuals until they are able

Drop-in centers can often provide help for people who might be unwilling to contact welfare services in the usual way. At this center in Sweden, social workers are available to help addicts gain access to housing and medical care.

to regain employment, a place to live, and stability in other aspects of their lives.

A drop-in center's goal is usually to empower patients with mental health and addiction problems and to educate, inform, and help them enrich their lives by providing them with a safe and supportive network. Staff and members usually strive to make each drop-in center a safe and comfortable place. This is a crucial element of how drop-in centers work; although individuals may have different needs, centers provide a powerful and positive peer influence that the substance user's previous lifestyle does not usually provide. It is important to remember that diseases like substance addiction can restrict a person's social abilities and skills. Consequently, it becomes essential that he or she has an opportunity to reconnect with others in a positive and safe environment that encourages healthy interaction and provides alternatives to using substances. Some of the people who become victims of addiction have already suffered from devastating losses, which may have occurred previous to substance use or while under the influence of substance use. The support of peers is considered a crucial part of a person's ability to process loss and to rebuild trust.

Joining

Membership at a drop-in center is as simple as writing a name in a book or being introduced to the staff, most of whom are usually volunteers. Memberships tend to be free or have a minimal charge. Members should be self-maintained and able to function without direct supervision or professional care, unless the center is providing treatment or is staffed adequately to provide other services that members need. Some centers ask their members to sign a membership agreement and abide by center rules at all times. Others are much more flexible. Regularly attending members of the drop-in center may also have the opportunity themselves to be involved in operation of the center. They help coordinate activities, self-help groups, meals, and meetings, and provide upkeep of the center. Transportation is not usually provided, but most of these centers are within a maximum 15- to 20-mile radius of any particular community. Some centers have funding from government grants or charitable

foundations that allows them to provide a certain level of transportation, with priority going to the handicapped and elderly, who can call a number prior to the opening time of the center to arrange a ride.

All patients of mental health and addiction services are encouraged to come by and visit the drop-in center in their area. Volunteers take part in and help spread the word about drop-in centers and their role in recovery from mental health and substance use diseases. Research has shown that centers such as these that offer peer support, advocacy, education, and so on, are a great help to patients in the empowerment and recovery process. Drop-in centers are not the same as psychiatric rehabilitation programs, and serve a different and vital support and advocacy function; they therefore should not be seen as treatment but as a recreational and sometimes vocational service. Also, consumer-run drop-in centers are staffed and directed by primary consumers, not by professional staff. While professionals can offer support and technical assistance in the development and on-going operation of drop-in centers, they do not usually staff or manage these centers.

Other types of centers

Drop-in centers are not unique to recovery from substance or mental health disorders; the concept is used in many other areas of life. For example, the Department of Transportation in the United States uses them to interact with local communities about road projects, and the Boy and Girl Scout movements use them as gathering centers for activities and information. Since 1985 drop-in centers have provided young people with an alternative support system emphasizing contemporary issues such as drug and alcohol prevention, teen suicide, teen pregnancy, gang awareness, and self-esteem building. Interactive games and arts and crafts can be offered. More important, drop-in centers are places where young people can develop friendships with peers and where healthy social alternatives are taught and encouraged.

M. KARAM-HAGE

SEE ALSO:
Continuum of Care • Halfway Houses • Hotlines • Support Groups

Drug Abuse Resistance Education

The aim of the Drug Abuse Resistance Education program (DARE) is to steer children and young adults away from drug abuse by providing information and contact with positive role models.

In 1983 Los Angeles Police Department chief Daryl Gates founded Drug Abuse Resistance Education, or DARE, to address increasing incidences of drug-related criminality. Its long-term goal was to reduce crime by encouraging young people to lead drug-free lives, and so to reduce the drug-taking population and its associated criminal activity. The original organization has since evolved into DARE America as other countries have also adopted the program.

DARE America is a not-for-profit organization that is independent of the government and receives only a small part of its funding from federal sources. Most of its funding is from private donations.

Each year around 26 million school students and 50,000 law-enforcement officers participate in DARE America in 300,000 classrooms in all 50 states. Internationally, DARE programs benefit a further 10 million young people in 44 countries.

Immediate goals

The DARE curriculum now covers tobacco, alcohol, drugs, violence, and personal safety. Information and encouragement are provided on how to avoid the negative influences of substances while focusing on personal strengths and abilities. Exposure to positive role models is a key aspect of DARE, and these role models include teachers, parents, and police officers from the local community. The intention is to encourage students to follow their example and keep away from drugs and involvement in gangs.

DARE in practice

DARE programs bring together local schools and local law-enforcement teams to educate students about the dangers of drugs and violence and the effects these can have on a young person's life. This cooperation has a positive impact on community relations and helps develop familiarity between the officers and young citizens of a city or town. At the beginning of each program, students are required to sign a pledge to keep their bodies drug free. Students

then undertake weekly hour-long lessons, using workbooks to record the outcomes of each lesson. At the end of the 10-lesson program a culmination ceremony is held. Students receive T-shirts, pins, and certificates identifying them as DARE graduates.

DARE is organized around curricula that list topics to be covered for each year from kindergarten to 12th grade. The DARE scientific advisory board reviews these curricula on an annual basis, and contributions from the DARE law enforcement advisory board, schools, and local government officials help ensure that any new information on personal security and drug abuse becomes incorporated into the program. There have been occasional curriculum revisions to reflect improved knowledge and understanding of substance abuse by young people. The 2003 revision condensed the courses from 17 to 10 weeks. In 2007 curriculums were added on prescription drug and over-the-counter drug abuse.

The central message of DARE is "no use," which has meaning in both English and Spanish (in Spanish, *no use* means "do not use"). This message is reinforced by discussions of the immediate harm that can arise from lack of judgment under the influence of drugs and by advice on strategies for anger management and avoiding violent confrontations and situations that could lead to abduction. DARE instructors also emphasize the importance of finding safe pastimes as alternatives to drug abuse.

Staff and training

More than 50,000 police officers are trained to lead DARE classroom sessions. Selected officers receive 80 hours of training in educational techniques to help them work effectively in schools. The employment of local police officers as instructors lifts the burden of drug education from teachers.

A parent-training program is also being introduced throughout the United States to help parents talk with their children about things they have learned in the school-based DARE lessons. Outside school hours, programs such as DARE + PLUS and DARE

Dance allow educational establishments to offer middle-school students the chance to participate in safe and enjoyable after-school activities. These programs require that a number of local community volunteers, school staff, and law-enforcement officers work together after hours on school campuses.

In addition to instructor training for law enforcers, DARE provides student kits that include workbooks, brochures, bumper stickers, song cassettes, books, and parents' guides. Multimedia tools include *DARE Safety Tips Starring Retro Bill,* in which Bill Russ plays a caricatured 1950s teenager introducing tips on street safety and drug avoidance.

How successful has DARE been?
For more than 20 years, DARE has received praise from all levels of government up to the president. In cooperation with its sponsors, DARE has given more than one million U.S. dollars in funding to support participating law enforcement agencies.

Presidential praise and high-profile funding initiatives have been instrumental in nurturing public awareness of DARE. Consequently, many people perceive the DARE program to be a worthwhile assault on problems that detract from the quality of life in the United States.

The program is not without critics, however. Despite the widespread popularity of DARE among parents and educators, some critics point to the lack of hard scientific evidence that DARE works. If the aim of DARE is to reduce drug abuse, they say, statistics often show that it is not working. The collection of accurate statistics for drug consumption is notoriously difficult, therefore, concrete evidence against or in favor of DARE is hard to find. Moreover, the benefits brought by teaching awareness of road safety and street hazards are equally difficult to quantify, as are the benefits of promoting self-esteem among school students and improving relations with law enforcement agencies.

There have also been complaints that DARE programs exclude parents from DARE classes. Some parents worry that their authority is being undermined by DARE workers teaching resistance strategies in sessions that are closed to parental inspection. Another concern is that adults are sometimes portrayed as drunks and drug takers. Other parents are surprised by the fact that the

A 13-year-old student from Arlington, Virginia, makes a speech at a 1989 DARE Day reception in the Rose Garden of the White House in the presence of U.S. president George H. W. Bush, Washington, D.C.

program originally dealt only with illicit drugs and not with the two most heavily abused drugs, alcohol and tobacco, although this has now been remedied. Many parents take issue with the notion that self-esteem can be taught rather than learned through experience or overcoming challenges.

DARE remains popular despite its critics, and it is especially popular with students who participate in sessions. The DARE initiative is likely to continue, provided criticism does not discourage its sponsors from supplying funds. In the future, however, DARE may evolve or be replaced by another program that can demonstrate clearer benefits to society.

W. INGLISS

SEE ALSO:
Children • Hotlines • Peer Influence • Prevention

Drug Testing

Drug testing is used by employers, schools, and the justice system to determine whether people have been using drugs. Testing methods can range from simple home-testing kits to sophisticated laboratory assessment techniques.

Urinalysis, the oldest approach for the detection of illicit substances, first began in the late 1960s. It was initiated by the U.S. Department of Defense to address the growing problem of marijuana and heroin use by military personnel in Vietnam. During the early 1980s, the criminal justice system began using drug testing with the intention of identifying drug addicts and abusers before they could do further harm. Other federal, state, and local agencies followed suit, including the Federal Bureau of Investigations. With statistics showing that 15 to 25 percent of employees either use drugs at work, or come to work under the influence of drugs or alcohol, workplace testing followed several years later. In 1986 President Reagan signed into law regulations governing drug testing and abuse in the workplace with the hopes of eliminating drug abuse within the labor force. This act set out the basic structure for preemployment, random, and probable-cause drug testing. Over these years, the collection and testing procedures and cutoff levels (minimum concentrations of a drug required to report a sample as a positive result) were established, and the technology evolved.

Opposition to drug testing has been intense and challenged legally all the way to the U.S. Supreme Court. The Supreme Court has upheld government drug testing for U.S. Customs agents and railroad employees involved in accidents or safety violations, the basis being that the safety of the nation's transportation outweighs employees' right to privacy.

Urine testing

While urinalysis may be the most common, reliable, and cost-effective method for testing for the presence of drugs in the human system, there are a variety of test options available. Each method has unique strengths and weaknesses regarding the procedures for collection and the information obtained from the test.

Urinalysis detects the presence of substances from hours to days following ingestion but cannot determine the amount originally taken. For heavy regular use of marijuana, urine testing may detect the presence of the substance for as long as six weeks. Urine testing allows the detection of infrequent or recent single use of substances. It also offers the ability to perform dozens of tests on a single specimen. The collection procedure is invasive of a person's privacy, as it must be completely observed. If not properly monitored, drug users can substitute another individual's clean urine or otherwise tamper with the urine specimen. Of all types of samples, urine is the most easily adulterated. Methods for detecting adulteration will be covered in detail later.

Urine-testing methods fall into two types: instrumental and noninstrumental. Both use an initial screening technique with a confirmatory follow-up test. Instrumental testing involves the use of instruments and machines to sample, measure, and provide a numeric test result. The samples can be conveniently stored for additional testing at a later time, which is especially helpful in legal situations in which verification of initial results is needed.

Noninstrumental testing requires manual sampling and observation, and produces a positive or negative result at the point of collection. Noninstrumental tests are used in the field by police officers, as well as for home drug testing by parents. There have been improvements in noninstrumental test devices in recent years. While this type of test does not provide the detailed information of the instrumental tests, it does provide quick and relatively accurate results. Supplies for noninstrumental tests are easily stored and used; however, specific provisions need to be established to avoid problems with the storage of specimens and retrieval of test results for court situations.

Blood testing

Blood testing is the most accurate form of testing. It provides relatively specific information regarding the degree of an individual's impairment. It allows measurement of the actual amount of substance in the blood. This type of test can only detect use

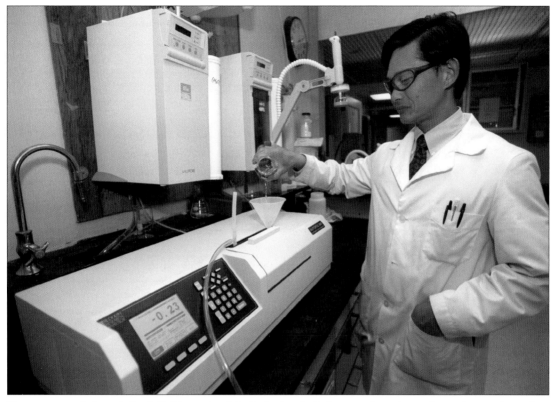

The presence of drugs in body fluids can be detected using techniques such as chromatography, spectrometry, and immunoassay. This type of equipment can determine the exact nature of substances in the sample and the concentrations present, from which it sometimes can be calculated how long ago the substance was taken.

within the previous two to three days for most drugs. After that period, substances have been flushed out. While there are some advantages to blood testing, such as the near impossibility of adulteration, it is generally the least used and recommended form of drug testing. The materials and specific skill required for this type of testing make it costly, which can be prohibitive for many settings. In addition, it is a highly invasive procedure, and there is often pain associated with the needle. There is also the risk of the tester contracting a blood-borne infectious disease, such as hepatitis or AIDS, during collection and handling of the specimen.

Hair analysis

As technology has led to the creation of more powerful testing instruments, the sample types have also changed. Hair is one of the most contemporary sample types. This is a noninvasive procedure that

detects the presence of substances from weeks to months, sometimes even years, following use. Going beyond a simple positive or negative result, hair testing is also able to reveal historical patterns of use or nonuse over a given time period in relation to hair growth.

Body hair is a repository for the toxins that are carried through the body by the blood. As a substance is introduced into the body, toxins are deposited throughout the body until they are flushed out. When toxins are sent to the hair, however, they are deposited into the hair follicle, which supplies the root of the hair shaft with nourishment; thus the toxins become trapped within the hair shaft until it is cut off. Hair grows out of the body at an average rate of one-half inch per month. Because it takes approximately five days for drugs to show up in a person's hair, and because hair sampling detects drug use occurring over such an extended period of time, it is unsuitable for use in proving drugs as a definite cause of an incident or accident.

Hair testing has the advantage of being difficult to adulterate and is the cleanest for collection. It requires cutting about 120 strands of hair from an inconspicuous place at the back of the head and sending the sample to a laboratory for analysis. If there is no hair available from the head, or if it is damaged, hair from any other location on the body may be used. Results are usually returned within a few days.

Hair testing is the most sensitive test, revealing use that has occurred within the past three months, including regular marijuana use. One-time or sporadic marijuana use may go undetected, but hair analysis is still more effective than urinalysis in identifying low-level drug use. Hair testing is virtually impossible to defeat, although results can be affected through contamination of samples and may be biased by the hair type or ethnicity of the individual being tested. For example, hair with darker pigments seems to absorb drugs more readily than blond or bleached hair. There is nothing a subject can do to dilute the sample, and washing, bleaching, or coloring will not affect the hair shaft contents. Temporary short-term abstention cannot empty the system of the substance. Since the donor need not handle the sample, it is virtually impossible to substitute someone else's hair for the sample. It is the most effective and accurate of the drug testing options. The most significant disadvantage of the hair-testing methodology is the high cost of the technology required for analyzing the samples.

Other tests

Human sweat is another source of substance-use information. Sweat samples are collected by placing a collection patch on a subject for a specified period of time, generally between 10 and 14 days. Many consider the length of the collection period to be overly invasive. Since the patch is worn for multiple days, it provides a longer period for detection. Unfortunately, as with other forms of testing, sweat samples are unable to provide information about the degree of impairment. Many believe that this type of test can be easily adulterated. Since the subject cannot be fully observed by the collector for the entire collection period, the patch could be removed

and transferred to a substance-free person to wear until just prior to the time the subject is to return for removal. This would, ultimately, deliver an adulterated or fictitious sample. Because sweat sampling is also subject to individual variations in sweat productivity, the subject may also remove the patch during the testing period without detection by the collection professional.

Saliva and oral drug tests are becoming more common. The opportunity for detection begins immediately. Sample collection is easy, less invasive, and more dignified than urine and blood testing. Saliva collection simply involves swabbing the inside of the subject's mouth; it does not require special instrumentation or training, and collection locations are flexible. If properly obtained, saliva tests are virtually cheat proof. Saliva testing can detect the presence of cocaine, opiates, methamphetamines, and Ecstasy for up to two to three days, but generally only detects what the subject has taken or ingested within approximately the last 24 hours. Unlike sweat, saliva can provide information on the degree of impairment. The costs for saliva testing are similar to urine testing. There are significant limitations with saliva testing; it may be subject to contamination from smoking or ingestion of other substances. In addition, saliva tests reveal only very recent or current marijuana use.

A form of testing rarely heard of in the public sector is fingernail sampling. As with hair, fingernail samples can accurately detect drugs of abuse. A significant disadvantage of fingernail sampling, however, is that fingernail clippings are generally between five and six months old by the time they have grown out enough to be collected. The delay between substance use and sample availability means that fingernail samples would provide little insight as to recent use of drugs, making it unsuitable as a test for proving a causal relationship between drug use and a specific incident. Despite its limitations, fingernail sampling has shown some value and is gaining acceptance in postmortem settings.

Testing methods

Drug tests can be valid tools for confirming abuse and in helping people maintain treatment compliance. In the 1980s, it was misunderstood, misused, and abused. Legally prescribed drugs,

DRUG HALF-LIVES AND DETECTION PERIODS

Drug	Half-life*	Detection period
Heroin	60–90 minutes	Less than an hour
Morphine (heroin metabolite)	1.3–6.7 hours	Opiates generally detectable for 2–4 days
Cocaine	0.5–1.5 hours	Few hours
Benzoylecgonine (cocaine metabolite)	5–7 hours	3–5 days
Methamphetamine	12–34 hours	2–3 days
Amphetamine (methamphetamine metabolite)	7–34 hours	2–3 days
Delta-9-tetrahydrocannabinol	14–38 hours	Blood levels fall 90% within 1 hour
Delta-9-tetrahydrocannabinoic acid (marijuana metabolite)	6 days	Few days up to 6 weeks depending on frequency of use
Phencyclidine (PCP)	7–16 hours	2–3 days
Barbiturates	8–48 hours	1–4 days (short acting)
	24–96 hours	2–3 weeks (long acting)
LSD	3–5 hours	1–3 days
Benzodiazepines	Few hours to several days	Up to 6 weeks
Alcohol (ethanol)	Levels fall by 15–18 mg/100 ml/hour	1.5–12 hours depending on peak blood concentration
Anabolic steroids		
Dianabol (oral)	4.5–6 hours	Up to 3 weeks
Winstrol (oral)	9 hours	Up to 3 weeks
Equipoise (injected)	14 days	Up to 3 months
Deca-durabolin (injected)	15 days	Up to 9 months

* Half-life is the length of time it takes for the concentration of the substance to fall by half. For example, if someone takes 0.1 grams of cocaine, after an hour there will be 0.05 grams of unmetabolized cocaine in the body. After a further hour the concentration will drop to 0.025 grams, and so on, until the cocaine is either converted to metabolites or excreted.

Table compiled using figures from the United Nations Office on Drugs and Crime and the National Institute on Drug Abuse. Figures are for detection in urine unless otherwise specified.

foodstuffs (for example, poppy seeds), and environmental factors resulted in false positives but were not considered. In the present day, all positives must be confirmed by a second procedure.

There are two widely used technologies for drug testing; immunoassay and gas chromatography–mass spectrometry. Immunoassay uses antibodies that specifically bind to drugs and their metabolites in the urine and other body fluids. Immunoassay technologies offer quick, accurate, and relatively inexpensive results. Immunoassay test kits are readily available through multiple vendors. This technology is generally used for initial screening.

Gas chromatography–mass spectrometry, or GC-MS is a technique generally used to confirm positive immunoassay results. This highly sensitive technology is able to distinguish between two substances with similar properties. The GC-MS technology can be used with any of the sample types. It is currently the most confirmatory procedure for most substances.

Every drug has two cutoff levels that must be reached for positive detection. The first cutoff, generally performed with immunoassay technology, is the higher of the two, which means a higher level of a substance may be present before the test is considered positive. The confirmatory test, or GC-MS, is more sensitive and is considered positive with lower levels of the substance present. If a substance is present but falls below the cutoff level, it is considered negative.

In addition, forensic standards for sample collection and handling have been improved and standardized. The collection and transfer of urine, blood, or saliva from the subject to the container must be witnessed. There are chain-of-custody procedures and documentation that verify the handling of the specimen through every step until it reaches the laboratory.

While drug testing generally covers the most commonly used drugs, including marijuana, cocaine, opioids, methamphetamine, and phencyclidine, it is also possible to test for particular substances such as inhalants and tobacco. Testing for inhalants is a more complicated process and must be completed by a forensic expert. The testing uses a urine or blood sample, though blood is preferred. The sample is used to analyze the gases emitted as the result of inhalant use. The vapors can be volatile, which often makes results inconsistent. To date, no quick point-of-contact test has been developed to detect the use of inhalants.

The presence of nicotine can be detected through a variety of means. In many states, drug courts are considering the restriction of tobacco use by underage youths. Nicotine can remain in the system for a lengthy period, depending on the frequency of use.

Urine and blood testing can be used to test for alcohol, urine being the better of the two. However, because it has a relatively short life span in the body, alcohol is generally not tested for in the above methodologies. Instead, breathalyzers are used for alcohol testing. Breathalyzers are reusable and are relatively inexpensive. The U.S. Department of Health and Human Services, the Department of Transportation, or the state toxicologist establish calibration standards for breathalyzers. Technicians who are trained in the use and interpretation of breath alcohol results must administer the test, which involves the individual blowing a strong, steady breath into a plastic tube attached to the breathalyzer machine. As the individual exhales, alcohol molecules are released with carbon dioxide molecules. The number displayed on the breathalyzer screen is the ratio of blood alcohol concentration to breath alcohol concentration. The ratio of breath alcohol to blood alcohol is 2,100:1; that is, 2,100 milliliters of breath will contain the same amount of alcohol as 1 milliliter of blood. If a person's blood alcohol concentration (BAC) measures 0.08, then there are 0.08 grams of alcohol per 100 milliliters of blood.

Breathalyzers are subject to contamination from residual smoke remaining in an individual's lungs. Therefore, a smoker must wait a minimum of 8 to 10 minutes after smoking to be tested on a breathalyzer. Additionally, a breathalyzer should not be used in any environment where there is ambient smoke present. Exposing the testing machine sensors to any type of ion generator, such as those found in contemporary air cleaners and filters, may also produce inaccurate results and provide a false positive reading.

Tampering with tests

There is much speculation about the efficacy of drinking large quantities of water to dilute drugs and metabolites enough so that they fall below the positive threshold, as well as other ideas on how to trick the tests. Water loading is one of the most common adulteration techniques and one of the most difficult to detect. Technicians are aware of attempts to beat the test and are experienced in detecting whether this technique has been used. The best way to find it is to run parallel tests for levels of

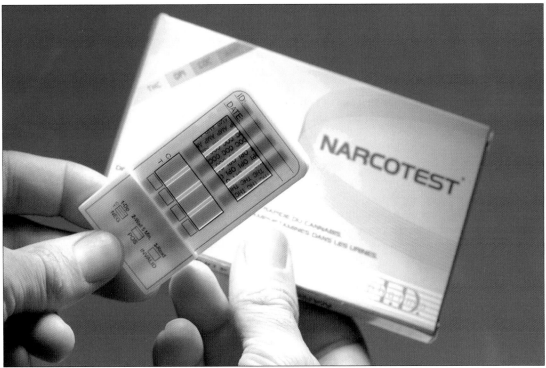

There are many drug-testing kits available that test for commonly abused drugs, such as marijuana, cocaine, opiates, and amphetamines. These tests are usually in the form of chemically impregnated strips that are dipped into urine and show a color or a line that indicates the presence of the drug being tested.

a natural metabolite, creatinine, which will be low if urine has been diluted.

Some individuals will attempt to beat the test by adding common household products to the specimen. These include such things as bleach, drain cleaner, or peroxide to change the chemical composition of the urine. There are products marketed as being able to provide a negative result despite the presence of substances. While some of these methods may work with an unskilled tester, there are ways to detect them all, including the use of the confirmatory GC-MS test.

Some individuals will attempt to beat the test by substituting someone else's urine, which they know to be substance free. This is made nearly impossible if established protocols for specimen provision observation and chain-of-custody procedures are followed thoroughly. In addition, collectors should observe the color, appearance, and temperature of each specimen, as well as attend to any unusual odor, that may warn of tampering.

While these are the most common methods used for adulterating urine, there are a variety of others. Every day there are new ideas for ways to beat tests administered in the workplace, sports, and the crim-inal justice system. There are Web pages and pub-lications devoted to the topic. Such efforts to deceive are risky, however. Laboratories have the option to conduct specimen-validity tests at their discretion. Specimen-validity tests are used to test for dilution and adulteration. Incorrect results can occur, but most laboratories have procedures in place to ensure that they meet legal and forensic requirements. The only sure way to beat a drug test is to not use drugs.

P. L. TORCHIA

SEE ALSO:
Arrestee Drug Abuse Monitoring Program (ADAM) • Driving While Impaired • Employee Assistance Programs • Intervention • Sports • Workplace

Drug Use, Life Patterns

Drug use is not constant through life. The majority of people who try drugs and alcohol will eventually limit or end their use. For others, drugs can become a cycle of abstinence and relapse.

Most people have some kind of drug-using pattern in their lives. There are people who do refrain from using any psychoactive (mood-altering) drugs, including caffeine, alcohol, tobacco, and over-the-counter painkillers, but they are almost certainly in the minority. In some Western cultures, drug use (in the widest sense of the term) can start quite young. Children in wine-drinking cultures, such as those of France and Italy, are often introduced to diluted wine at a very early age as part of family socializing. Use is controlled, and there are social norms to which people adhere in an attempt to limit any damage. For the most part, however, young people encounter drugs such as alcohol and tobacco at around the age of 11 or 12 as part of a set of unapproved activities away from the sight of adults. This clandestine drug use can have serious consequences when substances such as volatile inhalants are involved. Young children are attracted to inhalants because they are cheap and easy to obtain. To avoid detection, children tend to use drugs in out-of-the-way places, which increases risk, as they may not be found in time in case of overdose or emergency. Some studies conclude that those young people who start early with alcohol and tobacco are more likely to try illicit drugs.

With illicit drugs, there is a sharp peak in the statistics around the age of 14, when teenagers are most likely to experiment with marijuana. For the most part, this use will be the only illicit drug that the majority of young people will try. Marijuana has been the most popular illicit drug for many years. If young people do go on to try other drugs, these are most likely to be Ecstasy, amphetamines, or poppers (amyl nitrite). Relatively few younger teenagers are involved in cocaine, crack, or heroin.

Why do young people try drugs?

Drug use by young people has been variously described as a part of growing up, as a testing of boundaries, or as a form of rebellion. Actually, there are many factors influencing drug use by the young. Some young people who use drugs may be self-medicating to escape problems at home or school; others may be motivated by the desire to be part of a group. Drug use is not confined to those with problems or low self-esteem. Nor should it be assumed that all children start using drugs because of peer pressure. Although the need to fit in with others in a group is strong during adolescence, there may be other influences at work, such as social and environmental conditions, psychological problems, or drug use by other members of the family. However, research suggests that if onset of use can be delayed, the individual is less likely to face serious drug problems later.

Escalation theory

The escalation theory of drug use claims that once an individual starts using marijuana, he or she will search for an ever more potent high until the individual ends up injecting heroin or smoking crack. Undoubtedly, most heroin users have smoked marijuana at some point in their lives. This, however, does not necessarily indicate that smoking marijuana leads to heroin use. In fact, many marijuana smokers never go on to take other drugs.

There is, however, evidence that the age at which use of marijuana begins is related to later use of potentially more dangerous drugs. Figures reported by the National Survey on Drug Use and Health (formerly the National Household Survey on Drug Abuse) show that the highest prevalence of heroin, cocaine, and nonmedical prescription-drug abuse over a lifetime occurs among the group that began using marijuana when they were aged 14 or younger (*see* graph, p. 136). Of those who smoked marijuana when they were under 14, 62 percent went on to use cocaine. This tendency decreases as the age of initiation increases. Of those who began smoking marijuana after the age of 20, 16.4 percent went on to try cocaine. For people who have never smoked marijuana the figure drops to less than 1 percent.

Recreational use

Some people will move from experimental or occasional use to something more regular, which some experts call recreational use. This change in use is often tied into older adolescence in which the teenager is now frequenting clubs and music venues, usually on the weekend, perhaps taking drugs such as amphetamine and Ecstasy (together with alcohol) as part of that experience. Drug use here can ebb and flow. Many people feel that, after the initial novelty, they need to take a break to recuperate. This is especially true of the stimulant drugs, where even weekend-only use can take its toll, leaving people tired and depressed as a result of neurotransmitter (chemical messenger) depletions in the brain, which may take several days to return to normal.

From problem to addiction

At what point does recreational drug use become a more serious problem? Some drug experts would say that use of any drug, however small the quantity or however infrequently used, constitutes a problem. Many people seem to be able to control their use (for example, the person who has a few beers at the end

The use of alcohol, cigarettes, and marijuana are all seen by teenagers as markers that they are growing up. While these substances might be viewed as harmless or fun, the earlier that use begins, the more likely a teenager is to go on to other drugs.

of the working week) and come to no obvious short- or long-term harm. Setting such limits is not true for everybody. There are thousands of people for whom recreational drug use becomes a major problem in their lives, escalating in quantity and frequency of use. Once drug use becomes the most important thing in a person's life—to the detriment of job, family, and friends—then he or she may have a dependency problem.

Whatever the drug, the person in this situation could be trying to escape from some ongoing problem in his or her life. Chronic drug problems are more likely to occur in areas of social and economic deprivation but are not exclusively the domain of urban poverty. The middle-class child of emotionally or physically absent parents can just as easily end up in drug treatment as the homeless teenager.

The prognosis for people with chronic drug problems is not easy to determine. Under medical supervision, detoxifying from heroin, for example, is not that difficult or life threatening, although the experience is not pleasant. As the jazz musician Charlie Parker remarked, "They can get it out of your body, but not out of your mind." In other words, the real challenge is not coming off drugs, but staying off. Addiction is a chronic relapsing condition, and people will often try many times before finally becoming drug free, in much the same way that it frequently takes people several attempts to give up smoking.

Why is giving up drugs so hard? There are many reasons. Often addicts cannot imagine a life without drugs, or, after recovery, they return to their old drug-using friends because they have nowhere else to go. Another reason is that the individual has yet to find a way of dealing with the problems that underpinned the addiction. One survey conducted in the United Kingdom looked at what happened to a group of users attending a clinic over a period of 15 years. Very roughly, a third were still using, a third had given up drugs, and a third had died.

Stopping use

The age range of most chronic users is approximately 25 to 35. If they have survived that long, a number of users will "mature out" of even the most serious drug use in their thirties—sometimes without ever having attended a drug-treatment program. It could be that the user has found a new relationship, moved to another part of the country, changed his or her lifestyle, or just decided that enough is enough.

The same applies to more general, less chaotic drug use. In the main, the peak years for drug use are between the ages of 16 and 25. After that, interest tails off as careers and family responsibilities take on more importance. In other words, drug use for most people is associated with a certain lifestyle or time in their lives, and when that period has passed, so has the interest in drugs. At the same time, researchers note the lowering age of first use of drugs at one end of the spectrum and the fact that some people are carrying on their recreational drug use well into their thirties and beyond.

There have been very few long-term studies of drug use among the aging population. While current drug use data generally show a declining trend from a peak use at the age of 20, there is a small secondary peak among the age group that started their drug use in the 1960s. There is also evidence that the current midlife groups (the baby boomers born between 1946 and 1964) are maintaining a higher level of alcohol consumption than previous groups of the same age. These findings are reflected in the increasing numbers of people aged 55 and over who are entering treatment for alcohol abuse for the first time. Other data compiled by the Substance Abuse and Mental Health Services Administration show that abuse of prescription tranquilizers and sedatives, although low, increases with age. Indeed, estimates of the numbers of people aged 50-plus who will require treatment for addiction problems have doubled from 2.5 million in 1999 to 5 million in 2020.

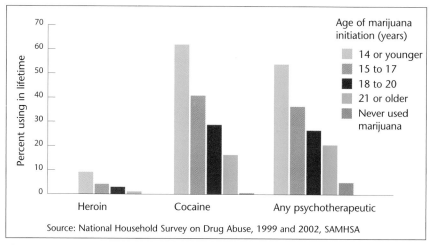

Source: National Household Survey on Drug Abuse, 1999 and 2002, SAMHSA

This graph of the prevalence of lifetime and past-year use of heroin, cocaine, and prescription drugs used for nonmedical purposes among adults aged 26 or older shows that the younger a person is when he or she first tries marijuana, the more likely that person is to go on to abuse other drugs later in life.

Gender

In general, men use more drugs than women and outnumber women in drug treatment services by around 2:1 for hard drugs and 3:1 for alcohol and marijuana. Generally, teenage girls are slightly older than boys when they initiate use of any drug, although the numbers of both sexes starting drug use are roughly equal for marijuana and alcohol. Girls are slightly more likely to use prescription drugs than boys, who are more likely to abuse inhalants. However, there have been concerns expressed in both the United States and the United Kingdom about the increasing levels of smoking and binge drinking among young women. Concerns have also been expressed about elderly women (60-plus), one in ten of whom drink more than the recommended limit of one drink a day. Women of this age are more vulnerable to the effects of alcohol and are also more likely to be prescribed sedative drugs for depression. This combination can lead to an unexpected addiction without any actual abuse of either substance that frequently goes unrecognized by health professionals.

H. SHAPIRO

SEE ALSO:

Adolescents and Substance Use • Drug Use Subcultures • Elderly • Gateway Drugs

Drug Use Subcultures

Drugs have been used by different subcultures throughout history. Such subcultures generate their own patterns and rituals of use, including peer group determinations of appropriate and excessive use of drugs.

Historical references to beer and wine date back thousands of years. Ancient records of early civilizations such as those of the Egyptians and Mesopotamians contain references to alcohol and drug use. Historical records of ancient Rome document times of moderation with regard to alcohol use, as well as times of excess. Beer and wine were both used in ancient cultures for medicinal and social purposes and for religious rites. Throughout the historical record there is also evidence of societal attempts to control the misuse of alcohol through social and financial sanctions and a variety of temperance movements.

In addition to alcohol use in ancient cultures, there is also evidence of the use of psychoactive substances such as marijuana and opium. Archaeological evidence suggests that opium plants were cultivated in Switzerland 6,000 years ago. Ancient Egyptian and Greek records document the use of opium poppy juice as a sedative. Opium poppy juice was also used to cure insomnia, coughs, hysteria, digestive ailments, and pain. Evidence of ancient drug dependence is difficult to find, but based on modern knowledge of the addictive properties of opium and ancient references to the dangers of opium overuse, it may be assumed that as long as opium has been used, it has probably also been misused.

Marijuana plants have been documented in Chinese literature for more than three thousand years. Ancient Chinese medical texts describe the use of marijuana for arthritic conditions, rheumatism, and menstrual difficulties, among other complaints. Marijuana use in India is recorded as early as 446 BCE by Herodotus, who describes a religious ritual in which participants intoxicated from marijuana would have visions and howl with pleasure. The use of such psychoactive substances continued, primarily for medicinal and religious purposes, up until the mid-nineteenth century, by which time their use had spread throughout the world. Other psychoactive substances, such as coffee, tobacco, and coca, were also gaining popularity. In England in the mid-

seventeenth century it was reported that Charles II ordered that all coffee houses be closed in response to concerns regarding the excessive use of coffee.

Wherever there is evidence of alcohol or drug use, there is also evidence of specific subcultures that support and maintain the habitual use of these substances. Throughout the centuries institutions such as the following have had their own phases of popularity: taverns, gin joints, coffee houses, opium dens, gentlemen's clubs, crack houses, and shooting galleries. All of these establishments have been created and have existed to serve a purpose, namely to provide a place where groups of like-minded people congregate to use a specific substance.

The 1960s in the United States saw the emergence of increasing numbers of drug use subcultures, particularly among what became known as the "hippie movement." The hippie subculture became associated with alternative lifestyles that included, in many cases, drug use. Since that time many Western societies, including the United States, have witnessed the growth of drug-using subcultures. These subcultures have various identities and geographic locations, but they all have in common the substance use that binds their members to one another.

Rituals

Drug rituals are important for users because of the general lack of social acceptability toward drug use. The rituals associated with substance use help create independent social systems in which drug users find acceptance. These rituals form a common bond and increase cohesion within groups of drug users. Each time a ritual is enacted, the bond among the drug users is strengthened, and their adherence to the beliefs and values that support the ritual is reinforced. Rituals are often comfort inducing, and drug users will return to those patterned behaviors, seeking the comfort of their initial use.

Experienced users of hallucinogens will often have a pattern of preparation before taking a drug that ensures that the user will have a positive outcome.

Such rituals may include fasting prior to use (some hallucinogens produce nausea), avoiding certain foods that interfere with the drug's metabolism, ensuring a warm and secure environment, playing certain types of music, being in a calm frame of mind, and having another person present to talk the user down in the event of a bad trip. Among some cultures such rituals become ceremonialized and are used in celebrations, for example, the taking of ibogaine by the Bwiti cult of west Africa, or for religious or social gatherings, such as the smoking of peace pipes or use of peyote by Native Americans.

Group rituals

Many rituals are enacted in group settings. This is somewhat contrary to the normal tendency of substance users to operate in isolation from others. People generally crave contact with other people. Group rituals allow substance users to participate in social activities without being stigmatized for their drug use. One example of a group ritual that supports the use of substances is a rock concert. Certain types of music are stereotypically associated with drug use more than others, and the rock music

of the 1960s and 1970s provides such an example. Large concerts drew thousands of music fans with an alternative purpose of using drugs in an attempt to experience the music on a deeper level. Similar associations exist between marijuana and reggae. The trend continues with the use of drugs such as Ecstasy and ketamine by the rave and club generation.

Criminal group behavior can become part of a drug-using subculture when money is needed to purchase drugs. Robbing houses for liquor and cash is sometimes the necessary and customary activity that makes it possible for a group of friends to gather for a night of partying with alcohol and other drugs.

Social sanctions for drug taking

Drug users tend to form alliances and connections with other drug users in an attempt to normalize behaviors (rituals) that society discourages. As previously mentioned, drug use is illegal in the United States and in most of the world. Drug users can experience both legal and social sanctions. Social sanctions include limiting access of drug users to social activities that do not involve the use of illegal drugs. An example might be a large wedding where

Hell's Angels chapters are one example of a group of people that have their own codes and values on drug and alcohol use, thus creating a subculture within society.

alcohol is flowing freely. In Western countries, this free use of alcohol is legal (as long as age requirements are adhered to) and an expected part of the celebration. The introduction of illegal substances into this scenario, however, would not be accepted, and a drug user would possibly be ostracized from the occasion. This experience might reinforce the substance user's allegiance to his drug-using companions, who see nothing wrong with substance use. The differences in social acceptability of drug use create divisions between those who use or abuse alcohol and those who use drugs. In most cases, it is socially acceptable to use alcohol. Using drugs is socially unacceptable in most circles and consequently not tolerated.

Disapproval of uncontrolled use

The uncontrolled use of substances is discouraged throughout most of society. Even in societies where alcohol use is widespread and commonplace, the uncontrolled use of alcohol is generally viewed as a sign of moral weakness. Uncontrolled use may also be viewed as an indication of a flawed character. This pattern reinforces the subculture of alcohol users who are unable to control their consumption. People who use alcohol in a socially acceptable manner or not at all have a low tolerance of people who seem unable to control their use of alcohol. People who use or abuse alcohol but who do not use illegal drugs have a low tolerance for people who use drugs. Likewise, people who use illegal drugs in a controlled manner have a lack of tolerance for people using drugs in an uncontrolled manner. These distinctions create different groups among drug users. Further distinctions are made between those who use different types of drugs and those whose method of ingestion differs from others. Examples of these distinctions include marijuana smokers who view crack smokers as different from themselves or people who smoke crack who view people who inject heroin as distinct from themselves. Each of these groups creates a unique subculture comprising the rituals that support and maintain it.

Characterizations of subcultures

In the early twentieth century, the term *drug addiction* was coined to describe any illicit use of drugs. However, the term did not discriminate between different patterns of use or the effects of different types of drugs. In the 1930s, the term *habituation* was introduced to discriminate between those drug users with a physical addiction and those drug users without a physical addiction. *Addiction* began to be applied to those drug users who experienced illness or withdrawal when they stopped taking the drug. *Habituation* more commonly referred to those drug users who were psychologically dependent but not physically dependent on a drug. In the 1960s the World Health Organization (WHO) began to discourage the widespread use of the terms *habituation* or *addiction* and adopted the term *drug dependence*.

Drug dependence was defined as the physical or psychological effect of a drug characterized by a compulsion to continue to use the drug despite negative physical or emotional consequences. The use of the drug may or may not be accompanied by an increased tolerance to the drug or by physical or psychological symptoms of withdrawal.

The term *addict* was originally introduced to describe those with a physical addiction to alcohol or drugs. The term *junkie* was coined to describe those persons who were using "junk," or opiates. In general, the societal view of a junkie involves someone who is injecting a street drug such as heroin or cocaine. In some circles, prescription drug users are known as pill junkies, but *junkie* is primarily reserved for injecting drug users. The societal view of an addict is much more inclusive and includes anyone who is addicted to his or her use of alcohol or drugs. Society tends to have a greater acceptance of those persons who use alcohol and prescription drugs as compared with those who use illegal drugs.

One of the primary issues when considering the controlled use of drugs is legality. At this time in the United States and in most other countries, it is illegal to use most types of drugs unless they are prescribed by a physician. Prescribed drugs can be as easily abused as street drugs, but there is not the same stigma attached to their use. In the past few years there have been several controversies regarding the abuse of prescription medications, including narcotic pain relievers such as oxycodone and others. Oxycodone is legal to use in the treatment of

Weddings are a typical example of a social situation where drinking alcohol in the form of toasts is part of a group ritual. While a degree of mild drunkenness may be tolerated at such events, loss of self-control is likely to be viewed as unacceptable behavior by the majority of the group.

pain when prescribed by a physician, but it is as easy to misuse or become addicted to as any other opiate. Addiction to narcotics of any kind can have devastating consequences, but there seems to be a greater acceptance of those addicted to alcohol or prescription drugs.

Public perception of drug users

Public perception of drug users varies widely and has shifted considerably during the twentieth century. In the early part of the century, access to opiates and cocaine was not restricted to medical purposes. The Harrison Narcotics Act of 1914 made the use of opiates and cocaine illegal unless prescribed by a physician. Physicians were limited in the amount of these powerful drugs they were permitted to prescribe, and many physicians were indicted on criminal charges for overprescribing. With one legislative act, the use of opiates and cocaine became a criminal offense, and those persons addicted to these powerful substances became criminals instead of medical patients. Addiction began to be widely viewed as a moral weakness or as an outward sign of internal

psychological deficits. These views further strengthened the criminalization of addiction, and the United States began to experience a sharp growth in prisons built to house, detoxify, and rehabilitate these addicts.

The founding of Alcoholics Anonymous in 1933 and Narcotics Anonymous in 1953 commenced the most long-standing and effective treatments to date for alcoholism or drug addiction. These programs are based on a disease model of addiction that views the substance use as a physical, mental, and spiritual disease. Acceptance of the disease model varies. The public at large still struggles with the view of an alcoholic or drug-addicted person as suffering from a medical disease. Legislative policies support the view that there is a moral or character deficit operating in people who abuse alcohol or drugs. The social and moral stigma of belonging to a subculture is a reality in the lives of those who use drugs.

D. E. BIRON

SEE ALSO:
Addictive Behavior • Peer Influence

Dual Diagnosis

A number of drug users are found to have a psychiatric illness alongside their substance use disorder. Accurately diagnosing which of the problems is the main disorder can have a significant impact on treatment and recovery.

Many people who abuse drugs or alcohol also experience significant psychiatric problems. Dual diagnosis is a term used to describe cases in which two disorders occur in an individual at the same time. However, the fact that a person has two disorders does not necessarily mean that one problem caused the other, although this possibility must be considered. For example, if a person were diagnosed with alcoholism and liver disease, an observer might conclude that the two problems are related because liver disease is much more common in people who have abused alcohol for years and, importantly, the toxic effect of chronic alcohol use on the liver is well understood by medical science. So, in this case, two disorders occurring in the same person are probably related with one causing the other. However, we can also easily imagine someone having two disorders at the same time that are not necessarily related at all. For example, if a person suffers from nearsightedness and has the flu, there would be no reason to think that these disorders are related, because no biological or statistical link can be made between the two conditions.

When two disorders are occurring at the same time, questions about their relationship are of interest to practitioners and researchers alike. Questions arise about the effect one disorder may have on the other and whether the presence of the two disorders changes how the individual should best be treated. Comorbidity is another term used to indicate dual diagnosis and sometimes is reserved for cases where it is understood that one of the disorders is causing the other. One important clue as to whether two disorders are related in some way is to see if having one affects the risk (this is, the likelihood) of having the other. As mentioned, people who abuse alcohol have liver disease at a much greater rate than do non-problem drinkers, whereas individuals who are nearsighted have no more risk of contracting the flu than do those who are not nearsighted. Therefore, it is reasonable to assume alcoholism and liver disease are related in some important way while the flu and vision problems are not.

How common is dual diagnosis?

To understand how frequently dual diagnosis occurs in a population, researchers use a discipline called epidemiology (the study of patterns in the occurrence of diseases). There are some basic terms used in epidemiologic studies that are important to understand. First, an *index disorder* is the disorder being used as a reference or starting point. For example, to find out how many individuals with a substance use disorder also have a psychiatric diagnosis, the substance use disorder would be used as the index disorder. *Base rate* refers to the rate (or percentage) of a given disorder in a specific population. So, for example, the base rate of substance use disorder might be different for the population of people who have a psychiatric disorder compared to the population of people who do not have a psychiatric disorder. For example, if the percent of people with a substance use disorder among those with a psychiatric disorder was three times greater than the percentage of people with a substance use disorder among those who do not have a psychiatric disorder, we would conclude that there is a statistical association between having a psychiatric disorder and having a substance use disorder. The last key term is *odds ratios*. An odds ratio (often identified by the initials OR) indicates if there is a different likelihood (odds) that someone will have an index disorder if they have a second disorder versus if they do not have the second disorder. So, for example, an OR of 1 indicates the risk for the index disorder is the same whether or not the second disorder is present, indicating that the two disorders are not statistically related, while an OR of 2 indicates that the odds of having the index disorder is doubled when the second disorder is present compared with when it is absent. In the latter case, the two disorders would be statistically related because having the index disorder increases the chances of having the second disorder.

In the case of psychiatric disorder and substance abuse, epidemiology has been used to study the

TABLE 1: Twelve-Month Odds Ratios of Mood and Anxiety Disorders with Substance Use Disorders			
	Any Alcohol Use Disorder	Any Drug Use Disorder	Any Substance Use Disorder
Any mood disorder	2.6	4.9	2.8
Major depressive disorder	2.3	4.2	2.5
Mania	3.5	7.4	3.9
Any anxiety disorder	1.7	2.8	1.9
Panic Disorder with Agoraphobia	2.5	6.0	3.1
Panic Disorder without Agoraphobia	2.0	3.4	2.1
Social phobia	1.7	3.0	1.9
Specific phobia	1.6	2.3	1.6
Generalized anxiety disorder	1.9	4.6	2.3

Source: Grant, B. F., Stinson, F., Dawson, D., Chou, S., Dufour, M., Compton, W., Pickering, R., and Kaplan, K. (2004). Prevalence and co-occurrence of substance use disorders and independent mood and anxiety disorders: Results from the National Epidemiologic Survey on Alcohol and Related Conditions. *Archives of General Psychiatry*, 61, 807-816.

national rates of the disorders both separately and together to judge whether there is a statistical association between the two. The epidemiologic studies most widely used to show the frequency of co-occurring substance abuse and psychiatric disorders are the National Epidemiological Survey on Alcohol and Related Conditions (NESARC) survey, the Epidemiologic Catchment Area (ECA) survey, and the National Comorbidity Survey (NCS). Information from these surveys is readily available on the web.

One thing these surveys makes clear is that certain kinds of psychiatric problems have a very strong statistical relationship to substance use disorders. While there are a large number of different types of psychiatric disorders, these are often organized within broader groupings. One broad grouping, *internalizing disorders*, refers to psychiatric problems that center on feeling too sad ("depression") or scared/worried ("anxiety") or that center on feeling too good ("manic"). Common internalizing anxiety disorders include symptoms like anxiety attacks (panic disorder), debilitating shyness (social anxiety disorder), or excessive worry (generalized anxiety disorder). Mood disorders are another grouping that falls within the internalizing disorders and includes debilitating sadness (major depressive disorder) and mania (bipolar disorder). A lot of research has focused on the association of internalizing disorders and substance use because they are both among the

most common disorders found in the various epidemiological surveys.

The first step to understanding the epidemiology of dual diagnoses is to see if the ORs are elevated (above a value of 1) for the association of particular disorders with substance use disorders indicating that the two problems are statistically associated. These ORs are shown for the internalizing disorders in Table 1. The ORs are elevated from as low as 1.6 for specific phobia (e.g., like fear of heights) and substance or alcohol use disorder to a high of 7.4 between mania and drug use disorder.

Tables 2 and 3 show the rates of overlapping mood and anxiety disorders and substance use disorders found in the NESARC sample. In Table 2, it is apparent that the rates of anxiety and mood disorders are much higher among individuals with substance abuse disorders. Conversely, Table 3 shows that rates of substance use disorder are lowest among those with no anxiety or mood disorder (that is, in the general community) but is substantially elevated among those with an anxiety or mood disorder.

The epidemiological data show that having either a substance use disorder or any of several common internalizing disorders increases the risk for the other. However, this does not show with any certainty how or whether one type of disorder causes the other in the direct way that alcoholism causes liver disease. Research looking at which disorder tends to start first

TABLE 2: Twelve-month rates of mood and anxiety disorders among those with and without a substance use disorder		
	No Substance Use Disorder	Substance Use Disorder
Rate of anxiety disorder	11	17
Rate of substance use disorder	7	19

TABLE 3: Twelve-month rates of substance use disorders among those in the general community versus those with an anxiety disorder versus those with a mood disorder		
	Community	Anxiety Disorder	Mood Disorder
Rate of substance use disorder	9	15	20

can help to disentangle cause and effect but it turns out that either a substance use disorder or psychiatric disorder can start first in people who have both problems. Therefore, it remains possible that either condition can contribute to the cause or worsening of the other and it is also possible that both conditions are caused by a common source (e.g., a shared underlying genetic risk). Although learning why psychiatric disorders and substance use disorders often co-occur remains an important goal for researchers, a practical question that can be studied is how dual diagnosis affects treatment.

How dual diagnosis affects treatment outcome

To determine the best options for treatment, researchers must take into account the way that the disorders may impact one another. Two basic issues emerge: the effect of a psychiatric disorder on the course (that is, the combination of symptoms, severity, and response to treatment) of a substance use disorder; and the effect of a substance use disorder on the course of a psychiatric disorder.

In patient populations, co-occurring psychiatric problems have been shown to increase the level of substance use (number of days of use), the number of hospitalizations, and the risk for relapse to substance abuse. There is also evidence that an increase in the severity of a psychiatric disorder may have a negative impact on the substance abuse disorder and on how well substance abuse treatment works.

As one may expect, substance use disorders complicate the course and treatment of psychiatric disorders. Research shows that substance use dis-

orders are linked to more severe psychiatric symptoms, higher rates of relapse to the psychiatric disorder, more hospitalizations, more visits to the emergency room, and noncompliance with treatment regimens for the disorder.

One common problem is that practitioners who treat common psychiatric problems (e.g., primary care doctors and psychiatrists) do not always check their patients to see if they have a problem with drug or alcohol use. Similarly, practitioners who specialize in substance abuse are not always knowledgeable about psychiatric problems. Because of this, treatment for one or the other problem can be incomplete and less effective when the other disorder is not identified and also treated. Research suggests that for dually diagnosed patients, both problems must be treated to achieve the best outcome. Increasingly, practitioners are becoming cross-trained to recognize and treat patients with dual diagnosis. This requires expertise in diagnosis and treatment.

Diagnosis of co-occurring disorders

Given what research shows about outcomes when psychiatric and substance use disorders co-occur, accurate diagnosis to decipher the disorders and prescribe appropriate treatment seems particularly important but may also be especially challenging. To start, diagnosis of dual disorders is complicated by the fact that different means of assessment may produce different diagnoses. For example, it has been shown that clinical interviews, research interviews, chart reviews, and clinical consensus (all common means of diagnosing patients in treatment settings) vary in their ability to detect co-occurring disorders. The general consensus is that a structured diagnostic interview produces the most reliable diagnosis in cases of dual diagnosis, but questionnaires that ask detailed questions about problems in both areas can also be useful and efficient.

Also, it has been found that individuals with current substance abuse disorders are less reliable reporters of psychiatric conditions (such as psychosis, anxiety, and depression) than those with past substance abuse or with no abuse history. The accuracy of patient self-report may be compromised by psychiatric condition, withdrawal states, or prolonged substance abuse. Individuals can find it hard to distinguish between symptoms caused by psychiatric disorders, such as depression and anxiety disorder, and similar symptoms that can be caused by substance abuse itself (for example, from withdrawal).

Interviewers, too, may struggle with accurately diagnosing psychiatric disorders when substance abuse is present. For example, individuals with depression have shown an increase in symptoms when actively consuming alcohol and a marked decrease during withdrawal and abstinence. In cases like this, findings suggest that diagnosis and treatment planning may be more accurate if conducted after the patient has begun a period of abstinence. After a diagnosis has been determined, practitioners face the question of deciding the optimal treatment.

Treatment options for co-occuring disorders

Treatment of co-occurring psychiatric and substance abuse disorders may fall under one of three models: parallel (both treatments occur at the same time), serial (one treatment takes place before the other), and hybrid (programs addressing both problems are integrated into a single treatment). A common scenario of parallel treatment may occur when a person with a substance use disorder and a psychiatric disorder is attending Alcoholics Anonymous or Narcotics Anonymous while receiving appropriate therapy for his or her psychiatric problem. Alternatively, a person might receive serial treatment if the symptoms of his or her substance abuse need to be managed before a clear diagnosis concerning psychiatric disorder can be made. A third potential type of treatment is considered a hybrid. In a hybrid care setting, a special treatment that is just for the

dually diagnosed is conducted. Such programs have been rare but are becoming increasingly common.

Hybrid treatment of dual diagnosis is a promising approach, primarily because it addresses the special needs of individuals with co-occurring disorders. For example, these patients need to understand the ways that their disorders impact one another. For a person receiving treatment for alcohol abuse and panic disorder, a substance abuse counselor may describe the symptoms of withdrawal to the patient, while a therapist explains that the symptoms of withdrawal and panic are closely linked. A hybrid approach has been characterized by higher retention of patients, ability to persuade patients of the relationship between the two disorders, and assessment sensitive to the nature of dual diagnosis.

Reviews of the literature on treatment models for dual diagnosis conclude that, although there is support for the model of integration (hybrids), scientific studies are necessary to provide evidence and further develop specific types of treatment. One example of this type of study is currently underway. Matt Kushner, a psychologist at the University of Minnesota, found evidence that alcoholism patients who were also diagnosed with an anxiety disorder were more likely than those without an anxiety disorder to return to drinking after they received alcoholism treatment. He is presently conducting a study to see if a treatment for anxiety, integrated with traditional alcoholism treatment, will help these patients to remain abstinent. Preliminary results that are being prepared for publication found that such hybrid treatments produce a superior outcome to substance abuse treatment alone.

Investigations into the dual diagnosis of chemical dependence and psychiatric disorders have found this combination of conditions to be a common and challenging problem that warrants increasing attention by researchers. Treatments specifically designed for individuals with co-occurring substance abuse and psychiatric disorders may provide the best chance for recovery from both diagnoses.

M. G. KUSHNER, E. MAURER, S. SLETTEN

SEE ALSO:

Alcoholism • Alcoholism Treatment • Antisocial Personality Disorder • Depression • Diagnosing Substance Abuse • Mental Disorders • Treatment

Elderly

Drug use is often regarded as a problem that affects the young. There is, however, a growing number of people who become addicted to alcohol and drugs in old age, although this problem is often overlooked by relatives and physicians.

Historically, most people have believed that alcohol and drug abuse were not issues of significant concern in the elderly population. It was generally believed that most alcoholics and drug addicts died long before old age, or spontaneously recovered through maturity. In the twenty-first century, however, persons age 65 and older constitute the fastest growing segment of the U.S. population. Not only is science prolonging the lives of adults in general, but it is also keeping substance abusers alive longer than ever before. As longevity increases, so do age-related stresses. These stresses may include loss of a partner, loss of physical functioning, exhaustion of financial resources, and loss of independence, to name only a few. Some studies show the prevalence of drinking problems in seniors as high as 49 percent.

As the elderly become psychologically and physically stressed, their risk increases for coping through substance abuse, especially through alcohol misuse. Misuse involves not only alcoholic beverages, but also over-the-counter medications that are high in alcohol content, such as cough suppressants. Illicit substance abuse in the elderly has been virtually nonexistent, but those battling cocaine, heroin, and marijuana addictions are increasing as the baby boomers bring these habits with them into their later years. Abuse of prescription medication does exist, though most is unintentional. Alcohol and prescription drug misuse affects up to 17 percent of older adults. Often, misuse of medications occurs because of difficulty reading labels or in managing multiple medications received from different physicians. The most common prescription medication addiction is to benzodiazepines and tranquilizer drugs, such as Valium and Xanax. However, alcohol use remains the primary problem for most in this age group.

The consequences of alcohol misuse are increased for the geriatric population. Alcohol can cause changes in the heart and blood vessels, which could dull the pain that may warn of a heart attack. Missing these early warning signs can place a person at increased risk for a major cardiac event. There are also changes in the body, especially the brain, that come with aging, which may result in a reduced ability to absorb and dispose of alcohol, as well as increased sensitivity to its effects. Older people have a decreased amount of body water in which to dilute the alcohol. Because alcohol is water soluble, it has a stronger and longer effect on the geriatric body. With age there is also a decrease in gastric alcohol dehydrogenase enzyme, which plays a key role in the metabolism of alcohol. The decrease in this enzyme results in alcohol being metabolized more slowly. Again, this adds to the risk of alcohol having a stronger and longer effect. It also increases the strain placed on the liver, increasing the risk for cirrhosis and other liver diseases. In addition, many medications, prescription and nonprescription, have a detrimental effect if mixed with alcohol. Not only is alcohol misuse a risk for seniors under these conditions, but unintentional overdose also becomes a significant risk.

For some time, research has shown that alcoholism increases the risk of suicide attempts. A study published in the 2003 issue of *Alcoholism: Clinical & Experimental Research* also reveals that suicide completion appears to increase with age. Younger adult alcoholics are more likely to make medically serious suicide attempts—those defined as requiring hospital admission of up to 24 hours. Middle-aged and older alcoholics, however, are at greater risk of dying from suicide attempts.

Recognizing alcohol abuse

There are two types of senior alcohol abusers. Chronic abusers are those who bring their alcohol problem with them into later life. They begin drinking most often in their twenties and thirties and continue into their geriatric years. Nearly two-thirds of older alcoholics are in this group.

Situational abusers are those who begin drinking because of stress. Women more frequently fall into this category. Because they have a shorter history of problem drinking, they tend to have fewer health problems than their early onset counterparts.

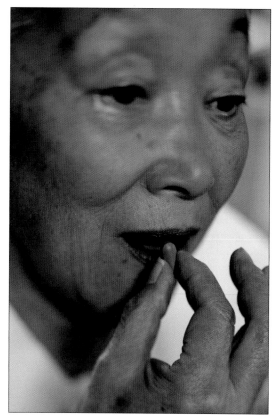

Elderly women represent a hidden population of substance users since they are more likely to keep their drug and alcohol use secret.

These drinkers often appear too healthy or normal to raise suspicions about drinking problems. Therefore, health care providers frequently miss their drinking as a concern.

It is not unusual for a diagnosis of substance abuse to be missed, regardless of the type of drinker. Physicians, in general, do not recognize the risks of the problem in the elderly population. Often rushed for time, doctors may not listen carefully to their senior patients and may miss cues that warn them of the issue. Complaints or changes in health status are often attributed to the aging process. More common is the mistaken assumption that older patients are nondrinkers. Studies have shown that less than half of alcoholics over 65 are diagnosed. Symptoms of alcohol abuse or dependence may also be mistaken for signs of other illnesses, especially with geriatrics. For example, injuries from falls while intoxicated may be mistaken or accepted as a fall because of the coordination problems and lack of mobility that often accompany aging.

Many seniors receive medications from multiple physicians (for example, a family physician and various specialists), making it difficult to adequately monitor their medication dosages. By age 65, most seniors take between two and seven prescription drugs, which significantly increases their risk for alcohol-medication interactions. Alcohol has a negative interaction with at least half of the 100 most frequently prescribed medications the elderly patient takes. In a 1993 study by Forster and colleagues, the combination of alcohol and over-the-counter pain medications was the most common source of adverse reaction in senior patients.

Clues to the problem

Patterns are one of the most significant clues of alcohol misuse, especially patterns in the frequency or nature of accidents and injuries. Alcoholics are 16 times more likely to die as a result of a fall, and 10 times more likely to suffer burn injuries. The incidence of hip fractures in the elderly increases with alcohol consumption.

Because most people retire prior to an age when they are considered truly elderly, there are no work-related problems to warn of a drinking or substance-abuse problem. Indications such as chronic tardiness or lack of workplace productivity are not present if the person is not employed.

Legal issues are not likely to arise as a warning sign. Hesitant to compromise an older person's independence, police may be less likely to file legal charges against an older person found to be driving under the influence or violating some other related law, which enables the use and problems to continue. In addition, many seniors no longer drive at all because of vision or other physical problems, thus eliminating this legal issue as a warning sign.

Women pose a special challenge when attempting to identify substance use in the elderly. They account for a larger portion of the geriatric population but a minority of older identified substance abusers. Older women tend more vigilantly to conceal their use because the stigma associated with drinking is greater for them. In order to help hide their use, they drink less often in public, which makes them less likely to drink and drive. There is also a proportionately larger population of older women who never learned to drive. Elderly women are more likely to live alone, which is an advantage in concealing patterns of use. Compared with men, women have less insurance coverage and less supplemental income, such as a pension, so they are more likely to live in poverty and less likely to be seen in medical treatment facilities where staff may recognize warning signs.

For some, embarrassment will prevent the individual from admitting the extent or consequences of his or her drinking. Many in this age group consider such issues as private matters. At other times, physicians recognize the signs but are reluctant to make a diagnosis because they are uncertain about the type of treatment to recommend, or whether it will be successful. Contrary to popular belief, senior substance abusers can be treated as aggressively as their younger counterparts. Seniors often respond more positively to treatment and have a better recovery rate because they tend to stay in the treatment program. They should be involved in counseling and given unconditional support.

As with any other age, there is no definitive list of signs that indicates an elderly person is drinking or abusing some other substance. There are, however, some signs that can alert outsiders to the need to further evaluate the possibility. Even if not frequently seen in a medical setting, most seniors have interactions with many others in their daily activities. Staff of day-care centers, social club members, pharmacists, clergy, or home repair or meal delivery personnel all have opportunities to observe seniors, especially those who are home-bound, for possible problems. These individuals could be trained to look for warning signs of substance abuse, including an increase in the occurrence of accidental injuries.

Certain medical problems, such as pancreatitis, hepatitis, cirrhosis, ulcers, and some types of cancer, can also be evaluated as warning signs of possible alcohol or substance misuse. Again, none of these is conclusive, and each may be the result of some other problem. It is important to discuss concerns openly with the individual, to speak with family or relevant significant others when possible, and to continue to closely monitor the individual.

Screening for abuse

There are no definitive rules governing the timing of screening for substance use in the elderly. In general, if there are physical changes or any type of major life change (for example, retirement, death of a spouse), screening should be considered. Depending on the setting, alcohol screenings can be integrated as part of other routine health screening questions. Screening should always be done in a confidential, nonthreatening, and nonjudgmental manner. Physicians and emergency personnel should also be more alert for repeat patients and should make discussions about alcohol use part of their routine care for every patient. Older patients should be advised to have no more than one alcoholic drink per day, with a maximum of two drinks on any drinking occasion. Limits should be even lower for women.

In the event that a screening is positive for alcohol or other substance abuse, the issue should be approached with care, and the effects of the use on the patient's health and functional status clearly and calmly discussed. The areas of concern most likely to motivate a senior patient into addressing the problem are physical health, loss of independence, and financial security. It is also important to follow up any concern with reassurance that the problem is correctable, and that reduction or cessation of use will improve the individual's life. Since reduction is often not sufficient for correcting substance abuse issues, emphasis should be placed on abstinence. If the person is resistant to abstinence, advising him or her to cut down, or changing potentially addictive medications may be a start. Treatment options need to be thoroughly explained and the patient given opportunities to ask questions and discuss concerns. The existence of co-occurring medical or psychiatric disorders will influence treatment options, priorities, and outcomes. In addition, it is important to have an established strategy for responding to denial or compliance issues. It often takes repeated contacts before a patient is willing to accept a referral for treatment.

P. L. TORCHIA

SEE ALSO:
Alcoholism • Drug Use, Life Patterns

Employee Assistance Programs

Workers with alcohol or other drug problems can have a detrimental impact on the efficiency of an organization or business. In response, many companies have set up services that can help an employee overcome substance abuse.

An Employee Assistance Program (EAP) is a mental health, work, life, and organizational consultation service provided to employees through their workplace. Increasingly used by private and public organizations since the mid-1950s, EAPs have grown from their earliest identity as alcohol-based problem intervention services to present-day comprehensive programs that address a wide range of personal and work-related concerns. EAP services are paid for by the employer and are offered to employees and their families free of charge. There are many different EAP structures, but EAPs generally resemble one another in a number of respects.

Professional counseling can be useful in resolving substance use problems that may be interfering with an employee's work and relationships.

Employees facing challenges that might detract from their performance at work can, at least, get a confidential assessment and referral for further help from an EAP. The financial investment in an EAP is offset by savings on costs that would otherwise be incurred by the organization due to employees who struggle with substance abuse, eating disorders, compulsive gambling or shopping, or other problems.

Focusing on substance abuse alone (and substance abuse represents a relatively small percentage of an EAP's overall scope), some of these costs include those associated with later-stage addiction-related depression or other psychiatric disorders. Physical disorders such as cardiovascular or liver disease, HIV, and AIDS not only cause increased absenteeism and greater medical disability claims, but also contribute to rising health care premiums for all employees. Substance-involved employees further decrease organizational productivity through their impaired work performance, lowering of group morale, and high employee turnover. Substance abuse and other forms of behavioral addictions such as gambling can lead to misuse or embezzlement of organizational funds. Intoxicant use on or off the job can result in workplace or motor-vehicle accidents, violence, and various forms of harassment that pose significant liability risks to large and small businesses alike.

An EAP is generally considered to be either internal or external. An internal EAP's staff is hired by and is accountable to the organization for which it provides services. An external program is contracted out by the organization and is administered as a separate entity. The best-used EAPs often provide confidential consultation on-site; however, some employees prefer to travel to an outside location or to use the EAP by telephone. Increasingly, EAPs are offering on-line services such as addiction self-assessments and on-line consultation.

EAPs generally employ clinicians with advanced degrees in social work, psychology, or medicine.

Some hold a Certified Employee Assistance Professional (CEAP) credential. Others may hold certifications as substance abuse specialists. Regardless of their credentials, EAP consultants are expected to have specialized knowledge pertaining to mental health and addiction, organizational functioning, and human resources.

Accessing services

Most EAPs are accessed on a voluntary basis only. Clinicians are required to follow licensure, state, and federal regulations that protect the confidentiality of all participating clients; this confidentiality may be breached only in cases of significant threat to the safety of the client or that of others. Some EAPs that work in safety-sensitive settings have special exceptions to the usually stringent confidentiality requirements. In all cases, it is standard practice for the EAP to inform each client of its confidentiality policy before the consultation begins, and to make each employee aware of the uncommon situations in which EAP consultants are required to disclose confidential information.

Services provided by EAPs vary widely, according to the cost to the employer. Basic services include the assessment of an employee's concern and referral to mental health professionals or other resources, including addiction treatment, emergency, rehabilitative, legal, financial, housing, family support, and elderly or dependent care services. Some EAPs are integrated into the organization's medical and mental health benefits, and will provide psychotherapy as a part of a comprehensive health care package offered to employees.

Before, during, or after the initial meeting, some EAPs may collect demographic information or satisfaction ratings from their clients. This information is used to analyze the EAP's effectiveness; the identities of all participants remain confidential. Other EAPs keep minimal or no records. By the end of the assessment process (typically, one to three meetings), the EAP consultant makes recommendations for further steps. It is the EAP's role to identify accessible, affordable, and appropriate resources to assist the client further if needed. Matching treatment providers to client needs, finances, and preferences is an important function of an EAP. For a female client with an addictive disorder and a history of domestic violence, this might mean identifying accessible female therapists with special expertise in addictions and post-traumatic stress disorder, referring the client to affordable child-care providers, and identifying safer housing resources.

Many EAPs provide short-term (one to six sessions), solution-focused counseling, or intermittent consultations about an ongoing situation. For example, an employee who is concerned about someone's drug use might receive support and coaching from an EAP consultant to help the drug-involved person to decide to seek treatment. Alternatively, a recovering employee with a manager who does not trust or support the recovery process may seek ongoing coaching from the EAP to improve that working relationship.

Workplace relationships

Consultation with supervisors and managers is a critical component of an EAP. When a manager is concerned about an employee's substance use, he or she may be educated by the EAP about the nature of addiction, its impact on the workplace, and the supervisor's role in both support and nonpunitive intervention. Managers can be helped to speak sensitively to troubled employees, to refer them to the EAP for evaluation, and to structure formal agreements that stipulate further evaluation or treatment as a condition of continued employment. In such cases, the EAP is often responsible for the case management of an employee who is in treatment; this management can include confirming continued participation in treatment services, determining readiness to return to the workplace, and facilitating reintegration or back-to-work plans.

EAPs are generally not considered part of an organization's disciplinary process. However, an EAP might provide consultation to management and the human resources department regarding an employee who requires disciplinary action for problems involving performance, conduct, or attendance. The EAP can help management recognize any contributing mental health or addiction problems, to anticipate and respond to potentially problematic reactions to the initiation of discipline, and to consider strategies to support the employee in accessing treatment for an existing problem. The EAP can coach management to establish or clarify relevant

Managing stress at work can help prevent employees from seeking relief in alcohol and illegal drugs.

policies and communicate these to all employees. The EAP can help coordinate an employee's leave of absence for substance-abuse treatment. Upon the employee's return (and with that person's full consent), the EAP can assist the employee to reintegrate into the workplace. The EAP can remain available both to the employee and management for further support or consultation as needed. Some organizations automatically refer a troubled employee to the EAP at the beginning of any disciplinary process. Because of confidentiality requirements, the referring supervisor may never know the outcome of this referral.

EAPs can play an important role in the promotion and maintenance of employees' overall well-being. For instance, psycho-educational seminars can target the needs of a workforce facing specific challenges such as organizational change, layoffs, or relocation. On-site stress management seminars offered to all employees can contribute to workplace relapse prevention strategies for those who are in early or long-term recovery from an addictive disorder. Workshops about substance use, abuse, and addiction can help employees recognize warning signs of problematic use in themselves or others, and to understand organizational policies that can support employees seeking help.

EAPs offer support to staff groups who are anticipating or responding to any form of crisis. For example, employees might be distressed over the news of a coworker's drug-related arrest, or the fatal car accident caused by an intoxicated manager. Some smaller, long-standing work groups might have questions about how to support a colleague when he or she returns from treatment for a gambling disorder. Increasingly, incidents such as workplace violence and terrorist events have highlighted the important role of the EAP in helping organizations to regain stability in the aftermath of trauma.

Whatever the type or structure of an EAP, it is a resource to employees at all levels, from part-time workers to company presidents. EAPs are vital components of organizations that recognize health promotion as a direct contributor to productivity and organizational stability. Finally, EAPs continue to uphold the tradition of promoting education and sensitivity about addictive disorders, and in assisting employees at all stages along the path to recovery.

N. COSTIKYAN

SEE ALSO:
Counseling • Workplace

Family Environment

Having a substance abuser in the family can create difficulties for its other members. How such families cope with substance use can depend on the protective or risk factors that underlie family structure and cohesion.

Substance use disorders (SUDs), also referred to as alcohol and drug abuse or dependence, affect almost one in five people. These disorders cause serious problems with the affected individual, the family, and society. SUDs are associated with higher rates of

- serious injuries or death from falls, or auto, boat, train, airplane, and other accidents due to impairment caused by substance effects
- medical diseases caused or worsened by substance use or methods of use (for example, using dirty needles to inject drugs)
- accidental or purposeful overdoses of alcohol or other drugs
- occupational impairment, such as the inability to find or keep a job, or working at lower paying jobs
- psychiatric illness, such as mood, anxiety, psychotic, personality, eating, or other disorder
- higher rates of suicidal and violent behavior
- problems with the law (arrests and convictions for crimes, which are often committed under the influence of substances, or in order to get money to pay for drugs)
- divorce, spouse abuse, child abuse or neglect, loss of family and social relationships, or serious conflicts in relationships.

The costs to society of SUDs and the problems they cause are in the hundreds of billions of dollars. These include the costs of medical care, lost productivity, and services needed to address problems caused or worsened by SUDs (for example, imprisonment, welfare to support families when the addicted person loses a job, and lost wages). Clearly, the family is adversely affected in many ways by SUDs.

Effects of SUDs on the family system

Substance disorders impact the whole family as well as individual members. However, not all families are affected in the same way. The specific effects are determined by the severity of the SUD, the presence of other serious problems with the substance-abusing family member, the behaviors of this family member, the support available within and outside the family for its members, and the personality of the non-SUD family member. For example, exposure to traumatic events, violent behavior, or the presence of a serious psychiatric illness in addition to the SUD creates an additional burden for the family. Members worry about their own safety or the mental well-being of the affected member.

Some family members are more psychologically resilient than others and will be less adversely affected. Other family members get help and support from trusted adults such as other relatives, teachers, rabbis, ministers or priests, or friends, which helps offset some of the negative effects that substance use disorders can have on an individual.

The family system is affected in many ways. Communication is often impaired, since family members often do not talk openly about the substance use problem. The family atmosphere is often tense and anxious because members worry about what to expect from the impaired relative. Roles within the family are also affected. For example, the substance abuser's spouse may assume the roles of both mother and father to the children. Or an older child may assume a parental role to help protect and take care of younger siblings, which adversely affects the development of the older child.

Normal family activities and rituals, including family meals, recreational activities, and celebrations, may be affected as well. For example, a father's alcoholism may prompt a child to complain that holidays and birthdays were ruined by his drinking. The child of a substance abuser may be continually embarrassed by the parent's behavior and may witness many arguments and fights. In addition, the child may experience problems caused by the economic hardship of loss of employment by the substance-abusing parent.

Impact on individual family members

Many studies show that individual family members, including children, are affected by a family member's SUD. A group of researchers at the Center for Drug Abuse Research of the University of Pittsburgh Medical School have been studying sons of drug-abusing fathers for more than 15 years. They compared these sons to those in families in which the father did not abuse drugs. The sons of drug abusers were found to be at higher risk for conduct problems, aggression, impulsivity, inattention, irritability, and heightened motor activity. These children also had lower IQ scores, poorer performance in school, and impairments in the part of the brain involved in planning and reasoning.

An unfortunate consequence of substance use is that some family members deny or minimize the problem or secretly hope it will go away. Others cover up or enable the substance use by bailing the person out of trouble or taking over his or her responsibilities. If a husband calls his wife's office to report that she is sick when she is actually impaired by alcohol, he gives the message that he is willing to lie to protect her from the consequences of the SUD.

Or, if a parent helps a child get out of legal trouble caused by driving under the influence of alcohol, the child may not get the message that there is a serious problem. He or she may be protected from the consequences of substance use and will be more likely to repeat the behavior in the future.

The emotional or psychological well-being and the physical health of family members are often affected. Parents often feel responsible for their children's substance abuse, unable to cope, and powerless to help. This is evident in the comment made by a father who said, "I blamed myself for my son's addiction. What often went through my mind was if only I had done this or that differently, maybe he wouldn't have this problem. It was just awful."

Children from families in which a parent has an alcohol or drug problem are at higher risk for these problems than are children from families in which SUD is not present. These problems include alcohol or drug abuse, depression or an anxiety disorder, conduct disorders, and school-related problems. Margaret Cork studied 116 children, aged 10 to 16, of alcoholics. Her assessment was that 43 percent of these children were very seriously hurt, 49 percent

Children can become upset by a parent's behavior while under the influence of alcohol or drugs. Younger children may not associate a parent's actions with substance use and think instead that they are to blame.

were fairly seriously hurt, and 8 percent were slightly hurt by their parent's alcoholism. Specific effects on children reported by Cork are shown in the box at right.

Another researcher, Edward Nunes, compared children of opiate-addicted parents with those whose parents did not have an addiction. Children of opiate addicts had significantly higher rates of school problems, disruptive behavior disorders, anxiety disorders, and depression.

The pain of children comes through very clearly in the types of comments made by children of parents with an addiction: "it (mother's drug addiction) made me sad and afraid"; "I was too embarrassed to bring friends home"; "it (father's alcoholism) upset me and my brothers"; "I feel I lost my dad to drugs and my mom to my dad's addiction." As a result of the rate of mortality associated with drug use, many children lose a parent as a result of addiction. The consequences can be devastating to the family.

Not all members are affected adversely by a substance use disorder within a family. There are protective factors that help offset some of the potentially negative effects and help the member build resiliency. These factors include connectedness to family, school, and the community. More than 20 years of prevention research has found a number of specific protective factors that reduce risk of substance abuse, violence, delinquency, school dropout, risky sexual behaviors, and teen pregnancy. These include the following:

- strong and positive family bonds
- parental monitoring of activities and friends
- clear rules of conduct, which are consistently enforced
- parental involvement in the lives of their children
- success in school performance
- bonds with school and religious organizations
- conventional norms about drug use (that is, believing that drug use is wrong, not desirable, and will contribute to problems).

While SUDs contribute to many problems for families and individual members, positive outcomes occur as well. Family members may develop resiliency, independence, good relationships within and outside

EFFECTS ON CHILDREN OF A PARENT'S DRINKING

- Family relationships were hurt (98% of cases studied).
- Children felt unwanted (97%).
- Relationships outside the family were hurt (96%).
- Children felt unsure of self or lacked confidence (94%).
- Children felt ashamed or upset (77%).
- Children were constantly angry (65%).
- Children worried about being different (63%).
- Children felt anxious about the future (61%).
- School work was affected (47%).
- Children felt burdened by too much responsibility (42%).

Source: Cork, M., *The Forgotten Children*, 1969

the family, and may bond together to cope with the stresses associated with SUDs. Most family members experience a combination of negative and positive effects. Some members are stronger and are able to tolerate difficult situations more easily than others.

Conclusions

Substance use disorders have an impact on family systems as well as individual members. These effects vary from mild to severe. Children who have a parent with an SUD are at higher risk for substance use disorders, mental health disorders, and academic problems. Families can also overcome the emotional burden experienced when an SUD problem is present. Participation in professional treatment, self-help programs, or both can provide emotional help and comfort to the family. Family members can learn specific tools to cope with a loved one's SUD as well as how to deal with their own feelings and reactions.

D. C. DALEY

SEE ALSO:

Children • Family Therapy • Protective Factors • Risk Factors • Support Groups • Treatment

Family Therapy

Families often bear the brunt of a substance user's addiction and can suffer related problems as a consequence. By including family members in therapy programs, many of the issues can be addressed and help can be given.

Substance use disorders (SUDs) create a burden for the family unit as well as individual members. Family mood or atmosphere, communication, interaction among family members, relationships to the outside world, financial condition, and quality of life may be adversely affected by an SUD. Involvement in professional treatment and mutual-support programs offers families an opportunity to become educated about SUDs, learn what they can and cannot do to help their loved one, and learn what family members can do to help themselves. While some family treatments focus primarily on helping the family help the member who has the disorder, most programs focus on the needs and problems of family members.

There are a number of approaches to treatment for the family in which an SUD exists. These may involve a single session with the family or multiple sessions over months or longer. While family approaches can be used with both adolescents and adults, it is the preferred treatment for adolescents. The different family treatment approaches are discussed below.

Intervention with the family and substance abuser

This approach helps families convince or pressure the member with the SUD to engage in treatment by using an "intervention." An intervention is an interactive process that involves a counselor meeting with the family (and other significant people) to discuss the substance problem and how best to get the affected member to agree to enter treatment. Several meetings may be held with the counselor to prepare the family for the actual intervention. The preparation process involves educating the family; providing family members with an opportunity to share their specific experiences regarding their loved one's SUD; identifying specific emotional, behavioral, and spiritual effects of the SUD on each family member; and determining what specific treatment to recommend once the formal intervention is held. This process also involves a practice session during which each member shares his or her written list of observations of the substance user's behaviors as well as the impact on the family member. The intervention planning group also anticipates resistance from the member with the SUD and practices ways to respond so that angry and hostile reactions are controlled, for example, "I understand you believe that you can stop drinking on your own, but we feel strongly that you need treatment," or, "We know you don't like the idea of going to a rehab program, but it can really help you. Remember, you tried to quit using drugs twice before on your own, but it didn't work. We want you to go for treatment, which we can help you to get, and to stay off drugs."

Once this preparation is finished, the counselor and family meet with the person to give feedback on the substance problem, how it has affected others, and how others feel about it. This intervention group then gives a specific recommendation for a treatment program and helps make the arrangements. If the substance-abusing family member refuses, consequences are laid out. For example, a spouse may tell her alcoholic husband, "I will no longer live with you if you choose not to get help for your drinking problem." Parents may tell their adult daughter, "If you refuse to get help for your cocaine problem, you will have to move out of our house. Also, we will no longer lend you money or help you pay your bills." The idea behind an intervention is to give the affected person an understanding of the reality experienced by others, along with consequences for failure to get help. Several variations of this approach have been used to help both adult and adolescent substance abusers enter treatment. While these approaches do not succeed in every case, they increase the likelihood that the affected person will agree to get help and will enter a treatment program.

Family counseling or therapy

Many forms of family therapy or counseling exist to help individual family members, couples, and the extended family deal with the SUD. Family

Counselors play a key role in intervention strategies for dealing with a substance abuse problem in the family. The counselor will discuss how the problem is affecting each member of the family and offer advice on how to deal with issues and ways to help the substance user recognize that he or she should enter treatment.

treatment aims to educate the family about causes of SUDs, effects on the impaired member, treatment, causes of relapse and ways to reduce relapse risk, and recovery support programs, such as Alcoholics Anonymous or Narcotics Anonymous. The family is also educated about professional treatment and self-help resources for families. Treatment helps the family address specific problems caused by the SUD. It also focuses on teaching the family what they can and cannot do to help their loved one. Perhaps most important, treatment helps the family learn to make changes to better manage the emotional burden. Some specific examples of the outcome of family treatment include learning to accept rather than deny the SUD and its negative impact on the family, reducing enabling behaviors in which the substance abuser is not exposed to consequences for alcohol or drug use, dealing with emotional reactions (for example, anxiety, anger, depression, fear, guilt, and shame) often felt by family members, establishing healthier forms of communication within the family,

and learning to detach from the substance user and to focus on one's own needs instead.

Family therapy sessions may be held with individual family members, the entire family, or subgroups of family members. Some clinics use multifamily groups in which several families meet with therapists for educational and counseling sessions.

Residential family programs

Some residential rehabilitation programs for addiction offer intensive family education programs for loved ones. These may be offered weekly for several weeks or they may be offered daily for up to a week. Such programs aim to educate the family, provide members with support, and help them begin learning how they can change their behaviors and help themselves. These family programs include a variety of treatment activities such as:

- *Educational groups.* These not only provide information but instill a sense of hope that change is possible. Educational groups provide a framework for understanding addiction, codependency (see box at right), and recovery for the entire family.

- *Therapy groups with several different families.* These groups provide participants with the opportunity to discuss issues such as the impact of the SUD on the family unit and its members, feelings (anger, hurt, pain, confusion, guilt, shame), behaviors (covering up or enabling the SUD, isolation from friends and relatives), and problems (dealing with violence, relapse of the member with the SUD). The goal is for family members to focus on their own experiences and feelings, and to get help and support for themselves rather than focus on the member with the SUD.
- *Family therapy sessions.* These provide each family the opportunity to work together on issues of concern. Such sessions usually include all family members, including the person with the SUD.
- *Individual therapy sessions for family members.* Some programs provide family members with the chance to talk one-on-one with a therapist.

Children often become withdrawn from friends and may suffer depression or behavioral problems as a result of a parent's drinking or drug use. Addressing the emotional needs of these children is an important part of family therapy.

During such sessions, the family member can discuss feelings, reactions, and concerns. In some instances, this will lead to a recommendation for ongoing treatment for a significant personal problem such as clinical depression.

- *Mutual support groups.* Family members are introduced to Al-Anon, Narcanon, and other types of groups, which are resources they can use for long-term recovery.

Some family residential programs are referred to as codependency programs. Codependency refers to the process of becoming so focused on the family member with the SUD that the family member fails to take care of his or her own needs. Instead, the codependent's life revolves around the SUD member, just as that member's life revolves around alcohol or drugs. Codependency programs were designed to help the family member help him- or herself.

Recovery for family members

Professional treatment programs encourage family members to get involved in family support groups to aid their ongoing recovery. Family support groups include Al Anon, Narcanon, Alateen, Alatots, Codependency Anonymous, and Adult Children of Addicts. Most of these mutual support programs are for adults; Alateen and Alatots are for teenagers and children respectively. All of these programs are based on the twelve-step program of Alcoholics Anonymous (AA). The "tools" of AA are adapted for families. These tools include attending meetings with other family members, reading recovery literature, using the 12 steps, getting a sponsor, and learning the slogans of the program (for example, "one day at a time," "this too shall pass," and "let live and let God"). Members who continue their recovery over the long term often sponsor newcomers by mentoring them. They help the newcomer learn about and use the self-help program, attend meetings together, and provide support to the newcomer who faces difficult emotions and problems caused by his or her relationship to an addicted family member.

All programs involve family members helping each other understand addiction and the impact on the family, and learning how to cope with both the affected family member as well as one's own reactions. Members learn to deal with feelings of anger, fear, hurt,

CODEPENDENCY

The concept of codependency originated from a phenomenon called co-alcoholism, a recognized pattern of behavior that occurs among the families of alcoholics. As the drinker falls further into alcoholism, family members begin to mirror some of the alcoholic's behavior patterns in order to gain some sense of self-worth and identity. Often, codependents are driven by a belief that they are somehow responsible for the failure to control or stop the substance use. This tendency can also affect treatment if the codependent tries to take on too much responsibility for the user's recovery, such that the substance user begins to rely on the codependent rather than on him- or herself to give up the addiction.

Codependency has a number of characteristic components that can be seen in most substance users' families. One is the sacrifice of an independent identity in an attempt to gain the approval of others. This may be related to fear of abandonment if others know how the codependent is feeling. Codependents are also afraid of rejection and will do anything to keep others happy, even to the extent of keeping the substance user from the negative consequences of his or her addiction. Loss of identity and feelings of responsibility for the user often result in the codependent having low self-esteem, which is reinforced every time the codependent fails to control the user's behavior.

Another common characteristic is compulsive behavior, which may manifest as a need to keep the family together, eating disorders, obsessive cleanliness, gambling, and so on. Compulsions can be a way of creating a sense of drama or a means of blocking deeper feelings in order to avoid confronting the pain of the loved one's addiction.

Denial, the key obstacle to the recovery of substance users, also affects codependents. Both think that the substance use can be controlled by willpower. Refusal to accept the problem and the perceived shame it brings lead codependents to deny that both they and the substance user are unable to cope with the addiction.

distrust, and depression in constructive ways. They learn to detach and reduce or stop enabling behaviors that cause them distress. Perhaps most important, family members learn to stop denying the addiction or its impact on their family and their individual lives. They learn to accept that the abuser's alcoholism or drug addiction is not their responsibility, and that their lives have become unmanageable as a result of living with an addicted family member. These family members also learn to take care of themselves by focusing on their emotional, social, and spiritual needs. Support programs help them discover that they cannot focus all of their efforts on their addicted loved one.

Conclusions
Substance use disorders affect the whole family as well as individual members. These effects may vary from mild to severe. Children who have a parent with an SUD are at higher risk for substance use or mental health disorders and academic problems.

Families can play a critical role in helping the substance-abusing member enter treatment. They can also support this member by attending sessions and offering help.

Families can also overcome the emotional burden experienced when an SUD problem is present. Participation in professional treatment and self-help programs have provided emotional help and comfort to many families. The evidence is clear: no one is left unharmed by a loved one's substance abuse. On the other hand, participation in treatment and support groups provides family members with specific tools to cope with a loved one's SUD as well as deal with their own feelings and reactions.

D. C. DALEY

SEE ALSO:
Addictive Behavior • Counseling • Employee Assistance Programs • Family Environment • Intervention • Support Groups • Treatment

Flashbacks

Flashbacks are unexpected returns to a hallucinogenic drug experience that may have happened months or years before. While the cause of flashbacks is unknown, evidence suggests that they may be linked to the sensory distortions of a bad trip.

Drug-related flashbacks happen when someone who has previously used a hallucinogenic drug, such as LSD, Ecstasy, mescaline, cannabis, ayahuasca, or "magic mushrooms," reexperiences something from the original drug experience even though the drug is no longer present in the body. A flashback can occur weeks, months, or even years after taking the drug and may last from just a few seconds to a number of minutes. Flashbacks are brief fragments rather than a complete replay of a previous trip, which may have lasted for hours.

Drug flashbacks are often triggered by something such as an image, a sound, a smell, or even an emotion that helps provide a link to a previous hallucinatory experience. In some extreme cases, however, a flashback can be completely unexpected and result in an intense visual reexperience of part of the original hallucination and can cause the individual trauma and debilitation. Most reported flashbacks are milder than this and present themselves in the form of perception and sense distortions of the surrounding environment. For example, time may seem to slow, stand still, or speed up; space (rooms, buildings, and so on) distorts; emotions can be felt intensely and overwhelmingly; and taste, smell, sound, and sight may be heightened and experienced in unusual ways, such as "feeling" colors.

Not all users of hallucinogenic drugs experience flashbacks. Studies vary, but it appears that around 25 to 30 percent of people who use hallucinogens later experience some kind of flashback, although this percentage does appear to be significantly higher among those with a preexisting psychiatric illness.

What causes a flashback?
Exactly what causes a flashback is not entirely clear. Some have argued that the use of drugs such as LSD causes temporary or even permanent changes to the

Flashbacks can re-create the experiences of a previous trip, including spatial distortions, bright colors, or intense sounds. The unexpectedness of a flashback may cause distress, especially if the original trip was disturbing.

brain, while others point to explanations that are more social and psychological in nature.

While it may be the case that flashbacks result from some temporary or even permanent change to the brain, this theory is, as yet, unproven. Even if drugs such as LSD do change the brain and bring about flashbacks, it is probably only a contributory factor. The mental state of the individual who uses the drugs and the context in which the drug is used also appear to be important, as does the way that the brain itself (even when there are no drugs present) can respond to traumatic or unusual events. Flashbacks appear to be linked to bad trip experiences. Because hallucinogens alter the user's perceptions of sight, sound, touch, and emotion and can make the user see or feel "outside" or beyond his or her previous range of experience, it is not surprising that some people become scared and find the trip traumatic. With LSD and other hallucinogens, it is impossible to stop a trip once it has started, so the trip, whether good or bad, must be seen through to its conclusion. That fact alone may increase fear, especially if the user feels like he or she is losing control during the trip.

Managing flashbacks

One of the things that is known about LSD use is that a bad trip is far less likely to happen when the user is in a positive frame of mind, emotionally stable, not anxious, and where the environment is soothing (for example, familiar music playing, gentle lighting), and at least one other experienced user is present to help the user "manage" the trip. In this type of setting, someone who is starting to feel disturbed about what he or she is experiencing may be "brought down" by the experienced user asking the novice to focus on things that are more familiar, effectively calming the user. Conversely, where LSD and other hallucinogens are used either by a lone individual or by the inexperienced with little or inappropriate support, the experience may be more traumatic. Thus, an approach that helps emotionally stable users to understand and control what they are experiencing appears less likely to produce the type of sensory distortion that leads to trauma. The comparative lack of reports of long-term negative effects from hallucinogen use by those who use them traditionally or ritually (for example, where

hallucinogens such as peyote or ayahuasca are used as part of religious ritual and where use is tightly controlled and managed as part of a spiritual event) suggests that this may be the case. What it also suggests is that the experience of an uncontrollable, frightening, and traumatic trip can induce a flashback to that experience.

Understood in this way, a drug-induced flashback may be similar to the nondrug-related experience of those with post-traumatic stress disorder (PTSD). PTSD is something that sometimes happens to individuals who experience an event that is physically or emotionally shocking (for example, soldiers who have been involved in combat or witnessed horrific events, or the witnesses or victims of violence or serious accidents). One of the symptoms of PTSD is flashbacks to aspects of the original trauma—an event that was so out-of-the-ordinary and intense that the experience imprints itself onto the individual, who then later (usually with triggers of some kind) can involuntarily recall the experience emotionally and visually. It may be that a bad trip is recalled in just such a way.

The advantage of understanding flashbacks as a reaction to events in which sensory overload occurs is that it can, at least partially, explain negative, neutral, and positive flashbacks of varying degrees of intensity. This theory could also provide an explanation for why flashbacks are reported from users of a variety of hallucinogens. If flashbacks were the result of chemically induced changes to the brain, it would be surprising to see all hallucinogenic drugs produce flashbacks in the same way, since many of the hallucinogens affect the brain in different ways.

Although the American Psychiatric Association has adopted a clinical definition of flashbacks as hallucinogen persisting perception disorder, the definition excludes many experiences that would be considered flashbacks by users and appears to have been based on research carried out largely on individuals with existing psychiatric ailments. It is likely that a more encompassing and reliable clinical definition will be developed in the future.

R. COOMBER

SEE ALSO:
Trauma and Addiction

Gateway Drugs

The theory that marijuana acts as a gateway to other illicit drug use is a popular but controversial idea. Evidence is beginning to show that exposure to dealers and early use of alcohol and tobacco may also play a part.

The term *gateway drug* refers to a drug that, when used, leads to the use of another, generally more harmful drug. Many people view marijuana as a gateway drug since most opiate and cocaine users have used marijuana prior to their opiate and cocaine use. People who subscribe to the gateway drug theory believe that drug users progress to ever stronger drugs to satisfy a growing need. Having experienced the high of marijuana, they are no longer satisfied and require something stronger. Cocaine may satisfy this need until they need something even stronger, for example, heroin.

Identifying whether marijuana—or any other drug—is a gateway drug is important in respect to establishing a credible and effective drug policy. If marijuana is indeed a gateway drug, then reducing its availability, or better still eradicating it altogether,

Teenage exposure to drugs often begins with being offered tobacco, marijuana, or alcohol by a friend. Progression to using stronger drugs may depend on whether the teen comes into contact with a dealer.

would reduce the number of opiate and cocaine users. However, if marijuana is not a gateway drug, then eradicating it would have little or no effect on opiate and cocaine use.

Teenage drug use

The evidence from almost all countries throughout the world suggests that drug use, both licit and illicit, is on the increase. It also suggests that the majority of this increase is among the young and that the age of initiation of drug use is getting lower, with some preteens using drugs regularly. Results from the 2009 National Survey on Drug Use and Health, which is sponsored by the Substance Abuse and Mental Health Services Administration (SAMHSA), show that after gradually declining from 11.6 percent in 2002 to 9.3 percent in 2008, the rate of past month illicit drug use among 12 to 17 year olds increased to 10.0 percent in 2009.

The consequences associated with adolescent substance use are high. Alcohol-related road traffic accidents are a leading cause of mortality among young people, and marijuana has also been associated with road traffic accidents. Longer-term problems include diseases such as cancer and cirrhosis, addiction, and legal trouble. Also, in the short term, there are problems of low achievement at school, which can have a profound effect on the career prospects of the individual and on the economy in general.

Studies of alcoholics have shown that early onset of drinking is associated with the severity of the problem in later life. Part of the reason for that appears to be that as adolescents mature they learn coping mechanisms and strategies, and they form social networks that also help with the problems of life. Both of these factors have a protective effect against forming an addiction, and they help in the recovery process for anyone who does become addicted. Someone who is drinking heavily from an early age is less likely to develop coping mechanisms or a supportive social network.

A further problem of adolescent substance use is lack of maturity. Adolescents tend to be physically smaller, less emotionally mature, and less practiced in handling the effects of psychoactive substances. Thus they may become intoxicated to a greater degree much more quickly. In recognition of this fact, pilot programs in both the United States and Australia experimented with different alcohol limits for driving for adolescents and adults.

Gateway concepts

The original idea behind the gateway drug theory came from evidence gathered from opiate addicts. Researchers would take a drug history going back to the addict's initial drug use and, in most cases, marijuana would be the first drug used. By examining the sequence of events, these drug histories are consistent with the view of marijuana as a gateway drug. There is, however, a fundamental flaw in this logic. While it is true that for most drug users their first illicit drug is marijuana, there are many more marijuana users who never progress to other illicit drug use. Examination of the statistics of drug use reveals that around 20 percent of the population have tried illicit drugs. In the vast majority of cases (in excess of 84 percent), the drug is marijuana. The actual number of opiate and cocaine users constitutes less than 1 percent of the population. Thus while some marijuana users may progress to other drugs, the majority, around 95 percent, do not.

A second piece of evidence that undermines the view that marijuana is a gateway drug comes from the Netherlands. For decades Amsterdam has had a policy of allowing "brown cafés" to operate. These are establishments where marijuana can be bought and consumed on the premises. In a gateway theory, such an easy availability of marijuana should lead to high numbers of opiate and cocaine users. In fact, the numbers of opiate and cocaine users in the Netherlands have not gone up but have decreased, one of the only countries in Europe where this is the case. Such evidence cannot be reconciled with a gateway theory.

Exposure theory, a weaker version of the gateway theory, suggests that progression from marijuana to other drugs is not caused by the need for a stronger drug but is instead facilitated by opportunity. It is obvious that an individual cannot indulge in drug use if the drug is unavailable. In order to obtain marijuana, an individual needs to come into contact with dealers, many of whom will be selling other drugs as well as marijuana. Exposure theory suggests that marijuana use increases the probability of other drug use by exposing the user to criminals who also sell cocaine, heroin, or amphetamines.

More recent evidence, gathered by studying schoolchildren over a number of years, has reawakened interest in the gateway theory. However, instead of implicating marijuana, the evidence points to the use of licit drugs such as alcohol and tobacco. It was found that between tenth grade and twelfth grade there was a marked increase in substance use. However, heavy tobacco users (more than half a pack a day) in tenth grade were significantly more likely to be using tobacco, alcohol, marijuana, and cocaine in twelfth grade. Also, tenth graders who were binge drinking (more than five drinks at a time) were significantly more likely to be using other substances in twelfth grade. There were also gender differences; illicit drug use was more likely to occur in binge-drinking males and heavy-smoking females.

Conclusion

Current thinking about gateway theory suggests that there is a progression in the types of drugs used. However, that progression is certainly not inevitable and it is not caused by the need for stronger drugs. It is believed that using substances at a young age—even so-called legal substances are illegal when used by minors—can expose someone to the opportunity to obtain other drugs. Therefore, it may well be legal substances that represent the gateway, rather than marijuana or other illicit drugs. In terms of policy, this finding suggests that more effective legislation and education regarding tobacco and alcohol may have a greater impact on future drug use than more stringent laws regarding marijuana.

J. MCMAHON

SEE ALSO:

Adolescents and Substance Abuse ● Drug Use, Life Patterns

Glue Sniffing

Despite more than 50 years of reported glue sniffing, there is still a poor understanding of its causes and consequences. However, as awareness grows, a number of new initiatives to address this practice are underway.

The principal constituent of glue is toluene, a clear, colorless liquid with a distinctive smell. It is a common solvent and is found in a number of other commercial products including paints, paint thinners, nail polish, and rubber. Other solvents in glue include hydrocarbons, esters, ketones, and chlorinated compounds. These solvents are all volatile, so they turn from liquids or semisolids into vapors at room temperature and mix with the air. As such, glues are classified as volatile substances or inhalants.

Who sniffs glue?

Glue sniffing first came to public attention in the 1950s and continues to be an issue for young people. Although individuals of all ages are reported to abuse inhalants, teenagers and young adults account for a large portion of inhalant abusers in the United States. A national survey of 12- to 17-year-olds found that about 10 percent had used inhalants, with 4 percent reporting use in the previous year and 1 percent in the past month. Glue was the most commonly used inhalant by this age group, with about 4 percent reporting at least one use. However, surveys of high-school students in the United States, United Kingdom, and Australia have found even higher rates of inhalant use (between 15 to 25 percent), although these studies did not specifically differentiate glue sniffing from use of other volatile substances.

There are few gender differences in the rates of glue sniffing among younger students, although regular use is more common among older adolescents and in those seeking treatment. The majority of glue sniffing is experimental, with users partaking five times or less. Yet there are groups of young people who become regular and chronic users. This is more common among disadvantaged and high-risk youth, including young people from poorer socioeconomic backgrounds, juvenile delinquents, and young people with behavioral problems, as well as school dropouts.

Glue is one of the first substances abused by young people. Its cheapness, legality, and wide availability make it easy for teenagers to develop an addiction.

Acute effects of glue sniffing

Glue and other inhalants may be abused by "sniffing," "huffing," or "bagging." Sniffing involves inhaling directly from the glue canister or from a material covered with glue. Some users hold the material over their nose or mouth (huffing), while others breathe directly from a glue-filled paper or plastic bag (bagging). Typically, sniffing is associated with experimental use, while bagging is more common among regular users, who are seeking higher concentrations of inhaled vapors.

Glue sniffing results in short-lived euphoria, excitation, and light-headedness. Intoxicated users feel less inhibited, making them more likely to act impulsively or take risks. Continued use leads to dizziness, sleepiness, slurred speech, blurred vision, and headaches. At this stage, users may appear confused or begin responding to hallucinations. Further use or higher doses may result in unconsciousness, seizures, and coma, as the solvents within glue depress the central nervous system. Deaths related to suffocation while bagging have also been reported. Accidental injury is common and is related to impulsive risk taking and impaired motor skills while intoxicated.

Why sniff glue?

Inhalants, such as glue, are typically one of the first drugs that young people misuse. Inhalants are cheap, loosely regulated, readily accessible, and provide a rapid high. Experimental use is typically short-lived and is usually motivated by curiosity or peer pressure. Most young adolescents who continue to misuse glue do so in small groups, and peer factors are extremely important in ongoing use. Chronic glue sniffers typically have histories of numerous social difficulties, disadvantaged backgrounds, and high levels of psychological problems, suggesting that some young people may use inhalants to cope with emotional and social distress.

Dangers and complications of glue sniffing

Chronic glue sniffing is associated with significant toxic effects, causing widespread and long-lasting damage to the nervous system and other vital organs, including the kidneys, liver, and lungs. Repeated use or high doses may result in unconsciousness, seizures, coma, heart failure, and death. Permanent damage to a number of brain and nervous-system structures have been reported, including peripheral nerves and the cerebellum, resulting in problems with speech, vision, hearing, poor balance, and numbness. In addition, cognitive deterioration (decreased mental ability) may occur over time, resulting in impairments in attention, learning, and memory, or even dementia. Abuse during pregnancy has been associated with significant risks, including spontaneous abortion, premature labor, and infant malformation.

Glue sniffers, like other inhalant users, have increased rates of delinquent behaviors, criminality, and sexual risk-taking behaviors as well as difficulties at school. Conflict at home is common, as are other family problems. In addition, rates of depression and behavioral problems are high, and glue sniffers as a group have significant rates of suicidal thoughts and attempts. Follow-up studies have found that inhalant use (including glue sniffing) is associated with a poor long-term prognosis. This group has elevated rates of alcohol or other substance use, particularly injecting drug use, as well as high levels of legal involvement and mental health problems, for example, anxiety and learning disorders.

Treatment

Young glue sniffers are difficult to identify and typically do not seek treatment. As such, there is little available information on the treatment of glue sniffing and other inhalant use. However, prevention campaigns have played a role in reducing rates of inhalant use in the United States. In addition, several countries have placed restrictions on the sale of some volatile substances and have provided retailers with strategies to decrease the availability of inhalants to young people.

Although there is a lack of clear treatment recommendations for young glue sniffers, there is a general consensus that this group should receive a thorough assessment of their physical, psychological, social, and neuropsychological state. However, most glue sniffers are only brought to medical attention as a result of injuries or complications related to intoxication and may be reluctant to accept ongoing treatment. It is therefore important to work closely with the young person and his or her family to begin to unravel the difficulties that they face. Involvement of key staff members within the school setting may also be appropriate given the high rates of difficulties at school. In addition, a number of community programs aimed at involving young people in alternative activities have been developed. Basic training in social and health skills and the development of less deviant peer networks have also been promoted. Supported withdrawal has been recommended for some chronic glue sniffers, and prolonged periods of detoxification have been suggested given glue's long-lasting effects within the body. For those young people who are not ready to reduce their drug use, a number of harm-minimization strategies, such as using less toxic types of glue, have been recommended in an attempt to reduce the dangers associated with ongoing use.

D. I. LUBMAN, L. HIDES

SEE ALSO:
Adolescents and Substance Abuse ● Peer Influence ● Suicide

Halfway Houses

Drug users who have received some form of treatment for their addiction often spend time in a halfway house before they rejoin the community. By doing so, addicts can make changes to their life that will help prevent a relapse.

A halfway house is a facility that provides a drug-free environment for individuals recovering from drug or alcohol problems who are not yet able to live independently. There is no formal definition of a halfway house, and whether an establishment is designated as such can depend on the licensing provisions of the state in which it is situated. In terms of licensing, some states make little or no distinction between halfway houses, recovery homes, or other forms of residential facility.

Halfway houses are usually located in the community but vary in the degree to which they are integrated into community life. There are also significant differences in the size of each establishment, the levels of funding and sponsorship, and whether or not they are state regulated. Treatment philosophies often differ, and some former users are there voluntarily while others are forced to attend under some form of court order. Some halfway houses specialize in drugs or alcohol or both—others are for a more general category of ex-offenders. There are facilities that take only adolescents, women, or specific ethnic groups. In some establishments, people are expected to have been abstinent at least for a few days, while others offer detoxification services. Staff arrangements also differ; some halfway houses are run by former users and are informal, others are run by professional staff on more structured lines.

Halfway houses are also used as part of a sequence of treatment known as continuum of care. After an addict has received treatment in a therapeutic community or prison, he or she will be encouraged to spend up to six months in a halfway house. Doing so enables the former user to reestablish family ties, find work and housing, or improve educational skills while retaining a support system that can intervene if there is any threat of a return to drug use. Studies have shown that offenders who follow a continuous sequence of treatment involving a halfway house are less likely to return to drug use or commit drug crimes that will return them to prison.

Oxford House movement

One well-established facility is known as Oxford House. The first one was set up in Silver Spring, Maryland, by J. Paul Molloy in 1975. The state was planning to close down a publicly funded halfway house due to lack of money. The residents decided to run the place themselves and worked out a democratic process for sharing expenses. Members wrote an operations manual as to how the place would be run, and agreed that anybody caught using drugs or alcohol would be asked to leave the house.

Eventually this first house had a surplus of funds, which were used to rent a second property, and the Oxford House movement spread. The name Oxford was an acknowledgment of the role that the Oxford movement played in the development of Alcoholics Anonymous, and the Oxford Houses follow AA principles without being formally affiliated. The principles that the house must be democratically self-run, that the house membership is responsible for all household expenses, and that the house must expel any member who uses alcohol or drugs remain as the guiding principles for all Oxford establishments.

There are now more than 800 Oxford Houses in the United States, with others in Canada and Australia. Three or more Oxford Houses within a 100-mile (160 km) radius comprise an Oxford House chapter. A representative of each house in the chapter meets with the others on a monthly basis to exchange information, to seek resolution of problems in a particular house, and to express that chapter's vote on larger issues.

These and other facilities are advertised under a variety of names, including halfway houses, recovery homes, sober living, and transitional living. The Internet has extensive links to the hundreds of establishments that exist across the United States.

H. SHAPIRO

SEE ALSO:

Continuum of Care • Prison Drug Use and Treatment • Therapeutic Communities

Harm Reduction

Drug users face many risks associated with their habit. Reducing the impact of drugs on users and others in society is the goal of harm-reduction programs, but this approach is controversial.

Harm reduction is becoming increasingly popular for its practical approach to drug abuse problems. Programs that embrace harm reduction are grounded in a public health philosophy rather than the more traditional approach based on criminal law, which is focused on eradicating drug use. Harm reduction sees drug use as an inescapable fact that must be dealt with in practical terms rather than a moral or criminal matter. As a result, harm reduction aims to reduce harm to users and society rather than eliminate or reduce drug use itself.

The harm-reduction movement in the drug field began to grow stronger from 1990 onward, as public health professionals responded to the spread of AIDS among injecting drug users. People saw the new viral epidemic as a greater threat to health than drug use itself and recognized that providing clean needles was a practical way to save lives.

In the broadest sense, harm reduction is seen as a logical approach by people with very different views on drugs and drug control policy. The idea of reducing harm is accepted by liberal reformers who are opposed to what they view as the hopeless effort to eliminate drug use altogether. The idea is also acceptable to more conservative observers who favor adopting punishments for drug use that may include sending drug users to prison. When the idea is so broadly interpreted that imprisonment and other forms of punishment are considered harm reduction, however, its original meaning is too distorted to be of much value in shaping drug policy. In an attempt to solve this problem, experts and policy advocates in the drug field have tried to come up with a more specific definition that could bring about a more general consensus.

Most people in the field now agree, for example, that harm reduction must provide workable options that focus on the health of the user. This position takes the middle ground between the policy extremes of allowing completely free access or demanding the total suppression of drug use. Unlike traditional abstinence-based programs, harm reduction is neutral about the long-term goals of intervention. Shorter-term goals that can actually be achieved are considered more important if they reduce harm, even if drug use continues. While not ruling out abstinence in the longer term, the harm-reduction position is that if people will not or cannot give up their drug use, they should be encouraged to reduce any harmful consequences to themselves and others. Harm-reduction programs thus accept that some people may continue to use drugs. This makes them very different from programs requiring abstinence, which should not be considered harm reduction.

Types of harm reduction

The earliest days of the harm reduction movement began in the early twentieth century when doctors in Britain prescribed heroin for addicts. These early efforts at harm reduction are supported by a study of a similar program that was successfully introduced in Switzerland in the mid-1990s. It was found that with daily provision of heroin in a controlled safe environment, drug-related deaths and crime are reduced, and the addict is able to establish a more normal way of life. By the 1960s, concerns began to emerge about the health risks associated with the widespread use of the legal drugs tobacco and alcohol. Later efforts to prevent the spread of AIDS among and by injecting drug users spurred calls to develop an integrated public health response to the problems posed by both illegal and legal drugs alike.

As with illegal drugs, harm reduction for tobacco and alcohol products focuses on both health risks and social harms resulting from their problematic use. Advising smokers to cut back, use filters and water pipes, or smoke lower-tar cigarettes allows smoking to continue while reducing the volume of cancer-causing inhalants. Another strategy suggests that higher nicotine cigarettes lower the level of harmful smoke inhaled by providing the desired drug effect sooner. Public health campaigns and restrictions to protect nonsmokers from passive or secondhand smoking are current interventions that might be justified in broader terms of social harm reduction. Harm-reduction initiatives for alcohol similarly target the most immediate risks to drinkers and those around them. Effective intervention by bar staff, use of shatterproof glasses, and designated driver campaigns are examples of programs that target common harms associated with public drinking.

For the chronic alcoholic who ends up on the street, one homeless shelter in Toronto, Canada, dispenses a measured dose of wine at regular intervals. The hostel does so because it recognizes that some alcoholics will not accept shelter if they are expected to abstain from alcohol. This designated "wet" hostel provides a safe place for problem drinkers to drink alcohol in an environment supportive of more moderate consumption. Related outreach strategies offer health care and information to street addicts who inject heroin, cocaine, and other illicit narcotics. Needle- and syringe-exchange programs and safe injection sites in some large cities help stave off disease and bring drug users into contact with health workers and treatment providers. Giving out bleach kits to inmates in prisons to promote the use of clean drug-injection equipment is another example of how harm reduction reduces the harm of prohibited drug use in certain settings.

For occasional users of MDMA (Ecstasy) and other club drugs used at dance parties, on-site inspections in some clubs in the Netherlands provide information about the chemical contents and purity of these illicit drugs. Rave scene participants themselves have played a role in promoting greater knowledge and safer drug consumption. Flyers distributed at local events and information shared globally on the Internet are much like the earlier "flight guides" that circulated among devotees of LSD and in other psychedelic subcultures.

Compared with heroin, cocaine, and other addictive drugs that are generally agreed to be more harmful, the most widely used of all illicit drugs, marijuana, is seldom discussed in specific terms of harm reduction. Although it is always the first drug for which law reform is proposed during any discussion of drug policy, harm reduction tends to focus on problems with the law rather than marijuana-use practices. It is increasingly suggested that the drug either be decriminalized or penalties reduced to limit the harm of its continued criminal-

Harm reduction strategies can range from the provision of clean needles to the setting up of rooms where addicts can take drugs more safely.

ization. Specific recommendations that have been adopted vary widely, from the sale of marijuana in coffee shops in the Netherlands to small fines against those charged with possession in some U.S. states, parts of Australia, and in Canada.

What these options have in common is the aim of reducing the financial cost to society of enforcing laws that have not been shown to reduce marijuana use. A reduction in harm to the otherwise law-abiding young user is realized by avoiding the stigma of a criminal record that may compromise future employment opportunities and other potentially serious individual consequences. Despite its low addiction potential and few adverse behavioral and health effects at low-use levels, marijuana is not without health risks, however. To reduce the risk of lung damage due to smoking, a harm-reduction approach recommends public education to diminish customary practices such as deep inhalation and breath holding or mixing marijuana with tobacco.

Considering the prevalence of marijuana use by smoking, developing technology for consumption of the drug in a form that is safer is highly desirable from a public health perspective. Innovations such as marijuana vaporizers, beverages, lozenges, skin patches, and other forms of delivery might be encouraged to eliminate the respiratory hazards. By urging safer drug-use practices in terms of personal health as well as the settings and circumstances of drug use, harm reduction suggests that when properly informed and treated with respect, drug users will behave responsibly and seek to reduce potential harms to themselves and others.

Harm-reduction education

A harm reduction approach to drug education acknowledges that many young people will use drugs at some stage in their lives, making it vital that students acquire knowledge and skills that will help them make informed decisions about drug use and minimize harmful effects. While harm reduction does not encourage, condone, or condemn the use of drugs, it does seek to inform about, rather than against, drugs. It also considers benefits as well as risks in the context of where drug use actually takes place. From this point of view, providing biased or incomplete information to prevent young people from taking drugs limits the credibility of drug education and makes it counterproductive. Although research shows that providing accurate drug knowledge is more effective than scare tactics and forced abstinence, implementing harm-reduction education has proved difficult.

While harm reduction has gained increasing acceptance, its full integration into drug education would mean shifting focus—from the problem of drug use as viewed by adults, to problems with use as experienced by adolescents. More generally, despite their logical appeal, there are major impediments to the adoption of harm-reduction programs and policies. Most developed Western nations have adopted international conventions that hold firm to the ideal of eradicating illicit drug use.

Subscribing to harm reduction involves accommodating drug use, which could be seen as a weak form of compromise. To promote harm reduction, as opposed to waging war on drugs, accepts the fact that continued drug use is inevitable, which, for some, may make drug use appear to be an acceptable behavior.

To those who believe that life should be lived without the use of drugs, harm reduction would appear to invite even more drug use. People who indulge in such reckless behavior as using drugs must accept the harmful consequences of their actions. From this point of view, helping people reduce the dangers of drug use only reinforces undesirable behavior. Advocates of harm reduction counter these moral objections by providing scientific evidence in support of their perspective. The successful stating of the case for harm reduction in some circumstances suggests that a level of agreement based on rational assessment may be said to exist despite value differences.

Increasing support for harm reduction may thus be inevitable. With more and better research seeking practical solutions to drug problems, policies that allow for better targeting of harm will surely follow. Although most people do not take illicit drugs and dislike the fact that other people do, the practice may still be endured or tolerated on grounds of necessity. While harm reduction has proven to be the immediate solution to public health crises, such as the HIV epidemic among injecting drug users, it remains controversial. From some perspectives, allowing drug use to continue while reducing the harm it may cause is both morally suspect and counterintuitive.

Despite important successes in harm reduction, however, even well-established harm-reduction initiatives face resistance from staunch prohibitionists who believe that strict drug controls and abstinence through treatment are the only acceptable long-term solutions. The future of harm reduction is thus a matter of debate. It remains to be seen to what extent harm reduction can make scientific reasoning a predominant perspective in the value-laden context of drug policy debates.

A. HATHAWAY

SEE ALSO:

Needle Exchange Programs • Public Health Programs

167

Heart and Circulatory Diseases

The heart is one of the human body's most vital organs, but it can be significantly harmed by the use of recreational drugs. The blood circulatory system can also be negatively influenced by drug use.

Drugs can be taken in a variety of ways—smoking, injection, or ingestion—but to produce their recreational effects, they ultimately need to reach their final destination, the brain and spinal cord (central nervous system). The circulatory system, in which blood carries oxygen, nutrients, and other vital chemicals to all the organs and tissues of the body, delivers drugs and their metabolites to their targeted site of action or the brain. If the drug is able to cross the blood-brain barrier—the protective mechanism that prevents toxic substances from harming the brain—it will react with receptors in the brain and trigger a response. Sometimes these responses affect the way that the heart and circulatory system function, for example, increasing the heart rate or increasing or decreasing the blood pressure. If the use of drugs is constant, such changes to the way the heart and circulatory system respond may lead to permanent damage. On other occasions, drug use may cause a sudden and fatal system failure.

The heart and circulatory system

The heart is essentially a hollow, cone-shaped pump that sits between the lungs. The heart is responsible for pumping blood to every organ and cell in the body, including the lungs, where the blood gives up carbon dioxide (which is discharged during exhalation) and takes up oxygen (acquired during inhalation). The heart has three distinct layers: a smooth, inside lining called the endocardium; a middle layer called the myocardium; and an outer, fluid-filled sac called the pericardium.

The heart is divided into four chambers: two atria (the right and left atrium) and two ventricles (the right and left ventricle). The atria receive blood entering the heart. When they contract, blood is pumped into the ventricles, which push blood away from the heart with enough force to ensure that it can travel throughout the circulatory system.

The atria and the ventricles are divided by valves, which ensure that blood flows in only one direction.

Valves also protect the outlet of the ventricles into the arteries, ensuring that blood does not flow back from the circulatory system into the heart until it has completed its journey to the lungs or around the body. The pulmonary valve is sited at the exit of the right ventricle and the aortic valve is at the exit to the left ventricle, pumping blood into the body's main artery, the aorta. The atria contract simultaneously, as do the ventricles. When the atria stop contracting and the ventricles begin their contraction cycle, blood is forced back against the valves that separate the atria and the ventricles, forcing them to close (systole). As the valves close between the ventricles and their arteries, the ventricles relax (diastole).

There are three types of blood vessels: arteries, veins, and capillaries. Arteries and veins are surrounded by a layer of smooth muscle, although the layer that surrounds the arteries is much thicker and contains more elastic fibers. The extra elasticity and thickness is needed because arteries have to expand to take blood as it is pumped from the heart, and then contract to squeeze this blood into the veins as the heart relaxes.

Arteries carry blood away from the heart, and veins carry blood back toward it. As a general rule, arteries contain oxygenated blood and veins deoxygenated blood. The exceptions are the pulmonary arteries, which leave the right ventricle for the lungs and carry deoxygenated blood, and the pulmonary veins, which carry oxygenated blood back from the lungs to the heart. Arteries branch to become smaller arterioles, which in turn branch to become capillaries, which form thin webs of blood vessels called capillary beds. The exchange of oxygen and carbon dioxide between the blood and the cells of the body takes place in these capillary beds.

On the return circuit to the heart, capillaries thicken and merge to become venules, which merge to become veins. Because the blood is no longer under the same amount of pressure as in the arteries, veins contain valves to ensure that the blood flows in one direction and does not pool or flow back into the

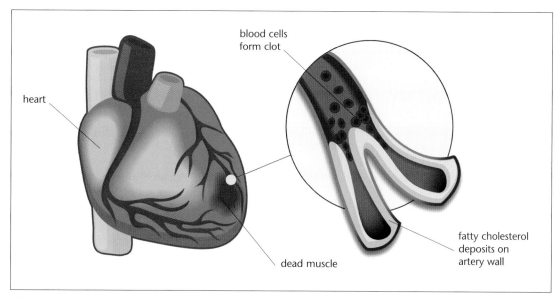

A heart attack occurs when the arteries become blocked by fatty deposits of cholesterol. If the vessels narrow too much, the blood cells are unable to pass through and form a clot. If blood is prevented from flowing, the area of muscle fed by the artery dies and reduces the heart's ability to function properly.

legs under gravity. If the valves break down, varicose veins are formed.

The heart also has its own individual blood vessels, called the coronary arteries, which serve solely to provide this vital organ with its own blood supply. The coronary veins return blood from the heart muscle directly to the right atrium.

High and low blood pressure

Blood vessels produce a resistance to blood flow, and the pumping of the heart against this resistance creates blood pressure, which enables blood to circulate around the body. There are two measurements in a blood-pressure reading: systolic and diastolic, systolic being the highest pressure produced by the heart when it contracts to pump blood, and diastolic, the lowest pressure when it relaxes. Normal blood pressure for a young person would usually be described as around 130 over 80, that is, a systolic pressure of 130 and a diastolic pressure of 80. Blood pressures of more than 160 over 100, common with the use of stimulant drugs, are described as high.

Permanently raised blood pressure increases the risk of blood clots and damage to the blood vessels. It can lead to structural changes, causing the vessels to thicken and deteriorate so the heart has to work harder to push blood through, leading to cardio-vascular diseases such as heart attack, angina, stroke, kidney failure, eye conditions, and circulation problems. Often there is no single obvious cause for high blood pressure, although it tends to run in families. This type of high blood pressure is known as essential hypertension. Many kidney diseases also cause high blood pressure, and those with kidney disease are at high risk of developing heart disease and circulation problems.

Low blood pressure, or hypotension, is normally defined as below 90 over 60. When blood pressure is too low, the flow of blood to the brain and other vital organs becomes inadequate and the sufferer may faint, become light-headed or, in severe cases, experience circulatory shock leading to permanent organ damage or even death. Hypotension is usually the result of low blood volume, which can be caused by sweating, not eating or drinking regularly or enough, or the effects of various drugs, including diazepam (Valium) and amitryptyline.

Heart and circulatory system diseases

Diseases of the heart and circulatory system caused by smoking, alcohol, and drugs such as cocaine include coronary heart disease. This term is used for a variety of conditions caused by an interrupted or reduced flow of blood to the heart resulting from a buildup of fatty deposits (atherosclerosis) in the coronary arteries, or the formation of a blood clot (thrombosis).

When the artery walls narrow as a result of atherosclerosis, the flow of blood to the heart muscle is reduced, so when the heart is under stress, during periods of rapid heartbeat, pain is experienced (angina). If a coronary artery blocks completely, a section of heart muscle will no longer be able to access oxygenated blood and will start to die—this is a heart attack (myocardial infarction). Other possible effects include cardiac arrhythmia, an abnormal heartbeat.

Peripheral vascular disease is a range of abnormal conditions of the vessels outside the heart, usually resulting in narrowing of arteries in the extremeties, particularly the legs and feet. If these vessels become blocked by clots, oxygen and nutrients may be prevented from reaching tissues, and the tissue will start to die. For example, blockage of an artery in the leg may lead to gangrene in the foot.

Drugs such as amphetamines can also be responsible for the formation of blood clots. A clot on the lungs is called a pulmonary embolism. Clots can occur when blood passing through the deepest veins flows so slowly that it forms a solid clot, known as deep-vein thrombosis (DVT). A stroke occurs when a blood clot blocks or breaks a blood vessel or artery, preventing blood flow to an area of the brain.

Although the effects occur in the lungs, pulmonary edema is usually due to cardiac failure; if a failing heart is unable to pump all the blood being returned to it, fluid leaks from the blood vessels into the air spaces (alveoli) of the lungs. Cardiomyopathy causes the heart to become enlarged and pump less strongly.

Drugs and their effect on the heart

Alcohol is known to have an effect on the heart, even at moderate levels of drinking. Chronic alcohol consumption can increase blood pressure. Cardiac arrhythmia is also commonly found during acute alcohol intoxication in people who otherwise have no cardiac problems. Cardiac patients may be even more sensitive to acute alcohol consumption.

The hearts of chronic alcohol users showed abnormally high internal pressures, which could not be compensated for by increasing forward blood flows. Ultrasound techniques have also shown that the hearts of chronic alcohol users cannot relax normally or their chambers fill properly with blood. Autopsies of such subjects have shown evidence of fibrosis—development of abnormal tissue—and scarring of the heart muscle.

Many heavy drinkers have a higher incidence of heart attacks, even in those without significant coronary disease, possibly through scarring of the coronary arteries or through blood clots forming spontaneously inside them. Alcoholic cardiomyopathy is a recognized direct toxic effect of excess alcohol consumption. Symptoms include weakness and fatigue, swollen neck veins, and swelling of the legs and feet—classic signs of heart failure. One study of a group of alcoholics with symptoms of heart failure found that those who abstained survived several years, while all those who continued drinking died.

Heavy alcohol consumption has been shown to cause rapid and irregular heartbeat. This irregularity and the impairment to the heart's pumping ability that alcohol has been shown to cause are two of the major causes of death following a heart attack. Alcohol may also interact negatively with medicines prescribed to treat heart diseases.

A stroke is caused by bleeding into the brain (area shown in red). Strokes are common among cocaine users because the drug sends the blood pressure so high that it can burst weak blood vessels.

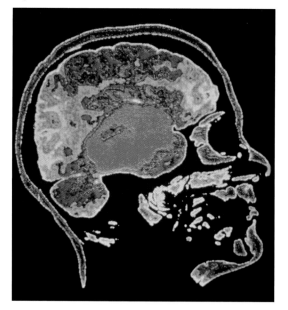

RISKS OF INJECTING

Injecting drug users risk contracting a number of conditions that do not affect other drug users. Infective endocarditis is an infection of the tissues of the heart, usually one of the heart valves. It is a progressive disease, characterized by frequent obstructions of blood vessels (embolisms) and severe heart valve deterioration, which can be fatal. The disease can be caused by using nonsterile needles or unusual methods of injection. Its symptoms include fevers of unknown origin, weight loss, heart murmurs, pneumonia, and blood cultures that test positive for candida, *Staphylococcus aureus* or *enteroccocus*, or gram-negative bacteria. Around 25 percent of cases of infective endocarditis are fatal, and major complications occur in up to 80 percent of patients. Groin injection can also lead to deep-vein thrombosis (the formation of blood clots).

Regular injection of drugs can also result in veins collapsing and scarring through overuse. They can also become blocked over time if drugs have been cut with insoluble substances or pills have been crushed for injection. There is no way at the present time to reverse the process. Skin abcesses can also form around the injection site if it is not cleaned before injecting. Dirty equipment can also cause the blood itself to become infected with septicemia (blood poisoning).

Pill fillers and other substances in cut street drugs often clump to form emboli in the pulmonary arterioles, leading to pulmonary hypertension. Amphetamine use can cause polyarteritis, an inflammation of the arteries, which can become necrotic and lead to tissue loss. This sometimes results in the blockage of blood vessels in the brain (cerebrovascular occlusion) and stroke.

Stimulant drugs

Stimulants such as cocaine and amphetamines generally result in increases in the blood pressure and heart rate, and can disturb the rhythm of the heartbeat. Amphetamines stimulate the production of epinephrine and norepinephrine in the body, which increases the heart rate and blood pressure, creating a risk of cardiac arrhythmia, and of heart attack in angina sufferers. Overdoses can lead to death from arrhythmia or pulmonary edema. Studies have found that amphetamines promote coagulation of the blood, which can lead to blood clot formation in the arteries, and subsequent stroke or heart attack.

Ecstasy (MDMA), which is related chemically to amphetamine, may trigger heart attacks, according to a case study. Ecstasy overdoses can also cause high blood pressure and cardiac arrhythmia, and the drug can reduce the pumping efficiency of the heart. Cases of stroke following use of the drug have been reported. Ecstasy is readily absorbed into the bloodstream, but once in the body it interferes with the ability to break down the drug. Consequently, additional doses can produce unexpectedly high levels in the blood, which could worsen the cardiovascular effects.

Cocaine has many medical side effects relating to the heart, including acute impairment of the blood supply to the heart and heart attacks, as well as hypertension, accelerated arteriosclerosis, ruptured aorta, cardiomyopathy, cardiac arrhythmia, and sudden death. The drug has two separate effects on the heart and vascular system: it causes an accumulation of catecholamines (such as epinephrine, norepinephrine, and dopamine), increasing their release from the brain and spinal cord, and blocks their reuptake at nerve endings. The result is a severe stimulation of the heart muscle and vascular smooth muscle, causing increases in heart rate, blood pressure, heart contractions, blood vessel constriction, and resistance of blood vessels to blood flow.

Cocaine also has an anesthetizing effect on cardiac tissue. It can prevent the movement of vital ions such as sodium and potassium, which are needed to provide the electrical stimulation that enables the heart muscle to contract. The result can be an abnormally slow heart rate or pumping failure. Tests have shown that inhalation through the nose can cause a significant reduction in coronary blood flow, or a sudden constriction of the blood vessels. Healthy patients exposed to chronic cocaine use have been found to develop acute cardiac dilation and heart failure, with symptoms clearing up if the user abstains from the drug.

Chronic cocaine use may also lead to a sudden rupture of the aorta, which is normally fatal. Most cocaine-related deaths, however, are from cardiac arrhythmia. In combination with alcohol, cocaine may be even more dangerous, metabolizing to coca-ethylene, which makes the combination of cocaine and alcohol considerably more lethal than either on its own. Studies have also shown that there is an association between the amount of cocaine taken and the risk of stroke, and long-term use of cocaine may on its own lead to coronary artery disease.

Other substances

Heroin and other opiates slow the rate of breathing, which can bring about respiratory failure and cardiac arrest. They also slow the heart rate and reduce blood pressure and may be linked to pulmonary edema. The most serious effects of heroin on the heart and vascular system result from one of the primary modes of use—injection—which can lead to infective endocarditis or deep vein thrombosis.

Glue and solvent sniffing, most often of butane lighter fuel or toluene-based glues, can disturb the rhythm of the heart and lead to sudden death. Cardiomyopathy is a rare effect.

Gangrene in this patient's right leg is a condition that can arise as a result of peripheral vascular disease. Smokers are at particular risk of losing a limb if a clot forms and restricts blood flow to the extremeties.

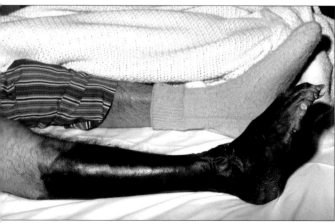

Anabolic steroids can affect cholesterol levels by lowering high-density lipoprotein (HDL) cholesterol, which protects the heart. They also cause small increases in blood pressure, and some studies suggest that users can develop a harmful enlargement of the heart that can persist even after use has stopped. Heart attacks and strokes have been reported in users of anabolic steroids, but more studies are needed to determine what the increased risk may be.

Smoking

Smoking is a major cause of heart attack, stroke, and peripheral vascular disease. It doubles the risk of heart disease and trebles the chances of dying before reaching retirement age. Smokers have a 70 percent greater risk of death from coronary heart disease than nonsmokers. Smoking is known to promote the formation of fatty deposits on artery walls by increasing blood cholesterol levels and reducing the rate of good HDL cholesterol compared to LDL (low-density lipoprotein) cholesterol. Smokers also have higher levels of fibrinogen, a protein that makes blood clot by clumping platelets together.

Smoking causes the heart rate to rise by as much as 30 percent during the first ten minutes. Nicotine raises blood pressure; blood vessels constrict, forcing the heart to work harder. The carbon monoxide in tobacco smoke reduces the blood's ability to carry oxygen. All of these effects make smokers vulnerable to a range of coronary heart diseases including heart attack, stroke (11 percent of all stroke deaths are thought to be smoking related), aneurysm (the ballooning and thinning of an artery wall), and peripheral vascular disease.

Marijuana can increase heart rate by up to 50 percent, and a link has been suggested between the drug and heart attacks in people with preexisting heart conditions. People over the age of 45 are five times more likely to have a heart attack in the hour after they smoke marijuana. Marijuana also contains many of the same chemicals found in cigarettes, which increase the risk of heart disease.

L. STEDMAN

SEE ALSO:
Alcoholism • Harm Reduction • Liver Diseases • Lung Diseases • Medical Care • Pregnancy and Fetal Addiction • Smoking

Hereditary and Genetic Factors

There is much debate about whether addiction to drugs or alcohol can be inherited. While it is unlikely that one specific gene is responsible, it is possible that there are a number of genetic influences on addiction.

It has long been observed that alcoholism seems to run in families. Research has shown that first-degree relatives (such as children or siblings) of an alcoholic are three to four times more likely to have an alcohol problem than those of nonalcoholics. Whether this tendency is inherited or is the result of being in an environment where alcohol is a constant presence, or a combination of both, is an ongoing area of research. If a genetic (inherited) link can be found, it may pave the way to identifying those who are at greatest risk of developing alcoholism or drug addiction and may lead to better treatment methods.

The risk of developing an addiction or substance use disorder (SUD) is not the same for everybody. Risk differences may be related to many factors, including individual characteristics (biochemical, physiological, psychological) and environmental influences, such as drug availability or the attitude of peers or family toward drug use. Genetic studies are being conducted to find out the causes of these differences, mainly focusing on genes but also taking into account environmental influences. Genes are the individual parts of the genetic code carried in DNA (deoxyribonucleic acid) and contain the program for the development and function of the organism. Variants of genes, called alleles, cause differences in the way these specifications are expressed, including those related to the risk for disorders.

Traits and phenotypes
Gregor Johann Mendel's success in discovering the laws of inheritance in the mid-1860s was to a large degree due to his selecting clearly defined traits (such as flower color) with distinct phenotypes (such as purple or white flowers). A phenotype is the way in which a gene is expressed physiologically, and can generally be observed. Mendel worked with relatively uncomplicated traits—the color and skin texture of peas—in determining the basic patterns of inherited traits and phenotypes. Genetic studies of substance use disorders are complicated by differences in the causes and symptoms of the disorder. In addition, different drugs are often used at the same time, which results in a large number of potential symptoms and drug combinations. To deal with such complexity, human genetics uses the idea of liability to a disorder.

The term *liability* was introduced to human genetics for traits that are not inherited (according to Mendel's laws) but nevertheless run in families. Liability was defined as the whole combination of circumstances that make a person more or less likely to develop a disease (that is, how vulnerable he or she is to a disease). This trait is quantitative, similar to that of weight or stature, but, unlike these directly measurable traits, is difficult to observe. Another example of an unobserved trait is intelligence, which is indirectly measured by the intelligence quotient, or IQ. People who have variations of liability that are above a certain point, called the threshold, are likely to be diagnosed with an SUD.

Multifactorial disorders
Since the differences in liability to substance use between different people are caused by many factors, it is classed among a group of disorders that are described as multifactorial, or complex. Factors include individual genetic differences, environmental factors, and possibly their interactions. The alleles of the genes influencing SUD liability in an individual determine the person's genetic predisposition to the disorder. Different alleles of these genes determine differences in the structure or the rate of metabolism of hormones, receptors, enzymes, or other proteins and, therefore, the biological systems that participate in drug-related processes. Genetic investigations of SUDs use a wide variety of methods that allow the study of all these systems, from the molecular level (gene structure and function) to complex physiological reactions of the nervous system and the brain, individual variations in personality and behavior, and family and social factors. In humans, these investigations can be subdivided into behavioral genetic and molecular genetic research. Behavioral

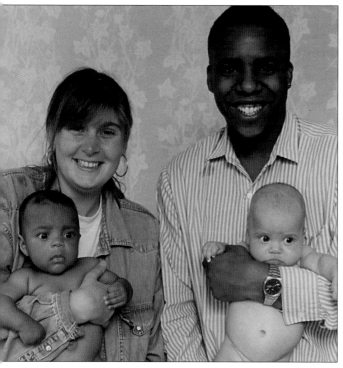

These fraternal twins show how variable genetic traits can be. Although they can have up to 50 percent of their genes in common, these children look markedly different, each having inherited different genes for skin color from their parents.

genetics has been used to conduct research in families, twins, and adopted children to estimate the contribution of genetic and nongenetic factors to individual variation in liability to alcoholism. Molecular genetic studies attempt to determine the areas of the genome (the complete set of genes an organism has) that are related to variation in liability, or test the role of particular genes in individual phenotypic differences.

Heritability of SUD liability

Heritability is a concept used to examine the relative contributions of genes and environment to variation in a specific trait. Genetic variation has been shown to play a substantial role in the diagnosis of the presence or absence of an SUD. Heritability, varying for different disorders, has been estimated to reach as high as 80 percent in both men and women. An adoption study in women showed a pattern of rela-

tionships between biological family background and SUD outcome similar to that in men, with strong associations between a SUD and antisocial behavior in the biological parents and drug abuse in their offspring. Parallel results from twin studies of alcoholism show heritability estimates reaching 70 percent in men and 60 percent in women. Adoption studies of alcoholism have shown that the risk for alcoholism in the offspring of alcoholics is higher than in the children of nonalcoholics, even when they are separated from their biological parents early in life.

Genetic components of variation in liability to alcohol and drug use disorders, substance use and smoking, as well as nicotine and alcohol dependence, have been shown to correlate, suggesting that alleles of the same genes contribute to variation in the risk for SUD in general. A biological background of alcohol problems predicted increased drug abuse in adoptees. However, there was no relationship found between the types of substances abused by the biological parent and by the adopted child.

Role of the environment

In determining the role of environment in differences in substance abuse liability, adoption research has identified several environmental factors, such as divorce or marital disharmony and psychiatric disturbance in the adoptive family, to be associated with increased drug abuse in adopted children. One twin-family study showed that an environmental factor of parental loss increases risk of alcoholism. Another example of influential environmental factors revealed by adoption studies is that siblings can have a substantial effect on adolescent alcohol use. Research suggests that people with an alcoholic sibling have about a 40 percent chance of becoming an alcoholic. There was also shown to be a significant correlation in alcohol use if nonrelated adopted siblings were the same sex and similar in age. The influence of religion within the family is another environmental variable that can protect against the risk for developing a substance use problem.

Behavioral genetic studies

Behavioral genetic studies have demonstrated that phenotypic variation in liability to substance use disorders is determined by variation in individual genotypes as well as by differences in environmental conditions. The two main methods used to estimate genetic and environmental components of phenotypic variation are twin and adoption studies.

The twin method is based on the differences between genetic similarity in the pairs of identical twins and fraternal (nonidentical) twins. Identical twins have exactly the same genes because they develop from the same zygote (fertilized egg). Any differences that arise within an identical twin pair result from environmental influences that are unique to each member of the pair, for example, if they are separated when young and grow up in different households. Their similarities arise from their identical genotypes (genetic sequences) and environmental factors that act on both twins in the same way (that is, if they grow up together). In contrast, the fraternal twins, developing from two zygotes, share on average only half of their genes in common. If substance use is influenced by genetics, then studies of identical twins will show that they both either use or do not use drugs, while pairs of fraternal twins will show more occurrences where one twin uses drugs and the other does not. The absence of differences in intrapair similarities between identical and fraternal twins would suggest that any phenotypic variation observed is caused by environmental factors.

Studies on the offspring of twins have showed how genetic differences are affected by environmental factors. Children of a substance-abusing identical or fraternal twin are at a high risk of using drugs themselves because of the environment in which they are being raised and the strong likelihood of inheriting genes associated with substance use. Children of a nonusing identical twin have a lower environmental risk than their cousins but share the same high genetic risk because their parents have identical genes. In contrast, the children of a nonusing fraternal twin of a substance abuser have a low environmental risk and only an intermediate genetic risk of becoming users.

Adoption studies are based on the fact that all similarities between adoptive parents and children result from a shared environment, whereas almost all similarity between biological parents and their adopted-away children is genetic. If genetic factors are involved, adopted children of alcoholics will be more likely to develop alcoholism as adults.

It should be noted that heritability of liability to an SUD may not be related to the causes of the disorder in an individual case, and may change with changes in the environmental conditions and the genetic pool of the population that may occur in time. A low heritability of a trait does not mean that genes have nothing to do with its development. In fact, it may indicate that the trait is under strict genetic control, so no genetic variation is allowed by natural selection.

It is important to know how inheritable liability to an SUD is because it indicates a possibility of finding genes that would explain this genetic contribution of phenotypic variation. It would also help determine any environmental factors that are capable of changing the liability phenotype.

It can be concluded that twin and adoption research provides convincing evidence that genetic variation contributes to individual differences in the risk for SUD, and, to a large degree, is shared in common between liabilities to addictions related to specific drugs. These genetic studies also suggest that environmental influences play an important role in liability variation.

Animal studies

Animal studies allow researchers to change both genes and environment at will. These studies include not only hybridization and selection experiments, but also studies of knockout and transgenic animals, which allow the effects of controlled gene inactivation (knockout) or the insertion of a gene (transgenic) to be observed.

A number of provisional markers and candidate genes are identified as being associated with various drug-related behaviors and reactions to drugs. Animal model data point to certain neurobiological systems in drug-related behaviors, confirm the results obtained in humans, and can serve as additional support for candidate genes. For instance, DRD2 (dopamine receptor D2) knockout mice (those with the inactivated DRD2 gene) have a total suppression of rewarding behavior with morphine but a normal response when food is used as a reward. The DRD4 knockout mice display elevated sensitivity to cocaine, methamphetamine, and alcohol, thus perhaps pointing at a possible component of common SUD liability. Most of this promising research, however, is still only provisional.

Molecular genetic studies

The observation that SUDs and associated traits seem to run in families suggests the existence of genetic polymorphisms (when a gene assumes several alleles among a population) contributing to variation in individual liability phenotypes. The two main general approaches applied in the search for these polymorphisms are linkage and association studies.

Linkage studies relate transmission of liability in families (for example, parent-offspring similarity for the presence or absence of an SUD) to the inheritance of genetic markers (variable sites in the DNA molecule whose position is known). Association studies try to discover the relationship between particular genes and the liability to the disorder. The genes are selected because of known information about their role in the nervous system and response to drugs obtained from other fields of study.

The majority of positive findings in SUD genetic research have been obtained using association methods. It should be noted that virtually all such findings have failed to be reproduced in some of the studies by other investigators. It is thus possible that some findings are positive by chance only. Nevertheless, many of the nonreplications have occurred in the samples from populations different from those in which an association was found originally. This leaves open the possibility of differences between populations, related to the genetic structure of the population (for example, differences in the frequencies of relevant genotypes), environmental conditions, and interactions between them. For instance, the aldehyde dehydrogenase (ALDH2) gene contributes to variation in the risk for alcoholism in East Asians. This gene encodes an enzyme that helps metabolize alcohol. An allele of the ALDH2 gene that causes a very low activity of the enzyme prevents the development of alcoholism in a large proportion of the East Asian population, since it causes a very unpleasant flushing sensation. This allele, however, does not influence this risk in other populations where it is absent.

Much interest has been attracted to genes related to the dopamine system. Dopamine is one of the chemicals used by the nervous system for transmitting signals between nerve cells. Dopamine plays a role in the sensation of pleasure, generally called "reward," including that obtained with drugs. The

Transgenic mice are being used to determine whether certain genes have an influence on addictive behavior.

reward pathways for different drugs, to a large degree, share the same structures of the brain. Some studies have found an association between the genes involved in the dopamine system and SUD liability (for instance, DRD2, DRD4, and DRD5 genes), while others failed to demonstrate any association.

There is growing evidence about the contribution of nondopamine mechanisms and interactions between them that could be critically important both in natural and drug-related reward as well as in other components of drug response. These mechanisms are related to neurotransmitters, such as serotonin, GABA, glutamate, and other numerous potential targets. This evidence widens the range of genes that may be influencing variations in SUD liability. Recent data also show gene-environment interaction, that is, when the relationship between a gene and SUD liability may differ (become stronger or weaker) depending on the environmental conditions.

It is important to note that any gene related to the risk for SUD cannot be called an "SUD gene." Even if there were a gene strongly related to SUD liability, its function has nothing to do with SUD, which develops as a result of voluntary drug use. Variation in such a gene would most likely be related to the normal genetic and behavioral variation in the population. Genetic data, moreover, indicate that the genetic contribution in SUD liability variation is due to a large number of genes, each playing a small role.

M. VANYUKOV

SEE ALSO:

Biopsychosocial Theory of Addiction • Causes of Addiction, Biological • Research, Medical

Heroin Addiction Treatment

Heroin is one of the most difficult drugs to give up. Withdrawal can trigger many unpleasant physical symptoms that make the addict reluctant to try to overcome addiction. A combination of treatments can provide the best outcome.

Heroin addiction may seem a modern problem, but opium has been abused for thousands of years. The first opium harvest was recorded as long ago as the seventh century BCE in Assyria, and opium poppies were reported to be widely cultivated throughout neolithic Europe. Heroin is an artificial derivative of morphine, which is derived from opium, and it was first synthesized in 1897. Heroin is more fat-soluble than morphine, enabling it to pass easily through the membranes that surround the brain. Consequently, the drug induces a rapid high, which is one of the qualities that makes heroin extremely addictive.

Problems resulting from opiate addiction have been evident for the past 300 years. The British writer Thomas de Quincey (1785–1859), in his book *The Confessions of an English Opium Eater*, eloquently discussed the difficulties of stopping opiates, describing his addiction as if being bound by heavy chains. Opium was widely used as an analgesic during the U.S. Civil War, producing thousands of addicts, and its unrestricted sale during the nineteenth century led to serious social problems in both the United States and the United Kingdom. Although legislation at the beginning of the twentieth century reduced the availability of opiates to the general public, heroin addiction has remained a problem ever since. Lifetime prevalence rates for heroin use average 1 percent in Western countries but increase to 4 to 6 percent in young people (aged 18 to 30) in larger cities within the United States, Europe, and Australia.

Not all individuals who use heroin become dependent on it. Among those who use heroin regularly, around 10 percent stop within one year and another 2 to 3 percent become abstinent in each subsequent year. In fact, 10-year follow-up studies show that approximately 30 percent of heroin users become abstinent. For the remaining 70 percent,

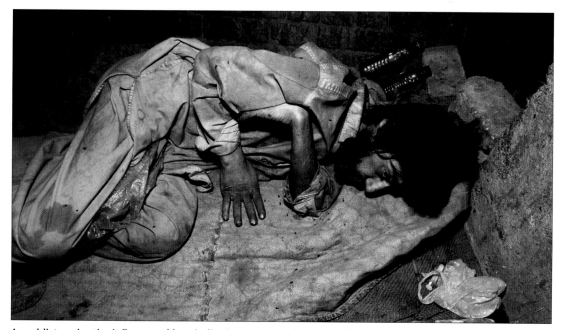

An addict under the influence of heroin lies in a street in Quetta, Pakistan. Facilities for treating addicts in developing countries are extremely basic and usually involve unmedicated withdrawal.

outcomes include ongoing active drug use, imprisonment, or death. Mortality rates are typically 1 to 2 percent per year. In addition, approximately one-third of individuals who undergo treatment are able to reduce associated drug-related harms, while the remaining two-thirds continue to experience ongoing negative consequences.

The diagnosis of heroin addiction

Before an individual enters treatment, he or she is formally assessed against the criteria set out for a diagnosis of substance dependence. In the United States, these criteria are laid down in the *Diagnostic and Statistical Manual of Mental Disorders* of the American Psychiatric Association (DSM-IV, 1994). The symptoms presented by a heroin user determine the level of use and whether it is classed as abuse, harmful use, or dependence. Chief among these symptoms are the development of tolerance, withdrawal effects, and physical and psychological dependence on the drug. Frequent heroin use leads to the development of physical dependence, in which the user experiences tolerance (needing greater amounts of heroin to achieve the same effect) or withdrawal symptoms (severe flulike symptoms and agitation) if heroin use is ceased.

A person is also addicted to heroin when he or she becomes psychologically dependent on the drug. Psychological dependence occurs when the user begins to experience a persistent overwhelming urge to use heroin, even at the expense of other activities. This difficulty in controlling use substantially influences an individual's ability to function in society. An addict may abandon important social, occupational, or recreational activities in the pursuit of further heroin use, even though he or she is aware that continued use is causing significant physical, psychological, and social harm. Addicts find it difficult to cut down use and experience significant cravings, especially in situations or places where they previously used heroin. Even if an addict does manage to stop using heroin, the cravings become more intense, and the majority of users return to use within several weeks. This cycle of recurrent drug use makes heroin addiction a chronic relapsing condition.

Physical dependence on heroin is serious and is usually associated with severe morbidity and a high risk of death. Street heroin is often a mixture of pure

heroin and other substances, such as talc, starch, baking powder, glucose, or quinine. The additives can be harmful, contributing to such complications as collapsed veins, tetanus, abscesses, and damage to the heart, lungs, liver, and brain. Heavy heroin use also frequently results in poor nutrition because the individual focuses more on obtaining heroin than following a healthy lifestyle. Intravenous heroin is also associated with an increased risk of infection with blood-borne viruses (for example, hepatitis B, hepatitis C, and HIV) through the sharing of needles with other intravenous drug users.

The high risk of death among heroin users is also related to the illicit nature of the addiction. Individuals are unaware of the purity of the heroin they have been sold, so are at risk of overdosing. When taken in overdose, the heroin user becomes unconscious and stops breathing. Unless the overdose is treated promptly with an opiate antagonist (which blocks heroin's effects), the individual will die from asphyxiation.

In addition to the physical complications, heroin addiction leads to significant psychosocial problems for the affected individual. School, work, and family life are frequently disrupted, and significant legal and financial problems can arise. Heroin addiction can also often have an impact more broadly than on the individual alone, affecting friends, families, the local community, and society in general. Family conflict is common, especially when demands are made on parents by their heroin-addicted adolescent for money, or when the young person engages in a life of crime, violence, or prostitution to support a heroin habit. Bereavement and grief are also common within these families, especially given the high mortality rates among heroin users.

Problems of heroin withdrawal

When an individual uses heroin regularly, tolerance to the drug develops. Tolerance indicates that the body is adapting to the acute effects of the drug, so that higher doses are needed to achieve the same effect. When heroin is not available, the body must readjust to functioning without it. This readjustment is called withdrawal and lasts several days to weeks. Withdrawal symptoms include watery eyes and a runny nose, sneezing, yawning, sweating, agitation, irritability, gooseflesh, hot and cold flashes, loss of

COMMON SYMPTOMS IN HEROIN WITHDRAWAL	
Time since heroin use	Symptoms
Within 12 hours	Sweating
	Sniffling nose
	Sneezing
	Watery eyes
	Yawning
Within 24 hours	Gooseflesh
	Hot and cold flashes
	Loss of appetite
	Agitation, anxiety, restlessness
2 weeks to 1 month	Most symptoms have subsided except insomnia, fatigue, and agitation. Cravings for heroin may still persist.

appetite, abdominal cramps, diarrhea, nausea and vomiting, aches and pains (for example, in the back or calf muscles), headache, insomnia, and fatigue. Cravings and urges to use heroin are particularly strong and make withdrawal especially difficult (*see* table, above).

Not all heroin users experience the full complement of these symptoms. Symptom severity and the length of the withdrawal experience can vary between individuals. Factors that influence the severity of withdrawal symptoms include how the person feels about withdrawing from heroin (that is, what he or she expects to experience in withdrawal), how much heroin has been used, and how long he or she has been using heroin regularly. Poor general health or nutritional state can also make the withdrawal experience more difficult, as can an unpleasant or unstable surrounding environment, especially when trying to abstain from further use.

Withdrawal symptoms, especially the physical symptoms, usually peak within two to four days and settle by five to seven days, but individuals may continue to experience problems with sleep, anxiety, and cravings for several weeks or months. High rates of relapse remain prominent during this time, with approximately 70 percent using heroin within six weeks of withdrawal, although not all relapse to dependent use. Heroin withdrawal is rarely fatal, though individuals may experience considerable distress with associated severe complications, such as major depression or suicidal behavior.

Problems of relapse

Although a person can overcome the physical aspects of heroin dependence (that is, following a successful withdrawal), it is extremely difficult for an individual to remain abstinent from heroin in the longer term. The individual may frequently relapse and may need to undergo repeated attempts to reduce his or her heroin use. Each time this happens, the addict can learn something new about himself and his ability to cope without the drug.

Types of treatment available for heroin addiction

There are a number of different types of treatment used for heroin addiction. These include self-help, withdrawal treatment, individual and group counseling, outreach, peer support, psychotherapy, and pharmacotherapy. Matching the individual with the most appropriate treatment intervention is very important. Availability and ease of access to various treatment methods also influences treatment choice. Choosing the most appropriate treatment method requires an assessment of the specific goals that the heroin addicted individual has in mind, as well as an assessment of the degree to which the person is physically dependent on heroin. The latter indicates whether withdrawal treatment or whether maintenance pharmacotherapy should be considered.

Self-help programs

Self-help programs for heroin addiction include Narcotics Anonymous, among others. Most of these programs are based on the Alcoholics Anonymous model and focus on abstinence from heroin as the primary goal. These programs are voluntary and provide regular and informal support to addicted individuals, with meetings arranged in a number of public places. They provide an opportunity for indi-

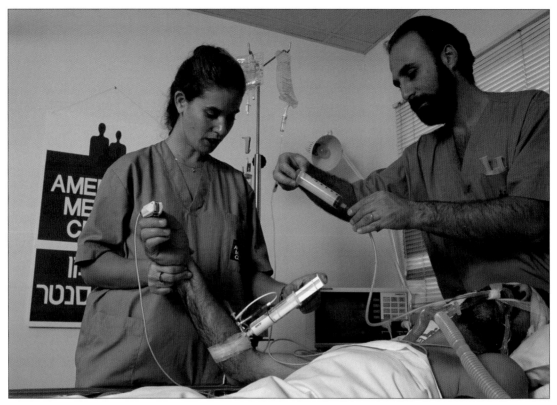

A heroin addict undergoing treatment is given naltrexone, an opioid antagonist, which blocks the action of opiates in the brain. Naltrexone is a long-acting medication that does not produce any pleasurable effects. It is sometimes given in place of methadone because it does not cause dependence.

viduals to share their experiences as drug users, reflecting on their lives and the consequences they have experienced as a result of their drug use. The strength of self-help programs is thought to lie in the support provided to members through the regularity of meetings, routines followed, and anonymity of individuals attending. Research into the effectiveness of self-help programs is limited but shows that although there is a high drop-out rate in the preliminary stages, for those who persist with the program, regular weekly participation helps maintain abstinence. Self-help programs also beneficial when used in combination with other treatment methods.

Withdrawal treatment and detoxification
Some individuals undergo withdrawal from heroin without assistance; however, others prefer the support of treatment services. Treatment services

assist individuals to complete heroin withdrawal safely and with minimal discomfort. A service may be provided in inpatient, outpatient, or home-based environments. Treatments can be classified as medicated or unmedicated. Unmedicated withdrawal, or "cold turkey," relies on providing a supportive calm environment to ease symptoms. Medicated heroin withdrawal may be divided into several different types, and not all are available in every country. They include symptomatic medications, for example, drugs that reduce the physical withdrawal symptoms, such as antinausea drugs, antidiarrheal agents, medications for musculoskeletal pains, and clonidine. Other medicated treatments include gradually reducing doses of prescribed opiates (such as methadone or buprenorphine), or the use of opiate antagonists such as naltrexone to precipitate and accelerate the withdrawal episode. Withdrawal treatment for heroin addiction rarely results in long-term abstinence from the drug, and hence is not appropriate as a solitary treatment. Instead, it helps ease withdrawal and provides a break from the adverse physical, psychological, and social harms related to heroin use. Interventions for heroin addiction that are more appropriate in the longer term include counseling and residential rehabilitation.

Maintenance pharmacotherapy

Maintenance or substitution pharmacotherapy is the provision of continuing opiate medication to prevent relapse to heroin use. The underlying rationale for this treatment is that it replaces illicit, erratic heroin use with a prescribed, legal drug, thereby enabling the individual to gain stability in his or her life and experience the associated improvements in physical health, relationships, and emotional well-being. Maintenance also removes the need to engage in criminal behavior to support the heroin habit. The prescribed medication is typically an oral therapy, so that addicted individuals do not need to continue their injecting behavior, thus reducing associated risks. The most well-known maintenance pharmacotherapy for heroin addiction is methadone, but the much safer opioid buprenorphine is offered in some countries as an alternative substitution medication.

Behavior-change interventions

Behavior-change interventions aim to provide individuals with the capacity to change their patterns of drug-related behavior and to maintain these changes over time. For example, individuals may be taught how to cope with distress or other unpleasant emotions, or may learn new social skills. These interventions also include learning to reduce the risk of relapse and deal more effectively with cravings or urges to use heroin. There are a number of behavior-change interventions for heroin addiction, including individual or group counseling, relapse prevention training, stress management, social-skills training, cognitive behavior therapy, and therapeutic communities.

Therapeutic communities are based on long-term residential treatment. Individual programs differ, but they are generally highly structured and have specific rules. The emphasis is on self-help, with the participants themselves acting as the main agents for change. It is important to note that length of time in treatment is a significant predictor of outcome. Because long-lasting behavior change is the aim, residential stays as long as a year or more might be necessary. Therapeutic communities are often located in areas where external influences are limited, for example, in rural settings.

Various psychotherapies, including psychoanalysis and psychodynamic psychotherapy, have been used to assist individuals to change long-standing patterns of heroin addiction. These interventions are not routinely offered within drug treatment settings, but they are indicated in the management of some individuals, such as those with long-standing psychiatric or behavioral disorders.

Outreach

Outreach intervention aims to access hidden populations of heroin-dependent individuals uncovered through community-based street work. The objectives of individual outreach programs differ across services, but in general, the aim is to actively seek out a target group of heroin users and engage them in such a way as to give them the opportunity to access treatment or other assistance (for example, with health-related matters, finances, or accommodation). Contact may occur on the street or other public places, or where the heroin user lives.

Importance of the therapeutic relationship

It is important to bear in mind that whatever the treatment method, a critical factor in the treatment of heroin-addicted individuals is the therapeutic relationship between the individual seeking help and the person providing support or treatment. In fact, in many circumstances, a genuine, supportive, and empathetic therapeutic relationship is more important in delivering successful outcomes than the specific intervention offered.

Y. BONOMO, D. I. LUBMAN

SEE ALSO:
Addictive Behavior • Cognitive Behavior Therapy • Cold Turkey • Craving • Detoxification • Diagnosing Substance Abuse • Drug Use, Life Patterns • Harm Reduction • Needle Exchange Programs • Overdose • Relapse • Treatment • Withdrawal

Hotlines

Hotlines provide an invaluable service for people who have problems with drugs or who need information about how to find help for their loved ones. Hotlines have the advantage over other health services of being anonymous, confidential, and accessible.

There are many subjects that people find hard to talk about face-to-face with a doctor or a counselor. Individuals may feel embarrassed or may be concerned that there might be breaches of confidentiality, especially where a young person is concerned. Appointments are usually necessary to see health professionals, and invariably there is a delay in accessing services. Often, general help and advice is all that is needed, but locating the right kind of information can be difficult. To help deal with these problems, there are special telephone services offering free, confidential advice and information that can direct people to more specialized help, sometimes on a 24-hour basis.

Accessibility can be particularly important because problems seem to be magnified at night, when no other help is immediately available. These services give basic information about drugs, or they can help locate local drug-treatment services. There are also hotlines or helplines for parents who have special concerns, and other services that specialize in legal advice.

Drug-related hotlines are sometimes run by government agencies or, more often, by charities and voluntary agencies. One of the most famous hotlines in the United States, 800-Cocaine, was started by Mark Gold, a physician, and took its first call on 6 May 1983. At the time, cocaine had a relatively benign image both in the media and popular culture and in medical circles. Gold observed, however, that increasing numbers of people were coming to see him with cocaine problems. Once the hotline was set up, thousands of people phoned in with stories about problematic cocaine use, many of them middle- and upper-class users who would not have dreamed of going to a drug-treatment agency.

In the United Kingdom, the government runs a telephone hotline called Talk to Frank. Originally called the National Drugs Helpline, it was renamed to be more user friendly. The charity Release runs both a legal advice line and a special line for those

DRUG-RELATED HOTLINES

- National Drug and Alcohol Treatment Routing Service: 1-800-662-HELP (4357)
- Narcotics Anonymous World Services: (818) 773-9999
- Al-Anon/Alateen Family Group Headquarters: 1-800-344-2666 or 1-888-425-2666
- The Alcohol Hotline: 1-800-ALCOHOL
- Marijuana Anonymous: 1-800-766-6779
- National AIDS Hotline: 1-800-232-4636
- Substance Abuse and Mental Health Services Administration (SAMHSA): 800-SAY-NOTO

with heroin problems. Hotlines run by the police or other enforcement agencies have been set up to enable individuals to inform the police about illegal activities, the location of premises where drugs are sold, or the names of dealers. The police in London have run a campaign called Rat on a Rat that encourages confidential calls about drug dealers. The U.S. Drug Enforcement Administration runs a number of hotlines for information about drug-smuggling activities.

Hotlines no longer refer just to telephones. Agencies and organizations can answer queries via Web sites and e-mail. The Samaritans found that contacts from young men increased substantially when they introduced an e-mail service. This type of service is valuable for those who feel inhibited about talking to an actual person. Help via text messaging on cell phones is a possible next step.

H. SHAPIRO

SEE ALSO:
Alcoholics Anonymous • Narcotics Anonymous • Support Groups

Intervention

Intervention to make an individual accept that he or she needs help with an addiction is often a method of last resort. Professional help is required to ensure that the process is carried out safely and effectively for all concerned.

Vernon Johnson first experimented with the intervention technique in the early 1960s. The technique, known as "The Johnson Model," which has been successful with drug and alcohol abusers, has seen little change over the years. Johnson believed that forceful confrontation is necessary in order to penetrate the barriers of denial. The most significant development with the process is the recognition that intervention is applicable to a broader range of issues and environments than alcohol and drug abuse. As the application of interventions has increased, some have made refinements to the original techniques.

Intervention may be employed for any self-destructive behavior, such as alcohol or drug abuse, eating disorders, gambling, computer addiction, and even with a senior citizen who is no longer able to appropriately care for himself independently. Done correctly, an intervention is carried out with respect and care, and does not pass judgment.

Intervention should not be the first response to problematic situations. Other avenues of help should be explored and attempted first. These include making a direct request of the person to seek help. The intervention is a final effort to save an individual from self-destruction.

The intervention process

Everyone who is meaningful to the individual is a candidate for inclusion in the intervention process. However, intervention may be undertaken with as few people as the individual and one other person. Elderly people or others with delicate health issues may be excluded to minimize the effects of potential stress upon them. Children can be powerful members of the intervention team. If managed appropriately, children's participation can be very beneficial to them as well as to the dysfunctional individual.

An intervention is very methodic in its structure. It begins when a family member, friend, or other significant person deems that the matter has reached a breaking point and other efforts have failed to help the person change his or her behavior. A professional experienced in intervention is consulted. The professional helps in determining the people involved, the location, and other details. These are delicate matters and should not be undertaken without the advice of someone suitably qualified. Because each family structure and situation is different, the scope and approach to the intervention will vary accordingly.

It is not uncommon for friends and family to be initially apprehensive and confused about taking this step. Because no one can predict with certainty how the person will react, family and friends may fear that the person will be angry with them. The goal of the initial meeting with the intervention professional is to prepare the group for a more cohesive and focused event. Participants are educated about the loved one's dysfunction, identify others who should be involved in the intervention, explore treatment options, and plan what will be said at the intervention. This process often involves several meetings, usually over a brief period of one to two weeks. The dysfunctional individual is not aware of these meetings.

At the intervention, the group gathers at an agreed location, which may be the individual's home, place of employment, church, or other appropriate venue. As a group they approach the person. The professional leader is present to ensure that the process unfolds in a safe and orderly manner. The group explains its concerns to the individual, including how the dysfunction has affected each person and the type of relationship each would like to have with him or her in the future. Sharing and expressing these thoughts and feelings gives purpose to the reopening of old wounds and allows family and friends to receive the support needed to resolve their hurt and anger. The ultimate goal of this step is to ask the addict to accept help now; arrangements for care have already been made. Hopefully, after hearing all that is said by those present, the individual realizes she can no longer hide her problem, nor wishes to, and finally accepts help.

An employer may also initiate an intervention. Perhaps a key employee develops one of the self-destructive habits listed above, for example, alcohol abuse, and it is interfering with her ability to perform to expectations. It can be very costly to terminate a key employee. Perhaps she is a valued employee, one who has been with the company for a long time, or even a friend. In these situations it is far better to correct the problem and keep the employee.

When performing an intervention in the workplace, the same principles apply as for family interventions. It is vital that the intervention is done properly. The employer must act only within the confines of the law and professional ethics, and with respect. To ensure this, an experienced professional should be consulted. An intervention should not be delayed once a decision has been made for its implementation. Executive interventions bring the unique considerations of legal implications, potential public relations issues, disclosure issues, and return-to-work matters.

Other types of interventions

In addition to the classic interventions discussed above, interventions may also take one of three other orientations, or be a mixture of these strategies. The first is a simple intervention, which may be little more than an individual who matters to the dysfunctional person making a request that the behavior change. This should always be the first step. Often, it is enough to set change in motion.

On occasion, an intervention may result from a crisis situation in which a person is in immediate danger to himself or others. In this case, the objective is to calm the crisis and create safety for all involved. Stabilized circumstances can often create an opportunity to convince the individual to accept help.

The final option is a family system intervention. This intervention focuses on changing the behavior of family members, whose actions may promote dysfunction. The family members maintain their changed behavior regardless of whether the person agrees to treatment. By doing so, the family may have a tremendous influence over the dysfunctional person.

Once the intervention has been completed, it is anticipated that the individual will accept treatment for his dysfunction. As part of the preparation process, a treatment program should already have been identified and arrangements made for immediate admission upon the patient's acceptance. The choice of treatment depends on the type of dysfunction, the current severity of the dysfunction, and many other criteria. In most cases, the initial treatment occurs in an inpatient setting.

If the individual refuses to enter treatment, there are usually established consequences that go into effect. His employment may be terminated, his spouse may separate from him, and other family support may be withdrawn until the individual agrees to get help. These consequences are not designed to punish the individual for his dysfunctional behavior but rather to give the family and friends control over their own responses instead of trying to control the individual's behavior. This type of tough love approach is not always part of the intervention, but it is typically recommended.

In the early 1980s, William Miller developed a theory of Motivational Interviewing. He challenged the viewpoint that denial was an inherent part of dysfunctional behavior. Instead, he proposed that it was the confrontational techniques of intervention that elicited the reaction of denial. Miller's approach focuses on the desire or willingness of the client to change, based on the stages of change as defined by Prochaska and DiClemente in 1982. The identification of the individual's readiness to change prescribes the counselor's course of action. The main point of Motivational Interviewing is that the professional should meet the client at his stage of readiness, not force the client into accepting something he is not ready for or interested in receiving. This approach is based on the philosophy that motivation for change occurs when a person perceives a discrepancy between where he is and where he wants to be.

Generally, other methods of intervention are rooted to one of the approaches described above. Regardless of the method, the identified patient is always in charge of his or her own motivation. As such, some patients will accept treatment as a result of an intervention and be successful in their recovery. Others will spontaneously improve without professional help. Still others will never accept any type of intervention and will remain the victim of their dysfunction.

P. L. TORCHIA

SEE ALSO:

Counseling • Employee Assistance Programs • Family Therapy • Treatment

Jellinek Classification

There have been many attempts to define alcoholism since the concept was first recognized. One of the most influential figures in the field of alcohol addiction was E. M. Jellinek, whose classification of alcoholic types is still in use.

Elvin Morton Jellinek (1890–1963), a cofounder of the Center of Alcohol Studies at Yale University in 1943 (now housed at Rutgers University in New Jersey), has had a profound influence on modern conceptualizations and understandings of alcohol abuse and alcoholism. He was a central figure, especially throughout the 1940s and 1950s, in the establishment of a scientific approach to the study of alcohol problems.

Early attempts to classify alcoholism

The classification of alcoholism did not receive systematic attention from professionals until the 1800s. The German physician Carl von Bruhl-Cramer wrote about the alcoholic's dipsomania, or drink-seeking compulsion, in 1819. In 1845 the French psychiatrist Jean Esquirol described drunkenness within a psychiatric context. The first use of the term *alcoholism* is attributed to the Swedish physician Magnus Huss in 1849. During the following 50 years, these efforts at classification continued, with particular attention to inebriety, dipsomania, and dependence as disease processes.

In the first half of the 1900s, most of the writings on classification focused on two constructs: addiction and dependence (particularly physical, as opposed to psychological, dependence). Much less attention was placed on other potentially important aspects of alcohol misuse, including its psychological, medical, and social consequences. A shift from this predominating focus on the physical aspects of addiction and dependence did not emerge until the mid-1950s, during which time Jellinek was developing his classification system for alcohol-use disorders.

Jellinek's concept of alcoholism

Jellinek's conceptualization of alcoholism is presented in his classic text, *The Disease Concept of Alcoholism*, which was published in 1960. As a starting point, Jellinek defined alcoholism as "any use of alcoholic beverages that causes any damage to the individual or society or both." The descent into

E. M. Jellinek's work on defining types of alcoholics was key to the establishment of the disease theory of addiction, which dominated the view of substance abuse disorders for many years.

alcoholism could be characterized by four stages. In the presymptomatic stage there are no problems in controlling alcohol use. This is followed by an early warning stage, during which the drinker suffers drunken episodes and blackouts, and the crucial stage, in which the drinker increasingly fails to control the urge to drink. The final chronic stage involves lengthy drinking binges accompanied by increasing mental and physical problems. Jellinek then proceeded to propose multiple "types" or "species" of alcoholism, each identified by a Greek letter to avoid the use of labels that might be controversial or that could have negative repercussions for alcohol misusers. Jellinek's types of alcoholism were called alpha, beta, gamma, delta, and epsilon.

Alpha alcoholism was proposed to represent excessive drinking for purely psychological reasons, particularly to relieve bodily or emotional pain. This drinking style, while viewed negatively by society as a whole, does not lead to "loss of control" drinking or to an "inability to abstain," both of which are described below. Physical dependence on alcoholism does not occur in alpha alcoholism, although psychological dependence is typically evident. The usual consequences associated with this type of alcoholism are impaired relationships with family and friends, work problems (including absenteeism), and nutritional deficiencies. Jellinek did not view alpha alcoholism as an illness in the traditional sense of the term, nor did he believe that it necessarily would lead to other types of alcoholism.

Beta alcoholism entails heavy drinking that results in damage to physical health, such as abnormal or degenerative nervous conditions, stomach disorders, or liver problems. Such consequences may occur, Jellinek thought, in the absence of either physical or psychological dependence on alcohol. Beta alcoholism, for example, might emerge from heavy drinking that occurs in a social group or society where heavy drinking is the cultural norm, and especially when the social group has poor nutrition. Thus, beta alcoholism is mostly associated with physical health consequences.

Gamma alcoholism was proposed to describe that species of alcoholism in which tolerance, physical dependence, and loss of control over drinking are evident. Loss of control over drinking is demonsrated by a situation in which the individual, once drinking, appears unable to restrain or end his or her consumption during that drinking episode. Among gamma alcoholics, there is a clear progression from psychological to physical dependence.

Gamma alcoholism is the type of alcoholism most often thought of when people refer to alcoholism. Further, gamma alcoholism is associated with the most serious kinds of drinking consequences, including physical, social, and psychological impairments. It is the predominant form of alcoholism in most Western societies.

Delta alcoholism, Jellinek's fourth species, is similar to gamma alcoholism, with one important distinction. Delta alcoholics, unlike gamma alcoholics, rarely, if ever, have periods of abstinence from alcohol—even for just a day or two. In this regard, delta alcoholism is characterized not so much by loss of control over drinking, but instead by an inability to abstain from alcohol. If the delta alcoholic tries to abstain, he or she experiences severe withdrawal symptoms.

The last species proposed by Jellinek was epsilon alcoholism, or bout drinking, which previously was called dipsomania. Epsilon alcoholics engage in what might be called periodic alcoholism. As such, they have occasional periods of alcoholic drinking, during which serious negative consequences often result. Jellinek identified epsilon alcoholism as the least understood species of alcoholism.

Jellinek did not suggest that his five species of alcoholism were fully inclusive. In fact, he felt certain that other species of alcoholism existed, and that with further study they would be identified and classified.

New approaches to classifying alcohol use disorders
In the years since Jellinek's landmark text, the predominant focus on classifying alcohol misuse has been on two broad categories: alcohol dependence and alcohol abuse. The best examples of this approach to classification are the fourth edition of the *Diagnostic and Statistical Manual of Mental Disorders* (DSM-IV; American Psychiatric Association, 1994) and the tenth revision of the *International Classification of Diseases and Related Health Problems* (ICD-10; WHO, 1992). A diagnosis of alcohol dependence within these similar systems is made when several indications are evident. Examples include tolerance to alcohol, withdrawal symptomatology, impaired control over drinking, continued drinking despite ongoing negative consequences, and compulsive use of alcohol. The less severe diagnosis of alcohol abuse (called harmful use of alcohol in the IDC system) is made when the person exhibits a pattern of drinking that causes impairment to physical or mental health. However, the symptoms or consequences experienced do not meet the criteria established for a diagnosis of alcohol dependence.

G. J. CONNORS

SEE ALSO:
Alcoholism • Binge Drinking • Diagnosing Substance Abuse • Disease Theory of Addiction

Liver Diseases

The liver plays an important role in the metabolism of drugs. Even though it processes toxic substances as part of its function, the liver can be damaged by alcohol and other drugs that interfere with its ability to eliminate them.

The liver is the largest organ inside the body and performs a large number of tasks that impact all the systems in the body. As a consequence, liver disease or impairment can have widespread effects on virtually all other organs and systems. The major functions that the liver performs are:

- storage of vitamins, sugars, fats, and other nutrients from food
- building chemicals that the body needs to stay healthy
- breaking down harmful substances, such as alcohol and other toxic chemicals
- removing waste products from the blood
- providing sufficient quantities of vital chemicals needed for other system functions.

Liver metabolism

The body is continually exposed to toxic substances that are derived from the environment. The body can also produce toxic substances during normal metabolism or as a result of disease. Some of these substances are hormones and drugs that, once their function or functions are performed, must be removed from the body to avoid toxicity. The liver is the most important organ involved in the removal of these harmful substances, and thus it is necessary for survival.

The liver transforms toxins into more water-soluble molecules that can be easily excreted into the bile or urine. For most substances, their metabolism results in the overall loss of their activity. However, in some cases, liver metabolism causes the activation of a substance. For example, some drugs require hepatic (liver) activation to work properly. With other substances, hepatic metabolism can result in by-products that are toxic or carcinogenic and thus are harmful.

The metabolism, or biotransformation, of toxic substances occurs in two stages:

Phase I: Functional reactions. In the first phase a drug can undergo oxidation, reduction, or hydrolysis. These reactions transform the substance into a metabolite. Through such reactions, the drug or substance is transformed into a more water soluble molecule that is easy to eliminate in urine.

Oxidation occurs primarily through a hepatic enzyme group known as the cytochrome P450 enzymes. The system is genetically influenced—some people lack certain types of these enzymes—and in addition can be stimulated or inhibited by many factors, including drugs and chemical poisons. As a result, oxidation of chemicals can vary widely from one person to the next, affecting the metabolism of drugs, with important clinical consequences. For example, chronic exposure to substances that can stimulate cytochrome P450, such as alcohol, will increase the system's ability to biotransform other drugs. As a consequence, an individual may have to take a higher dosage for the drug to work. Chronic alcoholics typically require higher doses of sedatives

The hepatitis B virus, seen here (right) as a cluster of round particles attacking a liver cell, causes a highly infectious disease that can lead to a number of conditions affecting the functioning of the liver. The virus can remain in the body and lead to liver cancer and cirrhosis.

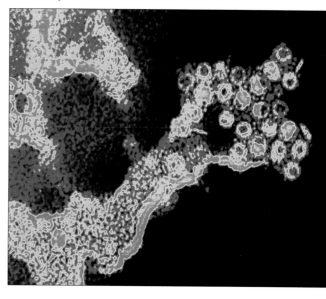

because their chronic exposure to ethanol has increased their ability to biotransform medication. In contrast, drugs that inhibit cytochrome P450 activity will reduce the liver's ability to biotransform medications. As a result, the individual must take lower doses in order to avoid a buildup of drugs that may be toxic.

Reduction is not as common as oxidation. The most important reaction is the reduction of nitro groups ($-NO_2$), for example, in the breakdown of benzodiazepines into amines ($-NH_2$). Alcohol is usually broken down by dehydrogenase reactions, in which hydrogen atoms are lost, first to produce acetaldehyde and then acetic acid.

Phase I prepares the substance for the second phase of reactions, which are the conjugation with other water-soluble molecules.

Phase II: Conjugation reactions. During this phase, one or more polar molecules are added to the drug or to its metabolites to transform them into more soluble molecules so they can be excreted. (A polar molecule has an unbalanced distribution of electrical charge. When bonded with another polar molecule, it will form a solution.) The polar substrates added to the drug molecule are also produced by the body (for example, glucuronic acid, sulfate, glycime, and glutathione). This process occurs in the smooth endoplasmatic reticulum within liver cells, and the most important substance involved in this process is glutathione. Glutathione is a peptide that is capable of binding important harmful compounds. During this process, the glutathione is depleted and must therefore be regenerated through sulfur compounds that occur in food.

Liver disease

Alcohol and drug use can cause major problems with the liver. Use of drugs can place the user at risk in numerous ways. When an individual gets high, he or she may engage in behaviors that he or she would not otherwise consider (for example, having unprotected sex). Some substances can directly damage the liver (such as alcohol); with other substances, the way in which they are used promotes other risks (for example, injecting drugs). When a disease impairs liver function, such as in advanced cirrhosis, the metabolism of drugs also becomes compromised, and the liver's ability to

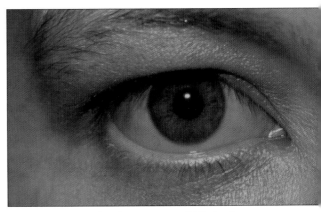

Jaundice is caused by the presence of bile in the blood and is a sure indication of problems with the functioning of the liver. Bile is greenish yellow in color and can turn the skin and whites of the eye pale yellow. It may also cause severe itching.

remove drugs and toxins from the bloodstream is greatly reduced.

Hepatitis, an inflammation of the liver, is one of the most common diseases that damage the liver. It can be caused by several viruses called hepatitis A, B, C, D, or E. These viruses cause acute, or short-term, viral hepatitis. Hepatitis B, C, and D viruses can also cause chronic hepatitis, in which the infection is prolonged, sometimes lifelong. Alcoholic hepatitis arises from the toxic effects of acetaldehyde on the structure of liver cells, which causes them to become inflamed and prompts an antibody response.

Effects of alcohol on the liver

Most people who drink heavily are likely to have globules of fat accumulate in their liver cells, leading to a condition known as fatty liver. The reasons this happens are not fully understood, but it is thought that when alcohol is present, the liver burns alcohol, rather than fat, for energy. The condition has no outward symptoms, although examination by a doctor may show that the liver has become enlarged and tender, and blood tests may show elevated enzyme levels. The condition can be reversed by abstinence and is not dangerous, but it is a warning that liver function is being compromised.

Excessive alcohol use can result in cirrhosis. *Cirrhosis* is a medical term that means "scarring of the liver." With cirrhosis, large parts of the liver become damaged and cannot be regenerated satisfactorily. Scarring occurs because acetaldehyde, one of the metabolites of alcohol, is toxic to liver cells. The cells become inflamed, die, and are replaced by scar tissue. The liver tries to repair itself by forming nodules of new cells, but because these are surrounded by scar tissue, the blood vessels servicing the cells become compressed. The increase in pressure can cause some of the veins to become enlarged, making them prone to rupture and hemorrhage. This is sometimes shown by blood being vomited.

Cirrhosis does not always show symptoms in people with alcoholic liver disease and may only be detected by medical examination. However, some people may show signs of jaundice as bile leaks out of the liver and into the blood, turning the skin and the whites of the eyes yellow. Others may build up fluid in their extremeties (edema) or abdominal cavity (ascites). Ascites can make the sufferer look pregnant and is an uncomfortable condition but it does not cause problems unless an infection occurs.

Cirrhosis can have an impact on the immune system generally, making the alcoholic more susceptible to infections. The spleen may also enlarge as a result of increased hepatic blood pressure. The blood itself may show a decrease in the levels of vital clotting factors, which is an added risk if hemorrhage occurs. The alcoholic may also beome anemic. Although the nodules can sustain liver function if the individual stops drinking, if he or she continues to drink, the outcome can be fatal without a transplant.

Other common causes of cirrhosis include hepatitis, especially hepatitis B and C. In the absence of alcohol use, most chronic liver disease among injection drug users is mild and is probably a result of infection by hepatitis C. However, the combination with alcohol can lead to severe liver disease for injecting drug users. For example, cirrhosis can be seen in young alcoholics and injecting drug users, while typically cirrhosis does not occur until the infected persons reach their fifties or sixties.

Hepatitis A

Hepatitis A (HAV) is a viral infection caused by eating food or drinking water that has been contaminated by feces from an infected person. The typical symptoms are similar to the flu, and the person may feel tired and fatigued, have a fever, and become jaundiced. HAV can affect anyone and occurs in situations ranging from isolated cases to widespread epidemics, but it is rarely life threatening. Only around 15 percent of HAV-infected people have prolonged or relapsing symptoms that extend longer than a nine-month period. Once a person has had hepatitis A he or she cannot contract it again, and there is no chronic (long-term) infection.

The people most at risk of transmission are the household contacts of infected people, the sexual contacts of infected people, men who have sex with men, injecting and noninjecting drug users, and people traveling to countries where hepatitis A is common. Basic hygiene procedures should be observed to prevent infection, such as always washing hands with soap and water after using the bathroom, changing a diaper, or before preparing and eating food. Short-term protection can be achieved by an injection of immunoglobulin two weeks before the risky period or prior to contact. The best protection against hepatitis A is the HAV vaccine.

Hepatitis B

Hepatitis B (HBV) is one of the most serious forms of hepatitis and is far more infectious and therefore more common than HIV, the virus that causes AIDS. Contracting HBV results in a lifelong infection, with the possibility of liver cancer and finally liver failure and death. Chronic hepatitis B can lead to scarring or cirrhosis, which can result in cancer of the liver. HBV symptoms include fatigue, abdominal pain, loss of appetite, nausea, vomiting, joint pain, and jaundice. However, around 30 percent of people infected with HBV have neither signs nor symptoms. Death occurs in 15 to 25 percent of chronically infected people.

HBV is transmitted by contact with infected blood or bodily fluids. HBV can be spread by unprotected sex, sharing needles, or accidental injury from a needle. An infected mother can pass HBV to her child during childbirth through exchange of bodily fluids. The people most at risk of transmission are people who have multiple sexual partners or unprotected sex, injecting drug users, those in contact with chronically infected persons, infants born to infected mothers, health care workers, hemodialysis patients, and anyone who had a blood transfusion during surgery prior to 1990 (before blood donations were routinely screened for the virus).

The best form of prevention against HBV is to not engage in risky behaviors, such as unprotected sex; injecting drugs; sharing needles, water, or other paraphernalia; or sharing of personal care items such as razors or toothbrushes. Tattooing or body piercing also present a risk and should always be carried out by a professional who follows good health practices. Pregnant women should be tested for hepatitis B and, if infected, the child should be given the hepatitis B immunoglobulin and vaccine within twelve hours after the birth. Health care workers are advised to get vaccinated against hepatitis B and to follow routine barrier precautions and needle disposal safety. The best protection is the HBV vaccine.

Hepatitis C

Hepatitis C (HCV) is spread by contact with the blood of an infected person. The symptoms of hepatitis C are fatigue, dark urine, abdominal pain, loss of appetite, nausea, and jaundice. Around 80 percent of infected people will display no signs or symptoms. It is common for people with chronic hepatitis C to have liver-enzyme levels that go up and down, with periodic returns to normal or near normal. Some sufferers have a liver-enzyme level that is normal for more than a year, but they may still have chronic liver disease. Around 70 percent of HCV-infected persons have chronic liver disease, although fewer than 3 percent of deaths occur as a result.

Risk of HCV occurs when blood or bodily fluids from an infected person enters the body of a person who is not infected. HCV is spread by sharing needles, water, or other equipment when injecting drugs; through accidental contact with contaminated needles; or passage from an infected mother to her baby during birth. People at risk for HCV infection might also be at risk for infection with hepatitis B virus or HIV (human immunodeficiency virus). Although HCV can be spread by sexual transmission, it is rare. No vaccine exists against HCV.

Hepatitis D

Hepatitis D (HDV) is a defective single-stranded RNA virus that requires the help of HBV to replicate (copy itself). HDV infection can be acquired either as a co-infection with HBV or as a superinfection (reinfection with a slightly different strain of the disease) of people with chronic HBV infection. Chronic HBV carriers who acquire HDV super-infection usually develop chronic HDV infection.

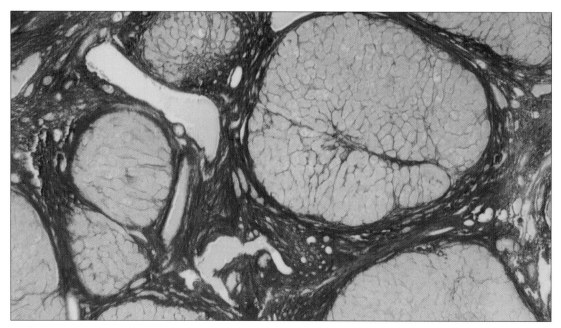

Cirrhosis of the liver can be diagnosed by performing a biopsy. In the sample shown above, the individual liver cells (yellow) are becoming isolated by scar tissue (red), which makes it harder for the liver to function.

ACCIDENTAL OVERDOSES

With the exception of alcohol, most drugs that are abused are not directly toxic to the liver, although injuries are sometimes reported among cocaine and solvent users. While the liver usually converts drugs into less active or harmless metabolites, some drugs are changed into more active forms. Codeine, for example, is converted into morphine, and cocaine becomes the more powerful cocaethylene if taken with alcohol.

A particularly dangerous change occurs with acetaminophen (paracetamol), a common ingredient in painkillers such as Tylenol. The change can produce a potentially lethal effect. At normal recommended doses, acetaminophen rarely causes problems, but if overdosed it can result in acute liver failure. Someone who disregards the dosage instructions and takes large quantities over several days may also precipitate liver failure. Alcoholics may also face an increased risk when using acetaminophen because even low doses can cause severe damage to an already compromised liver.

Another complication arises from the use of codeine in some acetaminophen preparations. Although acetaminophen itself is not psychoactive, many people abuse prescription painkillers for their codeine content. However, large quantities may need to be ingested to produce a high, and the abuser may inadvertently suffer an overdose from the acetaminophen content. While most people who overdose will be found and taken to the hospital for adminstration of acetylcysteine, the antidote to acetaminophen, drug abusers may not.

Other drugs may not work properly if the liver is damaged. People taking sedatives can experience an exaggerated effect because the liver cannot eliminate them quickly. A similar effect occurs if sedative users are also taking the anti-ulcer drug cimetidine, which inhibits liver enzyme function. Barbiturates, on the other hand, can stimulate liver enzymes to eliminate other therapeutic drugs more quickly. This may have a deleterious effect on anyone taking anticoagulant drugs following a stroke or drugs for heart disease.

Long-term studies of chronic HBV carriers with HDV superinfection have shown that 70 to 80 percent have developed evidence of chronic liver disease with cirrhosis, compared with 15 to 30 percent of patients with chronic HBV infection alone.

The risk for HDV transmission is similar to HBV. The greatest risk is through sharing needles when injecting drugs and through job-related needle exposure. Sexual transmission of HDV is less efficient than for HBV. Transmission from mother to baby is rare because HDV is dependent on HBV for replication. However, no products exist to prevent HDV infection of people with chronic HBV infection.

Hepatitis E Virus (HEV)
Hepatitis E (HEV) is transmitted in much the same way as hepatitis A virus. Hepatitis E virus, however, rarely occurs in the United States. The symptoms of acute hepatitis E are similar to those of other types of viral hepatitis and include abdominal pain, anorexia, dark urine, fever, jaundice, malaise, nausea, and vomiting. No evidence of chronic infection has been detected in long-term follow-ups of patients with hepatitis E.

Summary
Most people know that the liver acts as a filter and can be harmed by alcohol. Liver specialists suggest that men should have no more than two drinks a day, and women, one a day. Even this conservative estimate may be too much for some people.

One of the most remarkable accomplishments of the liver is its ability to regenerate. Three-quarters of the liver can be removed and it will grow back in the same shape and form within a few weeks. However, with severe damage the only option is a transplant.

J. S. WOODS

SEE ALSO:
Alcoholism • Medical Care • Overdose • Toxicity

Lung Diseases

The lungs are one of the most vital organs in the body. Their delicate structure and precise functioning can be compromised by substances found in smoke, which can lead to debilitating diseases and even death.

Many drugs harm the lungs and can cause severe respiratory problems. The delicate tissue in the lungs is damaged by smoking drugs such as tobacco, crack, and heroin, with long-term use leading to an increased risk of lung infection and various breathing-related disorders.

Function and structure of the lungs

The lungs are the organs that people use for respiration, the process in which oxygen is brought into the blood and used to fuel body functions, while carbon dioxide is released into the air. Oxygen is needed for a variety of life-supporting functions, the most important being releasing energy from food. Carbon dioxide is a waste product of this

process and must be removed efficiently to avoid suffocating the organism.

Evolution has made the human lungs and surrounding chest a highly efficient structure for breathing. A typical person can inhale around 250 cubic inches (4 liters) of air in one breath, but normally takes in only about 30 cubic inches (half a liter). Moreover, each person breathes in and out from 15 to 25 times a minute throughout his or her life, usually without being aware of doing so. Air is pumped into and blown out the lungs by a set of specialized muscles around the chest cavity. Intercostal muscles lie between the ribs and alter the shape of the chest to help inhalation and exhalation; the diaphragm is a sheet of muscle at the bottom of

This close-up shows the tiny hairlike projections called cilia that cover the surface of the trachea (windpipe) and bronchi. Cilia line cells that secrete mucus in response to substances in smoke that irritate the lungs and move in a sweeping motion to keep the air passages clean. Tar from cigarettes can clog the cilia, preventing the lungs from clearing other harmful irritants.

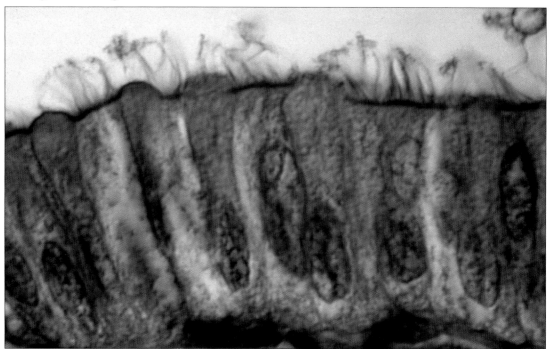

the chest that, when contracted, moves down to suck air into the lungs.

Air enters the body through the mouth and nose, and then goes into the trachea (windpipe). As air travels down the trachea, it passes the larynx, or voice box, which contains the vocal cords. The trachea continues deep inside the chest and then branches into two bronchi, which channel the air into the left and right lungs. Inside each lung is an intricate network of millions of tiny branching tubes called bronchioles. Each of these tubes ends in a little air sac, or alveolus, which is covered by tiny blood vessels. Gases can easily cross into the blood through the thin walls of these alveoli, making the lungs very effective for exchanging the gases oxygen and carbon dioxide between the air and blood. In total, the surface area of these tiny sacs is around 110 square yards (90 m²)—about the size of a basketball court.

Drug intake through the lungs

For any psychoactive drug to have an effect, it must reach the brain, where it affects the neurochemical processes that regulate how a person feels, behaves, and perceives the world. In practice, the most efficient route to the brain is through the bloodstream, although some painkillers called epidurals are injected straight into the spinal cord. There are several ways that a drug can enter the blood, which include directly injecting the drug into a vein; eating or drinking a drug; snorting powder up the nose; and inhalation through the mouth and nose into the lungs.

Drugs that are absorbed through the lungs must be either a gas or a vapor. Some substances are obtained in this form and are just sniffed or inhaled directly, such as nitrous oxide ("laughing gas") and inhalants from solvents or aerosols. Others need to be burned to release fumes of their active chemicals, which are then inhaled, a practice called smoking. The properties of the lungs that make them efficient for breathing and absorbing oxygen, such as a large surface area and a good blood supply, also make them an extremely effective method for delivering drugs into the body. For example, crack cocaine provides a more rapid hit than cocaine powder because crack is smoked, while cocaine powder is usually taken through the gums or nasal lining, which provides a slower method of absorption.

Pulmonary diseases

The most common symptoms of lung disease include chronic coughing, possibly producing blood; chest pain or tightness; a shortness of breath; and wheezing. These symptoms can signal one of a number of possibly life-threatening disorders.

Asthma is a condition in which the airways are very sensitive to certain triggers, such as cold air, dust, exercise, stress, viral infection, and airborne irritants, such as marijuana or cigarette smoke. Muscles around the lung passages constrict when exposed to these triggers, narrowing the airways and making it difficult to breathe. Asthma is often accompanied by swollen and inflamed lung tissue, which also hampers breathing. Common effective medications include steroids to reduce the underlying inflammation and bronchodilators to relieve an attack. Even with these medications, around 5,000 people die every year in the United States of asthma, out of nearly 17 million asthma sufferers.

Bronchitis is an inflammation of the airways that causes swelling of the lung tissue and excessive mucus production. A brief episode of acute bronchitis often follows a cold or flu, producing a chest cough. When this condition continues for months and years, it is described as chronic. Bronchitis is also accompanied by shortness of breath and if allowed to deteriorate can result in a severely disabled patient who has difficulty walking without supplementary oxygen. Treatments include bronchodilators, oxygen from portable tanks, and lung transplantation. Cigarette smoking is the main cause of chronic bronchitis.

Emphysema is a disease that occurs when the tissues of the alveoli break down and no longer absorb oxygen properly. It is usually preceded by chronic bronchitis, with which it is collectively called chronic obstructive pulmonary disease (COPD). Patients suffering from emphysema have a chronic cough and difficulty breathing. Bronchitis further exacerbates the disability caused by the disease. Treatments are similar to those for chronic bronchitis. COPD is a leading cause of death in the United States, totaling nearly 120,000 fatalities a year from around 10 million sufferers.

Lung cancer arises when a group of malignant cells, known as a tumor, grow uncontrollably. The cancer's effects usually go unnoticed until the tumor

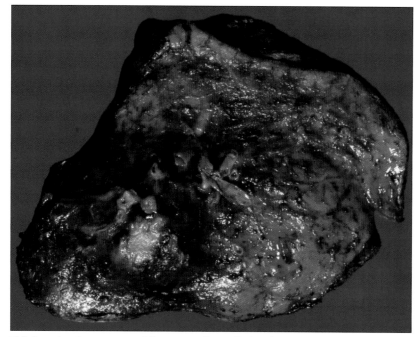

This lung has been removed from a smoker suffering from cancer. The lung is blackened by tar and has been hardened by the cancer, making it difficult for the lungs to expand and for the patient to draw breath.

has become widespread throughout the lungs or has reached another organ. Symptoms of advanced lung cancer include chest pain; difficulty breathing; a persistent cough or wheeze, perhaps producing blood; weight loss; and susceptibility to pneumonia. Lung cancer is fatal unless detected in its early stages, when it can be treated by surgically removing the tumor, radiation therapy, and chemotherapy. Cigarette smoking causes most lung cancer cases in the United States. Cancer is the second leading cause of death in the United States, with lung cancer itself causing around 160,000 deaths every year.

Pneumonia is a serious infection of the lungs, in which the alveoli become blocked by fluid and pus. This obstruction of the air sacs makes breathing and thus absorbing oxygen difficult. Many agents can cause pneumonia, such as bacteria, viruses, and inhalation of some chemicals. Symptoms include fever, severe chest pain, a chest cough, and sometimes bluish lips from insufficient oxygen in the blood. Treatment includes taking antibiotics and getting adequate rest. Alcoholics, heroin addicts, and other people with weakened immune systems are particularly at risk of contracting pneumonia.

When fluid accumulates in the lung and causes difficulty breathing, pulmonary edema results. While edema is often a complication of a heart attack, it can also result from direct lung injury caused by heat, poisonous gas, or a severe infection. The symptoms of pulmonary edema include difficulty breathing, anxiety, a feeling of drowning, gurgling sounds when taking a breath, coughing, and blood in the sputum. Although pulmonary edema is treatable with supplemental oxygen and a breathing tube, some patients eventually require long-term use of a breathing machine.

Pulmonary embolisms are blood clots in the lungs. Such clots are serious and often life threatening, since they can block blood flow in large areas of the lungs. Some symptoms of an embolism are pain in the chest, back, shoulder, or upper abdomen; shortness of breath; wheezing; and painful breathing. Treatment is by supplementary oxygen and drugs to relieve blood clotting.

Respiratory depression and failure

Respiratory depression is a slowing of the breathing rate and is a side effect of sedating drugs. These drugs affect the mechanisms of the brain that control breathing. A degree of respiratory depression follows standard doses of such drugs and is not harmful unless the person taking the drug has an existing breathing problem. However, at high doses the breathing rate slows to such an extent that the level of oxygen in the blood can become dangerously low, or carbon dioxide too high, which can induce a coma and then death. Drugs that cause respiratory depression include the opioids, such as morphine or heroin, and depressants, such as barbiturates or alcohol. Combinations of drugs often cause accidental overdoses, a common example being alcohol with barbiturates. Further, the medical painkiller morphine is sometimes given in extremely high doses, although for terminally ill patients this is seen as an acceptable risk.

Respiratory failure occurs when the lungs fail to absorb enough oxygen or remove enough carbon dioxide to support life. While often the final stage of a chronic lung disease, respiratory failure can also be caused by an overdose of opioids or alcohol. Respiratory failure can also happen after a pulmonary embolism, which blocks blood flow to an area of the lungs. Treatment is by supplemental oxygen, mechanical ventilation, and action against the cause of the respiratory failure.

Substances that cause lung or throat disease

Many inhaled or smoked substances damage the lungs by being either corrosive, irritating, or poisonous to the sensitive tissue. Other drugs carry with them carcinogenic chemicals that cause throat or lung cancer.

Alcohol is a nervous system depressant. Regular heavy consumption or use with another nervous system depressant, such as heroin or tranquilizers, can lead to shallow, depressed respiration that in severe cases causes coma and death. Long-term alcohol abuse also suppresses the immune system, giving a greater chance of contracting respiratory infections such as pneumonia.

Marijuana, also called cannabis or hashish, is usually taken into the body by smoking. Smoking marijuana causes similar damage to the throat and lungs as tobacco smoking but can cause particular damage to the mouth and throat because marijuana smoke is hotter. The practice of holding the smoke in the mouth also prolongs its contact time with the soft tissues. Adverse health effects include an increased risk of emphysema, chronic bronchitis, and throat or lung cancer.

Crack is the freebase crystalline form of cocaine and is smoked instead of snorted. Cocaine powder decomposes at a relatively low temperature, which makes it unsuitable for smoking. Crack, however, can be heated in a flame with little decomposition. Crack fumes damage the delicate tissue of the lungs, and short-term use often leads to a chest cough, chest pain, and exacerbation of asthma. Long-term crack use inflames lung tissue, possibly leading to chronic bronchitis, pulmonary edema, and a high risk of contracting pneumonia.

Inhalants, such as solvents or aerosols, are common household chemicals that are sniffed or inhaled through the nose or mouth. High concentrations of inhalants can cause asphyxiation and then unconsciousness or death. The sudden expansion of aerosol gases as they depressurize can also rupture the lining of the lung, leading to a collapsed lung. Frozen-tissue injuries and sores in the mouth and throat are also common occurrences.

Opiates, which include opium, heroin, and morphine, are highly addictive narcotics that can be either smoked or injected. In large doses, opiates strongly depress respiration, which can lead to death by respiratory failure. Opiate smoking also damages the lungs, causing an increased risk of emphysema, chronic bronchitis, and throat or lung cancer. In the long term, opiates suppress the immune system, making respiratory infections such as pneumonia more probable.

Tranquilizers, such as the benzodiazepines and barbiturates, are nervous system depressants that are usually legally prescribed, although they can also be bought illegally. Prescribed doses are used to relieve anxiety or promote sleep by slowing excitatory processes in the brain that control automatic functions, such as breathing. An overdose depresses respiration, slowing breathing and possibly leading to unconsciousness or death. Tranquilizers are dangerous in combination with alcohol, since both drugs suppress respiration.

Tobacco contains nicotine, which is usually consumed through smoking but can also be chewed or sniffed. Tobacco smoking is extremely damaging to the mouth, lungs, larynx, and respiratory system. Smokers have very high rates of chronic bronchitis or emphysema, and tobacco smoke can also trigger an asthma attack. Meanwhile, tar in the tobacco is highly carcinogenic and causes lung, throat, and other cancers. It has been estimated that more than half of long-term tobacco smokers die from their habit, totaling around half a million people every

N. LEPORA

SEE ALSO:
Liver Diseases • Medical Care • Mortality Rates • Smoking • Toxicity

Medical Care

Drug users have to cope with more than just their addiction. Often users are beset by a number of other medical conditions that compromise their health. Trying to get the necessary help for these problems can be daunting.

As well as the emotional, financial, and legal problems of being a drug user, there are many health issues that need to be faced. Serious users are often quite ill for much of their lives as a result of the drug's own effects, the way that drugs are used (especially injecting), and the fallout from a chaotic lifestyle—everything from poor diet and infections to mental illness and homelessness.

Problems with drugs

The lack of quality control in the world of illegal drugs makes it impossible for a user to know the purity or strength of the drugs being used. If, for example, a batch of heroin is too strong, then the user could overdose and either die or end up in the hospital. Some users reportedly became very ill when they injected heroin that had been buried in the ground prior to sale and had become infected with soil bacteria. Drugs might also be cut with substances

not meant to be injected, or the drug itself might be a tablet not intended to be crushed and dissolved for injecting. Such adulterations can block veins and cause gangrene, and there are many cases of users having limbs amputated as a result. Chronic users of amphetamine and those on long-term methadone prescriptions often have dental problems because of calcium being leached out of the body in the first instance and the sugar content of methadone in the second. Long-term use of drugs such as crack and amphetamine can cause severe mental health problems including psychosis and paranoia.

Problems with methods of using drugs

Injecting is by far the most dangerous way of using drugs because of the risk of infection and of contracting blood-borne diseases such as HIV and hepatitis. Many injecting drug users need to seek medical assistance because of abscesses and blood

Patients arriving at the hospital with drug-related injuries can generally get emergency treatment, but basic medical care and access to treatment programs may be denied unless the user has insurance or Medicaid.

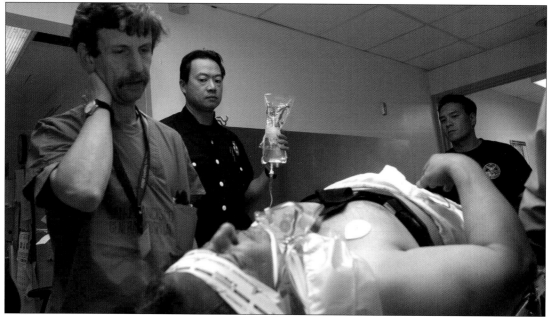

poisoning, which can be fatal if not properly treated. Sometimes users will accidentally hit an artery trying to find a vein—again this needs immediate medical attention to prevent acute blood loss.

Physicians are seeing an alarming rise in the number of drug users with serious liver disease caused by hepatitis C. People with hepatitis C can remain without symptoms for many years before they realize they are ill. Many people in the 1980s experimented with injecting heroin—some just once—when the drug became popular. Twenty years later it is this group of people who now find themselves with serious liver disease. Fortunately, there are medications now available that can eradicate the hepatitis C virus from the body, although these treatments do not work for everybody. Chronic users of crack cocaine frequently have a number of respiratory problems, including wheezing and a persistent cough caused by smoking the drug.

Problems of the drug-using lifestyle

Most chronic users do not have settled lives with secure accommodations and regular nutritious meals. Drug users often are in a generally poor state of health. They may need the services of many different professionals, including doctors, nurses, and dentists. Users also need to be in contact with drug-treatment services for prescriptions and possibly for psychosocial counseling. Women drug users who become pregnant require pre- and postnatal care. Some chronic drug users (both men and women) become prostitutes in order to pay for drugs. Aside from HIV, these drug users put themselves at risk of contracting a wide range of sexually transmitted diseases. Some drug users also have serious mental health problems and need the assistance of mental health workers.

Accessing care

There are many problems faced by drug users who try to access specialized and general medical care services. Dealing with administration and bureaucracy can be daunting. It often can be particularly problematic for drug users to keep regular appointments. Trying to get people to attend treatment clinics is one of the biggest problems in caring for drug users. One initiative that is being tested is the addition of drug-treatment services to

mobile clinics that provide medical care to areas with large populations of out-of-treatment heroin addicts. Such clinics report success in managing to reduce cases of tuberculosis among drug users.

Another problem is that many areas have few drug-treatment services. The facilities that do exist may have long waiting lists. This can be very disheartening for somebody who has finally faced up to the fact that he or she needs help, only to be told to go away and come back in three weeks' time. Delays are a particular problem for crack cocaine users, who are often looking for immediate respite from chaotic and dangerous situations.

Drug users with a co-occurring mental disorder can fall through the health care net because drug treatment services cannot handle the mental health problems, while psychiatric services are unable to deal with chronic drug use. The problem is compounded when these patients self-medicate with illegal drugs to offset the often traumatic side effects of drugs legally prescribed to deal with major psychiatric illness.

The attitude of some health and social welfare professionals can actively discourage users from coming forward for help. Medical staff may consider drug users undeserving of treatment. Pregnant drug users often avoid prenatal care because of disapproval of their lifestyle by hospital staff, and also the fear that their babies will be removed from their custody.

The relationship between drug users and physicians—both general and drug-treatment physicians—can be especially troubled. This dynamic is almost unprecedented in medical care. Usually people go to the doctor because they are ill. Although the patient may not know what is wrong, he or she relies on the doctor to correctly diagnose the problem and prescribe the right drug at the right dose.

In the case of the chronic heroin user, for example, the patient may know exactly what is wrong. Addicts may actually know more about their condition than a general physician; they know which drug they need and they are not necessarily looking to be "cured." Doctors find themselves under pressure to dispense drugs and report that users employ a variety of ruses to extract a prescription, frequently going from doctor to doctor to build up a bigger supply. Many users say that they plead with drug-treatment doctors to increase levels of methadone so that they do not

EMERGENCY DEPARTMENT VISITS

Data on the number of drug-related visits to U.S. emergency departments are collected by the Drug Abuse Warning Network (DAWN) for the Substance Abuse and Mental Health Services Administration (SAMHSA). Figures from reporting hospitals in 2009 show that there were more than 658,000 drug-related visits, most involving more than one drug. The most frequently reported drugs were:

Alcohol (in combination): 519,650
Cocaine: 152,631
Marijuana: 125,438
Heroin: 43,110
Stimulants: 17,511
Methamphetamine: 12,106
PCP: 10,927
Ecstasy: 9,062
Amphetamines: 6,787
LSD: 1,188
Inhalants: 1,045

have to top up their drug intake with illegal drugs. Doctors often refuse such requests.

A new system that is being studied in California combines medical care with addiction treatment by a primary care physician. Although integrated treatment is more expensive at around $1,500 for a course of treatment per patient, it may prove more cost effective in the long term. Early results have shown that people treated by this method are three times more likely to remain abstinent than those in traditional programs. Patients also expressed greater satisfaction with their treatment.

Emergency care

Few addicts seek treatment for their health problems. However, there may be occasions when the use of drugs results in the addict needing emergency medical care, usually as the result of an overdose or an accident. Overdoses occur when someone has taken too large a dose of a drug or has mixed it with one or more other substances. The impact that an overdose can have on the body is severe and can cause the failure of vital systems such as breathing, heart function, or temperature control. Unless the doctor knows that a particular substance has been taken, he or she will initially have to assess the patient by observing the symptoms while waiting for tests to confirm a diagnosis. Such delays can be crucial in providing the correct treatment. Use of multiple substances presents further difficulties to medical staff, as one set of symptoms may mask others that may be more critical, or can lead to complications with medication. Attempts by addicts to go through unsupervised withdrawal may also result in emergency admissions to the hospital if symptoms suddenly become acute. Withdrawing from chronic alcohol abuse is especially dangerous and should not be attempted without medical help.

Accidents are common among drug users either as a result of a loss of control of motor functions or from changes in perception of the risks in their environment. Traffic accidents are common, both from drunk or drugged driving or by intoxicated users walking into the road. Phencyclidine (PCP) and other hallucinogenic drugs can make some users feel invincible, leading to reckless behaviors, such as trying to "fly" off buildings. Alcohol and stimulant drugs can prompt aggressive behaviors that result in violence and require hospital treatment for wounds and broken bones. Medical treatment to deal with the toxic effects of drugs taken in suicide attempts should be followed by psychiatric evaluation to address the underlying cause that led to the attempt.

A final problem that users face is that while medical insurance will cover the costs of addiction treatment, few, if any, drug users with a chronic habit can afford insurance. Hospital emergency rooms treating overdoses frequently have to discharge patients with long-term drug-use problems immediately after treatment because the patient does not have the money or insurance to enter a treatment program. For the funded places that are available, the patient may face a lengthy wait, during which he or she will continue drug use or risk overdose again.

H. SHAPIRO

SEE ALSO:

Clinics • Continuum of Care • Public Health Programs • State Agencies • Treatment Centers

Mental Disorders

Many people who are referred for treatment of substance abuse problems are also assessed for co-occurring mental health disorders. Substance abuse can mask underlying psychological difficulties or may be an attempt to self-medicate.

The term *disease* generally is reserved for conditions with a known, detectable, or observable physical change process, such as a virus or bacteria. The term *disorder*, on the other hand, is reserved for clusters of symptoms and signs associated with distress and disability (impairment of functioning), yet whose cause is unknown. Most mental health conditions are referred to as disorders rather than as diseases because diagnosis rests on the presence of most or all symptoms in the clinical symptom check lists made up by experienced psychiatrists (medical doctors specializing in mental health) and psychologists (nonmedical mental health specialists, usually with a doctorate degree). Not all mental disorders are purely psychological in origin; some can have a physical basis, for example, depression may result from neurotransmitter imbalances, and some dementias can be caused by cerebrovascular disease.

The primary reference for symptom lists, or criteria, used to identify mental disorders is the *Diagnostic and Statistical Manual of Mental Disorders*, fourth edition (DSM-IV; American Psychiatric Association, 1994). The DSM-IV provides a common language for professionals in mental health to discuss the different mental disorders that individuals may have. Mental disorders in the DSM-IV are thought of as "clinically significant" because people who have them experience distress (for example, painful or disturbing symptoms), disability (impairment in important areas of functioning such as work, school, or family life), or a significantly increased risk of suffering death, pain, or an important loss of freedom.

Even when DSM-IV symptoms are present, a number of other issues must be considered before a diagnosis is made. For example, a diagnosis is not made if the symptoms can be attributed to a culturally appropriate response to a particular event, such as the death of a loved one. Also, even though the cause of many mental disorders is unknown, a diagnosis is not made unless the symptoms are considered as an expression of dysfunction that is specific to the person (behavioral, psychological, or biological dysfunction) rather than something external to the person, such as atypical behavior resulting from religious or sexual orientation. Before making a diagnosis, clinicians must also determine whether drugs or alcohol may be causing the symptoms.

Four different broad categories of mental disorder are summarized below, including internalizing disorders, externalizing disorders, personality disorders, and psychotic (or thought) disorders.

Types of mental disorders

Internalizing disorders are so-called because the focus of the difficulty is primarily internal to the person suffering with the condition. Disorders involving anxiety and depression are typical internalizing disorders. There are different types of anxiety, each associated with a different anxiety disorder subtype. For example, experiencing repeated unexpected attacks of fright is associated with the anxiety condition called panic disorder. Social anxiety (also known as social phobia) can be a problem for people who are afraid of being judged negatively by others. Feeling constantly worried for long periods is typical of generalized anxiety disorder, and a fear of being contaminated by germs or dirt is common in obsessive-compulsive disorder.

Depression is also a common internalizing disorder. Major depression can include symptoms such as sadness or irritability, a lack of interest or energy, hopelessness, feelings of worthlessness or inappropriate guilt, psychomotor agitation or retardation, or disturbance in sleep, appetite, or concentration. Experiencing these symptoms on occasion does not necessarily mean an individual has a mental disorder. For example, reactive depression is an internalizing problem that does not rise to the level of "disorder" but is nonetheless a common and unpleasant condition (*see* box p. 202). Common treatments for internalizing disorders include cognitive behavior therapy, which examines and changes thoughts and behaviors that promote anxiety and depression, and medication, for example,

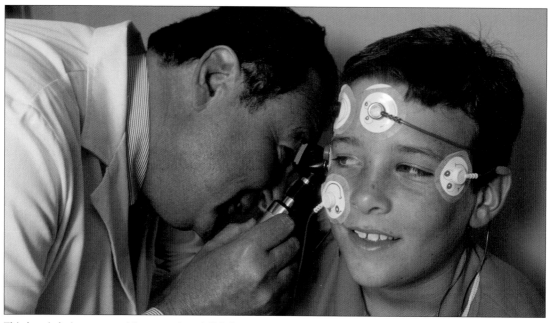

This boy is being assessed for attention deficit hyperactivity disorder, a common externalizing disorder in young children. Many ADHD sufferers try illicit drugs in an attempt to relieve their symptoms.

serotonin reuptake inhibitors (SSRIs), such as Prozac and Paxil.

Externalizing disorders are so-called because unlike internalizing disorders, the focus of the difficulty is primarily external to the person suffering with the condition. Externalizing disorders often involve unruly, disruptive, or illegal conduct. Typical externalizing disorders include attention deficit hyperactivity disorder (ADHD), conduct disorder, antisocial personality disorder, and substance abuse disorders. Externalizing disorders often involve aggression toward people or animals, destruction of property, deceitfulness or theft, and violations of school or home rules. Among the more common externalizing disorders are individuals with ADHD, which affects 3 to 5 percent of school-age children and adolescents. There is a higher proportion of boys than girls with ADHD (3.5 boys to every girl with this problem), and boys are more likely to be referred for treatment as a result of aggressive and antisocial behavior. Typical treatments for externalizing disorders include behavioral programming, such as contracts for important rewards and punishments based on observable behaviors that are targeted for change, and medications such as Ritalin.

Psychotic/thought disorders refer to conditions in which a person loses contact with reality in one or more senses for an extended period of time. This loss of contact with reality can include hallucinations (false perceptions of sight, sound, taste, or feel), delusions (demonstrably false beliefs that are nonetheless believed completely), or withdrawal into a private world (nonresponsive to external stimuli). While there can be many causes of a single psychotic episode, for example, from drug use, longer-term psychotic states can be caused by the disorder schizophrenia. Schizophrenia is characterized by profound disruption in thought and feeling, affecting the most fundamental human attributes: language, thought, perception, affect, and sense of self. Individuals diagnosed with schizophrenia can experience intermittent or ongoing psychotic episodes, which include hallucinations and delusions. The DSM-IV criteria for schizophrenia includes "positive" symptoms, such as delusions, hallucinations, and disorganized speech, and "negative symptoms," such as the apparent absence of emotion (flat affect), disruptions in speech, and difficulty with or an inability to initiate goal-directed activity. Men are more likely to develop this disorder than are women and it tends to begin early in adult development (age 15 to 25). The onset of the disorder for females can sometimes be much later (age 25 to 35). Schizophrenia affects about one person in 100 but is somewhat more common among those with a close relative who has schizophrenia. For example, 40 to 50 percent of people with an identical twin who has schizophrenia will also develop the disorder. Those with an aunt or uncle with schizophrenia have around a 3 percent risk for this disorder. There have been significant advances recently in the medication treatment of schizophrenia, including the new class of drugs called atypical antipsychotics.

Personality disorder. A diagnosis of personality disorder is considered when a persons' characteristic style of dealing with others, themselves, and the world is ineffectual, maladaptive, and a source of discomfort to the person and those around him or her. Those who struggle with a personality disorder often have great difficulty dealing with other people.

DSM AND THE INTERNATIONAL CLASSIFICATION OF DISEASES (ICD)

DSM is known as the *Diagnostic and Statistical Manual of Mental Disorder* because it evolved from attempts by the U.S. census to gather statistics about people in mental hospitals. In 1840 the U.S. Census recognized only the single disorder of "idiocy/ insanity," but seven disorders were listed by 1880. After World War II (1939–1945), the World Health Organization (WHO) began for the first time to include mental illnesses in its International Classification of Diseases (ICD), the definitive worldwide guide to illnesses of all kinds. Shortly afterward, in 1952, the American Psychiatric Association (APA) published its own catalog of mental disorders, the first *Diagnostic and Statistical Manual* (DSM-I). Several versions of DSM have been published since then; DSM-IV was published in 1994. The ICD system also continued to develop in parallel and is currently in its tenth version (ICD-10).

A deeply ingrained, inflexible pattern of relating, perceiving, and thinking serious enough to cause distress or impaired functioning is the basis of a personality disorder. One such style, for example, includes inflexibility, rigidity, and an inability to respond to the changes and demands of life. Although they typically feel that their behavior patterns are "normal" or "right," people with personality disorders tend to have a narrow view of what is appropriate to the setting, which can lead to difficulties in participating in social activities. In order to be diagnosed with a personality disorder, an individual must demonstrate several specific criteria, again listed in the DSM-IV.

Personality disorders are usually recognizable by adolescence or earlier, continue throughout adulthood, and become less obvious throughout middle age. For the most part, the different types of personality disorders affect children, adolescents, and adults equally. Treatment for personality disorders is difficult and not always effective. Psychotherapy that aims at making an individual more aware of how his or her thinking and behavior style affect others, as well as encouraging new styles of thinking and behavior, is a typical treatment approach. Research and practitioners do not agree whether it is possible to change someone's personality style, but most do agree that those with personality disorders can be taught to cope better in spite of having a dysfunctional personality style.

Dual diagnosis

Accurately diagnosing mental disorders is more difficult than diagnosing many general medical disorders since there is rarely a definitive lesion, laboratory test, or abnormality in brain tissue that can identify a specific psychiatric condition. The diagnosis of mental disorders often rests with the patients' reports of the intensity and duration of symptoms, signs from their mental status examination, and clinician observation. The diagnosis is often further complicated by the presence of one or more mental disorders in the same person.

Individuals that have two mental disorders or medical conditions can be said to be dually diagnosed, or comorbid. Although some people make subtle distinctions between the terms *dual diagnosis* and *comorbidity*, for the purposes of this discussion, the terms are considered to be same, and here the term *dual diagnosis* will be used. When a person is dually diagnosed, it is common to assign one diagnosis as the primary condition and one as secondary.

Primary and secondary disorders in dual diagnosis
The difference between primary and secondary mental disorders has several possible meanings. Some meanings for "primary mental disorder" in a dually diagnosed pair of disorders include the disorder that began first, the disorder that is the most severe, the disorder requiring the most attention or resources in treatment, and the disorder for which an individual has sought help. For example, if an adolescent was depressed and abusing alcohol, the first focus of treatment may be the symptoms of depression if the individual is having suicidal thoughts. Alcohol abuse may be the main focus of treatment if this behavior was interfering with important life functions (for example, drinking rather than going to school or work) and the depression was less severe. Another approach to this problem is to try to determine whether one of the disorders has caused or is maintaining the other. For example, if the treatment model suggests that alcohol abuse is causing depression (either chemically or through disrupting the individual's life), then the conclusion might be to treat the alcohol disorder with the expectation that the depression will clear up once drinking stops.

Secondary drug and alcohol model. This model would include individuals who first experience a mental disorder that then contributes to the development of problematic drug and alcohol use. If a mental disorder such as depression precedes the use of substances, the abuse of substances may result from a misguided effort aimed at controlling the depression through drinking or using drugs (sometimes referred to as self-medication). In addition, some researchers have found that individuals diagnosed with a major depressive disorder are more likely to have a strong urge to use alcohol when experiencing heightened symptoms of depression or increased levels of distress. Therefore, treating the symptoms of depression (when primary) could help to prevent individuals from developing secondary alcohol or drug disorders.

REACTIVE DEPRESSION

Reactive depression, also known as adjustment disorder with depressed mood, is the most common form of mood problem in children and adolescents. In this type of internalizing problem, depressed feelings are short-lived and usually occur in response to some negative experience, such as a rejection, a slight, a letdown, or a loss. Children may feel sad or sluggish and appear "in a world of their own" for periods as short as a few hours or as long as 2 weeks. However, mood improves with a change in activity or an interesting or pleasant event. These temporary mood swings in reaction to minor problems or obstacles are not regarded as a form of mental disorder.

Individuals with externalizing disorders can also exhibit secondary drug and alcohol problems as explained by this model. For example, individuals diagnosed with conduct disorder, who are more likely to exhibit high risk-taking behaviors, tend to use larger amounts of marijuana and alcohol, which contributes to higher rates of violence, in comparison with individuals who do not have conduct disorder. Individuals with antisocial personality traits who were also diagnosed with alcohol abuse were identified as having higher tested rates of impulsivity. Impulsivity involves a tendency to engage in behaviors without proper regard for consequences or inherent risks. In 2003, Lynam and Whiteside suggested that alcohol abuse could be part of a general tendency to engage in harmful behaviors that relieve negative emotions in the short term but lead to detrimental long-term consequences.

Individuals with psychotic disorders can also fall under the scope of the model. It has been suggested that individuals with schizophrenia who are abusing substances may be attempting to medicate their symptoms, especially the so-called negative symptoms, which include a lack of motivation and an inability to experience pleasure. The reward system in the brain uses the neurotransmitter dopamine, and its malfunctioning is apparently the cause of at

Antisocial and risk-taking behaviors, such as underage or drunk driving, can often be indicators of future substance use in adolescents.

least some schizophrenic symptoms, both positive (chiefly hallucinations and delusions) and negative. Alcohol, marijuana, and cocaine may facilitate dopamine transmission in these circuits, producing a short-lived sense of well-being. The price is a long-term deterioration in functioning and a poor outcome for individuals with schizophrenia.

Secondary mental disorder model. This model describes dual diagnosis relationships in which an alcohol or drug disorder contributes to the development of a mental disorder. The severe symptoms of withdrawal from alcohol or drugs can be confused with the presence of a mental disorder, or symptoms may persist beyond an extended period of abstaining from alcohol use, resulting in the development of a mental disorder. In this model, symptoms such as depression, anxiety, eating disorders, or other behavioral manifestations are secondary to the primary problem of substance abuse. It is well-known, for example, that abuse of drugs such as cocaine and amphetamine can cause high levels of anxiety and panic attacks in the short term and can cause paranoia, hallucinations, and antisocial behavior with chronic use. Alcohol and drug abuse may also lead to significant negative consequences that, in turn, cause stress-sensitive mental disorders, such as anxiety or psychotic disorders. This is especially true in individuals who are predisposed (have a family history of mental disorders) to psychiatric difficulties. Also, as noted, withdrawal from chronically abused drugs has been associated with the symptoms of anxiety, depression, and psychosis.

One big question that has not yet been resolved is whether psychiatric symptoms caused by alcohol and drug use will clear up automatically when the abuse stops. While research does not clearly answer this question, clinical reports suggest that in some such cases, discontinuation of drug or alcohol use also relieves the psychiatric symptoms with no additional treatment, but in other cases the psychiatric problems caused by drug or alcohol use take on a life of their own that continues even during periods of abstinence.

C. DONAHUE, M. G. KUSHNER

SEE ALSO:
Antisocial Personality Disorder • Attention Deficit Disorder • Compulsive Behaviors • Conduct Disorder • Depression • Diagnosing Substance Abuse • Dual Diagnosis

Mortality Rates

The number of deaths resulting from the use of illicit drugs can only be estimated. Many deaths might be attributed to a wide range of other causes that are a consequence of drug use rather than being directly caused by drugs.

There is a range of problems for those who use drugs. Death is by far the least likely, but it is the one that attracts most attention and, naturally, causes most concern. Deaths from Ecstasy produce newspaper headlines, although the risk of fatality is around 1 in 100,000 in the United States, and sports and traffic accidents claim more teenage lives every year than do illegal drugs. On the other hand, some forms of drug-related death go relatively unreported. For example, in the United Kingdom, since the late 1980s, there have been at least 350 deaths related to the use of Ecstasy (MDMA). For the first ten years of interest in Ecstasy, every death was headline news, including the death of Leah Betts in 1995, which prompted the launch of an anti-Ecstasy campaign. In recent years, however, deaths related to Ecstasy have hardly been reported, although they still occur.

Direct drug-related deaths
There are two main types of drug-related death: direct and indirect. Deaths that occur as a direct result of taking a drug or combination of drugs are normally referred to as an overdose. With depressant drugs such as alcohol, heroin, or sleeping pills, an overdose can happen when key functions of the body such as respiration are depressed or slowed down sufficiently to the point that breathing stops and the individual dies. In depressant overdoses, the cough reflex is also suppressed, so if the individual is unconscious yet still alive, he or she may vomit but be unable to remove the vomit from the back of the throat by coughing, and thus suffocate. An overdose fatality is more probable if drugs are mixed; a number of heroin users might have survived their heroin overdose if they had not been drinking alcohol at the same time.

Heroin users might be especially at risk of overdose if they have had a period of abstinence when their tolerance has dropped. When the individual uses the drug again at the same dosage level as before, his or her body is unable to cope with such a large quantity. For this reason, overdose is quite common in heroin-using offenders soon after release. Overdose can also occur if an especially strong batch of drugs hits the streets or if the drugs are contaminated in any way.

With stimulant drugs such as cocaine, amphetamines, or amyl nitrate, users might suffer cardiac arrest as a direct result of the impact of these drugs on the heart and circulatory system.

Indirect drug-related deaths
Indirect deaths are not the immediate result of consuming drugs but rather those that occur as a consequence of having a drug habit that exposes individuals to the risk of dying in some other way. These risks might occur through the acquisition of an infectious disease such as HIV. There may be complications arising from an infection acquired

Alcohol and drugs are responsible for a large number of driving incident fatalities, either as a result of driver impairment or from an intoxicated pedestrian wandering into oncoming traffic.

DRUG-DEATH TRENDS IN THE UNITED STATES

- Drug-related death rates increased about five-fold from 1990 to 2007
- In 2007, overdose deaths were second only to motor vehicle crash deaths as the leading cause of unintentional death
- Since 1999, deaths caused by opiate-based pain relievers have risen more than any other drug-related deaths, followed by cocaine and heroin
- In 2007, states in the southwest and Appalachian region had the highest drug-related death rates in the United States, while

- California and New York were among the lowest
- In the decade of the 1990s, California and New York had among the highest rates of drug-related deaths
- Overdoses by males occur at twice the rate for females
- The most vulnerable age for overdoses appears to be between 38 and 54
- Tobacco- and alcohol-related deaths far outstrip deaths related to illicit drug use by a factor of at least 20 and 5, respectively

through long-term drug misuse, for example, hepatitis, which causes liver failure or cirrhosis and can be caught by using infected needles. The world of illicit drug dealing is violent, and unknown thousands of people have died in drug-related gun crime and violence of every kind. Finally, there are accidents (including road traffic) arising from impaired judgment as a result of consumption of drugs, whether prescribed or illicit.

Mortality statistics

One would imagine that it would be easy to determine how many people die from illegal drug use every year. However, the figures are only an estimate for a number of reasons.

The main reason is that total figures are not collected centrally. The most reliable source of mortality data for the United States is collected by the Drug Abuse Warning Network (DAWN), which collects both emergency room admissions and mortality statistics on an annual basis. However, these figures are collected only by "participating death-investigating jurisdictions," which for 2008 included 544 medical examiners in 36 states. Not only are the figures not a total of all drug deaths in the United States in a given year, they do not even represent the figures for one city because not all the jurisdictions for one city contribute data. The point of collecting these data is to monitor trends rather than to calculate the total number of deaths in a year.

Overall, the drug death jurisdictions only cover about one third of the population.

There are other reasons that accurately attributing a cause of death to drugs or drug-related consequences may be problematic. The pathology reports may be inconclusive concerning the degree to which any particular drug might have been a contributing factor in a drug death. For example, if somebody is involved in a car accident and marijuana is found in the victim's blood, should the cause of death be considered related to drug use? It might be if the person had just smoked the drug. However, if the individual's last dose was two weeks before the accident, it is most unlikely that marijuana is implicated in the death, even though the drug is still present in the body.

There are also issues surrounding the way in which individual coroners and medical examiners deal with drug cases. There are some coroners who might too readily attribute deaths to drug use as a platform for promoting general warnings about the dangers of using drugs. Conversely, some coroners may be reluctant to make a determination that the death is drug related out of concern for the feelings of the family. Instead, the coroner may leave the cause of death unresolved.

H. SHAPIRO

SEE ALSO:
Driving While Impaired • Overdose • Suicide

Multiple Addiction

For many people, drug use is not confined to a single substance. Combinations of legal and illicit drugs can complicate the action of any one drug in the body and may make addiction difficult to diagnose and treat.

Multiple addiction commonly refers to an addiction involving two or more drugs. With growing recognition of other forms of reward-directed behavioral disorders (for example, addictions to food, sex, gambling, or shopping), the term may also apply to people with both substance use disorders and one or more of these other impulse-control or compulsive disorders. In regard to substance use, multiple addictions may indicate addictions to different drugs taken separately, or to a combination of drugs used at the same time. Psychiatrists use the related diagnostic term *polysubstance dependence* when an individual demonstrates drug-use patterns consistent with substance dependence involving three or more substances as a group, not including caffeine or nicotine, over a 12-month period.

In recent decades there has been a growing awareness that drug addiction is frequently complicated by the use of more than one substance, and in many populations multiple addiction is so common as to represent the rule rather than the exception. The high prevalence of multiple addictions represents a significant challenge for the treatment of addictions, since in many cases treatment regimes and health care systems are tailored to address only one type of drug of abuse. Research on the neural causes and effects of addictions is often complicated by subjects who use multiple substances, making it difficult to determine how particular brain changes reflect the action of a specific drug. However, with growing research on multiple addictions, more effective treatments are being developed, and new insights about the causes of addictions are emerging.

Forms and causes of multiple addiction

An array of biological, psychological, and social forces operate together as causes of multiple addictions. While examples of virtually all possible combinations of abused drugs may be found in some individuals, certain combinations of substance use disorders are observed more often than others. Studies of these combinations and their common patterns of development in individuals provide clues about how underlying biopsychosocial forces contribute to multiple addictions.

Epidemiological surveys show that the earlier one type of drug use begins (typically in adolescence or early adulthood), the more likely an individual is to experiment with and develop a substance use disorder involving multiple substances. These trends also correlate with an increased severity of addictions to one or more drugs diagnosed in adulthood. These observations have been suggested as strong evidence in support of a gateway theory of drug abuse, in which the use of one substance, often a legal recreational substance, for example, nicotine or alcohol, or one popularly regarded as a relatively safe illegal drug—marijuana—leads to use and disorders involving "harder" or more potentially dangerous

Many people continue to smoke and drink while taking a prescription drug, unaware that doing so might interfere with how the drug works. The combination of alcohol with some drugs, especially tranquilizers, can lead to overdose and even death.

drugs, such as cocaine or heroin. Evidence put forward for the gateway phenomenon suggests that either the properties of gateway drugs may themselves cause the progression to other drugs, or that individuals at increased risk for use and abuse of gateway drugs are also at increased risk for using harder drugs. Evidence for the first view relates to the concept of cross-sensitization, in which the addiction processes, once initiated by the repeated use of one drug, might produce a nonspecific acceleration of the addiction process in association with other drugs. A likely mechanism for cross-sensitization is suggested by findings that most addictive drugs share a common capacity to induce release of the neurotransmitter (chemical messenger) dopamine into the nucleus accumbens, a brain region involved in motivation. Repetitive drug-induced stimulation of the dopamine system plays a key role in brain changes that create an increased desire to acquire and use an addictive drug. Since many types of addictive drugs share this dopamine-mediated process, exposure to one drug may alter or increase the motivational responses to another drug taken at some future time.

Evidence for the second premise also relates to the common mechanisms of various abused substances to produce addictions via incremental brain changes in motivational systems. However, in this case, the increased risk for developing substance use disorders lies in individuals who have a genetic or neurobiological vulnerability for a more rapid progression of the addiction process in the brain, regardless of which type of drug might be initially used. Studies suggest that such heightened vulnerability may correspond to various forms of childhood- or adolescent-onset mental illness, or may heighten a tendency to engage in risky behavior. From the standpoint of both biological arguments, the typical gateway drugs (nicotine, alcohol, and marijuana) happen to be the first drugs used because they are simply more widely available, condoned, and used by larger segments of society. In this way both biological and social factors may work in concert leading to common patterns of progression from the use of gateway drugs to multiple addictions.

Factors that drive multiple addiction
Differences in the availability and permissiveness of society toward different addictive drugs are important factors in the both the prevalence of single types of substance use disorders and common combinations of multiple addictions. Substance use disorders involving the legal drugs nicotine and alcohol represent by far the most common types of single drug addictions, while addiction to both drugs in the same individual represents the most common form of multiple addiction. The high rates of combined use of nicotine and alcohol in public venues throughout society, including bars, restaurants, casinos, and play an important role in the high prevalence of this form of multiple addiction. Other frequent combinations are substance use disorders involving nicotine and marijuana, alcohol and marijuana, or nicotine and alcohol and marijuana, which also may be related to the high prevalence of marijuana use alone as the most frqeuently abused illicit substance.

Biological and psychological factors pertaining to the psychoactive or motivational effects of different substances when used simultaneously may also contribute to the higher prevalence of particular drug combinations in multiple addictions. For instance, cocaine and alcohol are a frequently observed combination. The intoxicating effects of cocaine can produce uncomfortable levels of paranoia, anxiety, and excitation, which might be reduced or controlled by the use of alcohol with its sedative and relaxing effects. When cocaine is taken with alcohol, chemical processes in the body transform cocaine and alcohol molecules into a new compound called cocaethylene. Like cocaine, this compound causes dopamine release in motivational systems, but the compound is broken down more slowly and remains in the body longer. Alcohol thus extends the psychoactive or motivational actions of cocaine, leading to greater use of the combination. In addition, the capacities of both cocaine and alcohol alone to cause dopamine release in the brain's reward systems may produce an amplification of their addictive effects when used in combination, as a variant of cross-sensitization described previously.

In many populations, subgroups with addictions involving two or more illegal drugs can be identified, often in combination with the use of the legal substances nicotine and alcohol. One such combination is cocaine and heroin, which when taken simultaneously by injection into the bloodstream is referred to as a "speedball." This combination represents a severely addictive form of drug use for several reasons: the highly addictive potential of each drug taken separately; possible cross-sensitization interactions of both drugs taken in combination; the intravenous form (representing the most addictive manner of drug intake since significant drug levels in the brain are rapidly achieved); and the combined psychoactive properties of these drugs, which tend to maximize their pleasurable effects while canceling out their respective aversive (off-putting) effects (that is, the aversive stimulating effects of cocaine are counteracted by the depressant effects of heroin).

Multiple addictions involving two or more illegal drugs are also seen because an individual who demonstrates a willingness to acquire and use one illicit drug, despite the negative potential consequences, is more likely to use other illegal drugs despite risk of similar consequences. In addition, illegal drug dealers often promote access and sales of more than one illegal substance, thus increasing the availability of different types of drugs that may generate addictions. In some instances dealers concoct specific drug combinations for sale as a single substance of abuse. For example, in the late 1990s in the northeastern United States, a popular combination known to users as "Illy" consisted of marijuana cigarettes laced with phencyclidine (PCP) and soaked in a solvent such as gasoline or embalming fluid (formaldehyde).

Risks of multiple addictions

A fundamental aspect of multiple addictions is that the regular use of several substances carries a greater risk of potential psychiatric, medical, and social consequences than might be observed with single substance dependence. Because the intoxication or withdrawal effects of a variety of abused substances can produce symptoms similar to one or more of the major psychiatric syndromes, the regular use of multiple substances may increase the likelihood of being diagnosed with one of these disorders. Some drug combinations can result in states of intoxication marked by unusual, unexpected, or unstable perceptual and emotional disturbances not encountered in single drug use. These multiple drug-induced symptoms can induce violent acts or suicide, or produce such impairment in judgment as to cause behavior leading to traumatic injury and death. In some cases,

multiple addictions worsen psychiatric disorders already present before the substance use, and in other cases, the drug use goes unreported to mental health care workers while causing psychiatric symptoms, diagnostic confusion, and the unnecessary or unhelpful prescription of multiple psychiatric medications. For instance, insomnia is a common symptom of alcohol, cocaine, and opiate abuse. When this drug use is not reported to or observed by physicians, patients may be prescribed antidepressant or sleep-aid medications, some of which may themselves be addictive, or which may have dangerous effects when combined with recreational drugs. Multiple addictions may also produce a larger array of potential long-term brain changes, including those that represent the generation of more severe addictions, and those that have other long-term emotional and cognitive consequences. For instance, the chronic use of cocaine and alcohol carries both the risk of brain damage from strokes inherent to cocaine use and the risk of dementia associated with drinking alcohol.

Multiple addictions involve a greater risk of accumulating medical problems. Both smoking and heavy alcohol use are associated with accelerated heart disease, and their combined use increases the risk of certain types of cancers, particularly oral and esophageal cancer. For many drug combinations, the medical risk is more immediate and is associated with the simultaneous use of multiple substances. Because many addictive drugs are broken down by similar metabolic processes in the liver, it is possible for the intake of one drug to retard the natural breakdown of another, leading to higher-than-usual drug levels in the body as a risk for accidental overdose. In addition, many drugs used in combination can act synergistically in their effects on the heart, vascular system, and breathing, increasing the risk for sudden death. Combinations of alcohol and other central nervous system depressants such as opiates, benzodiazepines, or barbiturates are particularly well-known as lethal combinations, since they have repeatedly been implicated in the premature death of many famous people. Overdoses of multiple substances represent a greater risk for death even after emergency treatment is initiated; it is more difficult to identify the drugs involved and to treat their combined effects, since the clinical signs and symptoms typical of overdose of one drug may be masked by the presence of another. In addition, drug combinations may represent a greater health risk because many of their short- and long-term psychiatric and medical consequences may not have yet been fully described by medical researchers.

The social consequences of multiple addictions are often greater than for unitary addictions. In many cases, the presence of multiple addictions indicates a more generally severe addiction syndrome, resulting in greater financial loss (due to job loss or spending on drugs) and raising the risk of homelessness. Financial deprivation, along with the greater psychiatric and medical illnesses incurred with multiple addictions, increases the likelihood of the breakdown of families and peer groups. Because patients with multiple addictions often use one or more illegal substances, a greater risk of arrest and imprisonment is incurred.

Treatment of multiple addictions

With increasing recognition that patients treated for substance dependence often have several forms of habitual drug use, research and treatment methods have taken on new importance. However, these efforts face several challenges. Much of the available research data and treatments for addictions focus on single addictions, even though in many instances the research subjects or patients themselves actually have multiple addictions (for example, an alcoholic smoker who is part of a brain-imaging study examining the effects of alcohol addiction). Also, the greater severity of psychiatric, medical, and social problems renders this patient population less capable of maintaining participation in long-term research and treatment. Considerable gaps in knowledge about the optimal treatment for the various combinations of multiple addictions leave important questions unanswered. For example, there is not yet a general consensus about whether patients should be encouraged to stop all forms of their drug use at once, or whether they should progress toward abstinence in several stages, one drug at a time. This uncertainty relates to observations that in some patients, cessation of one form of drug use may decrease the use of other drugs, while in other patients cessation of one drug increases the use of others. In intensive abstinence programs, such as those involving substitution

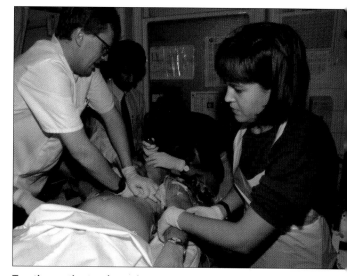

Treating patients who arrive at emergency rooms poses difficulties for medical staff. Some drugs show very similar effects when used in combination or may exacerbate the metabolism of others.

treatments, for example methadone clinics, continuing treatment is often contingent upon drug-free urine testing. It is not clear whether patients with repeated positive drug tests for nonopiate addictive drugs, such as cocaine or marijuana, should also be discharged from treatment, as are patients with continuing opiate use.

Despite these clinical uncertainties, the similarities of the addiction syndrome suggest that many of the methods applicable in the treatment of various unitary addictions may also apply to multiple addictions. For example, many of the group therapy–oriented approaches used in Alcoholics Anonymous are also useful for patients with multiple addictions. Motivational Enhancement Therapy (MET), a form of one-on-one psychotherapy supporting abstinence and relapse prevention behavior for single addictions, may also prove useful. Similarly, medications such as naltrexone for opiate or alcohol addiction may also show benefit for multiple addictions.

R. A. CHAMBERS

SEE ALSO:
Addiction • Causes of Addiction • Compulsive Behaviors • Drug Use, Life Patterns • Dual Diagnosis • Sensitization • Treatment

Narcotics Anonymous

From its modest beginnings as a small movement, Narcotics Anonymous has expanded to become a worldwide organization, offering nonjudgmental help and therapy to anyone suffering from addiction.

Narcotics Anonymous (NA) is an international, community-based association of recovering drug addicts. NA was inspired by Alcoholics Anonymous (AA) in the late 1940s, and meetings started in California in the early 1950s.

Like AA, NA began in the United States as a small organization that has grown and spread to more than 130 countries around the world, with more than 58,000 weekly meetings, and publications in more than 40 languages. The aims of NA are very much the same as those of AA; members meet weekly to help one another abstain from drug taking. NA describes itself in a pamphlet known as "the White Booklet" as "a nonprofit fellowship or society of men and women for whom drugs had become a major problem. We …meet regularly to help each other stay clean….We are not interested in what or how much you used…but only in what you want to do about your problem and how we can help."

Twelve steps

In NA, members work through the process of remaining free from drug use by sharing their experiences, offering each other support, and by following a set of principles outlined in the Twelve Steps and the Twelve Traditions. In AA, the focus is on a single addiction, namely an addiction to alcohol. Members attending NA, however, may have addictions to a wide range of different drugs that have different effects on the user. Also, they may be addicted to not one but a combination of drugs. An important difference between the Twelve Steps used by AA and those used by NA is in the wording of the first step. For AA the step states that "We admitted we were powerless over alcohol." Initially NA altered the first step to state that "We admitted we were powerless over drugs" but this was later altered to "We admitted we were powerless over our addiction." This significant change was made to remove drug-specific terms when it became apparent that the different drugs that members had taken led to confusion at meetings. Also, it was thought that

the new wording reflected the concept of addiction as a disease, as well as focusing on the common ground between drug users.

Twelve Step programs emphasize the need for individuals to develop a spiritual awakening, which may or may not be aligned with an established religion but includes the belief in God or a "higher power." Some critics have argued that emphasizing spiritual beliefs may deter addicts who are atheist or agnostic from becoming involved with NA.

Other aspects of the Twelve Step program include the importance of engaging in a thorough mental self-examination, making amends for wrong actions, and helping other drug addicts to recover from their addiction. In addition to the Twelve Steps, NA employs a system of sponsorship in which an experienced member works with a new member to help him or her maintain abstinence.

Abstinence is the key

NA regards drug addiction as a disease and considers the best method of dealing with this disease to be total abstention from drug taking rather than controlled use, in which occasional or limited drug taking would be acceptable. Addicts are encouraged to share the successes and difficulties they have faced in remaining free of drugs. NA limits itself to this form of mutual help and does not provide members with professional counselors or medical services.

In order to focus on its main aims, NA also follows a policy of avoiding controversy and thus makes no comment on a variety of issues, from those relating to medicine and religion, to drug legalization, and syringe programs. NA also avoids commenting on other organizations that offer help for drug addicts. NA does, however, cooperate with other organizations, such as churches, hospitals, correctional facilities, and with the voluntary sector. Groups are run by members who take turns opening and closing the meetings. The group meeting often takes place in rented spaces in civic, public, or religious buildings.

Recovering heroin addicts attend a church service in Warsaw, Poland. Acknowledging belief in a higher power, such as God, and developing spiritually are key steps in an NA recovery program.

The necessity for anonymity

One important aspect of self-disclosure practiced in NA is anonymity. The program states that "Anonymity is the spiritual foundation of all our traditions, ever reminding us to place principles before personalities." Members therefore introduce themselves to the group using only their first name.

Anonymity is important in NA as a means of encouraging humility and avoiding egoism. In addition, this policy reduces any fears that members may have of the likely social or legal consequences if they admit to their addiction. In accordance with this policy, there are no records of attendance at meetings, which, however, makes it difficult to judge the effect of NA programs. Anonymity also extends to the presentation of public information for television and newspapers. While members may choose to participate at events in the public arena, the disclosure of full names or having publicity photographs taken are considered a violation of the tradition, which states that "Our public-relations policy is based on attraction rather than promotion;

we need always maintain personal anonymity at the level of press, radio, and films."

In countries where NA groups are well established, a local service committee, comprising delegates elected by local groups, may offer a range of services such as telephone information, presentations on the NA program to treatment or correctional facilities, and the distribution of NA literature. NA literature has been translated into many languages (more than 40 in 2011, with more planned), reflecting the worldwide spread of this organization. In countries where many groups have been established, regional committees may exist to coordinate the local service committees. On an international level, NA holds an assembly known as the World Service Conference, where delegates establish guidelines for the entire organization.

P. G. THOMPSON

SEE ALSO:

Alcoholics Anonymous • Step Programs • Support Groups

National Institute on Alcohol Abuse and Alcoholism (NIAAA)

The National Institute on Alcohol Abuse and Alcoholism is one of the centers that are part of the National Institutes of Health (NIH). NIAAA supports most of the research conducted on alcohol abuse in the United States.

The National Institute on Alcohol Abuse and Alcoholism supports and conducts biomedical and behavioral research on the causes, consequences, treatment, and prevention of alcoholism and alcohol-related problems.

NIAAA traces some of its roots back to the founding in 1935 of Alcoholics Anonymous (AA). Prior to this, alcohol abuse was considered either a moral weakness, a sin, or a criminal behavior. The establishment of recovery organizations such as AA represented the beginning of a reconsideration of alcoholism less as a failure of willpower and more as an illness requiring treatment.

Scientific and medical organizations supported this concept, and a growing research effort, as well as the establishment of scholarly publications directed at alcoholism, slowly began to recast the public perception of alcohol abuse and alcoholism as problems that would yield to scientific study. In addition, educational organizations such as the National Committee for Education on Alcohol (founded by Marty Mann, the first woman to recover through AA) began recasting alcoholism as a disease.

Major medical and mental health organizations, including the American Medical Association and the World Health Organization, began to focus increasingly on health care dimensions of alcoholism. In the 1960s the American Psychiatric Association and the American Public Health Association formally designated alcoholism as an illness, even as public opinion clung to the view of alcohol abuse and alcoholism as a moral issue.

On July 30, 1969, the first hearing of the Special Subcommittee on Alcoholism and Narcotics was held in Washington, D.C. Among those testifying at this event were Marty Mann and William G. Wilson (also known as "Bill W.," one of the founders of AA). Wilson's testimony before the Senate Alcoholism Subcommittee hearing was pivotal, along with a series of other hearings in which the members of the subcommittee listened to testimony from scientists, alcoholism treatment providers, religious leaders, and recovered alcoholics. Based in part on these hearings, on May 14, 1970, Senator Harold E. Hughes (himself a recovered alcoholic) introduced a bill that was intended to establish a comprehensive federal program that would address the prevention and treatment of alcohol abuse and alcoholism. On December 31, 1970, President Richard Nixon signed into public law the Comprehensive Alcohol Abuse and Alcoholism Prevention, Treatment, and Rehabilitation Act of 1970. This legislation placed NIAAA as a part of the National Institute of Mental Health (NIMH), with Morris Chafetz as its first director. NIAAA, NIMH, and NIDA (National Institute on Drug Abuse) were established as sister institutes within the Alcohol, Drug Abuse and Mental Health Administration (ADAMHA) in May 1974. On July 10, 1992, the ADAMHA Reorganization Act made NIAAA an independent NIH institute. NIAAA receives funding for its activities through the federal budget appropriations process. NIAAA receives less than 2 percent of the total NIH budget to carry out its activities.

Mission

To achieve its mission of investigating the causes and treatment of alcohol problems, NIAAA works with a wide range of researchers, health care and treatment providers, universities, communities, businesses, and governments. NIAAA supports preventive interventions, epidemiology, and treatment research. Research is performed by intramural researchers, who work within the National Institutes of Health, and by extramural researchers at universities, medical schools, and centers throughout the country. Research sponsored by NIAAA has made a number of significant contributions to understanding and treating the causes of alcoholism:

- Identification of the neurotransmitter receptors and neural circuits that are targeted by ethanol, particularly neurons that use the neurotransmitters GABA, glutamate, and dopamine
- Identification of the genetic contributions to alcohol abuse and addiction. Through the Collaborative Study on the Genetics of Alcoholism and studies of groups with a predisposition to alcoholism, NIAAA-funded scientists have identified several chromosome regions that may contain genes that influence individual susceptibility to alcoholism
- Identification of the biological mechanisms of fetal alcohol syndrome (FAS), the country's leading cause of preventable birth defects, which suggests potential for pharmacologic and therapeutic interventions
- Understanding of the risks to major body organs, such as the heart and liver, by excessive ethanol consumption and treatments for these ethanol-related disorders
- Clinical trials of promising new drugs that prevent relapse or inhibit the desire to drink
- Prevention efforts aimed at adolescent drinking are a primary focus, as studies indicate that drinking at a young age increases the likelihood of life-long alcohol abuse and dependence.

NIAAA, in addition to sponsoring research, communicates research findings to the public through a number of initiatives, including the Research to Practice Initiative, Alcohol Screening Day, the Advisory Council's Subcommittee on College Drinking, and the Leadership to Keep Children Alcohol-Free. NIAAA strives to balance the responsibility of providing the most current information on alcohol abuse and alcoholism without sensationalizing research findings.

Almost 14 million U.S. adults meet medical criteria for the diagnosis of alcohol abuse or alcoholism, with approximately 6.6 million children under age 18 living in family environments where at least one parent is an alcoholic. Although alcohol is not regulated in the same way as illicit drugs, there is a significant societal impact of alcohol abuse and alcoholism. In the United States more than 100,000 people die each year of alcohol-related causes. NIAAA estimates that alcohol abuse has a

William G. Wilson, known as "Bill W.," was one of the founders of Alcoholics Anonymous. He was also instrumental in the process that led to the establishment of NIAAA and research into alcoholism.

societal cost of at least $185 billion. This figure includes direct treatment and health care costs (14 percent), reduced productivity of those who abuse (47 percent), and productivity losses due to premature death (20 percent). Costs associated with traffic crashes and criminal activity account for around 9 percent each.

Research into alcoholism has moved forward in tandem with the acceptance of alcoholism as a medical disorder. The mission of NIAAA has evolved over the years to emphasize basic research into the root causes of alcohol abuse and alcoholism as well as the dissemination of research results, in an ongoing effort to translate these basic research findings into prevention and treatment strategies.

Proposals have been made to merge NIAAA with the National Institute of Drug Abuse (NIDA). Proponents justify this proposed merger on the basis of similar missions and scientific focus on addiction. Critics argue that drug and alcohol addiction each possess unique societal and scientific components that require individualized approaches and study.

D. W. GODWIN

SEE ALSO:
Alcoholics Anonymous • Alcoholism • Alcoholism Treatment • Binge Drinking

National Institute on Drug Abuse (NIDA)

The National Institute on Drug Abuse (NIDA) is one of the institutes and centers that are part of the National Institutes of Health (NIH). NIDA supports more than 85 percent of the world's research on drug addiction.

NIDA was established in 1974 as a federal agency for research, treatment, prevention, and data collection on the nature and extent of drug abuse. NIDA was initially part of an agency called Alcohol, Drug Abuse, and Mental Health (ADAMHA). NIDA's first mandate was data collection and research: from 1974 to 1992 the data collection was implemented by work on the Drug Abuse Warning Network (a system of information gathering based on hospital visits and reports from medical examiners and coroners), and the National Survey on Drug Use and Health (a survey tracking specific illicit substance abuse trends). The research mission was located in the Addiction Research Center, a center within a United States Public Health Service hospital in Lexington, Kentucky. The Addiction Research Center was a research unit of the hospital that was created in 1935 to study heroin addiction among prisoners and others who voluntarily admitted themselves for treatment. The Addiction Research Center became NIDA's first internal research program.

The mission of NIDA shifted more toward research when, in 1981, the United States Congress legislated the Alcohol and Drug Abuse and Mental Health Services block grant program. The responsibility for delivery of prevention and treatment services was shifted to individual states. NIDA maintained primary responsibility for supporting and conducting research on drugs of abuse. Alcohol is covered by a separate organization, the National Institute on Alcohol Abuse and Addiction (NIAAA). Additional legislation expanded the NIDA's role in disseminating research findings to states, localities, and community organizations around the country. In October 1992, NIDA became one of the National Institutes of Health under the ADAMHA Reorganization Act. The organization receives funding from the United States government through the budget appropriations process. Out of the approximately $27 billion NIH 2003 budget, NIDA received approximately $968 million to underwrite its activities.

Mission

The mission of NIDA is to focus the scientific resources and expertise of the nation on the problem of drug abuse and addiction. This mission has two main parts—research and the dissemination of research findings. To fulfill the research responsibility, NIDA supports and conducts research across a broad range of disciplines. This goal is accomplished through two programs. The first is an Intramural Program of staff scientists who work within NIDA in areas such as molecular biology, drug discovery, behavioral science, and brain imaging. The second is called the Extramural Program, and in this program individual scientists from across the nation may apply for grant and contract funding to carry out research that is consistent with the core mission of NIDA.

NIDA-sponsored research has had a broad impact on the understanding of the processes of drug abuse and addiction. Research supported by NIDA addresses fundamental questions about drug abuse, including tracking trends in emerging drug use, understanding the mechanisms underlying how drugs work in the brain, and developing and testing new drug prevention and treatment strategies. Among specific accomplishments attributed to NIDA research and support are the identification of the regions of the brain and the molecular targets of every major drug of abuse, including the opiates, cocaine, PCP, and THC (the active ingredient in marijuana).

Work has also been carried out to develop neurobehavioral models that characterize drug-taking behavior in order to improve treatment and rehabilitation methods. Efforts to improve drug therapies have included support for the development of three medications for the treatment of opiate addiction (LAAM, buprenorphine, and naltrexone), which NIDA shepherded through the Food and Drug Administration's approval process. Treatments have also been developed for newborns withdrawing from narcotic exposure in the womb. NIDA further pioneered the use of drugs used to treat depression and other mental disorders in drug users to improve therapy for addiction. NIDA-sponsored scientists were the first to recognize the link between HIV and intravenous drug abuse, and led innovative community-based research on prevention strategies.

Research into the mechanisms of addiction has verified physiological studies identifying brain regions (and has identified new circuits) involved in craving, reward, euphoria, and other effects of addictive drugs. Key studies on tobacco have demonstrated the addiction potential for nicotine, and led to the development of the scientific basis for nicotine gum and skin patches as therapy. It has also been shown that prenatal exposure to cigarettes and marijuana have long-term effects on the brain.

New areas of addiction research are being pioneered in the fields of genetics and immunology. Among the successes achieved by NIDA scientists are the cloning of the genes for the major drug receptors for nearly all drugs of abuse, an important step in understanding how drugs affect brain circuits. Mice have been genetically engineered to eliminate or "knock out" certain drug receptors, showing how drugs affect certain brain circuits. Rats have been immunized against the psychostimulant effects of cocaine, which some scientists believe may lead eventually to a vaccine against the addicting power of cocaine.

Public role

In fulfilling its responsibility to disseminate the findings of its varied research endeavors, NIDA has become a clearinghouse for the most up-to-date information available on drugs of abuse and societal drug use trends. NIDA and other agencies discover what drugs are being abused by characterizing trends in drug use through the use of surveys and data collection. NIDA supports the collection of data on drug abuse patterns through the Monitoring the Future Study (an ongoing study of the behaviors, attitudes, and values of

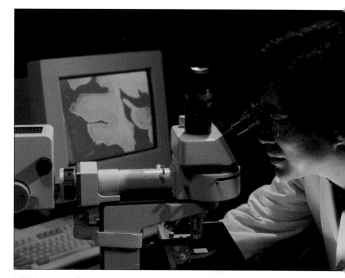

NIDA research into neural pathways yields clues about reward mechanisms and the process of addiction.

American secondary school students, college students, and young adults). NIDA has also compiled information on its Web site on commonly abused drugs. The organization also monitors general and emerging drug use trends through periodic meetings of its Community Epidemiology Work Group, which reviews trends in major metropolitan areas.

In communicating research findings to the general public, NIDA strives to explain the known hazards of drug abuse and addiction without sensationalizing or overinterpreting dangers that are still under active investigation. This is sometimes a difficult balance to achieve, and NIDA is not without critics. While the mission of the organization has shifted over the years toward the basic science of drug abuse and addiction, its research and dissemination efforts have led to many new and improved strategies for prevention and treatment. In 2003, a National Academies panel recommended a study to merge NIDA with NIAAA, with the justification that the missions of the two agencies overlap. This proposal has gathered support, but the two organizations remain separate in 2011.

D. W. GODWIN

SEE ALSO:

Addiction • American Society of Addiction Medicine (ASAM) • Causes of Addiction • Research, Medical

Needle Exchange Programs

Providing clean needles to injecting drug users has been a controversial policy in many countries. However, reductions in the number of infections among drug users prove that the practice has health benefits.

Needle exchange programs (NEPs) arose from the concept of harm reduction in dealing with drug problems. This concept assumes that it is impossible to stamp out all illegal drug use, so a useful strategy in dealing with some of the problems of addiction is to try to reduce the harm caused by activities associated with drug use. One of the most dangerous ways to use drugs is to inject them. Intravenous use gets the drug into the system extremely quickly and, because all the drug is injected at the same time, the person is more likely to overdose. Another problem is that people who inject drugs tend to share needles and syringes with other users. Sharing drug paraphernalia puts users at risk of contracting HIV (human immunodeficiency virus), hepatitis, and other blood-borne diseases. The idea behind needle exchange programs is that they provide free, clean, and sterile equipment so that users do not have to share.

Background

The idea to provide clean needles was first tried in the Netherlands in 1983. Dutch health workers realized that they could not eradicate all injecting drug use. At the same time, there was great public concern about HIV, and it was known that injecting drugs was a key risk factor in acquiring the virus. The Dutch, swiftly followed by the United Kingdom and other countries, decided that it was more important for the community at large to stop the spread of HIV than it was to get people off drugs, so NEPs were set up to provide clean equipment. The idea worked. Over the years, the Netherlands and the United Kingdom have had some of the lowest HIV rates among drug users in Europe, compared with countries such as Spain, which had many drug injectors but no NEPs.

Benefits of needle exchange

Based on evidence collected worldwide, including that from programs operating in the United States, NEPs have been shown to reduce unsafe injection practices, curtail transmission of HIV/AIDS and hepatitis, increase the safe disposal of used syringes, and help injecting drug users obtain drug information, treatment, detoxification, social services, and primary health care. Many users who access NEPs have never used any other drug-treatment service. The research also showed that access to sterile syringes does not encourage people to increase drug use or to start injecting drugs. Nor does access to sterile syringes hinder other drug treatment efforts.

Although politically committed to a "drug-free world," the United Nations has recommended a comprehensive package of prevention and care for injecting drug users that could include such harm-reduction measures as access to clean needles and syringes. Most health professionals working in the drugs and AIDS fields around the world (including developing countries), health academics and researchers, and national and international medical organizations and charities recognize the value of NEPs as one of a range of measures to reduce the harm caused by drugs.

Opposition to NEPs

In the United States, the Centers for Disease Control and Prevention estimates that 24 percent of all AIDS infections can be related to injection drug use. The Substance Abuse and Mental Health Services Administration estimates that around 400,000 Americans may be injection drug users.

However, despite these figures and the research evidence from around the world, the U.S. Congress has restricted the use of federal funds for NEPs, fearing that the implementation of NEPs would encourage substance abuse by sending the message that injection drug use is endorsed and promoted through the distribution of clean needles. However, since 2010, the ban on federal funding has been modified so that programs are eligible for federal support, subject to provisions regarding the location of such programs. Yet there is also a feeling among some politicians and organizations that harm

Some needle exchange programs are run by outreach workers who go into the streets to find drug users who may be reluctant to come into a center. Collecting needles also prevents other people from accidental injury— HIV can linger for up to four weeks in a discarded syringe.

reduction as a concept is defeatist and also that it is being used as a back-door route by those who want to legalize all drugs.

Despite restricted federal funding, the North American Syringe Exchange Network (NASEN) estimates that there are 184 NEPs operating in 36 U.S. states. These often provide drug-treatment referrals, methadone clinics, peer education, and HIV prevention programs. However, those who attend NEPs have at times risked arrest. In 2002 New York City police were ordered to stop arresting and charging drug users who participate in state-approved hypodermic needle exchange programs. The court found that police were charging users with drug possession based on the residue of drugs found in used needles and with illegal possession of hypodermic needles and syringes.

The problem was caused by the contradiction of New York penal law sections criminalizing needle and drug possession and sections of the New York

public health law that empower the state health commissioner to establish a number of needle exchange pilot projects and to designate classes of people who are allowed to obtain needles and syringes without a prescription and who carry cards to say they are in the program. The goal behind the pilot projects was to reduce the transmission of HIV and other diseases through the sharing of dirty needles among users, who were given cards that attested to their participation in the program, which were supposed to shield them from arrest.

Attempts at the deregulation of syringe sales have been generally hampered by state-level drug paraphernalia and prescription laws. However, among the states that have officially recognized NEPs, possession of needles and syringes obtained from the program would not be illegal. The exemptions may be written into state laws, may arise from judicial decisions, or merely be acknowledged in police practices or through prosecutorial discretion. In general, if a state or city authorizes a NEP, this is usually considered to overrule any countervailing paraphernalia regulations.

Examples of state action are evident in Maine, Minnesota, and New York, which changed their drug paraphernalia and prescription laws to allow over-the-counter purchase of up to ten syringes; Rhode Island has legalized pharmacy sales of syringes and set no limit on how many may be purchased. According to one survey, since Connecticut changed its paraphernalia laws in 1992 to allow for possession and sale of up to ten syringes, needle sharing among injecting drug users dropped by 40 percent, and needle-stick injuries to police decreased by 66 percent.

Types of programs

Drug agencies run different types of NEPs. The majority are at fixed sites—either set up specifically for the exchange of needles and syringes or as part of existing treatment facilities. A key part of the NEP initiative is to encourage people who have never accessed a treatment service to come forward. To that end, outreach workers will go out into the community to encourage people to come into their local service. Some agencies run mobile vans that tour the community dispensing clean equipment and advice on hygienic practice.

As well as drug agencies, many local pharmacies are involved in the program. The sale of syringes in pharmacies has allowed drug users in areas that cannot sustain NEPs to access clean needles. Access to sterile syringes through pharmacies can ensure that clean equipment is available where there is strong local resident opposition to the establishment of a dedicated facility. There is also a population of drug users in need of sterile needles who may not feel comfortable attending NEPs because they are reluctant to be identified as injecting drug users.

Pharmacy sale is standard throughout western Europe, much of central and eastern Europe, Australia, Canada, New Zealand and, increasingly, in the United States. Many pharmacies also sell special packs that include syringes, alcohol swabs, and other sterile items, such as cotton and water, which are often shared by drug users. Many packs also contain condoms and HIV prevention information. Some European countries have installed vending machines to dispense syringes at low cost.

Different agencies also have different rules about the meaning of "exchange." For some, this means one-for-one; others allow users to take as many as they want in the hope that they will give out extras to other users. A study of one NEP in Canada found that it was failing in its objective to reduce levels of HIV and hepatitis because it was not giving out enough equipment.

The need to give out sufficient needles and syringes was underlined in a document produced by the British Columbia Center for Disease Control in 2003 that gives guidance to those running NEPs. "In order for clients to use a clean needle for every injection it is necessary that NEPs provide that particular client with a sufficient number of needles to achieve this recommended standard. A consequence of this may be that the NEP distributes more needles than it retrieves or gives the client more needles than he or she has to exchange."

Impact on public health

Needle exchange programs have had an undoubted impact on the health of the drug-injecting population. The National Institutes of Health expert panel on HIV prevention has reported reductions in risk behavior of 80 percent, with an estimated drop in incidence of HIV of more than 30 percent among injecting drug users. Studies have also shown that NEPs do not encourage drug use among participants or attract first-time drug users. The majority of people using the services are older men who have been injecting for some years.

Providing clean needles comes at a cost. Estimates of needle use reveal that every injecting drug user goes through around 1,000 needles a year. At a cost of around a dollar per syringe, NEPs are still viewed as cost effective. Including the other prevention measures provided, the cost per HIV infection prevented by NEPs is calculated at $4,000 to $12,000. However, this amount is considerably less than the $190,000 it has been estimated it would cost public health services to treat a drug user infected with HIV.

H. Shapiro

Neurotransmission

The brain works by means of a system of chemical messaging called neurotransmission. Addiction can occur when this finely tuned system is upset by chemicals that mimic or interfere with the way this process operates.

Neurotransmission is the process of transferring a message from the axon of one nerve cell, across a junction called the synapse, to a neighboring nerve cell or muscle. This message is transmitted by a chemical substance called a neurotransmitter. Neurotransmitter release, diffusion, reuptake, and postsynaptic action all occur in a delicate balance that allows normal brain communication—but it also forms the basis of the brain's response to illicit and therapeutic drugs. When this balance is disturbed by drugs, the compensatory changes made by the brain to restore function contribute to addiction.

Chemical communication in the nervous system

Many nerve cells generate waves of electrical activity called action potentials. Action potentials are the means by which a message is sent rapidly across large distances in the brain. These electrical waves are caused by the opening of tiny channels that are embedded along the membrane of the nerve cell in response to the buildup of charged ions near the membrane. Once triggered, the action potential can maintain itself as it travels along a thin neural extension called an axon. Action potentials that originate at the cell body of the nerve cell can travel along the axon, but they cannot leap from one nerve cell to another. Without an additional step, nerve cells could not communicate with each other, and the human brain could not function. Action potentials are converted from electrical impulses into chemical messages that pass between nerve cells. Different parts of the brain use an arsenal of brain chemicals to send different types of messages to the receiving neuron.

After traveling from the cell body to reach the end of the axon (also called the nerve terminal, or presynaptic terminal), action potentials trigger the release of neurotransmitters at a junction where the nerve cell and its neighbor come very close together—this junction is called the synapse. The neurotransmitter rapidly diffuses across a narrow fluid-filled space between the two cells that is called the synaptic cleft. This space is only about 10 to 30 nanometers wide, so the neurotransmitter molecules can quickly cross the space between the axon and the neighboring nerve cell. Once the journey is complete, the neurotransmitter binds to proteins called receptors that are embedded in the postsynaptic membrane of the adjacent nerve cell. Depending on the neurotransmitter, this binding may result in either stimulation or inhibition of electrical impulses in the neighboring cell. The neurotransmitter may be quickly inactivated within the synapse either through the breakdown of the neurotransmitter by enzymes, or through the reabsorption (reuptake) of the neurotransmitter by the axon, employing transporter molecules located on the cell membrane in order to recycle the neurotransmitter.

Neurotransmitters may cause rapid changes in the excitability of the neighboring neuron, a process called the postsynaptic response. This usually occurs in the form of a postsynaptic potential (PSP). The response is usually excitatory (EPSP) or inhibitory (IPSP) to the neuron, making it more likely (in the case of the EPSP) or less likely (in the case of the IPSP) that the next neuron in the chain will generate an action potential. In muscle tissue, contraction results in response to the neurotransmitter.

Role of calcium in releasing neurotransmitters

The release of the neurotransmitter is a tightly regulated process. The region of the synapse includes the presynaptic nerve terminal that is filled with packets of the neurotransmitter, the synaptic cleft, and the postsynaptic neuron. The presynaptic terminal is specialized to convert the electrical action potential signal into a chemical signal. When action potentials flow into the terminal membrane, the strong depolarization triggers the opening of a cluster of calcium channels. When these channels open, calcium ions (Ca^{2+}) flow into the terminal. Near these clusters of channels, the local concentration of Ca^{2+} may increase nearly a thousandfold.

Studies have demonstrated that calcium must reach a rather high concentration to trigger neurotransmitter release, and that release only occurs very

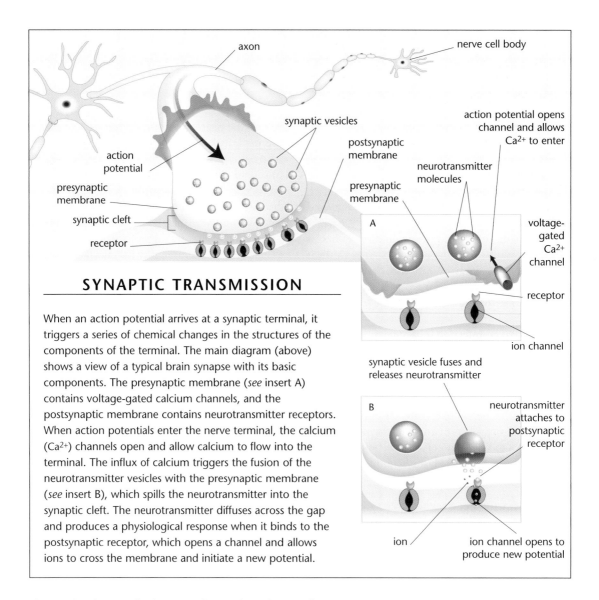

SYNAPTIC TRANSMISSION

When an action potential arrives at a synaptic terminal, it triggers a series of chemical changes in the structures of the components of the terminal. The main diagram (above) shows a view of a typical brain synapse with its basic components. The presynaptic membrane (*see* insert A) contains voltage-gated calcium channels, and the postsynaptic membrane contains neurotransmitter receptors. When action potentials enter the nerve terminal, the calcium (Ca^{2+}) channels open and allow calcium to flow into the terminal. The influx of calcium triggers the fusion of the neurotransmitter vesicles with the presynaptic membrane (*see* insert B), which spills the neurotransmitter into the synaptic cleft. The neurotransmitter diffuses across the gap and produces a physiological response when it binds to the postsynaptic receptor, which opens a channel and allows ions to cross the membrane and initiate a new potential.

close to the clusters of voltage-gated Ca^{2+} channels in the nerve terminal. All neurotransmitters, except for neuropeptides, are made in the terminal, where they are contained in packets called vesicles. The vesicles are composed of neurotransmitters contained in a bubblelike sac made of a lipid bilayer that is embedded with proteins. Ca^{2+} causes the vesicle to move close to the presynaptic terminal to dock and fuse with the terminal membrane (this process, called exocytosis, occurs in many cells). There are several proteins associated with the vesicle that are thought to be involved in vesicle docking and fusion. One possible target of this flood of Ca^{2+} is thought to be synaptotagmin, which is a vesicle protein that becomes involved in the vesicle-docking complex that brings the synaptic vesicle membrane and the presynaptic membranes close enough together to fuse. Ca^{2+} is thought to induce a change in the shape of synaptotagmin that, in conjunction with other proteins, leads to the formation of a fusion pore, through which the neurotransmitter is released from the presynaptic terminal to cross the synaptic cleft. If many action potentials invade the synaptic terminal in quick succession, more calcium flows in through the channels that, in turn, results in a flood of neurotransmitter release. After rapidly diffusing across the synaptic cleft, the neurotransmitter binds to a postsynaptic receptor (either on a target muscle, a blood vessel, or a nerve cell). Receptor binding may also occur at receptors (called autoreceptors) of the terminal releasing the neurotransmitters, which modulates the amount of transmitter released.

Types of neurotransmitters

The specificity and physiological action of a neurotransmitter is determined by its chemical structure and the structure and response of the receptor proteins to which it binds. Many drugs of abuse share structural similarities to common neurotransmitters, or they control the duration of neurotransmitter response by modulating the levels of naturally occurring neurotransmitters at the synapse. Neurotransmitters have a variety of chemical structures, but they can be divided into two main categories—small molecule transmitters and neuropeptides. Though many volumes have been written about the neurotransmitters, their basic properties can be briefly summarized:

Biogenic amine neurotransmitters. The biogenic amines include the catecholamines (dopamine, norepinephrine, and epinephrine), as well as serotonin and histamine. All catecholamines are derived from the amino acid tyrosine. They are part of the same biochemical pathway and their structures are, in many cases, separated by the action of a single enzyme. The enzyme tyrosine hydroxylase converts tyrosine to dihydroxyphenylalanine (DOPA), which is in turn converted to dopamine through action of the enzyme DOPA decarboxylase. Dopamine can be converted into norepinephrine and finally epinephrine. Though not amino acids themselves, histamine and serotonin are derived through enzyme modification of amino acids (histidine and tryptophan, respectively).

Amino acid neurotransmitters. Amino acid neurotransmitters include glutamate, the most prevalent excitatory amino acid neurotransmitter in the brain (more than half of the brain's synapses use glutamate), and gamma-aminobutyric acid (GABA), the dominant inhibitory amino acid neurotransmitter (used by about one-third of the brain's synapses). Glutamate release results in rapid excitation of nerve cells that possess glutamate receptors. GABA release results in rapid inhibition in nerve cells containing GABA receptors, making it less likely that these cells will generate action potentials.

Acetylcholine. Acetylcholine is the neurotransmitter used by motor neurons that extend from the spinal cord to form synapses with muscles. Acetylcholine release at these "neuromuscular junctions" causes

RECOGNIZING NEUROTRANSMITTERS (THE FIVE Rs)

A set of classic criteria known as "the five Rs" dating back to the 1920s has been developed to determine whether a substance should be considered a neurotransmitter. These criteria can be summarized by the following conditions:

- The substance *resides* in the presynaptic neuron. The neurons contain the transmitter and the appropriate enzymes to synthesize it.
- It is *released* in response to presynaptic activity.
- *Receptors* for the substance are present in the synapse, which can be shown through the pharmacological blockade of the receptor with known antagonists. Receptors may also be detected with antibodies that are raised to recognize and bind to the receptors.

- *Removal* or termination of the transmitter action occurs through active mechanisms such as enzymes, reuptake by presynaptic terminals, and uptake by postsynaptic neurons.
- *Replication* of the effects can be achieved by stimulating the neural pathway of the candidate substance or by the application of the substance.

These criteria provide a good fit for most neurotransmitters; however, exceptions exist in the brain, including the gaseous neurotransmitter nitric oxide (NO). This chemical is generated by an enzyme when it is needed, rather than being stored in vesicles, and diffuses across membranes, rather than relying on normal neurotransmitter release mechanisms.

muscle contraction and movement. This neurotransmitter is also released by cells that are part of the diffuse brain stem pathways controlling arousal and attention. Acetylcholine is usually considered to be excitatory if it attaches to nicotinic receptors, but inhibition can occur through activation of muscarinic receptors (the names "nicotinic" and "muscarinic" refer to chemical agents, nicotine and muscarine, that have been used to segregate the functions of the receptors from each other).

Neuropeptides. Neuropeptides are transmitters that are first synthesized at the cell body, shipped out to the synaptic terminal, and released from large vesicles that are located away from the small-molecule neurotransmitters. This location, within the terminal but away from the active zones, suggests that peptides are probably released when action potentials are invading the presynaptic terminal at particularly high rates. Peptides are made from large, propeptide starter molecules, which may be broken down into smaller neuroactive molecules, some of which are also peptides. The opioids are a type of peptide that are particularly important in drug abuse and addiction. Morphine is the active ingredient of opium that binds to opium receptors.

The others. Other substances do not fit neatly into the criteria defining neurotransmitters. These include substances such as nitric oxide (NO), which is made in response to activity of a calcium-dependent enzyme. NO is not packed into vesicles, nor does it require vesicle docking, but is instead made on demand. Unlike the classic neurotransmitters, which are locally released, NO diffuses freely across cellular compartments and can even be made on the postsynaptic side of the synapse to diffuse to the presynaptic terminal.

Basic types of neurotransmitter receptors

Neurotransmitter receptors are proteins that are embedded in the nerve cell membrane. Neurotransmitters bind to the receptor and cause a physiological change in the nerve or muscle cell. Many drugs act through their ability to mimic the form and functional interaction of neurotransmitters with receptors.

There are two fundamentally different types of neurotransmitter receptors—ionotropic receptors and metabotropic receptors. Ionotropic receptors are relatively large protein complexes that form ion channels. These channels perform the same essential role as the Ca^{2+} channels—allowing ions through the

LONG-TERM SYNAPTIC RESPONSES TO DRUGS

Synapses have several control points that modulate the release and turnover of neurotransmitters. Under normal conditions (A) the effect of a neurotransmitter, such as dopamine or serotonin, released into the synapse is terminated by enzymes, through the reuptake (reabsorption) of the neurotransmitter back into the presynaptic terminal, or through autoreceptors that reduce the degree of neurotransmitter release (or combinations of these mechanisms). Drugs of abuse upset these control mechanisms. Part of cocaine's acute effect (B) is thought to involve blockade of the reuptake transporter that is responsible for removing dopamine from synapses. In response to cocaine, dopamine is thought to

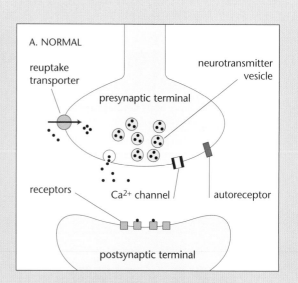

accumulate in the synapse and strongly stimulate dopamine receptors. Prolonged use of cocaine (C)

membrane. The difference is that these channels will not pass ions in the absence of a neurotransmitter, but the binding of a neurotransmitter to a region of the receptor induces a change in the shape of the channel that causes it to open and permits ions to flow down electrochemical gradients. Ion flow ceases when the transmitter disengages, or if the receptor becomes desensitized.

Metabotropic receptors are receptors that do not directly trigger the opening of ion channels but instead are linked to so-called second messengers. (Second messengers are chemicals within the cell that can modify the activity of the cell.) Metabotropic receptors are composed of a single polypeptide and possess numerous regions that pass in and out of the cell membrane. Binding of a neurotransmitter induces a change in the shape of the protein that allows the receptor to interact with G-proteins in the neural membrane. G-proteins may affect ion channels laterally through the membrane, or through functional coupling with the second messengers within the cell.

The description of synaptic transmission so far has centered on ionotropic receptors, which turn chemical signals (presynaptically released neurotransmitter) into electrical signals (postsynaptic potentials, or PSPs). The postsynaptic potentials produced by opening or closing ion channels may excite or inhibit the cell. In contrast to the rapid changes caused by activating ionotropic receptors, metabotropic receptor effects tend to be slow in building and in turning off, and some are considered to be neuromodulatory, modifying the electrical activity of other inputs. Their influence on the cells depends in part on the type and number of second messengers with which they interact.

Many neurotransmitters activate both ionotropic and metabotropic receptors. A notable example is acetylcholine, known to have both fast excitatory effects through nicotinic receptors and slow modulatory effects through muscarinic receptors. Other examples include GABA and glutamate, which are not classically thought of as neuromodulators. In many cases, both ionotropic and metabotropic receptors can be present at the same postsynaptic site, providing an even more potent variety of postsynaptic responses. Some neurotransmitters, such as dopamine and norepinephrine, activate only metabotropic receptors. A given neurotransmitter may be excitatory or inhibitory and may act rapidly or slowly, depending on the activated receptors.

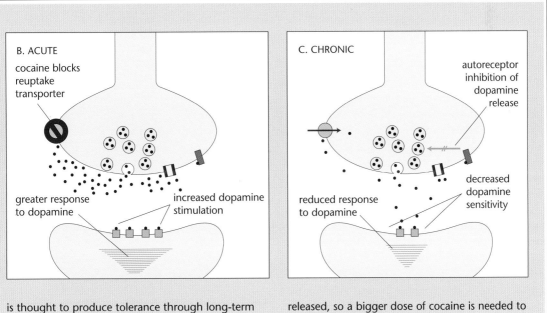

is thought to produce tolerance through long-term changes in sensitivity to dopamine. Less dopamine is released, so a bigger dose of cocaine is needed to produce a euphoric effect.

The synapse and drugs of abuse

Research has shown that the synapse is an important target of many drugs and that changes in the operation of the synapse may support drug addiction. Cocaine is a prime example of an addictive drug that affects the physiology of synapses.

Normally, neurotransmitters are removed from the synaptic cleft by transporter protein molecules that reabsorb them back into the presynaptic neuron. There are transporters that interact with many drugs, including cocaine, amphetamines, and antidepressants. Cocaine reduces the activity of monoamine transporter proteins, blocking the reuptake of dopamine, norepinephrine, and serotonin. This blocking prolongs the duration of monoamine-mediated synaptic potentials. Monoamine autoreceptors may further inhibit the release of monoamine neurotransmitters.

A major pathway in the brain that is greatly affected by cocaine is the pathway between the ventral tegmental area (VTA) to the region of the brain known as the nucleus accumbens, considered part of the brain's reward pathway. When normal pleasurable events occur, dopamine is released at the dopamine-containing synaptic terminals that communicate with nucleus accumbens neurons. Cocaine blocks the removal of dopamine from the synapse, causing it to accumulate. This buildup of dopamine produces overstimulation of receiving neurons, intensifying the euphoria associated with cocaine abuse. As the abuse of cocaine continues, the receptor proteins that comprise the synapse are thought to adapt to compensate for the abnormal stimulation, a process called tolerance. Neurons are thought to respond to the additional dopamine stimulation by reducing the available dopamine receptors and by autoreceptors reducing the amount of endogenous dopamine release. This change has two major consequences. First, with greater adaptation, normal modes of pleasurable stimulation lose their impact in daily life. Second, higher frequency of cocaine use occurs and higher doses are used in an effort to produce the same euphoria achieved with the first use of the drug. The action of amphetamine at the synapse is more complex but involves reversing the transport of dopamine out of the terminal. In mice in which the transporter has been "knocked out," or deleted with molecular biological techniques, amphetamine does not increase synaptic dopamine levels.

Ethanol abuse also involves significant changes to the synapse. Ethanol has many targets within the brain, but two in particular involve fast synaptic transmission. Gamma-aminobutyric acid (GABA) is the major inhibitory neurotransmitter in the brain, and GABA-like drugs are used to depress the firing of neurons. Alcohol acts in part by mimicking the effect of GABA at these synapses, binding to GABA receptors and inhibiting neuronal signaling. Alcohol also inhibits the major excitatory neurotransmitter, glutamate, particularly at the N-methyl-D-aspartate (NMDA) class of glutamate receptor. Alcohol abuse produces tolerance in part by changing the sensitivity of postsynaptic receptors. This may occur for both GABA and glutamate through changes produced by alcohol in the presynaptic terminals. These changes may promote GABA or glutamate release into the synapse. Similar to the response of dopamine synapses to cocaine, excess GABA or glutamate may transform normally functioning synapses by disturbing the normal balance of mechanisms that control neurotransmitter levels within the synapse.

The future for addiction research

As with many psychiatric disorders, at the most basic level drug addiction is a malfunction of neurotransmission occurring at synapses. Although understanding a disruption of a chemical balance at such a fine scale may seem daunting for designing effective treatments, there are many reasons for optimism. "Knockout" mice that are deficient in certain receptors and transporters are beginning to provide important clues about the structural changes that the synapse may undergo in the transition to addiction. Drug-induced changes to genes and proteins can be measured by using new scientific technologies, which is leading to improved physiological, behavioral, and molecular findings. The overall goal of research directed at the synaptic disruption caused by drugs of abuse are treatments that will blunt or block the addiction process and the painful process of withdrawal, and thereby ease the path to recovery.

D. W. GODWIN

SEE ALSO:
Sensitization • Tolerance

Nicotine Replacements

Attempts to stop smoking can require a great deal more than willpower alone. The symptoms of withdrawal can be alleviated by using products that deliver nicotine in a safe manner without the harmful effects of tobacco.

Regular use of tobacco products, such as cigarettes, cigars, chewing tobacco, or snuff, produces nicotine dependence, which is characterized by a persistent use of tobacco despite knowledge of the harm it causes and a desire to stop. A major reason that tobacco use is difficult to stop is the emergence of nicotine withdrawal, the body's reaction to a dropping level of nicotine that was previously maintained by regular tobacco use. When an individual stops using tobacco, nicotine is no longer being delivered to the brain, and the body reacts to this sudden change. That reaction is called withdrawal. Nicotine withdrawal can make people feel irritable, frustrated, anxious, depressed, and restless. It also often increases appetite and craving and can lead to difficulties sleeping and concentrating. Nicotine withdrawal usually peaks within several days but can last up to four weeks, varying in severity from person to person.

Because nicotine withdrawal is the body's reaction to the absence of nicotine, the only sure way to stop withdrawal is to use nicotine again. Returning to tobacco use will very quickly diminish the unpleasant symptoms of withdrawal. In fact, people who use tobacco products learn this before they ever try to quit. For example, a tobacco user will begin to feel mild symptoms of withdrawal within a few hours of his or her last cigarette. This cues the smoker that his or her nicotine levels are dropping and tobacco must be used again soon to keep such symptoms from escalating.

The knowledge that using nicotine again will eliminate withdrawal is a key reason that quitting smoking, or any tobacco use, is difficult. In order to quit, an individual must be able or willing to fight through nicotine withdrawal until it finally ceases. How difficult that is depends on the person and the amount of tobacco used daily prior to quitting. With little exception, nicotine withdrawal after quitting is a difficult and unpleasant experience, and the inability to deal with it is the most commonly reported reason for returning to tobacco use within a few weeks of quitting.

Using nicotine to quit tobacco use

With so many people reporting that nicotine withdrawal leads them back to tobacco use after quitting, a number of treatments to lessen withdrawal have been developed. The goal of these treatments is to get nicotine to the brain through methods less harmful and addictive than tobacco products. Therefore, these treatments are termed nicotine replacement therapies (NRTs). The rationale behind NRTs is that if nicotine can be administered in safer and less addictive ways than it is through tobacco products, nicotine withdrawal, and in turn the difficulty of quitting, can be reduced.

Tobacco products deliver nicotine to the brain very quickly and in large doses, both of which make nicotine highly addictive. NRTs deliver lower doses of nicotine to the brain through slower absorption methods, thus drastically reducing the potential for addiction through such products. NRTs also allow individuals to use nicotine without being exposed to the thousands of chemicals, many of which are cancerous, that exist in tobacco products. These chemicals, such as tar, are the elements that make tobacco products so dangerous to health; NRTs, which are devoid of these ingredients, are safe.

Types of nicotine replacements

NRTs come in several forms, some of which are available over-the-counter (without a prescription) at drug stores, and some of which must be prescribed by a physician. These include nicotine gum, lozenges, patches, nasal sprays, and inhalers. These NRTs were developed mainly to help people quit smoking. Their effectiveness as cessation aides for individuals who use other types of tobacco products has not been well established.

Nicotine gum and lozenges

Nicotine gum was developed in 1984 and was the first NRT. Lozenges, which are sold separately but function in a similar manner to the gum, are a later development. Originally obtained only with a

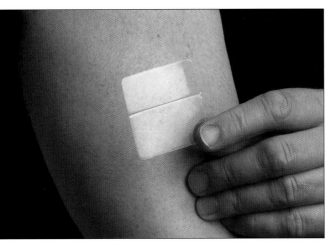

Nicotine patches are easy to use since they can be left in place throughout the day.

doctor's prescription, nicotine gum and lozenges are now widely available over the counter in both 2 milligram and 4 milligram doses and in multiple flavors. The dose and number of pieces used by individuals is, as with all NRTs, based on the level of tobacco use prior to quitting. In general, one piece of gum or one lozenge is used every 1 to 2 hours, with the time between use gradually increasing as treatment continues. Individuals are advised to follow a decreasing schedule of use for three months, which has proven more effective than using these products randomly. Unlike chewing gum, the nicotine gum is chewed briefly and slowly until a peppery taste is evident in the mouth. It is then placed between the cheek and the gum line to facilitate the absorption of nicotine through the oral mucous membranes, called buccal absorption. The gum creates a tingly feeling where it is placed. When that feeling subsides, the gum must be chewed again until the peppery taste returns, at which point it is placed again. The lozenge is used similarly, with slow dissolving and intermittent placement of the lozenge on different sides of the mouth.

The advantages of using nicotine gums and lozenges are that they are easily transportable and fairly discreet methods of NRT. The most common side effect of these NRTs is a sore throat. Chewing gum too fast or swallowing saliva too often can increase this effect and can lead to hiccups and stomachache. Eating the lozenge or swallowing too frequently while the lozenge dissolves leads to the same negative side effects. Additionally, proper use of both gum and lozenges requires consistent compliance throughout each day, which some individuals find frustrating. As a result, users often underdose with nicotine, due to misuse or lack of diligence in using these products, and they experience withdrawal.

Nicotine patches

The nicotine patch was developed in 1991. This NRT allows for gradual absorption of nicotine transdermally (through the skin). Nicotine patches are available over the counter and come in several doses, typically 21 milligrams, 14 milligrams, and 7 milligrams. A new patch is applied each day to a new area of the body, anywhere above the heart. The most common schedule for using the nicotine patch is a "step down" method. Individuals start with the highest dose needed, based on their previous tobacco use. After several weeks, they step down to a lower dose. This stepping-down process continues until the patch is no longer needed, typically after 3 months.

The nicotine patch is the most discreet method of nicotine replacement, since patches can be easily concealed under clothing. This method also leads to better compliance than most NRTs because it requires only that the person remember to put on a new patch each day. The patch has the added benefit of maintaining nicotine levels 24 hours a day, so individuals do not experience early morning withdrawal. Nicotine can, however, disrupt sleep; therefore, the patch can lead to difficulty falling asleep, night waking, and vivid dreams. Patch users can also experience mild skin irritation.

Nicotine nasal sprays

The nicotine nasal spray was developed in 1996 as a method of delivering nicotine through the nasal membranes of the nose. This method is available only by prescription. One bottle of spray contains 100 doses of nicotine and is typically used one or two times per hour. The spray bottle works similarly to common cold sprays. The nozzle is inserted in the nostril while the user's head is tilted back. The bottle is sprayed, and the nicotine solution must sit in the nasal cavity to be absorbed. Sneezing or sniffing it into the sinus cavity, where it is poorly absorbed, decreases its effectiveness.

The nicotine nasal spray delivers a larger dose of nicotine compared with other NRTs. Nasal absorption of nicotine is also more rapid than both buccal or transdermal methods. For this reason, some people, particularly those who used large amounts of tobacco prior to quitting, find this NRT to be the most helpful. On the negative side, the nicotine nasal spray can lead to sinus infection if it is used improperly. Individuals often report experiencing nasal irritation and temporary changes in smell and taste that go away with continued use. Also, because the nasal spray delivers a somewhat larger and more rapid dose of nicotine than other NRTs, it is thought to have some potential for addiction. However, this potential is very low compared with that of tobacco.

Nicotine inhaler

The nicotine inhaler was developed in 1997 and is available only by prescription. It is unique among NRTs in that it was designed to simulate the behavioral actions of smoking. A small white mouthpiece, slightly larger than a cigarette, is used to hold a cartridge containing nicotine. The nicotine can be inhaled through the mouthpiece, simulating puffing on a cigarette. The nicotine vapor enters the mouth and is absorbed buccally. At least 80 puffs must be taken from one cartridge to absorb 2 milligrams of nicotine over a 20-minute period. The number of cartridges used is reduced until the inhaler is no longer needed.

A positive feature of this method is that the simulated action of smoking a cigarette appeals to many smokers who miss the feel of a cigarette in their hand and the action of puffing. Typically, 6 to 16 cartridges are initially used per day, so that up to 7.3 hours a day of puffing might be needed to help reduce withdrawal. Therefore, this method of nicotine replacement is time consuming and not a particularly efficient way of getting nicotine. However, the side effects are generally mild and include some throat or mouth irritation and a cough that disappears after repeated use of the inhaler.

Effectiveness of NRTs

NRTs significantly increase success rates among individuals attempting to give up smoking. As stated above, the effectiveness of these products to help individuals quit other types of tobacco use has not been well established. In formal studies, approximately 15 to 20 percent of those who use NRTs during an attempt to quit are still abstinent from cigarettes one year later, compared with approximately 5 to 10 percent of those who attempt abstinence with a placebo (a product that looks like the NRT product but does not have any nicotine). Quit rates are even lower in those who stop without any cessation aids. Thus, although the absolute quit rates may seem disappointing, NRTs clearly have a positive effect on quitting smoking.

Why NRTs sometimes fail

There are three main reasons that NRTs still fail for many people. The first is simple human error. With the advent of NRTs being offered over the counter, people who use the patch or gum no longer get proper instructions for use from health care providers. Those who buy the gum or patch often do not use the product enough, leading to underdosing, which reduces effectiveness. Across all NRTs, compliance is another common error, such as forgetting to use it or using it randomly rather than following a schedule, all of which also lead to lowered effectiveness. The second reason that NRTs often fail arises from the slow speed with which they deliver nicotine, which, although a necessity to maintain safety, prevents these products from providing some of the rapid mood-elevating effects of nicotine when consumed by smoking. Thus, smokers recognize that smoking produces some effects of nicotine that they cannot get from an NRT. Finally, the most common reason that NRTs fail is that, while they clearly help reduce nicotine withdrawal, they do not help with other elements of quitting that can lead to relapse. Specifically, people report that cues associated with past tobacco use, such as the sight and smell of tobacco, friends who still use, and stressful emotional states often lead them back to tobacco use after they have quit. For this reason, nicotine replacement products are often more effective when used in combination with psychotherapies that teach methods of dealing with these triggers.

C. A. CONKLIN, K. A. PERKINS

SEE ALSO:
Smoking • Smoking Cessation • Withdrawal

Overdose

The users of most types of drugs face the risk of an overdose. Usually, overdoses are the accidental result of overconsumption, mixing drugs, or unexpected side effects. Prompt action is necessary to prevent fatalities.

An overdose is the accidental or intentional use of a drug in an amount higher than normally used, such that it produces toxic or lethal effects. However, not all overdoses are the result of taking too much. Overdosing can happen in various circumstances:

When drugs are mixed, they can produce an effect known as potentiation, in which the effect of one drug is augmented by the activity of another. Non-lethal doses of sedatives have killed people because they were taken with alcohol, both of which depress breathing. Alcohol is one of the most dangerous mixers with many types of drugs.

Injecting drugs presents a particular risk of overdosing because it puts a large amount of drug into the body all at once with no way of controlling it. In some heroin overdose cases, the drug reaches the brain so fast that the body shuts down before all of the drug can be injected.

Another risk occurs when tolerance to a drug has dropped. A high number of people who go into prison as heroin users come out clean because of the difficulty of being able to inject heroin in prison. Consequently, their tolerance to the drug drops. After release, the addict may immediately go back to using heroin at his or her previous levels, and the body is unable to cope with what is now a high dose.

Unknown side effects are another problem. Not everybody reacts to a drug in the same way. A good example of this is Ecstasy. Millions of people have tried the drug, but some have died. Ecstasy affects the way the body regulates temperature, and the user can become very overheated. If this happens when the person is dancing in a hot club environment without regular breaks and liquid intake, the temperature of the body can spiral out of control and the person may die.

An underlying medical condition of which the user is unaware may also result in a fatality. For example, somebody with an undiagnosed heart condition could die from the effects of a powerful stimulant drug such as cocaine, which increases the heart rate and can cause irregularities in heart rhythm.

Victims of an overdose should be placed in the recovery position to prevent further injury and choking. Resuscitation may be necessary if the patient is not breathing or if the heart has stopped beating.

WHAT TO DO IN THE EVENT OF AN OVERDOSE

- Call an ambulance immediately.
- If there is no other injury, move the person to a safe place free from any hazards.
- If the person has collapsed, put him or her into the recovery position and make sure that there is nothing blocking the airway.
- If the person stops breathing, use CPR (cardiopulmonary resuscitation).
- Do not leave the person alone; wait for the ambulance so that the paramedics can be made fully aware of what has happened.
- If any of the drug is still available, give it to the paramedic. It will help the medical team to identify the problem and give the correct treatment more quickly.

Lack of quality control in street drugs is another source of problems, especially when the drugs bought are poor or (paradoxically) very good quality. Drugs are not usually cut with dangerous substances, because dealers want their customers to come back. However, users have little idea of what they are buying. Sometimes, a batch of powder or pills might be unusually strong, and users may inadvertently take more of the drug, thinking that they are taking their normal dose.

Symptoms and treatment
Physical symptoms of a drug overdose will vary depending on the drug, but will include abnormal breathing, slurred speech, lack of coordination, slow or rapid pulse, low or high temperature, changes in pupil size, heavy sweating, drowsiness, delusions or hallucinations, aggressive behavior, seizures or tremors, lips turning blue, and unconsciousness.

There are various antidotes to drugs and other methods that can be used in overdose situations. Injections of naloxone are a standard treatment for heroin overdose, as naloxone binds with opiate receptors without activating them, thus preventing many of heroin's more serious effects, such as respiratory depression. Patients who have taken prescription drugs or an oral illicit drug can be made to vomit if they are still conscious by using an emetic. Alternatively, they may have their stomach contents pumped out. Tranquilizers may be administered for severe psychosis and delirium caused by hallucinogens or cocaine. Somebody suffering from a bad trip can often be talked down gently in a quiet room with subdued lighting.

Of course, not everybody who overdoses dies. A person might be admitted to a hospital overnight for treatment and then released the next day relatively unharmed. However, while many victims of drug overdose recover without long-term effects, there can be serious consequences. Some drug overdoses cause the failure of major organs, such as the kidneys or liver, or failure of whole systems, chiefly the respiratory or circulatory systems.

In the United States, the Drug Abuse Warning Network (DAWN) logs all emergency room (ER) drug admissions. Between 2001 and 2009, the number of admissions rose from around 1.6 million to just over 2 million. Alcohol in combination with other drugs topped the list for admissions, followed by cocaine, marijuana, and heroin. The actual number of deaths from illegal drugs in the United States annually is between 20,000 and 30,000, which compares with more than 400,000 from tobacco-related illnesses. There are no comparable ER figures for Europe, but the latest report from the European drug monitoring center indicated that between 1990 and 2006, there were around 135,000 drug-related deaths recorded across the 15 countries of the European Union. Most deaths are related to heroin overdoses.

Prevention
The best way to avoid an overdose is not to take drugs at all. Beyond that, there are ways of avoiding overdose situations or those situations that could become fatal: never take medications intended for somebody else; do not mix drugs; do not inject drugs; if drugs are being taken in a group, all those involved should look out for each other; and act immediately if somebody becomes unwell.

H. SHAPIRO

Peer Influence

It has long been thought that adolescents may be pressured into using drugs through the influence of friends in their social peer group. Alternative theories propose that teenagers choose to take drugs to conform with a group's ideology.

Adolescence is a time when teenagers begin to identify more closely with friends than with their parents. They declare their independence through shared styles of clothing, activities, or experimentation with substances.

One of the most enduring and pervasive theories on drug initiation is that of peer pressure, the idea that children start taking drugs because of pressure from their peers. This article will examine this theory and some aspects of how it may affect drug use.

Developmental theories suggest that the most powerful influence on shaping our personality and nature comes from our parents. It is our parents, in particular our mothers, who share and guide our early experience, our first steps, first words, and so on. However, parental influence tends to wane temporarily as a child enters adolescence. During adolescence, parents and children become more psychologically and physically distant from each other: physically distant because the adolescent spends increasing amounts of time away from the family and the family home, usually with friends of his or her own age; psychologically distant as the parent's and adolescent's range of interests diverge. In developmental terms, this distancing is part of the normal process of growth and maturation. It creates opportunities for an adolescent to extend his or her ideas and to try new experiences away from adult influence or judgment. However, peer pressure has acquired negative connotations; the media and popular literature are full of discussions about peer pressure and advice on how to save the adolescent from the insidious force that comes from peers.

Why do adolescents start using drugs?

There is no definitive answer to this question, as there are a number of reasons that adolescents start to use drugs, from curiosity and rebellion to the environment and coping with problems, or any combination of these elements. What is known is that about 50 percent of drug use, legal and illegal, begins between the ages of 15 and 18 years. Some of these factors can help explain why adolescents start using drugs.

Environment. One could argue that those brought up in areas of multiple deprivation, little money, and few prospects of employment, education, or a good future are at an increased risk of drug use and abuse. Drugs can offer an escape from the despair and boredom that these adolescents experience and can even offer a career path as a dealer—after all, the risks may be high but so too are the profits. While there may be more people from deprived areas who choose this path, the evidence suggests that drug users span the full spectrum of social class and demographic area. Many of the traditional boundaries between the affluent and the deprived are falling as drug use becomes more egalitarian. For example, crack and heroin use was far more prevalent in deprived areas in the 1980s, while Ecstasy and cocaine use was common in the more affluent areas. Subsequently differences between the social classes may lie less in the range of available drugs and more in the resources that people possess to alleviate the worst effects of drugs; for example, those with greater finances do not need to commit crimes to feed their habits, and those with more social support are less likely to become addicted or to stay addicted for as long.

Coping with problems. Another commonly given reason for drug use is that it is used as a "crutch," that is, it is used to help cope with trauma. Researchers have also found that initiation of drug use generally occurs during major changes in a person's life, for example, moving from junior to senior high school, or going to college, or getting a job. There would also appear to be a significantly large group of adolescent drug users who come from families where there is either little stability or there is active conflict leading to separation or divorce. Drug-using adolescents also appear to be low achievers; however, that could be a consequence rather than a cause of drug use. Also, while coping may provide a plausible explanation of maintenance and even escalation of drug use, it has limited utility as an explanation of initiation.

Curiosity and experimentation. Adolescence is a time of discovery about oneself and the outside world. Research has shown that it is a pivotal time cognitively as attitudes move from the childlike to the mature. For example, research on attitudes toward alcohol has found that, prior to age 12, attitudes tend to be negative, viewing alcohol as something to be avoided. However, after the age of 12, these attitudes change to become positive and more like those of an adult. As part of these changes, adolescents will experiment to discover what they enjoy. Thus, they may try smoking, drinking, and perhaps drugs.

Rebellion. Since adolescence is a time for experimenting, part of that experimentation can involve testing the boundaries and rules of society. Part of growing up involves finding out who we are in relation to others, that is, in what ways we are the same and in what ways we differ. Adolescence is the time where conformity is eschewed in favor of rebellion and a declaration of uniqueness, characterized by clothes, music tastes, speech, and behavior. Since the adolescent believes that he or she has now "invented" life, sex, and values, the teachings and warnings of adults regarding certain behaviors, such as those involving sex and drugs, may be ignored in favor of the new mores. This cycle has repeated for generations, the only difference now being that the menu of substances that can be used to express rebellion has greatly increased, from legal substances such as alcohol and tobacco to illicit drugs.

Peer pressure

As stated above, peer pressure has been one of the most frequently invoked reasons for the initiation of drug use. The question is how to define peer pressure and whether this pressure is emotional or physical. What is known is that adolescents and, for that matter, humans of all ages are influenced by their peers. Fashion is an obvious manifestation of peer influence. How else could one explain some of the clothes worn or hairstyles sported in the past? Although we may cringe now when we see old photographs, the styles seemed not only fine at the time but we may have felt differentiated from and excluded by our friends if we had not followed the fashion. Much of youth fashion and culture is bound up with experimentation and rebellion and is a fairly harmless part of the process of maturing. The mechanism that drives it is, ironically, conformity. While rebelling and stating their uniqueness, most adolescents are aware of the very strict boundaries that govern inclusion in their selected group. However, this is mostly an informal process. Would that kind of influence be enough to initiate drug use, or is there a more powerful and insidious force at work among adolescents? Some researchers suggest a different explanation.

Peer pressure or peer preference?

Alternative theories suggest that, rather than being pressured by peers, adolescents instead exercise choice, and that a better explanation may be "peer preference." Adolescents choose the groups to which they want to belong. If that group takes drugs, then part of the admission cost may be to indulge in the same behavior. One can observe that there are usually a number of adolescent fashions in vogue at

Parental involvement in a teenager's life can be a key factor in building resistance to peer pressure about taking drugs and other negative behaviors.

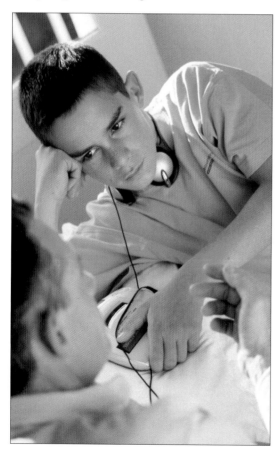

any given time. The followers of each of these fashions usually have a dress code, a musical taste, and a set of behaviors. To gain membership in such a group usually requires the individual to adopt some of the characteristics of the others. If part of the behavior of the group entails drug taking, then that may be a consideration that is addressed as part of the admission process.

Of course neither of these theories, peer pressure or preference, are mutually exclusive. Just because one has chosen a particular group does not mean that the group cannot or will not exert some influence on its members. This is especially true during early to middle adolescence, when the group may still be trying to define itself, and what is considered acceptable behavior within the group may be changing. The group may grow more daring or extreme in its behavior and there may be influence on more reticent members to participate. The theory of peer preference, while plausible, also assumes that there are a number of groups from which to choose, an assumption that may be correct in larger urban environments but not in small communities.

Combating peer influence

Assuming that peer influence is indeed a major cause of initiation into drug use, what measures can be taken to minimize its effect? Most commentators would suggest that the process of inoculating against peer pressure should begin when the child is very young. Two basic ingredients are required: strong values and a good sense of self as an independent and valuable person. These ingredients are dependent on the main caregivers, usually the parents. Discussing drugs (including alcohol) at an early age is advisable—parents should take responsibility rather than simply leaving drug education to schools. Parents also need to be aware of and monitor their own alcohol and drug use, since adolescents are extremely sensitive to parental substance use.

Parents also need to help their children to value their own choices and opinions. If teenagers are to resist peer influence, then they need to feel confident that their own decisions are correct for them. This requires an ongoing process starting at a young age: expecting adolescents to make difficult choices when they have never before had the opportunity is almost certainly unrealistic.

Harnessing peer influence for prevention

Drug education is beginning to take advantage of the putative power of peer influence. For many years psychologists and educators have recognized that the status of the educator is as important as the message that is delivered. Advertisers rely on the same principle when paying celebrities to endorse their products. More recently, this same strategy has been used in drug prevention programs. However, rather than celebrities, it is adolescents themselves who deliver the message.

Much of the information in drug prevention programs had previously been delivered by teachers and the police, knowledgeable educators of high status. However, evaluations of these programs suggested that they were not very effective. Reasons given for the lack of effectiveness concerned the message and, perhaps more important, the message giver. Adolescents felt that some of the messages being delivered were exaggerations because the information conflicted with their personal or vicarious experience. For example, one approach was to emphasize the dangers to health from drug taking. These messages were at odds with the fact that most adolescents had taken drugs or knew someone who had taken drugs with no ill effects. Therefore the message, however otherwise accurate, often fell on deaf ears. The second problem was the message carrier. While the police and teachers may have impeccable credentials to deliver factual information, there was a generation gap that further called their credibility into question.

One solution was to recruit recovering drug users to teach drug education. Their credibility was not in question and they were usually closer in age to the adolescents they were teaching. Unfortunately this strategy was not as successful as had been hoped. The problem with this approach was that few adolescents saw themselves as people who would succumb to addiction.

Finally, two solutions suggested themselves— change both the message and the deliverer of the message. Changing the message consisted of being pragmatic; if young people are going to take drugs, despite being warned of the dangers, then perhaps they need to be taught about harm reduction, that is, how to make drug taking safer. This part of the solution has not been universally adopted, as it is viewed by some as condoning, if not actually encouraging, drug use. However, it does allow the topic of social norms to be discussed—how common drug use actually is and what sort of quantities are being used. This important information is omitted from a "just say no" type of program. The second component of the solution is much less controversial —peer-led drug education.

Adolescents can be selected and trained to deliver a program of drug education. This strategy should avoid the problems of credibility so redolent when adults in authority deliver the program. The success of the strategy depends very much on the selection process. For this approach to be a success, the peer educators delivering the program must be malleable enough to deliver the program as designed. They need to have good communication skills and must be drug free themselves. To be taken seriously by their peers, they need to be respected by them. This is not an easy process but it is one that has proved to be very effective. A number of studies have shown that giving adolescents the opportunity to help and learn from each other encourages feelings of self-worth and efficacy in resisting pressures to take drugs. Not having adults conduct sessions also allows adolescents to discuss their attitudes and experiences more openly. Another finding is that acting as a peer leader can transform the school performance of some teenagers who may have been underachieving or feeling alienated.

Overall effect of peer influence

Peer influence is apparent in all aspects of one's life. It can be particularly strong in adolescence when youths are still trying to discover who they are. Peer influence can also provide a positive effect on drug use, not only in peer education; a minority of adolescents use illegal drugs so most groups in fact support abstinence. Although peer pressure has been cited as a main cause of drug use, peer preference suggests an opt-in system whereby adolescents choose those who will influence them.

J. MCMAHON

SEE ALSO:
Adolescents and Substance Abuse • Dependence • Prevention • Self-esteem • Vulnerability

Pharmacology

Pharmacology is the science dealing with the interactions between chemicals and systems in the body. Understanding how substances react is vital to the way that drugs are used and the effects they will produce, both good and bad.

The science of pharmacology is extremely broad. Pharmacology deals with numerous aspects of drugs, including their history, where they come from, how they are made, their physical and chemical properties, the effects of drugs (biochemical or physiological), how drugs work, how they are handled by the body, what diseases they affect, and what other uses there may be for the drugs. Since drugs may be defined as any chemical or even biological agent that can affect a living organism, the general area of pharmacology extends well beyond humans. However, this review will be restricted to the area of pharmacology as it relates to people.

While most interest in pharmacology centers on drugs that are useful in the prevention, diagnosis, or treatment of human diseases, the pharmacological study of drugs is also relevant to the areas of household and industrial health as well as drug abuse. The former area deals with drugs that may play a role in environmental pollution as well as potential poisonings that could occur at home or at work. The latter area, drug abuse, deals with the inappropriate use of drugs that are taken illegally or in excess for their pleasurable effects.

Aspects of pharmacology

There are many subdivisions of pharmacology. These include pharmacokinetics, pharmacodynamics, clinical pharmacology, and toxicology. While there is a certain amount of overlap among these areas, conceptually they help us understand the intricate nature of the complexities of pharmacology.

The area of pharmcokinetics deals with how drugs are handled by the body. Much of pharmacokinetics is described by the acronym ADME, which stands for absorption, distribution, metabolism, and excretion. In examining the absorption of a drug, the scientist is interested in how and how much of a drug that a person consumes actually gets into the bloodstream and tissues. When a drug is given intravenously, all of what is given gets into the bloodstream. However, most drugs are taken orally,

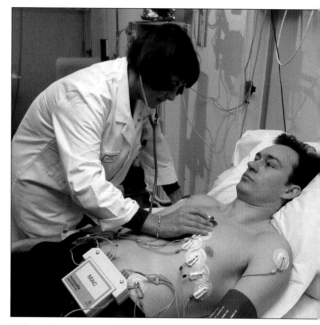

Before drugs are allowed to be used by the public they are carefully assessed to determine whether they have any harmful effects on the body.

in which case the drug must be absorbed across the lining of the stomach or other parts of the gastrointestinal tract, that is, the small or large intestine. Once the drug is inside the body, it is then carried around the body through the bloodstream to the various tissues and organs of the body. This process is called distribution. While in the bloodstream or in the tissues, a drug may be altered by the body. This process, called metabolism, usually happens through enzymes changing the chemical nature of the drug. The metabolism of drugs may be quite variable. Some drugs undergo quite extensive metabolism within the body, while others may not be metabolized at all. Finally, the body must excrete or dispose of the drug or its metabolites (breakdown products). The usual route of excretion is into the urine or feces. However, other routes of excretion may include exhaling the drug or metabolites through the lung or sweating, that is, excretion through the skin.

While pharmacokinetics may be viewed as answering the question of what the body does to the drug, the area of pharmacodynamics is concerned with the issue of what the drug does to the body. Again, the drug itself may affect the person, or it may be a metabolite of the drug that has the major effect on the person. In many circumstances, it is both the drug and its metabolites that have pharmacodynamic effects on people. In order to understand the pharmacodynamics of drugs, the researcher relies heavily on a variety of other sciences, such as physiology and biochemistry. For example, two pharmacodynamic effects of narcotic analgesics such as morphine or oxycodone are pain relief and constipation. Understanding these effects requires insight into the physiology of both pain and gastrointestinal peristalsis, or movement of food through the stomach and intestines.

When the pharmacokinetics and pharmaco-dynamics of a drug have been determined, it is then important to study the interrelationships between these two areas, called pharmacokinetic-pharmaco-dynamic interactions, sometimes abbreviated as PK/PD. For example, it can be useful to understand what concentrations of a drug in the bloodstream (pharmacokinetics) produce certain effects on the body (pharmacodynamics). This sort of information is crucial in determining what doses of drugs are appropriate to prescribe.

Variations in effect

When dealing with the pharmacology of drugs in humans, the area of clinical pharmacology is crucial. The same drug may have different effects on men than on women, the elderly than on the young, and on people of different races, such as Caucasians or Asians. In addition, if a drug is metabolized or excreted by the liver or kidneys and those organs are not functioning properly, the dose of the drug may have to be altered, or perhaps the drug cannot be used at all. The absorption of a drug may be very different if the drug is taken on an empty stomach or with food. Numerous questions such as these are studied by the clinical pharmacologist. Understanding all these potential factors is important before a drug can safely be given to a particular population. Thus, even though a drug may be approved for adults, it is usual to study at a minimum its clinical pharmacology in children before the drug is given to children.

Unexpected effects

One of the greatest concerns in the use of drugs in humans is the area of side effects, or adverse reactions. The study of toxicology, frequently considered an area of pharmacology, concerns understanding the effects of drugs other than the intended therapeutic ones. Before a drug is given to a human, it is studied fairly extensively in animals to determine the toxicology profile, usually in two species of animals. While the toxicology in animals is not necessarily predictive of what the adverse effects will be for people, it does give some insight into which organ systems may be most affected by the drug, as well as the types of side effects that may occur in humans. If a drug is very toxic in animals, it may never even be tried in humans. Specific areas of toxicology that are studied in animals include embryotoxicity and genotoxicity. There is concern for all drugs that they do not alter the patients' genes, or in the case of pregnant women, adversely affect the fetus. Ultimately, the toxicology of any drug must be studied in humans to be certain it is safe in humans. When an adverse reaction is common, it can usually be noticed very quickly when the drug is given to people. However, some adverse reactions to drugs occur very infrequently. These reactions can be extremely difficult to detect and may not become obvious until even thousands or tens of thousands of patients have been treated with the drug.

Thus, the purpose of pharmacology is to help understand both the intended use of a drug as well as the potential problems or side effects of a drug. Pharmacological studies are usually the first to be carried out in humans during the prolonged process of drug testing. These studies are of immense importance in the decision-making process to determine which drugs will ultimately be useful in the detection, prevention, or treatment of disease.

M. NADEL

SEE ALSO:
Dosage • Toxicity

Pregnancy and Fetal Addiction

Drug use during pregnancy poses distinct risks to a developing baby. Not only can the baby suffer a wide range of cognitive and physical abnormalities, it may also spend the early weeks of its life with symptoms of drug withdrawal.

Everything that a pregnant woman eats, drinks, smokes, or otherwise puts into her body goes into her unborn baby's body, too. As in the mother, every substance has an effect on the baby's brain and body. The difference between the mother and the baby, however, is that the baby's brain and body are still developing. While the mother may be destroying a couple of million used brain cells, the baby may never get the chance to develop them.

Drug use during pregnancy is the single most preventable cause of birth defects, mental retardation, and developmental disorders in the United States today. Despite knowledge of the risks, as many as 1 in 5 pregnant women drink alcohol and, in some areas of the country, nearly 1 in 4 pregnant women smoke cigarettes. Undoubtedly, drug use during pregnancy is a significant public health problem.

Risks for drug users becoming pregnant

The ages of childbearing and the ages of greatest risk for alcohol and other drug abuse are nearly the same (ages 15 to 44). Alcohol and most drugs of abuse affect judgment and decrease inhibitions. Some drugs, for example, cocaine, can actually stimulate sexual desires. These combined effects set the stage for unplanned and unprotected sexual encounters, leading to pregnancy. Women who are addicted to alcohol and other drugs are at an increased risk of being involved in prostitution or using sexual favors to get drugs. They are also at greater risk for contracting sexually transmitted diseases (STDs), including HIV, and for being victims of physical and sexual abuse.

Problems of addiction during pregnancy

Addiction to alcohol and drugs is no different for the pregnant woman than it is for anyone else. A woman will often reduce her drug use once she finds out she is pregnant, but the addictive properties of the drug will usually prevent her from quitting completely without treatment. Addicted pregnant women often suffer from inadequate nutrition, medical problems such as pancreatitis, hepatitis, toxemia, numerous infections, and anemia. All place the unborn baby at increased risk for problems with growth and development.

Prenatal care

Prenatal care is the most effective strategy for intervening in the life of the pregnant addicted woman. Unfortunately, many addicted women do not seek prenatal care until late in the pregnancy, if at all. Pregnant substance users are often suspicious of becoming involved with the health care system for fear that they will lose custody of their children or that they will be identified to the authorities as a drug user.

Some women who do seek prenatal care are never identified as drug users until pregnancy complications develop or until the baby's delivery because health care providers have not asked about drug or alcohol use. Many pregnant users will time visits to clinics around their drug use so as to test negative if blood or urine samples are required. All women receiving prenatal care should be asked about their history of drug and alcohol use, their partner's history, and their family's history. Even if a woman states that she is not currently using any drugs or alcohol, she may relapse into drug use again during the course of the pregnancy; therefore, she should be asked about use at every prenatal visit.

It is in the health interests of both mother and child that a woman should try to stop using drugs during pregnancy. Treatment can take the form of accessing outpatient clinics or therapeutic communities, or pursuing methadone maintenance for opioid addicts. Pregnancy can often be a way to persuade a female drug user into treatment, although many feel that there is a lack of understanding by medical staff about their addiction and social or welfare problems. Psychosocial counseling should ideally be carried out by experienced professionals who can support the pregnant user and encourage her to attend medical appointments.

Effects of various drugs on the unborn baby

Just as different drugs have different effects on the user, drugs have various effects on the unborn baby. Drugs can affect the baby either directly, by destroying tissue and cells, or indirectly, by interfering with the mother's body and its ability to provide the growing baby with blood, oxygen, and adequate nutrition. The severity of these effects is not necessarily dependent on the amount of the drug used or at what point in the pregnancy the drug was used—and not all babies exposed to drugs will experience these effects. However, most pregnant drug abusers use a number of different substances, increasing the risks that the baby will experience harmful effects from those drugs.

Alcohol. Alcohol affects the growth and development of the brain and central nervous system. As a result, babies are at increased risk for problems with their growth in the mother's womb and will be born small for their gestational age. These babies are prone to heart abnormalities and bone (skeletal) malformations, particularly of the head.

The terms *fetal alcohol syndrome* (FAS), *alcohol-related birth defects* (ARBD), and *alcohol-related neurodevelopmental disorder* (ARND) have been defined to describe the physical and neurological effects of prenatal alcohol use on the child. The box on page 238 provides more specific information on these effects.

Amphetamines. Also known as "speed," amphetamines speed up the development process but do not allow the baby to grow and the brain to develop normally. The result is a higher rate of miscarriages and stillbirths. Babies born to women who use amphetamines during their pregnancy are usually born prematurely and are small. These babies also tend to have small heads, an indicator of an underdeveloped brain.

Cocaine. The effects of cocaine on the baby are similar to those of amphetamines. For these babies there is a significantly higher rate of miscarriage, stillbirth, and premature births. Additionally, there is a high risk of the placenta separating from the mother's uterus, reducing or cutting off the blood

Drinking and smoking present risks to a developing baby. Research has shown that even low levels of fetal alcohol can cause intellectual difficulties and behavioral problems later. Women who smoke during pregnancy are likely to continue after the birth, further exposing the baby to the harmful effects of tobacco.

FETAL ALCOHOL SYNDROME (FAS)

Fetal alcohol syndrome (FAS), a term coined in 1973, describes a pattern of physical and neurological features associated with children born to mothers who drank alcohol during pregnancy. In 1996 the definition of FAS was refined into five categories of alcohol-related effects. This was necessary because not all children born to women who drank during pregnancy demonstrated all of the signs of FAS, but had some. Conversely, there were children who demonstrated all of the signs of FAS, but the mother's drinking during pregnancy could not be confirmed. In order to help researchers and clinicians speak the same language, the following categories of alcohol-related birth effects were defined:

Category 1: FAS with confirmed maternal alcohol exposure
- Heavy regular or episodic (binge) drinking by mother during pregnancy
- A pattern of facial abnormalities: small head, small eyes, skin folds at corners of eyes, flat midface, short and flat nose, thin upper lip, and no ridge (philtrum) between the nose and the upper lip
- Growth retardation: low birth weight, slow growth or weight gain over time, disproportional weight-to-height ratio
- Central nervous system (CNS) abnormalities such as small head size and abnormal brain structures or neurological symptoms of CNS

impairment such as poor motor skills, hearing loss, and poor eye-to-hand coordination.

Category 2: FAS without confirmed maternal alcohol exposure
- The same pattern as Category 1 except mother's drinking during pregnancy is unknown.

Category 3: Partial FAS with confirmed maternal alcohol exposure
- Maternal drinking during pregnancy
- Some facial features described in item 2 above
- And any of the following:
  Growth retardation, as in item 3 above, CNS abnormalities, as in item 4 above, or behavior or learning problems that cannot otherwise be explained.

Category 4: Alcohol-Related Birth Defects (ARBD)
- Maternal drinking during pregnancy
- One or more birth defects (bone deformities, heart, kidney, vision, or hearing defects).

Category 5: Alcohol-Related Neurodevelopmental Disorder (ARND)
- Maternal drinking during pregnancy
- CNS abnormalities, such as those in Category 1, or
- Behavior or learning problems that cannot otherwise be explained.

supply to the baby. This results in a lack of oxygen to the baby and can result in a stroke or bleeding in the baby's brain, causing permanent brain damage. As with amphetamines, babies born to mothers who used cocaine during their pregnancy are small, and will experience some level of drug withdrawal.

Heroin. Heroin directly affects the chemistry of the brain, both in the mother and the unborn baby. The baby will experience growth retardation in the womb and may be born prematurely. These babies also tend to be very small and have small heads. These babies

will experience severe withdrawal symptoms that may require medical detoxification from the drug, similar to an adult who is in withdrawal from heroin.

Marijuana. A mother who smokes marijuana during pregnancy exposes her unborn baby not only to the brain-altering chemicals in the drug but also to oxygen depletion as a result of inhaling the smoke. These babies tend to be born prematurely and are very small. They may experience shakes and tremors, tend to have respiratory problems, and will be prone to infections and colds.

Sedatives. This family of drugs depresses the central nervous system, slowing everything down. The result for the unborn baby is growth retardation in the womb, small size, and very little activity. Because sedative drugs take a long time to be eliminated from the body, withdrawal symptoms may not appear until the baby is one to three weeks old. Until withdrawal begins, the baby will sleep more than other babies and will be hard to wake. The baby will not be very active and will not want to eat as often as it should, resulting in a condition called "failure to thrive," which can lead to the death of the infant.

Tobacco. The primary risk of smoking during pregnancy is the lack of oxygen to the baby caused by the reduction of oxygen in the mother's lungs. This is caused in two ways: first, smoking reduces the ability of the mother's lungs to absorb oxygen and to release carbon dioxide; and second, tobacco smoke contains carbon monoxide, which replaces oxygen in the bloodstream and starves the body of oxygen. This lack of oxygen prevents the baby's brain from developing and functioning properly. It also causes problems in the development of the lungs and circulatory system (heart and blood vessels), leading to respiratory problems and heart defects in the baby. These babies are more prone to die from Sudden Infant Death Syndrome (SIDS) within the first year of life.

Problems during delivery

The most common problem during delivery of the baby for women who use drugs is premature delivery. Because labor is unexpected, women may wait until the labor is very advanced before they go to the hospital, and may deliver the baby before proper medical help is available. Additionally, there is an increased risk of breech presentation, meaning that the baby has not turned in the mother's womb to be delivered in a normal position, head first. In breech presentation, the baby's leg, arm, or buttocks enters the birth canal first, making it difficult for the baby to be delivered without medical help. Without quick and proper medical intervention, the baby is at high risk for birth trauma, such as broken bones, dislocation of joints, or even death. In some drug users the placenta may separate prematurely from the mother's womb or rupture, depriving the baby of oxygen from the mother's bloodstream.

Another common problem, especially among marijuana users, is meconium staining. Meconium is the first bowel movement that a baby has after birth. Meconium staining is caused by the baby eliminating the meconium while still in the mother's womb. When this happens, the meconium may float around in the amniotic fluid and can be aspirated (inhaled) into the baby's lungs at the time of delivery. This is very dangerous and may be fatal.

Postnatal care

Most women and babies are hospitalized for 24 hours after a baby is born, unless there are medical complications. Hospitals do not systematically conduct drug screens on mother or baby, and even if they did, the drugs might not be detectable. The drug-exposed baby usually goes home with the mother, and drug-withdrawal symptoms may not appear for several days. Depending on the severity of the symptoms, the mother may return to the hospital or go to the pediatrician because the child is not feeding properly or is showing symptoms of withdrawal.

Addicted newborns

Normal newborn babies are able to interact with their caregiver and their environment from the time they are born. They respond to faces and voices, they can comfort themselves by drawing their hands to their mouths and sucking, and they can follow the movement of an object with their eyes for short periods. These skills improve as they get older. The amount of time spent crying increases during the first 6 to 8 weeks after birth, then crying time decreases as they get older. Similarly, the length of time they sleep at one time increases as they get older.

Drug-exposed newborns do not interact well with their environment or their caregivers. They may be sensitive to light or noise, will avoid looking at their caregivers, and may become agitated and cry when being held or even touched. They go from sleeping to crying with no intervals between, and they are unable to comfort themselves. They do not have a regular sleep-wake cycle and may sleep for only short periods (1 to 2 hours) at a time. When they are awake, they are crying.

These babies have a lot of feeding difficulties. Some problems are caused by the excessive crying, which causes gas to build up in the baby's stomach, causing pain. For some babies, there is a lack of coordination of the suck and swallow reflex. The baby may suck constantly but is unable to swallow the formula or breast milk. This excessive sucking when not feeding also leads to gas in the stomach, causing pain and crying. Often the mother will think that the baby is hungry because of the constant sucking and will overfeed the baby, leading to frequent vomiting and diarrhea.

These types of problems will continue until the baby is 4 to 6 months of age, making caregiving very difficult and exhausting. These babies do not bond well with their caregivers, and the reverse is also true. When mothers (or caregivers) do not bond with their babies, the baby is at an increased risk for child neglect and abuse.

Managing withdrawal

Symptoms of drug withdrawal in newborns depend on the type of drug, how recently the unborn baby was exposed, and how much was used over time. How long a drug stays within the body depends on the drug and the body's metabolism of the drug. Infants have a slower metabolism rate than do adults, have less blood volume, and lack certain enzymes that break down the substances in their blood; drugs will therefore stay in their bodies for longer periods of time and may not be detectable using standard drug-testing procedures. Because of this, withdrawal symptoms may not occur for 1 to 3 days for drugs such as alcohol, cocaine, and heroin, or as long as 1 to 3 weeks for barbiturates or sedative-type drugs.

Withdrawal symptoms can be categorized according to the body system in which they are manifested. As all drugs affect the central nervous system (CNS), withdrawal also affects the CNS. Common CNS symptoms include agitation, high-pitched crying, stiffness of the legs, arms, neck, and back, tremors or jitteriness, overactive reflexes, and small seizures or sudden jerks of legs or arms. The withdrawal symptoms related to the autonomic nervous system (the system that regulates involuntary actions in the body) include sweating, sneezing, yawning, rapid breathing rate, and poor body temperature regulation. Vomiting, diarrhea, lack of coordination of sucking and swallowing when feeding, excessive

sucking, excessive feeding, and stomach and intestinal gas are all withdrawal symptoms related to the gastrointestinal system.

Treatment of withdrawal depends on the severity of the symptoms. Medical professionals who are familiar with drug withdrawal in infants use a monitoring system in which they rate the severity of symptoms at regular intervals. If the symptoms persist and the infant fails to feed properly, medical intervention is required. Two medications commonly used to detoxify babies are tincture of opium and phenobarbital. For opiate-type drugs, such as heroin, tincture of opium is given in very small quantities every four hours for 2 to 3 weeks, gradually reducing the amount administered over time. For alcohol, cocaine, and sedative-type drugs, phenobarbital is administered every 8 hours in small doses, gradually decreasing the dose over 1 to 2 weeks. Even with medical detoxification, the symptoms of withdrawal can last 4 to 6 months.

Management of withdrawal symptoms requires recognition of the baby's needs. Because the baby reacts negatively to stimulation (light, noise, touch), the child needs to be kept in a dark, quiet environment. Sometimes white noise (soft music or the hum of an electric motor, or even a vacuum cleaner running in another room) can soothe the baby, as he or she was accustomed to muffled noises while in the womb. Likewise, the baby in the womb is accustomed to the movement of the mother, so slow rocking, swinging in an infant swing, or car rides can be comforting to the baby experiencing withdrawal. The stiffness of a baby's arms and back prevent a baby from being able to pull its arms to its face to suck on its fists, making the baby unable to comfort itself. One comforting measure is to swaddle the baby by wrapping a blanket tightly around its body, with its arms wrapped against the body.

Problems with vomiting and diarrhea can be reduced by feeding the symptomatic baby frequent feedings of small amounts, burping often. Use of a pacifier is recommended to comfort the baby and to alleviate the gas built up by excessive sucking. The caregiver should be prepared to deal with the baby's short sleep cycles, but should try to get the baby to sleep at regular intervals and to extend those intervals as normal babies do. Finally, the caregiver needs to recognize when she or he is losing

Children born with fetal alcohol syndrome suffer brain damage, growth problems, and have distinct facial characteristics. With a caring and supportive environment, many of the difficulties they face can be overcome.

patience with the baby, and should have another adult available to lend a hand or provide breaks from caregiving responsibilities.

Long-term outlook for addicted babies

Research continues to be done to determine the long-term effects of prenatal exposure to alcohol and other drugs. Drug-exposed babies who experienced muscle stiffness as a symptom of withdrawal may have some delays in the development of fine and gross motor skills (reaching, grasping, rolling over, sitting on their own), but they usually catch up to normal children by 6 months of age. The same is true for their physical growth, particularly babies who are born prematurely. Most premature babies will remain small during the first year, but tend to grow normally after that. Language skills should develop normally, unless there is severe mental impairment or hearing loss.

Long-term negative effects of prenatal drug exposure are manifested mainly in the child's intellectual functioning and behavior. There is a higher rate of mental retardation (IQ less than 70) in children prenatally exposed to drugs. The majority of

these children, however, are not mentally retarded, but may experience other learning problems.

Current research has shown that brain structures and brain functioning in children prenatally exposed to cocaine and methamphetamines are different from those of normal children. These affected brain structures are those that enable children to control their impulses and to sustain attention to tasks. These changes in the brain may be the reason that many drug-exposed children are diagnosed with attention deficit hyperactivity disorder (ADHD) and conduct disorder.

Finally, children who were prenatally exposed to drugs, including tobacco, are at greater risk of developing substance use disorders as they grow older. They are more likely to experiment with substances of abuse at earlier ages, and to become addicted. This behavior may produce the next generation of drug-exposed babies.

M. D. REYNOLDS

SEE ALSO:
Children • Social Services • Treatment • Withdrawal

Prevention

Some young people present a greater risk for drug addiction than others. However, a combination of preventive measures and legal controls can have a significant impact in reducing levels of drug use in teenagers and young adults.

Teaching children and young adults about the dangers of drugs is an essential component of the curriculum in most schools. While this approach does have an effect, research has shown that the message that drugs are harmful must be reinforced every few years if its impact is not to diminish.

Work in prevention is designed to stop substance use problems before they begin. When applied to young people, the goal of prevention is to sustain their abstinence from alcohol and other drugs. For adults, the goal can be safe or moderate use, as is the case with alcohol; restricted medical use, as with prescription drugs; or abstinence, as with illicit drugs. The field of public health commonly refers to prevention at this level as primary prevention.

Primary prevention is usually differentiated from intervention, or secondary prevention, which is focused on early detection and reduction of substance use problems that have already begun. The goal is to prevent further use. In turn, tertiary prevention focuses on preventing any further progression of alcohol and other drug problems and reducing problems associated with established patterns of substance use or addiction. When used alone, the term *prevention* refers to primary prevention, usually with children and teenagers in mind.

A fundamental decision is whether to target high-risk individuals whose characteristics are predictive of future substance use problems or to apply broad-based strategies that will reduce substance use by the general population. A mix of both is needed, but population-level approaches should predominate. High-risk individuals are more likely to experience problems due to substance use, but they constitute a relatively small percentage of the population. Those at lower risk are less likely to experience problems, but given their far greater numbers, they will usually generate more cases than do the high-risk individuals.

Risk and protective factors

Developing an effective prevention program first requires an understanding of the multiple factors that contribute to patterns of substance use. Prevention experts often distinguish between risk factors, which make substance use more likely, and protective factors, which inhibit substance use.

Risk and protective factors can be classified according to the social ecological level at which they operate: individual, interpersonal, institution, community, or society. Prevention programs seek to reduce the influence of risk factors while augmenting the influence of protective factors.

Many risk and protective factors operate at the individual level. Key risk categories include genetic predisposition; personality traits, including impulsivity, need for stimulation, rebelliousness, and emotional stability; behavioral problems, including aggression and other high-risk behaviors; learning disabilities; poor problem-solving skills; weak social skills; and low self-esteem.

There are other individual-level factors more directly tied to substance use. Teenagers are less likely to use alcohol, tobacco, and other drugs when they know basic facts about their serious negative consequences, especially short-term effects; believe that substance use would jeopardize their personal health and safety; and perceive substance use as being inconsistent with their own values or self-image. Young people who know how to turn down peers who encourage them to experiment with substance use are also at less risk.

At the interpersonal level can be found family and peer group factors. Key protective factors include strong and nurturing family bonds, coupled with parental involvement in their children's lives, clear rules of conduct that are consistently enforced, and parental monitoring of children's activities and their peers. In contrast, a disorganized home environment greatly increases risk, especially when one or both parents are substance abusers, mentally ill, or physically or verbally abusive.

Association with peers engaging in deviant behavior, especially substance use, greatly increases risk. Recent research also has underscored the perception of broader social norms as a critical factor. Investigators have repeatedly shown that many teenagers tend to overestimate how many of their peers use alcohol, tobacco, or other drugs. Such misperceptions are associated with greater substance use.

At the institutional level, a key protective factor for young people includes a strong bond with school, which promotes identification with teachers and contributes to academic success. Such bonds are greater when the school has an orderly and safe environment and when teachers communicate high expectations and provide emotional support. Schools that fail to enforce rules related to substance use put students at greater risk. Teenagers with strong ties to religious organizations are also less likely to engage in substance use.

Communities present greater risk when they are economically disadvantaged. Other negative factors include high crime rates, a high density of alcohol outlets, an active drug trade, and gang activity. Community disorganization and a large number of transient residents also increases risk, while greater social capital—formed by a rich mix of neighborhood institutions and community-sponsored activities—provides a higher level of protection.

Protective communities make available afterschool programs for young people. These programs offer opportunities for teenagers to work with adult mentors, receive academic tutoring, and develop protective knowledge, attitudes, and skills, while also providing a structured environment during afterschool hours, a time of especially high risk for substance use when parents work and children are left unsupervised.

Broad societal factors are also important to consider, including cultural norms, economic conditions, and public policy. Media influences are especially noteworthy. Advertising for alcohol, tobacco, and prescription drugs normalizes substance use, and even abuse in the case of alcohol. Entertainment films and television programs reinforce this message by persistently depicting illegal or abusive substance use without portraying the negative consequences of this behavior.

Prevention programs

Substance use prevention programs can be broadly conceived as attempting to increase the strength and impact of protective factors while decreasing the strength and impact of risk factors. Determining which factors are the most critical and how best to address them has been the subject of intensive study since the 1970s.

The years following the 1970s have seen a marked change in the direction of substance use prevention. Early school-based health education programs focused on providing young people with knowledge about positive and negative health behaviors. Educators believed that this knowledge, combined with students' self-interest, would lead to healthy decisions to avoid substance use. Research eventually made clear that this approach, when used alone, is of marginal value.

Another early approach was affective (or emotional) education, which was based on studies showing a relationship between initiation of substance use and self-esteem, attitudes, and personal values. These programs focused on activities designed to promote a positive self-image, interpersonal skills, and improved decision making by clarifying personal values and analyzing the consequences of substance use in light of those values. Research on this approach generated disappointing results.

Attention then turned to the social pressures that prompt teenagers to use alcohol, tobacco, and other drugs. This next generation of programs focused on social-skills training so that students could recognize and successfully resist both overt and covert pressure to engage in substance use, especially peer pressure. To motivate students to apply these skills, these programs also included information on the immediate, rather than long-term, consequences of substance use and corrected students' misperceptions of peer substance use norms. Such programs often culminated in students making a public commitment to apply their new skills outside the classroom and to remain substance-free. Selected programs

Prevention through advertising campaigns often focuses on reversing misconceptions of the effects of drugs and the level of use by young people. Scare tactics can have a negative effect if they exaggerate what teenagers experience in their own environment, but concentrating on actual facts in a consistent manner can get the message across.

targeting preteens and young adolescents have produced short-term success in reducing cigarette and marijuana use but appear to have been less successful in reducing alcohol use. Without refresher programs in later years, the positive effects of these education programs have proved to be short-lived, often lasting only one or two years.

Over time, prevention experts began to realize that educational programs would continue to have limited effect if they failed to take environmental context into account. In retrospect, it was unwarranted to expect teenagers to say "no" to substance use if their environment continued to say "yes." It is not enough to rescue individual teenagers from the dysfunctional environments in which they are growing up. Also needed are efforts to diminish risk factors and enhance protective factors in the environment.

Environmental management

Environmental management is a term used to describe a wide range of prevention strategies that focus on changing the physical, social, economic, and legal environment in which young people make decisions about substance use. One of the clearest lessons from the field of public health is the value of environmental change in reducing mortality and morbidity due to high-risk behavior, including substance use. The principal vehicle for creating environmental change is policy development and stricter enforcement at the institutional, community, and societal levels.

Consider the case of youth alcohol use. The National Institute on Alcohol Abuse and Alcoholism (NIAAA), a U.S. federal agency that funds alcohol research, issued a report in 2002 with evidence-based recommendations on how to curb heavy drinking and its consequences among college and university students. All five recommendations were examples of environmental management:

Increased enforcement of minimum legal drinking-age laws. Laws to increase the minimum legal drinking age have been a major success in the United States, with substantial decreases reported in alcohol consumption and alcohol-related traffic accidents. This is the case even though enforcement of the age restriction laws has been patchy. More important, studies show that increased enforcement can substantially reduce sales to minors. By extension, NIAAA urged college and community officials to apply a variety of measures to prevent underage drinking, including, among others, cracking down on false age identification (fake IDs), eliminating home delivery of alcohol, and keg registration.

Implementation and enforcement of other laws to reduce alcohol-impaired driving. The best available estimate is that nearly 80 percent of alcohol-related fatalities among U.S. college students are the result of traffic accidents. In response, NIAAA stated that campus and community officials should call for state laws that will lower the legal limit for adult drivers to 0.08 percent BAC (blood alcohol concentration), set legal BAC limits for drivers under age 21 at 0.02 percent BAC or lower, and permit administrative license revocation after DUI (driving under the influence) arrests. NIAAA also recommended greater enforcement of existing laws, including the use of sobriety checkpoints and targeted patrols.

Restrictions on alcohol retail outlet density. The density of alcohol outlets is related to alcohol consumption and alcohol-related problems, including violence, other crime, and health problems. NIAAA noted in its report that restrictive local alcohol control policies and local zoning and land-use planning ordinances have been shown to reduce alcohol outlet density and consumption.

Increased prices and excise taxes on alcoholic beverages. The effect of price on alcohol consumption is well documented. Studies have shown that when the price of alcohol is increased many alcohol-related problems, including fatal traffic accidents, go down. Price variations especially affect young people, even

Enforcement of measures to control underage drinking or drug use is an effective strategy in reducing consumption. If students know that they will be prosecuted for trying to buy alcohol under age or for drunk-driving offenses, they will be less likely to take risks that will lead to arrest.

heavy drinkers. Price increases can come about by raising alcohol excise taxes. Another tactic is to work out cooperative agreements with local merchants to institute minimum pricing or to restrict or eliminate low-price drink specials.

Responsible beverage service (RBS) policies. RBS involves several policies to reduce alcohol sales to minors and intoxicated patrons at bars and restaurants, including checking for false age identification, serving alcohol in smaller standard sizes, limiting the number of servings per alcohol sale, restricting sales of pitchers, promoting alcohol-free drinks and food, eliminating last-call announcements, and cutting off sales to patrons who might otherwise become intoxicated. Studies suggest that such policies—reinforced by training for both managers and staff and by compliance monitoring—can reduce inappropriate alcohol sales significantly.

Environmental management can be applied to address other risk and protective factors, including efforts to offer and promote social, recreational, extracurricular, and public service options that do not include substance use and to create an environment that supports health-promoting norms. On campus, examples of specific ideas include providing greater financial support to student clubs and organizations that are substance free, expanding hours of operation for the student center, bolstering academic standards, and increasing faculty-student contact through revised advisory programs.

Prevention planning

A prerequisite to a successful program is a systematic planning process. Key steps include: a thorough analysis of the problem, including an examination of the physical, social, economic, and legal environment that drives substance use; outcome-driven strategic planning that outlines goals and objectives, specific activities designed to achieve those objectives, and the resources and infrastructure needed to support each activity; and a process and outcome data collection plan for evaluating the outlined program. Community mobilization involving coalitions of civic, religious, and government officials is now widely recognized as a primary means of organizing and implementing effective prevention.

In the United States, for example, the Community Prevention Trial (CPT) was implemented for five years in three small towns in California and South Carolina, with three additional communities serving as matched control sites. Community coalitions pushed for several environmental change strategies: responsible beverage service (RBS), zoning restrictions to reduce alcohol-outlet density, stricter enforcement of underage drinking laws to reduce youth access, and enhanced anti–drunk-driving enforcement, which included monthly sobriety checkpoints and use of passive alcohol sensors. Results included reduced alcohol sales to minors; a 6 percent decline in self-reported alcohol consumption; a 51 percent decline in self-reported driving after drinking; a 6 percent drop in single-vehicle nighttime traffic accidents (a proxy for alcohol-impaired driving); fewer drivers with BACs of 0.05 or higher; and a 43 percent decline in emergency room–reported assault injuries.

For Communities Mobilizing for Change (CMCA), part-time local organizers in seven small communities in Minnesota and Wisconsin worked with citizen groups in each community to identify and implement a variety of formal and informal policy initiatives that would make it more difficult for young people to obtain alcohol from both social and commercial sources. The organizers led their group through a multistage development process: conducting a needs assessment; forming a core leadership group; developing a strategic plan; building community awareness and support; implementing the action plan; institutionalizing the campaign; and evaluating campaign activities and outcomes. In CMCA communities, alcohol retailers increased age-identification checks and reduced sales to minors, while 18- to 20-year-olds were less likely to try to purchase alcohol, less likely to frequent bars, less likely to drink, and less likely to provide alcohol to other teens. Arrests for impaired driving also declined significantly among 18- to 20-year-olds.

W. DEJONG

SEE ALSO:
Adolescents and Substance Abuse • Binge Drinking • Biopsychosocial Theory of Addiction • Drug Abuse Resistance Education (DARE) • Intervention • Peer Influence • Protective Factors • Risk Factors • Vulnerability

Prison Drug Use and Treatment

Despite the fact that the majority of prisoners in U.S. jails have drug problems, little is done to cure them of their addictions. One reason for this situation is reversals of policy that have alternately provided or discontinued treatment.

When you consider that there is a relationship between drugs and crime, there must be a relationship between drug use and prisoners. Movies and television shows often portray prisoners using drugs while incarcerated. Actually, drug use in prison, while not as open and dramatic as depicted on television, is a constant problem, affecting everything from institutional violence to drug treatment programs to family visits. Research has shown, however, that it is a problem that can be reduced by active efforts by prison staff. Knowing something about the relation between prisoners and drug use can also be seen as a way to achieve a more effective use of prison resources.

Drug use and prisoners

According to the Bureau of Justice Statistics, 32 percent of state prison inmates and 26 percent of federal prison inmates in 2004 were under the influence of drugs when they committed their offenses. Further, 56 percent of state and 50 percent of federal inmates reported using drugs in the month prior to their arrest. These numbers do not consider the debilitating effects of long-term addiction to drugs and alcohol. The same report found that 53 percent of state and 46 percent of federal inmates met the criteria for drug dependence or abuse. The state of Pennsylvania assesses all of its inmates for drug addiction problems and finds that 92 percent need some form of substance abuse treatment. Yet a 2004 national survey of prison inmates found that only 39 percent had participated in drug or alcohol treatment during their current sentences. Further, most of those who did participate (27 percent) only reported involvement in a drug education (17 percent) or self-help program (26 percent). Only 9 percent received treatment in a dedicated residential program unit, while another 6 percent received counseling from a drug treatment professional. Thus, while more than 90 percent of prison inmates in Pennsylvania demonstrate a need for treatment, and 53 percent meet dependency or abuse criteria, most

do not get it, and most of those who do receive treatment get only limited and nonprofessional help.

We know that many inmates are drug abusers, but how many actually continue their use in prison? This is an important question because treatment professionals agree that you cannot effectively treat people who are currently practicing their addictions. While virtually everyone agrees that drug use in prison is a problem, numbers on the extent of users are extremely difficult to determine; drug use in prisons is severely punished when discovered, so inmates understandably do not talk about it. In the mid-1990s the Pennsylvania Department of Corrections began an extensive program to curtail drug use in its prisons. As part of the study, the department conducted hair sample drug tests on approximately 1,000 inmates. It found that 10.6 percent tested positive for some type of drugs. Breaking it down by drug type, 9.3 percent were using marijuana, 2.3 percent were using cocaine, and less than 1 percent were using opiates. Obviously, one out of ten inmates using drugs while incarcerated is a serious problem, for a variety of reasons.

As well as the obvious problem of people continuing their addictions to drugs inside prison, drug use can have consequences for inmates, prison guards, and relatives on the outside. Drugs come into the prison in various ways: they are passed to inmates during visits, thrown over the walls packed in tennis balls, hidden in objects and mailed in, stashed in hollowed-out heels of shoes worn to sentencing, and brought in by correctional staff. Once inside, the drugs enter into a black market that has a unique manner of functioning. Because inmates do not generally have access to cash, drugs must either be traded for commissary goods, or outside arrangements must be made. Sometimes inmates will have a friend or relative on the outside pay a friend of their inmate dealer. Other methods involve sending money to the prison commissary account of an inmate dealer. All of these methods present possible problems for an inmate user: commissary orders can

Although cigarettes are addictive, they are not seen as a problem in prisons, but rather as a way to reduce tensions. However, they are a valuable commodity and can be used to trade for harder drugs among inmates.

be lost, contacts on the outside can be missed, and people asked to send money may not do so. In an environment where resources are scarce, even small deals that have gone wrong can create serious problems. Such drug deals often lead to violent acts and contribute to escalating cycles of violence within the prison walls. Also, prison gangs are often involved in the prison drug trade, and their well-documented willingness to use violence as a tool feeds the connection to violence behind the walls.

Regarding treatment, the violence created by the prison drug trade makes it very difficult for inmates to change their behavior. If inmates do not feel safe walking down the halls or going to meals or classes or the exercise yard, they are likely to rely on the familiar patterns of criminal thinking and thus are not receptive to drug treatment. Drug use in prison therefore has both direct and indirect detrimental effects on both individuals and the prison environment.

Drug use in prisons does not have to be taken for granted. Knowing that 10 percent of inmates were using drugs, Pennsylvania set out to eliminate or at least curtail drug use in its prisons. A focused intervention beginning in 1996 dramatically increased the number of cell searches. K-9 dog units were used to sniff cells, common areas, and vehicles entering the grounds, for drugs. Scanning equipment was installed in visiting rooms, and more background information was required of visitors, resulting in an increase in the number of people denied visits. A new phone system was installed that allowed staff to monitor inmate telephone calls. Finally, the state increased its use of urinalysis among inmates from just under 30,000 in 1995 to over 100,000 in 1998. The results were both dramatic and far reaching. Hair analysis found that drug use declined from 10.6 percent in 1995 to 2.3 percent after 1998. Interestingly, most of the decline was in marijuana use, which fell from 9.3 percent to 0.8 percent. Use of cocaine and opiates declined but by a much lesser margin. The difference was probably caused by two factors: those addicted to these more powerful drugs were willing to go to greater lengths to obtain them; and cocaine and opiates are easier to smuggle, as much smaller amounts are needed to have an effect. Drug use in prisons, though highly problematic, is a problem that can be reduced through active interventions by correctional systems.

Juveniles, drugs, and incarceration

Reliable data on drug use in juvenile institutions are difficult to obtain, mostly because juvenile facilities tend to be smaller and are more likely than adult facilities to be short-term. A lot is known, however, about drug use by juveniles prior to their incarceration. According to the FBI, there were 134,610 juveniles arrested for drug abuse violations in 2009. As with adults, however, this is only part of the story. According to the Arrestee Drug Abuse Monitoring Program (ADAM), 60 percent of male and 46 percent of female juvenile arrestees sampled in 2002 tested positive for drug use. These numbers are actually higher than for adults, indicating that being under the influence may have a more detrimental effect—in terms of getting arrested—for juveniles than for adults.

Looking at the percentage of arrestees who are under the influence of drugs at the time of offense is useful, but another way to look at the numbers is to compare the drug use patterns of juvenile arrestees to that of the general population. The chart below shows past-year drug use by teenagers aged 12 to 17

COMPARISON OF DRUG USE BETWEEN IMPRISONED AND NONIMPRISONED TEENAGERS		
	Been in detention	Never been in detention
Any illicit drug	42%	21%
Marijuana	32%	15%
Cocaine	10%	2%
Heroin	10%	0%
Hallucinogens	12%	3%
Inhalants	8%	4%
Prescription drugs	21%	8%
Abuse or dependence	24%	8%

and whether they have ever been in a juvenile detention facility. As can be seen, those who have been in detention have a much higher likelihood of past-year drug use. Other research has shown much the same relationship in adult populations. While this tells us that drugs are a problem in relation to crime, it also provides an opportunity for treatment. One of the challenges in fighting any disease is gaining access to the affected population. The table clearly shows that juvenile justice practitioners are in constant contact with juveniles suffering from substance use disorders and therefore have access to the affected population. Through the application of substance abuse treatment, this correlation between drugs and crime can become part of the solution.

The debate over drug treatment in prisons

Most people would agree that prisons are conceived, built, and operated for the purpose of punishment. However, when it is considered that almost all of the people in prisons will eventually return to their communities, many would also agree that society benefits by doing its best to ensure that these people do not go back to prison. Many programs exist that aim to reform or otherwise increase the probability that offenders will lead crime-free lives after release, but perhaps none is more important than drug treatment programs. Unfortunately, as stated earlier, the majority of prisoners do not receive treatment or receive only a limited program. Before being too critical of the correctional system, however, one should be aware that the history of prison drug treatment in the United States has been subject to opposing points of view about its purpose and benefits.

While people have used various treatments for inmates since prisons were first built, the first organized drug programs were the narcotics treatment programs run by the U.S. Public Health Service in the federal prisons in the 1930s. By the 1950s rehabilitation had become a major goal of U.S. prisons, and programs ranging from vocational training and education to intensive psychological counseling were widespread, as were all manner of drug treatment programs.

As the political storms of the 1960s and early 1970s settled on prisons, two views emerged, both of which served to curtail the use of drug treatment.

Inmates at a state prison in Montana take part in a group therapy session at the facility's drug rehabilitation unit. These in-house programs are often followed by a stay at a halfway house after release to help prisoners reestablish connections with the community and maintain their drug-free status in a safe environment.

Some on the political left charged that rehabilitation amounted to thought control and that the structure of treatment programs took sentencing decisions away from judges and placed it with correctional bureaucrats. Justice, these critics argued, called for punishment for crimes, not conformity to standards. By seeking to rehabilitate prisoners, U.S. prisons were being used to mold socially acceptable citizens, not to punish. One example used was the case of Martin Luther King Jr. Were Dr. King deemed in need of rehabilitation because he had defied the law in the Birmingham civil rights marches, he would have been placed in a program in order to rehabilitate him. Critics argued that teaching people not to use drugs was inappropriate: the government could legitimately punish people for doing this, but to change their behavior through programming was likened to Siberian work camps or Chinese reform prisons.

The other criticism was less philosophical and more operational. Many states used indeterminate sentencing during this era, in which offenders were sentenced to a minimum and maximum term by a judge, with the actual time to be served determined by correctional officials or a parole board. These administrators took into account factors like participation in prison treatment programs when making release decisions. Thus, critics argued, offenders were serving sentences based not upon their crimes but upon what they did in prison and whether prison officials approved of their activities.

At the same time that critics from the left were attacking prison drug treatment for being overly oppressive, critics from the right were attacking it for coddling prisoners. Prisons were for punishment, these critics argued, not for dealing with offenders' addiction problems. As former Georgia governor George Wallace said, "If a criminal knocks you over the head on your way home from work, he will be out of jail before you're out of the hospital [because] some psychologist will say he's not to blame, his father didn't take him to see the Pittsburgh Pirates when he was a little boy." These "law and order" critics of treatment were increasingly working to curtail the use of drug treatment programs, arguing that they wasted taxpayer money on frills for criminals.

Into this growing political storm came the now infamous Martinson report, or as it was officially titled, *The Effectiveness of Correctional Treatment: A Survey of Treatment Evaluation Studies*. Published in

1975, the 735-page report reviewed over 200 studies on correctional treatment conducted between 1945 and 1967. While at least half of the studies reviewed had some positive effects on both recidivism and drug use, Martinson and his colleagues used stringent criteria and as a result were skeptical about the overall effectiveness of treatment programs. Their lengthy and detailed report was simplified by policy makers to one sentence: "With few and isolated exceptions, the rehabilitative efforts that have been reported so far have had no appreciable effect on recidivism." This approach, coupled with the dissatisfaction of those on the left for entirely different reasons, created the perfect storm against prison drug treatment and largely blew it out of American prisons for the next twenty years.

In spite of all this, there were a number of practitioners and scholars who believed that prison drug treatment could be effective in reducing recidivism and postprison drug use, and that attempting to do so was a worthy endeavor. Although not at the same level as the earlier era, prison drug treatment continued to develop and, as with any scientific approach to a problem, the treatments got better and the outcomes more positive. Indeed, certain criminological research began to show that "criminality" (the propensity to commit crime) and drug use were symptoms of underlying complex behavioral disorders that could not be properly addressed through short-term outpatient treatment, vocational rehabilitation, or periods of imprisonment.

With the increasing crime rates and explosion in U.S. prison populations in the 1980s and 1990s, more and more people began to argue that drug treatment for prisoners was vital. Research by James Inciardi and Steven S. Martin at the University of Delaware showed that intensive, residential treatment in a therapeutic community program had significant effects in lowering recidivism and postrelease drug use among offenders who received treatment, compared with a group of offenders with similar backgrounds who did not receive treatment. These researchers also found that it was important to continue treatment through the reentry phase. That is, offenders who had in-prison residential treatment coupled with a stay in a halfway house that followed the same treatment regimen had better outcomes than those who had only the in-prison treatment.

Research in the late 1980s and 1990s continued to demonstrate that short-term outpatient programs were not effective. When one considers that addicts have mostly been addicted for years prior to arrest and that the underlying disorders that led them down these roads are deep rooted, it is no surprise that short-term programs are relatively ineffective.

It seems in some ways that treatment policies have come full circle. Drug treatment for prisoners was begun in the 1930s because it was thought that addicts, if cured of their addictions, could become functional members of society. As discussed above, the ensuing decades saw that notion attacked from all sides and eventually rejected. In 1994 the federal government authorized the RSAT (Residential Substance Abuse Treatment) program for state prisoners. The program provides grants to state departments of correction to implement drug treatment modeled on the research findings of the previous decade, which indicated that, to be effective, programs:

- should be 6 to 12 months in duration
- should be residential (offenders live in the program) in a separate unit of the prison, where residents would have no contact with other inmates
- develop inmates' cognitive, behavioral, social, vocational, and other skills to address underlying substance abuse issues
- require postrelease urinalysis testing and preferably a stay in a transitional treatment program followed by aftercare

As of March 2011 there were more than 2,500 drug treatment programs operating in all U.S. states and territories, making drug treatment once again a major goal of U.S. corrections agencies. In 2011, President Barack Obama requested $30 million for RSAT programs.

D. J. O'CONNELL

SEE ALSO:
Continuum of Care • Halfway Houses • Rehabilitation • Relapse • Therapeutic Communities • Treatment

Protective Factors

There are many influences that can work against the development of drug or alcohol abuse. These protective factors are generally positive mechanisms that involve family, social, and cultural activities.

A protective factor can be defined as an event, experience, or characteristic that helps to protect against or decrease the likelihood that an undesirable outcome (for example, drug or alcohol abuse or addiction) will occur. Typically, the term *protective factor* is applied to individuals who are already in a high-risk group (that is, they are at high risk for developing the undesirable outcome). For example, if a child is born into an area where alcohol and drugs are easily accessible, and he has peers who use alcohol and drugs, and he is suffering from depressive symptoms, then he is at risk for abusing substances. Protective factors would involve positive events, experiences, or characteristics that would help to protect him from abusing substances. Protective factors serve to buffer the impact of risk factors that exist for a person or groups of persons.

Just as a risk factor such as easy access to drugs or alcohol does not guarantee that the undesirable outcome (drug abuse) will occur, a protective factor does not guarantee that it will not occur. Protective factors do, however, decrease the likelihood or the chance that the undesirable outcome will occur. Some scientists have tended to view protective factors as the mere opposite of risk factors, but this way of thinking has not proved particularly helpful. For some individuals, a risk factor (for example, having an addicted parent) may also serve as a protective factor. The outcome will depend on a number of variables, including biology, physiology, social and community factors, cultural elements, and age. In the following sections, common types of protective factors for addiction and their benefits will be discussed.

Common types of protective factors

Over the past few decades, researchers have identified the majority of potential protective factors for addiction. Thus, researchers now know what events, experiences, or characteristics serve to help protect high-risk individuals or groups of individuals from addiction. Protective factors can be divided into two major groups: external factors associated with broad societal or community characteristics; and internal factors related to characteristics within the individual.

Family has been shown to be one of the strongest sources of external protection against adolescent substance abuse. Family-related protective factors include having a positive attachment to the family, positive family support, healthy family relationships, strong bonds among family members, a commitment to the family, good communication, and a belief in family values. Children and adolescents who feel close to their family members and who feel supported by them are at a lower risk for substance use. In addition, positive family relationship characteristics of trust, warmth, and involvement have been shown to serve as protective factors against substance use. These important family relationships can serve to discourage substance use initiation and help protect adolescents and adults from addiction.

Education is another significant external factor. Educational attainment and academic achievement have been shown to help protect against substance abuse. Thus, children and adolescents who earn good grades, function well in school, and are actively involved in school-related activities are less likely to abuse substances. This connection between educational achievement and reduced substance abuse may be the result of less free time, clearer goals, or closer and more supportive relationships between students and their teachers and coaches. Having after-school activities, such as supervised youth services, that run contrary to substance use is also very important and protective for children and adolescents.

Spirituality and religiosity have been identified as protective factors against alcohol and drug abuse, as well. Religious or spiritual affiliation, attendance, and belief have all been found to be inversely related to substance use. This may be, in part, attributed to social support, activities, a sense of belonging, and the meaning that many find in religion or spirituality.

Taking part in after-school activities, such as sports, often gives teenagers something to focus on in terms of setting goals, teamwork, and keeping busy. By filling their time positively, teenagers are less likely to be drawn to drugs.

In addition to the external factors just described, there are a number of internal characteristics that can help protect against substance abuse. Individuals who have good self-regulation are often more protected against substance abuse than those with poor self-regulation. A person who can set a future goal (for example, obtaining an educational degree), which can help regulate and direct daily behavior and activities, will be more protected against activities that run contrary to that goal (alcohol and drug use). Some research suggests that children who are shy may be more protected against substance abuse because they are less likely to have drug-using peers. Certain genetic and biological factors—a genetic risk for addiction or enzymes that regulate alcohol metabolism—may also serve as buffers against alcohol and drug abuse.

It is important to remember that none of these protective factors provide immunity from developing an addiction. For different individuals, certain protective factors will be more or less salient than others, depending on a number of variables, including genetic, age-related, psychological, and cultural factors. The overall combination of these risk and protective factors can help mental health professionals understand how to best intervene and who is at most risk for substance abuse.

Protective factors and treatment

Protective factors are critical in reducing risk for alcohol and drug abuse. Knowledge of protective factors can be used to help design optimal treatment interventions that are tailored to the needs of each individual. For example, teenagers who have several risk factors and no protective factors may need a higher level of intervention in order to help guide them away from substance abuse. Protective factors such as improved family communication skills or after-school activities may need to be put in place as part of a comprehensive intervention. In addition, protective factors that already exist for a particular individual can be emphasized and strengthened as part of the intervention process.

Addressing one protective factor can also have a positive effect on other protective factors. Promoting one may lead to improvements in another. For example, enhanced family relationships and bonding may lead to improvements in academic achievement because the parents are assisting the child with homework. Enhanced academic achievement may subsequently lead to more positive peer relationships, which will further serve to help protect the individual from substance abuse.

S. E. BACK

SEE ALSO:
Adolescents and Substance Abuse • Biopsychosocial Theory of Addiction • Intervention • Prevention • Risk Factors • Vulnerability

Public Health Programs

Public health agencies are responsible for identifying risks that may have a significant impact on the health of the community. Among these are risks associated with drug and alcohol use that can harm the wider population.

The public health system is a broad range of services that extend from the local community to the world as a whole. The majority of public health programs are led by governmental agencies. Their mission is to promote the integration of public health and health care policy, to strengthen partnerships with community-based organizations, and to collaborate with hospitals, service providers, governmental agencies, businesses, insurance, industry, and other health care entities.

Many local agencies are moving toward the view that public health is more than the delivery of health care and public health services. The spectrum of this broader public health view also includes strengthening the social, economic, cultural, and spiritual fabric of the community. Both governmental agencies and community-based organizations have begun to embrace the view that problem solving in health care will not occur in isolation but in concert with solving the social, economic, and other challenges that exist in the community. Each of the fifty states has an agency that is responsible for public health, as do cities and counties at the local level. At the national level, public health is the responsibility of the Department of Health and Human Services usually working through the National Institutes of Health (NIH) and the Centers for Disease Control (CDC). Under the NIH are agencies or institutes that address specific public health issues, such as the National Cancer Institute or the Substance Abuse and Mental Health Services Administration. The World Health Organization (WHO) provides the same services as local public health agencies but on an international basis. Developing countries depend on WHO to help them monitor health, provide treatment, identify emerging problems, and develop public health policy.

Drug use and prevention

Since the mid-1970s many public health departments have undertaken the task of educating communities about drug use because of the health risks and social costs. The prevention of drug use is a relatively new discipline. Prior to this century the primary drug use problem in the United States was alcohol, as it is today. In the nineteenth century drunkenness was considered a moral failing and a threat to society and the growth of the new country. Drug users at that time were primarily dependent on opiates and were either professionals, housewives, or Civil War veterans. They were not perceived as being as dangerous as the drunkard. Although addiction to morphine was undesirable, it was considered a vice, like tobacco smoking.

It has only been since the mid-1980s that public health programs have begun to sponsor education about and prevention of drug use. While most communities primarily use a criminal justice approach in dealing with drug use, public health programs have begun to view drug use prevention as important to healthy communities.

Responsibilities of public health departments

The services that public health agencies provide can be broad or narrow, depending on the needs of the regions that they serve. Most public health departments monitor the health status of the community, which involves keeping track of infectious diseases and hazards, including biohazards. Hospitals and physicians are required to report certain diseases to the Health Department, which may initiate an investigation into the problem. This helps identify the extent of the problem, available health services, and treatment required, after which risks can be identified and a suitable policy established. The community is informed about the risks and educated as to where to go for treatment and the types of treatments that are available.

The main purpose of public health agencies is to:

- Monitor health status to identify community health problems
- Diagnose and investigate health problems and health hazards in the community

DIFFICULTIES OF PUBLIC HEALTH PROGRAMS

While public health programs may place importance on warning the community about using drugs, little has been done to educate those who are already using drugs about ways for them to remain healthy. During the first ten years of the HIV epidemic, public health departments failed to prevent intravenous drug users (IDUs) from sharing needles. The fear that HIV could be spread to the noninjecting heterosexual community through sexual transmission finally convinced many communities to initiate HIV-prevention programs aimed at IDUs. However, by the time this was decided, many IDUs were already infected and had been transmitting the disease to others for a number of years.

A further problem existed. In many areas, laws against drug paraphernalia made the sale or use of syringes to inject an illicit substance illegal. In New York City these laws resulted in the creation of shooting galleries where needles were used repeatedly, causing HIV rates to soar, such that within a six-month period, prevalence rates in some groups shifted from relatively low rates to more than 40 percent. It was this increase that convinced public health officials to initiate a needle exchange program and to allow pharmacies to sell syringes. This gave IDUs the tools to protect themselves and their families. Slowly, the HIV rates began to decrease among IDUs, who still remain the greatest group at risk for contracting HIV.

While HIV rates have been contained among injecting drug users, the hepatitis C virus continues to be transmitted at high levels. Hepatitis is many times more infectious than HIV and results in prevalence rates of 95 percent or more. Thus, large numbers of individuals, including those that may have injected drugs once or twice, are likely to be infected with hepatitis B or C or both.

Public health programs, while providing sterile needles, have yet to develop comprehensive education and risk-reduction programs for IDUs. The major message has been to "just say no," which is not practical for individuals addicted to opiates or cocaine, who often have no access to treatment. There is no effective medication for cocaine use, and most users relapse to using drugs very quickly. The needle exchange and other HIV prevention programs have shown that when IDUs are given clean equipment they will protect themselves from health risks.

- Inform, educate, and empower people about health issues
- Mobilize community partnerships to identify and solve health problems
- Develop policies and plans that support individual and community health efforts
- Enforce laws and regulations that protect health and ensure safety
- Link people to needed personal health services and assure the provision of health care when otherwise unavailable
- Assure a competent public health and personal health care workforce
- Evaluate effectiveness, accessibility, and quality of personal and population-based health services
- Conduct research on new insights and innovative solutions to health problems.

It is the responsibility of the public health system to develop meaningful education programs for drug users. Such programs should include warnings about the dangers of multiple drug use and the risk of overdose. San Francisco, for example, has begun to distribute naloxone, the medication given for an opiate overdose, to intravenous drug users and other users of opiates. Other organizations have begun to publish educational materials about what to do when someone overdoses. Many lives could be saved if these simple measures were more widely known and put into practice.

J. S. WOODS

SEE ALSO:

Harm Reduction • Needle Exchange Programs • State Agencies • World Health Organization (WHO)

Recovery

Getting over an addiction problem can be a long and difficult process. Relapses are a common feature of the recovery process, and trying to maintain abstinence may require several attempts before the addict achieves stability.

In all problems, but especially in addiction problems, how we define and view the problem will dictate how we view the recovery process. For example, if we view alcoholism as an incurable disease, then recovery must entail abstinence. There are, however, a range of possible definitions of the recovery process.

Many perspectives on alcoholism suggest that, while controlled or reduced drinking may indeed be an option, the safer option is probably abstinence. Although the recovery goal (abstinence or moderation) is the choice of the individual, most therapists would recommend that anyone showing signs of physical dependence (for example, withdrawal) or cognitive damage (such as memory lapses) should abstain. Research has shown that physically dependent or cognitively damaged drinkers have difficulty exercising control over their consumption for any prolonged period. However, abstinence does not come without its own problems—since the vast majority of adults drink to some degree, someone who is abstinent can be regarded as unusual, which may lead to situations in which the alcoholic is offered alcohol and is tempted to drink. Obviously, although these same problems can arise concerning drugs, the fact that drugs are less accepted, and thus less common, in society suggests that temptation may be less of a problem for drug users.

Problems of abstinence

One assumption that underlies the proposal that abstinence is the only, or best, recovery goal is that there is no cure for alcoholism. That is, the alcoholic may stop drinking and may remain abstinent, but if he or she were to take another drink, then the alcoholism would be as severe as ever. Thus groups like Alcoholics Anonymous (AA) argue that there is no cure, only an arrestment of the disease. Evidence for this position can be seen in the fact that many alcoholics who, after a period of abstinence, consume any alcohol relapse to binge drinking. It has been argued that this type of relapse shows that the alcoholic has a different metabolism from social drinkers. However, two U.S. researchers (Marlatt and Gordon) have proposed a different interpretation of these observations. Instead of viewing relapse as a physical reaction, they argue that it is actually a two-stage psychological reaction, triggered by a perception of failure to adhere to an absolute state. They named the reaction the "abstinence violation effect," suggesting that the abstinent alcoholic who takes a drink (a lapse) perceives this act as proof of being unable to control his or her drinking either through moderation or abstinence. This apparent recognition of "failure" sparks a negative emotional state and a full-blown binge (a collapse). In this theory, no metabolic mechanism is required to explain relapse; a negative state of mind can explain relapse to alcohol, drugs, smoking, or food binges.

One of the main problems with abstinence is that, as with all absolute goals, it is difficult to both achieve and maintain; hence addiction has been called a relapsing disease. Indeed, it is rare that someone manages to successfully give up any addiction the first time. It is more usual for the alcoholic, addict, or smoker to undergo numerous attempts before he or she is successful. However, relapse need not always be negative. Relapse can be a learning process that reveals places or situations that should be avoided, for example, sitting in a bar every night drinking soda with familiar drinking companions. It can also strengthen resolve, since overconfidence is recognized and the difficulty of changing is actually appreciated. Many alcoholics and addicts feel that they can stop or change their consumption behavior whenever they want, but when they actually try they relapse because they have underestimated the magnitude of the task. Thus relapse can lead to more effort and a positive outcome. However, for some it can have the reverse effect, as continual relapse can lead to feelings of helplessness and hopelessness, which can severely inhibit recovery. This is a dangerous situation that therapists need to address by trying to increase the client's self-efficacy, or the belief that he or she can achieve and maintain sobriety. Research has shown that higher self-efficacy is predictive of a positive outcome in treatment of addiction. Moreover, it has also shown that this self-efficacy can influence other behaviors and activities. That is, having changed a major part of their lives, alcoholics often succeed in changing other aspects of their lives in a more positive way, for example, relationships, employment, and education.

Self-help groups

Self-help groups can help the individual to remain abstinent. Of course, the fact that there is a shared goal among the members is helpful, as is the example of others staying sober through problems and hardships. A 1996 study, Project MATCH, the largest study of alcohol treatment conducted to date, found that attendance at AA meetings after treatment helped individuals to remain abstinent. This was particularly true for people whose social circle mainly consisted of heavy drinkers who may encourage the recovering individual to drink. In this case AA provided an alternative social circle, an abstinent one. However, this shared view of the world can also lead to problems in recovery, as will be discussed later in this article.

Psychological changes

Recovery is not just about the absence of, or reduced consumption of, alcohol or other drugs. If recovery is to be successful, then consumption changes need to be accompanied by considerable psychological changes. AA and the other twelve-step groups recognize this and offer a program to accomplish these changes. While some may regard the program as pseudo-religion, the steps in fact make up an extremely practical recovery package for an addict, a package that does not differ too greatly from other more secular cognitive behavioral programs.

That AA apparently places considerable stress on confession and making amends could certainly be construed as being proof that the program is religious in nature. However, substance use is functional, that is, alcoholics and addicts drink or take drugs for a reason, though the reason may differ from individual to individual and may change over time. For many addicts, the reason they give for substance use is to cope with guilt for things they have done or not done. It would then seem that a very practical way

Recovering alcoholics often feel that they have failed if they have a drink. Teaching them to understand that lapses are likely to happen during recovery can improve the chances of alcoholics achieving sobriety.

to deal with the situation would be to bring commissions or omissions into the open and then to attempt to patch up differences with those people who have been harmed. This strategy attempts to deal with the guilt and helps the alcoholic or addict feel more acceptable and accepted. Moreover, it also teaches the addict a new broad strategy of dealing with problems, situations, and people; that is, to face and deal with the problems rather than run or hide from them. This lesson should produce a cognitive shift in the addict that should reduce the reliance on alcohol or drug use for coping and hence make relapse less likely.

The twelfth step of AA ("Having had a spiritual awakening as the result of these steps, we tried to

257

carry this message to others and to practice these principles in all our affairs") is designed both to perpetuate the organization and to produce another cognitive shift in the recovering alcoholic. This last step perpetuates the organization by producing a culture of helping that helps sustain meetings and keeps them open for newcomers. For the individual recovering alcoholic or addict, it again produces a shift of focus from selfish introspection to caring and accepting responsibility for others.

Social

For many alcoholics and addicts, recovery can be a time of mixed emotions. On the one hand, there is the joy and pride of having overcome a life-crippling problem. However, on the other hand, recovery can represent the end of a way of life and the loss of friendships that have been built up over years of drinking and drug taking. The sadness of these changes should not be underestimated; indeed, some researchers have referred to a period of grief, in which the old way of life is mourned before the new way of life is fully adopted. However, after this mourning period, the alcoholic or addict would normally be expected to have a lifestyle that is much improved. Indeed, if it were not one would not expect the "recovery" to be very long lasting. Even if it is stable, adopting to this new way of life may be difficult for both the addict and the family.

One regular criticism of AA, and other self-help groups, is that the alcoholic or addict is encouraged to spend too much time at meetings and working with other addicts. While time spent at meetings or other AA activity may be beneficial in terms of recovery and remaining abstinent, it may cause conflict with the family. It has been suggested that in order to recover from one addiction the addict needs to develop another more positive one, for example, AA and meetings. Nevertheless, the family may feel now that the addict is no longer intoxicated that they have a right to expect some respect and attention. The addict may feel that the family is placing too many demands and is inhibiting his or her recovery. Old resentments may start to boil over, and relationships that have survived the heavy substance use years can break up at the recovery stage.

Part of the reason for this problem may lie in the expectations of the family and in particular the partner. He or she may feel resentful at having waited for the addict to recover and for the return to a life that is familiar with a partner who is also familiar. However, the intervening period of substance use may have wrought quite fundamental changes in the addict that the partner has not shared. Hence the old partner may no longer exist. Indeed, the old life may have been part of the reason that the alcoholic or addict used substances, and a return could be undesirable as it could precipitate a relapse.

The final danger in recovery is that having accepted the need to make changes in his or her life, the addict starts to believe that the partner and family also need to make changes. Again, this can be a source of conflict as family members point out that the addict has the problem, not them. Some partners may interpret this conflict as betrayal or an attempt by the addict to shift the blame for his or her overindulgence, instead of accepting the damage that he or she did. AA and other step groups have family groups Al-Anon and Alateen for partners and children of alcoholics; however not every partner or child wants to join these groups. Indeed, for many family members, the heartfelt desire is to return to some semblance of normalcy with the alcoholic or addict not using substances. Their definitions of normalcy may not include meeting the partners of other alcoholics and addicts or taking part in soul searching.

Some have argued that *recovery* is an inappropriate term. Recovery has connotations of returning to a previous state; they argue that the cauldron of addiction and the process of recovery have forged a new person, better in many ways than if he or she had not been addicted. What is certainly true is that many people do recover from addiction and lead fruitful, happy lives. However, it takes time; some argue that it takes two years for recovery to be stable. The early stages of recovery can be traumatic as the alcoholic or addict moves from a destructive, but familiar, way of life to a more positive, but strange, new life.

J. McMahon

SEE ALSO:
Abstinence • Alcoholics Anonymous • Alcoholism Treatment • Dependence • Relapse • Self-esteem • Step Programs • Treatment • Withdrawal

Rehabilitation

Rehabilitation centers are places where addicts are prepared to return to society. During rehabilitation, participants are taught skills they will need to meet the challenges of recovery and ongoing abstinence from drugs.

Rehabilitation, or "rehab," refers to a specific type of treatment program that aims to restore the addicted individual to health through the use of therapy (or counseling) and education. Rehab centers are designed for individuals diagnosed with an alcohol or drug dependence, whose lives have been disrupted by their addictions. Addiction can harm physical, mental, and spiritual health, family and social relationships, school or work performance, and the ability to be a responsible member of society.

Since addiction is a biological, psychological, social, and spiritual disorder, rehabilitation aims to help the individual begin to address problems in these areas. At the most basic level, the goal of rehabilitation is to help the addicted person get sober from alcohol or other drugs, and to begin to develop skills that will help him or her stay sober after treatment. Rehab centers also help the person create a long-term plan to address these domains of recovery.

Short-term rehab programs

Short-term programs include inpatient hospital and residential programs in which the person lives at the facility between two and four weeks. Although the length of stay is based on clinical criteria, it is also determined by the patient's insurance. Some insurance companies pay for very brief stays (a week or less), while others pay for longer stays (three to four weeks).

These programs offer counseling or therapy, education, and Alcoholics Anonymous (AA) or Narcotics Anonymous (NA) meetings. Most programs are designed for people with any type or combination of substance addiction. Some are designed for specific populations, such as adolescents, women, those involved in the criminal justice system, or those with co-occurring psychiatric disorders. Programs for adolescents usually last longer than those for adults, as do programs for individuals with coexisting psychiatric disorders.

Rehab programs are staffed by certified addiction counselors, social workers, psychologists, nurses, doctors, clergy, dieticians, recreational therapists, and aides. Many employ recovering alcoholics or drug addicts, who use their life experiences in addition to their clinical skills to help patients. Some rehab programs offer services to family members as well.

The person may enter rehab after being detoxified from alcohol or drugs, or directly if detoxification is not needed. The goals of a rehabilitation program include helping the person:

- Overcome denial of the addiction and accept the need to change
- Become educated about addiction and recovery
- Understand the relationship between substance use and life problems
- Begin to learn skills needed to meet the challenges of recovery (for example, managing cravings or emotions, using a support system)
- Accept the need for ongoing involvement in recovery
- Develop a relapse prevention plan
- Involve the family or significant others in recovery.

Any individual with an addiction can benefit from a rehabilitation program, especially if outpatient treatment has been tried and has not worked. The decision as to which type of program is best for a particular individual is made with the help of an addiction treatment professional.

A rehab program is just a beginning step in recovery. An addicted person is not likely to continue to make changes or remain sober without following through with other professional treatment or AA and NA meetings upon finishing a rehabilitation course.

Some participate in rehab only once, while others go through several courses over many years. If a person returns to treatment it does not denote failure: with chronic disorders like addiction, some experience more episodes of illness and require more help than others.

Life in a rehab center starts at six in the morning, when inmates shower and clean their shared rooms before starting a day of lectures, group therapy, and self-help sessions to overcome their addictions.

The rehab process

The size of a rehab center may vary from 20 to 100 or more beds. Most are for men and women, although some programs focus exclusively on one gender. Rehab patients usually room with each other to avoid isolation and to encourage sharing and mutual support.

One way to understand rehab is to review a typical day. After getting dressed, showered, cleaning up one's room, and having breakfast, the patient (or client) participates in a structured day with little free time. Many group therapy and education sessions are offered.

The treatment day begins with a community meeting in which rules and regulations and the schedule for the day are reviewed, new members in the center are introduced, and those leaving say good-bye and share their follow-up plans. A daily reading is reflected on and briefly discussed.

Several group treatments are held throughout the day. One type is a therapy group with 10 or fewer participants, which lasts one to two hours. The group members decide which personal concerns, problems, or recovery issues to discuss. Examples of issues

discussed include: motivation struggles; effects of addiction on physical, mental, or spiritual health; the effects of addiction on family and social relationships; what patients will miss about getting high; fears of living sober; depression, anxiety, anger, boredom, shame and guilt; pressures to use alcohol or drugs; cravings; relapse; reactions to and experiences with support group meetings; and problems specific to an individual (for example, what it is like to be addicted and gay, a woman, an African American, and so on).

Education groups (sometimes called psycho-education or skills groups) include lectures by professional staff, discussions, and videos on a topic relevant to addiction or recovery. Examples of topics include the effects of alcohol or a specific drug, symptoms, causes and effects of addiction, the process of recovery, addiction and the family, the twelve steps of AA or NA, handling social pressures to use substances, managing emotions in recovery, developing sober relationships, identifying early signs of relapse, and spirituality. These groups last an hour or more, and may include the entire community rather than small groups. Recreational and social activities are offered so participants learn to reduce boredom and have fun without using alcohol or drugs.

Family groups may be held weekly, which involve family members attending sessions along with rehab patients. Individual sessions are held throughout the week with counselors or other professionals, such as a dietician or chaplain. These sessions focus on specific issues or problems of the patient, a review of the rehab experience, or planning for recovery after rehabilitation.

Recovery assignments are given in the form of readings, writing in a journal, completing a work-book task, or practicing a new behavior. These assignments aim to provide education, to help the person to relate material to his or her life, and to plan how to change and solve problems. For example, a patient beginning rehab may be asked to write a detailed personal history of substance use and addiction, then share this with his therapy group. A patient completing the rehab program may be asked to identify potential relapse warning signs and strategies to handle these, and then share this with his group. Alternatively, a patient who has difficulty asking others for help and support may be asked to reach out and initiate discussions on recovery with at least two other rehab patients.

Meetings of AA and NA are usually held several days each week onsite or in the community. Patients are encouraged to use the tools of AA or NA in their ongoing recovery (sponsor, twelve steps, slogans, and so on).

Long-term rehab programs

Some addicted people need longer-term treatment in residential settings where they have continued access to education and counseling, as well as vocational training or counseling. These individuals are not ready to return to their communities after a short-term rehab. Alternatively, they may not have the necessary financial, social, or family support to put their lives back together. They need more time and help in making personal and lifestyle changes and in developing skills necessary for long-term sobriety.

Halfway house (HWH) and therapeutic community (TC) programs were developed for such people. A stay at an HWH usually lasts several months or longer, while residence in a TC lasts months to a year or more. Therapeutic communities are generally more intensive in their treatment and more psychologically demanding than HWH programs.

The goals of HWH and TC programs are to continue developing recovery skills, to help the addicted person pursue educational or occupational goals, to form a network of sober people, and to prepare for independent living. TC programs further aim to get the addict to make personality changes, which is a difficult and long-term process. These programs focus more on psychological and interpersonal change, whereas HWH programs focus more on offering a supervised environment in which vocational goals can be pursued.

In fact, TCs are "habilitation" programs because they help residents develop skills that are lacking (for example, skills in developing and maintaining healthy relationships, solving problems, planning for the future). A unique feature of TCs is their focus on promoting values such as citizenship, honesty, love, charity, altruism, and responsibility to others.

Therapeutic communities were established for chronic drug addicts who have difficulty staying off drugs and functioning in society. They were originally designed to last two years and required a major commitment from the recovering addict. A number of modified TC programs have now been set up that last several months to one year or longer.

Similar to the case of the person who completes a rehabilitation program, the addict or person who completes an HWH or TC program should have follow-up in an outpatient clinic or self-help program. This provides the opportunity to continue with sobriety and change.

What happens after rehab?

All patients who attend rehabilitation programs are encouraged to continue their recovery and attend groups such as AA or NA. Many will also continue receiving professional services, such as individual or group therapy, in an outpatient program. Those who successfully access these services and attend AA or NA programs have the best outcomes.

D. C. Daley

SEE ALSO:

Clinics • Continuum of Care • Halfway Houses • Recovery • Relapse • Therapeutic Communities • Treatment • Treatment Centers

Reinforcement

Reinforcement is a key stage in the process of addiction. If a person experiences a positive response to a drug-taking event, it is likely he or she will repeat it. A negative response, such as withdrawal, may also act as a reinforcing behavior.

Broadly, reinforcement theory attempts to explain the behavior of organisms by systematically analyzing the relationship (or *contingencies*) between the occurrence of a stimulus (a reinforcer) and changes in the subsequent probability of the behavior that preceded it. In the context of drug abuse and addiction, reinforcement describes the relationship between the behavior of drug seeking and drug taking and the consequences of that behavior, namely the biological and psychological effects of the drug.

Reinforcement learning was first systematically studied by the U.S. psychologist Edward L. Thorndike (1874–1949). Using a so-called puzzle box, Thorndike demonstrated that behaviors (for example, escaping from the puzzle box) that are followed by a pleasant consequence, for instance a food reward, have a higher probability of reoccurring in the future. It was the Harvard behaviorist B. F. Skinner (1904–1990), however, who most thoroughly studied and popularized the ideas of reinforcement learning, or what has become known as operant, or instrumental, conditioning. For his studies, Skinner developed a specialized test apparatus consisting of a chamber containing a lever (for rats) or a pecking key (for pigeons) that the animal could manipulate to obtain a food or water reinforcer. Much of the current research methodology and understanding of reinforcement learning comes from Skinner's meticulous work on how "behavior is shaped and maintained by its consequences."

Principles of reinforcement

Reinforcers that shape and maintain behavior fall into two general categories. First, positive reinforcers are stimuli that when presented increase the frequency of the behavior that precedes them. For instance, if a hungry rat receives a small amount of food reward after pressing a lever, the rat is more likely to press the same lever on future occasions to receive more food. Negative reinforcers, on the other hand, are stimuli that when removed increase the frequency of the behavior that precedes them. For instance, a rat will press a lever with increasing frequency if this prevents it from receiving a mild electric shock to the foot or some other aversive stimulus. Thus, although the psychological nature of positive and negative reinforcers are very different, their behavioral consequences are the same—they both increase the frequency of the behaviors on which they are contingent.

Two conditions produce the opposite effect—they decrease the frequency of behavior. First, when the presentation of aversive stimuli is made contingent on a behavior (that is, the behavior produces the stimulus), it typically suppresses the behavior. This is called punishment. Second, when previously reinforced behavior ceases to be reinforced, typically the behavior diminishes with repeated experiences with nonreinforcement. This is called extinction and, although it can be effective to suppress previously established (and undesirable) behavior, extinction is rarely permanent, and the behavior is readily recovered—a phenomenon called reinstatement.

Reinforcing stimuli such as food and water (positive) or electric shocks (negative) are called primary or unconditioned reinforcers because they are intrinsically able to reinforce behavior. Other stimuli, however, acquire their reinforcer qualities by having been associated with a primary reinforcer. In this case, a previously neutral stimulus becomes a conditioned, or secondary, reinforcer. In the context of addictive drugs, for instance, drug paraphernalia (for example, syringes or pipes) or environments (such as a crack house) that have been associated with drug taking may thus become secondary reinforcers that exacerbate drug taking or trigger relapse in recovering addicts.

Finally, an important variable in reinforcement learning is the schedule of reinforcement. Simple schedules of reinforcement can be classified into two categories. In the ratio schedule of reinforcement, the reinforcer is presented only when a certain number of responses have been performed. In the interval schedule of reinforcement, on the other hand, the number of responses is irrelevant and reinforcement is given after a certain amount of time has elapsed. Both ratio and interval schedules can also vary in whether the ratio or interval of reinforcement is regular (fixed) or is variable. In the laboratory, variations in the schedule of reinforcement have a profound and predictable impact on rates and patterns of reinforced behavior.

Reinforcement models of addiction

There are two general reinforcement models of drug addiction. Traditionally, the action of drugs as negative reinforcers has been the central focus in addiction research. According to this view, drug use is maintained not because of the state

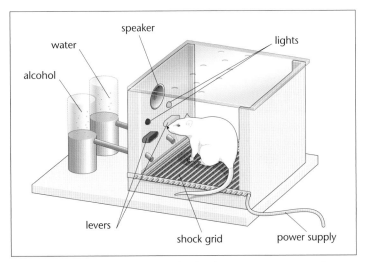

The Skinner box is used to test behavioral responses to cues such as lights or sounds. The animal learns to press the lever that will deliver food, water, or a drug. It can be further conditioned by the input of a negative stimulus such as a small electric shock to the feet.

that the drugs produce, but because the aversive symptoms associated with drug withdrawal are alleviated by taking the drug. Indeed, many addicts suffer from symptoms of physical and psychological distress upon cessation of drug intake. Additionally, drug-associated secondary reinforcers can trigger withdrawal-like states. Drugs may also be used to self-medicate preexisting aversive states such as anxiety or depression, explaining the comorbidity between these disease states and addiction.

More recent formulations have focused on the role of drugs as positive reinforcers. Thus, a positive reinforcement view of addiction suggests that drugs sustain self-administration because of the state they produce, not because they prevent or alleviate drug withdrawal. Most prominent among this category of explanations is the theory that the positive reinforcing effects of drugs are due to their pleasurable or euphoric effects. Thus, drugs are addicting because they produce a pleasurable feeling. Furthermore, drug-associated stimuli become secondary reinforcers, not because their absence can trigger withdrawal symptoms, but because they evoke druglike pleasurable effects that act to further motivate drug-seeking and taking behavior.

Although an increasing number of researchers have begun to question the usefulness of positive and

negative reinforcement views as explanatory models of drug abuse and addiction, the principles and methodology of operant conditioning have been, and still are, widely applied to the study of drugs of abuse and addiction.

Methods of assessing drug reinforcement

A number of procedures have been developed to study drug reinforcement. Arguably the least complicated of these is the conditioned place preference test. This procedure involves several trials in which the animal is injected with the drug, paired with placement in a distinct environment containing various cues (for example, tactile, visual, or olfactory). The animal thus develops an association between the reinforcing effects of the drug and specific environmental cues. When tested in the drug-free state, approaches to and the amount of time spent in the compartment associated with the drug injection are used as indicators of drug reinforcement.

However, the most common technique for assessing drug reinforcement is the self-administration procedure using operant chambers. This technique allows direct measurement of the reinforcing effects of drugs of abuse and, with the development of intravenous catheter implantation

263

techniques in different laboratory animals, it has become relatively easy and quick to evaluate the reinforcing effects of various drugs. Typically, in these studies a behavioral response such as lever pressing is followed by intravenous drug delivery using an infusion pump. The ability of the drug injection to directly reinforce behavior is determined by measuring operant lever-pressing rates and patterns.

Over the years, a large number of paradigms have been developed using drug self-administration procedures. For instance, drug discrimination procedures, in which animals can choose between one of two drug injections, can be used to assess differences in reinforcer efficacy. Also, animals can be tested for acquisition and maintenance of drug intake under different schedules of reinforcement. More recently, models have been developed to study the factors involved in regulation and escalation of drug intake. Drug self-administration procedures can also be used to assess the role of drug-associated stimuli in drug seeking and taking (that is, secondary reinforcement). By explicitly pairing cues (for example, discrete light or tone stimuli) with drug infusions during the drug-taking phase, the ability of the secondary reinforcers to maintain a response in the absence of drug reward (that is, under extinction conditions) can be measured. Finally, a number of laboratories interested in mechanisms underlying relapse have been studying the ability of drugs or drug-associated secondary reinforcers (or other stimuli) to reinstate extinguished lever pressing.

A number of procedures exist that indirectly measure the reinforcing effects of drugs. These methods are based on the notion that the reinforcing effects of drugs are dependent on neural substrates underlying other primary reinforcers, and thus should interact with these. In particular, addictive drugs appear to enhance or facilitate brain stimulation reward. This technique involves surgically implanting stimulating electrodes in brain regions where electrical stimulation is reinforcing (into dopaminergic neural circuits, as described below). Animals are trained to press levers to receive brief pulses of electrical stimulation to certain brain areas. Addictive drugs enhance the reinforcing impact of such electrical stimulation, providing a measure of the reinforcing effects of drugs.

The physiological basis of reinforcement

Using the above methods, investigators have been able to investigate the neural substrates underlying natural and drug reinforcement. The common currency for most rewarding and reinforcing stimuli appears to be activation of the mesotelencephalic dopamine system, comprised of neuronal pathways originating from the substantia nigra and ventral tegmental area—nuclei within the midbrain—that project to a forebrain area called the striatum, in particular to its ventral part containing the nucleus accumbens. Consistent with this idea, a large number of studies have shown that interfering with these dopamine systems decreases the motivational and reinforcing impact of stimuli. For instance, antagonist drugs, which selectively block the receptors for the dopamine neurotransmitter, or complete surgical destruction of the dopamine neurons using neurotoxins, impair operant lever-pressing for food, electrical brain stimulation, or intravenous drugs. These same manipulations also disrupt drug-produced conditioned-place preference. Furthermore, using a complicated form of the self-administration technique in which drugs are self-injected directly into the brain, rats will self-administer drugs into the appropriate portions of the dopamine system.

Based on these types of findings, it is now generally accepted that dopamine systems play a key role in the rewarding and reinforcing effects of various natural chemical and drug reinforcers. That is not to say that other brain areas are not involved in some way in these effects. There is mounting evidence, for instance, that a small region called the amygdala is critical for secondary reinforcement. Also, brain regions such as the prefrontal cortex, hippocampus, and subthalamic nucleus now appear to be involved. The emergent picture, therefore, is that the brain substrate underlying reward and reinforcement consists of a complex neural network involving interactions between various subcortical and cortical regions important for motivation, learning and memory, and decision-making processes.

H. CROMBAG

SEE ALSO:

Addiction • Addictive Behavior • Aversion • Conditioning • Dependence • Reward

Relapse

Giving up drugs or alcohol is not easy. Many addicts who have undergone treatment find that they are tempted back to their old ways. Teaching them to recognize and understand triggering factors can help avoid relapses.

Relapse to drug and alcohol use is most often associated with crime, arrest, and incarceration but can happen to any recovering addict. The return to drug use touches the very fabric of society and impacts children, parents, spouses, schools, employers, and perhaps every social structure and institution known today. As such, the cost is innumerable. Although there are a vast number of treatment services aimed at relapse preventive measures, the many and varied approaches to relapse prevention are based on one's definition of relapse and the factors that perpetuate relapse, prevent relapse, identify relapse risks, and define relapse-coping strategies. To further complicate matters, relapse education, prevention, risks, and strategies may vary from one treatment population and service provider to another. The variables involved in relapse are extensive, for example, age, delinquency, ethnicity, income, education, employment, gender, health, and so on.

Definition

There are various definitions applied to the term *relapse*. Several noted drug and alcohol treatment experts define relapse as a single drug-using event. Others define relapse as a psychological process that develops over a period of time and subsequently results in drug or alcohol use. Some professionals and recovering individuals also note that people cannot relapse if they have not sincerely begun to recover—physically, psychologically, and socially.

Although the term *relapse* varies with regard to application, the terms *lapse* and *relapse* are differentiated more clearly. In general, a lapse, or slip, is most often associated with a single drug- or alcohol-using incident, while a relapse, or setback, is most often associated with a return to a regular pattern of use. While the difference in terms may or may not seem significant, the interventions to restore abstinence contrast drastically. For example, a lapse that involves a single drug- or alcohol-using incident may actually have a greater psychological impact, rather than a physiological impact. Therefore, the planned intervention would most likely focus on guilt, shame, or remorse rather than physical withdrawal factors, or anxiety and depression caused by expected consequences from a pattern of drug or alcohol use and the resulting loss of employment, family breakups, criminal acts committed to purchase drugs, or wrongdoings committed while under the influence of drugs or alcohol.

Factors that lead to relapse

Renowned drug and alcohol treatment researchers George DeLeon and S. Swartz note that drug addiction is a chronically relapsing condition, and as such, in most cases relapse will occur despite treatment. Although contributing factors concerning relapse may vary between researchers, social workers, prison officials, and so on, most would agree that major relapse-contributing factors include: availability of drug and alcohol education specific to relapse triggers; post-acute withdrawal; biochemical factors; insufficient support systems; inadequate employment; people, places, and things; environmental issues; negative association; unresolved family issues; and transitional support. Failure to implement a comprehensive relapse prevention plan that includes these features may therefore contribute to a relapse.

All too often, treatment providers tailor their approach to relapse by their specific treatment philosophy or by way of the funding source's goals or concerns. Generally, a tailored or specific approach is appropriate when considering therapeutic interventions; however, the diverse components of relapse itself demand a comprehensive and broad-based approach. For example, a prison treatment program may focus on transitional concerns such as housing and employment, while a short-term residential program may choose to focus on the development of a twelve-step self-help support system. Others may choose to specifically focus on environmental and biochemical factors.

While consideration of each aforementioned relapse component is essential, professional addiction counselors must rely on credible client intake and assessment instruments to establish a treatment plan to support relapsed clients. While most professional counselors agree that a biopsychosocial or data-gathering questionnaire is paramount, the resulting information merely provides assistance to create a general client profile and subsequently establish a treatment strategy. In brief, there are no readily available instruments to measure a client's biochemical reaction once he or she is back in the community.

Unfortunately, addicted individuals do not understand the physiological sensation they may experience as a result of going back to their former drug-using environment. All too often, these individuals give way to old feelings and influences and resume their drug use. As such, it is best to educate the client as to what he or she can expect regarding all relapse-contributing experiences. A personalized strategy aimed at reducing relapse is usually best, yet at the same time a specific approach may inadvertently restrict a client's education.

Relapse prevention

As noted, one of the most effective ways to prevent relapse is to provide the client with a thorough knowledge of relapse-contributing factors. It is also essential to teach relapse prevention skills, preferably by way of an experiential method such as role playing. Role-playing and role-reversal techniques are a good way to develop relapse-prevention skills. For example, a client might identify his or her specific relapse triggers and stage a situation that has previously caused a relapse. Other members of the group might serve as characters that the client has contact with, such as family members, employers, drug-using associates, and so on.

It is also important to include or to establish a sober support system when role playing and to identify anticipated obstacles that might prohibit the individual from accessing these systems. Likewise, continuum-of-care arrangements should be clear regarding the objectives and services offered and the manner in which to ask for assistance.

Identifying risks

The identification of relapse risks can also be helped by educating individuals about relapse-contributing factors. Once the individual has been taught that temptation may arise in social, physiological, psychological, environmental, and familial circumstances, he or she can learn to avoid situations and emotional triggers that could lead to relapse. Generally speaking, most recovery-oriented support groups have adopted slogans that deliver a positive message and remind recovering individuals of presenting risks, such as "stay away from people, places and things," "if you always do what you always did you will always get what you always got," "pick up the telephone and call your sponsor before you pick up a drug," and so on. People who have gone through recovery have testified that recounting these thought-provoking phrases has actually helped them maintain their sobriety or prolong their abstinence. A client's previous relapsing experiences also provide a basis on which to assess a client's current risks.

Coping strategies

Terry Gorski, a well-respected drug and alcohol educator, is best known for his comprehensive educational approach to relapse prevention, which includes a specific focus on coping strategies. Most educators would agree that relapse prevention entails the ability to cope with or handle situations that might cause or perpetuate relapse. In brief, while knowledge is required to identify potential relapse-contributing factors, preplanned responses and a host of coping strategies and skills are required to maintain abstinence.

One such strategy may require that the recovering person engage in a deep-breathing exercise when confronted with an anxiety-producing situation that may include seeing large sums of money, a former drug-using associate, or drug paraphernalia. Another situation may require an exercise that uses self-talk and positive imagery to reduce the anxiety. Other circumstances may require that the relapse-prone individual develop patterned responses in an effort to curtail negative conversations. All in all, coping strategies are based on the individual's own knowledge of what might trigger a relapse.

R. A. BEARD, D. J. O'CONNELL

SEE ALSO:
Abstinence • Addictive Behavior • Counseling • Craving • Recovery • Treatment

Research, Medical

Drug addiction is a complex problem that is known to have medical, chemical, and behavioral components. A great deal of research is underway to determine the biological bases that may lead to effective addiction treatments.

Drug addiction, defined as overwhelming and compulsive involvement with the use of a drug, involves complex interactions between biochemical processes, individual and group psychology, and social customs and mores. Scientists and physicians studying addiction are using the different research methods and approaches employed by molecular cell biology, neurobiology, and behavioral psychology. These research approaches share the view that there is a common, progressive aspect to the process of addiction. This model postulates that an individual uses a drug and obtains pleasure or reward that reinforces usage. This is referred to as the acute drug state. Continuing drug use leads in some cases to the development of tolerance, sensitization, and the dependence of the chronic drug state. Desire to exit from the addicted state and cessation of drug use leads to withdrawal symptoms during the short-term abstinence phase. However, it is widely recognized that persistent cravings can lead to stress-induced relapses from any established long-term abstinence state.

All psychoactive drugs "short-circuit" normal perception of the environment by acting directly on the brain to influence emotional state and behavior. Directly administered psychoactive drugs are clearly novel features of human evolutionary experience. In bypassing the adaptive information processing systems that have evolved over evolutionary time, drug taking can give the brain abnormal signals that it would not naturally receive. Thus psychoactive drug abuse would appear to be unlikely to help an individual maximize adaptation to the natural environment or enhance his or her "biological" fitness.

The heavy physical and psychological toll that drug addiction exerts on individual addicts lends general support to this somewhat crude evolutionary biological interpretation of addiction. Evolutionary insight can guide experimentation but is rarely useful in the practical treatment of addiction, and it is clear that psychoactive drugs can alleviate certain forms of mental illness and distress. Nor is it realistic to ignore the fact that psychoactive drugs such as caffeine and alcohol are widely used in human societies and are known to induce pleasures that are considered safe when used in moderation. Most current biomedical research on the causes and mechanisms of drug addiction is therefore not centered on the deep issues of human evolutionary biology but is concerned with trying to gain knowledge that can be used in the prevention and treatment of addiction.

The molecular and cellular basis of drug addiction

The molecular and cellular approach to understanding addiction seeks to discover the mechanisms that are involved in the interaction between the drug molecule and the brain cells. This approach also seeks to understand how persistent exposure to drugs causes adaptations that alter the function of the brain and to learn whether these alterations are temporary or permanent. The early stages in the process, that is, the acute drug state induced by opiates such as morphine and heroin, are probably the best understood in molecular detail.

On initial contact, all opiates stimulate the adenosine monophosphate pathway in neurons, a process commonly described as "up-regulation of the cyclic AMP (cAMP) pathway." The process is not simple, since acute opiate exposure also seems to down-regulate the cAMP pathway in some neurons, while chronic opiate exposure induces a compensating up-regulation of the cAMP pathway in other neurons. Up-regulation boosts the amount of other brain enzymes such as adenylyl cyclase and cAMP-dependent protein kinase A. Thus chronic up-regulation of the cAMP pathway actually opposes acute opiate down-regulation (inhibition) of the same pathway, and this seems to be the biochemical basis for drug tolerance. After removal of the opiate, the chronic drug-induced up-regulation of the cAMP pathway may explain why dependence, withdrawal, and craving for opiates occur.

These events are now known to occur in a single pathway deep within the brain, often referred to as the mesolimbic dopamine reward system of the locus coeruleus. This is the major center for noradrenergic nerve transmission in the brain. Stimulation of this pathway appears to be a common property of many and perhaps all highly addictive substances for humans, including opiates, cocaine, and alcohol. Up-regulation of the cAMP pathway in the locus coeruleus increases the rate of "firing" (neural transmission events) by these brain neurons. Increased locus coeruleus activity is also a characteristic feature of drug withdrawal symptoms.

The research findings of many groups indicate that addictive substance-induced up-regulation of the cAMP pathway is also occurring in other regions of the brain, such as the cerebral cortex and the hippocampus. Unnaturally high and persistent overstimulation may account for some of the more damaging and long-lasting effects of drug addiction. Interestingly, it has been proposed that such drug-induced alterations in the preexisting patterns of biochemical neurotransmission could be similar to the type of alterations in brain activity that have been proposed to account for other highly significant but

Discovering how drugs work in the brain requires the use of sophisticated technology such as this positron emission tomography scanner, which can be used to detect areas of the brain that become activated when different drugs are introduced into the body.

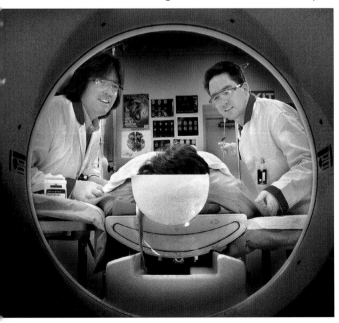

poorly understood properties of the human brain, such as long-term memory.

Memory and long-term adaptations in the brain are also proposed to involve stable changes in the patterns of gene expression in the brain. Gene expression is the biochemical term for the conversion of the DNA-encoded genetic information into enzymatic and structural proteins, via translation of messenger RNA, a short-lived copy of the DNA information. Changes in gene expression lead to changes in brain signaling (neurotransmission) and rerouting of connections between neurons. Long-term drug use can cause profound changes in brain metabolism, the number of receptors available for the drug of addiction, the patterns of gene expression, and the ways in which individuals respond to signals, or "cues," from the environment. The addicted brain thus becomes significantly altered by the persistent drug availability.

Research on drug addiction behavior

A key unanswered question about addiction stems from the observation that many people at some time self-administer a potentially addictive drug, but few people become addicts. How does use become addiction, and why are some individuals more susceptible than others? It is possible to carry out observational social research on this question, but scientifically testing theories of possible causes on humans is unethical as it would involve experimental administration of dangerously addictive drugs. Nonhuman animal models for drug addiction have been developed, and since the classic studies of Weeks in 1962, it has been known that rats will repeatedly perform certain actions that result in the intravenous delivery of potentially addictive substances. Most animals will self-administer nearly every drug that is abused by humans to the extent of redirecting their activity to drug use in preference to natural rewards such as food, water, and sex. The notable exception to mammalian drug preferences seems to be a nonhuman lack of interest in hallucinogens.

Research published in 2004 by Deroche-Gamonet, Belin, and Piazza at the Institute of Neuroscience in Bordeaux has exploited the rat model to gain more understanding of why certain individuals progress from occasional self-administration to the compulsive use that characterizes true addiction. They approached the problem by trying to define the diagnostic criteria that characterize human addiction and then testing to see whether rats, when allowed to self-administer intravenous cocaine, ever develop human-type addictive behaviors.

The first criterion of human-type addictive behavior was whether any rats ever continued to seek the drug even when it was unavailable. An experiment was designed to permit the measurement of this behavior by giving a green signal above a hole. When the green light is on, if the rat pokes its nose into the hole five times, intravenous cocaine is given through a tube inserted into a vein. This line is attached in such a way that the rat is able to move freely within the confines of the box. A red light above the hole indicates that the drug will not be fed into the rat, however many times it pokes the hole. Normal rats will learn to poke only when the green light is on. However, other rats can be selected who will continue to work for cocaine that they desire, but do not receive, when the red light is on.

The second human-type addictive behavior sought in this rat drug self-administration model was a very high motivation to get a drug, that is, a drug craving-type behavior. This criterion was measured by progressively increasing the frequency of nose poking (work) that has to be done to receive a dose of intravenous cocaine. At some point, around 30 to 50 nose pokes for most rats, the effort appears to exceed the benefit received by the rat and it ceases to work for the cocaine dose. However, a subset of rats will work significantly harder (up to 200 nose pokes) to obtain the cocaine dose.

The third human-type behavior sought was the continuing quest for a drug even when the drug was associated with a type of pain or punishment. This aspect of addiction behavior was approximated in the rat box by observing whether the rats would continue to work for intravenous cocaine, even when an additional blue light indicted that the cocaine delivery will be accompanied by an electric shock administered through a foot plate that the rat must step on. Again, while the great majority of the rats will learn that the blue light signals co-administration of the electric shock and cease to nose poke for cocaine, a few rats will continue to work for cocaine, despite the pain.

The novelty of these experiments is that the rats showed symptoms of addiction that were not initially present but developed over time in a minority of the rats. Only after at least one month of short self-administration experiences in the box, or after prolonged drug-access sessions, did some rats show signs of developing the more extreme behaviors that we associate with human addiction. Furthermore, although all rats would self-administer cocaine, 41 percent did not fulfill any of the three criteria of human-type addiction, 28 percent fulfilled only one criterion, and 14 percent showed two symptoms. Seventeen percent displayed all three symptoms of "human-type" cocaine addiction, a similar proportion to that actually occurring in humans. The experiment reveals that despite equal access and similar drug intake in all subjects, addiction behavior appeared in relatively few rats. This seems to imply that it is the combination of long exposure to the drug with some factor intrinsic to a minority of rats that leads to addiction rather than one of these factors acting alone. This research finding could have significant implications for how we view and treat human drug addiction.

It is surprising that the same drugs of abuse can induce addiction-type behavior across the animal kingdom. This striking observation seems to strongly support the hypothesis that these drugs are stimulating major neurological pathways that activate reward and pleasure sensations that have been conserved through mammalian evolution. It therefore seems likely that these novel and more realistic animal models of drug addiction can be of real value in future neurophysiological and neuro-biochemical experiments designed to understand the molecular mechanisms of transition into drug addiction and the genetic basis for differences in susceptibility to drug addiction.

Is drug addiction a brain disease?

Illegal drug users and particularly addicts are viewed with ill-concealed horror and contempt by essentially all human societies. The most tolerant view is that the addict is a victim of a difficult upbringing or social situation. More common is the attitude that drug addicts are weak or bad and immoral people without the self-control to restrain their self-absorbed obsession. At its most extreme, there are

GENETIC TECHNIQUES

One of the biggest advances in addiction research has been in the field of genetics. Many scientists believe that some people are more susceptible to developing addictions than others and that certain behaviors and disorders may have a genetic basis. The decoding of the human genome and the development of new genetic tools has enabled scientists to investigate processes such as tolerance, sensitization, and dependence at the cellular and molecular level. One group has identified more than 400 different genes that are affected by long-term cocaine abuse. Research into alcohol and opiates is expected to find similar patterns. By identifying marker genes for addiction, researchers hope to develop therapeutic drugs that will prevent craving and relapse.

Genetic engineering has led to the development of animals that have had certain genes inactivated so that the role of these genes in addiction can be determined. These "knockout" techniques are used to test responses to a wide variety of drugs at the molecular, cellular, and behavioral level. By selecting a particular gene, such as one that is responsible for producing a neurotransmitter receptor or one that makes a protein that transmits signals within cells, scientists can determine what contribution a gene makes in modifying the body's response to a drug. For example, alcohol is known to increase levels of dopamine, the chemical that promotes pleasurable feelings in the brain's reward system. However, chronic use of alcohol depletes the number of D2 dopamine receptors, blunting the response. It is thought that alcoholics increase consumption to try to overcome this lack of reward. Transgenic rats that have had some of their D2 receptors knocked out show a preference for alcohol over water. By using gene therapy techniques, in which a virus is used to carry a replacement gene to target cells, the rats were able to produce more D2 receptor proteins and showed a marked drop in alcohol consumption. Such a treatment may one day be applicable to human alcoholics. Other scientists have developed "knockin" mice that show an increased sensitivity to nicotine that they hope will lead to better understanding of nicotine abuse and addiction.

many who feel that penal incarceration is the most appropriate form of treatment for drug addicts.

Essentially all who study drug addiction at present conclude that the available scientifically collected data support a view that addiction is an illness, caused by specific, drug-induced alterations to the brain. Long-term use of addictive drugs clearly causes detectable pathology. The major organ affected by the process of addiction is the brain, although there may be extensive damage at secondary sites, for example, cirrhosis of the liver following chronic alcohol addiction. In this sense, drug addiction is a brain disease, although obviously major social and historical factors ensure that it is not treated as an illness like any other. The most important new findings in addiction research are the increasing weight of scientific evidence for the special susceptibility of the mammalian brain to a few types of small drug molecules that appear to mimic the brain's highly evolved neural transmission pathways in particularly rewarding and potentially addictive ways.

Drug addiction thus appears to be a problem that is best addressed by a primarily scientific and medical approach, defining science as common sense used systematically to choose between alternative proposals and medicine, as science harnessed to healing the sick and distressed. It is possible that a more widespread adoption of this viewpoint, which excludes no therapeutic method proven to be effective, would at last pave the way for more humane attitudes and more effective public policies toward drug addicts.

D. E. ARNOT

SEE ALSO:

Causes of Addiction, Biological • National Institute on Alcohol Abuse and Addiction (NIAAA) • National Institute on Drug Abuse (NIDA)

Reward

The reward system of the brain evolved to provide a pleasurable sensation for maintaining vital functions such as eating, drinking, and sex. This system is also triggered by drugs and plays a key part in the process of addiction.

It is generally assumed that humans as well as other organisms engage in behaviors that have rewarding consequences. That is, if a specific behavior is followed by pleasurable feelings, the experience of these feelings will serve as positive reinforcement so that the behavior will be repeated in the future. This argument is often used to explain why drug addiction develops. In other words, individuals keep taking drugs because the drugs produce rewarding feelings, which are as pleasurable, and sometimes even more pleasurable, than the feelings produced by natural rewards, such as food, water, or sex. Although appealing because of its simplicity, this view blurs important differences between reward and reinforcement that are crucial to our understanding of the psychological and neurobiological processes involved in drug addiction.

Reinforcement

Reinforcing stimuli are events that follow responses and change the probability that these responses will occur in the future. This change occurs because reinforcing stimuli have the ability to enhance the formation of memories about the situations in which they are encountered, that is, the stimuli that precede a given response, the response itself, and the consequences of the response. Such memories increase the probability that, in the presence of certain stimuli, the response leading to reinforcement will be repeated in the future. It is important to note that this action of reinforcers is not dependent on their rewarding properties; it simply refers to their ability to enhance the storage of information in the brain. It is known from animal studies, for example, that electrical stimulation of certain brain regions following an experience can improve the memory of that experience, even though the stimulation lacks some of the intrinsic motivational properties. Also, some stimulatory drugs, such as strychnine and pentylenetetrazol, will enhance memory formation, but there is no evidence that either of them has rewarding properties. Amphetamine, on the other

hand, is an example of a stimulatory drug that has memory-enhancing functions and is also rewarding. Animal studies, however, have indicated that the memory-enhancing and rewarding actions of amphetamine can be dissociated by injecting this drug directly into different brain regions, which is consistent with the notion that reinforcement and reward can be independently processed in the brain.

Reinforcing stimuli have another major function: they motivate behavior by conferring conditioned motivational properties on previously neutral stimuli. In other words, one effect of introducing a reinforcer into a learning situation is to confer motivational power to previously nonmotivating stimuli. This process appears to be dependent on the reinforcer's action on a circuitry composed of specific brain regions. Much of what is known about the biological mechanisms of reinforcement is based on studies showing that rats can be trained to press a lever for tiny electrical jolts to specific regions of the brain, a phenomenon known as intracranial self-stimulation (ICSS). On the basis of pharmacological, neuroanatomical, and electrophysiological studies, it has been determined that the mesocorticolimbic dopaminergic (DA) system is central to ICSS. Furthermore, rodents and nonhuman primates can be trained to self-administer intravenously a number of drugs that are typically abused by humans, such as amphetamine, cocaine, heroin, morphine, and marijuana. The mesocorticolimbic DA system is also central to drug self-administration.

The core of the reinforcement circuitry in the mammalian brain contains at least three neural elements: first, a descending pathway originating in the front of the medial forebrain bundle and projecting rearward to dopaminergic neurons in the ventral tegmental area; second, an ascending dopaminergic pathway originating in the ventral tegmental area, projecting upward and forward through the medial forebrain bundle onto neurons in the nucleus accumbens, prefrontal cortex, septum, amygdala, and hippocampus; and third, a descending

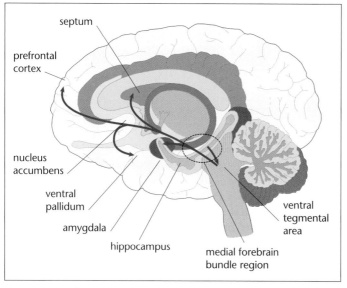

septum

prefrontal
cortex

nucleus
accumbens

ventral
pallidum

amygdala

hippocampus

ventral
tegmental
area

medial forebrain
bundle region

Dopamine pathways in the brain stimulate areas responsible for memory, motivation, and pleasure, which form the reward system.

components are learning, affect or emotion, and motivation.

Learning is essential to the acquisition of information relating stimuli, responses, and their rewarding or aversive consequences. This knowledge is then used for predictions about expected rewards, for making anticipatory responses, for guidance by environmental cues, and for goal-directed actions. Some learning about rewarding stimuli is quite basic. This would be the case for reward prediction whereby a conditioned stimulus reliably predicts the occurrence of an unconditioned rewarding stimulus, leading an organism to exhibit preparatory responses before the presentation of the reward. Alternatively, specific instrumental responses to stimuli predicting rewarding outcomes may be strengthened by response-contingent reinforcement. Other learning about rewarding stimuli may be more complex. This would be the case when forming cognitive representations of situations that combine predictive and causal relationships between stimuli, responses, and rewarding outcomes, and which are ultimately used to guide explicit goal-directed behaviors.

The consumption of a reward also has affective components. In the context of drug addiction, however, it is important to note that the subjective emotional reaction to rewards may be dissociated from conscious awareness and from actual behavior. For example, experimental evidence has indicated that drug addicts will exhibit behavior reinforced by drugs such as stimulants and opiates, without being aware of doing so, and for drug doses that produce no discernable subjective effects. Also, it is fairly well-known that drug addicts typically complain about the reduction of pleasure associated with their drug use and express a strong desire to stop using, yet they keep self-administering compulsively. These and other observations have led psychologists to make a distinction between the affective and motivational consequences of rewarding stimuli.

The conscious pleasure associated with a reward has been equated to the subjective affective reaction

pathway originating in the nucleus accumbens and projecting to the ventral pallidum. It appears that the dopaminergic fibers in this circuitry are crucial to the motivational properties of most reinforcing stimuli. In fact, both natural reinforcers and addictive drugs have the ability to enhance, although by different neurochemical mechanisms, dopaminergic activity in the nucleus accumbens. However, in contrast with the dopaminergic response to natural reinforcers, which habituates (becomes less responsive) with repeated exposure, drugs of abuse activate dopamine transmission without any loss of the rewarding effect. It has been hypothesized that this process abnormally strengthens stimulus-drug associations, thus resulting in the attribution of excessive motivational value to discrete stimuli or situations where drugs are available. Viewed this way, therefore, drug addiction is the expression of the excessive control over behavior acquired by drug-related stimuli as a result of abnormal associative learning following repeated stimulation of dopaminergic transmission in the nucleus accumbens.

Reward

Not only is reward different from reinforcement, but it also contains multiple psychological components involved in different aspects of drug addiction. These

it produces and has been termed *liking*. Examples of objective affective reactions of liking or "disliking" include a number of facial expressions displayed by mammals as a reaction to different tastes. Thus, sweet tastes typically produce tongue protrusions, while bitter tastes elicit gapes. It is interesting to note that dopaminergic activity in the mesocorticolimbic dopamine system is neither necessary nor sufficient to the experience of liking. Thus, a number of pharmacological manipulations that enhance or disrupt dopaminergic activity in this system have no effect on facial reactions to various tastes. This may explain why dopamine-receptor antagonists, at doses that do not produce gross motor and motivational impairments, generally have no effect on the feelings of pleasure associated with the use of amphetamine or the smoking of cigarettes in humans.

Motivational consequences

The motivational consequences of reward, on the other hand, have been termed *wanting*. Of course, rewards that are liked are usually also wanted, but nevertheless the two processes are dissociable. This motivational component of reward is termed the *incentive salience,* and it transforms the sensory information of a stimulus (sight, sound, smell, and so on) by giving it an attractive or desirable quality. The incentive value of rewards can be attributed to other stimuli, turning them into motivational magnets that elicit similar behaviors. For example, a crack-cocaine addict searching a table for unused crystals may have a response if he or she comes across spilled sugar or salt. Incentive salience, or wanting, unlike liking, is crucially dependent on dopamine activity in the mesocorticolimbic dopamine system.

Many of these learning and motivational processes are severely disturbed by chronic exposure to drugs of abuse. Furthermore, drug addiction is not a static phenomenon and, similar to other behavioral problems with biological determinants, there are different components that take part in the cycle as addiction takes hold. Within this cycle, reinforcement and reward processes change drastically. Positive reinforcement occurs when presentation of the drug increases the probability of a response to obtain the drug again. This typically occurs in the initial stages of addiction, when drugs have strong rewarding properties. With repeated use, however, negative reinforcement becomes more frequent as drugs are used to alleviate a drug-generated aversive state (drug withdrawal). At this point, use becomes a "coping strategy," and the rewarding effects of drugs become secondary to their ability to alleviate withdrawal. Crucial to the transition from positive to negative reinforcement is the disruption of an allostatic state.

Allostasis is defined as the process of achieving stability through change, and an allostatic state is defined as a state of chronic deviation of the regulatory system from its normal operating level. Chronic drug use is believed to directly alter brain systems involved in reward and reinforcement. It also activates neurochemical and hormonal responses aimed at compensating for these drug-induced alterations. Thus, from the drug addiction perspective, allostasis is the process of stabilizing reinforcement and reward functions by recruiting changes in the neural systems that process these functions. It is hypothesized that with chronic drug use these adaptive processes fail to return within the normal range, leading to further disruptions that make the allostatic state grow and induce additional drug use.

Such disturbances of the reinforcement and reward systems are believed to compromise the functioning of various neurotransmitter systems, including the dopamine and the natural opiate systems (endorphins and enkephalins), in specific components of the mesocorticolimbic system such as the nucleus accumbens, amygdala, and prefrontal cortex. Furthermore, brain and hormonal stress systems are also recruited, which induces abnormal activation of corticotrophin-releasing factor stress hormone and the norepinephrine neural systems. It is argued that the manifestation of this allostatic state as compulsive drug taking may be the result of activation of neural circuits in the cortico-striatal-thalamic system. These circuits are believed to be implicated in other repetitive or obsessive-compulsive behavioral disorders.

F. LERI

SEE ALSO:
Addiction • Causes of Addiction, Biological • Craving • Dependence • Reinforcement • Sensitization • Tolerance • Withdrawal

Risk Factors

The likelihood of becoming addicted to drugs is not the same for everybody. There are, however, a number of factors that have been identified as indicative of risk potential in children and adolescents.

The concept of risk factors first emerged through studies on public health, when researchers and scientists became interested in trying to learn more about what increases a person's risk for developing certain physical diseases. A risk factor can be defined as an event, experience, or characteristic that increases the likelihood that a particular outcome of interest (for example, cancer, obesity, or addiction) will occur.

A risk factor for addiction can be defined as an event, experience, or characteristic that precedes the onset of addiction and has been found to increase the likelihood that addiction will develop. Thus, in order to be a risk factor, the event or characteristic must temporally come before the addiction and must make it more likely that addiction will manifest. Note that a risk factor does not guarantee that the outcome of interest will occur, it only increases the chances of it occurring. For example, eating a high-fat diet has been shown to be a risk factor for obesity, but that does not mean that people who eat a high-fat diet will always become obese. The final outcome will depend on a number of other factors, such as how often they exercise, their metabolism, or genetic factors. Similarly, a risk factor does not necessarily cause the outcome of interest. It may only increase the likelihood that the outcome of interest will occur, for whatever reason. In the following sections, different types of risk factors for addiction and the role of intervention in reducing those risk factors will be discussed.

Types of risk factors

Researchers have identified a number of different types of risk factors for addiction. These can be subsumed under three broad risk factor categories: the person, the social situation, and the environment he or she inhabits.

Risk factors concerning the person include, for example, having positive beliefs about substance use, having expectations that the substance use will be beneficial in some way (for example, it will make him or her feel more confident or decrease feelings of anxiety), and lower perceived risk of negative consequences from using substances. In addition, certain types of behavioral characteristics and temperaments, such as a high degree of sensation seeking, impulsivity, aggression, and the inability to delay gratification have been found to be risk factors for substance use. Finally, having certain types of psychiatric disorders, such as major depression, bipolar disorder, antisocial personality disorder, and post-traumatic stress disorder, also increases the risk for addiction.

Risk factors involving the social situation include, for example, having close attachments with people who use drugs, social norms that facilitate drug use, having peers who use drugs, and a lack of social support. In addition, a lack of coping skills (not knowing how to resist offers from others to use drugs, not being able to be assertive and stand up for oneself, feeling excessively shy with peers) can increase the risk of using substances.

Environmental risk factors for addiction include having easy access to drugs, the price or cost of substances, being exposed to and having positive beliefs about media portrayal of substance use, lack of support from parents, relaxed laws and regulatory policies concerning alcohol and drugs, and low exposure to prevention programs.

Some of the risk factors mentioned above can be directly targeted in intervention programs. Other risk factors exist that are much harder to target directly—such as having a family history of substance use, being genetically predisposed to addiction, distressed family functioning, a history of stressful life experiences, and the biological mother's prenatal use of substances—which must be counteracted more indirectly through intervention programs.

It is important to remember that none of these risk factors in and of themselves indicates that a person will develop an addiction. Typically, a person's risk for addiction will depend on the types of risk factors, the particular combination of factors, and the overall number of factors that are affecting him or her.

Fighting, aggressive behavior, and constantly getting into trouble, together with personality disorders and a pro-drug peer group, are among some of the risk factors for developing an addiction.

Role of intervention in reducing risks

A great deal of research has been conducted on learning how to reduce risk factors for addiction. One of the main reasons that studying risk factors is so important is that risk factors are a prime target for intervening early in the process of addiction. First, a risk factor must be identified. Then, interventions can be developed to help treat or minimize the risk factor, which will in turn help reduce the likelihood that the outcome of interest (in this case, drug addiction) will occur. For example, scientists and nutritionists know that a diet high in fat is a risk factor for obesity, so programs have been developed to help people decrease their fat intake, which then decreases their risk for obesity. The same is true for addiction. Years of research have helped to identify risk factors for addiction. Then, programs have been developed to help address and treat these risk factors, which in turn helps to decrease the likelihood that addiction will develop.

One of the most powerful aspects of interventions designed to target risk factors is that they have the ability to help prevent addiction from developing in the first place. These interventions are very different from interventions that are designed to treat an addiction that has already developed. In many ways, it can be more effective to address risk factors for an addiction that has not yet developed than it is to treat an addiction that has already developed.

Another, related reason that intervention programs are so important in reducing risk is that they help to identify individuals who are particularly vulnerable to developing an addiction later in life. Not everyone has the same level of risk. Once individuals who are at a heightened level of risk or susceptibility are identified, steps can be taken to help reduce that risk with the overall goal of preventing the onset of addiction for that person, or for that group of people.

S. E. BACK

SEE ALSO:
Adolescents and Substance Abuse • Biopsychosocial Theory of Addiction • Intervention • Prevention • Protective Factors • Vulnerability

Self-esteem

Self-esteem is the concept of how we see ourselves and rate our standing in the world. Positive and negative estimates of self-esteem are regarded by many researchers as important factors in the development and maintenance of addiction.

Popular definitions of self-esteem generally involve our assessment of our own worth. Having a high self-esteem will result in having a pride in oneself and behaving like an upright and law-abiding citizen. Conversely, having a low self-esteem can result in any number of antisocial behaviors from crime and violence to teenage pregnancy and drug abuse. Clearly, low-self esteem is a debilitating and powerful force. In recognition of this position, most drug prevention education attempts to "inoculate" adolescents against low self-esteem to prevent drug use and abuse. The question remains, however: is there any truth in the above view or is it merely a myth? There are two main problems with this view of drug use: a definition of what self-esteem is, and beliefs about how this mechanism works.

The first problem with the above theory is that there is no clear consensus on a definition of self-esteem. It is seen variously as a generalized feeling about one's identity and place in the world, or as an assessment based on judgments of self in a number of areas of performance. To clarify, the first position, self-esteem as a generalized feeling, views self-esteem as being an emotional reaction that is generally more or less positive. It is based on a global view of the self that biases how we view specific aspects of ourselves, for example, intelligence or physical attractiveness. The second position suggests that self-esteem is actually made up of a cumulative judgment of all of these other aspects of ourselves. Thus, in this second view, one may have high self-esteem in some areas but not in others, whereas in the first view, self-esteem is either entirely high or entirely low. There is no clear consensus, and both views have strengths and weaknesses.

In the "common sense" view of drug use, low self-esteem leads to young people using drugs as a crutch to compensate for a poor view of themselves and, in turn, drug use prevents adolescents from building and maintaining self-esteem. Does the evidence support such a view? The answer to this question, unfortunately, is not simple. It would appear that

Spraying graffiti "tags" that are recognizable to their peers is one way that adolescents may try to establish an identity and self-esteem among a like-minded group.

studies of alcohol and drug abusers have shown that they have low self-esteem. This is certainly true of dependent drug users. So does this support the compensation, or common sense, view? Actually, it does not. It has been found that low self-esteem is a consequence of drug use, not a cause.

The common sense view suggests that adolescents who have low self-esteem are attracted to drugs because drugs will make them feel good, or at least less bad, about themselves. Thus adolescents with high self-esteem will have no (or, at least, less) need or reason to take drugs. As an explanation, it is, at least superficially, highly plausible as it provides a mechanism, low self-esteem, that "causes" drug use and provides a prevention and treatment strategy that should be acceptable to all sections of the population, namely, improve the way adolescents view themselves and they will become model citizens.

The main problem is that the evidence points in the opposite direction. Rather than adolescents with low self-esteem using drugs as a crutch, it would appear to be the adolescents with high self-esteem who are using drugs. Research has shown that early use of cigarettes, alcohol, and drugs are all related to high levels of self-esteem. Initiation of early substance use appears to require a level of confidence and maturity that is not generally found in children who have low self-esteem. Confidence is required to mix with other more mature substance users in order to both acquire the substance and learn how to administer it. Contrary to the popular view of drug users as solitary figures cut off from society and their peers, almost all drug use is surrounded and governed by a rich and unique culture. For example, there are many types of marijuana and many ways to ingest it. The most common way is obviously smoking, but even with smoking there are conventions on how to roll the marijuana cigarettes or prepare pipes, for example, whether tobacco is used, what type, and how much. There are conventions concerning the method of smoking—how to inhale deeply and hold the smoke—and also about sharing. All rituals and customs need to be learned and observed if the adolescent is to fit into the group and also secure his or her supply.

Protection and maintenance

Although high self-esteem does not appear to have a protective effect against initiation of drug use and indeed appears to have the opposite effect, it does have a positive effect against the dilatory consequences of prolonged use. There is a link between low self-esteem and alcohol or drug use; the research suggests that addiction or dependence on a drug leads to low self-esteem. Part of the reason may be the feeling of not being in control of one's life but rather feeling as if a substance (or the need for a substance) is controlling one's decisions or behavior. These feelings of dependence on a substance can seriously erode the self-esteem that one possesses and these negative feelings can in turn lead to more drug use, as the person seeks comfort. Thus low self-esteem may have a role in maintaining drug use. Where high self-esteem does appear to have a protective effect is in regard to the erosion of self-esteem. Research shows that people who have the highest self-esteem at the beginning of drug taking tend to be more robust in respect to developing addiction, that is, they continue to have a good level of esteem and tend not to use drugs to obtain comfort. Alternatively, self-esteem appears to have a protective effect from the more extreme psychological and emotional problems often associated with addiction.

Self-efficacy

A concept related to self-esteem, self-efficacy has been found to be very important in the treatment of addiction problems. Self-efficacy is one's estimation of being able to perform a particular behavior or set of behaviors; for example, drug refusal self-efficacy would be the ability to refuse, or resist taking, a drug. Self-efficacy is usually measured under a variety of conditions; for example, feeling good, feeling bad, when encouraged by friends, at a party, and so on. People low in (drug refusal) self-efficacy under certain conditions—for example, when feeling low, would be at high risk of relapse when this condition is present. However, knowing the high risk situations allows the treatment to be tailored to address the deficit by giving the person strategies to deal with these situations. Having a strategy then increases self-efficacy, and, if the situation is successfully handled, further increases self-efficacy. Thus dealing with situations gets easier as success breeds success, which breeds self-efficacy. This success in self-efficacy in turn feeds back into self-esteem estimates, and the person feels more positive.

While popular opinion often cites low self-esteem among adolescents as a primary cause of drug use, the evidence does not support this view. Instead, addiction and dependency would appear to erode self-esteem. The resultant low self-esteem can maintain use, although a high initial self-esteem may provide some protection against this process. Thus high self-esteem does not appear to be a protective factor against initiation of substance use but instead protects against becoming addicted or the more severe consequences of addiction. Self-efficacy, however, is an important factor in recovery and treatment.

J. McMahon

SEE ALSO:
Adolescents and Substance Abuse • Dependence • Peer Influence • Prevention • Vulnerability

Sensitization

Some drugs lead to tolerance, a condition in which more of the drug is needed to produce the same response. However, the reverse of this process, sensitization, can also occur and may play a key role in maintaining drug use.

Much of our understanding of how addictive drugs affect behavior and the brain comes from studies in which laboratory animals are exposed to the drug only once. However, when given the opportunity, people and laboratory animals are likely to self-administer certain drugs repeatedly and sometimes compulsively. For that reason, it is important to understand how the effects of drugs change when they are administered repeatedly. It is well-known that repeated drug administration often results in a decrease in the responsiveness (or tolerance) to some of the drug's effects such that higher doses are needed to produce the same effect. The ability of morphine to suppress pain or of amphetamine to suppress food consumption decreases with repeated and prolonged exposure. The role of tolerance in the development of physical dependence and the role of physical dependence in withdrawal in sustained drug use has been a focus of research on addiction for many decades.

Less appreciated is the fact that not all drug effects involve tolerance and that other effects work in opposite ways. Thus, rather than showing a decrease, some drug effects show an increase with repeated exposure such that lower and lower doses are required to produce the same effect. This phenomenon is known as reverse tolerance, or sensitization. Since the 1990s the phenomenon of sensitization has received much attention among addiction researchers and many think that sensitization plays an important role in the development and maintenance of compulsive drug use and in the high rate of relapse observed in drug addicts even after extended periods of abstinence.

Behavioral sensitization

In a typical laboratory study examining sensitization, a constant dose of a drug is given repeatedly and the behavioral response to successive injections is measured. With this type of treatment procedure, there is a progressive enhancement in the ability of the drug to produce psychomotor activation as indicated by an increase in locomotor hyperactivity

and stereotyped behaviors (typically repetitive head and limb movements). If different doses are then administered to generate a dose-effect curve, subjects who are already sensitized to the drug typically show a shift in the dose-effect function for psychomotor activation indicating that in sensitized subjects lower doses are required to produce a response comparable to that of drug-naive (placebo-treated) subjects.

Although sensitization has most thoroughly been studied and characterized using psychomotor stimulant drugs, for example, cocaine and amphetamine, there is substantial evidence that sensitization also occurs with repeated exposure to other abused or addictive drugs, including opiates (morphine and heroin), nicotine, alcohol, methylphenidate, Ecstasy (MDMA), and phencyclidine (PCP).

For practical and ethical reasons sensitization is most often studied in rats and mice. However, sensitization with psychomotor stimulant exposure has been shown in many species ranging from flatworms (planarians) and fruit flies (*Drosophila melanogaster*) to rabbits, cats, dogs, and nonhuman primates. Most important, there is now evidence of amphetamine-induced psychomotor sensitization in drug-naive human subjects. It appears, therefore, that sensitization is a common consequence of repeated exposure to drugs that have a high abuse potential in most species of animals, including humans.

Features of sensitization

Sensitization is a complex and rich phenomenon with many interesting features. First, and probably most striking, is how long sensitization persists after the drug treatments have ceased. In rats, for instance, behavioral sensitization to amphetamine's stimulant effects has been found as long as one year after the last drug exposure. Thus, it may well be that once sensitization is induced it will last for the life of the subject. Consistent with this notion, human amphetamine addicts have been found to be hypersensitive to the effects of amphetamine even after years of abstinence. Second, there is enormous individual variation in the susceptibility to sensitization, even in laboratory animals. Some subjects show rapid and robust sensitization even after a single injection of drug, whereas others sensitize very little or not at all. Third, when sensitization is produced by repeated exposure to one drug, a sensitized response is often seen to different drugs as well (cross-sensitization). Thus, preexposure to amphetamine often makes subjects hypersensitive to the effects of morphine. Cross-sensitization can also occur between drugs and nondrug stimuli, in particular, environmental stressors, such that drug preexposure makes subjects hypersensitive even to mild stressors, and vice versa.

Sensitization of motivational processes

Most studies showing that repeated administration of drugs of abuse produces sensitization involve some measure of the psychomotor activating effects. However, it is now known that not only do the psychomotor stimulant effects of drugs sensitize, but so do their motivational and rewarding effects. For example, prior exposure to a variety of addictive drugs increases the likelihood that animals will subsequently acquire a drug self-administration habit as well as increase the effort that animals are willing to exert to obtain the drug. Also, sensitized subjects are more likely to acquire a preference for places that become associated with drug administration.

However, the ability of sensitization to alter motivational processes is not confined to drug reinforcement and also applies to other aspects of motivation. For instance, animals sensitized to cocaine or amphetamine are more active in pushing levers when the response is reinforced by a stimulus previously associated with a natural reinforcer. Furthermore, the ability of stimuli that have been associated with natural rewards to influence goal-directed behavior is more effective in rats and mice previously exposed to amphetamine compared with control animals. These more general effects of drug sensitization suggest that drug-induced sensitization affects neurobiological reward processing in such a way that various aspects of reward learning become persistently altered; and compulsive drug seeking in addicts may be due to sensitization-related changes in the ability of stimuli

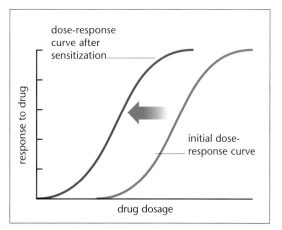

When a laboratory animal becomes sensitized to the effect of a drug, the dose-response curve shifts to the left, so that less of the drug is needed to produce the same effects.

to become associated with drug taking and seeking, thus reducing the likelihood that such stimuli will control behavior.

Factors that influence sensitization

Because sensitization affects motivational processes, and the possibility that these effects are critical for understanding addiction, much effort has been directed at identifying factors and circumstances that influence sensitization. Several factors have been identified, including gender-related, treatment-related, and environmental factors.

Gender-related factors. Female rats show more rapid and robust behavioral sensitization than male rats when repeatedly exposed to amphetamine or cocaine. This profound difference is not attributable to pharmacokinetic differences; it is more likely to result from complex interactions between the neurobiological actions of drugs and organizational (developmental) and activational effects of gonadal hormones (in particular, estrogen and testosterone). Sex differences in sensitization could explain differences in the pattern of addiction and relapse seen between male and female drug users.

Treatment-related factors. From laboratory studies we know that the pattern of drug exposure and the amount of time between drug exposures is an important factor in the susceptibility to sensitization. To produce robust sensitization, drug treatments must be given intermittently; and the more time between injections, the more robust the sensitization that is induced. Indeed, when drug injections are given close in time such that brain levels of the drug are chronically elevated, transient tolerance is more likely to occur.

Environmental factors. An important but poorly understood feature of sensitization is that its induction and expression are powerfully modulated by the circumstances surrounding drug administration. There are at least two ways in which environmental circumstances can influence sensitization. First, even when sensitization has been induced, in order for this hypersensitivity to be seen, the environmental circumstances at the time of testing must be similar to those during the drug preexposure phase. Thus, even small changes in the environmental context can profoundly influence whether sensitization is expressed or not. Second, the environmental circumstances can influence whether sensitization is actually induced. When amphetamine or cocaine are administered in the animal's living environment little psychomotor sensitization is often observed, even though these same doses will produce robust sensitization when given after the animal is placed in an unfamiliar or novel environment.

These examples of modulating factors demonstrate that sensitization is a complex phenomenon and not only the result of pharmacological factors. Similarly, we know that many people repeatedly try addictive drugs (for example, alcohol) but only a few actually develop a drug problem, suggesting that mere exposure to the drug is insufficient to explain addiction.

The neurobiology of sensitization

Since the mid-1990s substantial progress has been made in understanding the neurobiological basis of sensitization. Many cellular- and systems-level neuroadaptations have been reported in brain regions known to be important for drug-induced behavioral activation and reward. In particular, the neural system that involves dopamine projections from the midbrain to the nucleus accumbens, prefrontal cortex, and related neural circuitry, seem affected. For instance, sensitizing regimens of amphetamine or cocaine result in persistent increases in the subsequent ability of these drugs to increase concentrations of dopamine and glutamate in these regions—two neurotransmitter systems critically involved in psychomotor activation and reward. Also, sensitization has been associated with persistent structural changes in these regions as characterized by changes in the number and shape of neuronal dendritic processes. These findings are particularly interesting because dendrites are the primary sites of neurochemical information transfer between nerve cells, indicating that sensitization could involve a fundamental reorganization of the brain's neural circuits. Finally, many other cellular and molecular alterations have been reported as a consequence of sensitization. Whether any of these will turn out to be important or merely secondary to the above-mentioned alterations, remains to be seen.

Sensitization and addiction

In an influential review in 1993, Terry Robinson and Kent Berridge proposed the incentive-sensitization theory of addiction, the central tenet of which is that a state of hyperexcitability (sensitization) of the mesolimbic dopaminergic system might be the source of the cravings that drug addicts experience. They argued that potentially addictive drugs share the ability to produce long-lasting adaptations in neural systems that are normally involved in reward processes. As a result of these neuroadaptations, brain reward systems are rendered persistently hypersensitive ("sensitized") to drugs and drug-associated stimuli. Thus, the ability of drugs to produce sensitization-related changes in the brain's reward system may explain why the behavior of some drug users becomes increasingly directed at and controlled by drug and drug-related stimuli, even at the expense of other activities. Additionally, the persistence of sensitization may explain why addicts remain hypersensitive to the effects of drugs and are susceptible to relapse even after long periods of abstinence. It is because of this and because traditional positive and negative reinforcement accounts of addiction insufficiently explain addiction, that sensitization has increasingly become a central focus of drug researchers.

H. CROMBAG

SEE ALSO:
Causes of Addiction, Biological • Craving • Reinforcement • Reward • Tolerance • Withdrawal

Smoking

Smoking tobacco releases nicotine into the bloodstream, from where it quickly passes to the brain. Nicotine is a highly addictive substance that causes feelings of alertness and well-being, prompting the urge to keep smoking.

Cigarette smoking is drug use. The cigarette is the vehicle for administering the drug; the drug is nicotine, a mood-altering chemical found in tobacco. Unlike other drugs of abuse, both the administration and the drug are legal, yet lethal. One in every five deaths in the United States can be attributed to tobacco use. This represents more deaths than are caused by alcohol use, illegal drug use, motor vehicle accidents, homicide, suicide, and AIDS combined.

How tobacco is taken into the body

When tobacco is burned, the chemicals in it form into two types of matter: particulate matter, also known as "tar," and vapor or gaseous compounds. As a cigarette is smoked, some of the particulates, including the nicotine, attach to the mucous membranes in the mouth and nose. The nicotine is immediately absorbed into the bloodstream. The rest of the smoke travels down the bronchial tubes. These are lined with little hairlike cells, called cilia, which are designed to catch dirt and dust particles to prevent them from going into the lungs. Many of the tar compounds are caught in the cilia, and may be coughed up and spat out later, but many more, including the nicotine, continue the journey into the lungs. Once in the lungs, the nicotine is absorbed by tiny air sacs called alveoli. These are responsible for the exchange of oxygen and carbon dioxide in the blood. The nicotine is absorbed into the bloodstream and reaches the brain within 10 seconds of being inhaled.

In the brain, the nicotine moves through the capillary walls and into the spaces between the neurons, normally occupied by chemical messengers known as neurotransmitters. These neurotransmitters are responsible for communication between nerve cells. Nicotine acts like a neurotransmitter by interacting with acetylcholine receptors. This stimulates the neurons into firing off multiple nerve impulses, increasing the electrical activity in the brain, which results in feelings of alertness. The nicotine also triggers the release of other neuro-

Secondhand smoke is a considerable hazard to nonsmokers. This smoke contains hundreds of dangerous chemicals that are normally removed by the cigarette filter before the smoke is inhaled.

transmitters that are associated with feelings of pleasure and well-being, while it blocks or inhibits the release of an enzyme called monoamine oxidase B, or MAO-B. This enzyme is responsible for cleaning up the extra neurotransmitter substances between the nerve cells. When the MAO-B is blocked, the neurotransmitters continue to float around between the nerve cells, allowing them to continue firing off impulses. With repeated smoking, the brain adapts to this heightened activity but cannot maintain it without the nicotine. This process is what leads to addiction.

Typical quantities and potentiation

A cigarette manufactured in the United States contains 8 to 10 milligrams of nicotine and, under normal smoking conditions, a person's body absorbs 10 to 30 percent of it. However, cigarette manufacturers have found ways to increase the nicotine potency of the cigarettes, increasing the chances that the smoker will become addicted. One way is through the use of tobacco plants that have been genetically engineered to have a higher nicotine content. Another is through the use of chemical additives, such as ammonia compounds, which boost the body's absorption of the nicotine by changing its chemical composition. The addition of menthol to cigarettes may also contribute to the addiction process by reducing the irritation in the throat, leading to longer and deeper inhalation of the smoke into the lungs. Recent research also points to the possibility that menthol may increase the body's absorption of nicotine, affecting the release of neurotransmitters in the brain, making the cigarette more addictive.

Urges to smoke

Most smokers who try to quit find it difficult, not only because of the physical addiction to nicotine, but also because of the psychological addiction to the behaviors of smoking. Most smokers establish a pattern of behaviors that they associate with smoking, such as smoking after meals or while talking on the telephone. These smoking-related behaviors become associated with feelings of well-being and relaxation, making it more difficult to quit. These behaviors lead to urges to smoke, even when the brain does not need the nicotine.

Adolescents and smoking

Young people are likely to try smoking for the first time between the ages of 11 and 15 years, especially if they have friends, siblings, or other people in their immediate environment (such as home, school, work, or social activities) who smoke. Nearly one-third of young people who try cigarettes will become regular smokers by the time they are 18 years old. There tends to be a misperception that "everyone" smokes, making the person feel like he or she is left out of the group if he or she doesn't smoke. Cigarette advertisers know this and promote smoking as part

CHEMICAL

A cigarette is much more than tobacco and a filter wrapped in paper. A typical cigarette is a cocktail of chemicals. According to U.S. government figures, the six major cigarette manufacturers have listed nearly 600 ingredients that have been added to cigarette tobacco. The law requires only that the ingredients added to the tobacco are reported; therefore this list does not include chemicals and additives used in the paper or filter. The following is a description of what is really in a cigarette.

Paper
The white part of the paper is made up of cellulose that is bleached and dyed using unknown chemical agents. It is manufactured in two thicknesses, forming what are called "burn rings," which help determine how slowly the cigarette burns and how much smoke it produces while burning. The paper is treated with various chemicals, such as titanium, to keep the cigarette burning, to give the ash a more pleasant appearance, and to add aroma. The dyed paper covering the filter of the cigarette is called the tipping paper, which is coated with a substance to keep it from sticking to the smoker's lips. Add to this the glue that holds the paper together and the ink in which the brand name is printed. All of these substances are being inhaled by the smoker and those around him or her.

Filter
Filters were added to cigarettes in the 1950s in response to growing concerns about the health risks associated with smoking. The truth is that

of adventurous and glamorous adult activities. Research has shown that young people are more susceptible to the influence of cigarette ads than adults and that they associate smoking with popularity and relaxation and, consequently, are more likely to try smoking. Exposure to cigarette advertisements and other marketing techniques (promotional products, auto racing sponsorship,

CONTENTS OF A TYPICAL CIGARETTE

they do little to prevent the smoker from inhaling the particulates, or tar, or the vapor chemicals. In fact, how much tar and nicotine the smoker inhales is wholly dependent on the smoker. Even "light" and "ultra-light" cigarettes can deliver the maximum level of tar and nicotine depending on how the smoker holds the cigarette, how much of the filter is covered by the lips, or how frequently and how deeply the smoker draws on the cigarette.

The cigarette filter is made up of about 12,000 cellulose acetate fibers, a type of plastic used in photographic prints. These fibers are bonded together with a plastic glue called triacetin. Some filters also contain charcoal, which is supposed to reduce some of the toxic chemicals in the smoke. However, fiber fragments caused by the machine cutting of the filter to length, or charcoal dust in the charcoal filters, can come loose while a smoker is puffing on the cigarette, and the fibers or particles can be inhaled into the lungs with the smoke.

Most filters have a ring of tiny holes to allow fresh air in while the smoker is inhaling, thus reducing the amount of tar and nicotine inhaled with each puff. If the smoker covers these holes with his or her fingers or lips, they become useless in reducing tar and nicotine.

Tobacco
Cigarettes manufactured in the United States are made with a blend of bright, burley, and oriental tobaccos, but the majority of the tobacco used is not from the leaf of the tobacco plant but is a manufactured product called "reconstituted tobacco" in which the tobacco stems and ribs of the leaves are ground up with various chemicals and colorants, then dried in sheets, like paper. The paper is then shredded to make it smokable. Some manufacturers also use "expanded" tobacco, which is tobacco that is chemically bulked up to lower the cost of production.

Between 6 and 10 percent of the tobacco in a cigarette manufactured in the United States is a chemical additive. The manufacturers can add hundreds of ingredients to the tobacco to enhance the taste, moisture content, burnability, or pH of the cigarette. Although all of the additive ingredients listed are generally considered to be safe when used in food products that are eaten (ingredients such as menthol, brown sugar, caramel coloring, cocoa, corn syrup, licorice root, and glycerin), there is no indication that these are safe when burned and inhaled into the lungs. Indeed, glycerin, an ingredient added to keep the tobacco moist, becomes acrolein when burned, a known cancer-causing agent.

Burning tobacco produces as many as 400 to 500 individual gaseous compounds and at least 3,500 particulate compounds. The gaseous compounds have nitrogen, oxygen, and carbon dioxide as their major constituents, but also contain the following toxic or tumor-causing agents: carbon monoxide, benzene, formaldehyde, hydrogen cyanide, and others. In addition to tar and nicotine, the particulates in tobacco smoke include toxic substances such as seven known tobacco-specific nitrosamines, phenol, naphthalene, fluorenes, vinyl chloride, arsenic, and heavy metals such as nickel, chromium, cadmium, lead, and polonium-210.

cigarette brands smoked in movies) exerts a greater influence to try smoking than does peer pressure. However, young smokers experience nicotine addiction and withdrawal when they try to quit, even if they have smoked only a short time. The likelihood of experiencing these negative effects (difficulty concentrating, irritability, cigarette cravings) increases with the length of time the person has been smoking and the amount smoked, making it harder to successfully quit. Only about one-fourth of teenage smokers are successful at quitting.

Gender and racial differences
Smoking among women was once a rare occurrence; however, the rate of smoking among females is now approaching that for males. The rate of current

cigarette smoking in 2009 was only slightly higher for males than for females (9.2 percent for males vs. 8.6 percent for females) among youths aged 12 to 17.

The health consequences of smoking are also increasing among women. Until 1987 breast cancer was the leading cause of death from cancer among women. By 2004 it was lung cancer, and 90 percent of all lung cancer is caused by cigarette smoking. Women who smoke are also at greater risk of coronary heart disease, the number one killer of women. Smoking also negatively affects reproduction for women, causing problems with conception and fertility, increasing the risks of tubal pregnancies, miscarriages, and stillbirths. Smoking during pregnancy is also a known cause of premature birth and places the infant at increased risk of death from Sudden Infant Death Syndrome (SIDS). One of the reasons that many women start smoking is to control their weight; however, studies have shown that smoking is not associated with weight loss, although it does slow weight gain and decreases bone density, leading to increased risk of bone fractures. Another reason women start smoking is because they believe that smoking can help control negative moods, yet smokers are more likely to suffer from depression than nonsmokers.

Smoking is less prevalent among racial minorities, particularly African Americans, but the health risks are much greater for these groups. In 2009, 5.2 percent of African Americans aged 12 to 17 reported being current smokers, compared with 10.6 percent of Caucasian and 7.5 percent of Hispanics. Among young adults (aged 18 to 25), the rates are much higher, with 27.0 percent of African Americans reporting current smoking, compared with 40.5 percent of Caucasians and 29.9 percent of Hispanics. The three leading causes of death for African Americans—heart disease, cancer, and stroke—can all be attributed to smoking. Research has shown that African Americans metabolize nicotine at a slower rate than Caucasian and Hispanic people; it therefore stays
in their bodies for longer periods of time, contributing to a higher rate of nicotine addiction and, ultimately, to more difficulty quitting. The quit success rate for African Americans is about 8 percent, compared with 14 percent for Caucasians and 16 percent for Hispanics. Three out of four African

American smokers prefer menthol cigarettes, which also contributes to the addictive process. Finally, the tobacco industry spends a disproportionate amount of money advertising in African American communities and acting as corporate sponsors for many influential African American political, social, artistic, religious, and media organizations in the United States.

Passive smoking

The risks associated with smoking are not limited to the smoker. Environmental tobacco smoke (ETS), or secondhand smoke, is associated with about 38,000 deaths per year in the United States and contributes to over 1 million illnesses in children, including asthma, respiratory infections, and ear infections. ETS is a "Group A carcinogen" according to the U.S. Environmental Protection Agency, meaning that it is known to cause cancer in humans. The smoke that comes from the lit end of a cigarette (sidestream smoke) contains a greater concentration of cancer-causing chemicals than does the smoke that is inhaled through the filter end (mainstream smoke). These burning chemicals are readily absorbed through the mucous membranes of the nose and mouth.

The length of exposure is also a factor: while the smoker breathes in the mainstream smoke only while actively smoking, everyone living in a house with a smoker is constantly exposed to the polluted air. Children of smokers are particularly vulnerable because their lungs are still developing and they have a higher breathing rate. As a result, the concentration of nicotine in their blood is higher than that of adults who are exposed to ETS, making them more susceptible to smoking-related diseases.

There is no such thing as safe smoking. All cigarette smoking is dangerous to the smoker's health and to the health of everyone around the smoker. No one is immune to the negative health effects of smoking. The best way to avoid these health risks is to never start smoking.

M. D. REYNOLDS

SEE ALSO:
Gateway Drugs • Heart and Circulatory Diseases • Lung Diseases • Nicotine Replacements • Smoking Cessation

Smoking Cessation

Smoking tobacco is one of the most difficult addictions to overcome. There are a variety of methods to help people quit, but it may take a combination of nicotine replacement therapies and motivation techniques to achieve this aim.

Statistics show that every day in the United States more than 4,000 young people try their first cigarette, while another 2,000 become regular daily smokers. On this same day, nearly 1,100 people will die as a result of their smoking, and another 100 will die as a result of someone else's smoking. Meanwhile, 47,000 people will try to quit smoking, and maybe 2,800 will succeed.

There are many reasons people give for smoking—it relaxes them, it helps them to cope, and so on. These reasons narrow down to three: physical addiction, emotional connection, and behavioral habit. The three are intertwined to create a physical and psychological stranglehold on the smoker. Regular smokers are addicted to nicotine, a psychoactive drug that affects brain chemistry. The physical effect is a stimulation of nerve impulses, causing the smoker to feel more alert and better able to concentrate, an effect that cannot be sustained without continued smoking. Nicotine stimulates certain brain chemicals that create feelings of pleasure and well-being, leading to an emotional response to smoking. These "good feelings" become associated with certain behaviors of the smoker, such as smoking after meals or when talking on the telephone, which lead to the development of the habit. Successful smoking cessation strategies need to address all three aspects: the physical addiction, the emotional connection, and the behavioral habits.

Hypnotherapy is sometimes used to help people give up smoking. Women often find behavioral approaches more successful because their body chemistry does not respond as well to nicotine replacement therapies as does that of men.

Withdrawal

When the smoker quits, he or she removes the nicotine from his or her brain and the result is withdrawal. Some common withdrawal symptoms are cravings, irritability, fatigue, inability to concentrate, insomnia, and hunger. All of these are temporary and will fade as the brain eliminates the nicotine. Some people will experience a cough, mucous buildup in the nose and throat, dizziness, and even tightness in the chest. These are all a result of the lungs clearing out the smoke and will disappear within days. Most withdrawal symptoms can be overcome by employing good health practices, such as engaging in some form of gentle exercise, drinking plenty of water, avoiding stressful situations, and relaxing. Eating low-calorie, healthy snacks such as fruits and avoiding caffeine also help overcome cravings and urges. Use of alcohol should be avoided while quitting, as it reduces the person's inhibitions and may also be psychologically associated with smoking.

Motivation

Although no one can make someone else quit, they can help motivate the smoker to want to quit. Motivation is the first step to successful smoking cessation. To help someone take that first step, it is helpful to remember the "three Rs." First, the smoker needs to know that quitting is *relevant* to him or her. That is, it has a direct and specific effect on his life and the lives of the people around him. The second R is that the smoker needs to be *reminded* of the risks associated with continued smoking, both for her and the people she loves. The third R is to point out the *rewards* of quitting, again being very specific as to what these are for the individual. Chances are that the smoker will not instantaneously want to quit when confronted with the three Rs, but it will reinforce the reasons for quitting.

Independent quitting

There are many strategies available to help an individual quit smoking. Some people prefer to do it on their own, a method often referred to as cold turkey—to one day put down the cigarettes and never smoke again. There are people who have done this and never smoked again. Then there are people such as the author Mark Twain, who said, "Quitting smoking is easy. I've done it a thousand times." It is hard to stay off cigarettes without help.

Most self-directed smoking cessation programs involve a standard format. The smoker who wants to quit smoking needs to prepare himself to quit by:

- Setting a quit date
- Getting rid of all smoking paraphernalia, such as cigarettes, cigarette cases, lighters, and ashtrays
- Garnering support from friends and family members
- Planning for situations that might lead to smoking relapse.

The research on self-directed programs shows that they are of limited effectiveness for long-term smoking cessation as the quit rate is only about 5 percent. The benefit is that these programs are inexpensive and can be widely distributed. They are best used as information sources for those considering quitting. More formal intervention is necessary to improve the chances for success.

Assisted quitting

Behavioral treatments are the most commonly practiced smoking-cessation methods. These programs generally address the habit of smoking and the emotional aspects of smoking. Brief person-to-person interventions with a physician or other health care provider have shown some success in helping smokers to quit. The U.S. Public Health Service has developed a set of guidelines for physicians to help their patients quit smoking. These guidelines recommend the use of the "five As" at each visit. The five As are:

- *Ask* patients about smoking
- *Advise* all smokers to quit
- *Assess* their willingness to make a quit attempt
- *Assist* those who want to quit, and
- *Arrange* follow-up visits for those trying to quit.

These two-to-three-minute interventions have a success rate of between 5 and 8 percent, depending on how often the smoker received this advice.

Problem-solving and skills-training methods have been developed to direct the smoker who is trying to quit to use behavioral strategies to avoid situations that might lead to smoking, to cope with urges to smoke, to replace smoking behaviors with positive healthy behaviors, and to deal with nicotine withdrawal symptoms. This training has been shown to increase the success rate by as much as 50 percent, meaning that if 5 percent of smokers quit without this training, 7.5 percent will quit with it. Behavioral interventions that teach the smoker to recognize the cues that lead him or her to want to smoke (talking on the telephone, finishing a meal, and so on) have not been found to improve the quit success rate.

Some research has been done to look at the use of offering financial rewards to people who are able to remain abstinent from smoking. In this type of program, the instructor collects a fee from the participants at the outset of the program. At each session, if the participant has not smoked, a portion of the fee is returned to him. This system of motivating the person to become a nonsmoker via rewards is very effective in the short term but does not significantly improve long-term cessation rates.

One behavioral strategy that has improved quit success rates is the use of a social-support network to encourage and aid the smoker in his or her cessation. The support may come from family members or friends who enroll in the cessation program with the smoker, or through the use of a group therapy model, in which the group serves as one another's source of support. Both have been effective at improving long-term cessation by 30 to 50 percent. Still, the quit success rate is less than 10 percent.

A behavioral treatment that gradually weans the smoker from nicotine by either having the smoker use low-nicotine-yield cigarettes, or special filters, or just smoking fewer and fewer cigarettes over time has met with some success. However, there are many problems with this method, and it is generally conducted in combination with other methods. These nicotine-fading combination methods have long-term success rates varying from 25 percent to 44 percent, much better than any other behavioral treatment methods alone, because they address the addiction to nicotine and not just the emotional and behavioral components of smoking.

Pharmacotherapies

As physicians and pharmacists learn more about the influence of brain chemistry on behavior, new medications are being developed to aid patients in overcoming addictions. One of the most widely used medications to aid smoking cessation is the drug to which the person is addicted, that is, nicotine. Nicotine replacement therapies (or NRT) are used

Zyban (bupropion) is an antidepressant medication that works by reducing nicotine withdrawal symptoms in smokers. It is a successful treatment for around 30 percent of smokers trying to quit.

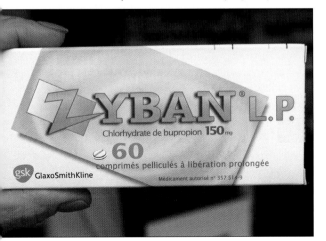

to relieve nicotine withdrawal symptoms, hence addressing the addiction.

NRT is available in several forms, and while most require a prescription from a physician, nicotine gum and the transdermal patch are also available over the counter. Nicotine gum was approved by the U.S. Food and Drug Administration (FDA) for use as a smoking cessation aid in 1984. Many studies have been conducted regarding the effectiveness of nicotine gum in helping individuals achieve long-term smoking cessation. The average quit success rate was 24 percent, and it was found to be most successful for people who are heavily addicted to nicotine. The nicotine patch became available in 1991. It delivers approximately 0.9 milligrams of nicotine per hour through the skin and should be used for a period of eight weeks. The long-term quit success rate is lower than the gum at 18 percent, and it cannot be used to curb sudden urges, unlike the gum.

The nicotine nasal spray offers a more immediate delivery of nicotine through the mucous membranes of the nose. One spray provides 0.5 milligrams of nicotine, with the recommended dose being 1 milligram (one spray in each nostril). The quit success rate with the nicotine nasal spray is 30.5 percent. The nicotine inhaler is a cigarette-shaped plastic tube that holds a cartridge containing 10 milligrams of nicotine and 1 milligram of menthol. It is recommended for use up to 12 weeks, then gradually decreasing use until cessation is complete. The smoker must puff on the tube 80 times to get the nicotine contained in one cigarette. Only a few studies have been done to measure its effectiveness; however, those show a quit success rate of 23 percent.

Two newer NRT methods are still being tested. One is the nicotine lozenge, which received FDA approval in 2002. Similar to nicotine gum, it delivers nicotine on an as-needed basis. The second new method is a nicotine tablet placed under the tongue that can last up to 20 minutes, delivering 2 milligrams of nicotine. It is recommended for people who are highly addicted to nicotine.

Bupropion SR (brand name Zyban) is an antidepressant medication that was approved by the FDA in 1997 for use as a smoking-cessation aid. Bupropion works by weakly inhibiting the reuptake of the neurotransmitters (chemical messengers) responsible for feelings of alertness and pleasure. It is available only by prescription, and the dose is 150 milligrams per day for three days, then increased to 300 milligrams a day for 12 weeks. The actual cigarette-quitting day takes place one to two weeks after starting the medication. Unlike nicotine, bupropion is not addictive but works to curb withdrawal symptoms. Bupropion is very effective at helping smokers quit, with a success rate of 30.5 percent.

No other medication has been approved by the FDA for smoking cessation. Nortriptyline, another antidepressant, has been tested. Like bupropion, the medication is started two to four weeks before the target quit date. Although the quit success rate is 30 percent, there are several negative side effects of the medication. Clonidine, a medication generally used for controlling high blood pressure, has also been tested as a smoking cessation aid. Patients start the medication several days before the quit day and continue for several weeks. Studies show the quit success rate to be 27 percent, but there are many unpleasant side effects, and many people do not complete the course of treatment.

Alternative therapies

When a person decides to quit smoking, he or she wants it to be immediate. The problem with addiction is that recovery is a long-term process. Many people invest in alternative methods with the hope that they can quit without really thinking about it. Hypnosis is one such method frequently promoted for smoking cessation. The hypnotherapist will use either a direct hypnotic suggestion to never want to smoke again, or suggestions that smoking will produce a negative reaction. There is also training in self-hypnosis to help smokers redirect their thoughts when the urge to smoke is greatest. Studies of the effectiveness of hypnosis for smoking cessation are inconclusive. Generally, it is most successful for people who are highly susceptible to hypnosis or when used in combination with other strategies.

Acupuncture is another alternative method for smoking cessation. The acupuncture does not create the desire for cessation but relieves the discomfort of withdrawal. The acupuncture needles are inserted into the outer ear. Some acupuncturists use clips or staples that the person wears for a period of time. Clinical studies of the method have found that it is no more effective than using nothing at all.

Aversive therapy is any method in which the therapist directs the smoker in behaviors that will make smoking unpleasurable, addressing the emotional component of smoking. One strategy is to have the smoker inhale deeply on a cigarette in rapid succession until the smoker becomes sick. Another requires him to smoke about twice as much as he normally would in a day, also resulting in making him sick. Another is to puff quickly without inhaling, resulting in breathlessness. All of these methods can have serious side effects (raising heart rates and blood pressure, raising carbon monoxide levels in the blood). Although they can produce quit rates as high as 40 percent when used in conjunction with other methods, the physical risks make them undesirable.

Relapse

Almost all smokers will lapse back to smoking at some point during their attempts to stop. The challenge is to prevent the lapse (having one puff or one cigarette) from becoming a relapse (back to the same rate of smoking as before the quit attempt). Most smoking cessation programs address the risks for relapse through helping the smoker identify high-risk situations for smoking and developing strategies for dealing with them. Risk factors for relapse include negative emotional states (depression, anger, boredom, weariness), being around smokers (especially family members who smoke), cravings, alcohol use, negative thoughts such as "I can't do this," and lack of alternative activities. Smokers who relapse generally return to their precessation level of smoking within a week and will often escalate the smoking to above the previous level.

The greatest successes at long-term cessation have been with combinations of behavioral and pharmacological treatments. However, no combination has been found to work for everyone. The smoker who is truly motivated to quit needs to find a combination of cessation methods that will address physical addiction, emotional connections, and the behavioral habits of smoking.

M. D. Reynolds

Social Services

Many people with addiction problems depend on welfare services for support. However, differences in funding and legislation can make it difficult for clients to gain access to the help they need.

When U.S. president Ronald Reagan told the story of a woman using government food stamps to purchase orange juice and spending the change to buy vodka as an attack on social welfare programs, he highlighted a major problem facing social services; namely, that many recipients are substance abusers. Social service programs in the United States grew out of the Great Depression, when millions of people were unemployed, homeless, and living near starvation. Prior to the 1930s, there was no safety net, or institutionalized government program to assist those who were destitute. During the Great Depression it became obvious that some form of assistance to the unemployed was needed, and the social welfare system was created. At that time, recipients were perceived as deserving the assistance they received. Subsequently, social services came to be seen as handouts, and recipients are often considered undeserving, especially if they are substance abusers. Indeed, as Ronald Reagan's story suggests, substance abusers sometimes use their government aid to further their addictions.

Though the question of whether substance abusers deserve social service assistance will not be debated here, the issue affects the way social service agencies approach substance abusers and is thus in the background of any discussion of the topic. The key questions for service providers include: how big a problem are substance abusers in terms of social services; how many of them are there and what special needs do they have; and which programs and policies are effective in dealing with these clients?

Numbers using services
Determining the number of substance users receiving social services is difficult because each state is responsible for its own social service delivery. As a consequence of different ways of defining substance use across states, differing systems, and confidentiality issues, there are no nationwide statistics kept on substance abusers receiving services. Funding cuts have made it more difficult to compile statistics, but studies conducted in the 1990s shed light on the issue. Data available from the National Survey on Drug Use and Health (formerly National Household Survey on Drug Abuse) show that people receiving social services are more likely to use drugs than those not receiving services. Twenty-two percent of those receiving services reported past year drug use in 1998, while 13 percent of those not receiving services reported past year use. Thus, when comparing social service clients to the general population, it seems clear that they are more likely to use drugs.

A different picture emerges from the National Study on Child and Adolescent Well-Being (NSCAW), which has collected data from a nationally representative sample of children in child welfare services. The NSCAW measures dependence rather than use, and finds much lower rates; for persons in welfare who retained custody of their children, 10 percent reported a problem with alcohol or drugs, and only 3.9 percent reported alcohol or drug dependency. Only 11 percent of caregivers whose children live at home with them had a substance abuse problem. This rate is similar to the percentage of children in the general population (11 percent) who are living with a parent who is alcoholic or needs treatment for illicit drug abuse.

It is thus difficult to truly determine the prevalence of substance abuse among those receiving social service benefits. While comparing the general population statistics of those using drugs to those receiving services is important, it is more important to know the proportion of those receiving services who are dependent on or addicted to drugs. Again, these data are difficult to compile. It is also important to differentiate those who have a disorder that causes them to receive services from those whose use occurs at the same time they are receiving services for other reasons. What is clear from data from the Department of Health and Human Services is that substance abuse is higher among long-term recipients, suggesting that while it might not always cause them to be there, substance abuse can keep people in social services for longer periods of time.

The reason substance abusers receive services for longer periods of time is largely due to the myriad problems they tend to bring with them in addition to being dependent on drugs or alcohol. These range from little work experience, low education levels, transportation issues (especially in rural areas), having a criminal record, homelessness, child care and domestic violence issues (especially for women), health problems, and co-occurring mental health disorders. Jon Morgenstern and his colleagues reported in 2003 on women receiving social services, comparing the needs of those who reported substance use disorder to those who did not. Women with substance use disorders face more problems such as unemployment, homelessness, current diagnosis of posttraumatic stress disorder, depression, past incarceration, and domestic violence.

Achieving independence

The overall goal of social services has always been to help clients achieve independence. The additional problems faced by substance abusing clients make this job even more difficult. Shrinking budgets and changes in social service practices that limit lifetime allowances for benefits make achieving independence both more difficult and more necessary for substance abusers. In the 1990s the federal government passed legislation limiting recipients of Temporary Assistance for Needy Families (TANF) to five years during the lifetime of any one individual. While it remains up to each state to decide how to meet that goal, in order to receive necessary federal assistance, states must comply. As a result of these issues, many states have formed partnerships with local substance abuse treatment programs in order to meet the goals of both systems.

According to the Welfare Information Network, substance abuse treatment shares the same goal as social services: independence. While social services seek independence through stable employment, treatment agencies seek independence from addiction for their clients. Obviously, substance abuse inhibits the ability to work, and stable employment is considered a key part of most recovery plans. Because these organizations were traditionally separate agencies, however, only recently have they begun working together and even then in spite of policies that serve to keep them apart.

Helping former addicts get back into employment is seen as an important step by social service departments. A stable work environment can provide a sense of self-esteem and make people less dependent on benefits.

In the 1990s Congress passed legislation that disqualified those convicted of a drug-related felony from receiving services for five years. Thus, those coming out of prison, most of whom have employment and housing issues—exactly the problems social services were created to address—were not allowed to access the services they needed. Other barriers were also placed in the way of providing services to substance abusers. Many states passed legislation that barred those known to be current drug users or practicing alcoholics from receiving services unless they were in treatment. The result was that clients quickly learned to lie about their circumstances. Clients would not inform their caseworkers of their legal problems and would hide their addictions from others. Doing so enabled clients to receive cash assistance and food stamps but, because their caseworkers were unaware of the underlying issues, clients were prevented from receiving the necessary assistance that could enable them to return to independence.

Linking services

Social service agencies subsequently began attempting to link substance abuse treatment with services. Partly driven by new rules that limit clients to five years of services and that require them to be in either a work or training-related activity within two years, agencies have begun to address substance abuse. By using drug testing, creative financing, and innovative programs, social services have integrated substance abuse treatment and social services. Many agencies have started to use urinalysis to test clients for drug use. This practice enables the agency to identify drug users, to monitor those in treatment, and to directly reduce drug use by sanction or threat of sanctioning. It is too expensive to test all clients, but most agencies will test those they suspect of using, and then mandate treatment for those who test positive.

Social service agencies often mandate drug treatment for those discovered with substance abuse problems. Social service clients do not have the money to pay for their own treatment, so agencies use a number of ways to provide it. Because of changes in the law, it is difficult for social service agencies to directly fund treatment, so many states partner with their health departments, which receive federal grants to provide treatment. Teaming health departments with social services works for both agencies. Social services have clients in need but lack money, while health departments do not have such ready access to the affected population as do social service departments.

While having on-site counselors is one innovative approach to substance using clients, numerous studies have shown that integrating social services, substance abuse treatment, and employment readiness programs increases the likelihood of a client achieving independence, both in terms of drug abuse and employment. A good example is the Casaworks for Families program at Columbia University that draws on local, state, and federal funding to promote a milieu in which many services work together. Clients are assigned a case manager who coordinates 6 to 12 months of intensive drug or alcohol treatment, job training or educational services, as well as parenting skills, personal health issues, and a host of family services. An evaluation of the program found that after 12 months in the program, 75 percent of participants had quit using drugs and 40 percent were working, compared with 16 percent working at the start of the program. Only 13 percent were still receiving cash assistance.

A final way that social services and substance abuse are intertwined is through foster care of children whose parents are incarcerated. There were 1.7 million children in 2007 who had a parent who was incarcerated. Data on the number of those in foster care are not reliable, but 2 percent of male and 11 percent of female inmates report having at least one child in foster care. Social service programs like Casaworks can have the added benefit of keeping some people out of prisons and their children out of foster care.

The creative work of professionals in the social services system has been able to overcome both their clients' unwillingness to seek help and policies that grew from labeling substance abusers as undeserving; these initiatives are providing services that, instead of merely removing clients from welfare lists, enable them to leave voluntarily by becoming independent.

D. J. O'CONNELL, T. C. O'CONNELL

SEE ALSO:
Continuum of Care • Public Health Programs

Sports

The urge to gain a competitive advantage can drive many athletes to take substances that can improve their performance. Sports organizations are having to develop sophisticated techniques to detect the use of drugs.

Most athletes train hard to be able to run or jump higher than their rivals. In doing so they must be careful not to take any food supplement or medicine that may be on the list of banned substances.

The use of substances to gain a competitive edge in sports has been of interest since ancient times. Olympic athletes in ancient Greece reportedly experimented with opium, mushrooms, and herbal potions to improve their athletic performance. Ancient Aztec runners consumed extracts from cactus plants as stimulants to reduce fatigue in long-distance events. In the 1800s, when the stimulants amphetamine, ephedrine, and strychnine became available, American and European athletes began using them. In the 1940s the male hormone testosterone and similar compounds were produced and subsequently used by athletes to increase muscle growth and strength. The term *doping* (derived from the Dutch word *doop* for a type of viscous opium juice) is typically used to denote the use of performance-enhancing drugs in sports.

The use of drugs by athletes in the modern era has become a prominent problem and concern. The use

and risk of stimulants became prominently exposed after a cyclist died during competition in the 1960 Olympic Games in Rome, a death that was associated with the use of amphetamine. Similarly, a cyclist in the 1967 Tour de France collapsed and died during the race, also attributed to the use of amphetamine. Anabolic-androgenic steroids became popular with strength athletes in the 1960s and 1970s and continue to be the most abused class of drugs in the modern Olympics.

Why athletes take drugs

Serious, competitive athletes desire to maximize their performance, not only from extensive training, but also from proper nutrition, adequate sleep, using the best equipment, and other rational means. This often includes the use of nutritional dietary supplements, such as vitamins and minerals. However, the desire, pressure, and incentives to succeed and win at any and all costs entices some athletes to resort to illicit means, including the use of performance-enhancing drugs. Wealth, prestige, and fame often accompany athletic success in society, where winners are regarded as heroes. Some athletes may feel that their only chance of winning or making it to the next level is by gaining an unfair advantage. Further, some athletes may feel compelled to use banned drugs because they believe that their competitors are using them.

Competitive athletes generally train with teams, partners, or groups. Hence, the pressure to keep up and improve is greater. If some members of the group use drugs to improve their performance, they may encourage the other members to do so as well. If the athlete is successful—whether or not the success can be attributed to drugs—the other athletes may feel that taking the same drugs will produce the same success. Some athletes have even been unscrupulously doped by their country, without their consent or knowledge, in order to produce winners in international competitions.

Effects of drugs on performance

An ergogenic drug is one that increases work output, and for athletes it is one that improves their performance. The following drug classes are commonly used by athletes as ergogenic aids: stimulants, narcotics, anabolic-androgenic steroids, diuretics, and peptide hormones. Although there are numerous other drugs, dietary supplements, and other products that are promoted to enhance athletic performance, scientific evidence to support many of these claims is notably lacking.

Stimulants include such drugs as amphetamine, methamphetamine, cocaine, ephedrine, and caffeine. Amphetamine and related compounds stimulate the brain and the heart. They can potentially improve athletic performance by increasing alertness, strength, endurance, and they can reduce fatigue. These drugs can also cause euphoria (a feeling of well-being), and they can increase confidence and aggression. Some athletes take drugs or dietary supplements that contain these substances to assist with weight loss.

The side effects of these stimulants can be serious, particularly at high doses or when different stimulants are taken together. Such effects include insomnia, restlessness, nervousness, irritability, rapid and pounding heart rate, abnormal heart rhythms, thermogenesis (increased heat production by the body), stroke, seizures, and death.

Narcotics are drugs that stem from opium or similar compounds. These agents are used in sports primarily to relieve pain or to increase the pain threshold. Other effects of narcotics include euphoria and an increase in the athletes' perceptions of their abilities (sometimes to the point of feeling invincible). Side effects of narcotics include nausea, vomiting, constipation, sedation, altered judgment, and mood changes. Long-term use can result in physical and psychological addiction, and overdoses can result in respiratory depression and death.

Anabolic-androgenic steroids are compounds that are similar in chemical structure and actions to the male sex hormone testosterone. These compounds are considered anabolic because they promote the growth of muscles and bones. They are also classified as androgenic because they have masculinizing effects too, similar to testosterone and other androgens. When combined with intense physical training and high-protein diets, these drugs can help increase muscle size and strength. Abusers of these agents often take more than one particular anabolic-androgenic steroid at the same time, a practice that is called stacking. In an attempt to minimize side effects, some abusers take anabolic-androgenic steroids for a specific period of time (usually 6 to 12 weeks), and then stop for a period of time. This process is referred to as cycling. Further, some abusers take higher and higher doses during the cycle, and then they taper the dose back down in increments, a method known as pyramiding.

Anabolic-androgenic steroids have complex effects in many organs and tissues. In addition, their presence in the body alters the regulation and secretion of other natural hormones because the brain and sex glands work in conjunction to determine the right balance of testosterone and other hormones to produce. In males, for example, since the body senses these compounds to be androgens, the brain signals the cells in the testes to pause from producing testosterone.

In males, side effects of anabolic-androgenic steroids include a decrease in the size of the testicles, enlargement of the prostate gland, a decline in the production of sperm, infertility, impotence, and changes in sex drive. Further, since these drugs are partially converted to estrogenic compounds (the female hormone), they can cause enlargement of the breasts in males. This is potentially irreversible and may require surgical treatment. In females, anabolic-androgenic steroids have a masculinizing effect, which includes the growth of facial hair, deepening of the voice, and baldness. Other effects in females include enlargement of the clitoris, menstrual irregularities, and changes in sex drive. Additional side effects of anabolic-androgenic steroids in both males and females include high blood pressure, acne, male-pattern baldness, fluid retention, elevated blood cholesterol, myocardial infarction (heart attack), strokes, and cancer. Changes in personality can occur, including aggression and hostility. In adolescents, these drugs may cause the bones to cease growing sooner than normal, which can result in a shortened growth span. Finally, these drugs may lead to addiction and dependence, especially when taken in high doses. Withdrawal can result in depression and suicidal thoughts.

IN THE GENES

For those desperate to improve their performance, new techniques developed for medical research could be used to enhance athletic achievement. Gene therapy, which is seen as a possible cure for cancer or multiple sclerosis, could also be used to boost the gene that produces natural erythropoietin in the blood. Existing tests can spot synthetic versions of erythropoietin but may not be able to detect genetically boosted natural production. There can be drawbacks. Too much erythropoietin can elevate blood pressure and result in a heart attack or stroke. Altering genes could aggravate such dangers, especially as the technique is still experimental. Antidoping agencies are trying to stay one step ahead by searching for tiny changes that occur when the body is exposed to certain genes, in the hope that these may then be detected in blood samples.

Diuretics are often referred to as water pills. These medications enhance water and salt excretion through the kidney and increase the production of urine. Thus, some athletes use diuretics to improperly "make weight" for sports that have weight classifications, such as wrestling, boxing, and weightlifting. Diuretics also have been used to dilute the urine of athletes who are using banned substances, with the hope that they can cheat or fool a drug test. Since urine drug tests require a minimum concentration to reliably and accurately detect a drug, diluting the urine can reduce the concentration of a drug below the detection threshold. However, since diuretics are often banned by sports agencies, the detection of a diuretic will result in a positive drug test. Side effects of diuretics include dehydration, mineral imbalance, cramps, weakness, and nausea.

Peptide hormones include naturally occurring hormones consisting of various amino acids. Some of these hormones have positive ergogenic effects, and their synthesis has made them available for abuse. Athletes have used human growth hormone, hoping to increase muscle size and strength, and they often combine this with the use of anabolic-androgenic steroids. Erythropoietin is a hormone that stimulates the production of red blood cells, which carry oxygen to muscles and other organs in the body. The use of synthetic erythropoietin provides a competitive advantage for endurance athletes, since their blood has a higher oxygen-carrying capacity. Other hormones have been used by athletes even though any ergogenic effects have not been scientifically proven. These highly active compounds can also produce undesirable or adverse effects. For example, adverse effects from the use of human growth hormone include depression, antisocial behavior, abnormalities in blood sugar and fats, heart disease, and a disorder known as acromegaly. Problems associated with the abuse of erythropoietin include high blood pressure, iron deficiency, convulsions, myocardial infarction, and stroke.

It is not the intent of the sports-governing bodies to deny athletes the use of medications needed to treat medical conditions. These organizations supply lists of banned and permitted drugs under their purview, and for some banned or restricted drugs there is a mechanism for the athlete and his or her physician to petition for a medical exception.

Staff at the 2000 Sydney Olympic drug-testing unit made routine analyses for a number of banned drugs. Random testing is the only way to ensure that cheating is stamped out in competitive sports.

Incidence of drug use in sports

The incidence of drug use in sports varies according to the sport and the level of competition. According to various studies and surveys, 4 to 11 percent of high school males and 0.5 to 2.5 percent of high school females have used anabolic-androgenic steroids. The use of these agents in college sports has ranged from approximately 1 percent to a high of 20 percent; the lower incidence was observed in more recent years after the institution of drug education and testing policies. During a recent survey of college athletes, the use of stimulants (amphetamines and ephedrine) was approximately 7 percent. Although rumors, claims, and anecdotal reports suggest that the use of anabolic-androgenic steroids and stimulants is prevalent in some professional sports (for example, football and baseball), the true incidence is not known. In one study, as many as 55 percent of elite weight lifters had admitted to the use of anabolic-androgenic steroids. In a review of the modern (1896–2002) summer and winter Olympic Games, there were 29 documented cases of the use of anabolic-androgenic steroids, 22 cases of stimulant use, and 7 cases of the use of diuretics. However, wide-scale drug testing at the Olympics was only instituted in 1972, and only since 1984 has it been technologically possible to rapidly and accurately test urine samples for a wide array of banned substances. Moreover, athletes are fully aware that drug testing will be conducted at Olympic events and are able to discontinue the use of drugs prior to testing. Some Olympic officials have estimated the incidence of doping to be about 10 percent, while some athletes, coaches, and trainers believe the prevalence to be much higher.

Drug testing of athletes

Drug testing (doping control) is one of the methods employed to deter the use of banned substances in sports. Drug testing aims to protect the health and safety of athletes and their competitors, and to maintain the dignity and integrity of sports by ensuring fair and equitable competition. Ideally, it also assures athletes that their competitors are not allowed to cheat, so they too will not feel compelled to break the rules.

Drug testing is routinely conducted on urine specimens; however, testing for the use of erythropoietin has consisted of both blood and urine tests. Urine specimens are used because the collection of samples is noninvasive, and because drugs and their metabolites are concentrated in the urine, which renders it easier to detect them. Testing is generally conducted just after a competition is completed. However, drugs such as anabolic-androgenic steroids are used during training and may not be detectable during competition if the athlete stops using the drugs long enough to allow them to clear from his or her system. Therefore, out-of-competition testing for these drugs is conducted at random times during the year and with short notice to the athlete.

Athletes who test positive for banned substances are subject to sanctions imposed by their specific sports-governing organization. Penalties generally include disqualification, and a number of Olympic athletes have had their medals stripped and records erased due to positive drug tests. Further, athletes who test positive for banned substances are usually banned from future competition for a specific amount of time.

P. J. AMBROSE

SEE ALSO:
Drug Testing

State Agencies

Providing treatment for drug addiction in the United States usually falls to the responsibility of individual states. Funding for programs is a joint venture between the federal government, the state, and counties or cities within the state.

Since the mid-1970s, growing attention has focused on providing drug treatment services through state networks because of regional organizational differences and the size of the United States. State agencies have a greater knowledge of the needs of their citizens in their respective areas. States and state agencies also coordinate services and funding from several sources, including the National Institutes of Health, Department of Health and Human Services, Centers for Disease Control, Substance Abuse and Mental Health Services Administration, National Institute on Drug Abuse, and National Institute on Alcohol Abuse and Alcoholism. Although subject to budgetary review and constraint, federal funding supports the majority of governmental funding, with the state and county or city providing a portion. State officials are involved in policy and decisions regarding federal money.

In every state there are a variety of programs that are involved in drug prevention and treatment. This provision has arisen since the 1970s as the use of drugs increased and drug abuse began to be recognized as a problem. Certainly the use of drugs was not new and, depending on the era, various groups have been affected by drug use, with the largest number of addicted Americans peaking at the beginning of the twenty-first century. The main difference from earlier eras is that until the 1960s drug use was prominent among older rather than younger age groups.

All states have one primary agency that is responsible for ensuring that citizens of the state have access to treatment, educating communities about drug use, and policy making. For the majority of states the agency responsible for drug-use issues is part of a larger agency, such as the state department of health. In larger states, or in states with a larger drug problem, drug use often has a separate agency (*see* table on p. 298). A state's view of drug use is often reflected by the agency that has oversight. It demonstrates the confusion that frequently arises about whether drug use is classified as a medical

condition. Some states may place an agency with the Department of Health or Public Health, while at the same time regarding drug use as a social and rehabilitative problem.

Federal oversight agencies

The primary federal agency involved with drug use and mental health is the Substance Abuse and Mental Health Services Administration (SAMHSA), which is an agency of the Department of Health and Human Services (HHS). SAMHSA was established in 1992 by an act of Congress, Public Law 102-321. Created to focus more attention on improving the lives of individuals with mental health and substance use disorders, SAMHSA is separate and distinct from the National Institutes of Health (NIH) or the National Institute on Drug Abuse (NIDA) or any other agency within the HHS.

SAMHSA interacts with the states, national and local community- and faith-based organizations, and public and private sector providers. SAMHSA's primary mission is to ensure that people with a mental health or addictive disorder and those individuals at risk have the opportunity for a fulfilling life that includes a job, a home, and meaningful relationships with family and friends.

As the substance abuse and mental health systems of services evolve, SAMHSA conducts research and then translates these findings into best practice with the goal of facilitating science-based knowledge to community-based services. State programs are supported through the block grant program, and discretionary grants are offered to implement programs and practices. It should be noted that in addition to the 50 states, various territories such as Guam, Puerto Rico, and the Virgin Islands receive funding, as does the United Indian Health Services, which oversees funding for Native American nations.

SAMHSA has three centers that carry out its mission and interact with state agencies, community-based programs, research centers, and nonprofit and private organizations. The Office of Applied Studies

Provisions made by states to combat addiction vary widely. Some may provide 24-hour hotline advice; others may only have limited funds for treatment.

collects, analyzes, and disseminates national data on practices and issues related to substance use and mental health disorders. The Center for Mental Health Services (CMHS) works to improve the quality of community-based services and make them more accessible. The Center for Substance Abuse Treatment (CSAT) promotes the availability and quality of community-based substance abuse treatment services.

What do state programs do?

Each of the 50 states and the various territories have some agency that is responsible for coordinating the various prevention and treatment efforts that are undertaken in the state. In general, it can be said that the greater the state's drug problem, the larger the agency. Nearly all state agencies have an educational or prevention branch that travels to schools and community-based programs and gives presentations. These programs are more effective than criminal justice agencies because the people providing the education are trained professionals who know not only about the criminal aspect of drug use but about treatment and the social issues that are often associated with drug use.

A second large part of most state programs is providing treatment, which includes outpatient counseling, residential, and medication-assisted treatment (such as methadone and buprenorphine). State agencies license programs and provide oversight to ensure that citizens are not being harmed. Many state agencies are also involved in the funding of these programs. Every year the federal government through SAMHSA carries out a needs assessment for each state and then provides funding. Usually the federal money does not cover all the treatment costs, and typically it is broken down to 50 percent federal money, 25 percent state money, and 25 percent local money. In some states, public medical assistance pays for drug treatment; in others, citizens are expected to pay for drug treatment themselves. This can be costly to individual citizens when one considers that drug addiction is considered a chronic relapsing medical condition.

State agencies are designated by SAMHSA to be the state methadone authority (SMA) and have oversight and licensing responsibility for programs in the state. This development followed changes in the federal methadone regulations and the change in oversight from the Food and Drug Administration (FDA) to SAMHSA. The SMA provides state oversight and technical assistance to methadone programs in the state and is involved in policy making and state regulation.

Many state agencies are involved in the training of professionals who work in the field and in the credentialing of persons who work in programs, such as counselors. Each state issues its own credentials, such as "certified substance abuse counselor." Professionals must maintain their credentials or they will not be allowed to work in a state-licensed program.

While each state agency's mission may sound similar, the ways in which their goals are implemented are as varied as the 50 states. Some state agencies are very small, having only a few employees, while other state agencies have offices throughout the state, a research division, a media and public relations division, and provide direct advocacy to citizens through an advocacy center, to name but a few spheres of activity. Some departments in the agency may address specific issues within the state, such as homelessness, a cocaine epidemic, an HIV epidemic, neighborhood youth programs, and so on. Some state agencies have had a local weekly cable program to educate their citizens about drug issues in the state.

VARIETY OF STATE JURSIDICTIONS

Department of Health	Mental Health and Addiction Services or Behavioral Health	Community Health
Arkansas		Michigan
Hawaii		
Nevada	Connecticut	**Social and Rehabilitative Services**
New Mexico	Idaho	
Pennsylvania	Indiana	Kansas
Tennessee	Oklahoma	
	Utah	**Children and Family Services**
Department of Public Health	West Virginia	
	Wyoming	Florida
Iowa		
Massachusetts	**Health or Human Services**	**Separate Agency**
Montana		
	Alaska (Social Services)	Arizona
Department of Mental Health, Mental Retardation, or Developmental Disabilities	Colorado	California
	Delaware (Social Services)	District of Columbia
	Minnesota	Illinois
	Nebraska	Louisiana
Alabama	New Hampshire	Maine
Georgia	New Jersey	Maryland
Kentucky	North Dakota	Missouri
Mississippi	South Dakota	New York
North Carolina	Vermont	Ohio
Rhode Island	Washington (Social Services)	Oregon
Virginia		South Carolina
		Texas
Source: *Monitoring the Future Study*		Wisconsin

Core issues for states

Each of the 50 states has core issues that have been developed with SAMHSA to take its goals from vision to practice. These priorities are linked to principles that help ensure that state programs will meet the highest standards, driven by a strategy to improve accountability, capacity, and effectiveness:

- Promoting accountability; SAMHSA tracks national trends and establishes measurement and reporting systems to monitor services.
- Enhancing capacity; by assessing resources, supporting systems of community-based care, and improving service financing and organization, SAMHSA promotes a strong, well-educated workforce and improves the nation's capacity for treatment and prevention services.
- Assuring effectiveness; at the federal level SAMHSA works to continually improve services by identifying and promoting evidence-based approaches to care and by providing technical assistance and workforce skills training.

J. S. WOODS

SEE ALSO:
Public Health Programs • Treatment

Step Programs

Many addiction recovery programs are based on a self-help system known as a step program. The concept was first developed for Alcoholics Anonymous, but its principles have found application in helping treat other addictions.

The last two decades of the twentieth century witnessed an explosion in the growth of self-help groups for all types of problems. One prominent researcher estimated that in the state of California alone there were 275 different self-help groups, including groups for addiction such as Alcoholics Anonymous and Gamblers Anonymous, and groups for mental health problems such as depression and agoraphobia. The growth of these groups accompanied an increased interest in alternative, or complementary, medicine.

The interest in self-help (or, more correctly, mutual help) groups was a reflection of a growing discontent with conventional medicine and the over-weaning reliance on medication as the answer to all problems. When celebrities openly began discussing their addiction problems and proclaiming their allegiance and gratitude to self-help groups, in particular Alcoholics Anonymous (AA), it became more acceptable to discuss addiction, leading some cynics to suggest that addiction was becoming a fashion accessory. Regardless of the hyperbole attached to the latest celebrity's revelations about his or her battle with drugs or alcohol, the publicity has had some benefits. To a large extent it demystified and destigmatized addiction problems and made people aware of a readily available source of help, the self-help group.

Origins

Step programs have been described as the instruction manual for addressing various behavioral problems, most famously alcoholism. This manual, or program, consists of a number of tasks, or steps, that need to be followed to recover from the problem. In its current and most recognizable form, the program consists of twelve steps (*see* box, p. 301), mainly because subsequent groups adopted the program as it was exemplified by AA. However, even in AA the program has not always consisted of twelve steps, as the organization's history reveals.

The man generally credited with the authorship of the twelve-step program is Bill Wilson, an American stockbroker and alcoholic. In his writings he describes his constant struggles and failures with alcohol until, in 1934, a friend took him along to a meeting of the Oxford Group, an evangelical Christian society. It was there that he found some basis for his personal sobriety and later made plans for what was to become AA. He found that the Oxford Group practiced a program based on a few simple principles: acceptance of powerlessness, honesty with self and others, making restitution, and seeking guidance through prayer and meditation. Bill found that by practicing these principles he no longer craved alcohol and began trying to spread the message to other alcoholics. The message, a modified six-step version of the Oxford Group's principles, was not particularly well received, and in 1939 Bill, with some help from other sober alcoholics, wrote the book *Alcoholics Anonymous* (the so-called Big Book). In this book he expanded on the six steps, and the program as practiced today was born. A 1941 newspaper article by Jack Alexander publicized the program, and the membership of AA eventually grew from around 100 to the worldwide fellowship of around two million that it is today. The apparent success of AA led to other self-help groups being organized along the same lines and adopting, with minor modifications, the twelve-step program. The earliest of these was Al-Anon, the group for the families of alcoholics, then Alateen, for the children of alcohol abusers. Similar groups for other addiction problems began to emerge, for example, Narcotics Anonymous and Gamblers Anonymous, and the spread has continued.

Key concepts

The key concepts of the groups continue to be the principles that Bill Wilson learned from the Oxford Group back in 1934. They include admission of helplessness, honesty, reparation, working with others, and prayer and meditation. These are principles that are often lost in a life of addiction, which is often characterized by dishonesty and selfishness. Supporters of the program argue that someone who adopts these principles and makes radical changes in his or her life can undergo a powerful transformation, and there are many personal stories to support this case.

While many people exhort the program as a transformer of lives, it is not difficult to find other reasons that AA and other step programs might work. The first reason is fellowship—all or most of the people attending these groups will be in a similar situation, hence the mutual support and practical advice will be both helpful and motivating. Second, AA meetings tend to be attended by members who have been sober for varying lengths of time, and the example of long-term sober members can be motivating. Third, there are the sayings of AA, which, although they have become rather clichéd, are both profound and powerful. Take, for example, the saying "one day at a time." Any counselor attempting to help someone with problems knows the value of breaking the problem into manageable pieces. This approach is precisely what is being advocated by this saying; that is, do what can be done today. Thus, twelve-step groups may work on multiple levels.

The program

It is usually suggested that when someone embarks on the twelve-step program he or she acquire a sponsor who will assist the person through recovery. The sponsor is normally someone who has been a successful member of the group for a long time and has also successfully completed the program. In AA (and groups tackling substance use) the goal is abstinence, although this can be a barrier for those who would like to be able to control their drinking. However, AA argues that this is an impossible goal, since alcoholics suffer from a disease that dictates that they can never control their drinking, a position not shared by all commentators on alcoholism. For some other addiction problems, regarding this predisposing condition as a disease is more theoretically problematic and is often glossed over, if not ignored. Much of the program, especially the early steps, consists of talking and attitude change. However, later steps entail actual behaviors, for example, making direct amends and carrying the message to others. Some AA members argue that one never completes the program and that it is an

Step programs rely on an experienced sponsor to help the recovering addict through difficult times.

ongoing process. Others argue that although one never finishes the program, steps 10 to 12 are used as a maintenance program.

Advantages and disadvantages

There are many advantages to twelve-step groups. First, they are free. A collection is taken, but this is a voluntary contribution, and there are no fees for membership or attendance. Meetings are plentiful; AA can be found in most towns and cities in the United States and in almost every country in the world. The same principles, if not practices, apply in all meetings; visitors are generally reassured by the familiar format. There is an emphasis on helping others to help oneself, so there tends to be a great deal of help available to newcomers and returning members.

There are two major disadvantages for some people with twelve-step groups—their religious nature and the creation of what can become a substitute addiction. As discussed above, twelve-step programs can trace their origin to the Oxford Group. It was from there that the concepts of confession (being truthful with self and others), surrender (to a higher power), penance (making amends), and prayer and meditation were derived. For AA detractors, and there are many, the historical and contemporary religious overtones are too strong for them to accept AA as a treatment program for themselves or others.

THE TWELVE STEPS OF ALCOHOLICS ANONYMOUS

Step 1	We admitted we were powerless over alcohol—that our lives had become unmanageable.
Step 2	Came to believe that a Power greater than ourselves could restore us to sanity.
Step 3	Made a decision to turn our will and our lives over to the care of God as we understood Him.
Step 4	Made a searching and fearless moral inventory of ourselves.
Step 5	Admitted to God, to ourselves, and to another human being the exact nature of our wrongs.
Step 6	Were entirely ready to have God remove all these defects of character.
Step 7	Humbly asked Him to remove our shortcomings.
Step 8	Made a list of all persons we had harmed, and became willing to make amends to them all.
Step 9	Made direct amends to such people when possible, except wherever to do so would injure them or others.
Step 10	Continued to take personal inventory and when we were wrong promptly admitted it.
Step 11	Sought through prayer and meditation to improve our conscious contact with God as we understood Him, praying only for knowledge of His will for us and the power to carry that out.
Step 12	Having had a spiritual awakening as the result of these steps, we tried to carry this message to alcoholics and to practice these principles in all our affairs.

Source: Alcoholics Anonymous (1976).

AA and other twelve-step programs have long argued that they are not religious, that instead the program is a spiritual one. They further argue that all references to God are nondenominational; however, the vast majority of members are Christian. There is no doubt in this more secular age that the apparent religious nature of AA and the twelve-step program is viewed by many as a barrier.

The second disadvantage is that many who join step groups can substitute attendance at these groups for their obsessions for substances or other behaviors. The aim of joining such groups is to change one's behavior, and these groups state that behavior change must come from a change from within. However, these changes are not always palatable to the family. For example, the recovering alcoholic may spend almost all of his or her time at meetings or helping newcomers. Or the individual may demand that, now that he or she has changed, the family must change as well. This type of new behavior can lead to relationship difficulties at a time when the family had thought that its problems were about to diminish.

Outcomes

It is difficult to state how successful AA or twelve-step programs are compared with other treatment regimes. It is true that there are millions of people around the world who would attest that they would not be sober today if AA did not exist. However, in terms of proof, this kind of evidence counts for very little. It has been difficult to conduct scientific research into AA because the anonymous nature of its organization means that there are no records of its members. Therefore it is difficult to know how many people attend AA meetings and never become sober or fail to complete the course. A 1996 study into recovering alcoholics, Project MATCH, tested three different types of treatment: cognitive behaviour therapy (CBT), motivational enhancement therapy (MET), and twelve-step facilitation (TSF). This study found that there was no difference in outcome between any of the treatments. However, it further found that attending AA following treatment, regardless of what treatment had been given, was associated with remaining abstinent. Although it should be stressed that TSF was not actually a twelve-step group but consisted of encouragement to join and a guided tour of the first five steps, nevertheless the study is hailed as the first evidence for the efficacy of AA.

J. McMahon

SEE ALSO:

Alcoholics Anonymous • Narcotics Anonymous • Recovery • Support Groups

Stress

Stress is a common occurrence in life. Sometimes it can be a positive influence, but it can have negative consequences if people begin to use addictive substances as a means of coping with stressful demands.

Stress is most concisely defined as the response to physical or psychological demands upon the body. More specifically, a state of stress involves various external and internal challenges to the body and brain, usually termed stressors. Stressors come in various forms. For example, a form of physical stress may be working a 12-hour shift or not getting enough sleep for an extended period of time. Psychological stress may be represented by academic deadlines, time commitments, or conflicts with family or friends. Not all forms of stress are negative. Positive events that are also stressful include graduating from school, starting a new career, and getting married.

Stressors cause many physiological changes in bodily function. Stress can activate the sympathetic nervous system, which is part of the body's "fight or flight" system. Activation of the sympathetic nervous system results in an increased heart rate, constriction of blood vessels, tense muscles, and dry mouth. Therefore, a body that is under chronic stress may be more prone to cardiovascular problems, ulcers, and suppression of the immune system. Emotional centers in the brain can also become active during stress, making concentration difficult. Another primary effect of stress on the body is the activation of the hypothalamic-pituitary-adrenal axis, otherwise known as the HPA or "stress axis" (*see* diagram).

Activation of the HPA axis begins with release of corticotropin-releasing hormone (CRH) from the hypothalamus into the portal system of the pituitary gland. CRH induces the release of adrenocorticotropic hormone (ACTH) from the anterior pituitary into the blood circulating throughout the body. Finally, ACTH enhances the release of cortisol into the blood from the adrenal glands, located just above the kidneys. Cortisol is often referred to as a stress hormone. The daily production of cortisol can rise markedly during severe stress to regulate the physiological effects of stressors. Chronic activation of the HPA axis and elevated levels of cortisol can be dangerous to human health. For instance, students are more likely to get sick during or after final exam

periods, since they endure a prolonged period of stress. Sustained stress and subsequent overactivation of the HPA axis can lead to critical long-term health complications, such as a weakened immune system, psychological disorders, and cancer.

Some people are more vulnerable to the biological and psychological effects of stress as a result of an inherited overactive neurobiological system. The combination of genetics and environment plays a pivotal role in the coping mechanisms and behavioral responses to stressors. A common model used to explain the relationship between genes and environment is the diathesis stress model. In this model, individuals inherit tendencies to express certain traits or behaviors that may be activated under conditions of stress. In this definition, the diathesis is genetic vulnerability and the stress is environmental exposure to general life events. For

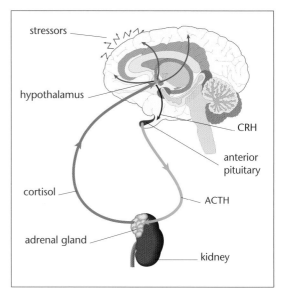

Once activated by external or internal stressors, the hypothalamus in the brain directs the pituitary gland to release the hormone ACTH into the bloodstream. ACTH induces the adrenal gland to release cortisol, a so-called stress hormone.

example, if two men are fired from their job one man may immediately search the Internet for new job leads, while the other man may develop a deep depression. Genetic vulnerability does not mean that an individual will definitely develop a disorder associated with a stressful situation—he or she is merely more prone to the psychological and biological effects of stress.

The most common behavioral responses to stress are maladaptive. These responses to stressors are often unconscious reactions at the onset of stress. However, conscious efforts to alleviate stress in a constructive manner, such as exercise, can be advantageous to a person's health. Examples of maladaptive responses include preoccupation, edginess, tension, negative affect, sleep disturbances, eating disturbances, and withdrawal from social situations. Conscious decisions to deal with stressful events can also be maladaptive and potentially harmful to one's health. For instance, after a hard day at work some people may go out for a few alcoholic drinks, or smoke cigarettes. This may initially be a way to cope with stress, but because of the addictive and rewarding properties of drugs of abuse, this coping mechanism can develop into an addiction and substance dependence.

Stress and drug abuse

As suggested above, stressful life events are a primary factor leading to drug abuse and dependence. Some scientists split the continuum of drug abuse into three stages: initial acquisition, maintenance, and relapse. Stress may contribute to all three of these levels.

Initially, drug abuse is often a coping mechanism for people during stressful situations. While alcohol and nicotine are the two legal drugs of abuse most often sought to cope with stress, illegal drugs such as marijuana, cocaine, and heroin are often used as a form of self-medication to alleviate stress. However, the acute effects of these drugs provide only minimal relief from stress. Therefore, individuals may continue abusing drugs in order to cope with or ignore their stress. However, drugs of abuse become physically addictive, and the individuals soon find themselves depending upon the drugs to ameliorate stressful events. This leads to the second phase in drug abuse: maintenance.

Maintenance refers to the stage in which a person continues abusing drugs after the initial acquisition period. At this point, various factors influence an individual's conscious or unconscious use of drugs. Stress may still be a contributing factor, but other determinants, such as physical addiction and dependence, have a greater influence over the continued abuse of drugs.

Once an individual becomes physically dependent upon drugs, abstaining from this behavior may prove to be very difficult, even after years of being drug free. The propensity for relapse is a very serious issue in the treatment of addiction. Stressful situations drastically increase the likelihood of drug-seeking behavior being resumed. For example, if a former alcoholic is faced with an acutely traumatic event, such as the death of a spouse, he or she may resort to dealing with this stress by having an alcoholic drink. This one seemingly insignificant exposure to alcohol may lead to a full relapse into drug abuse by triggering a state of craving. Likewise, a student who has recently recovered from cocaine addiction may want to return to college. Reexposure to academic stress, commitments, and the same social arenas significantly increases the probability of relapse.

Biologically, residual changes in the central nervous system following a period of drug addiction and subsequent abstinence may contribute to the vulnerability of relapse. Specifically, the HPA axis releases the stress hormone cortisol into the bloodstream during stressful situations. Increases in circulating cortisol are believed to contribute to the reinstatement of drug-seeking behaviors. Animal models of relapse have shown that exposure to stressful events, for example, an electric shock, increases the levels of corticosterone (cortisol in rodents). As a result, the animals begin to self-administer drugs. Blocking this increase by pharmacological manipulation reduces the likelihood of drug-seeking behavior and self-administration. Therefore, cortisol-blocking agents, such as CRH-antagonists, are being studied in human clinical trials as novel drugs to treat drug addiction and the propensity for relapse.

K. PHILPOT

SEE ALSO:
Causes of Addiction, Biological • Relapse

Suicide

Drug and alcohol use are often implicated in attempts at suicide. This can either be a direct link, in which drugs are used to cause death, or indirect, when attempts to self-medicate other symptoms result in overdose.

Although the risk factors for suicide are widely accepted as extremely complex and often interlinked, it is a fact that in the United States alcohol and illicit drugs are involved in around 50 percent of suicide attempts. Suicide has been measured as the eleventh leading cause of death in the United States, accounting for 1.2 percent of all deaths, and the second leading cause of death among 15- to 24-year-olds. Some 25 percent of successful suicides are drug abusers or alcoholics, and substance abuse is seen as the main factor behind the increased risk of suicide among people under the age of 30. The suicide rate among alcoholics was found to be 18 times that of nondependents in a key 1980s U.S. Epidemiological Catchment Area study.

The most vulnerable members of the population are the young and the elderly. Adolescents are particularly prone to depression and suicide: 28 percent of high school students have been found to have experienced severe depression—but nonabusers were also found to have the lowest levels of depression and suicidal thoughts. The 2007 report of the National Survey on Drug Use and Health, which periodically asks youths aged 12 to 17 if they have thought seriously about killing themselves, or have tried to kill themselves during the past year, found that 8.2 percent had experienced at least one major depressed episode in the past year. Those using any illicit substance other than marijuana were more likely to be at risk than abstainers.

Psychological factors either deriving from or predating alcohol and substance abuse also have to be taken into account, as do other factors such as age, sex, ethnicity, and social situation. For instance, alcoholics who commit suicide tend to be older, are more likely to be male, have a mood disorder, partner relationship difficulties, and other personal problems. In all cases, such risk factors may act cumulatively to significantly increase the chances of suicide.

An important study published in the American Journal of Psychiatry confirmed that family, childhood, personality, psychiatric, and physical risk factors contribute to suicidal behavior in cocaine-dependent patients. Polydrug abuse—the parallel use of other substances—was a very significant factor. Forty-nine of the 84 patients who had attempted suicide had a history of alcohol dependence (58.3 percent, compared with 34.6 percent among the group that had never attempted suicide), and 16 of the patients had a history of opiate dependence (19 percent, against 9.2 percent in the group that had not tried suicide). In all, 39 percent of the cocaine-dependent patients had made suicide attempts. The American Foundation for Suicide Prevention found that in one year 20 percent of victims under the age of 60 used cocaine just before committing suicide.

The fact that alcohol and drug-related behavior can lead to incarceration exacerbates the problem: a U.S. national study of jail suicides (1981) and a further update in 1986 showed that 30 percent of arrests for nonviolent crimes were alcohol- or drug-related. It also revealed that 50 percent of suicides died within 24 hours of incarceration, highlighting the possible role of withdrawal symptoms in suicide attempts, with isolation as an aggravating factor.

Co-occurring disorders

Mental health can be an important factor, and research from the United States has shown important links between bipolar disorder, substance abuse, and suicide. Studies have also made a strong, specific link between a particular type of bipolar disorder, substance abuse, and an increased risk of suicide. Psychological and social stressors were seen as extremely important additional risk factors. A study undertaken by the International Consortium for Research on Bipolar Disorders showed that substance abuse increased the risk of suicide by a factor of 2.2 among a group of severely ill people diagnosed with bipolar or nonbipolar major affective disorder. Studies have also shown that antisocial personality disorder and drug abuse, which often occur in genetically predisposed males who become alcoholics early in life, is also linked to suicide attempts.

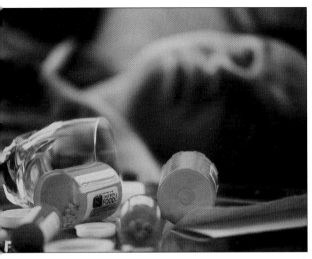

Prescription drugs are frequently used for intentional and accidental suicides, often combined with alcohol.

Alcohol and other substances

Most studies consistently support the view that substance abuse is strongly associated with a risk of suicide, particularly in young people. The substances most often implicated in suicide are alcohol, stimulants, and opiates. Recent studies disagree on whether there is a link, albeit weak, with extreme cannabis use. Use of cocaine, methamphetamine, and other stimulants is associated with high rates of completed suicide and suicide attempts. Opiates are also strongly linked with suicide—in an analysis of nine studies involving around 7,500 subjects, suicide among heroin addicts was found to be some 14 times more common than in nonusers. It is likely the statistics are clouded by other factors: drug abusers, particularly heroin addicts, often adopt high-risk behaviors that are likely to lead to death. Such fatalities may not be listed as suicides.

Alcohol may also play a part in suicides among nonalcoholics: heavy drinking during young adulthood was linked in a Swedish study of military conscripts to suicide in middle adulthood. Alcoholism increases the risk of death from many other sources, such as liver disease, accidents, and pancreatitis, but suicide remains the main cause of death. The 1980s San Diego Suicide Study, for instance, found that over 50 percent of 274 consecutive suicides had links to either alcoholism or substance abuse, although other contemporary studies into drug abuse–linked suicides showed that 5 percent were substance abusers, compared with up to 35 percent who were alcoholics.

This high level of coincidence is probably due to the strong link between alcoholism and major depression, which is 50 percent more common in alcoholics than nonalcoholics. Evidence from treatment programs suggests that alcoholics and drug abusers may drink to reduce feelings of depression, but that the initial state of well-being is replaced within hours by anxiety, depression, and increased suicidal thoughts. No cause-and-effect relationship between alcoholism or drug abuse and suicide has been established, but it may be that such substances reduce inhibitions and affect judgment to the extent that any suicidal thoughts are more likely to be acted on. Certainly, a report to Congress in the 1990s suggested that alcohol is linked to impulsive rather than preplanned suicide.

It is not only illicit drugs that have been linked with suicide: the antidepressant Paxil, known in Europe as Seroxat, was withdrawn as a prescription drug for young adults in European Union member countries after surveys linked its use among this particular group with a possible increased risk of suicide. The European regulatory agency covering such drugs, the European Agency for the Evaluation of Medicinal Products (EMEA), issued an advisory to member states suggesting that it be prescribed "with caution" to anyone under 30. The drug is a member of a group of drugs known as SSRIs, or selective serotonin reuptake inhibitors. The U.S. Food and Drug Administration has also warned that for this age-group, taking the drug could increase suicidal impulses.

Withdrawal from the use of steroids—taken by athletes and bodybuilders to enhance performance—has also been linked to an increased risk of suicide. Depression is known to be one of the major risks when ending use of these drugs. Researchers note feelings among former users of "paranoid jealousy, extreme irritability, delusions, and impaired judgment stemming from feelings of invincibility." Left untreated, depressive symptoms can last up to a year.

L. STEDMAN

SEE ALSO:
Depression • Mental Disorders • Overdose

Support Groups

After detoxification or treatment, many addicts face the difficult problem of maintaining abstinence from substance use. Support groups often provide a way for former addicts to help themselves stay away from drugs and alcohol.

Support groups for substance abuse have a long history. The first, Alcoholics Anonymous (AA), began in 1935 in Vermont as a self-help movement for alcoholics. In 1939 the basic text used today (entitled *Alcoholics Anonymous*) was published. This text contained the twelve steps to recovery and case histories easily recognized in today's AA support groups. Groups such as AA have helped millions of individuals attain and maintain their sobriety.

Many groups have modeled themselves after AA, including Narcotics Anonymous (NA), founded in 1947, and Gambler's Anonymous (GA), founded in 1957. There are also support groups for family members of someone who is chemically dependent (for example, Al-Anon, Alateen). These groups are found in most small and medium-sized towns, and there are often multiple groups in major cities. The Internet also houses these groups in the form of on-line chat rooms and twelve-step programs modeled after AA, and there exist multiple Web sites for group resources. The goal of all of these groups is for group members to help and support each other to achieve and maintain sobriety through abstinence.

Aims of support groups

Physicians, clinical psychologists, social workers, and counselors tend to agree that involvement in a support group is critical to successful recovery and maintenance of sobriety. Thus, support groups are typically recommended as aftercare and follow-up to detoxification or inpatient hospitalization and rehabilitation. Many individuals attend a substance abuse support group while they are in psychotherapy targeted at rehabilitation. Support group involvement thus serves as an important adjunct for more formal mental health treatment. Some individuals attend meetings every day or even twice a day, while others may opt for once a week or even once monthly.

Support groups are often anonymous, and members use only first names to protect their privacy. They are also open-ended, and group composition changes as members come and go. Typically, a support group will meet for 60 to 90 minutes, and the agenda for discussion is set by the group members. Attendance is often free of charge, especially for AA groups. Some recovering alcoholics and addicts attend support groups for years after detoxification in order to maintain their sobriety.

In general, support groups are different from groups emphasizing counseling or psychotherapy. They aim to support sustained changes over time rather than initiating personality changes, symptom reduction, or interpersonal change. For example, a substance abuser who is in a support group may seek the social support and experience with others to maintain sobriety. A therapy group often has the quite different goal of personality change or amelioration of symptoms such as depression, anxiety, bereavement issues, marital distress, or chronic illnesses. Further, many support groups are associated with self-help movements and are not led by licensed mental health professionals. The principle here is that the recovering person is the most suitable person to assist others in recovery, and that trained mental health professionals are less able to understand and cope with addictions if they have not been through the experience themselves.

Filling the gap

One major feature of a support group is that it is designed to help the person with the lifelong process of drug or alcohol rehabilitation. Thus, each support group may have a variety of goals that affect nearly every aspect of life. Goals may include, but are not limited to, education about chemical dependency and alternatives to using, recovery and relapse prevention, and school- or work-related issues.

Group members may discuss alternatives to using a substance, such as identification of other pleasurable activities that can be substituted for drug taking. This issue is important, since many addicts experience a sense of loss and a void when they stop using the substance. Substance abuse is time consuming, and when ceased, there is a need for replacement activities. For example, an alcoholic who spent three or four hours nightly in a bar will need to develop other activities to occupy those hours. Otherwise, the alcoholic may go to the bar out of habit or lack of other things to do, which increases the probability of relapse. This can be a difficult task, especially if such individuals have been abusing substances for a prolonged period of time. Group members can provide their personal insights about how to develop alternative activities while simultaneously acknowledging the difficulties in doing so.

Other goals for a substance abuse support group may include discussions about successes and difficulties associated with recovery, communication with other individuals experiencing similar problems, and decreasing feelings of isolation. It is believed that support group involvement helps the individual better understand his or her own addiction through listening to and empathizing with similar individuals. Further, feelings of shame and guilt associated with the substance abuse can be discussed with others who understand and can provide words of encouragement. Some discussions may be more confrontational than others, particularly when a group member seeks excuses for relapse or behaves in self-defeating ways. It is important for support group members to trust each other, despite varying opinions and confrontation, inasmuch as the overall goal remains that of helping each other stay sober.

Maintaining abstinence

As the group members form a bond with each other, an important function of a support group is to establish new relationships and have peer pressure to maintain sobriety. Many times the addiction results in estrangement from family and friends as the abuser comes to value the substance use over relationships, often damaging them irretrievably in the process. Further, it is common to avoid individuals formerly associated with the substance abuse, leaving a void in the person's circle of friends and acquaintances. Because of the estrangement and the need to avoid active users, there is a need to reconnect with nonusing individuals and form positive bonds. Group members can be honest with each other regarding their cravings for the substance and temptations to start using again, and this

honesty is typically experienced as emotionally positive. They can also reinforce each other's attempts to avoid the substance and help focus on positive aspects of sobriety. Providing help to another group member is gratifying and results in positive affect. Typically, the better a person begins to feel about himself or herself and others, the less the risk for relapse.

In terms of peer pressure to maintain sobriety, knowledge that other group members care about the individual's sobriety and would be disappointed if he or she used again can serve as an important deterrent to relapse. This knowledge can help the person avoid triggers or tempting situations. In fact, if the sobriety is recently gained, support group members may form a "buddy system" in which a member has a sponsor who can be telephoned when the individual is feeling tempted to use a substance. The sponsor may dissuade the member over the phone or meet in person to help him or her avoid obtaining the substance.

In terms of recovery and relapse, support group members may discuss issues and hazards associated with holidays or other triggers. They may discuss the need to avoid acquaintances and environments associated with the substance use or certain emotional states (such as sadness) that may increase their risk for relapse. However, a support group does not typically address the reduction of the sadness, but rather focuses on the link between this emotion, the risk of relapse, and how to avoid it. Along similar lines, the group may discuss how job stress contributes to relapse risk, as opposed to trying to ameliorate the source of the job stress.

Substance abuse support groups are likely to remain an important aspect of the recovery process in the future. Most professionals agree that they are effective in treatment and relapse prevention. Further, they have many positive advantages in addition to the major goal of abstinence. Support groups are readily available in almost any location and they welcome new members, making them generally a positive experience and a critical resource for recovering substance abusers.

J. L. JOHNSON

SEE ALSO:

Alcoholics Anonymous • Narcotics Anonymous • Step Programs • Treatment

Therapeutic Communities

Therapeutic communities are residential treatment programs that operate on a self-help basis. Peer influence, behavioral change, and acquisition of social skills are key components of this sometimes controversial method of treatment.

Therapeutic communities as drug treatment systems have long been a source of debate. Most often the term *therapeutic community*, or TC, has been associated with drug treatment programs that employ confrontation as a primary means of treatment. Another controversial aspect of TCs is their greater use of clients—referred to as community members—and recovering addicts as change agents, rather than professional personnel. Although the TC treatment process seems to lead to successful outcomes, the methodology is considered by many to be undefined. Despite the ongoing controversial issues and ambiguous features, TCs have been used as a credible means of substance abuse treatment since the mid-1960s, especially within criminal justice systems.

Therapeutic community defined

The first TC, Synanon, was founded in Santa Monica, California, in 1958 by Charles Dederich, a recovering alcoholic. As such, TCs continue to be fundamentally grounded in the Alcoholics Anonymous twelve-step, self-help philosophy. According to George DeLeon, director of the Center for Therapeutic Community Research, Synanon did not consider itself a treatment agency, but a "learning community." Correspondingly, present day TCs consider every experience or event within the TC environment as an opportunity to provide insight into the community member's attitude and behavior and as an opportunity for learning. In effect, the environment becomes the teacher, and the treatment setting or community a learning community.

Many researchers have sought to define what constitutes a TC. They generally agree that the basic model is an organized and structured community in which the staff and members interact to reinforce positive behaviors and social skills that will enable the recovering substance user to live a drug-free life when back in society. In particular, the community members' interactions within the specifically defined treatment system serve as the primary means of

treatment. In this regard, TCs differ in their approach to treatment from traditional drug and alcohol treatment programs. While traditional programs use professional personnel as teachers or catalysts for facilitating insight and change in the client, the TC uses the community and the treatment personnel—who often include recovering substance users—collectively as change agents. The community and the all-encompassing experiences within the TC environment become the teacher. Although TCs use professional personnel as well, all staff members are regarded as sources for help within the therapeutic environment.

Use of a therapeutic community

Most individuals admitted to TCs have extensive histories of substance abuse. Research conducted by the National Institute on Drug Abuse (NIDA) indicates that these individuals frequently have other severe problems, including multiple drug addictions, involvement with the criminal justice system, lack of positive support, mental health problems, antisocial disorders, and so on. In brief, these individuals' overall social and personal responsibilities have been hindered by their substance abuse. For them, recovery involves rehabilitation or relearning appropriate social skills. Some TC participants or community members may have never acquired an appropriate level of social functioning. Their participation in a TC may be their first experience with living in a disciplined or organized environment of any kind. For these individuals, the recovery process entails habilitation or learning acceptable social skills for the very first time.

One NIDA research study conducted between 1991 and 1993 showed that of the 2,315 admissions to residential TC programs, 80 percent met the diagnostic criteria outlined in the American Psychiatric Association's *Diagnostic and Statistical Manual of Mental Disorders* for cocaine dependence, while 45 percent met the diagnostic criteria for alcohol dependence. The NIDA study also reported that two-thirds of the admissions had involvement with the criminal justice system and that approximately one-third had been referred from the criminal justice system for treatment. Other statistics from this report indicate that one-third were women, approximately one-half were African American, and 60 percent had prior substance abuse treatment.

Therapeutic communities are used in numerous settings and for a diverse range of treatment populations. Overall, the TC approach can be modified to correspond with the targeted treatment population, for example, dual diagnosed populations, women, women and their children, juveniles, and men. TCs are also used in a host of settings, including detention centers, jails, prisons, and halfway houses. TCs can be structured as long term, usually consisting of a 12- to 24-month residential stay, and short-term or modified programs, usually consisting of a 3- to 6-month residential stay that may or may not include a continuum of care arrangement.

Key concepts

The primary concepts concerning TCs are based on self-help, reciprocal and mutual help, peer influence, community as method, and shared responsibility with respect to maintaining a therapeutic environment. Researchers and practitioners insist that the TC environment be conducive for change and, as such, must be physically and psychologically safe for its participants.

Prison-based TCs in particular need to remain isolated from the general population to accomplish this task. Positive social principles, such as honesty, industriousness, and a genuine commitment to the welfare of others, are strongly promoted and encouraged. Additional essential principles concerning the development and maintenance of a therapeutic environment require the use of appropriate confrontation techniques, behavioral limits, role modeling, learning through crisis, consistency, internalization of healthy values, open communication, social learning through social interaction, and consistent graduated sanctions, to name a few. The key concepts, although somewhat varied among substance abuse researchers and clinical practitioners, remain firm in that the treatment structure must function as a peer-driven system and that the community itself serve as teacher and primary change agent.

Life in a therapeutic community instills discipline and social skills, such as doing chores and attending group therapy sessions, as part of a structured day.

Programmatic functions

It is a well-established fact that there are a number of programs that promote themselves as TCs and yet fail to employ the most basic TC components and programmatic elements. In an attempt to be identified as a TC, many programs have adopted the descriptions "third generation" and "modified" TCs. All too often, the deficient outcomes and internal problems related to these treatment structures are passed on as another TC failure. Worse yet, the indiscriminate implementation of such structures contributes to the existing misunderstandings regarding TCs.

The programmatic components used within TC structures (*see* box p. 310) are systematically designed to bring about positive changes for treatment participants. Therefore, it is essential that management and clinical personnel understand the mechanisms associated with each component and their contribution to the environment and to individual community members as well. A lack of understanding of the basic theory of each activity promotes misuse of therapeutic concepts, perpetuates haphazard strategies, and often fails to provide an opportunity for individual growth. Knowledge

ELEMENTS OF A TC

In an attempt to clarify the components of a therapeutic community (TC), NIDA has adopted George DeLeon's "basic TC model," which identifies 14 components usually found in a typical TC. The following components are adaptable to various treatment settings:

- community separateness
- community environment
- community activities
- staff roles and functions
- peers as role models
- structured days
- work as therapy and education
- phase format
- TC concepts
- peer encounter groups
- awareness training
- emotional growth training
- planned duration of treatment
- continuity of care.

of TC structure, culture, philosophy, essential components, and associated mechanisms is therefore important for staff members.

Advantages and disadvantages

One of the advantages of criminal justice–managed TCs is the ability to support coerced treatment. Numerous studies have suggested that coerced clients do as well as voluntary clients. Steve Martin and James Inciardi of the University of Delaware Center for Drug and Alcohol Studies (CDAS) report that the one consistent finding among substance abuse researchers is that the longer a client stays in treatment, the better the outcome in terms of reductions in drug use and criminality.

Another advantage of operating TCs within correctional facilities is that there is also a drop in incidents concerning violence, drug use, and overall rule violations. The 2002 Sentencing Trends and Correctional Treatment in Delaware annual report indicated that the costs associated with operating

TCs were offset by reductions in disciplinary actions, reductions in security and correctional counselor staffing, and lowered maintenance costs. The report stated that there was an annual cost reduction of approximately $400,000.

The major disadvantage of TCs seems to be the lack of understanding regarding the methodology itself. While there is a general understanding as to the basic components and therapeutic elements, the process itself remains somewhat ambiguous. Developing a suitable framework for future TCs requires further study and a proper evaluation of existing TC theory and practice. Lack of expertise, inexperienced personnel, inability to select participants, lack of mental health professionals, staff burnout, and pressure to adhere to state licensure standards are other potential disadvantages to the efficient functioning of TCs.

Program outcomes

TCs have been evaluated from several different methods of research. Substance abuse research into drug abstinence is usually based on self-report or an examination of probation or parole records. However, the CDAS research projects use self-report and urine samples to determine project participants' abstinence. Ongoing studies show that the reductions in relapse and recidivism for TC graduates continue for a period of five years after release from prison.

A Delaware Department of Correction (DOC) comparison project shows that participants in the prison-based and halfway house continuum of care arrangement did better than the participants in the DOC-managed non-TC treatment program or the solely prison-based program regarding percent arrested for any felony within a 24-month period.

All in all, extensive research in North America, Norway, the United Kingdom, and a host of other countries strongly suggests that TC participants experience positive outcomes overall regarding drug and alcohol use, depression, employment retention, criminal behavior, rearrest, and recidivism.

R. A. BEARD

SEE ALSO:
Continuum of Care • Halfway Houses • Prison Drug Use and Treatment • Rehabilitation • Treatment

Tolerance

When a drug is taken for the first time, it can upset the mechanisms that the body uses to maintain its functional equilibrium. Over time, the body gradually adapts to the drug's presence. This process is called tolerance.

Tolerance can be defined as a decreasing responsiveness to a drug over time. In other words, a person who develops tolerance to a drug requires higher doses of a drug to achieve the same effect. For example, a person prescribed the opiate drug morphine for pain relief must slowly increase the dosage over time in order to maintain the pain relief. Tolerance can happen during an initial exposure to a drug, but more generally it is considered to happen over multiple drug doses. Like many phenomena involving the brain, the process and function of tolerance are not well understood. However, one general explanation of tolerance is that a drug alters the preset levels, or homeostatic "set points" of a variety of systems in the body. The function of these homeostatic set points is to keep the various systems of the body running at an optimal level. If a drug alters a body system in one direction, the body alters the system in the opposite direction in response, in an attempt to maintain the homeostatic set point. These actions of the body to oppose the effect of the drug lead to tolerance to the drug, requiring that more of the drug would have to be taken to overcome the effects on the body and cause the same net effect. The function of tolerance is to maintain biological homeostatic set points in order to keep the body running at optimal levels.

An analogy of tolerance and withdrawal involves being in love. In terms of mood, a person cannot always be manic or depressed but instead lives his or her life in a normal, "average" mood. The body is designed to achieve this balance so it can function normally. However, when someone begins a new relationship and falls in love with another person, he or she feels a euphoria, or giddiness—the presence of the other person produces a "high." Since that other person pushes one's mood out of the normal homeostatic set point, the body responds by acting on its physiological systems to oppose the effect of that other person, pushing the mood down to a normal level. Indeed, over time, that initial excitement fades until one feels more normal in the relationship and in the presence of that other person. This effect on mood is akin to drug tolerance. The body develops a tolerance to the euphoric effect of the other person in an attempt to maintain a functional, homeostatic set point. Now imagine what happens if the influence of the other person is suddenly taken away, for instance in a breakup of the relationship. The balancing, negative influence of the body's actions is unopposed by the positive effect of the other person, causing the overall mood to go in the other direction, and one feels sad or depressed. This is an example of withdrawal. The presence of the other person is taken away and one feels negative effects from having the actions of the relationship on the body taken away. Over time, however, the negative effect of the body on itself fades away in order to maintain the homeostatic set point and return the mood to its normal state of being.

Developing tolerance

Some types of tolerance take place rapidly within the first or first few exposures to the drug. This type of tolerance is called acute, or initial, tolerance. Acute tolerance is most often caused by the depletion of a substance in the body that is required to cause a drug effect. It does not even need to be a direct effect of the drug at its receptor, but an indirect effect, which then causes acute tolerance. For example, several drugs cause effects not by direct interaction with receptors in the body but instead by acting at other cellular sites to release substances that are stored in the body. These substances are inactive in their stored form, but once released by certain drugs they can activate their own receptors, causing a cascade of effects resulting in actions attributed to the drug. If these drugs are taken frequently enough to cause these substances in cells to be released faster than they can be replenished by the body, then they will be depleted. As the stored quantity of the physiological substances is reduced, the net effect caused by a certain dose of the drug is also reduced, resulting in acute tolerance. An example of acute

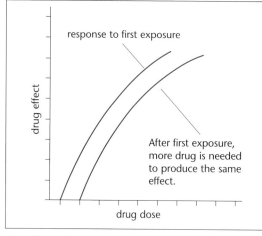

response to first exposure

drug effect

After first exposure, more drug is needed to produce the same effect.

drug dose

The effect of increasing tolerance requires larger doses to be administered to gain the same effect.

tolerance is the effect of morphine on flushing of the face, neck, and upper throat. Morphine causes the release of histamine, which is stored in various cells of the body, which results in this flushing. If small doses of morphine are given over long periods of time, this effect never diminishes. However, if large doses of morphine are given over a short time, this flushing effect rapidly diminishes because the stored histamine is depleted.

In contrast to acute or initial tolerance, a more slowly developing tolerance called acquired tolerance usually develops only over the course of many exposures to a drug. Acquired tolerance to a drug can take place in two different ways: either the concentration of the drug changes, or a decreased reactivity at a site of action in the body (usually through a decreased number of drug receptors) occurs. The first case of tolerance is called drug disposition tolerance, while the second is called cellular, or pharmacodynamic, tolerance. In drug disposition tolerance, a drug decreases its own absorption or rate of transfer across a barrier. For example, ingesting alcohol (ethanol) or barbiturates increases the activity of metabolic enzymes that degrade those drugs. However, disposition tolerance is minor compared with cellular tolerance (a decreased response of receptors). Cellular tolerance accounts for most of the tolerance seen for drugs that act on the brain to produce changes in mood and behavior. The manner in which cellular tolerance

takes place is not very well understood; however, it generally appears that there is some change or decrease in the activity of target cells in the brain that render them less sensitive to those drugs.

A good example of cellular tolerance to a drug is shown by ethanol. Even though ethanol increases the activity of enzymes that metabolize ethanol, this drug disposition tolerance is small compared with cellular tolerance induced by ethanol. This tolerance can be illustrated by an experiment in which a large amount of ethanol is given to two separate groups of rats. One group has become tolerant to ethanol through daily injections, while the other group has never been given ethanol before. The dose of ethanol is so large that both groups of rats rapidly become unconscious. However, the rats who have become tolerant to ethanol quickly wake up. The other group stays asleep for a much longer period of time, even though they have similar levels of ethanol in their bodies. These rats do not wake up until the level of ethanol in their bodies is much lower than that of the other group when they awoke. In the case of ethanol, it appears that cellular tolerance is caused by a reduction in the number of cellular targets to ethanol, particularly a receptor called the GABA receptor.

It appears that the development of tolerance may occur by several different mechanisms, and sometimes more than one form of tolerance may take place at the same time. As mentioned above, tolerance to ethanol can occur by both drug disposition tolerance (by altering the activity of metabolizing enzymes) and also by cellular tolerance (by changing the reactivity of brain cells). The same situation is true for morphine. Additionally, the amount of tolerance that takes place also varies from drug to drug. People can become so tolerant to morphine that a tolerant person can take a dose of morphine that is several times higher than the lethal dose for a nontolerant person. By contrast, although a person who has developed tolerance to ethanol will show fewer impairing effects from a moderate dose of ethanol than a nontolerant person, both individuals will be impaired almost equally by high, near-lethal doses of ethanol.

Another interesting point about tolerance is the phenomenon of cross-tolerance. If tolerance develops to a particular drug, that person will also have some tolerance to other similar drugs belonging to the same class, even though he or she has never been exposed to those other drugs. For example, a person who develops tolerance to morphine will also be tolerant to heroin, methadone, and other narcotics, but not to caffeine, alcohol, or other drugs in different classes. The cross-tolerance will disappear when administration of the drug that caused the cross-tolerance is stopped.

Relationship between tolerance and dependence

Drug dependence is a condition in which the drug user has a compelling desire to continue taking a drug to either experience its effects or to avoid the discomfort of the drug's absence. Drug dependence has two distinct independent components: physical and psychological dependence. Physical dependence refers to an altered or adaptive physiological state of the body in response to the long-term exposure to a drug. The effects of becoming physically dependent on a drug only become clear when the drug is abruptly discontinued or when an antagonist of the drug is given (an antagonist will block the actions of the drug on the body). Either one of these actions will result in a withdrawal syndrome, which is characterized by intense negative effects on the body. The severity of the withdrawal syndrome depends on the drug and the amount of dependence that has been induced. For example, withdrawal from barbiturates, narcotics such as morphine, and alcohol is very severe. In fact, withdrawal from alcohol and barbiturates can be lethal. These effects of withdrawal are so severe that a person who is dependent on these drugs will keep taking these drugs to avoid the withdrawal effects—a striking example of physical dependence. However, no physical dependence occurs with LSD, and no or only very slight physical dependence with marijuana; hence these drugs cause no withdrawal syndrome.

In contrast to physical dependence, all of the drugs of abuse, including LSD and marijuana, can cause mild to strong psychological dependence. Psychological dependence is characterized by an emotional or mental urge to keep taking a drug because the user feels the drug is necessary to maintain a sense of optimal well-being. The amount of psychological dependence depends on the personality of the user and the specific drug. This is a complex interaction and can lead to a compulsion to keep taking the drug. This compulsion is a big problem in drug abuse because it means the person has lost control over the drug, and the drug has taken control over the person. Some drugs such as marijuana cause no physical dependence, so psychological dependence is the only dependence factor involved in their abuse.

Many drugs that can cause dependence also cause tolerance, although these phenomena are different and may occur independently of each other. For example, tolerance occurs to nitrates such as nitroglycerin, which is taken for heart problems, but no dependence occurs with this drug. However, psychological dependence on drugs may occur even without any tolerance. In addition, some drugs may induce tolerance and psychological dependence without any physical dependence, as is the case for the hallucinogen LSD. However, drugs that cause physical dependence almost always induce some tolerance.

Environmental cues

An interesting facet of tolerance involves the effect of environmental cues on tolerance. Indeed, the setting in which the drug is taken has a large effect on the degree of tolerance achieved. If a drug capable of inducing tolerance is routinely taken in a specific setting, then exposure to that setting alone will cause a response in the body in the opposite direction as that of the drug. This effect of environmental cues on the body's response can be seen by comparing the effect of a drug in its usual setting against a new setting in which the drug is not normally taken. For example, a person in a retirement home is always given morphine for pain relief in a certain treatment room. For a change, one day that person is taken outside and given the same routine dose of morphine. In the absence of the environmental cues contained in the treatment room to oppose the effects of morphine, it is entirely possible that person could overdose from the treatment simply because of the unfamiliar environmental setting.

J. JAWORSKI

SEE ALSO:
Causes of Addiction, Biological • Craving • Dependence • Sensitization • Withdrawal

313

Toxicity

The majority of drugs, whether therapeutic or illicit, have a threshold point at which they become poisonous, or toxic, to the body. Toxic effects may manifest themselves as adverse reactions and, in the most severe cases, death.

The single biggest problem in developing therapeutic drugs is the occurrence of side effects, or adverse drug responses that are the undesirable manifestation of a degree of drug toxicity. When the toxicity cannot be removed by chemical modification of the drug, variation of the dose, or method of administration, and it clearly outweighs the therapeutic benefit of the drug, the development project must be abandoned. The economic loss to the drug developer can be very heavy, and the unpredictability of the appearance of drug toxicity, even late in the clinical development process, constitutes a major challenge to the pharmaceutical industry.

The evaluation of drug toxicity

After more than a century of experience with drug toxicity problems, the pharmaceutical industry and its regulators follow a well-established protocol to detect and evaluate the problem. If a drug is to be licensed for sale in the world's largest market, the

Extensive testing in animals and humans is required before any new drug can be prescribed. This testing helps eliminate any potential health risks and minimize side effects in patients.

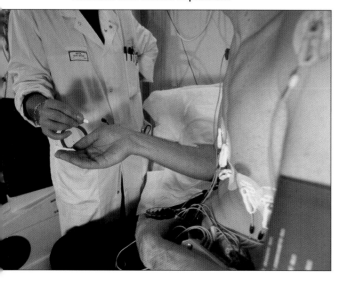

United States, a developer must submit a detailed body of pharmacologic and toxicologic information derived from preclinical studies in animals to the U.S. Food and Drug Administration (FDA). Equivalent bodies exist in Europe and Japan.

The developer or sponsor's objective is to obtain approval for investigational new drug (IND) studies in humans. The FDA must be satisfied that the levels of acute, subchronic, and chronic toxicity of the drug in experimental animals are such as to indicate that there is an acceptable, that is, very low, level of risk in allowing testing of the new drug in human beings. Among the assumptions underlying this process are that the effects of different drug doses in animal models will be generally similar to those in humans and that the high-dose administration experiments in animals will permit detection of potentially rare toxicity events in humans.

Detection of toxicity in animal models

The preclinical trial data submitted with the IND application must include studies on acute toxicity that determine the actual lethal drug dose. This is measured as the LD_{50}—the dose required to kill 50 percent of the experimental laboratory animals—and the LD_{90}—the drug dose that will kill 90 percent of the animals. These data must be obtained using at least three animal species, including one nonrodent species. Acute toxicity must be determined using at least two routes of drug administration, normally oral and intravenous or intramuscular injection.

Subchronic toxic effects of an investigational drug are measured using three drug doses, ranging from the expected normal therapeutic dose to levels high enough to produce toxicity. The duration of these tests is normally 90 days, with daily drug administration, if possible, via the route that will be used in any human study. At least two animal species must be used; laboratory testing of blood and urine to monitor drug and drug metabolite levels as well as physical examination of the animals are carried on continuously. After the end of the study, the animals are sacrificed and a full pathological examination of all animals is carried out to ascertain whether organs show signs of toxicity-induced damage.

Chronic toxicology testing in animals involves administering the new drug for the entire lifetime of the species. This can involve testing for up to two years in the case of laboratory rats and mice and longer for nonrodents such as rabbits. Three dose levels are used, ranging from nontoxic low doses to high doses that are expected to show some toxicity. Physical and laboratory tests on the animals are carried out continuously, and particular attention is paid to microscopic examination of tissue sections from periodically sacrificed animals. This examination is intended to detect potential tissue damage and induction of cancers. The effects of chronic drug administration on the reproductive organs and cycles of rats and rabbits are also studied.

Testing in cell cultures and nonanimal systems

So-called in vitro (Latin, meaning "in glass") toxicity studies can provide faster and cheaper data on toxicity and do not involve animal testing (in vivo studies). However, in vitro toxicity studies are not accepted as substitutes for animal testing, only as supplemental data. A very widely used test is the Ames bioassay for testing the capacity of a drug to cause mutations in bacteria. Bacterial mutagens are often, but not always, human carcinogens. Research has also exploited the large-scale study of proteins, or proteomics, particularly when the search for possible drug toxicity has moved into the human clinical testing stage and biological markers, such as urine proteins, can be compared between subjects.

Human clinical trials

If the animal testing data indicate that a new drug is sufficiently safe, then approval may be granted to initiate Phase I of the human clinical testing process. The clinical trial protocol detailing the conditions and personnel involved in the study must be approved by both a hospital Institutional Review Board (IRB) and by the FDA, which will then issue an IND exemption permit.

Phase I studies are primarily intended to test the safety of the drug and establish at what level of dose signs of toxicity first appear in humans. This involves giving the new drug to between 20 and 80 healthy male volunteers aged between 18 and 45. These volunteers must give their informed consent to the study protocol before they can participate in a clinical trial. The first step in the trial is administration of a single dose of the drug, followed by monitoring of all recipients for any sign of adverse reactions or toxic side effects. If no adverse reactions occur, the dose of the drug will be progressively increased to a predetermined level, or until evidence of toxicity is found. During this process the patient's absorption, metabolism, and urinary secretion of the drug will be closely monitored.

If satisfactory initial evidence that the new drug is safe is obtained, a Phase II clinical trial protocol will be submitted to the IRB, and a larger group of trial volunteers will be recruited. The objective of the Phase II clinical trial is to obtain the first set of data on the effectiveness of the drug in treating or preventing a specific disease or disorder, in addition to expanding the data set available on possible toxic side effects of the drug. Patient volunteers should, if possible, have no health problems other than the condition being treated. The study will randomize the treatment group, "blinding" the medical personnel administering the drugs from the knowledge of which patient is receiving the new drug and which patient is receiving the older, or prototype drug. If no prototype drug exists, a harmless, unrelated substance may be given as a placebo.

Phase II trials are the most crucial test of a new drug because they will verify if it is useful in treating its target disease or disorder, determine the best treatment dose (the optimal dose-response range) and assay the effects of long-term administration of the drug to affected and thus, in some degree, unhealthy human beings. The data from the Phase II trial will determine whether a new drug seems worth the expense and effort of proceeding to new and yet more extensive testing in larger human trial groups. Successful Phase I and II trials indicating that a drug is useful and without unacceptable toxicity will usually lead to Phase III expanded trials that will continue until the drug is licensed for sale. Phase III trials will involve thousands of patients and are intended to obtain further evidence that the drug is safe and effective. When the sponsor feels that sufficient trial data has been collected, a full New Drug Application will be filed with the FDA.

Most new drugs will not pass this rigorous testing process, and this is no doubt as it should be. However, unexpected clinical utility has also been discovered during clinical testing. Most famously, Sildenafil was originally intended to be a therapy for angina, but its effectiveness for treating erectile dysfunction was noted in clinical trials. This led to its ultimate, profitable reemergence as Viagra.

Drug toxicity management in clinical practice

It is frequently the case that a drug has known problems of toxicity, yet it remains the most effective treatment available for a serious condition. An example of this is the widely used immuno-suppressive drug cyclosporin A, employed to prevent rejection of skin grafts and organ transplants. Cyclosporin A is now known to cause kidney toxicity in nearly 40 percent of those treated. This toxicity is associated with increased secretion of calcium, resulting in calcification of kidney tubules that can lead to fatal kidney failure. Yet we do not have a better immunosuppressant than cyclosporin A, and many patients, particularly children with leukemia, will die without a bone marrow graft. Thus toxicity must be closely monitored and managed as well as possible by dose modulation, while research continues to produce safer drugs or, alternatively, drugs that can alleviate the toxicity of other essential but problematic drugs.

Unexpected toxicity problems

Many common adverse events derived from toxic drug side effects cannot be detected in animal models. These include depression, headaches, gastro-intestinal problems such as heartburn, and hearing problems such as tinnitus (ringing). Often such problems may be quite real, but occur only in a very small proportion of the human population. The preclinical and clinical testing process is relatively insensitive and is unlikely to detect adverse effects that occur in less than 1 in 1,000 of those who receive the drug. Thus there is a Phase IV clinical testing process, conducted after a new drug is approved and starts to become generally used. Such studies are termed ongoing studies in large populations.

Even after a drug has been on the market for some time, toxicity problems in a relatively small

ABUSE LIABILITY

The side effects produced by therapeutic drugs, while considered unwanted by drug developers, are often the reason that the drug is deliberately used for recreational purposes. For example, the euphoria produced by opiate painkillers is rarely felt by those experiencing physical pain but is immediately triggered by those using them for nonmedical purposes. New drugs that have an effect on the central nervous system undergo further tests to determine whether they have any potential or liability for abuse. Initial tests on animals are not always indicative, as some animals may not develop dependence toward a particular drug. Human trials are therefore necessary.

There are advantages to testing on humans: the subjective effects of many drugs are not always apparent from assessments of animal behavior. Humans can tell researchers what they are feeling or whether there is an unexpected reaction. Most of the volunteers used for these studies are experienced drug users who can assess whether the new drug has a greater or lesser potential for abuse than the one they know. Light social drinkers are also recruited to test combinations of alcohol with medications such as sleeping tablets or diet pills.

population may be severe enough to cause the withdrawal of a drug from sale. An example that came to light in 2004 was the discovery of an increased risk of heart attack and stroke events in those using Vioxx, an arthritis pain reliever. Despite the fact that the drug had been sold since 1999 and was used by more than two million people, this low-incidence toxicity effect was sufficiently serious to cause its manufacturer, Merck, to withdraw the product from the market.

D. E. ARNOT

SEE ALSO:

Dosage • Liver Diseases • Lung Diseases • Pharmacology • Research, Medical

Trauma and Addiction

Trauma and addiction are closely linked; trauma may be the result of addiction, or addiction may follow severe trauma. Although recovery can take a long time, with perserverance and support, it is possible.

In its simplest meaning, trauma is any event that causes distress and has lasting effects upon a person. There are two broad categories of traumatic events: mental trauma and physical trauma.

Mental trauma refers to the damage that can result from a frightening or emotionally trying situation, such as sexual abuse or the death of a loved one. Victims of mental trauma often experience severe psychological, emotional, and social problems. Physical trauma is any serious injury or shock to the body, sustained through accident or violence. Physical trauma can be life threatening and is a major cause of death among teens and young adults.

Trauma has a complicated relationship with addiction. In fact, doctors often cite trauma as both a cause and result of substance abuse and other addictions. For example, a person who undergoes an emotionally traumatic event might be more likely to develop an addictive disorder than someone who does not experience such trauma. In such a case, trauma is a precipitating factor in the development of addiction. Victims of mental trauma sometimes turn to substance abuse, compulsive gambling, or other behavioral addictions, such as compulsive sex or eating, to help cope with feelings of anger or despair. In other cases, trauma is the result of substance abuse. Because substance users can suffer from a lack of judgment, a person with a substance abuse disorder, such as heroin addiction, is more likely to sustain a serious physical traumatic injury than someone who does not use drugs. As a result, the majority of all traumatic injuries treated in emergency rooms involves alcohol or drugs.

Mental trauma and addiction

While the most effective and highly recommended treatment for mental trauma is often counseling under the guidance of a certified professional, such as a psychologist, victims of mental trauma sometimes try to find ways to escape the reality of their situation. One of the ways that victims of mental trauma attempt to cope with their feelings of hopelessness and despair is to turn to alcohol and drugs. While mood-altering substances can provide a temporary diversion to emotional stress, substance abuse can compound psychological problems. For example, suppression of mental trauma through alcohol or drug use interferes with a person's ability to progressively work through his or her problems. Because they are unable to adequately cope with their trauma while struggling with addiction, mental trauma victims are more vulnerable to addiction relapse upon recovery.

Post-traumatic stress disorder

Rates of addiction in individuals who have suffered mental trauma are notably higher than in the general population. This is especially true among people who suffer from post-traumatic stress disorder, or PTSD. The U.S.–based National Center for Post-Traumatic Stress Disorder defines PTSD as a psychiatric condition that can occur in people who experience severe mental trauma through life-threatening events such as military combat, natural disasters, terrorism, severe accidents, or personal violence, such as rape. People who suffer from PTSD often have trouble coping with their trauma and vividly relive their experiences through nightmares and flashbacks. PTSD can be a debilitating condition, affecting many aspects of a victim's daily life. Scientific studies have shown that individuals with PTSD are more likely to have multiple psychiatric disorders and more severe problems with addiction, increased hospital time, and higher potential for relapse. One possible explanation for the high rate of addiction among the PTSD-diagnosed population is the negative emotional states that are characteristic of PTSD. After severe trauma, individuals with PTSD can experience panic attacks and episodes of emotional distress. Thus, individuals with PTSD often self-medicate with alcohol and drugs to alleviate such feelings, and may develop substance use disorders. These negative emotions have also been shown to increase alcohol and drug cravings in

The majority of accidents that cause traumatic injuries involve alcohol or drug use.

PTSD-diagnosed individuals with a history of substance use. Victims of mental trauma are not only vulnerable to substance-based addiction but also to a variety of behavioral addictions. Because many victims experience mental trauma at a young age, behavioral and emotional development can be interrupted, and emotional needs can be left unmet. In such cases, a person who develops a behavioral addiction might not be suppressing angry feelings, but instead might be trying to meet his or her needs in a way that is familiar. For example, sexual abuse can cause shame and confusion in children, which can then lead to unhealthy sexual development during adolescence. A person in this situation might experience many failed relationships and low self-esteem and ultimately might develop a sex addiction. Because the traumatic event suppresses his or her ability to support healthy and loving relationships,

such a person then attempts to meet healthy needs in an unhealthy manner. Addiction can result when a mentally traumatic event robs a person of the skills to maintain a healthy lifestyle.

Physical trauma and addiction

The main risk factor for physical trauma is impairment by drugs and alcohol. Substance abusers experience increased risk for traumatic injury, including auto accidents, falls, burns, and drowning. Substance users are also at a greater risk of sustaining violent injuries, such as stabbings and gunshot wounds, due to accidents and drug-related violence. Also, people who experience trauma while under the influence of substances are often unable or unwilling to cooperate with emergency personnel. This can make injury diagnosis and treatment difficult for emergency physicians and trauma surgeons.

Scientific research has shown that people who continue to use alcohol and drugs after surviving physical trauma are more likely to experience additional traumatic injuries. At the same time, the reality of sustaining a traumatic injury can frighten a patient into recognizing the severity of the situation, and thus provide the motivation to seek treatment. For this reason, emergency and trauma physicians are in a unique position to intervene in the cycle of addiction and trauma. A patient who is admitted to a hospital with a traumatic injury often experiences a window of opportunity when he or she is more likely to talk and learn about addictive behaviors. At this time, physicians and hospital staff can inform patients about the available treatment options and can arrange for patients to enroll in counseling or treatment programs. If a physician recognizes symptoms of substance abuse in a patient, discussing and encouraging treatment could prevent the patient from experiencing future injuries.

There are barriers, however, that can prevent physical trauma victims from receiving treatment for substance abuse problems. For example, many emergency doctors and trauma surgeons focus solely on repairing injuries and do not believe that it is their responsibility to screen trauma patients for alcohol or drug use. Such doctors might take alcohol or drug intoxication into consideration in assessing the proper course of treatment for the patient's traumatic injury but would not use this information to identify patients with addiction problems. In addition, in the United States, the Uniform Accident and Sickness Policy Provision Law (UPPL) allows health insurance companies to deny coverage for any injury sustained while the victim was under the influence of alcohol or drugs. Any patient who receives a traumatic injury could be held responsible for large medical bills if tests prove he or she had alcohol or drugs in the bloodstream at the time of the accident. A patient faced with such a situation often cannot pay, thus creating a liability for the hospital. To avoid this situation, many trauma doctors do not screen their patients for drugs or alcohol, and so guarantee that insurance companies will cover costs. In this way, many patients who would benefit from alcohol or drug intervention fail to receive treatment and often return to the emergency room with additional potentially preventable traumatic injuries.

Treatment and recovery

Left untreated, addiction, whether substance-based or behavioral, can destroy the health and relationships of victims and their families. Treatment allows individuals to recover from addiction and return to a healthy lifestyle. While there are many steps involved in recovery, one factor is essential for the successful treatment of addictive disorders: the individual must be ready and willing to recover. The first step of admitting and accepting his or her problem is often the most difficult stage of recovery for a person struggling with addiction. For a victim of mental trauma struggling with addiction, recovery is often contingent upon psychotherapy for the underlying psychological problems associated with the traumatic event. However, because such therapy can be long and emotionally painful, simultaneous recovery from substance abuse can seem impossible. Similarly, a person who sustains repeated traumatic injuries attributable to substance abuse might not be ready to accept change. Repeated visits to the emergency room with addiction-related trauma could indicate severe substance dependence and resistance to advice and education offered by doctors and addiction specialists. Such a person might be at risk for a variety of other comorbid, or simultaneous, psychological problems, such as depression, that could also complicate recovery.

Treatment options

Once ready to recover, there are several treatment options for trauma victims struggling with addiction. Because addictions can plague individuals for decades, identification of an individual's problems and professional treatment are the options that offer the most long-term hope. Mental health professionals, such as psychologists, can help individuals manage emotional problems and prepare them for a program of recovery from addiction. Addiction recovery programs are diverse and can consist of inpatient care at hospitals or regulated care facilities, one-on-one outpatient therapy with a specialist or psychologist, or self-help sessions through organizations such as Alcoholics Anonymous (AA) or Narcotics Anonymous. The therapy selected depends on a patient's preferences. Inpatient therapy may focus on a patient's medical and biological needs, such as chemical detoxification or pharmacological treatment with drugs to reduce cravings. These programs can be demanding and require patients to leave their families for extended periods. Conversely, self-help programs require a patient to share feelings with large groups—a concept that makes some people uncomfortable.

Trauma victims can work within these options, and psychologists might use specialized diagnostic instruments to create customized treatment strategies for patients with both mental disorders and substance abuse disorders. There are support groups, such as Dual Recovery Anonymous (DRA), for people with both a chemical dependency and an emotional or psychiatric illness, which can help victims cope with addiction and mental health problems by sharing their feelings with others in a similar situation. Or, patients can explore their feelings in family therapy groups. Patients might have to explore several options before deciding on the path to recovery. Successful recovery depends on the realization that it requires patience, dedication, and perseverance. No treatment strategy is guaranteed to work for every patient, but with support, it is possible to break free from the cycle of trauma and addiction.

A. N. DONATO

SEE ALSO:
Clinics • Driving While Impaired • Medical Care • Recovery • Treatment

Treatment

Treating an addiction is not a straightforward process. The circumstances and problems surrounding the addiction are unique to the person and must be assessed for each individual. With the right program, addiction can be overcome.

Substance use disorders (SUDs) are experienced by more than 16 percent of adults in the United States. SUDs include abuse or dependence on alcohol, cannabis, cocaine and other stimulants, opiates, sedative-hypnotics, hallucinogens, inhalants, or the "club" drugs. Alcohol abuse and dependence are the most common of the SUDs. Many people with these disorders use multiple substances.

SUDs are associated with many problems for the affected individual. For example, more than 30 diseases are associated with alcohol problems. Intravenous drug use is associated with higher rates of HIV infections and transmission. SUDs cause or worsen numerous medical, psychological, family, social, legal, occupational, academic, economic, and spiritual problems. An untreated SUD can end in death or other negative consequences, such as losing a job or family, incarceration, or a severe medical or psychiatric disorder.

Substance use disorders also have many negative effects on the family and its members, including children. Family breakups and divorce are higher in families in which a parent has an SUD. Children who have one or both parents with an SUD are at increased risk for substance abuse, psychiatric disorders (anxiety, depression, or combined disorders), behavioral problems (for example, aggression or oppositional behaviors), and academic problems. These disorders cost society hundreds of billions of dollars each year as a result of lost productivity at work and the costs of medical, criminal justice, social and treatment services.

Treatment helps individuals restore their health and overcome or reduce other problems. Treatment also helps families overcome the emotional burden caused by SUDs.

Obtaining treatment
Most people with SUDs never receive treatment. While some are able to stop using on their own or with the help of mutual support groups such as Alcoholics Anonymous (AA) or Narcotics Anonymous (NA), others require professional treatment to help them stop using substances and make changes in themselves and their lifestyle.

The person with an SUD may enter treatment voluntarily or involuntarily as a result of:

- Realizing that substance use is a problem and help is needed.
- Taking the advice of a religious, health care or social service professional, attorney, teacher, coach, employee assistance counselor, boss, colleague, friend, loved one, or other concerned person. This advice may be actively sought by the person. Or, it may be offered by the significant other out of concern for the person with the SUD.
- Giving in to pressure from an intervention in which loved ones meet with the person with the SUD and share observations of substance use and impaired behaviors, as well as how they have been affected. A professional may or may not be present to guide this process.
- Agreeing to a legal mandate by the court related to a charge or conviction in which substance use was a factor. An attorney may be instrumental in persuading a client to get help with an SUD.
- Treatment can be effective even if not entered voluntarily. In fact, there are some advantages to having a legal mandate or pressure from an employer to seek help. Often, the person will initially seek treatment because of such pressure but will eventually come to realize a serious problem exists. Those who stick with treatment as a result of a mandate may eventually develop a desire to change as motivation shifts from external to internal.

Determining appropriate treatment
Treatment services recommended depend on the unique problems and needs of the individual with the SUD. The American Society on Addiction

Medicine (ASAM) recommends that treatment decisions be based on a comprehensive assessment of six dimensions of functioning. This assessment determines the severity of the SUD and related medical or psychiatric disorders and other significant problems, which in turn determines the level of care needed.

The assessment is conducted by a physician, nurse, psychologist, social worker, or counselor trained in addiction medicine who gathers information from interviews with the affected person, her family, significant others, a physical examination, and laboratory studies (for example, liver function levels, urinalysis, and blood-alcohol tests). The six dimensions that make up the assessment include:

- *Intoxication and withdrawal potential.* This potential determines if medically supervised detoxification is needed before engaging in rehabilitation or counseling.
- *Biomedical conditions and complications.* These conditions determine if treatment is needed in a medically supervised setting.
- *Emotional conditions or complications.* This element determines if treatment of a co-existing psychiatric disorder is required. If so, the person may be referred to a dual diagnosis treatment program.
- *Readiness to change.* Motivation or readiness to change has an impact on whether or not treatment recommendations are followed.
- *Recovery environment and social support.* The availability of supportive family, friends, or community groups plays a role in making treatment recommendations. Some environments are more (or less) conducive to recovery than others.
- *Relapse potential.* Prior attempts at treatment and recovery and history of relapses impact treatment decisions.

Continuum of care

Treatment requires a continuum of services that can meet the needs of people with different types and severity of SUDs. This continuum includes professional services specific for SUDs, services for other types of problems (for example, medical, vocational, educational, housing, economic, legal),

The treatment of addicts at the Thamkrabok monastery in Thailand may seem harsh by Western standards, but the method has saved many from continuing addiction. Five days of purging to rid the body of toxins are followed by several weeks of meditation and community involvement to build up the patient's willpower and resistance to returning to old patterns and lifestyles.

and mutual support groups such as Alcoholics Anonymous or Narcotics Anonymous.

ASAM recommends that treatment be matched to the problems of the individual with the SUD based on the assessment. Treatment settings from the least to most intensive include the following:

Outpatient counseling (OPT). Individual, group, or family counseling may be offered. Frequency of sessions depends on the needs and problems of the individual with the SUD and the concerns of the family. Individual counseling involves talking one-on-one with an addiction counselor, usually up to an hour at a time. Group counseling involves meeting with one or two counselors with a group of six to ten other individuals who also have SUDs, usually for one to two hours per session. Goals of outpatient treatment include: determining if an SUD exists and what to do about it; stopping substance use; making personal changes to support abstinence; learning to spot early signs of relapse; and dealing with problems contributing to or resulting from the SUD. Some attend only a few sessions, while others attend many sessions over several months or longer. Group counseling sessions are usually held weekly, while individual and family sessions may initially be held weekly, then reduced to less frequent sessions.

Intensive outpatient (IOP) or partial hospital (PH) programs. These programs have the same goals as outpatient counseling and are used with more severe types of SUDs. Individual, family, and group counseling may be offered as part of IOP or PH programs. IOP is less intensive than PH, and may involve the person attending a program 3 to 5 days per week, for up to 10 weekly hours of education and counseling. A PH program involves attending sessions 4 to 7 days per week, up to 20 weekly hours or more per week. Both IOP and PH each may last 2 to 6 weeks.

Ambulatory detoxification. Some clinics offer supervised detoxification in addition to OPT, IOP, or PH services. This service involves meeting with a nurse or doctor who monitors withdrawal symptoms and vital signs and provides counseling and education. Medications are used to help the person safely withdraw from alcohol or other addictive drugs. This service usually lasts just a few days. A major goal is to get the person being detoxified to remain in treatment. If withdrawal symptoms significantly worsen, the person may be referred to an inpatient detoxification unit in a hospital or rehabilitation program.

Residential rehabilitation programs. A primary rehabilitation program lasts up to three or four weeks; a halfway house program (HWH) lasts several months or longer; and a therapeutic community (TC) lasts several months to more than a year. All of these programs aim to provide education, support, and counseling to help the person with the SUD learn ways to stay sober and solve problems without relapsing to substance use. Many of these programs use addiction counselors who have personal experiences with addiction and recovery. Some, such as TCs that specialize in helping individuals with criminal histories, may also have counselors who are ex-prisoners.

A primary rehabilitation program provides a structured treatment day in which the person attends many treatments. These include recovery education groups, therapy groups, individual counseling, leisure or recreational counseling, and mutual support groups such as AA or NA. Clients are often given reading, writing, or workbook assignments to help them personalize the material covered during the treatment day. For example, a client may be asked to write an extensive personal history of alcohol and drug use (types, amounts, and frequency of substances used, as well as effects on oneself and others), and then share this with a counseling group. Peers then share their opinions on the seriousness of this person's SUD. A client nearing program completion may be assigned an interactive workbook task in which he or she develops a follow-up plan with the names, addresses, and telephone numbers of specific resources he or she will use to help stay sober (professional and self-help programs). This client may also be asked to list potential relapse warning signs and risk factors and what can be done to manage these without using alcohol or drugs.

While in an HWH, the client may get involved in vocational counseling and training or focus on academic issues (for example, getting a GED or finishing college). The HWH provides support and treatment to help the client pursue these other goals.

A TC program is generally more psychologically intense than other rehab programs. It is often used for those individuals whose lifestyle evolved around addiction and who have had problems with the law in addition to their addiction. Many residents of a TC have poor academic, occupational, and social skills and need help acquiring these skills, which are needed for success in life.

A TC aims to help the resident become part of a community in which people help each other by confronting and changing negative, unhealthy, and addictive behaviors, and acquiring more prosocial behaviors. In addition to teaching ways to manage recovery from addiction, a TC aims to teach values such as citizenship, honesty, love, charity, altruism, and responsibility to self, family, and others. This type of program is considered more "habilitation" than "rehabilitation" because many residents of a TC never learned some of the requisite skills needed to function responsibly and effectively in society.

BEHAVIORAL TREATMENTS

- Cognitive-behavioral therapy focuses on helping the client change beliefs and learn behaviors that are incompatible with substance use.
- Community reinforcement approach involves receipt of rewards or reinforcements for sobriety, along with personal and family counseling.
- Cue exposure teaches the person to control reactions to stimuli that trigger desires to use substances.
- In group drug counseling, several addicted individuals work together to learn about addiction and how to manage the day-to-day challenges of sobriety, for example, cravings and social pressures to use, or how to deal with upsetting emotions.
- Individual drug counseling helps the person learn to manage addiction through the use of twelve-step programs, building a recovery support system, and managing relapse warning signs and risk factors.
- MATRIX model (for methamphetamine and cocaine) provides a comprehensive program to manage addiction and reduce relapse risk.
- Motivational enhancement therapy helps the person develop motivation to change.
- Relapse prevention helps the person learn to identify and manage early signs of relapse and high risk factors.
- Social skills training (also called coping skills training) helps the person learn to manage relationship conflicts or internal conflicts (cravings, negative emotional states, thoughts of using substances).
- Family therapy and social network therapy engages members of the addicted person's family or social network, both to help the addicted person and to help themselves.
- Twelve-step facilitation therapy helps the person recover through involvement in AA or NA and the use of a sponsor, the twelve-steps, and other tools of AA.

Medical detoxification. This process occurs in a medically managed unit of a hospital or a medically monitored unit of an addiction rehabilitation program. The main difference between the two is that the former is for individuals with more severe withdrawal syndromes or those with significant medical or psychiatric problems in addition to an active addiction. Detoxification usually lasts 2 to 5 days and involves monitoring withdrawal symptoms, taking medications if symptoms warrant this, and participating in educational or counseling services.

While some individuals use only one type of service, others use multiple services, either during the course of their current episode or as a result of relapses following periods of sobriety. For many people, addiction is a chronic and lifelong disorder. Like chronic medical or psychiatric disorders, their addiction may require multiple episodes of treatment over time. Periods of recovery may be followed by recurrent episodes of use.

Behavioral therapies

There are many effective behavioral or psychosocial therapies and programs, medications, and combined approaches available to treat people with SUDs. Typical behavioral or psychosocial treatments are shown in the box at left. These approaches may be used in any of the levels of care described earlier. Although the theory behind each treatment model and the clinical techniques vary, all aim to help the affected person manage the SUD and make personal and lifestyle changes.

Medications

Medications help addicted people safely and comfortably withdraw from substances such as alcohol, opiates, or sedatives. Medicines used depend on the drugs to which the person is addicted.

Medicines may be used to take the place of the addictive drug. Methadone maintenance (MM) helps heroin addicts transfer their addiction from street drugs to methadone, which is administered and monitored in a licensed clinic. Nicotine replacement therapy in the form of gum, patches, or nasal spray helps some people stop smoking.

Antagonist or mixed replacement (agonist/ antagonist) medications are used for some opiate addicts. Naltrexone "antagonizes" the effects of heroin, so the addict does not get high if he or she ingests heroin while using it. Buprenorphine has both replacement and antagonist effects. It can be used to help the addict withdraw from heroin or other opiate drugs. Buprenorphine also helps the addict in maintenance therapy. Medications may be used to reduce craving among alcoholics and those addicted to smoking. Naltrexone reduces the alcoholic's craving, and buproprion reduces the smoker's craving.

Disulfiram (Antabuse) serves as aversive therapy for alcoholics. If the alcoholic consumes alcohol with disulfiram in her system (which stays in the system up to 7 to 14 days after the last dose), she becomes nauseous. This aversive reaction is a motivator for some alcoholics not to drink. The idea is to "buy the alcoholic time" so that she does not drink when craving alcohol. If she perseveres until disulfiram is out of her system, her craving to drink may subside.

Medications that eliminate or reduce psychiatric symptoms may lower the desire to drink or use drugs. Medications that improve mood or help organize thinking can indirectly support the client's resistance to use substances.

One of the practical problems some addicts face is the pressure from others in recovery to not use any drug, including a medication. Some misguided people perceive medications as the same as addictive substances and do not see their potential benefits.

Other services
To address other problems common among those with SUDs, a variety of services are needed. These include vocational assessment and training, case management, housing, and social services. Case managers help clients with SUDs with problems related to housing, transportation, applying for benefits, and accessing medical, psychiatric, or addiction services.

Principles of effective treatment
The National Institute on Drug Abuse (NIDA) has published principles of treatment that serve as an important guide to providing care for those with SUDs. Because no single treatment fits all individuals, NIDA recommends that a variety of levels of care and treatment approaches are provided. Treatment must be readily available and easily accessible, or the person may find reasons not to get

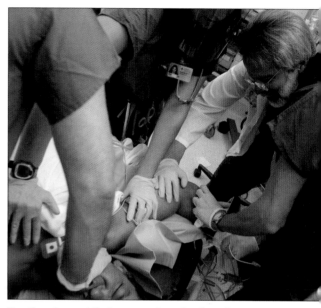

Treating drug addiction sometimes begins when an addict is rushed to an emergency room following an overdose. However, addicts often lack the resources to complete a proper treatment program.

the help he needs. It is also important that all the client's needs are assessed. Many with SUDs have medical, psychiatric, and psychosocial problems that require help. Treatment does not have to be voluntary to be effective. Clients mandated to treatment by the court or an employer often benefit from it. Although motivation is external at first, it may later shift to internal as the person realizes an addiction exists and develops motivation to change.

Once the client is part of a program, the treatment plan may need to be modified based on the changing needs and problems of the client. Treatment is an active process, and the focus can change over time according to the needs and problems of the person with the SUD. Adequate time in treatment is a prerequisite for the client to benefit. Less than three months in treatment is seldom effective, and outcome is often associated with time in treatment. The highest risk period of dropout and relapse is the first 30 days in treatment. Any co-occurring mental disorders should be treated in an integrated manner. The treatment plan needs to address both the substance and the psychiatric disorders, as an untreated psychiatric disorder can contribute to relapse.

Most treatment programs start with detoxification, which prepares clients for ongoing treatment. Once the client is clean, it may be helpful to monitor any further drug use during treatment, as external checking motivates some clients to stay sober. Urinalysis reports help identify recent use and provide the caregiver with information that can be used in counseling sessions. Treatment programs should also test for HIV/AIDS, hepatitis, and other infectious diseases. Counseling can then focus on helping the client to reduce behaviors that increase the risk of diseases, for example, using dirty needles, cotton, or rinsing water for IV users, unprotected sex, and sex with multiple partners.

Recovery can be a long-term process requiring multiple episodes of treatment. Addicted clients are no different from those with mental disorders in that some are sicker, have more difficulty with recovery, and need more professional services than others. Even after they finish professional treatment, many remain involved in recovery by attending mutual support groups such as AA or NA.

Special populations

Some programs are designed to help unique populations based on demographic or clinical characteristics. An entire program or a track within a program may address a single population, for example, pregnant women, clients in the criminal justice system, clients with co-occurring psychiatric disorders, African Americans, Native Americans, women, adolescents, the elderly, gays and lesbians, or multiple relapsers.

Self-help groups

Many people with SUDs recover primarily with the help of mutual support programs such as AA or NA. Others use both professional treatment and support groups. Professionals routinely teach their clients about these programs and facilitate their attendance. Many treatment programs offer on-site AA and NA meetings. AA and NA are fellowships of people who share their experiences, strength, and hope to help one another recover from addiction. Members help each other by providing education, support, and mentoring. Established members sponsor newcomers by helping them learn about the twelve steps and twelve traditions.

Treatment effectiveness

There is much scientific evidence that treatment for SUDs is effective. Positive treatment outcomes and examples from studies include:

- *Reducing or stopping substance use.* One major study found that at one-year follow-up, alcoholics reduced the percentage of drinking days per month from 80 percent to 20 percent, and reduced the average number of drinks per drinking day from 17 to 3.
- *Reducing or stopping high-risk behaviors that increase the risk of infectious diseases.* Many studies show greater reductions of HIV rates among treated clients compared with those who do not receive treatment.
- *Improved physical, mental, or spiritual health.* Treated individuals use fewer medical services after treatment and report a more positive mood than untreated individuals.
- *Improved family relationships.* Treatment helps families function more effectively and reduces their emotional burden. Mothers often reunite with their children after they get involved in treatment.
- *Increased ability to hold a job and fulfill responsibilities.* Opiate addicts on methadone maintenance show increases in rates of employment as a result of treatment.

Conclusions

SUDs are associated with many problems and increased rates of mortality. However, many effective behavioral treatments and medications exist to help individuals with SUDs and their families. A variety of professional services and mutual support programs are available to address this serious health care problem. It is clear from outcome studies that there are substantial benefits to treatment.

D. C. DALEY

Treatment Centers

Addiction treatment has a number of different components that vary with the needs of the client. By adapting established methods and adopting new techniques, centers can provide specialized treatment for a wide range of clients.

In the 1950s, the American Medical Association (AMA), the national professional organization for physicians in the United States, first recognized alcohol and drug addiction as a disease. Since that time, alcohol and drug dependence has received increasing attention, and treatment efforts have steadily improved. In this article, the most common types of services and programs offered to treat alcohol and drug addiction will be reviewed. In addition, several well-known and historically important treatment centers will be discussed in detail.

Provision of services

Treatment centers can vary widely in their approach to treatment and in the services they deliver. Types of centers include hospitals, private clinics, halfway houses, therapeutic communities, and prisons. Treatment is generally provided as a residential or outpatient service for a set period of time. Several basic treatment services are typically provided, including assessment, detoxification, medication management, and individual and group psychotherapy. Before 1990 alcoholics and drug addicts were treated in separate programs, but since the two programs were merged, the majority of substance abuse programs treat both types of addicts.

Most treatment programs for substance abuse in the United States are funded federally, usually through state grants, local or county agencies, or directly by the government. Just over a third of the costs are provided by private sector sources. Federal funding comes from the substance abuse block grant, which was $2.5 billion in 2004. Despite this level of funding it is estimated that a large number of people needing treatment are unable to access services. Difficulties arise primarily from a lack of treatment places, which creates waiting lists; facilities being sited outside affected communities; a reluctance to fund lengthy inpatient treatments; eligibility for Medicaid; and the limited availability of specialist services for certain populations. The general policy toward abstinence as a goal has also restricted the availability of harm reduction and methadone maintenance programs in some states. There are also issues with federally funded treatment over the lack of choice of the type of treatment offered, integration with other services (such as welfare and housing), provision of aftercare, and how states target their funding. In contrast, people with private health insurance generally have around 90 percent of their treatment fees paid and have a wider range of treatment providers to select from than those requiring government-funded assistance. However, the relapsing nature of addiction means that even insured addicts may face restrictions on how many times they can access treatment.

Elements of a treatment center

Treatment centers are set up according to the needs of their target community. Most provide a core outpatient and day care program with provision for or access to residential treatments. The majority of clients seeking treatment for drug or alcohol problems receive services on an outpatient basis (that is, they present for meetings or appointments at the clinic but do not reside there). Inpatient services are provided for clients suffering from severe psychiatric or medical conditions. Inpatient treatment allows the client to receive continuous care in a safe environment. It is, of course, significantly more expensive than outpatient treatment and is generally brief (for example, several days to weeks). Other functional components can include aftercare, community outreach, helplines or advice centers, and research programs.

The staffing of centers reflects the services offered. These usually include medical and psychiatric physicians and nurses, counselors and psychotherapists, social and family liaison workers, occupational therapists, and support staff. Halfway houses and therapeutic communities also employ recovered addicts as staff members.

When a person is first admitted to a treatment center, a comprehensive assessment is performed.

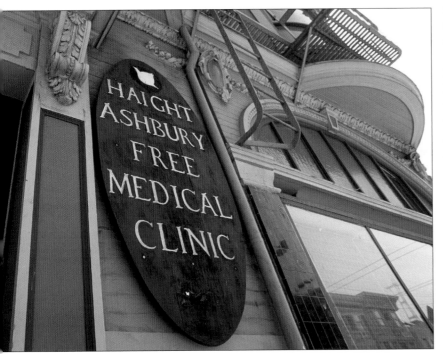

The Haight Ashbury clinic was set up in 1967 to provide free medical care to drug users in a nonjudgmental environment. Its innovative approach to drug treatment became a training ground for health workers studying addiction.

to decide whether the treatment plan needs to be modified to benefit the client.

Medication management
Following assessment and treatment plan development, therapeutic services are implemented. In addition to assessment services, most treatment centers offer medication management and psychotherapy. Generally, the medical director of the clinic oversees the pharmacological treatment (that is, medication treatment) of clients to ensure that they receive appropriate medications and are carefully monitored for side effects. In alcohol and drug abuse centers, medications such as Antabuse, naltrexone, or methadone are sometimes provided, when appropriate, to help decrease cravings for alcohol or drugs, discourage clients from using, and to help reduce the effects of withdrawal from drugs.

The majority of clients (76 percent of men and 65 percent of women) who enter drug and alcohol community treatment centers also have co-occurring psychiatric conditions that require medical and psychological treatment. Some of the most common co-occurring disorders are anxiety disorders (phobias, post-traumatic stress disorder) and mood disorders (major depressive disorder). Thus, medications may also be prescribed to address both the substance use disorder and any other co-occurring psychiatric conditions.

Individual and group therapy
Group therapy is the most common type of treatment offered for alcohol and drug dependence. Depending on the type of treatment center, a number of different types of groups may be offered. For example, some centers offer groups for women only, for men only, for adolescents, for men with domestic violence charges, for health care

This can sometimes require several visits to accomplish, and may include, for example, a urine drug-screen test, breathalyzer test, clinical interview, and physical examination.

Using all the information gathered during the assessment phase, initial decisions are made about the type of therapeutic services that will be the most helpful to the client. An individualized treatment plan is then developed for each client. The treatment plan is determined with the input of a number of different individuals, such as the clinician who performed the initial assessment, the medical director of the clinic, the client and his or her family members, and other treatment providers. The finalized treatment plan is discussed with the client to ensure that the client understands the plan, agrees with the plan, and feels that he or she will be able to comply with the specific details. The treatment plan is then reviewed periodically to ensure that the plan is being implemented correctly, to consider whether the plan is serving the client's needs and is resulting in improvements and treatment gains, and

professionals who are addicted to substances, for Spanish-speaking clients, or for family members of persons addicted to substances. Groups are often held on a weekly basis in outpatient settings and on a daily basis in inpatient settings.

There are a number of important advantages to group therapy. It is economical, costs the client less, and may be just as helpful as individual therapy for some clients. In addition, group therapy offers clients the opportunity to hear how other individuals in similar situations are coping with drug and alcohol problems, and to receive support from their peers. Finally, group therapy can help motivate clients, help battle against the social stigma of addiction, and remind clients with alcohol and drug problems that they are not alone.

Individual psychotherapy, which may be offered in addition to or in lieu of group therapy, also has several advantages. A key advantage is that it provides a more private, confidential setting, which can seem safer and less threatening to some clients. Some clients do not feel comfortable in group settings, particularly in the early stages of treatment. Thus, it can be helpful to start a client in individual therapy when he or she first enters treatment, and then work up to joining group therapy. Finally, individual therapy also has the advantage of being able to address and concentrate on one person's issues rather than many persons', as is the case in group therapy, and it provides a more individualized pace.

Examples of treatment centers

The Betty Ford Center. The Betty Ford Center (BFC) was cofounded by former first lady Betty Ford, wife of former U.S. president Gerald Ford. Prior to establishing the BFC, Betty Ford completed her own treatment for alcohol addiction. It was during her treatment that she realized the need for more specialized addiction services. Ford and ambassador Leonard Firestone cofounded the nonprofit BFC in California. BFC treats men and women, and offers inpatient services, residential day treatment, and outpatient treatment.

In the inpatient treatment program, clients live in one of the halls on the BFC campus. Ongoing medical and psychological problems associated with early recovery and abstinence are targeted in the inpatient treatment program. In the residential day

treatment program, clients live in housing that is off-campus, but they have assigned roommates and participate in daily activities at BFC. Typically, meetings and groups also take place on the weekends. In the outpatient treatment program, clients participate in daily meetings but live and work outside the center.

When clients first enter treatment at BFC, they receive detoxification, if necessary, and undergo further assessment, which is used to develop their individualized treatment plans. BFC offers several specialized programs addressing, for example, spirituality, children and family issues, and professional education. Treatment at BFC is based on the twelve-step philosophy, which is also the basis of Alcoholics Anonymous, a national, peer-led, outpatient organization. The twelve-step philosophy views spirituality as a basis for recovery from addiction. To this end, the BFC has a spiritual care program designed to assess and incorporate each individual's spiritual path into the treatment plan. Each client's spiritual concerns (for example, the meaning and purpose of his or her life) are identified and addressed during treatment.

The BFC emphasizes that numerous individuals are affected when a person is dependent on alcohol or drugs. They offer a four-day children's program for children aged 7 to 12 who have a family member with alcohol or drug dependence. During the program, children are taught about alcohol and drug dependency and they learn a variety of coping skills such as problem-solving skills and self-care activities. Parents are invited to participate during the latter part of the program. The BFC also offers a five-day family program to help support and educate adult family members.

Once a client has completed the primary treatment at BFC, plans for continuing or aftercare treatment are made. This need reflects the long-term treatment that is often necessary to fully recover from alcohol and drug addiction. Aftercare at BFC may include, for example, scheduled telephone contacts or local weekend retreats. The weekend retreats are held several times a year and involve workshops, lectures, and small-group activities.

Finally, a professional education training program is offered for treatment care providers. This program is designed to help treatment providers increase

Betty Ford set up her clinic after her own battle against addiction. A particular focus there is specialized programs for women, who often have different treatment needs than men.

awareness and understanding of alcohol and drug addiction and treatment skills.

Hazelden. Hazelden was established in Minnesota in the late 1940s by Austin Ripley. Ripley initially sought to establish a center for priests with alcohol problems, but this idea was expanded to include a broader client base. Since it first opened, Hazelden has expanded geographically, and additional treatment centers are now located in Florida, New York, and Illinois. Similar to the BFC, Hazelden was founded on the twelve-step philosophy. It has since incorporated other, multidisciplinary treatment approaches (spirituality, meditation, family) but maintains a twelve-step philosophy foundation.

Treatment at Hazelden begins with a diagnostic assessment and evaluation. For a comprehensive evaluation, individuals may come to Hazelden and stay for several days, during which time they complete a number of assessments (called a "battery" of assessments). Hazelden, like most treatment centers, promotes a goal of abstinence from all substances. They approach treatment in a holistic way, addressing issues related to the mind, body, and spirit. To accomplish this task, they have staff members with medical and counseling backgrounds, as well as those with expertise in fitness, spiritual care, and recreation.

Hazelden offers treatment for family members through its Hazelden Center for Youth and Families. A four-day parent program is designed to help support and educate parents and caregivers who have children or who are taking care of a young adult with an addiction. The program helps parents understand addiction, the effects of alcohol and drugs on the child's development, and new techniques for parenting children with addiction problems.

Finally, Hazelden offers a number of other specialty programs including, for example, a center for women's recovery and a meditation center. In addition, Hazelden has a research center, which monitors new advances in treatment outcome research so that these can be incorporated into the services being offered.

Haight Ashbury Free Clinics. The Haight Ashbury Free Clinics (HAFC) were founded in California in 1967 by David Smith. An initial goal of the HAFC was to provide free health care services to the drug-using counterculture community of San Francisco. Today, HAFC offers a number of programs designed to help treat addiction and associated problems. For example, the Oshun Center was developed by the HAFC in 1999. It is a 24-hour, 7-day-a-week drop-in center for women and their families. The services provided by the Oshun Center target substance abuse and relationship problems, such as domestic violence or childhood trauma, that often co-occur with substance abuse. Group and individual therapy are provided, as well as family counseling, crisis intervention, and advocacy.

A culturally specific treatment program developed by the HAFC is the Western Addiction Recovery House, a 20-bed treatment program specifically for African American men. Services provided there include assessment, substance abuse education and counseling, parenting classes, and job skills training.

S. E. BACK

SEE ALSO:
Clinics • Counseling • Drop-in Centers • Family Therapy • Halfway Houses • Medical Care • State Agencies • Therapeutic Communities • Treatment •

Vulnerability

It is hard to say exactly what makes an adolescent vulnerable to the influence of drugs. Researchers are discovering that a wide mix of biological, sociological, and enviromental factors may all play a part in the addiction process.

Why can some people use drugs or alcohol recreationally, while others develop serious problems? Can we predict which young people are at most risk of developing drug- or alcohol-related disorders? These questions concerning vulnerability or susceptibility to substance abuse and addiction have been the focus of significant research for several decades. Traditionally, research on vulnerability has focused on identifying risk factors that increase the probability of developing a substance use problem. More recently, however, there has been growing interest in the role of protective factors, which reduce vulnerability to substance use disorders (SUD). However, it is important to realize that vulnerability is not simply the culmination of risk and protective factors, as there are many elements that potentially contribute to the development of SUD (including genes and proteins, neuronal circuits, behavior, and social networks). To this end, researchers have now identified an array of biopsychosocial factors that are all associated with vulnerability to SUD.

Genetic and neurobiological vulnerabilities

Epidemiological studies have demonstrated that young people with a family history of SUD are more vulnerable than peers without a family history to developing later substance abuse and addiction. The evidence appears strongest for alcoholism, although other SUDs also appear to have a heritable component. While researchers believe that there are specific sets of genes that directly contribute to SUD, inheritable behavioral, personality, and temperament traits are also associated with an increased risk of SUD (for example, antisocial personality disorder). The role of genetic factors has been further explored using animal models. These studies have shown that certain genes are responsible for an animal's preference for different drugs, as well as their pattern of use. For example, by manipulating certain genes using "knockout techniques," in which certain genes are removed from the genome of the animal, researchers have been able to make some animals

Children may be drawn into addiction by drug-using friends. Peer influence is one of the strongest factors in starting and maintaining drug use.

compulsively self-administer drugs, while reducing use in others. As the functional significance of gene polymorphisms (variation in DNA structure) in behavior and their differential expression in addicted versus nonaddicted individuals is investigated more fully, we will better understand which genes are involved in vulnerability to substance abuse and addiction, and how they interact with neurobiology and behavior.

Another interesting area of neurobiological vulnerability is that of brain structure and function. We now know that a tremendous amount of structural and functional (cognitive and emotional) brain development takes place during the teenage years. In addition, animal studies have shown that the adolescent brain is more vulnerable to the neurotoxic effects of alcohol, and perhaps other drugs, than in adulthood. Studies in humans have shown that certain areas of the brain, particularly those in the frontal cortex (the areas involved in aspects of self-regulation, planning, complex attentional skills, impulse control) are still maturing during adolescence, and may be particularly susceptible to the long-term effects of alcohol and drugs. An arrest or disruption to the maturation of these brain regions and functions may in turn contribute to young people experiencing difficulties in regulating or ceasing substance use (as a result of problems with planning, attention, impulse control), particularly if they are already vulnerable (have a chronic mental illness, for example, or a strong family history of substance abuse). Studies investigating brain activity in children with a family history of alcoholism show abnormal electroencephalographic (EEG) activity, suggesting that brain processes are altered in at-risk individuals, although the significance of these results are yet to be fully determined. Finally, the rate and timing of puberty have also been implicated in SUD (through its influence on brain and social development), in which early puberty in girls and delayed puberty in boys are also identified as risk factors.

Cognitive and behavioral vulnerabilities

School-related behavioral and academic problems are also a major risk factor for SUD, with poor academic achievement, discipline problems, truancy, and school dropout all identified as risk factors. Young people with below average levels of intellectual functioning, or with language or other learning disorders, are also at risk. In fact, young people with a current SUD or who are at high risk of developing SUD have been found to have specific neuropsychological deficits on formal testing. These deficits in executive cognitive functioning (ECF) include tests of problem solving, attention, memory, and hypothesis generation. Lower ECF capacity is also a risk factor for SUD through its association with other behavioral risk factors, such as impulsive, aggressive, or antisocial behavior.

In terms of other behavioral risk factors, young people who have behavioral problems early (for example, a difficult temperament in infancy or oppositional, aggressive, or impulsive behaviors in childhood) are at increased risk of developing SUD, especially males. Childhood diagnoses of oppositional defiant disorder (ODD), conduct disorder (CD), and attention deficit hyperactivity disorder (ADHD) are also well-established risk factors for

youth SUD, as is early use of substances. A history of childhood bereavement or major illness, teen pregnancy, or childhood sexual, emotional, or physical abuse are also significant risk factors. In addition, a number of mental health disorders are also associated with predisposition to problematic substance use. Disorders such as depression, anxiety, schizophrenia, bipolar disorder, and obsessive-compulsive disorder have high rates of comorbid substance use, although the mechanisms underlying this increased vulnerability are complex and multifaceted.

Emotional and personality vulnerabilities

A number of personality traits have also been identified as risk factors for SUD, including negative affectivity/neuroticism (NA/N) and disinhibition/impulsivity (DIS/IMP). NA/N is characterized by a general tendency to experience life negatively and a difficulty in controlling one's mood, while DIS/IMP is associated with impulsivity, irresponsibility, risk taking, and sensation seeking. There is growing evidence to suggest that adolescent substance misuse and SUD result either from an attempt to reduce negative affectivity (arising from an individual's general disposition to experience negative mood states or being less tolerant to stressful life events, that is, NA/N) or as a result of an individual's disinhibited behavior or impulsivity. Furthermore, at-risk individuals high in DIS/IMP have also been found to experience significant reductions in stress when intoxicated, suggesting they may also be more vulnerable to stress-induced drinking and drug use.

Finally, low self-esteem is also commonly cited as a risk factor for SUD, even though there is little research evidence to support such an association. However, self-esteem is a difficult construct to study, and it is likely that both low self-esteem and substance abuse are linked through other risk factors. For example, several factors related to how individuals see themselves (that is, their self-concept) are also important risk factors for SUD. These include self-efficacy (how confident you are that you will succeed at a specific task), self-belief (how optimistic or pessimistic you are about yourself and the future), self-control (for example, how you control any aggressive tendencies) and social confidence (how you believe you get along with others and whether you make friends easily).

Environmental vulnerabilities

Understanding SUD also requires a consideration of factors within the individual's environment, and how they interact with more individually specific risk factors as mentioned above.

In recent years, there has been increased recognition of the role of family environmental factors in risk for SUD. Parental substance use and parental beliefs and attitudes that are conducive to substance use are important risk factors for SUD in young people. Twin and adoptive studies have also indicated that parental divorce, death, or mental illness also increase the risk of SUD in young people. However, while parental characteristics are important, parenting style and other factors in the family environment may have a bigger impact on subsequent SUD. Such factors include inconsistent child-rearing practices, communicating in a negative style, and a lack of emotional support within the family. A lack of parental supervision and monitoring are particularly important risk factors for SUD. Finally, how families use substances are important in determining adolescent expectations and patterns of use, as overt parental use may teach children that alcohol or drug use is an appropriate means of coping with adversity.

Participation in family and social events, such as going to church, is a protective factor against drug use. Strong family bonds help increase the resiliency of adolescents to say no to drugs.

Peer factors

Peer variables have universally been identified as the single factor most likely to predict adolescent substance misuse. Young people are usually introduced to substances by their peers, and peer substance use has consistently been identified as the most robust predictor of SUD. Other peer variables, including positive peer attitudes toward substance use, peer pressure or encouragement to use, and low sanctions against using are also important. Affiliation with a deviant peer group also contributes to continued substance use, as individuals fail to develop attitudes and values consistent with society at large. However, it is difficult to determine whether the association between peer variables and risk of SUD is related to peer influences to use or a preference for drug-using peers. Nevertheless, there is clear evidence of the importance of peer variables in youth SUD, as they are not only the most potent predictor of SUD but also mediate the influence of other individual and environmental risk factors.

Neighborhood factors

Factors in the neighborhood environment of young people, including poverty, high crime rates, homelessness, and low numbers of religious and cultural institutions have also been found to influence substance use outcomes. However, these factors do not invariably result in SUD among young people in these environments, as many of these young people do not develop SUD. As such, it is likely that neighborhood variables influence youth SUD through their interaction with other factors, such as peer, family, and individual risk factors (for example, higher number of drug-using peers, limited youth-specific social venues, parental mental illness, poor academic performance, and easier access to illegal substances in socioeconomically deprived regions).

Cultural and sociopolitical factors

Cultural factors also have an important role in vulnerability to SUD. Cultural and subcultural attitudes toward specific substances, appropriate situations in which to use, and even acceptability of intoxication have been noted to be important risk factors. For example, in Jewish culture, where alcohol is introduced early in a ritualized fashion and drunkenness is frowned upon, community rates of alcohol dependence are low. In contrast, in Irish communities, where alcohol is a central feature of social interaction, rates of alcoholism are significantly higher. This sharing of cultural norms may explain why ethnicity has been found to be a powerful predictor of substance misuse.

Other subcultures that may affect rates of substance abuse include deviant youth groups and even some amateur sports clubs. In these latter settings, heavy alcohol use may be encouraged by the shared ideal that alcohol intake is a sign of masculinity. Certain occupations are also more vulnerable to substance abuse, largely as a result of increased accessibility and availability, such as alcoholism among bar owners or abuse of anesthetic gases among dentists and anesthetists. Similarly, availability (including access and price) affects the pattern and level of alcohol and drug use in the wider community. Other institutional factors that affect community substance use include legislation, advertising, and regulation of alcohol or drug access and supply. For example, there are lower levels of community smoking in industrialized nations compared with developing countries following the introduction of smoking bans in the workplace and social venues, higher taxes on tobacco, limited advertising, and enforced legislation that prevents the sale of cigarettes to adolescents.

Protective factors

Since the 1990s there has been growing interest in the identification of protective factors that reduce vulnerability to SUD. However, these variables are not simply the opposite of risk factors; they also act to increase the resiliency of young people. Factors associated with lowered risk of substance use have most commonly been identified in the family environment of young people. Family bonding, including strong parental support and involvement, have most consistently been identified as a protective factor for youth SUD. Parental monitoring and supervision have also been identified as important protective factors, and there is some evidence that involvement with spiritual or religious organizations is also protective. More recently, a large body of work has identified "connectedness," or a strong sense of connection and closeness to parents, family, or other adults from school or other community-based institutions, as a critical protective factor for youth SUD.

While neurobiological and genetic protective factors are yet to be fully determined, there are examples of physiological protective factors within distinct ethnic populations. For example, a particular variant of aldehyde dehydrogenase (an enzyme involved in the metabolism of alcohol) that is linked to an aversive "flushing response" after drinking alcohol is found in a high proportion of people from China and Japan, resulting in low levels of alcohol misuse. However, while potentially protective, these factors do not work in isolation and are influenced by a range of other relevant risk factors. It has been observed that Asians with the enzyme variant who live in the United States have rates of alcohol use that are similar to those of their local communities.

Conclusions

Research since the 1970s has established a number of important risk factors for SUD in youth. Such factors include individual (for example, being male, family history of substance-related problems, mental health or behavioral problems, personality difficulties, history of abuse), family (parental drug use, family dysfunction), peer (peer drug use, low sanctions against use), and sociocultural variables (drug availability, cultural acceptance, community support), as well as specific protective factors (family bonding, parental supervision, connectedness). However, while this research has assisted in the development of prevention programs that combat risk factors and promote protective factors, we are still yet to develop a comprehensive understanding of the underlying causes and vulnerabilities to SUD.

There is now an increased emphasis on the need to understand risk and protective factors at the individual level. The interaction between a young person and his or her environment requires clear elucidation so that more targeted prevention programs may be developed to identify high-risk youth promptly and provide early intervention strategies.

L. HIDES, D. I. LUBMAN, M. YÜCEL

SEE ALSO:
Biopsychosocial Theory of Addiction • Causes of Addiction • Family Environment • Peer Influence • Protective Factors • Risk Factors

Withdrawal

Quitting some types of drugs can be difficult because of the physical symptoms that occur when the user stops taking the drug. This syndrome is called withdrawal and is a major obstacle in the difficult process of giving up drugs.

Some drugs induce a physical dependence, which is an adaptive state of the body produced by repeated drug administration. When a person becomes physically dependent on a drug, that person will experience intense averse physical disturbances, called withdrawal, when he or she stops taking the drug. In fact, the only way to measure physical dependence is to observe the degree of withdrawal symptoms. Generally, the effects of drug withdrawal are opposite from the effects of the drug itself. Most drugs of abuse produce a feeling of euphoria, thus withdrawal from these drugs produces a dysphoria, which is a feeling of anxiousness and misery.

The process and function of withdrawal is not well understood. However, it is generally agreed that a drug alters the preset levels, or homeostatic "set points," of a variety of systems in the body. These homeostatic set points maintain the functions of various systems of the body at an optimal level. If a drug alters a body system in one direction, the body then alters the system in the opposite direction in an attempt to maintain the homeostatic set point. This opposing action of the body is thought to result in drug tolerance, requiring that more of the drug must be taken in order to get the same effect. If the drug is abruptly discontinued, however, the body's response to the drug is now unopposed and the person experiences the opposite effects (withdrawal). The specific psychological and physiological symptoms of withdrawal depend on the specific drug that caused the dependency. Some drugs such as marijuana produce only a mild withdrawal syndrome, while other drugs such as the opiates and alcohol produce such a severe withdrawal that avoiding these effects is an important factor in the continuation of drug use. In fact, withdrawal from alcohol can be lethal.

Mechanisms behind withdrawal

There appear to be various ways in which a body opposes the effects of a drug. It is these opposing effects that result in withdrawal when drug taking is abruptly stopped. The first mechanism involves

Nicotine in cigarettes and caffeine in coffee can both produce withdrawal symptoms if use is suddenly stopped. Nicotine is notoriously difficult to give up, as cravings can last for many months, but symptoms can be alleviated by nicotine patches or gum.

modulation at a cellular level. There is a decrease in the production and release of the transmitter substances that the drug causes to be released. These transmitters activate certain molecules called receptors. These receptors are on nerve cells, and it is the activation of these receptors that results in the effects of the drug. In addition to decreasing the amount of neurotransmitters, the body also decreases the number of receptors. Both of these actions decrease the effect of the drug.

Withdrawal also involves a type of learning called behavioral conditioning. When a neutral stimulus is regularly followed by a stimulus that causes a response, the previously neutral stimulus begins to cause the same response by itself. Behavioral conditioning was established by Russian scientist Ivan Pavlov. Using dogs as experimental animals, Pavlov rang a bell just before showing food to the dogs. Over time, the dogs began to salivate at the sound of the bell itself, even without the presence of food. When a person takes a drug, the drug produces its effects on the body, which in turn cause the body to evoke its own compensatory response to the drug. Any environmental stimuli that are paired with the drug begin to be associated with the drug. This can include the room in which the drug is taken (for

example, a bar) and the drug paraphernalia (such as shot glasses, rolling papers, a needle, and so on). This environmental stimuli is akin to the bell in Pavlov's experiment. Thus, over time, the compensatory effects of the body to oppose the effects of the drug are elicited not only by the drug itself but also by the environmental stimuli. If a heroin addict enters a room where he or she normally takes the drug, these environmental cues will quickly cause withdrawal symptoms such as agitation, cramping, and dysphoria. The only way to get rid of these withdrawal effects is to wait for them to fade or to take more of the drug.

Withdrawal symptoms

The magnitude and type of withdrawal symptoms vary, depending on the drug taken. One of the important factors is the rate of disappearance of the drug from the body. Long-acting drugs take longer to leave the body, hence withdrawal from long-acting drugs has a delayed onset and is fairly mild. In contrast, shorter-acting drugs cause a withdrawal that is more intense but comparatively brief. After a person has become physiologically dependent on a drug, that person's body has responded by making adaptations that are directly opposite the effects of that drug. After the drug itself is removed, the withdrawal symptoms are also then directly opposite to the effects of the drug.

The effects of withdrawal from depressants of the nervous system are generally quite similar. These include alcohol, sedative-hypnotics such as barbiturates and benzodiazepines (including Nembutal and Valium), anxiolytics such as Xanax, anesthetics such as ether or nitrous oxide, and also substances that are inhaled, for example, glue and paint thinners. These drugs are used or abused for similar reasons: to decrease tension, reduce anxiety, and produce sedation. These drugs all depress the activity of the central nervous system (the brain and spinal cord). These drugs also have an additive effect with one another, and becoming dependent on one, for example, heroin, will cause cross-tolerance with other drugs in the same class, such as morphine or codeine. The withdrawal syndrome from general depressants is far more dangerous than that of other drugs and can even be fatal. Generally, symptoms appear within 24 hours after the drug is

---

TYPICAL WITHDRAWAL PERIODS

Alcohol
Mild symptoms peak within 12 to 24 hours and have largely subsided after 48 hours. Severe and potentially life threatening late withdrawal occurs between 72 and 96 hours after last drink.

Benzodiazepines
Symptoms can appear within hours, depending on half-life of drug, and can persist for several days. Untreated rebound symptoms may persist for months.

Opioids
Symptoms appear between 12 to 24 hours, peak after 4 days, and begin to subside after 7 days. Some withdrawal symptoms may persist for weeks or months afterward.

Stimulants
Binge use leads to exhaustive crash and intense cravings that may last 9 hours to 4 days. Withdrawal is mild but may be protracted, varying from 1 to 10 weeks, accompanied by craving.

Nicotine
Strong symptoms in first few days of withdrawal that usually diminish within a month. Some smokers may continue to feel symptoms for several months.

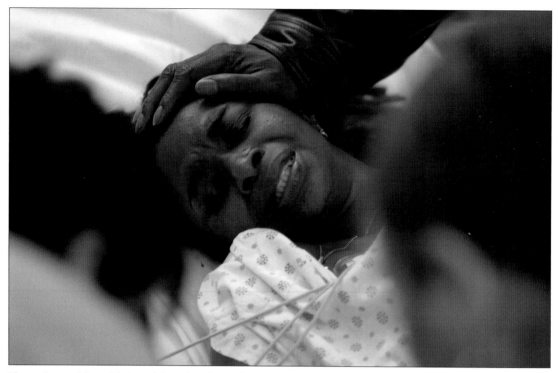

Planned or sudden withdrawal from heroin can be traumatic because symptoms begin as soon as a dose is missed and intensify over the following days. Administration of another opioid can help reduce symptoms, but this process must be carefully monitored, since the replacement may itself produce withdrawal.

discontinued, peak in 2 to 3 days, and last 7 to 14 days. The first few days of withdrawal from depressants are characterized by insomnia, headaches, anxiety, involuntary muscle twitching and tremor, sweating, intense dreaming, and nausea and vomiting. A few strongly dependent people go on to show later withdrawal symptoms in the following few days (these are called delirium tremens, or the DTs). People suffering from the DTs will have increasing agitation, general confusion and delirium, fever, vivid visual hallucinations (these are quite terrifying and often involve small animals such as rats, bats, or insects), and even seizures. The DTs are often fatal when they are not treated. Generally, treatment includes supportive care and administration of a long-acting depressant such as Valium. If this seems paradoxical, recall that the magnitude of withdrawal depends on the rate of drug disappearance from the body. Since all of the depressants cause cross-tolerance, a faster-clearing depressant such as alcohol is generally more

dangerous, and the withdrawal syndrome can be controlled at a slower, less dangerous rate with a longer-acting depressant such as Valium. Supportive care includes reassurance, keeping the patient warm, preventing dehydration, and reducing sensory stimulation by keeping the patient in a quiet, dimly lit room. Sometimes an antipsychotic is also prescribed to combat the hallucinations.

Drugs in the opioid class include morphine, codeine, heroin, and synthetic opioids such as meperidine (Demerol). Like the depressants, these drugs all cause a similar withdrawal syndrome, and cross-tolerance occurs among them. Hence, they can be freely substituted with each other to prevent or lessen the withdrawal syndrome. Withdrawal from opioids begins shortly after the next scheduled dose is missed, becomes more intense over the next few days, and then lessens over the next 7 to 10 days. Opioid withdrawal is similar to withdrawal from depressants, although this is not as severe. Symptoms include anxiety, irritability, restlessness, muscle aches, insomnia, sweating and flushing, nausea and vomiting, and fever. Treatment for opioid withdrawal usually includes giving another opioid, although this is not necessary, since this type of withdrawal is not as severe and is never fatal. Supportive care is helpful, however, and is similar to that for the depressants. It should be pointed out that withdrawal syndrome can be caused by giving an opioid antagonist such as naloxone or naltrexone (antagonists will bind to the active area on cells but not activate them, thus they compete with and can block the actions of opioids). This type of withdrawal is immediate, peaks in a half hour, and is much more severe.

Stimulant withdrawal

Drugs in the stimulant class include amphetamines, cocaine, and caffeine. Unlike the other classes, withdrawal from these drugs varies, depending on the specific drug. First, these drugs vary in their ability to produce a physiological dependence (although they all can cause a strong psychological dependence). Amphetamines (including Ecstasy) and cocaine do not really cause a physiological dependency, hence there is not a strong withdrawal syndrome with these drugs. It should be pointed out, however, that there are rebound effects to the stimulatory nature of these drugs. These effects can include a psychological and physical depression, lethargy, and a period of prolonged sleep, especially for amphetamine, which causes long-lasting wakefulness. In contrast to the amphetamines and cocaine, people can become physiologically dependent on caffeine, which can cause a withdrawal syndrome when it is discontinued. The most common caffeine withdrawal symptom is headache. Other symptoms include drowsiness, decreased energy and fatigue, impaired concentration, irritability, and decreased motivation. Caffeine withdrawal begins within 12 to 24 hours, peaks at 1 to 2 days, and can persist as long as a week. It is interesting to point out that caffeine withdrawal is an important issue when people have to undergo procedures where fasting is required, such as operations or various laboratory testing. It also is probably a factor when people are grouchy in the morning until they have had their tea or coffee. It probably even contributes to headaches and illness that people experience on holidays or weekends when their normal caffeine intake is altered.

Nicotine, marijuana, and psychedelics

Nicotine dependence comes on more slowly than dependence on other drugs, and its withdrawal syndrome varies in intensity among different people. However, while withdrawal from nicotine is not as physically severe as that from heroin, it is just as psychologically stressful. Many ex-heroin addicts who also quit smoking have said it was actually easier to give up heroin than nicotine. Withdrawal from nicotine usually includes increased eating (leading to weight gain), decreased heart rate, lack of concentration, lighter patterns of sleep or insomnia, anxiety, aggression, depression, and intense cravings for nicotine. Most of these symptoms disappear within a month, although the craving and weight gain continue longer, often as long as 6 months or occasionally longer. These symptoms can be relieved by exposure to nicotine, and different administrative routes of nicotine are helpful in quitting, including nicotine patches and gum. The symptoms can even be relieved temporarily by the taste or smell of tobacco. Unlike other drugs, withdrawal from nicotine is not directly related to dose. Heavy and light smokers both report equally severe withdrawal effects.

Unlike many other drugs, no marked withdrawal takes place from marijuana or psychedelics such as LSD. Withdrawal has only been seen after high, prolonged use of marijuana, and even then it is slight. The symptoms of withdrawal in a high-dose study using volunteers included a report by the subjects of "inner unrest," irritability, sweating, and restlessness. However, in a study where subjects were required to smoke only one marijuana cigarette per day for 28 days, no withdrawal symptoms were reported.

As a final note, it should be pointed out that drug withdrawal can be a factor in newborn babies of drug-dependent mothers. These babies will have the same symptoms as adults do and must be treated carefully to ease their withdrawal symptoms, which can persist for 4 to 6 months after birth.

J. JAWORSKI

SEE ALSO:

Addiction • Alcoholism Treatment • Detoxification • Heroin Addiction Treatment • Medical Care • Pregnancy and Fetal Addiction • Tolerance • Treatment

Workplace

The use of drugs in the workplace is an issue for many employers. Substance abuse has costs in terms of productivity and performance of employees, but workplace support can help many workers in overcoming their problems.

The Division of Workplace Programs, which is part of the Substance Abuse and Mental Health Services Administration of the U.S. Department of Health and Human Services, reports that substance use issues affect more than one in ten U.S. workers. A significant amount of illegal substance abuse takes place in the workforce, and some of this abuse occurs while at work or just prior to going to work. The belief that most people who use illicit drugs are unemployed and concentrated in impoverished parts of inner cities is a myth. A large-scale nationally representative study in the United States—*Worker Drug Use and Workplace Policies and Programs: Results from the National Household Survey on Drug Abuse*—showed that in 1997, 70 percent of the 9 million persons between the ages of 18 and 49 years who admitted using illicit drugs in the preceding month were full-time workers. The national survey for 2006 (now called the National Survey on Drug Use and Health) reported that 74.9 percent of current illicit drug users aged 18 and over were employed. Among full-time employees, 8.8 percent were current illicit drug users and 8.9 percent reported heavy alcohol use. The highest rate of past month illicit drug use was reported for employees aged 18 to 20 at 22.2 percent.

In the report for 1997, one-third of full-time workers were smokers, more than one-fifth reported binge drinking in the past month, and approximately 12 percent say they used illicit drugs during the past year. Among full-time workers aged 18 to 49, there were an estimated 6.3 million current illicit drug users and an estimated 6.2 million heavy alcohol users (drinking five or more drinks on one occasion five or more days in the past 30 days). Included in this number were 1.6 million people who abused both illicit drugs and were heavy alcohol users, for a total of 10.9 million people who were heavy alcohol users, illicit drug users, or both. Workers are three times more likely to report a dependence on alcohol than on illicit drugs. Male workers are twice as likely to be current illicit drug users and four times as likely to be heavy alcohol users as female workers. Substance abuse is more common in certain occupations and industries. Heavy alcohol and illicit drug use is highest among construction workers and food preparers. Auto mechanics, laborers, and light-truck drivers are among those more susceptible to alcohol use. In addition, tobacco use is more common among blue-collar workers than among white-collar workers.

Economic cost

Substance abuse can create hazards, not only for employees, but also for co-workers and the public. Substance abuse among transportation workers, for example, can endanger the lives of passengers and bystanders. In 1997 workers who reported current illicit drug use were more likely than those who did not report such use to have worked for three or more employers (9 percent versus 4 percent), to have voluntarily left an employer in the past year (25 percent versus 15 percent), and to have skipped one or more days of work in the past month (13 percent versus 5 percent). Workers who reported heavy alcohol use were about twice as likely as those who did not report such use to have worked for three or more employers in the past year (8 percent versus 4 percent) and to have skipped one or more days of work in the past month (11 percent versus 5 percent).

It is hard to measure the full economic burden of substance abuse on the workplace alone because of the society-wide spread of substance abuse. In general, the impact of substance abuse on the material welfare of a society can be estimated by examining the social and financial costs of law enforcement, lost productivity, treatment, prevention, and research, plus some measure of the quality of life-years lost, relative to a hypothetical scenario in which there is no substance abuse.

Employers can help their own bottom line, while at the same time reducing substance abuse, by clearly setting out in writing their policies regarding drug and alcohol abuse and encouraging substance abusers to enter treatment. The U.S. Congress expressed in the Drug-Free Workplace Act of 1998 that businesses should adopt drug-free workplace programs and that states should encourage businesses to adopt drug-free workplace programs. Many workplaces provide information regarding the use of alcohol or drugs. Some workplaces have a written policy regarding employee use of alcohol or drugs, and some provide access to employee assistance programs (EAPs) or some other type of counseling program for employees with alcohol or drug-related problems.

Testing in the workplace

In 1981, following a U.S. Department of Defense survey and precipitated by the crash of a navy plane on the deck of the aircraft carrier *Nimitz,* the U.S. Navy initiated a policy of zero tolerance to drugs and instituted a Navy-wide testing program. On September 15, 1986, President Ronald Reagan signed Executive Order 12564, which required each executive agency to establish a program to test federal employees in "sensitive positions" (broadly defined) for use of illegal drugs and to offer voluntary testing. The order also authorized testing for cause, as follow-up to counseling or rehabilitation, and at the pre-employment stage. The Drug-Free Workplace Act of 1988 requires federal government contractors to maintain drug-free workplaces. Urine is collected for federally regulated workplace drug-testing programs and for most private sector programs. In all, an estimated 33 million workplace drug tests are carried

---

EXCERPT FROM EXECUTIVE ORDER 12564 (15 September 1986)

I, RONALD REAGAN, President of the United States of America, find that:

Drug use is having serious adverse effects upon a significant proportion of the national work force and results in billions of dollars of lost productivity each year;

The Federal government, as an employer, is concerned with the well-being of its employees, the successful accomplishment of agency missions, and the need to maintain employee productivity;

The Federal government, as the largest employer in the Nation, can and should show the way towards achieving drug-free workplaces through a program designed to offer drug users a helping hand and, at the same time, demonstrating to drug users and potential drug users that drugs will not be tolerated in the Federal workplace;

The profits from illegal drugs provide the single greatest source of income for organized crime, fuel violent street crime, and otherwise contribute to the breakdown of our society;

The use of illegal drugs, on or off duty, by Federal employees is inconsistent not only with the law-abiding behavior expected of all citizens, but also with the special trust placed in such employees as servants of the public;

Federal employees who use illegal drugs, on or off duty, tend to be less productive, less reliable, and prone to greater absenteeism than their fellow employees who do not use illegal drugs;

The use of illegal drugs, on or off duty, by Federal employees impairs the efficiency of Federal departments and agencies, undermines public confidence in them, and makes it more difficult for other employees who do not use illegal drugs to perform their jobs effectively. The use of illegal drugs, on or off duty, by Federal employees also can pose a serious health and safety threat to members of the public and to other Federal employees;

The use of illegal drugs, on or off duty, by Federal employees in certain positions evidences less than the complete reliability, stability, and good judgment that is consistent with access to sensitive information and creates the possibility of coercion, influence, and irresponsible action under pressure that may pose a serious risk to national security, the public safety, and the effective enforcement of the law; and

Federal employees who use illegal drugs must themselves be primarily responsible for changing their behavior and, if necessary, begin the process of rehabilitating themselves.

out each year for U.S. employers. Aiming at improving precision in drug screening and making it harder for workers to cheat on urine tests, the Substance Abuse and Mental Health Services Administration (SAMHSA) issues revised rules that set specifications for alternatives to traditional lab-based urine tests, including lab testing of hair, saliva, and perspiration.

Current illicit drug users were more likely to report that their workplaces tested at hiring, randomly, upon suspicion, and post-accident in 1997 than in 1994. Despite its widespread use, drug testing has led to some controversy regarding reliability and validity, its effect on job applicants and current employees, and its legal status. Drug testing may have a deterrent effect, but this often comes at a high cost in the form of drug-testing expenses, employee turnover, and additional recruitment efforts.

Increasingly, illicit drug users have become much more accepting of drug testing in medium (25 to 499 employees) or large (500 or more employees) workplaces. For example, in 1994, 31 percent of current illicit drug users in medium establishments and 29 percent in large estab-lishments said they would be less likely to work for an employer who tests for drugs at hiring, while in 1997 only 15 percent in medium establishments and 7 percent in large estab-lishments said they would. In 1994, 41 percent of illicit current drug users in medium establishments and 48 percent in large establishments said they would be less likely to work for an employer who tests for drugs randomly, while in 1997 only 25 percent in medium establishments and 13 percent in large establishments said they would. Workers' attitudes toward workplace drug testing differ according to their drug-use status. In 1997, as in 1994, a larger percentage of current illicit drug users than nonusers said they would be less likely to work for an employer who tests for drug use upon hiring (22 percent versus 4 percent), randomly (29 percent versus 6 percent), upon suspicion (24 percent versus 10 percent), or after an accident (13 percent versus 4 percent).

Employee assistance and drug use prevention

Employee assistance programs (EAPs) have been used for three decades to reduce absenteeism, promote recovery, minimize relapse, cut treatment costs, and improve productivity among drug-using workers. Larger establishments were more likely to provide an EAP regarding drug and alcohol use. Three-fourths of those working in large establishments reported that their workplace had such a program, while only about one-fourth of the workers in small businesses said they had access to such a program. Of workers in mid-sized businesses, slightly more than half reported access to assistance programs. Belief in the efficacy of EAPs directly increased the likelihood of seeking help at an EAP. Greater perceived social support and supervisor encouragement increased the likelihood of going to an EAP both directly and indirectly.

Workplace drug testing is regarded as an essential demand-reduction component of a prevention program because it serves as a deterrent to continued use of illicit substances; provides a means to detect and, thereby, identify employees or job applicants who are using illicit substances; and assists employees in recognizing and admitting their abuse problems so that they may obtain the necessary treatment.

Workplace drug treatment is a critical way to reach those who need help. Increasingly, it is considered desirable that drug treatment should be covered at the same benefit level as other chronic relapsing disorders. In the United States, the Center for Substance Abuse Prevention (CSAP) offers a toll-free telephone consulting service through its Workplace Help line.

Workers' attitudes toward various drug-testing programs have changed over time. Although some controversial issues surrounding alcohol and drug testing at the workplace still exist, overall, the vast majority of workers worldwide are willing to work for an employer who has a drug-testing program. While future workplace intervention programs may benefit from this general attitude change, prevention and treatment efforts should engage in customized communications during implementation of the program, taking into account the variations in the different groups, such as the size of the workplace and the occupations involved.

Z. ZHANG

SEE ALSO:
Counseling • Driving While Impaired • Drug Testing • Employee Assistance Programs

World Health Organization (WHO)

The World Health Organization deals with all types of health issues, including that of substance abuse and dependence. It collates statistics from its member states that can be used by health workers all over the globe.

The World Health Organization (WHO) was founded in 1948 by the United Nations as its specialized agency for health. It is governed by 192 member states, representatives of which form the World Health Assembly. The Health Assembly makes WHO's major policy decisions and approves budgets. WHO's constitution states that health is not only the absence of disease or infirmity but is also the state of complete physical, mental, and social well-being. In the area of substance abuse, WHO's mandate includes: prevention and reduction of the negative health and social consequences of psychoactive substance use; reduction of the demand for nonmedical use of psychoactive substances; assessment of psychoactive substances so as to advise the United Nations with regard to their regulatory control. WHO is the only international agency that deals with all psychoactive substances, regardless of their legal status.

A number of different departments and bodies within WHO are responsible for achieving these aims. The Expert Committee on Drug Dependence, for example, advises the United Nations on regulatory control of psychoactive substances. The advice of this committee is given to the United Nations Commission on Narcotic Drugs, which then votes on whether a drug should be added to one of the lists of internationally controlled drugs, transferred to another list, or removed altogether.

The Department of Mental Health and Substance Dependence is concerned with the management of problems related to the use of psychoactive drugs. The tasks of this department are broken down into specific areas, such as the epidemiology of alcohol and drug use, substance use and HIV/AIDS, and the neuroscience of substance use and dependence. One of its key publications is its contribution to the *International Classification of Diseases and Related Health Problems* (ICD-10). Chapter V deals with the diagnosis of more than 300 mental and behavioral disorders, including those that relate to substance abuse. These classifications are used throughout the world as a means of assessing whether a person has developed a dependence on drugs as well as any other comorbid mental or behavioral symptoms that may relate to the problem.

WHO recognizes the importance of developing accurate and detailed sources of information on the epidemiology of drug use, particularly in developing countries where information may be limited. Extensive research carried out in many countries is used to create a thorough body of knowledge, which may then be consulted by policy makers and health professionals. In the case of the epidemiology of alcohol and drug use, for example, the *Global Status Report on Alcohol* presents data on alcohol consumption in 173 member states, while the *Guide to Drug Abuse Epidemiology*, produced in collaboration with the U.S. National Institute on Drug Abuse (NIDA), provides information on measures and methods that aid the assessment of national trends in drug taking. This guide is designed so that it may be adapted to a wide range of circumstances, including the limited medical resources and expertise that may be found in developing countries.

WHO works closely with a number of other organizations to improve existing knowledge on substance use. Research carried out, for example, with the Cochrane Collaborative Review Group on Drug and Alcohol Addiction aims to provide regularly updated information on the effects of prevention and treatment methods for psychoactive substances. Other activities of WHO include the exchange and dissemination of information through a variety of books, reports, and events, including conferences that target particular areas of concern and global awareness days.

P. G. Thompson

See Also:
National Institute on Drug Abuse (NIDA)

Resources for Further Study

BIBLIOGRAPHY

American Psychiatric Association (APA). 2000. *Diagnostic and Statistical Manual of Mental Disorders*. 4th ed. Washington, D.C.: APA.

Brick, John, and Carlton K. Erickson. 1998. *Drugs, the Brain, and Behavior: The Pharmacology of Abuse and Dependence*. New York: Haworth Medical Press.

Brick, John, ed. 2004. *Handbook of the Medical Consequences of Alcohol and Drug Abuse*. New York: Haworth Press.

DuPont, Robert L. 2000. *The Selfish Brain: Learning from Addiction*. Center City, Minn.: Hazelden.

Frances, Richard J., Sheldon I. Miller, and Avram H. Mack. 2005. *Clinical Textbook of Addictive Disorders*. 3rd ed. New York: Guilford Press.

Karch, Steven B. 2009. *Karch's Pathology of Drug Abuse*. 4th ed. Boca Raton, Fla.: CRC Press.

Liska, Ken. 2009. *Drugs and the Human Body*. 8th ed. Upper Saddle River, N.J.: Pearson Prentice Hall.

McKim, William A. 2003. *Drugs and Behavior: An Introduction to Behavioral Pharmacology*. 5th ed. Upper Saddle River, N.J.: Prentice Hall.

Spence, Richard T., et al. 2001. *Neurobiology of Addictions: Implications for Clinical Practice*. New York: Haworth Social Work Practice Press.

WEB RESOURCES

The following World Wide Web sources feature information useful for students, teachers, and health care professionals. By necessity, this list is only a representative sampling; many government bodies, charities, and professional organizations not listed have websites that are also worth investigating. Other Internet resources, such as newsgroups, also exist and can be explored for further research. Please note that all URLs have a tendency to change; addresses were functional and accurate as of April 2011.

Al-Anon / Alateen
www.al-anon.org
Al-Anon, which includes Alateen for younger members, helps the families and friends of alcoholics. It focuses on the importance of recovery and explains how to cope with the effects of problem drinking. The website operates in English, Spanish, and French.

Alcoholics Anonymous
www.alcoholics-anonymous.org
A fellowship of men and women who share experiences to help solve their common problems. The aim is to help other alcoholics achieve sobriety. The website operates in English, Spanish, and French.

American Society of Addiction Medicine
www.asam.org
An association of physicians dedicated to promoting research, educating health care workers, and improving the treatment of individuals suffering from alcoholism and other addictions.

Canadian Centre on Substance Abuse
www.ccsa.ca
CCSA is Canada's national addictions agency. It provides information and advice to help reduce the harm associated with substance abuse and addictions. There is a list of recommended reading to download on the topic of young people and drugs at *www.ccsa.ca/index.asp?ID=10*

Canadian Society of Addiction Medicine
csam.org
Policy Statements are available under Non-Member Services.

Center for Education and Drug Abuse Research
cedar.pharmacy.pitt.edu
Based at the University of Pittsburgh School of Pharmacy, Cedar's mission is to carry out long-term research into substance abuse. The research encompasses both genetic and environmental factors in abuse.

Center for Treatment Research on Adolescent Drug Abuse
www.miami.edu/ctrada/
CTRADA was established to conduct research on the treatment of adolescent drug abuse. It evaluates different treatments to develop a greater understanding of successful treatment factors.

Drug Enforcement Administration
www.usdoj.gov/dea
News bulletins, briefings, and background reports on a wide range of issues about illegal drugs. Part of the United States Department of Justice.

Food and Drug Administration
www.fda.gov
The FDA approves drugs for legal use in the United States. Information on over-the-counter, prescription, and generic drugs as well as the illegal use and trafficking of controlled drugs is available on this website.

Hazelden
www.hazelden.org
A not-for-profit organization, Hazelden helps those addicted to alcohol and other drugs. It provides treatment and care services, education, research, and publishing products.

Mothers Against Drunk Driving
www.madd.org
MADD's mission is to stop drunk driving, support victims of this crime, and prevent underage drinking. This website has the latest statistics on the impact of drunk driving, plus information on the laws, underage drinking research, and other issues related to MADD's mission.

National Center on Addiction and Substance Abuse
www.casacolumbia.org
CASA is based at Columbia University. It is the only national organization that brings together the professional disciplines needed to study and combat abuse of alcohol, nicotine, and illegal, prescription, and performance-enhancing drugs.

National Council on Alcoholism and Drug Dependence
www.ncadd.org
The NCADD provides education, information, and help to the public. This website has statistics, interviews with experts, and recommendations about drinking from leading health authorities. A nationwide network of affiliates can be accessed through the site.

National Inhalant Prevention Coalition
www.inhalants.org
NIPC promotes awareness and recognition of the problem of inhalant use. It campaigns on the issue, promotes the latest research, and can advise on individual local programs. The website operates in English and Spanish.

National Institute on Alcohol Abuse and Alcoholism
www.niaaa.nih.gov
NIAAA conducts and publishes research on alcohol abuse and alcoholism. Click on "Resources" for textual and graphical information.

National Institute on Drug Abuse
www.nida.nih.gov
This site provides information on particular drugs as well as statistics on drug use, treatment advice, and research.

The Partnership at Drugfree.org
www.drugfree.org
Successor to the Partnership for A Drug-Free America, the organization helps parents prevent, intervene in, and find treatment for children's drug and alcohol abuse.

Substance Abuse and Mental Health Services Administration
www.samhsa.gov
SAMHSA's website is an important resource for data, briefings, and reports. SAMHSA's Office of Applied Studies (*oas.samhsa.gov*) provides national data on drug-abuse issues.

Substance Abuse Treatment Facility Locator
findtreatment.samhsa.gov
This searchable directory, run by the U.S. Department of Health and Human Services, shows the location of treatment facilities around the country that treat alcohol and drug abuse problems.

Tobacco Free Kids
www.tobaccofreekids.org
This site offers news, research, and facts to discourage children from smoking. It presents the latest federal and state initatives and provides facts and figures on young smokers in each state.

United Nations Office on Drugs and Crime
www.unodc.org
The UNODC is a global leader in the fight against illicit drugs and international crime. The organization's website provides information on the fight against illegal drugs, including legislation passed by the United Nations.

University of Michigan Documents Center
www.lib.umich.edu/govdocs
A central reference point for government information: local, state, federal, and international. Includes news and statistics.

World Health Organization
www.who.int
The World Health Organization offers support to countries to prevent and reduce drug abuse. It presents recommendations to the United Nations about which psychoactive substances should be regulated. Information about substance abuse, including WHO projects, activities, and publications, is available at www.who.int/substance_abuse, including profiles of substance abuse by country.

Drug Table

COMMON NAME OR TRADE NAME	CHEMICAL, GENERIC, OR BOTANICAL NAME	STREET NAMES AND OTHER NAMES	TYPE OF DRUG
2C-T-7		Blue mystic, 7-up, beautiful, tripstasy	Phenethylamine
Acetorphine and etorphine		Elephant juice, M99	Opioid
Amyl nitrate		Aimies, boppers, pearls, poppers	Inhalant
Amytal	Amobarbital	Blues, blue heavens	Barbiturate
Ativan	Lorazepam		Benzodiazepine
Atropine			Belladonna alkaloid
Benzedrine	Amphetamine sulfate	Speed, bennies, amp	Amphetamine
Bufotenine	5-HO-DMT (5-hydroxy-dimethyltryptamine)		Tryptamine
Caffeine			Stimulant
Chloroform			Sedative/Inhalant
Cocaine	Cocaine hydrochloride	Coke, snow, blow, Bolivian marching powder, Charlie, big C, nose candy	Stimulant
Coca leaf	Erythroxylon coca	Coca	Stimulant
Codeine	methyl morphine		Opiate
Crack cocaine		Smack, rock	Stimulant
Demerol	Meperidine, pethidine		Opioid
DET	Diethyltryptamine		Tryptamine
Dexedrine	Dextroamphetamine (amphetamine sulfate)	Dexies	Amphetamine
Dilaudid	Hydromorphone	Hospital heroin	Opioid
DMT	Dimethyltryptamine	Businessman's LSD, Fantasia, 45-minute psychosis	Tryptamine
DOB	Brolamphetamine		Amphetamine
Doriden	Glutethimide		Sedative
Ecstasy	MDMA (3,4 methylene-dioxymethamphetamine)	XTC, love drug, Adam	Amphetamine
Ephedrine			Amphetamine
Equanil, Miltown	Meprobamate		Sedative
Erythropoietin		EPO	Hormone
Ethanol	Ethyl alcohol		Alcohol
Ether			Anesthetic/Inhalant
Ethyltryptamine	3-(2-aminobutyl)indole	ET, alpha-ET, love pearls, love pills	Tryptamine
Eticyclidine	PCE		PCP analog
Fentanyl		Jackpot, China white, TNT, friend, goodfellas	Opioid
GBL	Gamma-butyrolactone	Lactone, firewater, revivarant	Depressant/see GHB
GHB	Gamma-hydroxybutyrate	GBH, Georgia Home Boy, jib,liquid E (or X), organic quaalude, sleep	Depressant
Halcion	Triazolam		Benzodiazepine
Harmine and harmaline	Banisteriopsis caapi	Ayahuasca	Hallucinogen
Hashish	Marijuana	Gram, hash, soles, pollen	Hallucinogen
Heroin	Diacetylmorphine/diamorphine	Antifreeze, brown sugar, China white, gold, H, horse, shit, stuff	Opioid
HGH	Human growth hormone		Hormone
Ibogaine	Tabernanthe iboga		Hallucinogen
Isobutyl nitrate		Aroma of men, bullet, locker room, snappers	Inhalant
Jimsonweed	Datura stramonium		Belladonna alkaloid
Ketamine		Special K, cat Valium, jet, kit-kat, vitamin K	Dissociative
Khat	Cathine/cathinone	Somali tea, African salad	Stimulant

344

COMMON NAME OR TRADE NAME	CHEMICAL, GENERIC, OR BOTANICAL NAME	STREET NAMES AND OTHER NAMES	TYPE OF DRUG
Klonopin	Clonazepam		Benzodiazepine
Laudanum			Opioid
Levorphanol	(-)-3-hydroxy-N-methylmorphinan		Opioid
Librium	Chlordiazepoxide		Benzodiazepine
LSD	Lysergic acid diethylamide	Acid	Hallucinogen
Magic mushrooms	Psilocybin and psilocin	Musk, mushrooms, shrooms, Simple Simon	Tryptamine
Marijuana	Cannabis sativa	Pot, weed, grass, hashish	Hallucinogen
MDA	3,4 methylenedioxy amphetamine	Eve	Amphetamine/ Ecstasy analog
Mecloqualone	3-(o-chlorophenyl)-2-methyl-4(3H)-quinazolinone		Sedative/see Methaqualone
Mescaline	3,4,5-trimethoxy-phenethylamine	Buttons, cactus, mescal, peyote	Phenethylamine
Methaqualone	2-methyl-3-o-tolyl-4(3H)-quinazolinone	Quaaludes, ludes, 714s, sporos	Sedative
Methanol	Methyl alcohol	Meths	Alcohol
Methamphetamine		Crank, crystal, ice, meth, redneck cocaine, ya-ba	Amphetamine
Methcathinone	2-(methylamino)-1-phenylpropan-1-one	Cat, Jeff, ephedrone, bathtub speed	Stimulant
Morphine		God's drug, Miss Emma, morf, unkie	Opiate
4-MTA	4-methylthioamphetamine	Flatliner, golden eagle	Amphetamine
Nembutal	Pentobarbital	Yellow jackets	Barbiturate
Nexus	2-CB, BDMPEA	Bromo, spectrum, toonies, Venus	Phenethylamine
Nicotine			Stimulant
Nitrous oxide	NO	Laughing gas, buzz bomb, whippets	Inhalant
Noctec	Chloral hydrate	Mickey Finn, knockout drops	Sedative
Opium	Papaver somniferum	Poppy, Auntie, big O, Chinese tobacco, God's medicine, midnight oil, zero	Opioid
OxyContin	Oxycodone (14-hydroxy-dihydrocodeinone)	Oxy 40s/80s, hillbilly heroin, kicker, oxycotton	Opioid
Parahexyl			Depressant
Paraldehyde			Depressant
PCP	Phencyclidine	Angel dust, crazy coke, mad dog, ozone, rocket fuel	Dissociative
Prozac	Fluoxetine		SSRI
Restoril	Temazepam		Benzodiazepine
Ritalin	Methylphenidate	MPH, vitamin R, west coast	Stimulant
Robitussin	DXM (dextromethorphan)	Robo, Velvet, DXM	Dissociative/opioid
Rohypnol	Flunitrazepam	Forget-me drug, pingus, roofies, roaches, rope	Benzodiazepine
Rolicyclidine	PHP, PCPy		Dissociative/PCP analog
Scopolamine			Belladonna alkaloid
Serax	Oxazepam		Benzodiazepine
Talwin	Pentazocine		Opioid
Toluene		Tolly	Inhalant
TCP	Tenocyclidine		Dissociative/PCP analog
Thorazine	Chlorpromazine		Sedative
Valium	Diazepam		Benzodiazepine
Versed	Midazolam		Benzodiazepine
Vicodin	Hydrocodone		Opioid
Xanax	Alprazolam		Benzodiazepine

345

Index